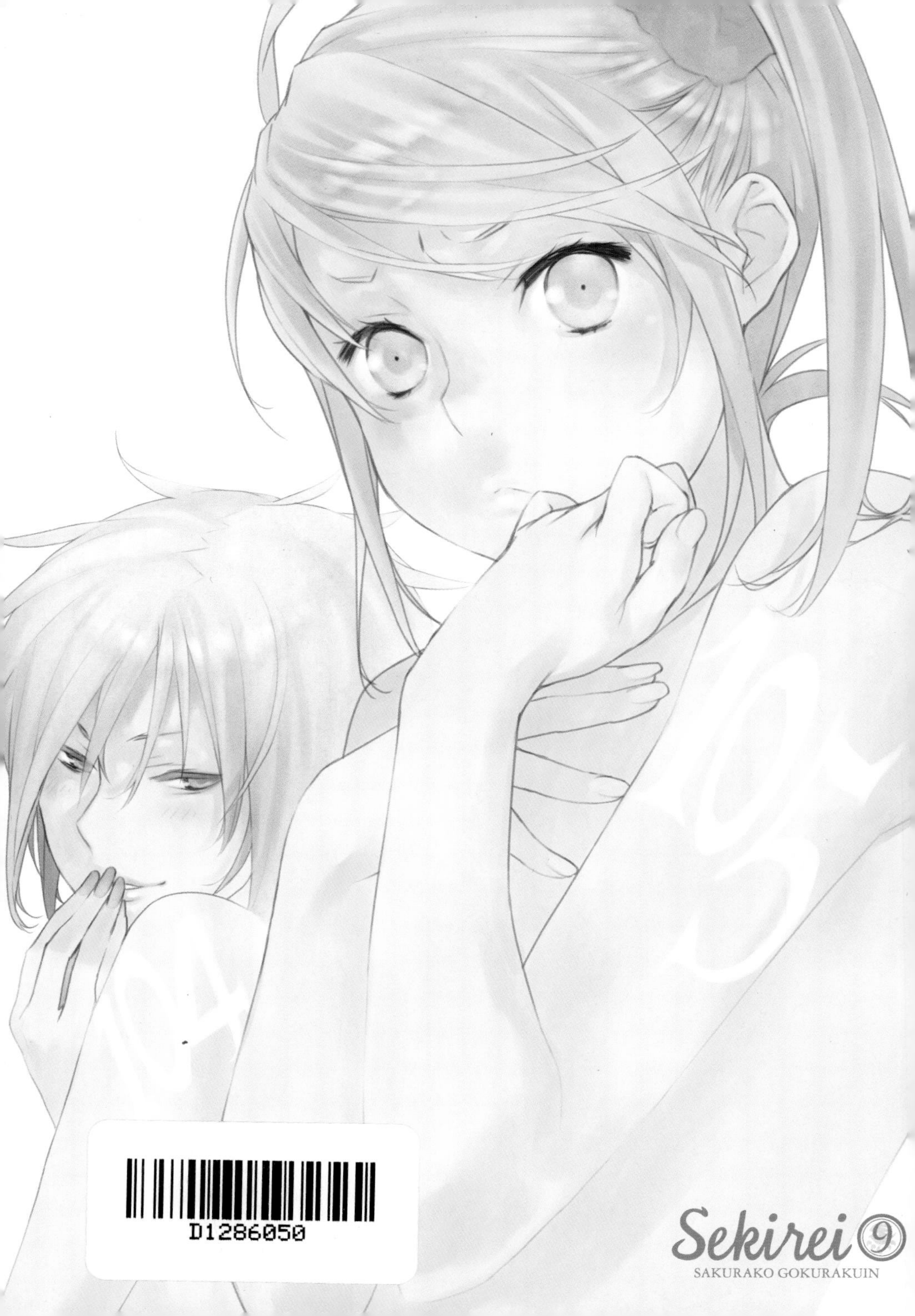
Sekirei 9
SAKURAKO GOKURAKUIN

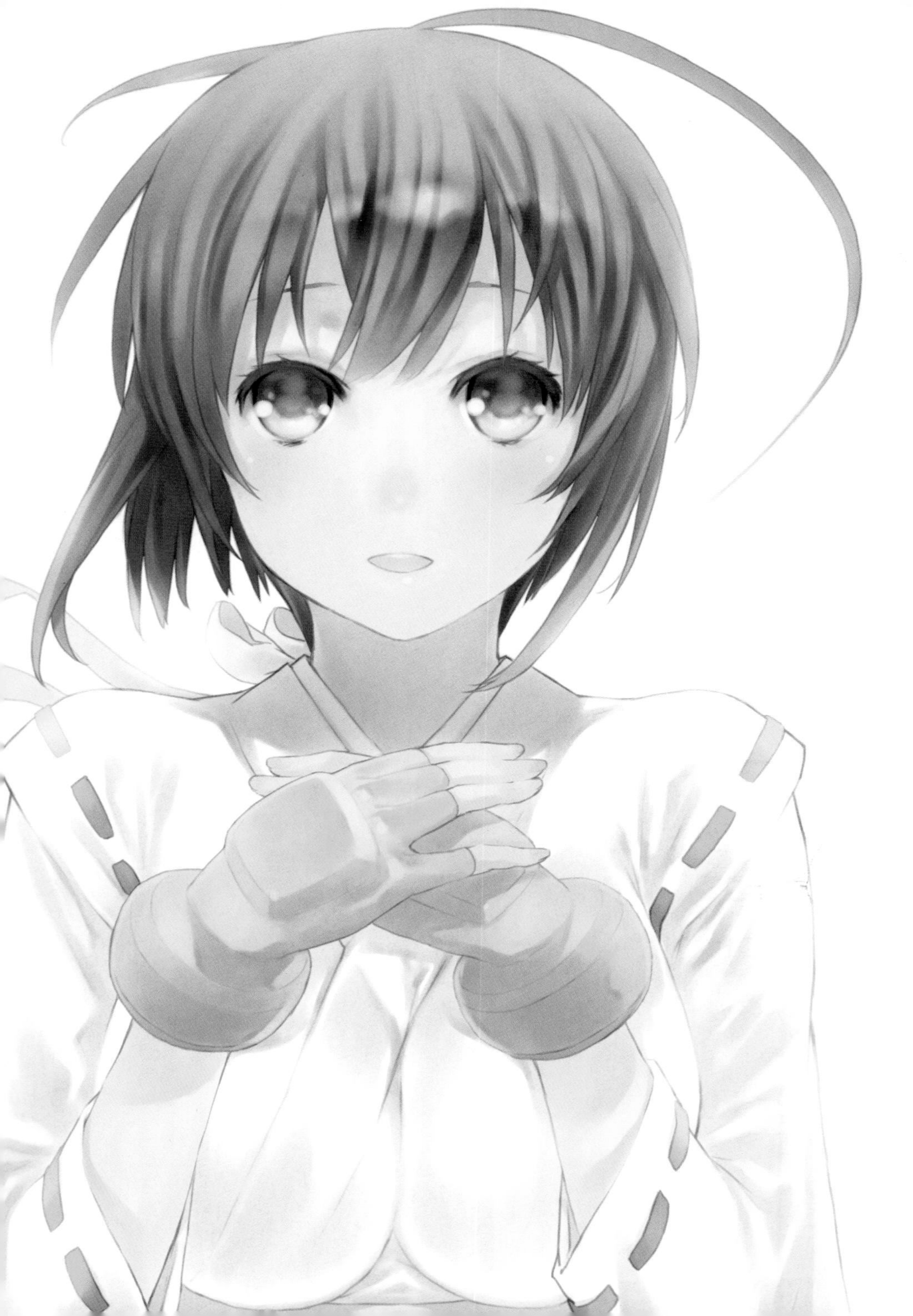

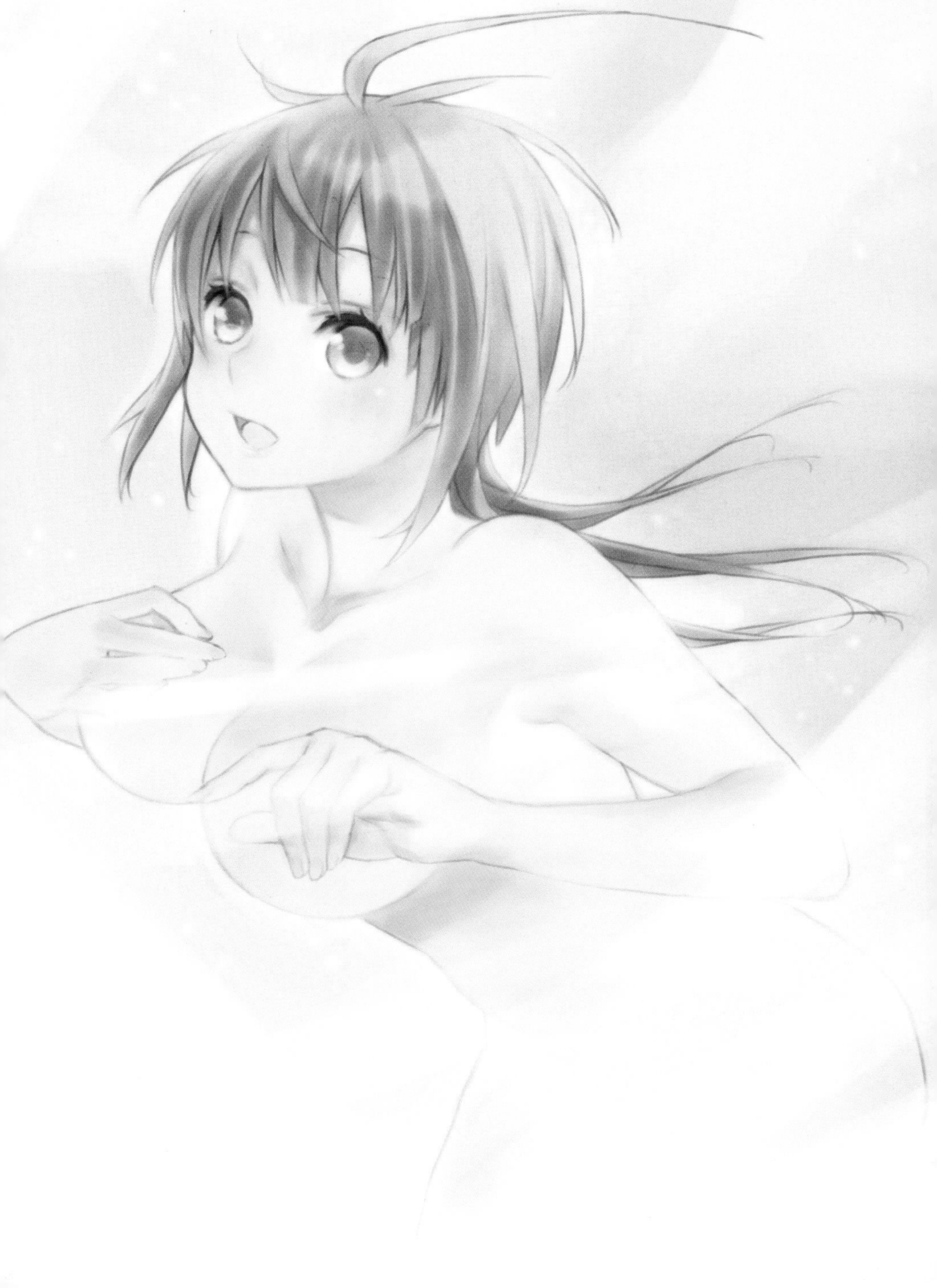

SEKIREI ⑨
Sakurako Gokurakuin

BY THE BONDS OF MY CONTRACT, SEND MY ASHIKABI'S WISH AND THE WISHES OF ALL SEKIREI TO THE HEAVENS!

CONTENTS

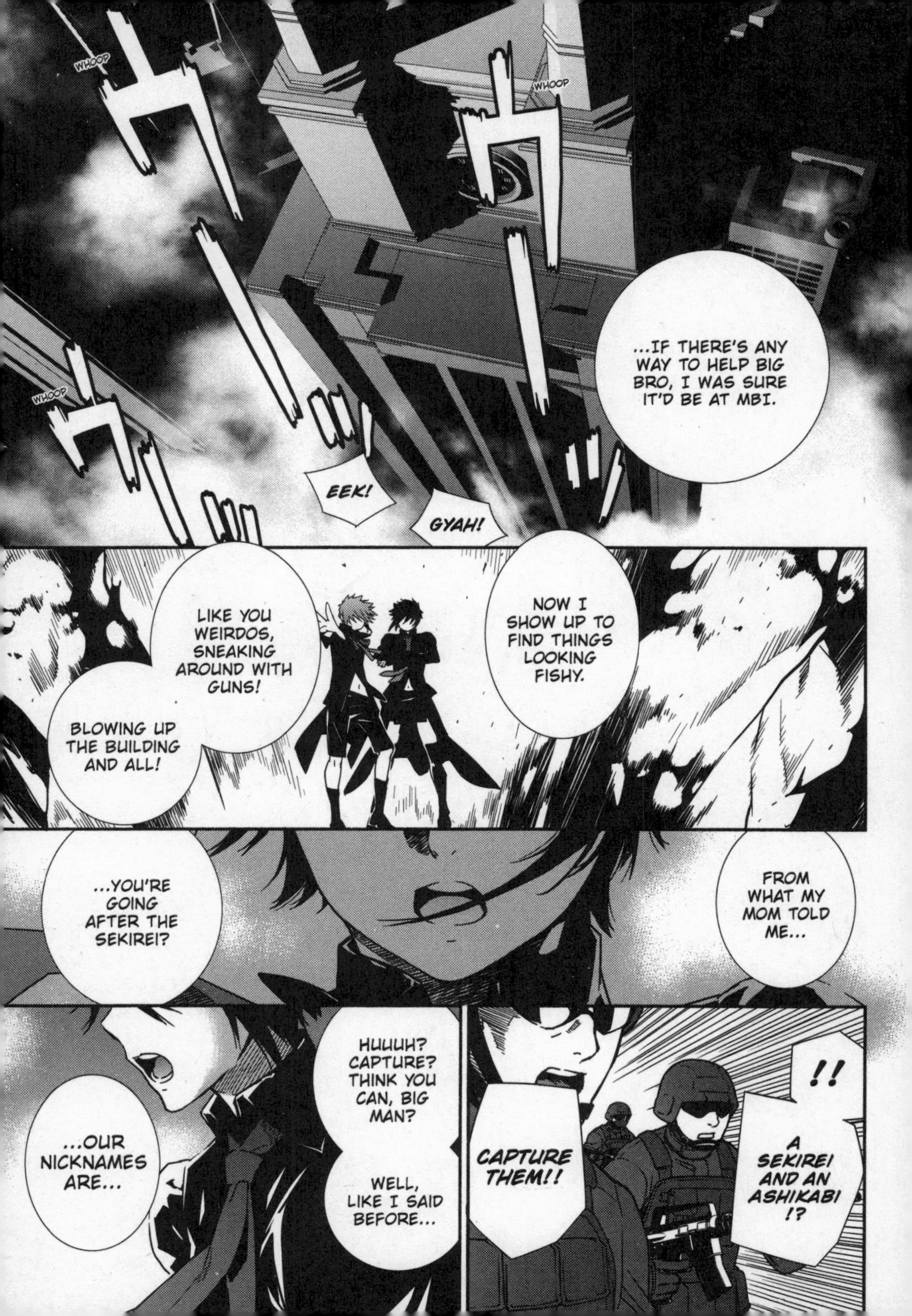
WHOOP
WHOOP
...IF THERE'S ANY WAY TO HELP BIG BRO, I WAS SURE IT'D BE AT MBI.
WHOOP
GYAH!
EEK!
NOW I SHOW UP TO FIND THINGS LOOKING FISHY.
LIKE YOU WEIRDOS, SNEAKING AROUND WITH GUNS!
BLOWING UP THE BUILDING AND ALL!
FROM WHAT MY MOM TOLD ME...
...YOU'RE GOING AFTER THE SEKIREI?
!!
A SEKIREI AND AN ASHIKABI !?
CAPTURE THEM!!
HUUUH? CAPTURE? THINK YOU CAN, BIG MAN?
WELL, LIKE I SAID BEFORE...
...OUR NICKNAMES ARE...

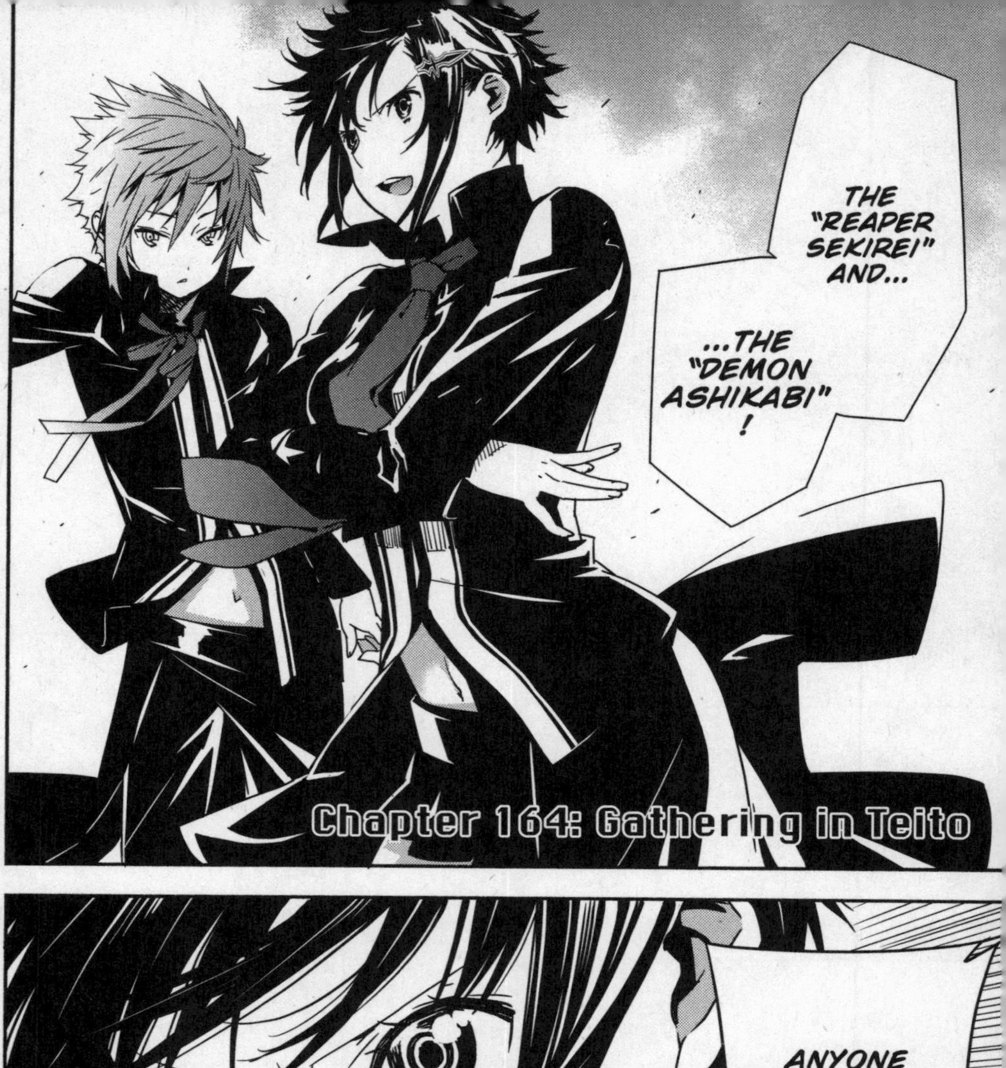
THE "REAPER SEKIREI" AND...
...THE "DEMON ASHIKABI"!
Chapter 164: Gathering in Teito
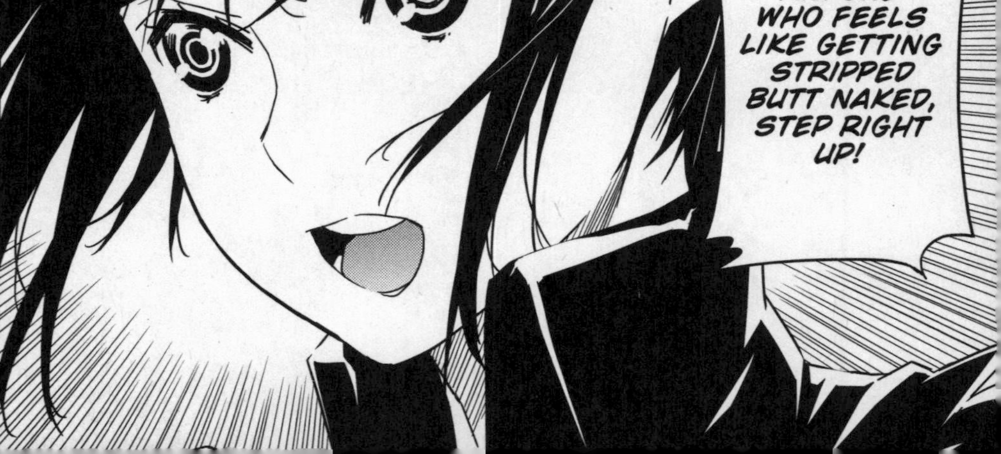
ANYONE WHO FEELS LIKE GETTING STRIPPED BUTT NAKED, STEP RIGHT UP!

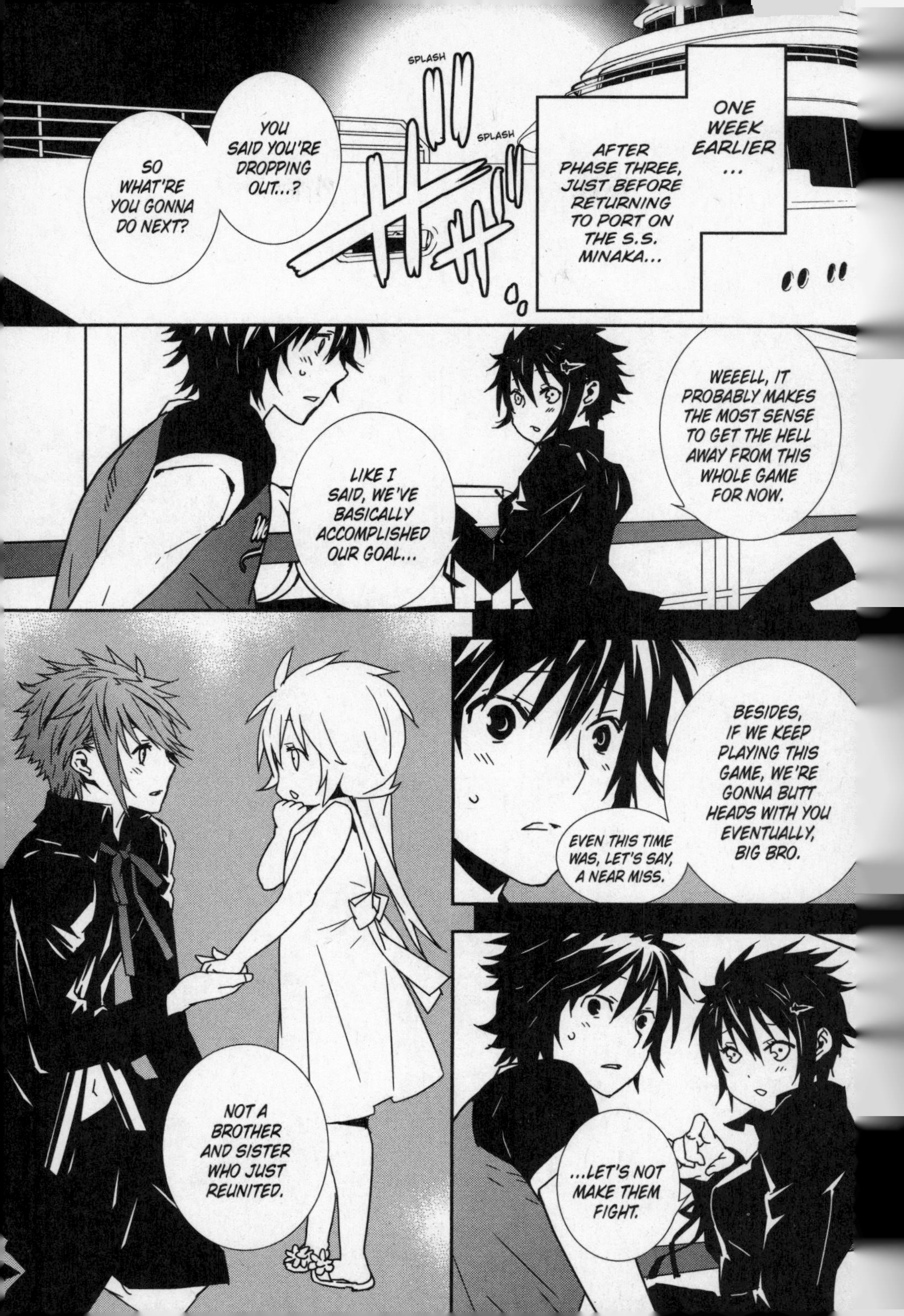
ONE WEEK EARLIER...
AFTER PHASE THREE, JUST BEFORE RETURNING TO PORT ON THE S.S. MINAKA...
SPLASH
SPLASH
YOU SAID YOU'RE DROPPING OUT...?
SO WHAT'RE YOU GONNA DO NEXT?
WEEELL, IT PROBABLY MAKES THE MOST SENSE TO GET THE HELL AWAY FROM THIS WHOLE GAME FOR NOW.
LIKE I SAID, WE'VE BASICALLY ACCOMPLISHED OUR GOAL...
BESIDES, IF WE KEEP PLAYING THIS GAME, WE'RE GONNA BUTT HEADS WITH YOU EVENTUALLY, BIG BRO.
EVEN THIS TIME WAS, LET'S SAY, A NEAR MISS.
...LET'S NOT MAKE THEM FIGHT.
NOT A BROTHER AND SISTER WHO JUST REUNITED.

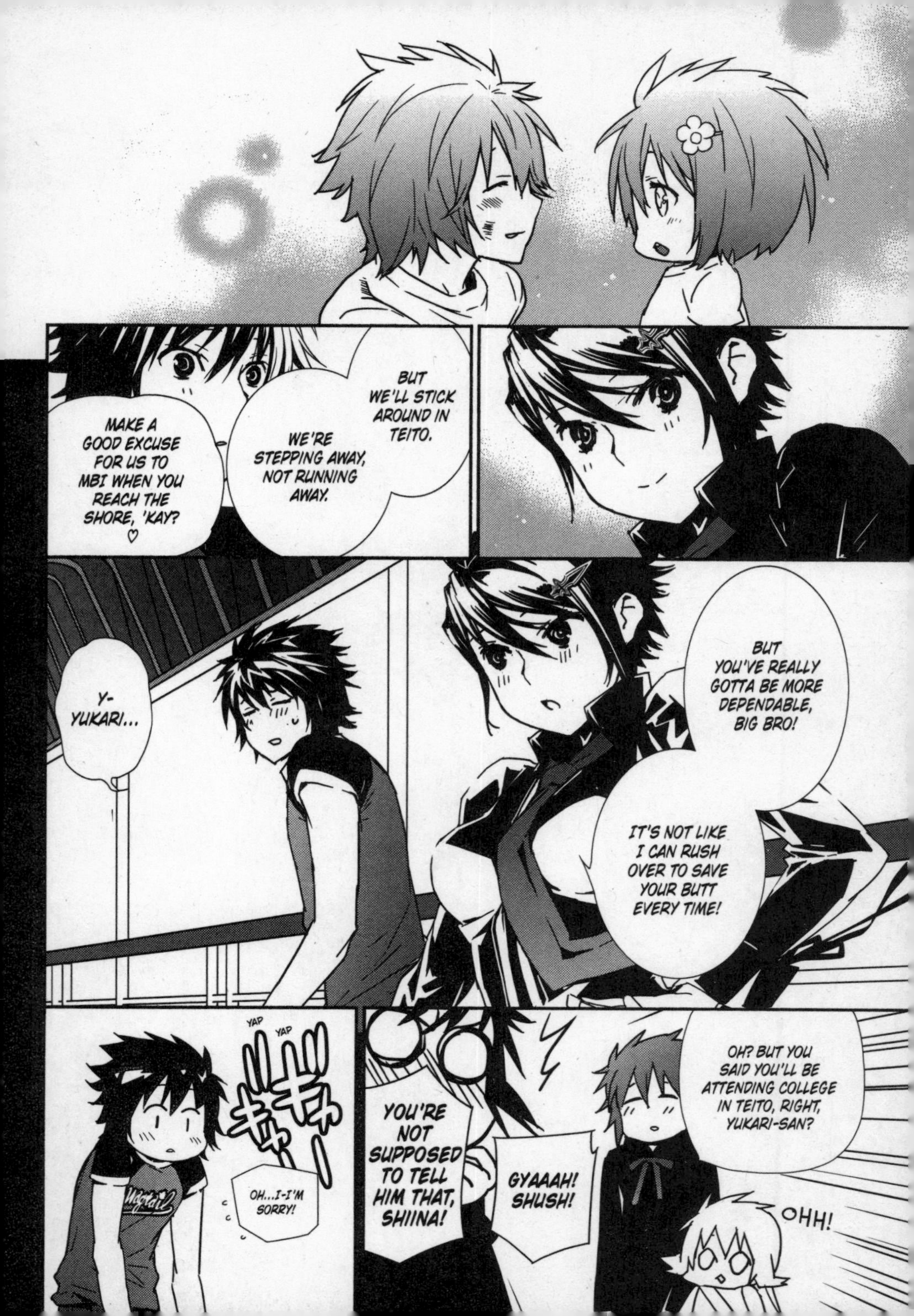
BUT WE'LL STICK AROUND IN TEITO.
WE'RE STEPPING AWAY, NOT RUNNING AWAY.
MAKE A GOOD EXCUSE FOR US TO MBI WHEN YOU REACH THE SHORE, 'KAY? ♡
BUT YOU'VE REALLY GOTTA BE MORE DEPENDABLE, BIG BRO!
IT'S NOT LIKE I CAN RUSH OVER TO SAVE YOUR BUTT EVERY TIME!
Y-YUKARI...
OH? BUT YOU SAID YOU'LL BE ATTENDING COLLEGE IN TEITO, RIGHT, YUKARI-SAN?
GYAAAH! SHUSH!
YOU'RE NOT SUPPOSED TO TELL HIM THAT, SHIINA!
OHH!
YAP YAP
OH...I-I'M SORRY!

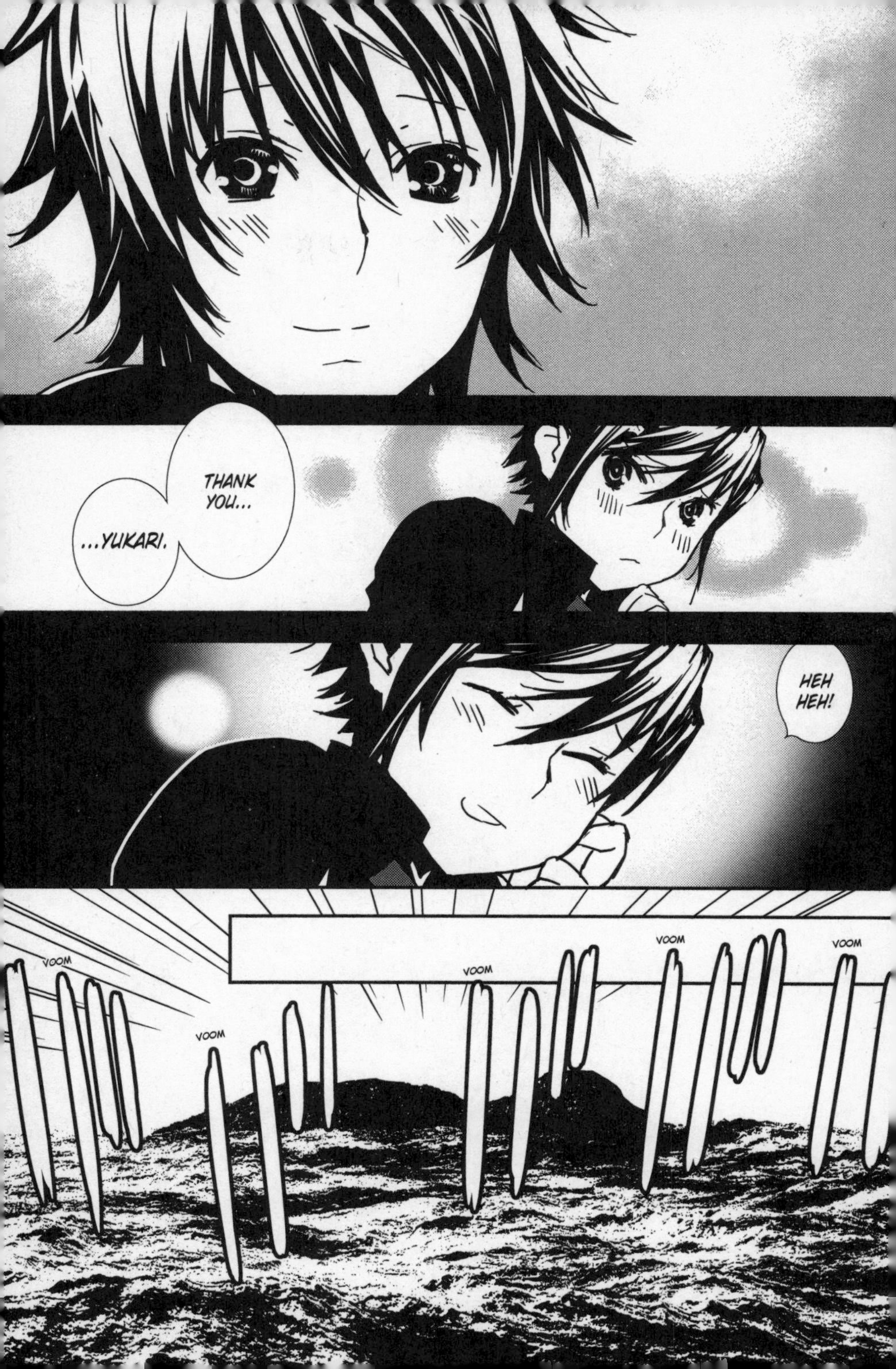
THANK YOU...
...YUKARI.
HEH HEH!
VOOM
VOOM
VOOM
VOOM
VOOM

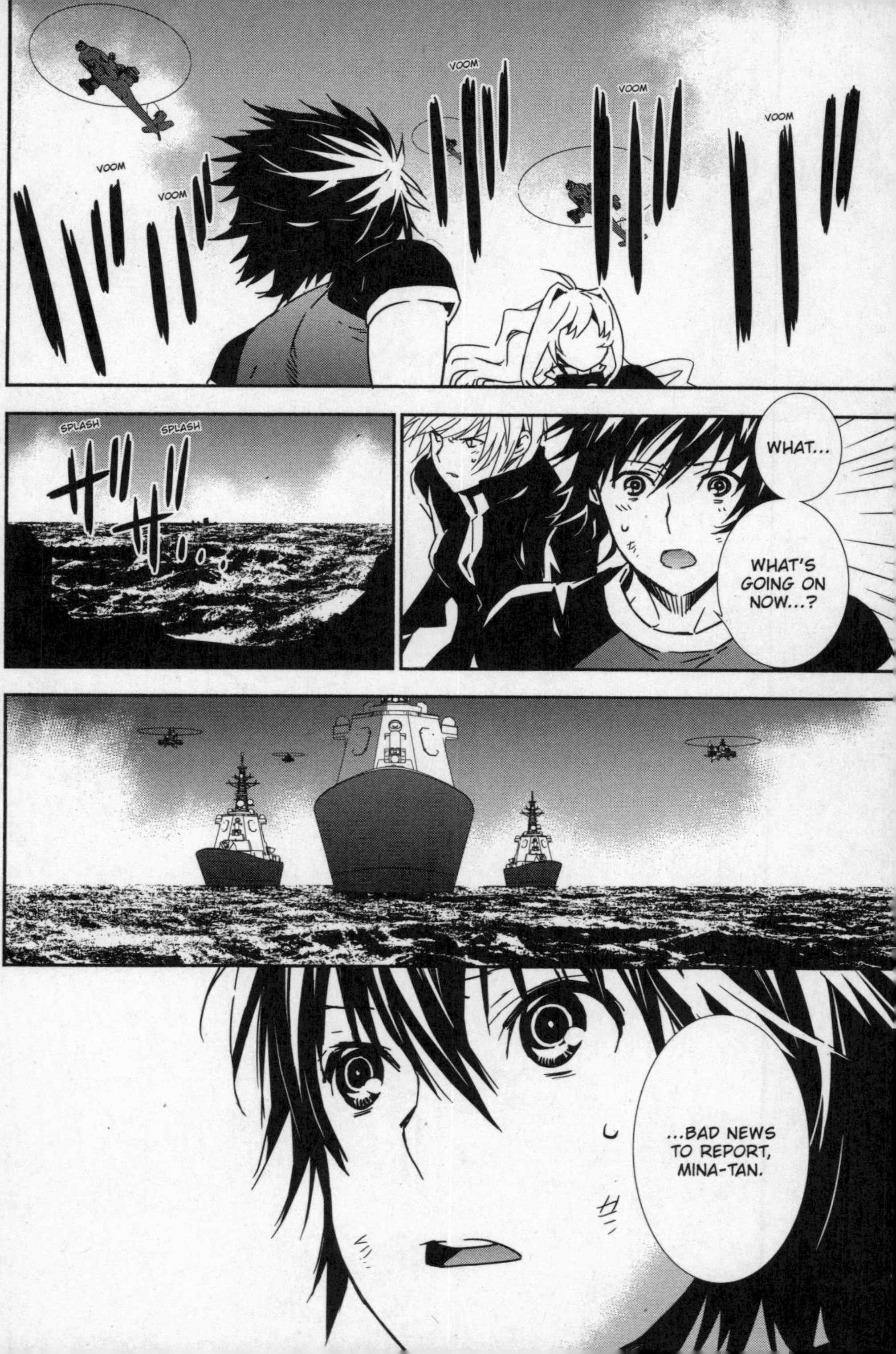
VOOM
VOOM
VOOM
VOOM
VOOM
WHAT...
WHAT'S GOING ON NOW...?
SPLASH
SPLASH
...BAD NEWS TO REPORT, MINA-TAN.

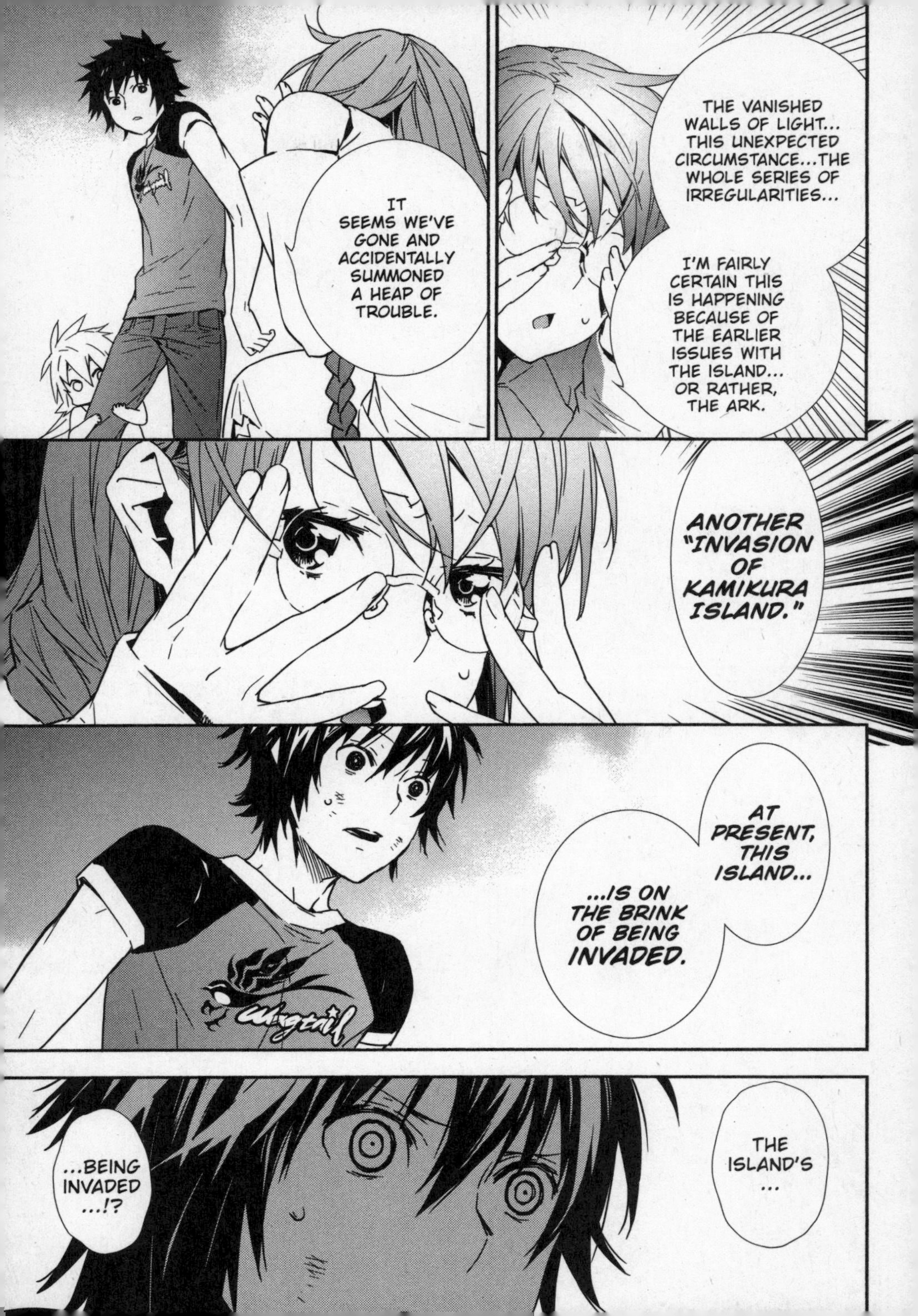
THE VANISHED WALLS OF LIGHT... THIS UNEXPECTED CIRCUMSTANCE...THE WHOLE SERIES OF IRREGULARITIES...
I'M FAIRLY CERTAIN THIS IS HAPPENING BECAUSE OF THE EARLIER ISSUES WITH THE ISLAND... OR RATHER, THE ARK.
IT SEEMS WE'VE GONE AND ACCIDENTALLY SUMMONED A HEAP OF TROUBLE.
ANOTHER *"INVASION OF KAMIKURA ISLAND."*
AT PRESENT, THIS ISLAND...
...IS ON THE BRINK OF BEING **INVADED.**
THE ISLAND'S...
...BEING INVADED ...!?

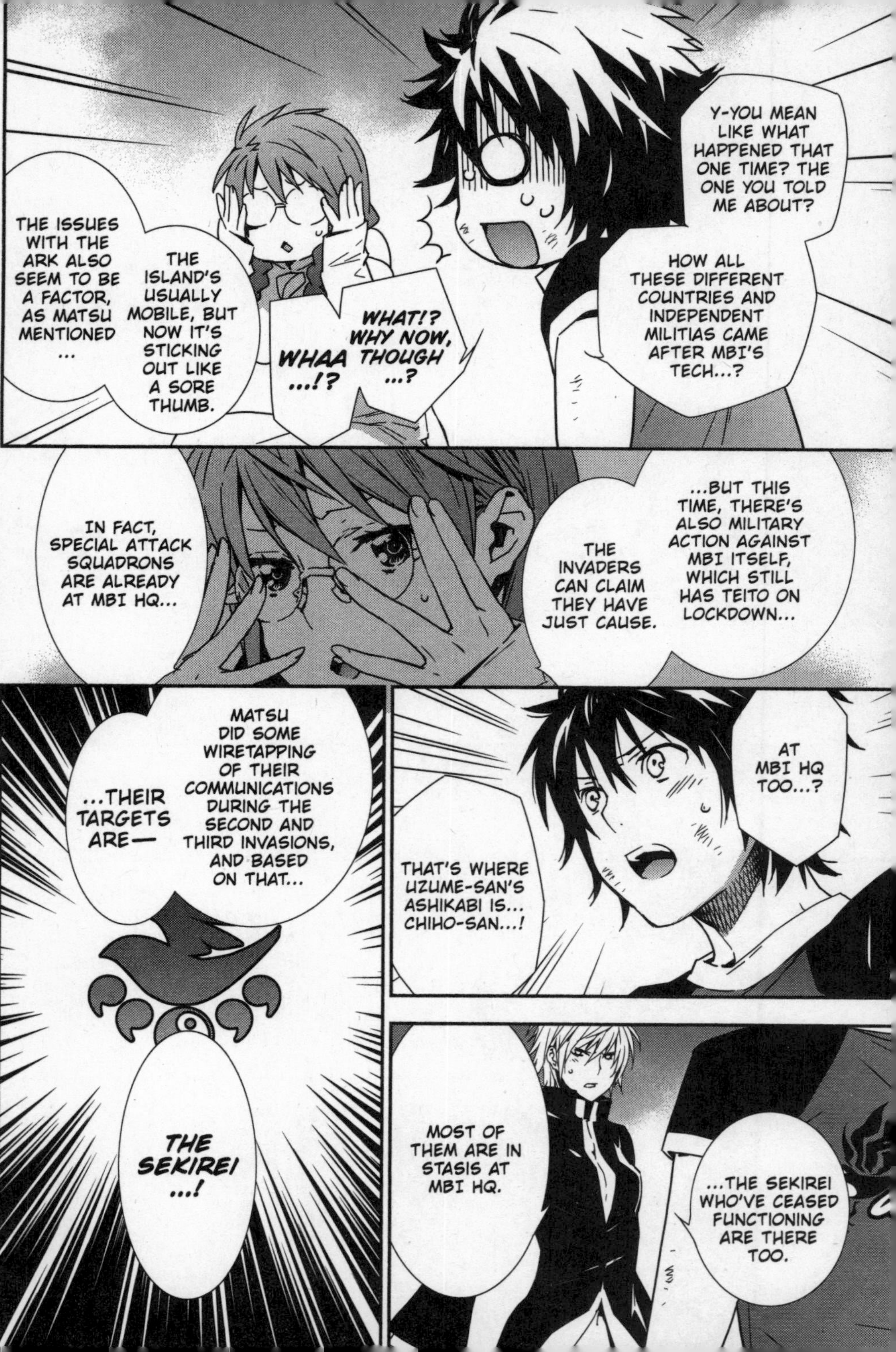
Y-YOU MEAN LIKE WHAT HAPPENED THAT ONE TIME? THE ONE YOU TOLD ME ABOUT?
HOW ALL THESE DIFFERENT COUNTRIES AND INDEPENDENT MILITIAS CAME AFTER MBI'S TECH...?
WHAT!? WHY NOW, THOUGH ...?
WHAA ...!?
THE ISLAND'S USUALLY MOBILE, BUT NOW IT'S STICKING OUT LIKE A SORE THUMB.
THE ISSUES WITH THE ARK ALSO SEEM TO BE A FACTOR, AS MATSU MENTIONED ...
...BUT THIS TIME, THERE'S ALSO MILITARY ACTION AGAINST MBI ITSELF, WHICH STILL HAS TEITO ON LOCKDOWN...
THE INVADERS CAN CLAIM THEY HAVE JUST CAUSE.
IN FACT, SPECIAL ATTACK SQUADRONS ARE ALREADY AT MBI HQ...
AT MBI HQ TOO...?
THAT'S WHERE UZUME-SAN'S ASHIKABI IS... CHIHO-SAN...!
...THE SEKIREI WHO'VE CEASED FUNCTIONING ARE THERE TOO.
MOST OF THEM ARE IN STASIS AT MBI HQ.
MATSU DID SOME WIRETAPPING OF THEIR COMMUNICATIONS DURING THE SECOND AND THIRD INVASIONS, AND BASED ON THAT...
...THEIR TARGETS ARE—
THE SEKIREI ...!

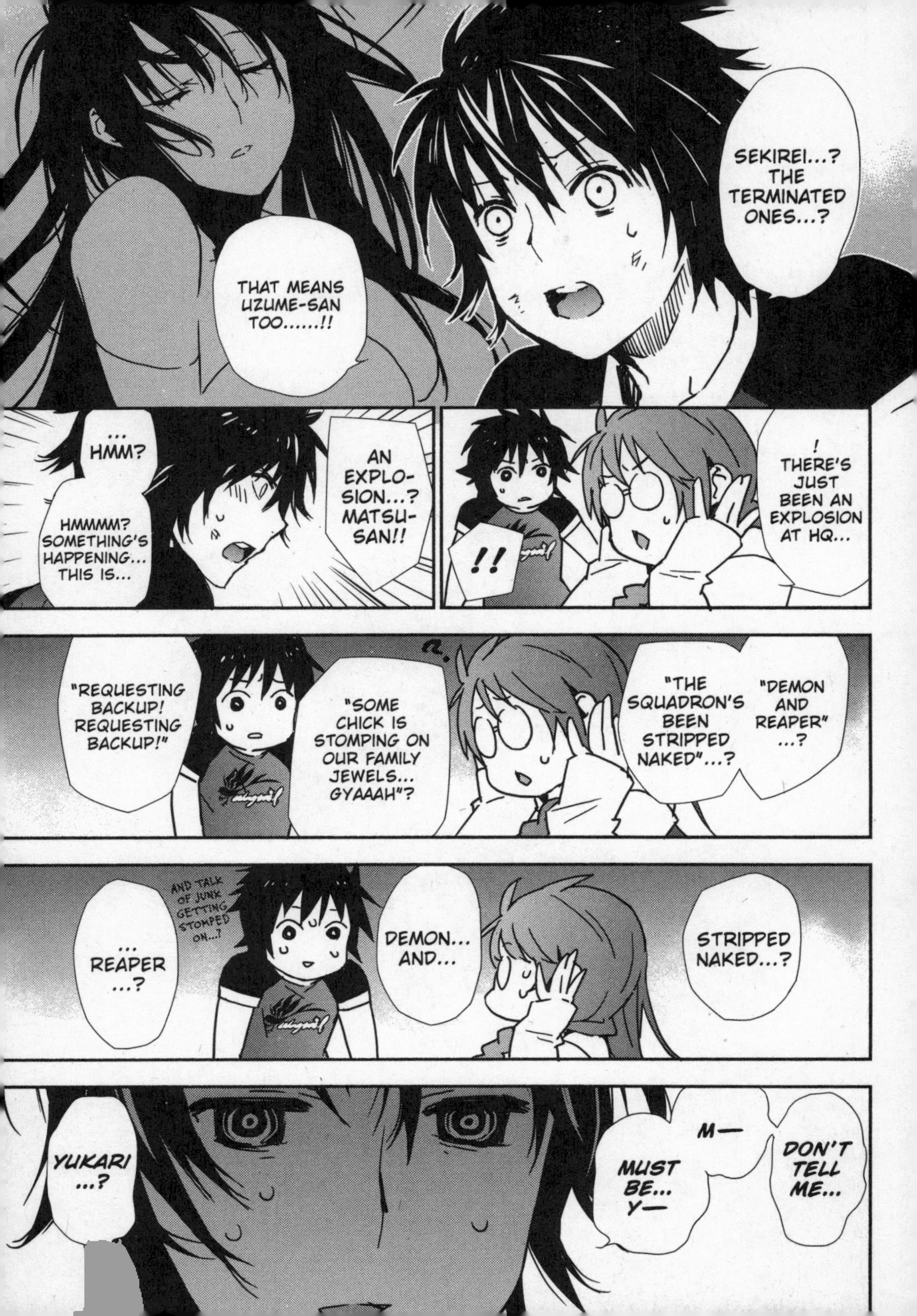
SEKIREI...? THE TERMINATED ONES...?
THAT MEANS UZUME-SAN TOO......!!
! THERE'S JUST BEEN AN EXPLOSION AT HQ...
!!
AN EXPLOSION...? MATSU-SAN!!
... HMM?
HMMMM? SOMETHING'S HAPPENING... THIS IS...
"DEMON AND REAPER"...?
"THE SQUADRON'S BEEN STRIPPED NAKED"...?
"SOME CHICK IS STOMPING ON OUR FAMILY JEWELS... GYAAAH"?
"REQUESTING BACKUP! REQUESTING BACKUP!"
STRIPPED NAKED...?
DEMON... AND...
AND TALK OF JUNK GETTING STOMPED ON...?
... REAPER ...?
DON'T TELL ME...
M—
MUST BE... Y—
YUKARI ...?

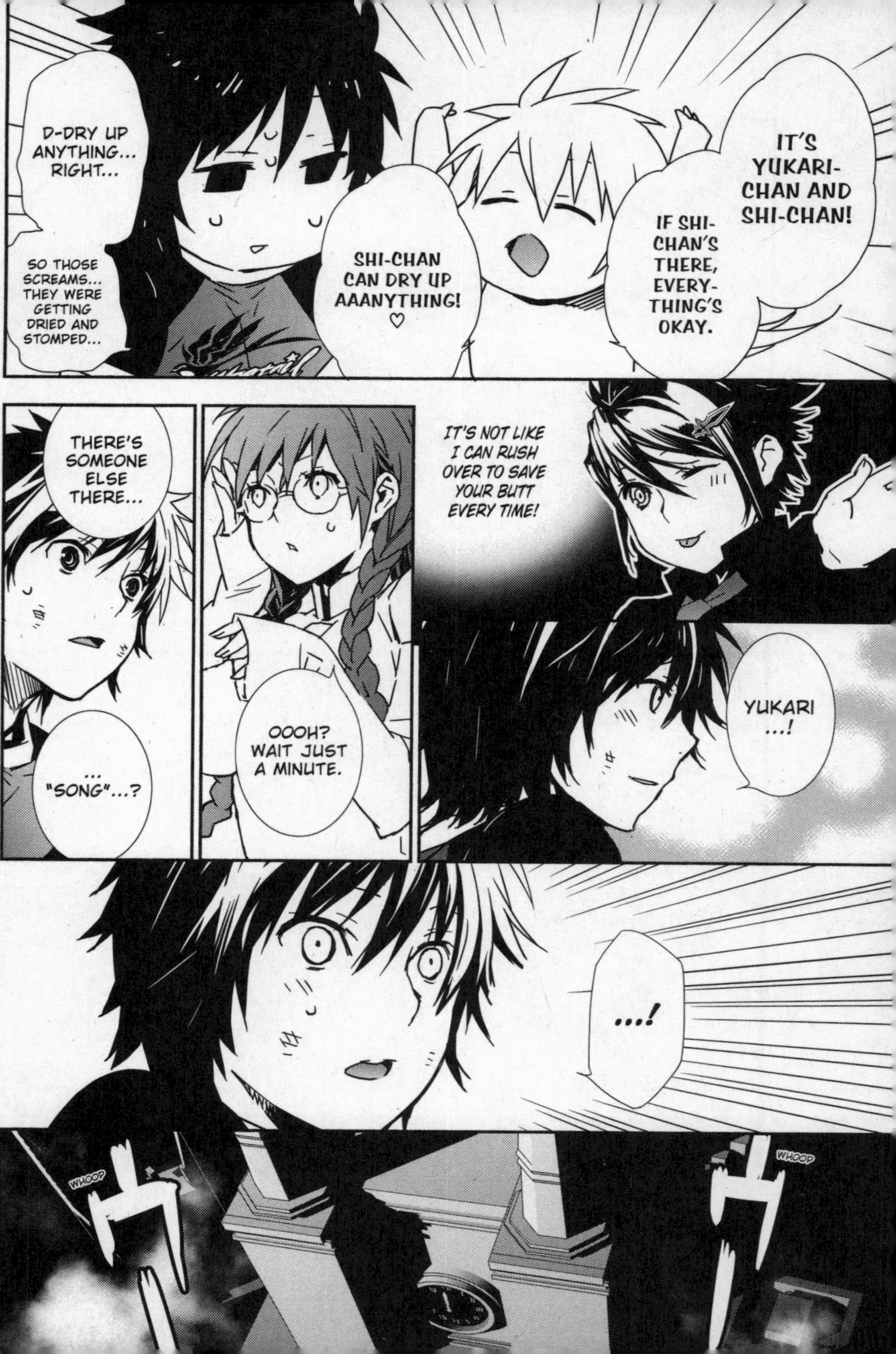
IT'S YUKARI-CHAN AND SHI-CHAN!
IF SHI-CHAN'S THERE, EVERYTHING'S OKAY.
SHI-CHAN CAN DRY UP AAANYTHING! ♡
D-DRY UP ANYTHING... RIGHT...
SO THOSE SCREAMS... THEY WERE GETTING DRIED AND STOMPED...
IT'S NOT LIKE I CAN RUSH OVER TO SAVE YOUR BUTT EVERY TIME!
YUKARI ...!
OOOH? WAIT JUST A MINUTE.
THERE'S SOMEONE ELSE THERE...
... "SONG"...?
...!
WHOOP
WHOOP

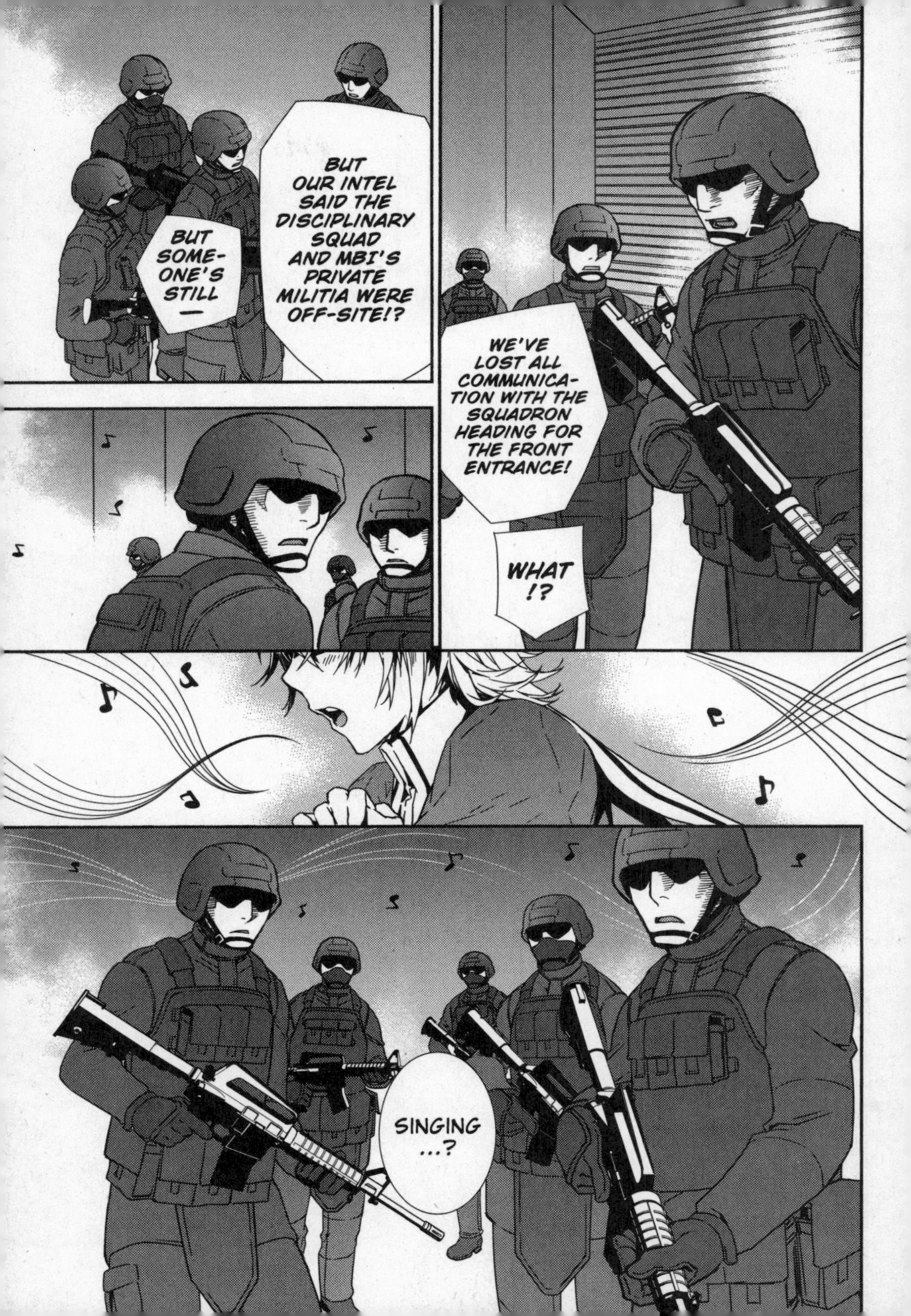
WE'VE LOST ALL COMMUNICATION WITH THE SQUADRON HEADING FOR THE FRONT ENTRANCE!
WHAT!?
BUT OUR INTEL SAID THE DISCIPLINARY SQUAD AND MBI'S PRIVATE MILITIA WERE OFF-SITE!?
BUT SOME-ONE'S STILL —
SINGING ...?

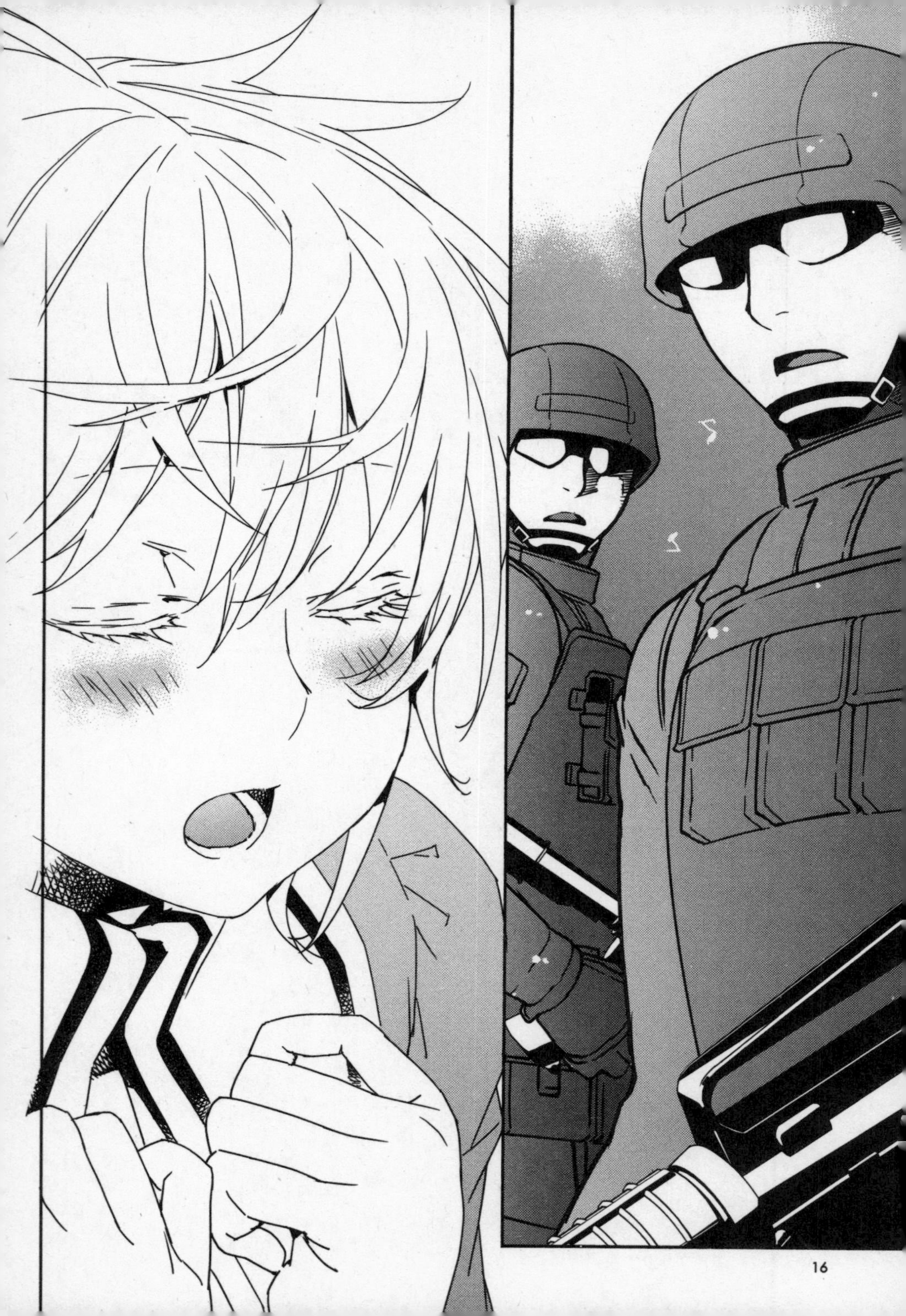

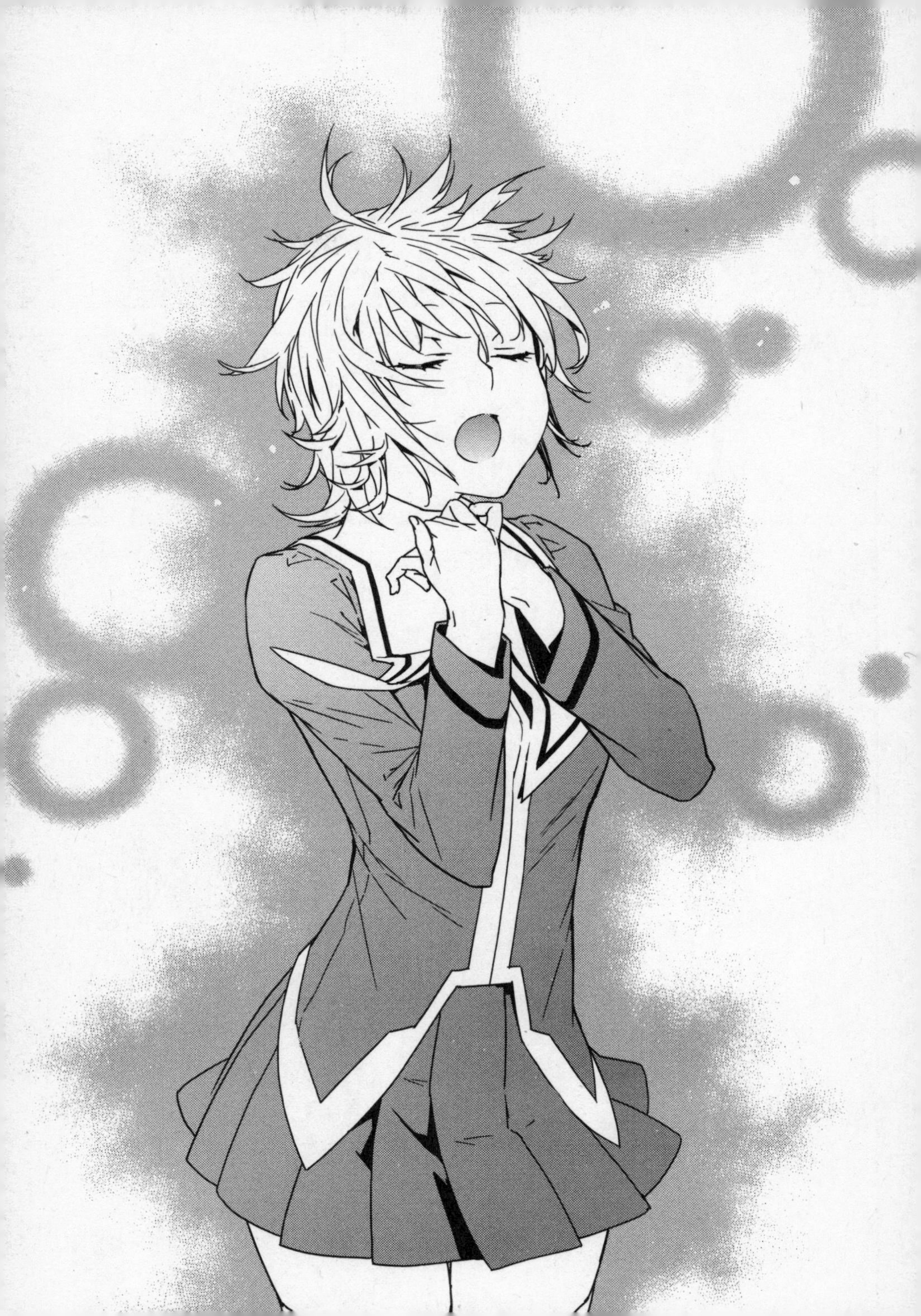

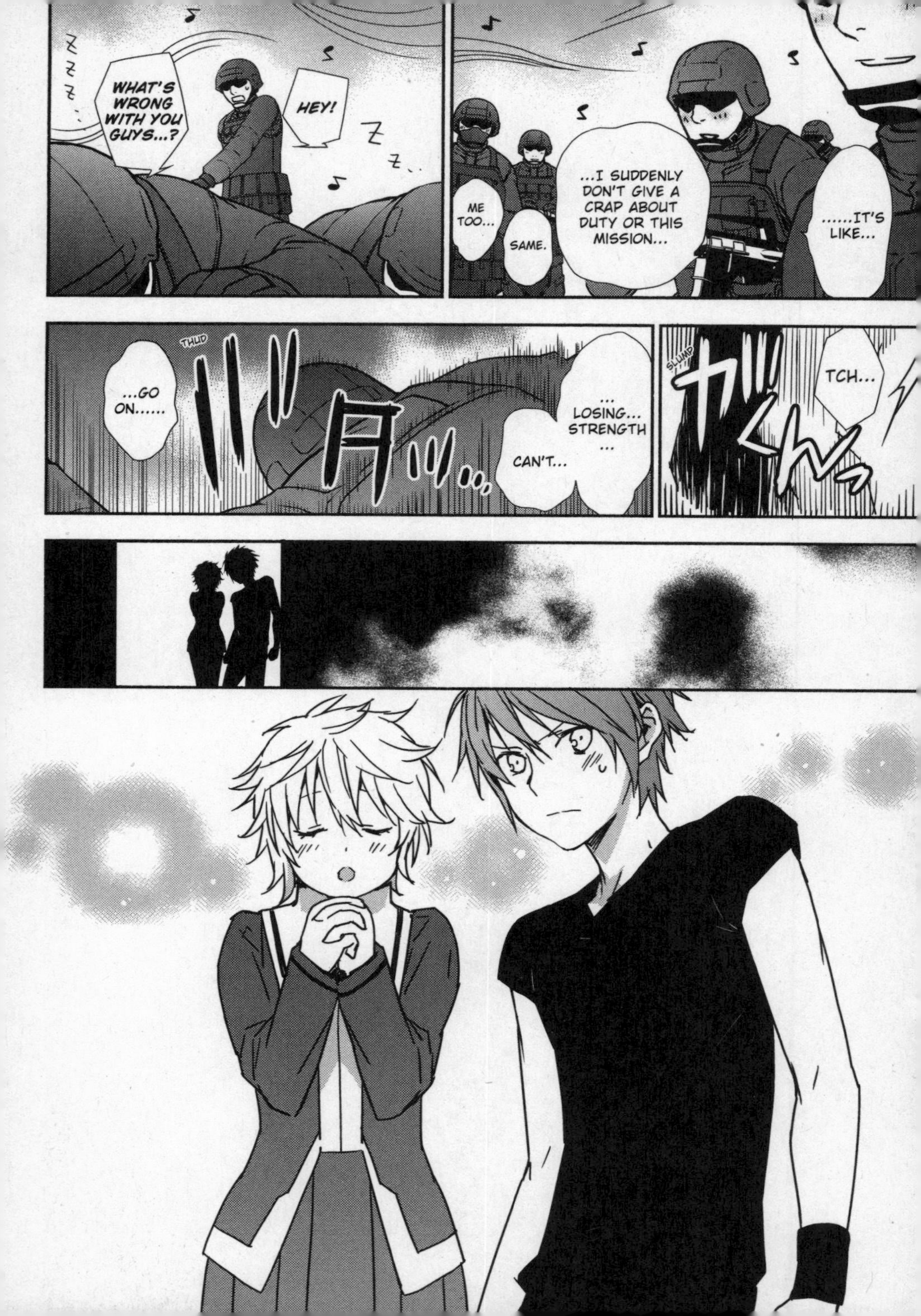

......IT'S LIKE...
...I SUDDENLY DON'T GIVE A CRAP ABOUT DUTY OR THIS MISSION...
SAME.
ME TOO...
HEY!
WHAT'S WRONG WITH YOU GUYS...?
SLUMP
TCH...
... LOSING... STRENGTH ...
CAN'T...
THUD
...GO ON......

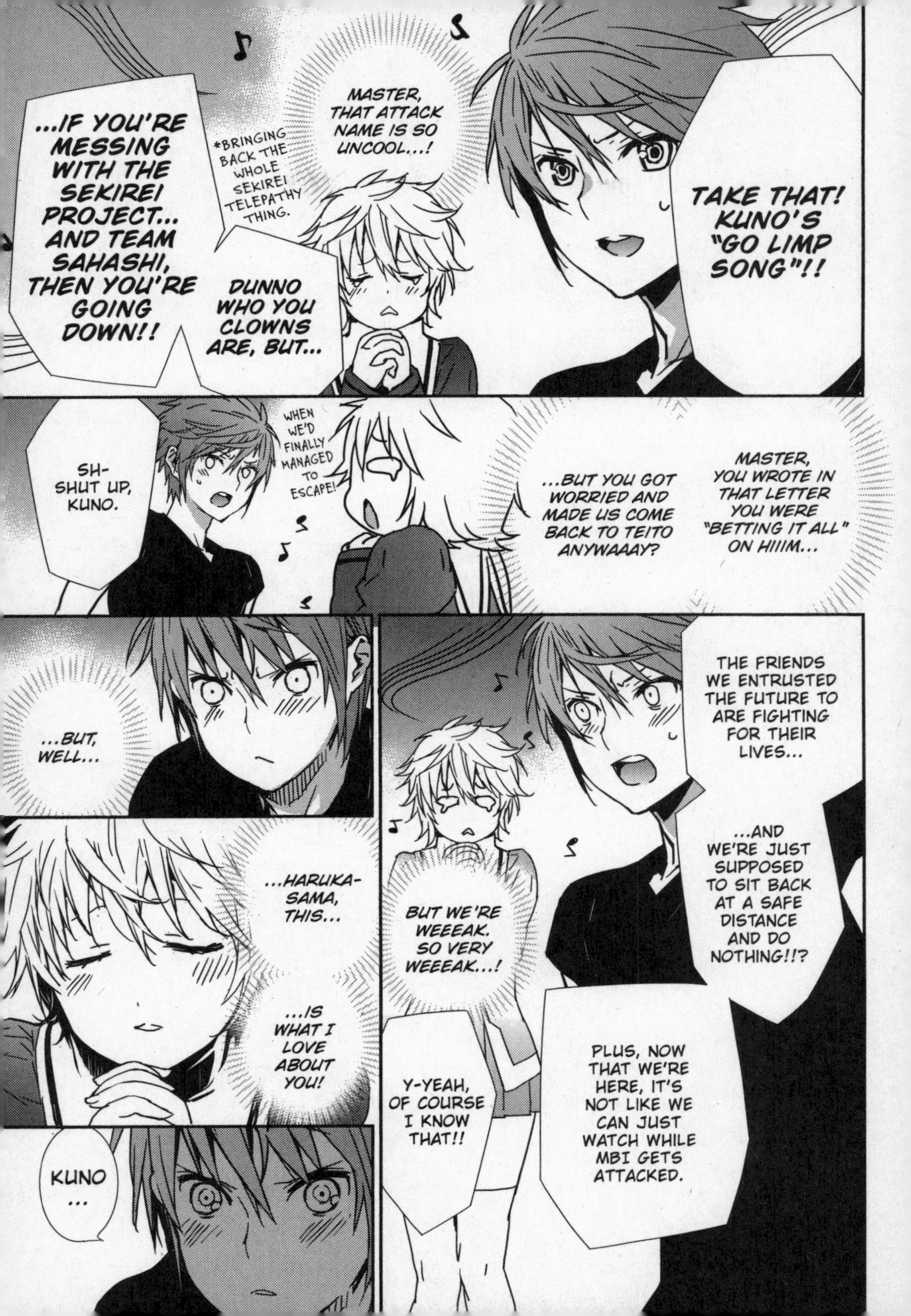
TAKE THAT! KUNO'S "GO LIMP SONG"!!
MASTER, THAT ATTACK NAME IS SO UNCOOL...!
*BRINGING BACK THE WHOLE SEKIREI TELEPATHY THING.
DUNNO WHO YOU CLOWNS ARE, BUT...
...IF YOU'RE MESSING WITH THE SEKIREI PROJECT... AND TEAM SAHASHI, THEN YOU'RE GOING DOWN!!
MASTER, YOU WROTE IN THAT LETTER YOU WERE "BETTING IT ALL" ON HIIIM...
...BUT YOU GOT WORRIED AND MADE US COME BACK TO TEITO ANYWAAAY?
WHEN WE'D FINALLY MANAGED TO ESCAPE!
SH-SHUT UP, KUNO.
THE FRIENDS WE ENTRUSTED THE FUTURE TO ARE FIGHTING FOR THEIR LIVES...
...AND WE'RE JUST SUPPOSED TO SIT BACK AT A SAFE DISTANCE AND DO NOTHING!!?
BUT WE'RE WEEEAK. SO VERY WEEEAK...!
PLUS, NOW THAT WE'RE HERE, IT'S NOT LIKE WE CAN JUST WATCH WHILE MBI GETS ATTACKED.
Y-YEAH, OF COURSE I KNOW THAT!!
...BUT, WELL...
...HARUKA-SAMA, THIS...
...IS WHAT I LOVE ABOUT YOU!
KUNO ...

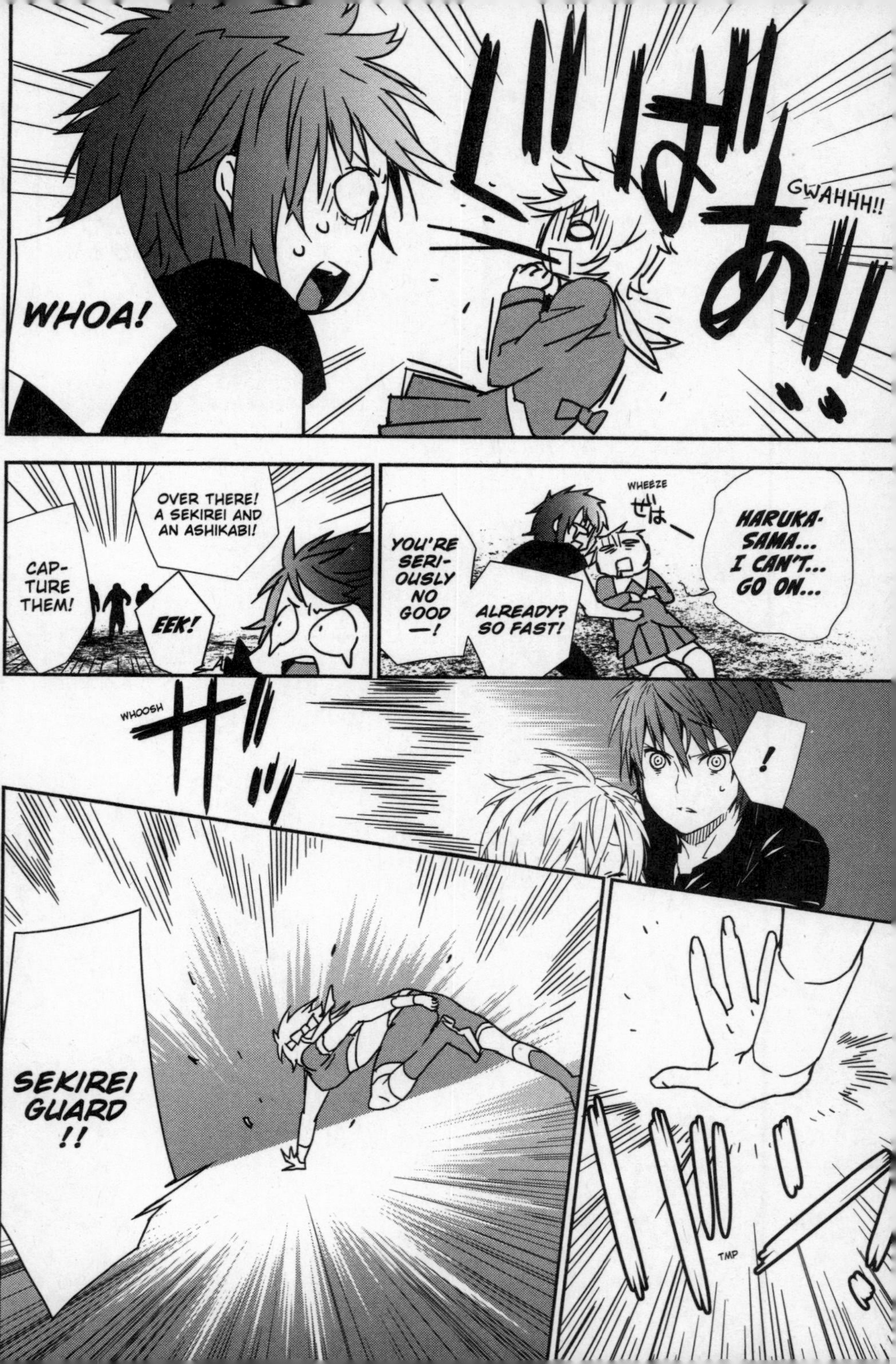
GWAHHH!!
WHOA!
HARUKA-SAMA... I CAN'T... GO ON...
WHEEZE
ぜは—
ALREADY? SO FAST!
YOU'RE SERIOUSLY NO GOOD—!
OVER THERE! A SEKIREI AND AN ASHIKABI!
EEK!
CAPTURE THEM!
!
WHOOSH
TMP
SEKIREI GUARD!!

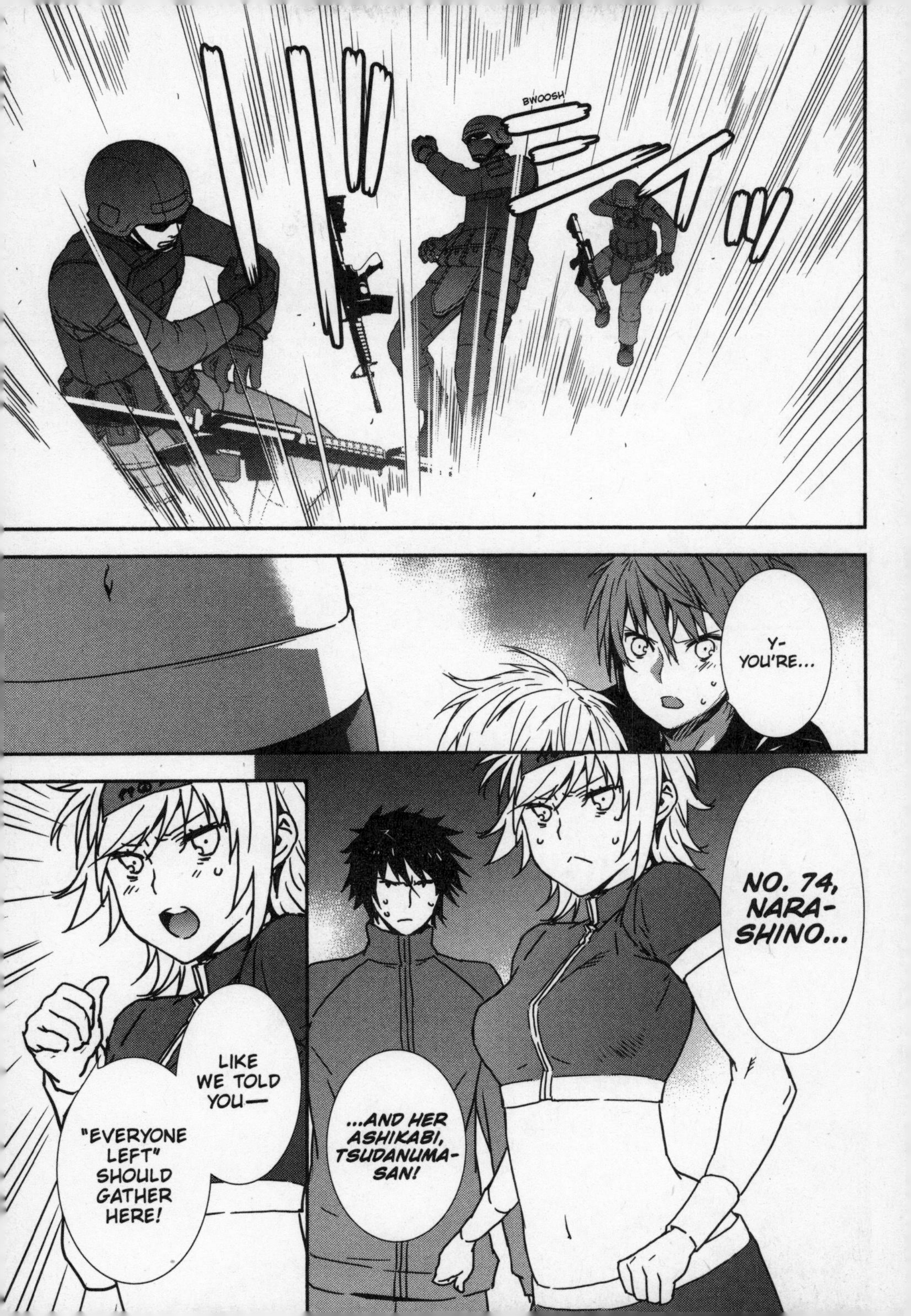
BWOOSH
Y-YOU'RE...
NO. 74, NARA-SHINO...
...AND HER ASHIKABI, TSUDANUMA-SAN!
LIKE WE TOLD YOU—
"EVERYONE LEFT" SHOULD GATHER HERE!

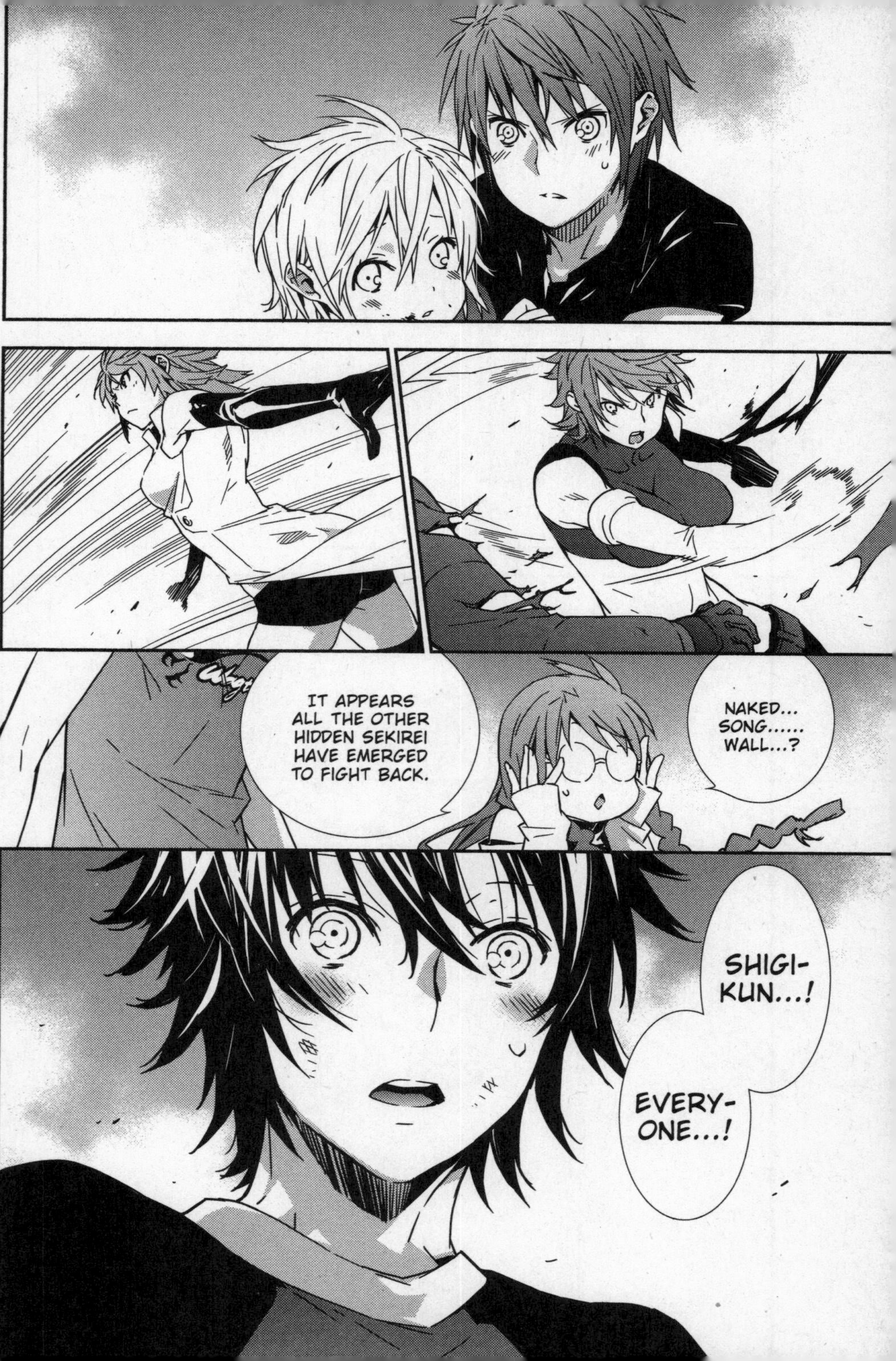
NAKED... SONG...... WALL...?
IT APPEARS ALL THE OTHER HIDDEN SEKIREI HAVE EMERGED TO FIGHT BACK.
SHIGI-KUN...!
EVERY-ONE...!

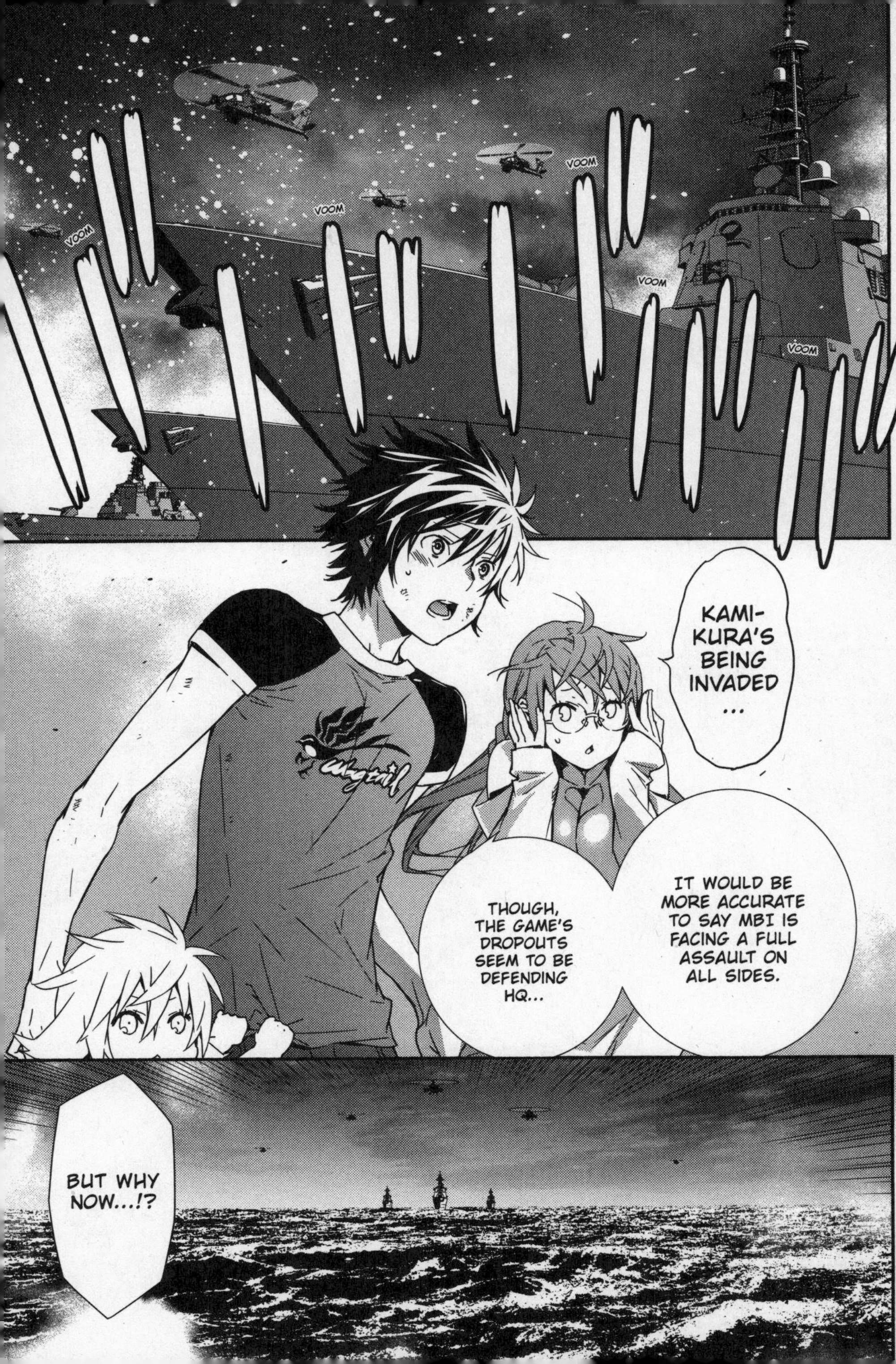
VOOM
VOOM
VOOM
VOOM
VOOM
VOOM
KAMI-KURA'S BEING INVADED...
IT WOULD BE MORE ACCURATE TO SAY MBI IS FACING A FULL ASSAULT ON ALL SIDES.
THOUGH, THE GAME'S DROPOUTS SEEM TO BE DEFENDING HQ...
BUT WHY NOW...!?

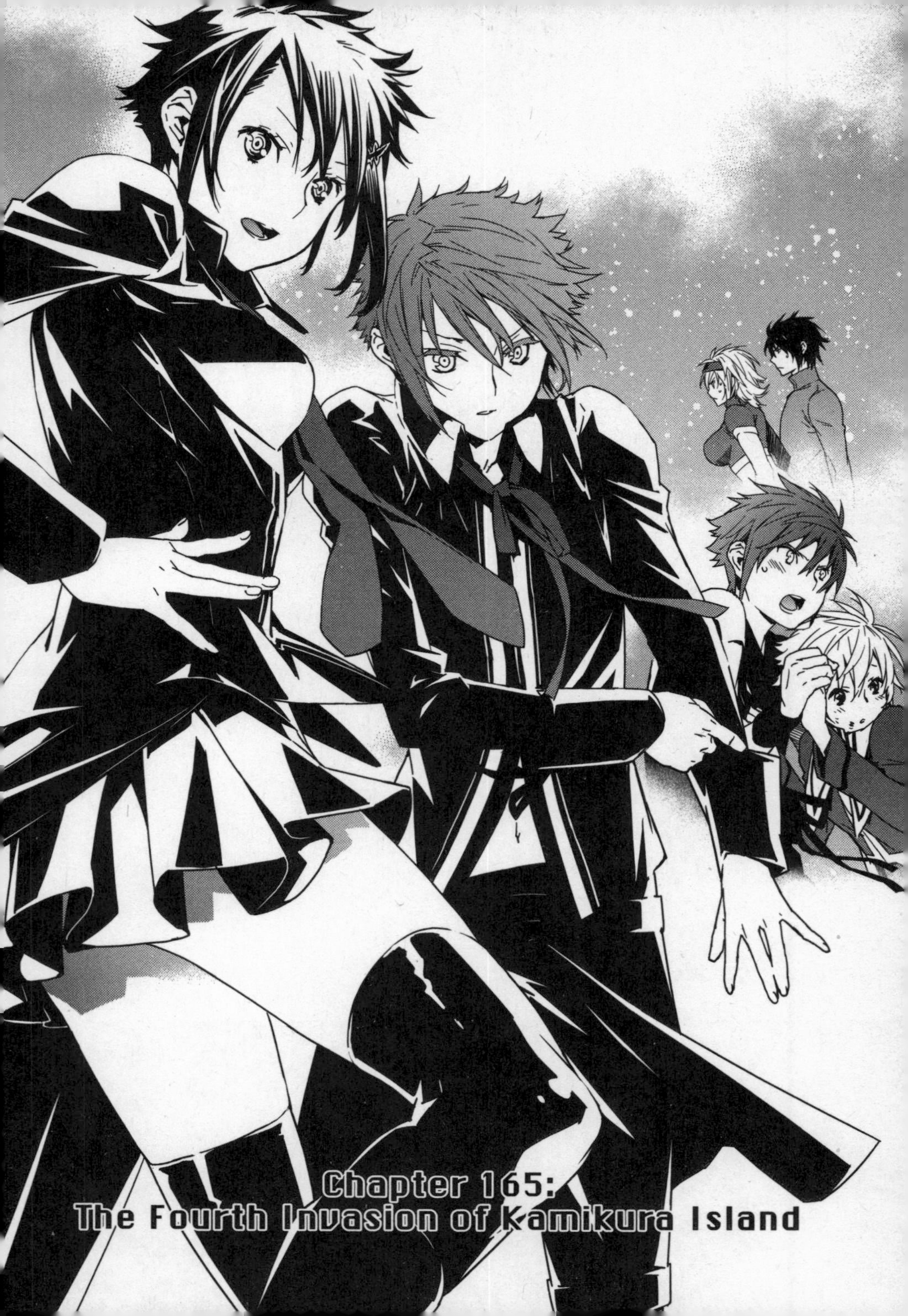
Chapter 165:
The Fourth Invasion of Kamikura Island

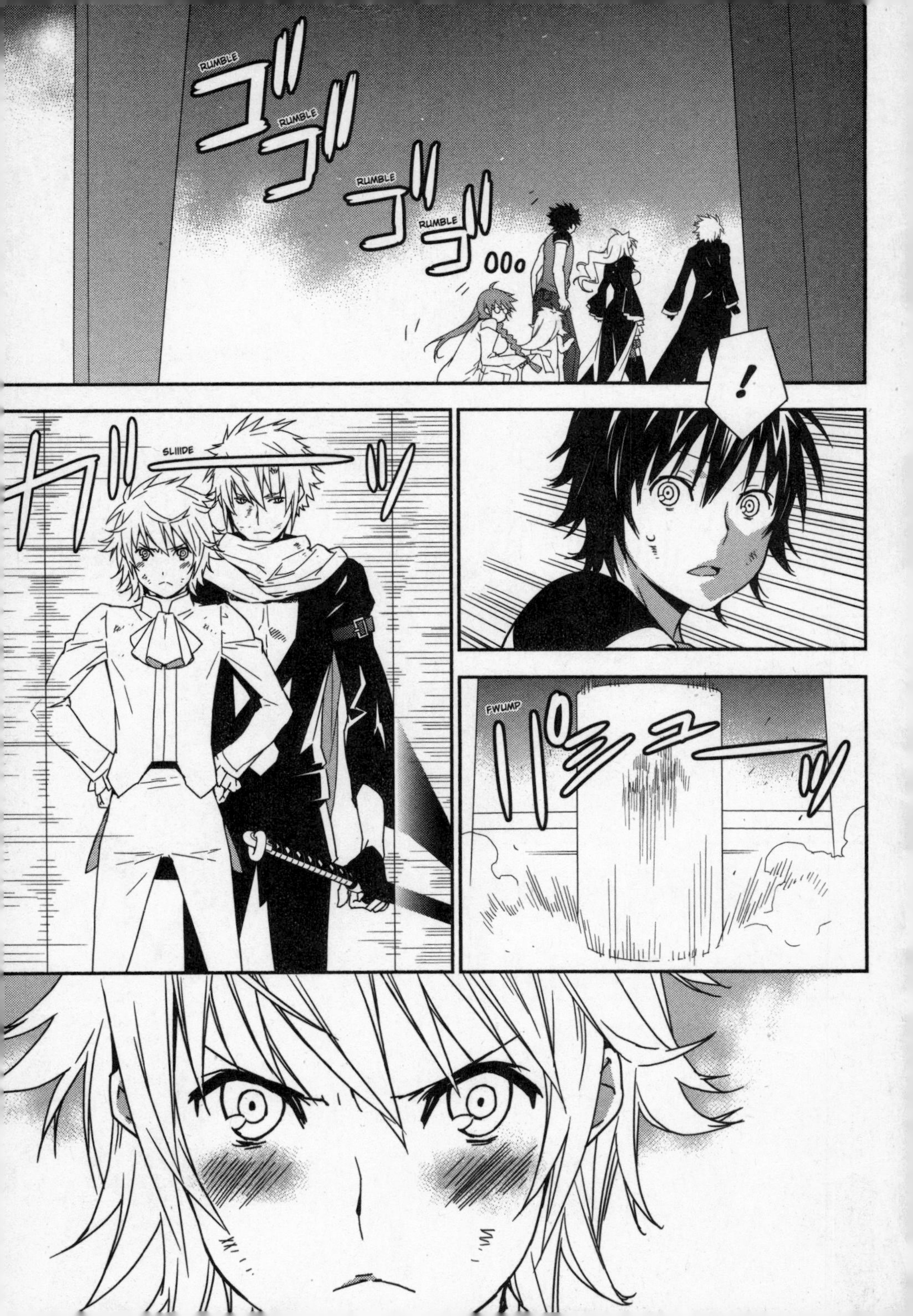
RUMBLE
RUMBLE
RUMBLE
RUMBLE
!
FWUMP
SLIIIDE

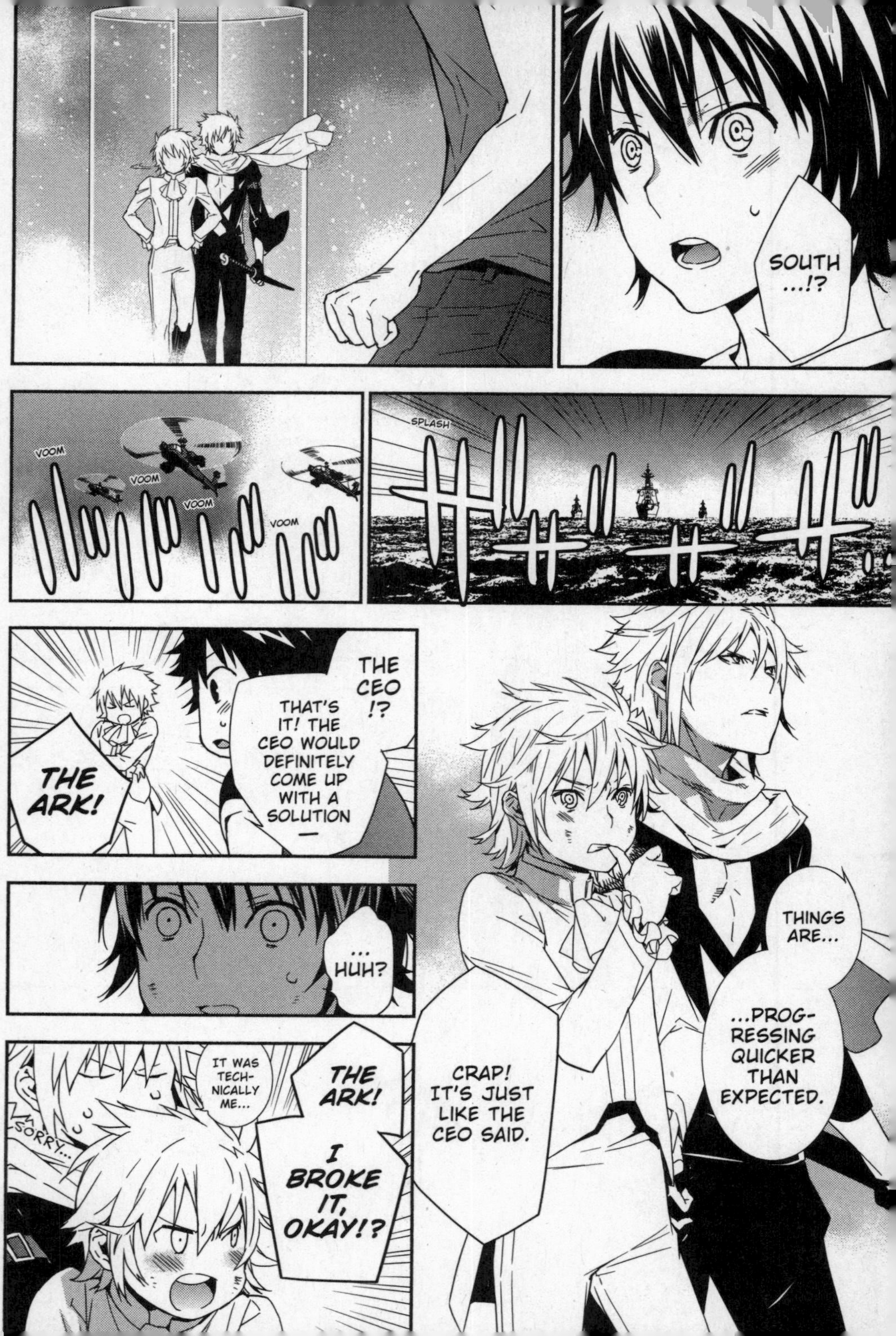
SOUTH ...!?
SPLASH
VOOM
VOOM
VOOM
VOOM
THINGS ARE...
...PROGRESSING QUICKER THAN EXPECTED.
CRAP! IT'S JUST LIKE THE CEO SAID.
THE CEO !?
THAT'S IT! THE CEO WOULD DEFINITELY COME UP WITH A SOLUTION—
THE ARK!
... HUH?
THE ARK!
I BROKE IT, OKAY!?
IT WAS TECHNICALLY ME...
SORRY...

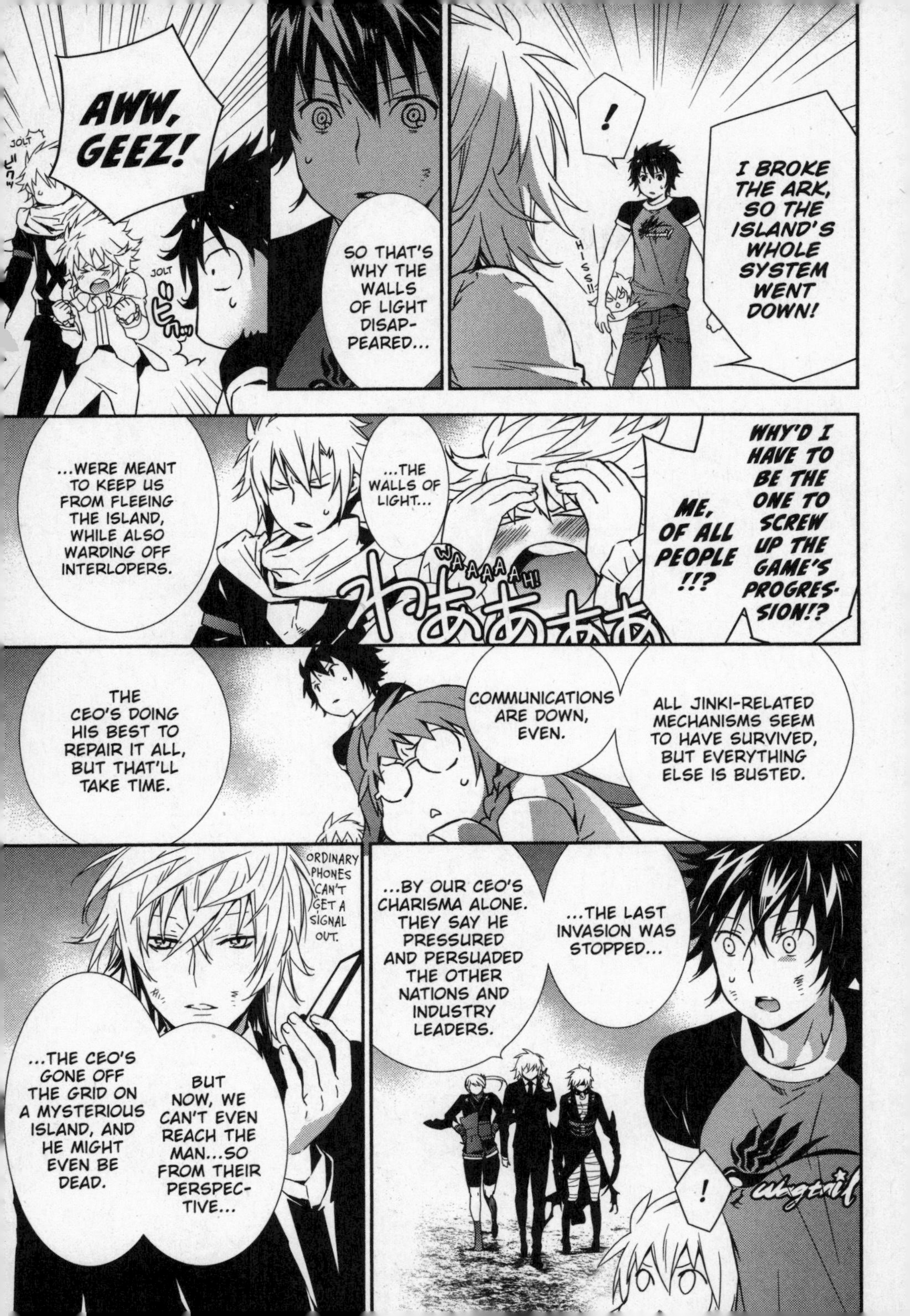
!
HISS!!
I BROKE THE ARK, SO THE ISLAND'S WHOLE SYSTEM WENT DOWN!
SO THAT'S WHY THE WALLS OF LIGHT DISAP-PEARED...
AWW, GEEZ!
JOLT
JOLT
WHY'D I HAVE TO BE THE ONE TO SCREW UP THE GAME'S PROGRES-SION!?
ME, OF ALL PEOPLE!!?
WAAAAAH!
...THE WALLS OF LIGHT...
...WERE MEANT TO KEEP US FROM FLEEING THE ISLAND, WHILE ALSO WARDING OFF INTERLOPERS.
ALL JINKI-RELATED MECHANISMS SEEM TO HAVE SURVIVED, BUT EVERYTHING ELSE IS BUSTED.
COMMUNICATIONS ARE DOWN, EVEN.
THE CEO'S DOING HIS BEST TO REPAIR IT ALL, BUT THAT'LL TAKE TIME.
!
...THE LAST INVASION WAS STOPPED...
...BY OUR CEO'S CHARISMA ALONE. THEY SAY HE PRESSURED AND PERSUADED THE OTHER NATIONS AND INDUSTRY LEADERS.
ORDINARY PHONES CAN'T GET A SIGNAL OUT.
BUT NOW, WE CAN'T EVEN REACH THE MAN...SO FROM THEIR PERSPEC-TIVE...
...THE CEO'S GONE OFF THE GRID ON A MYSTERIOUS ISLAND, AND HE MIGHT EVEN BE DEAD.

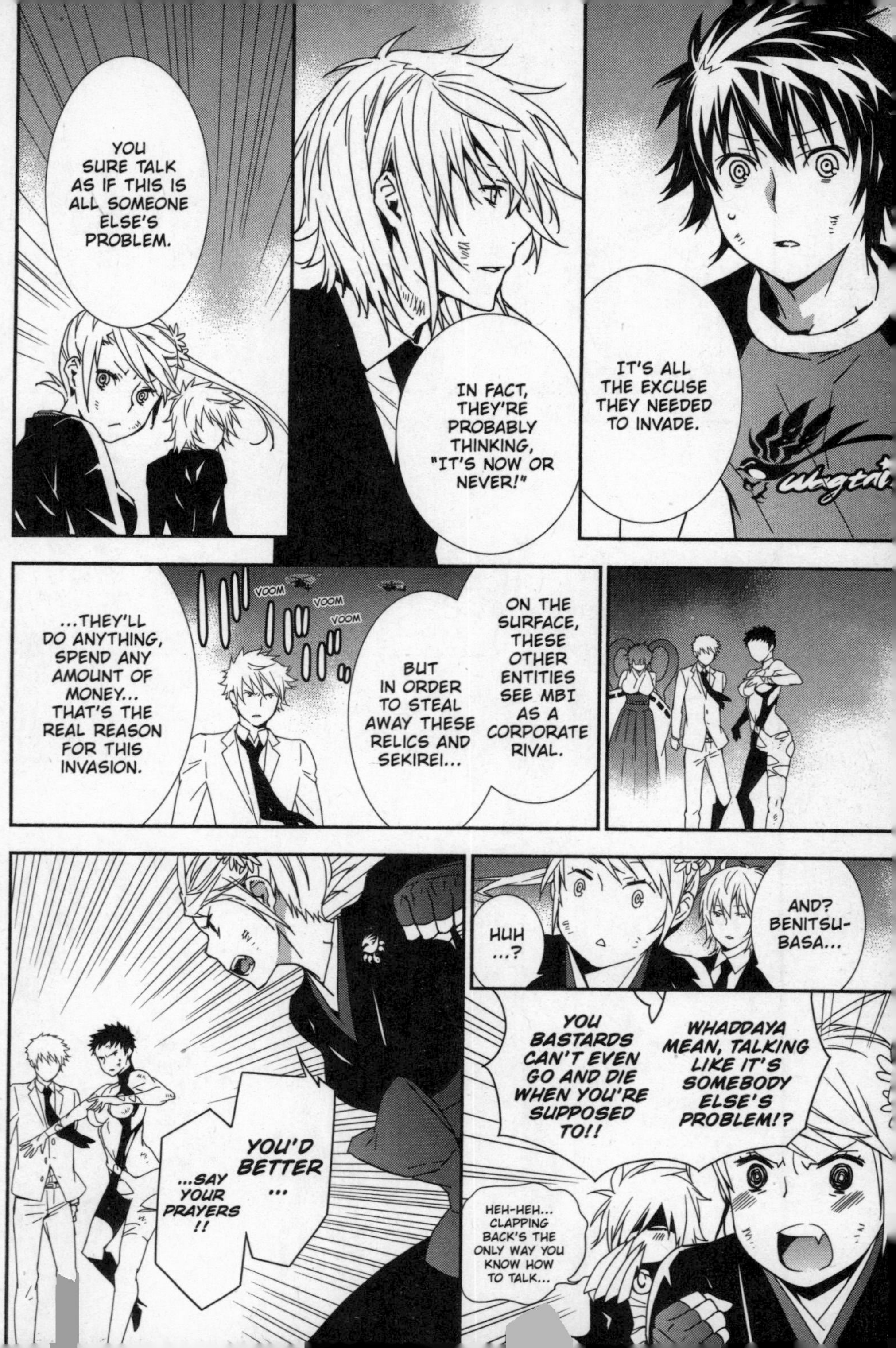

IT'S ALL THE EXCUSE THEY NEEDED TO INVADE.
IN FACT, THEY'RE PROBABLY THINKING, "IT'S NOW OR NEVER!"
YOU SURE TALK AS IF THIS IS ALL SOMEONE ELSE'S PROBLEM.
ON THE SURFACE, THESE OTHER ENTITIES SEE MBI AS A CORPORATE RIVAL.
BUT IN ORDER TO STEAL AWAY THESE RELICS AND SEKIREI...
VOOM
VOOM
VOOM
...THEY'LL DO ANYTHING, SPEND ANY AMOUNT OF MONEY... THAT'S THE REAL REASON FOR THIS INVASION.
AND? BENITSU-BASA...
HUH ...?
WHADDAYA MEAN, TALKING LIKE IT'S SOMEBODY ELSE'S PROBLEM!?
YOU BASTARDS CAN'T EVEN GO AND DIE WHEN YOU'RE SUPPOSED TO!!
HEH-HEH... CLAPPING BACK'S THE ONLY WAY YOU KNOW HOW TO TALK...
YOU'D BETTER ...
...SAY YOUR PRAYERS !!

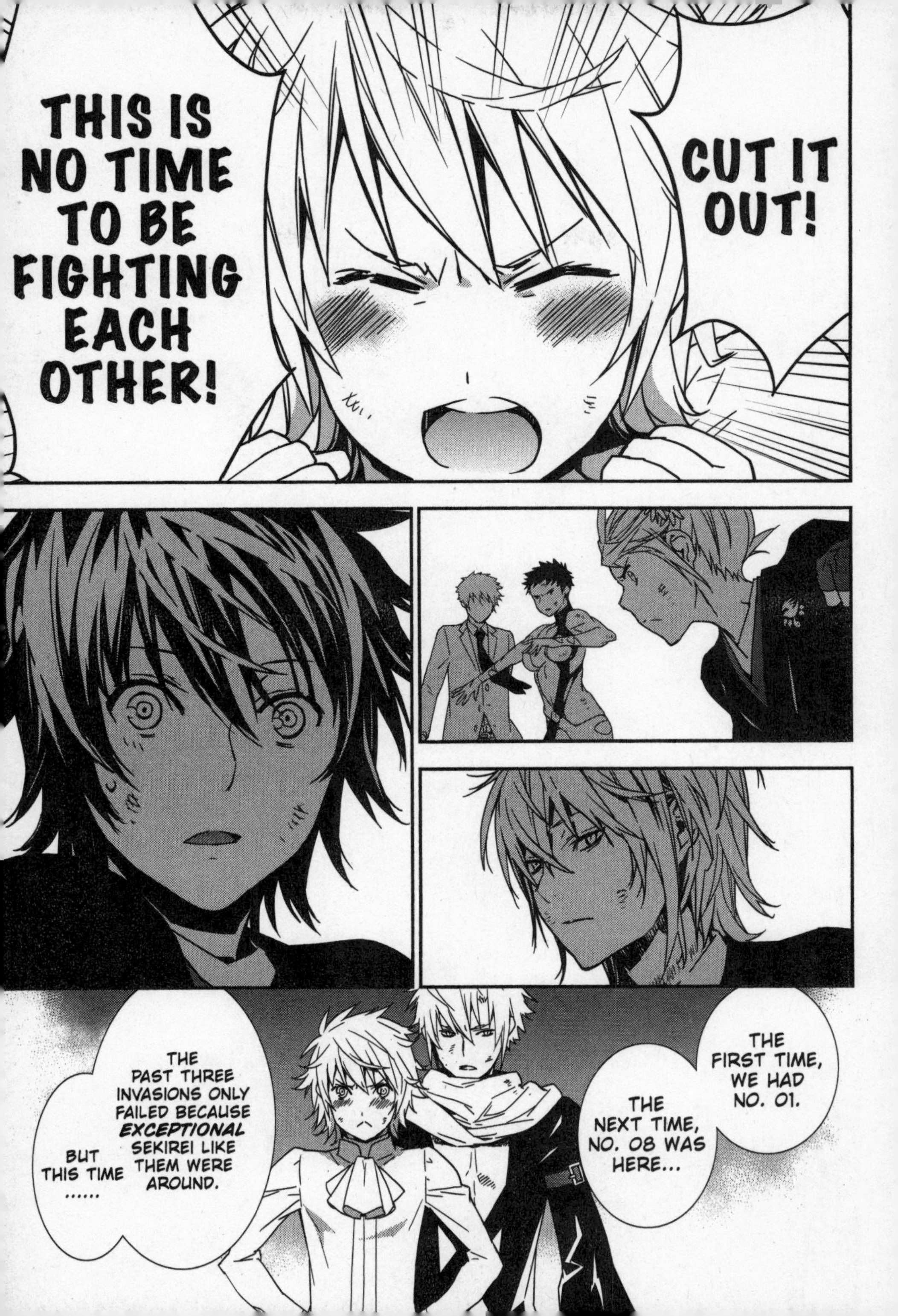
CUT IT OUT!
THIS IS NO TIME TO BE FIGHTING EACH OTHER!
THE FIRST TIME, WE HAD NO. 01.
THE NEXT TIME, NO. 08 WAS HERE...
THE PAST THREE INVASIONS ONLY FAILED BECAUSE *EXCEPTIONAL* SEKIREI LIKE THEM WERE AROUND.
BUT THIS TIME ......

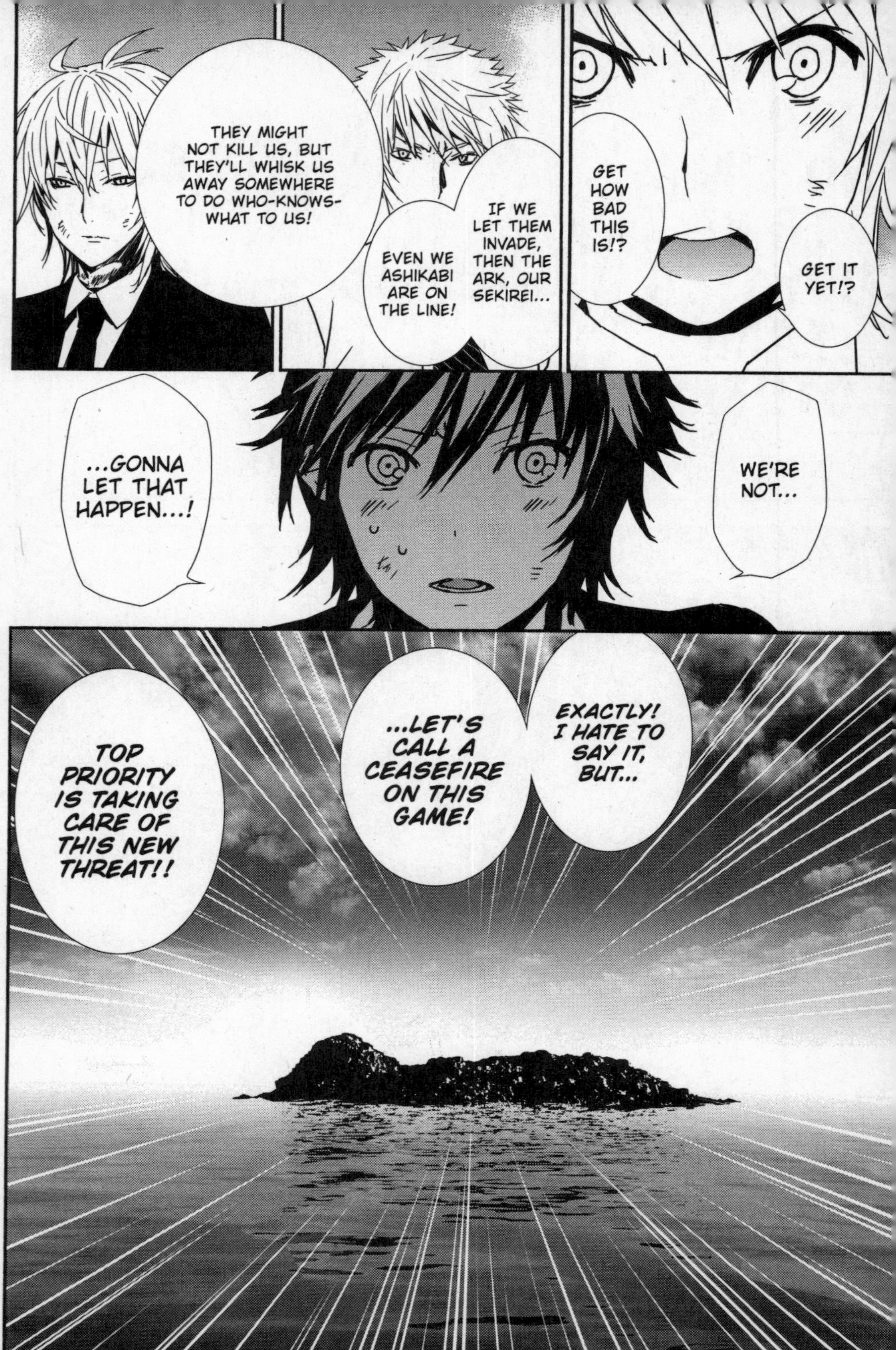
GET HOW BAD THIS IS!?
GET IT YET!?
IF WE LET THEM INVADE, THEN THE ARK, OUR SEKIREI...
EVEN WE ASHIKABI ARE ON THE LINE!
THEY MIGHT NOT KILL US, BUT THEY'LL WHISK US AWAY SOMEWHERE TO DO WHO-KNOWS-WHAT TO US!
WE'RE NOT...
...GONNA LET THAT HAPPEN...!
EXACTLY! I HATE TO SAY IT, BUT...
...LET'S CALL A CEASEFIRE ON THIS GAME!
TOP PRIORITY IS TAKING CARE OF THIS NEW THREAT!!

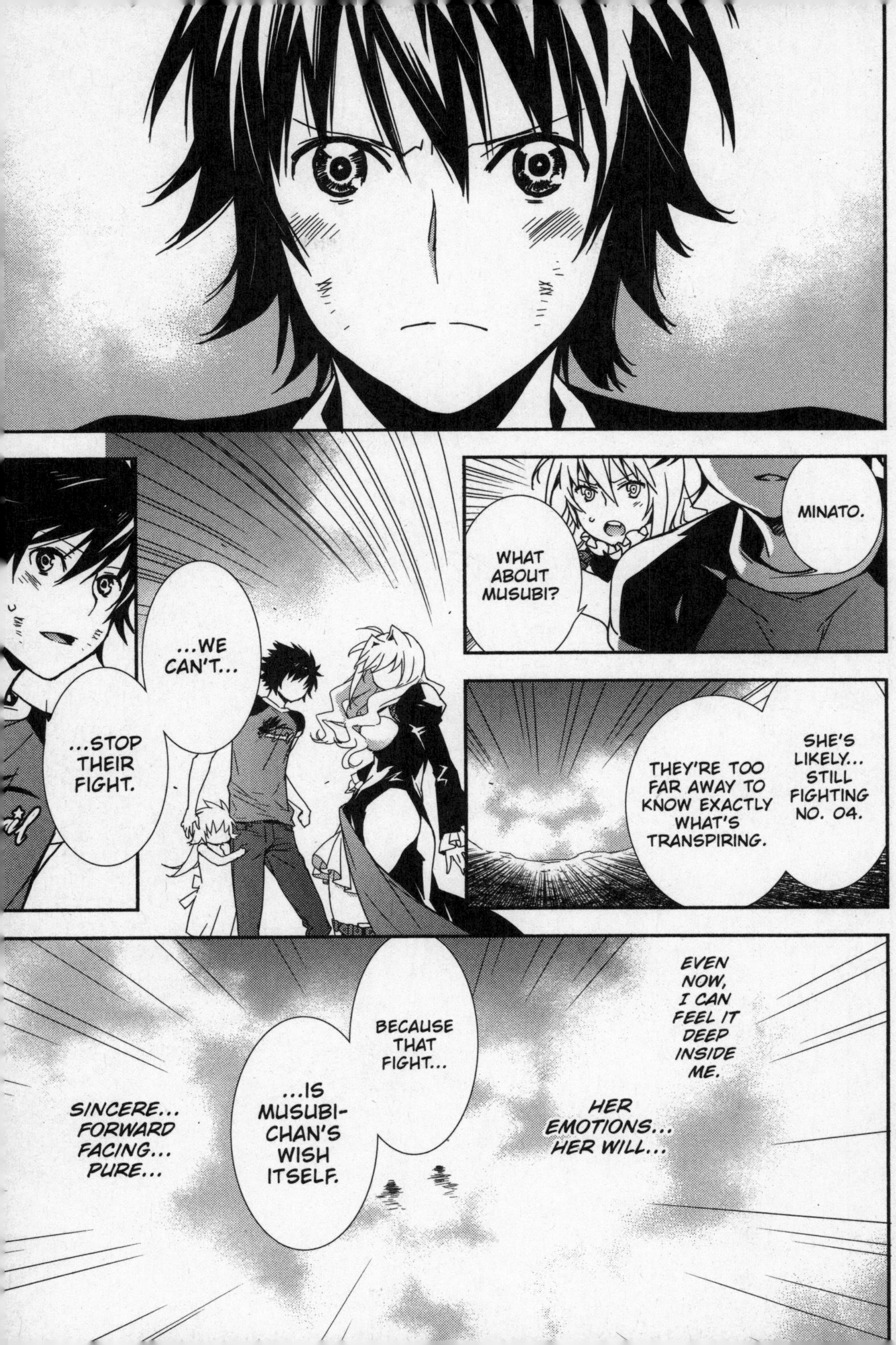
MINATO.
WHAT ABOUT MUSUBI?
SHE'S LIKELY... STILL FIGHTING NO. 04.
THEY'RE TOO FAR AWAY TO KNOW EXACTLY WHAT'S TRANSPIRING.
...WE CAN'T...
...STOP THEIR FIGHT.
EVEN NOW, I CAN FEEL IT DEEP INSIDE ME.
HER EMOTIONS... HER WILL...
BECAUSE THAT FIGHT...
...IS MUSUBI-CHAN'S WISH ITSELF.
SINCERE... FORWARD FACING... PURE...

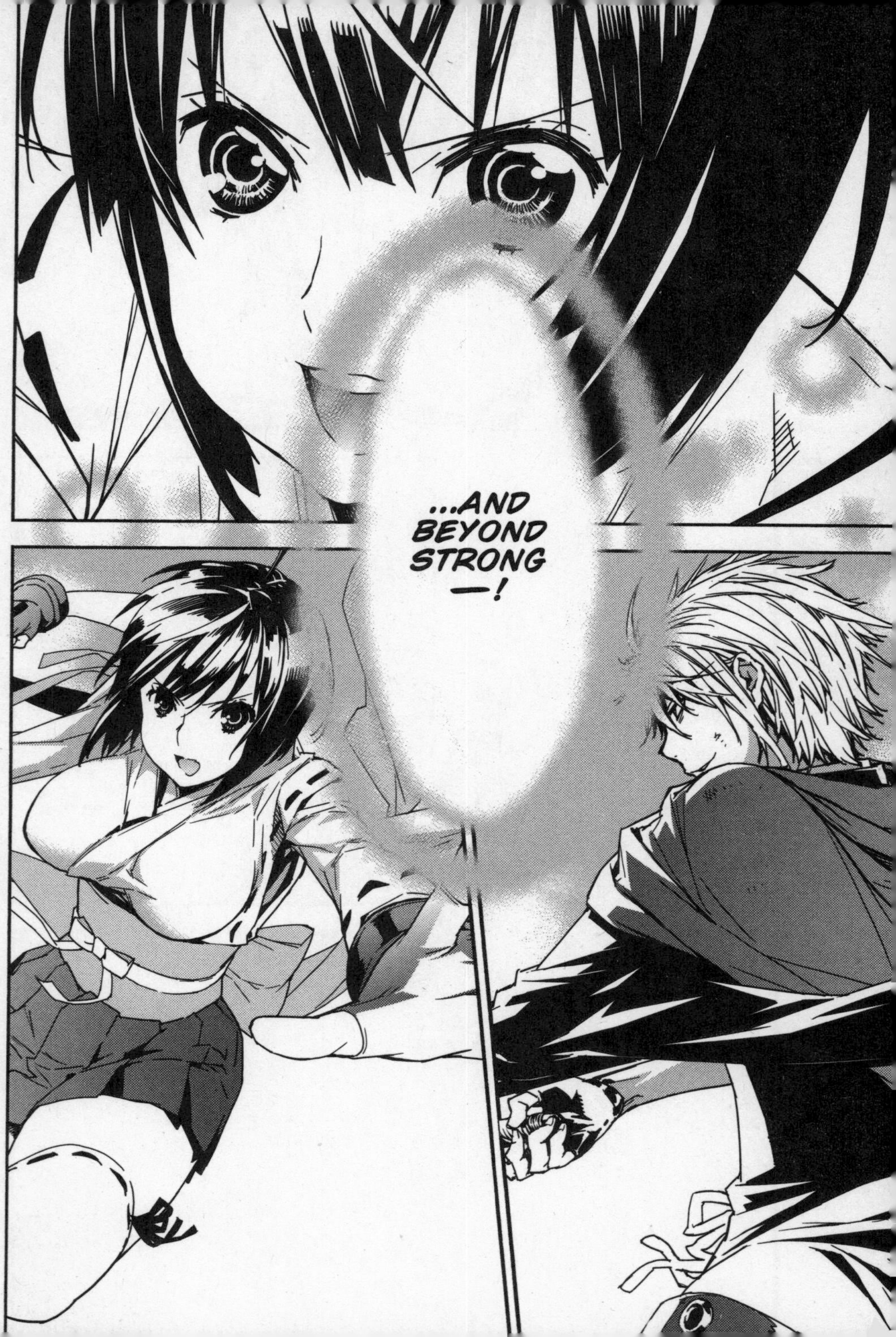
...AND BEYOND STRONG —!

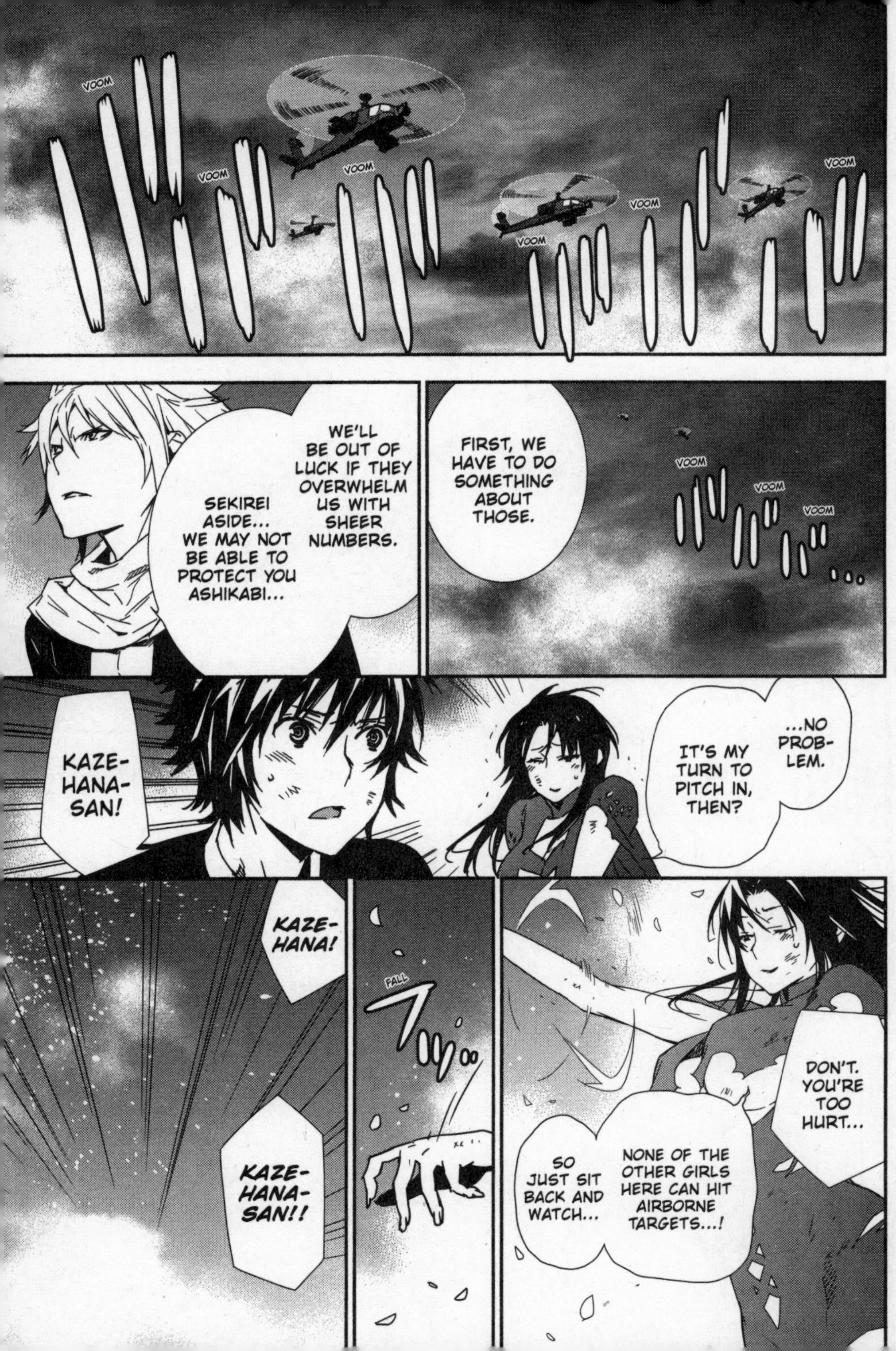
VOOM
VOOM
VOOM
VOOM
VOOM
VOOM
VOOM
FIRST, WE HAVE TO DO SOMETHING ABOUT THOSE.
VOOM
VOOM
VOOM
WE'LL BE OUT OF LUCK IF THEY OVERWHELM US WITH SHEER NUMBERS.
SEKIREI ASIDE... WE MAY NOT BE ABLE TO PROTECT YOU ASHIKABI...
...NO PROBLEM.
IT'S MY TURN TO PITCH IN, THEN?
KAZE-HANA-SAN!
DON'T. YOU'RE TOO HURT...
NONE OF THE OTHER GIRLS HERE CAN HIT AIRBORNE TARGETS...!
SO JUST SIT BACK AND WATCH...
FALL
KAZE-HANA!
KAZE-HANA-SAN!!

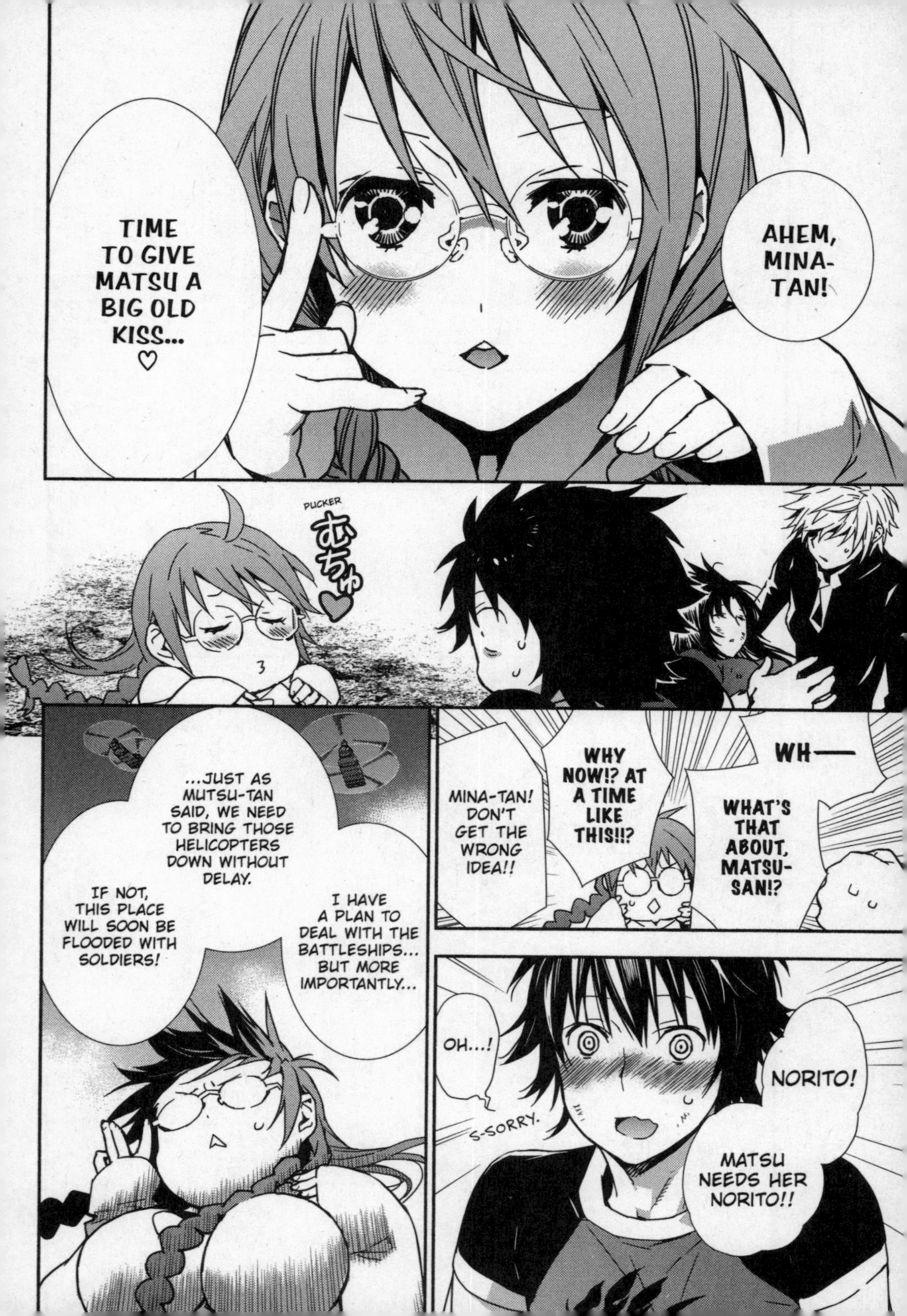
AHEM, MINA-TAN!
TIME TO GIVE MATSU A BIG OLD KISS... ♡
PUCKER
むちゅ
WH—
WHAT'S THAT ABOUT, MATSU-SAN!?
WHY NOW!? AT A TIME LIKE THIS!!?
MINA-TAN! DON'T GET THE WRONG IDEA!!
NORITO!
MATSU NEEDS HER NORITO!!
OH...!
S-SORRY.
...JUST AS MUTSU-TAN SAID, WE NEED TO BRING THOSE HELICOPTERS DOWN WITHOUT DELAY.
I HAVE A PLAN TO DEAL WITH THE BATTLESHIPS... BUT MORE IMPORTANTLY...
IF NOT, THIS PLACE WILL SOON BE FLOODED WITH SOLDIERS!

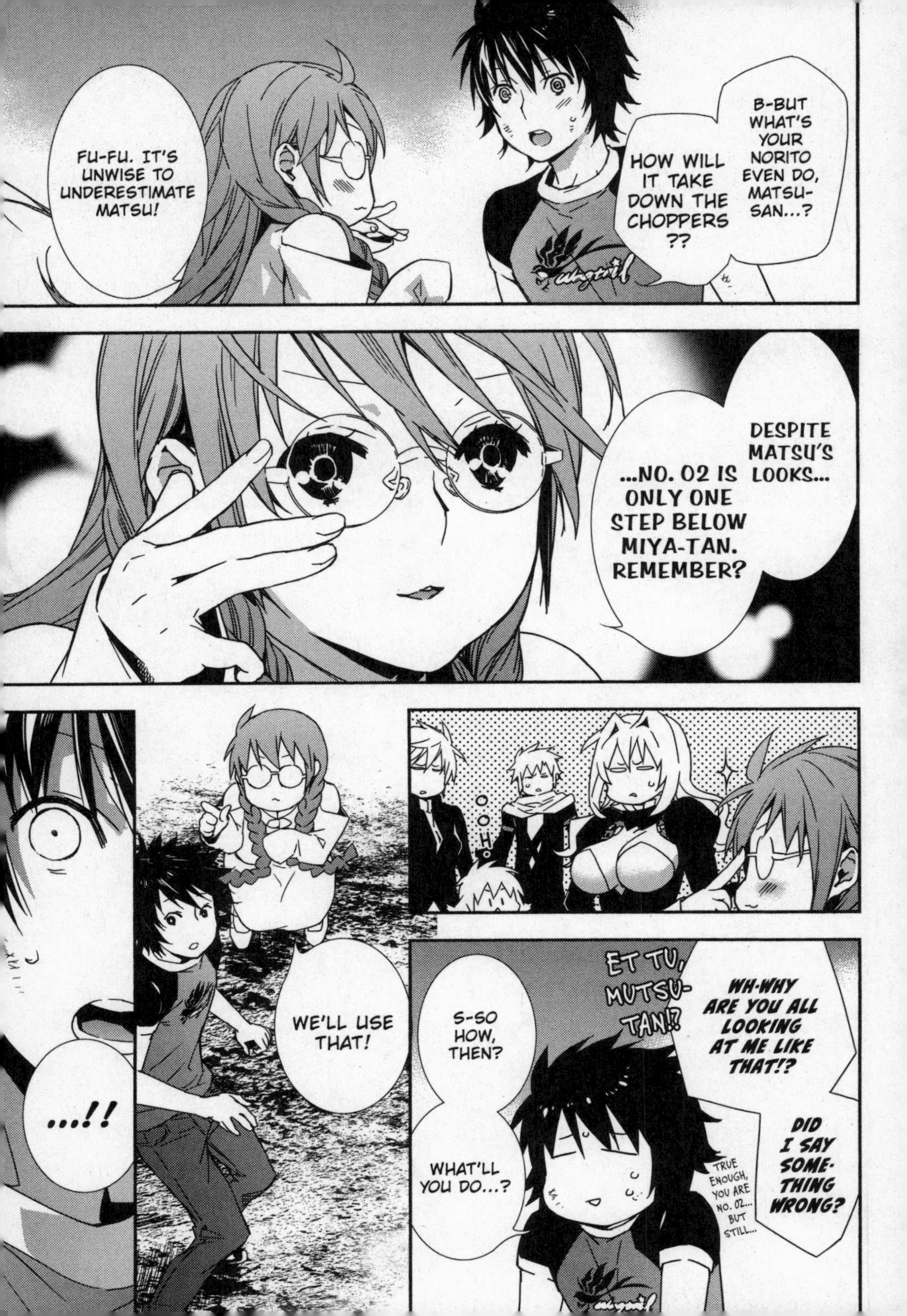

B-BUT WHAT'S YOUR NORITO EVEN DO, MATSU-SAN...?
HOW WILL IT TAKE DOWN THE CHOPPERS??
FU-FU. IT'S UNWISE TO UNDERESTIMATE MATSU!
DESPITE MATSU'S LOOKS...
...NO. 02 IS ONLY ONE STEP BELOW MIYA-TAN. REMEMBER?
OOH
WH-WHY ARE YOU ALL LOOKING AT ME LIKE THAT!?
ET TU, MUTSU-TAN!?
DID I SAY SOMETHING WRONG?
TRUE ENOUGH, YOU ARE NO. 02... BUT STILL...
S-SO HOW, THEN?
WHAT'LL YOU DO...?
WE'LL USE THAT!
...!!

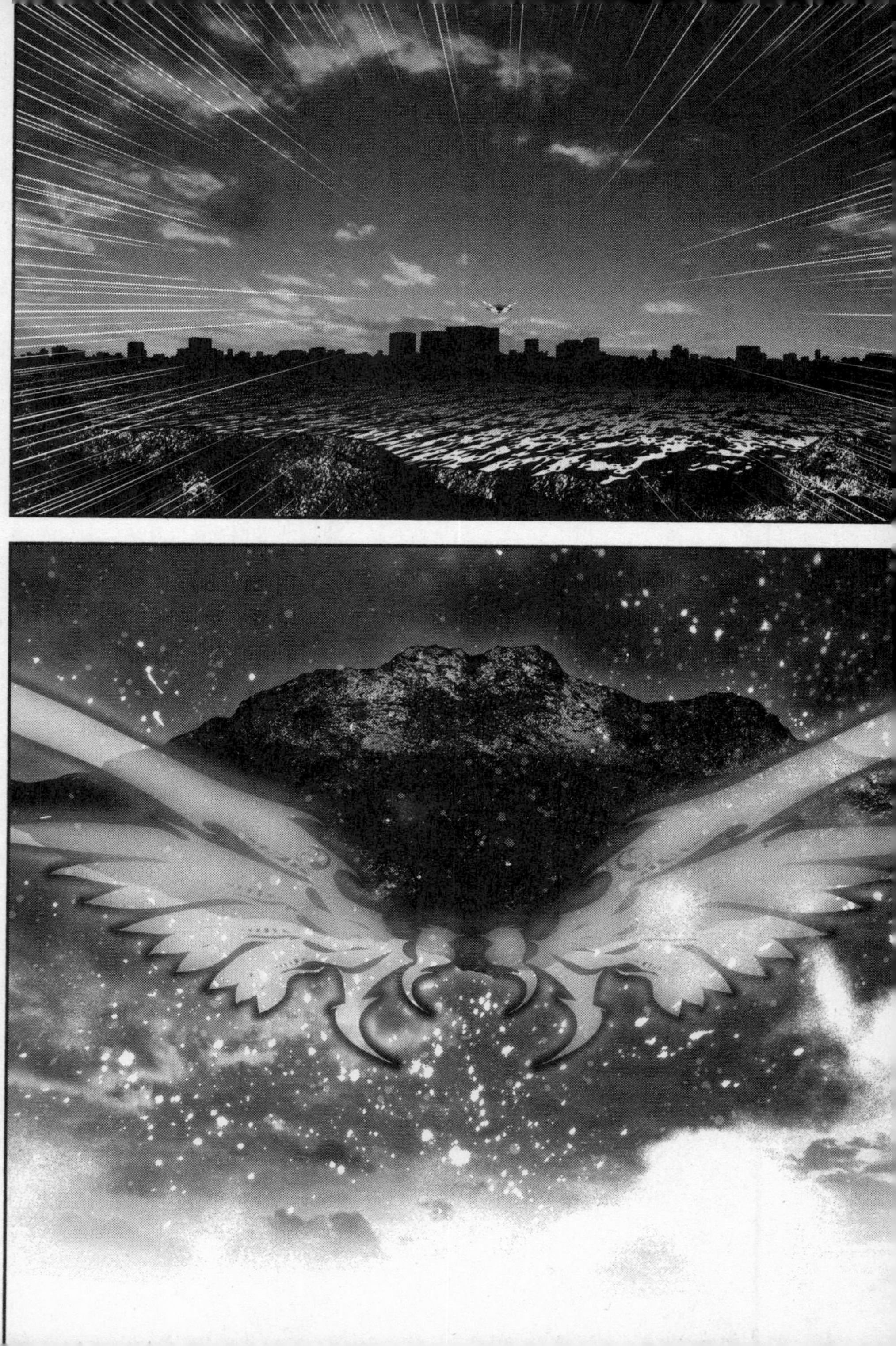

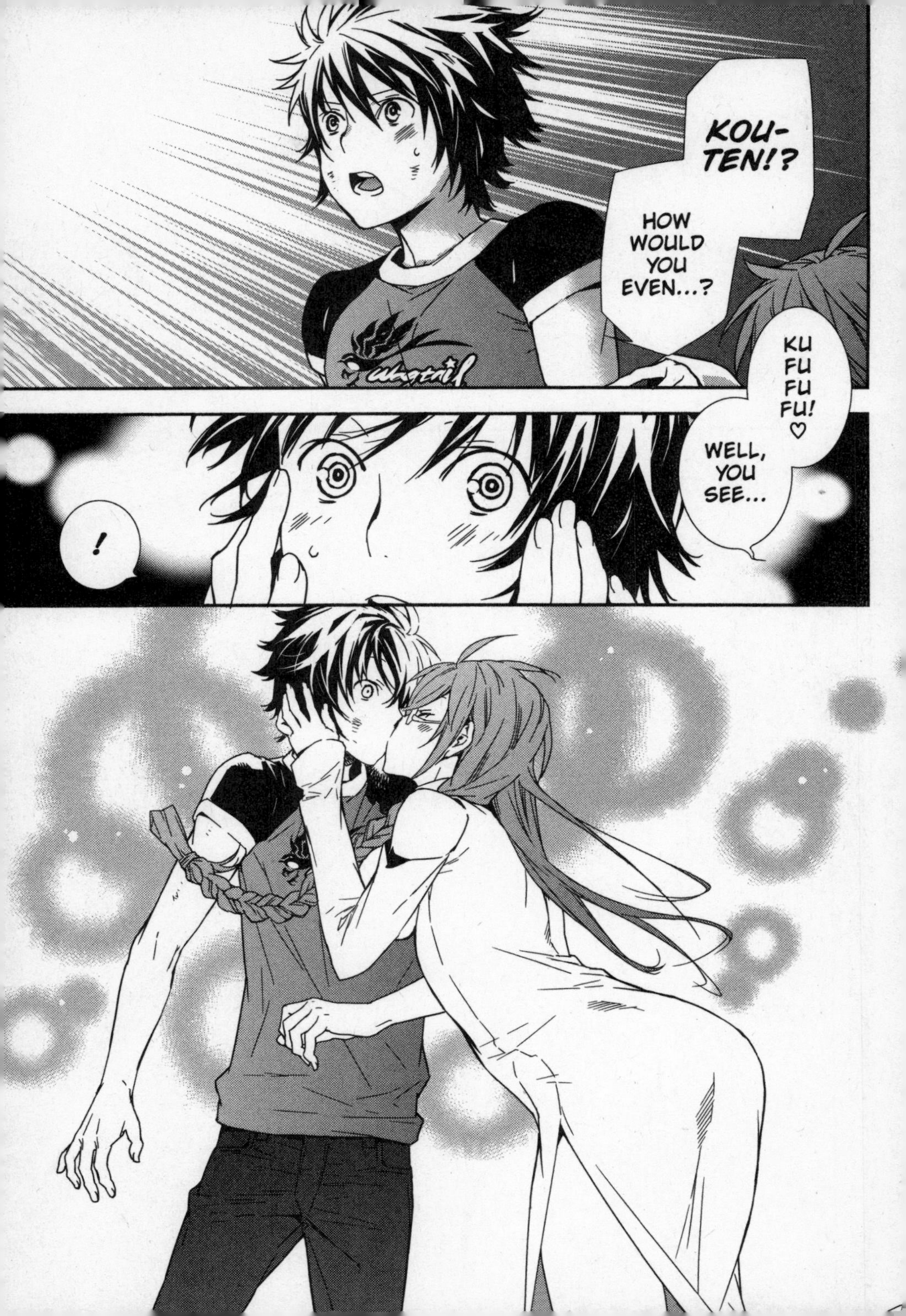
KOU-TEN!?
HOW WOULD YOU EVEN...?
KU FU FU FU! ♡
WELL, YOU SEE...
!

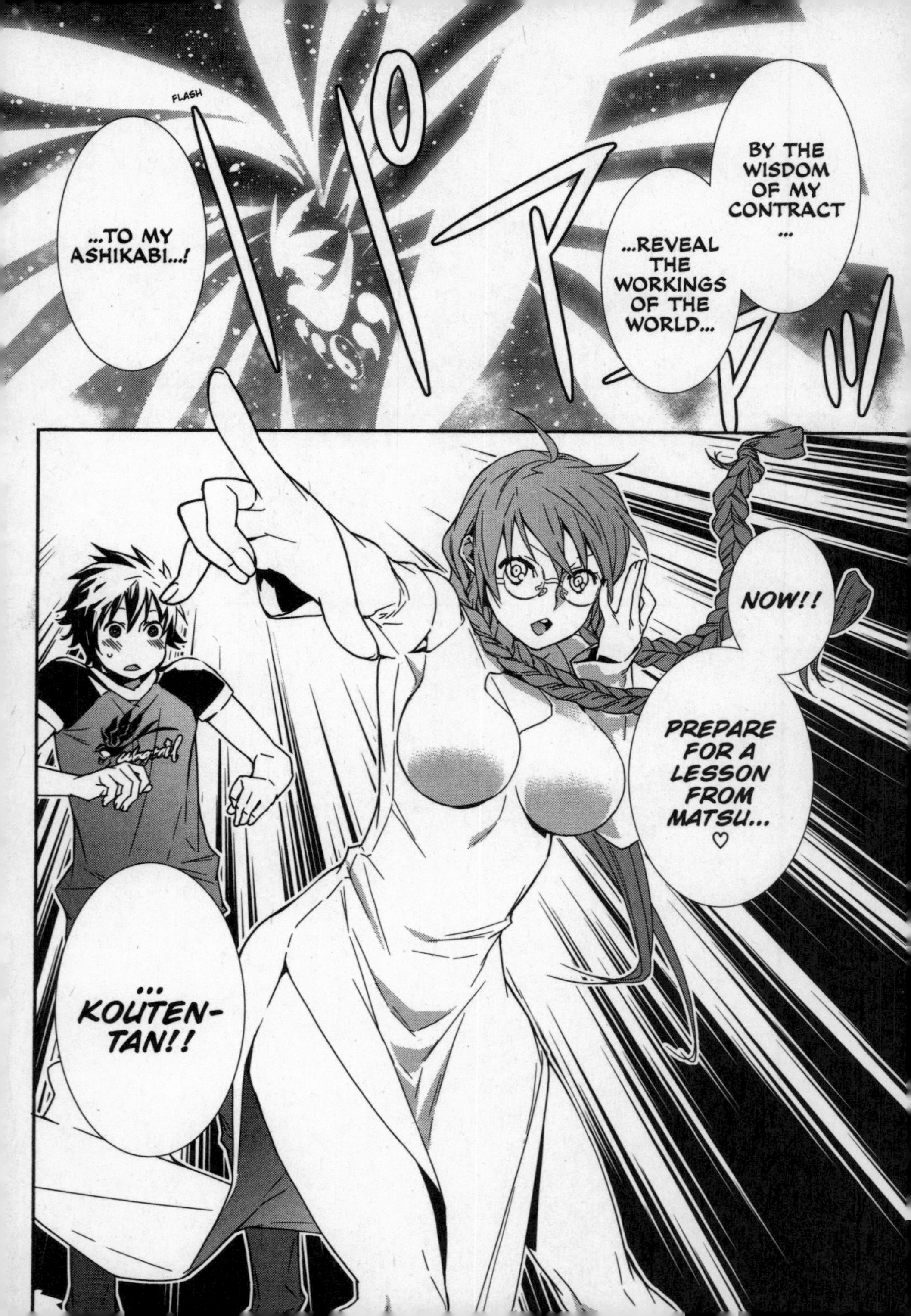
BY THE WISDOM OF MY CONTRACT ...
...REVEAL THE WORKINGS OF THE WORLD...
...TO MY ASHIKABI...!
FLASH
NOW!!
PREPARE FOR A LESSON FROM MATSU... ♡
... KOÜTEN-TAN!!

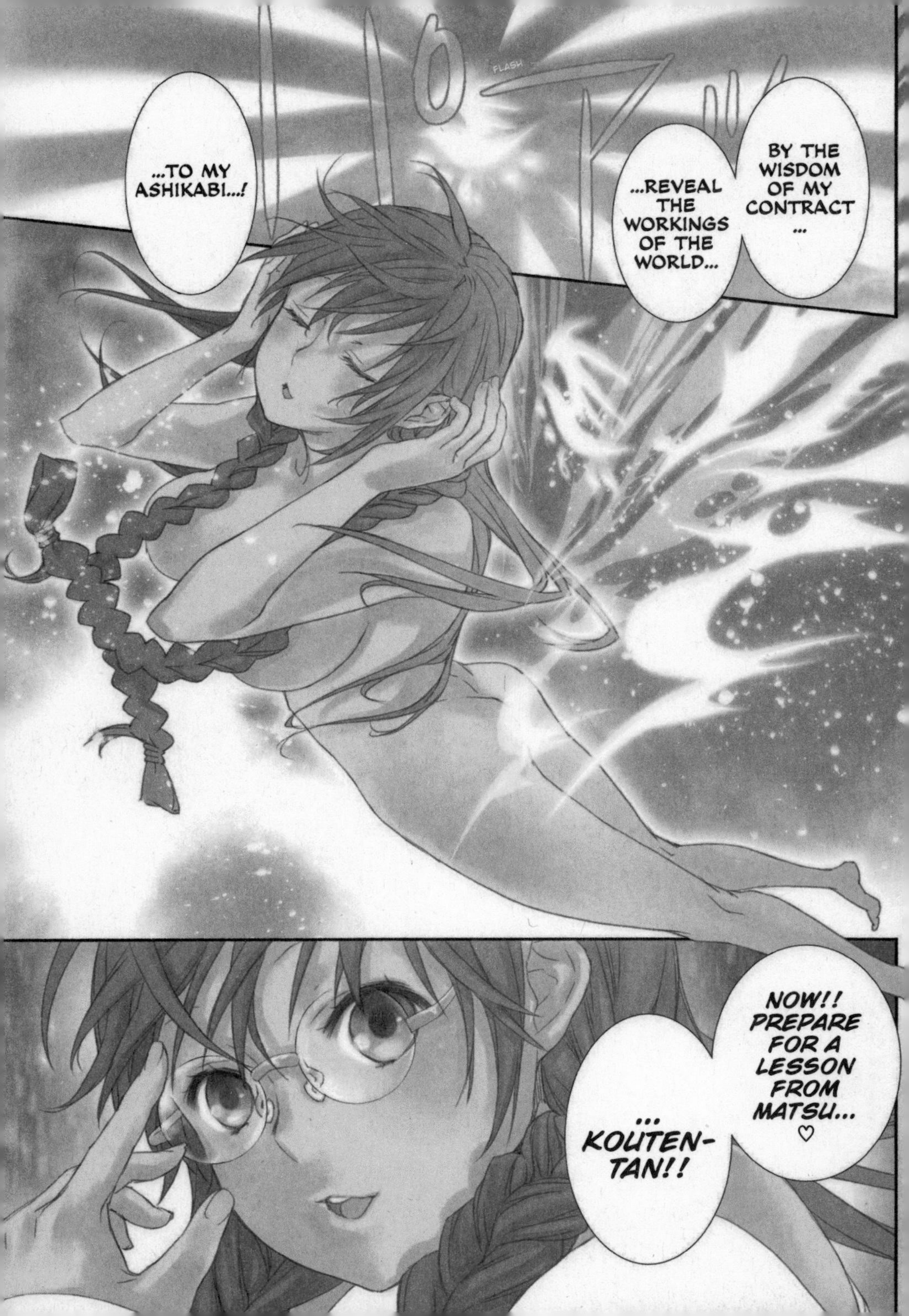
FLASH
BY THE WISDOM OF MY CONTRACT ...
...REVEAL THE WORKINGS OF THE WORLD...
...TO MY ASHIKABI...!
NOW!! PREPARE FOR A LESSON FROM MATSU... ♡
... KOÜTEN-TAN!!

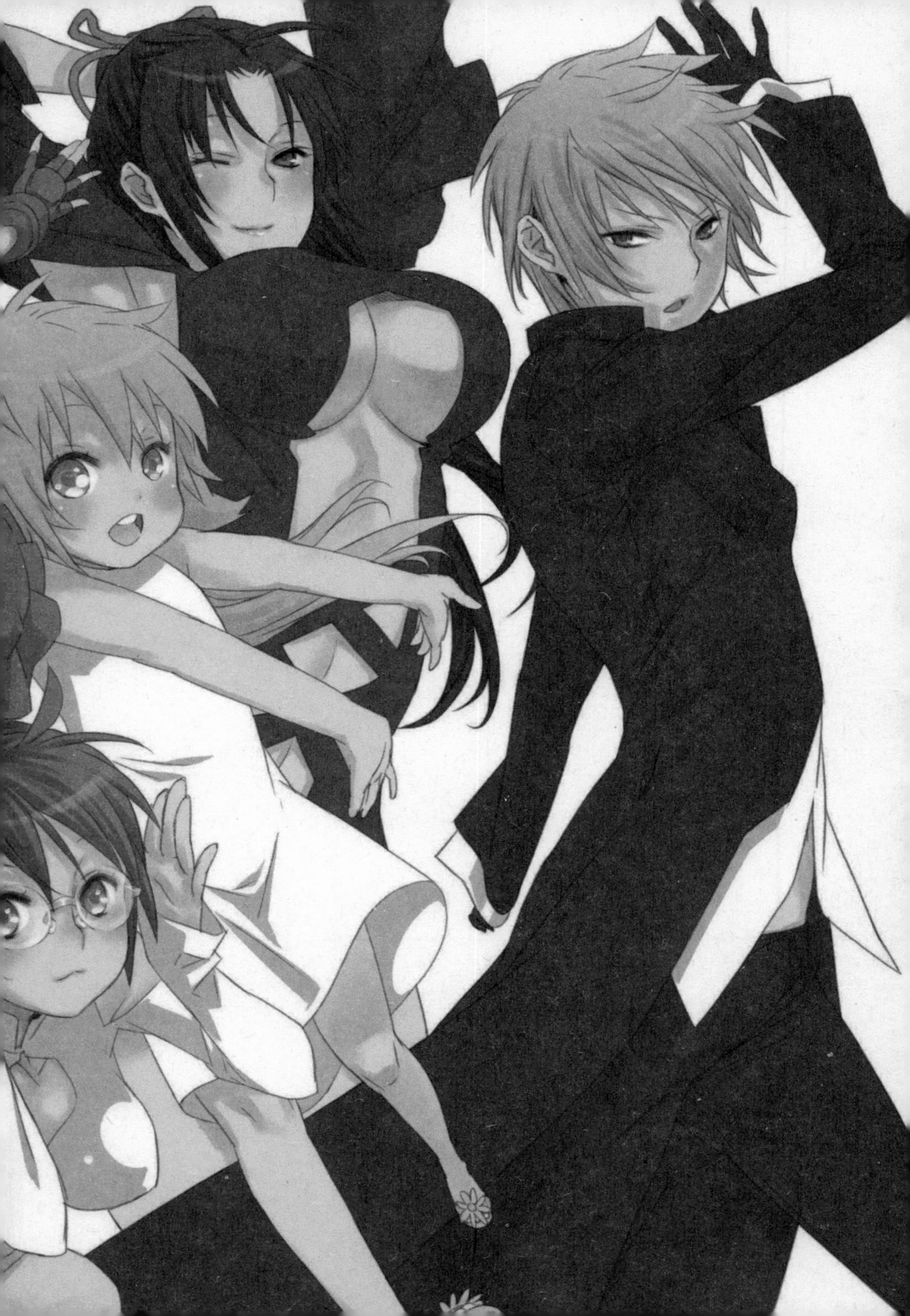

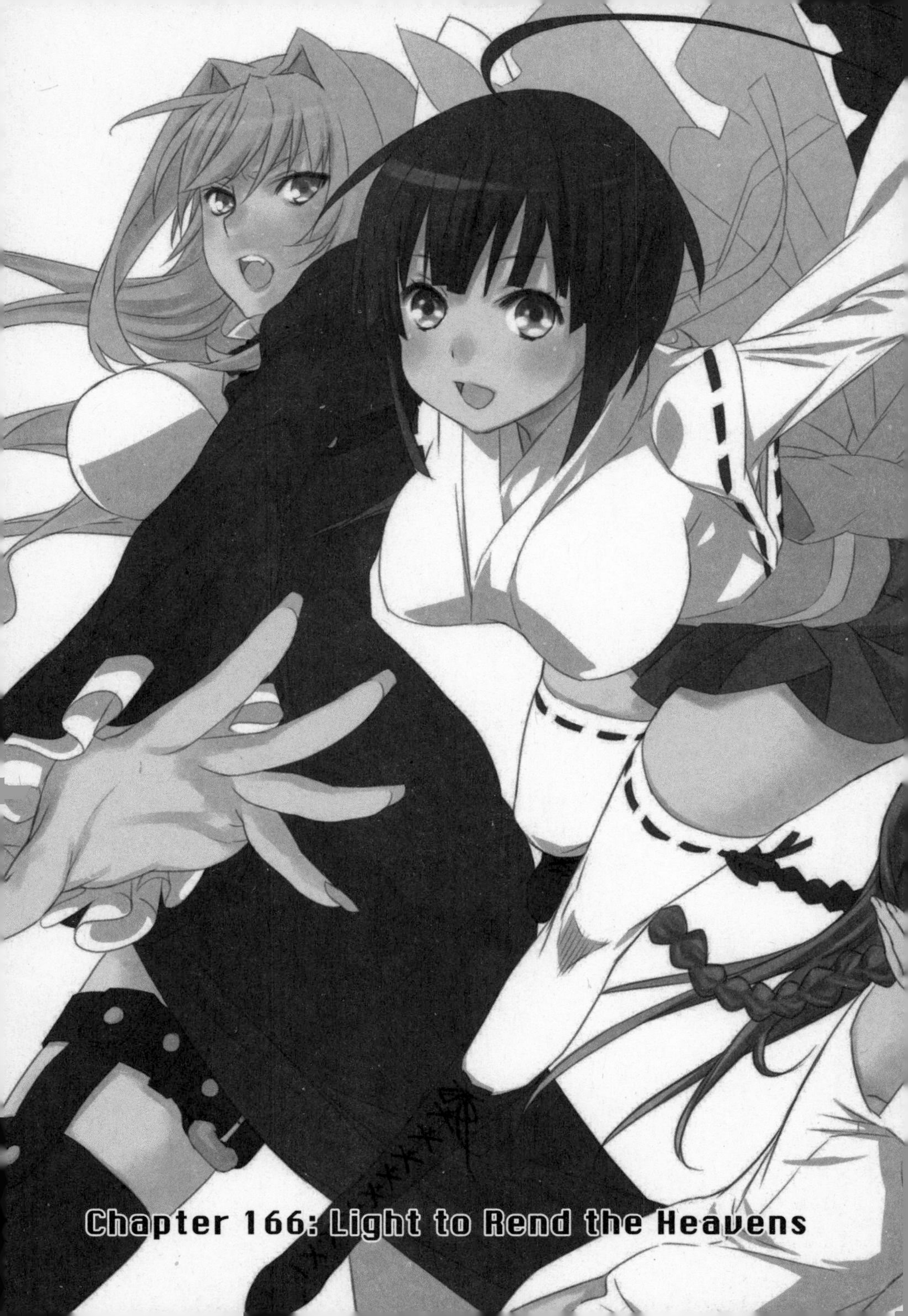

Chapter 166: Light to Rend the Heavens

#164: WHILE WE'RE AT IT, I'M INCLUDING SOME ORIGINAL CHARACTERS FROM THE ANIME.

THIS ONE DIDN'T SHOW UP, BUT SHE'S THE ASHIKABI TO THE ONE ON THE LEFT!

HAIR IS LONGER IN BACK

ABOUT 190 CM TALL

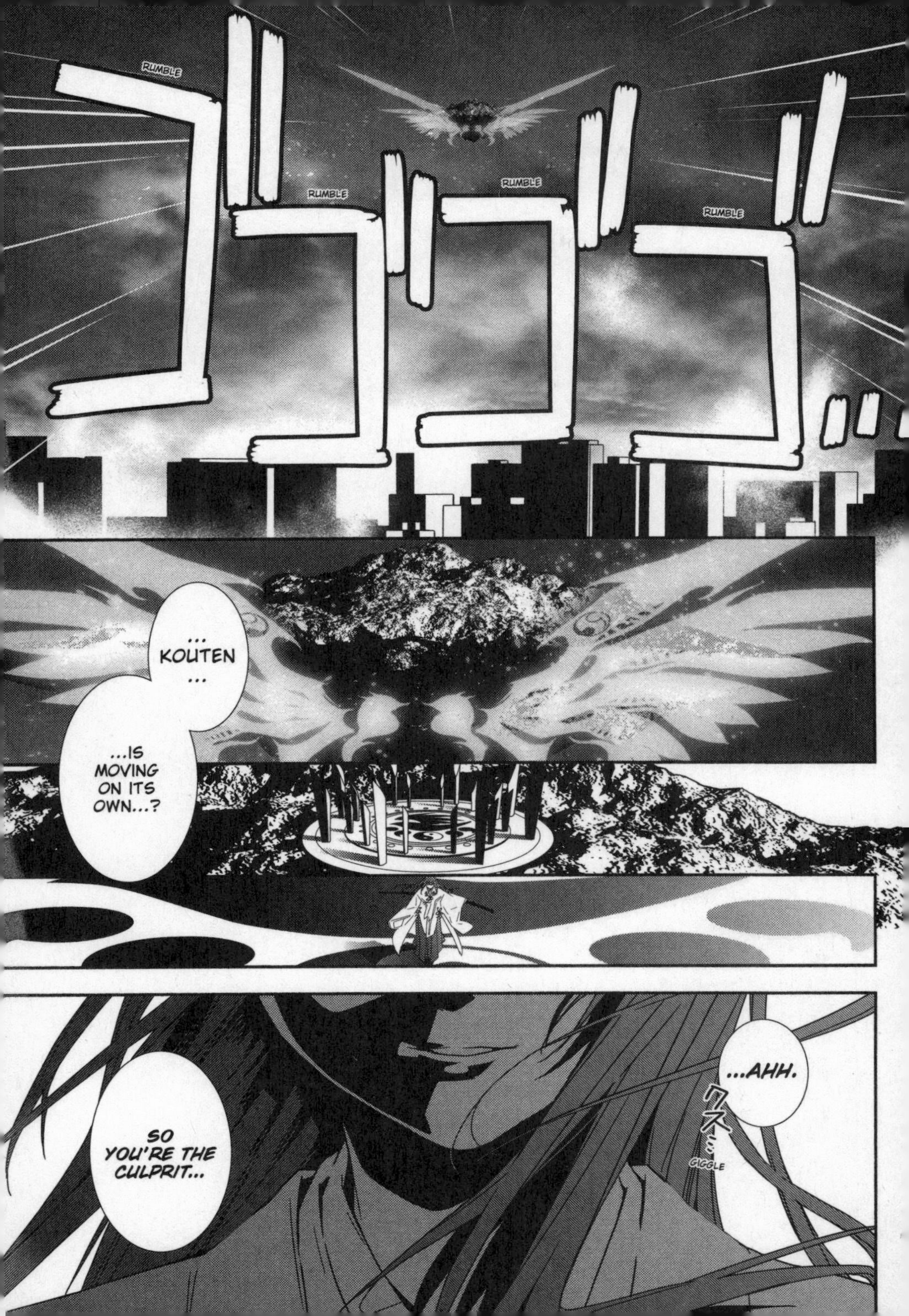
ゴゴゴゴ…
RUMBLE
RUMBLE
RUMBLE
RUMBLE
...KOUTEN...
...IS MOVING ON ITS OWN...?
...AHH.
クス…
GIGGLE
SO YOU'RE THE CULPRIT...

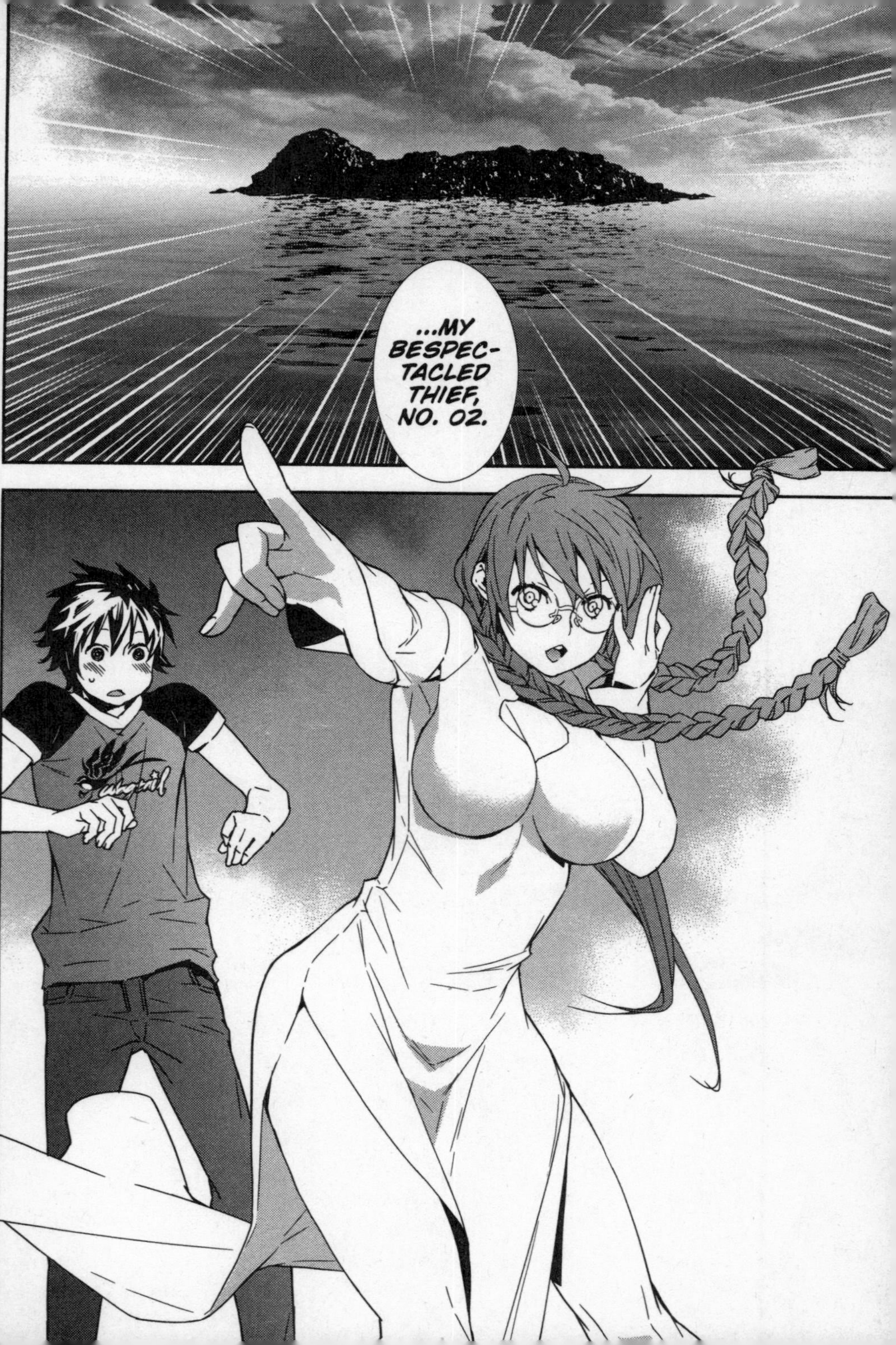
...MY BESPEC-TACLED THIEF, NO. 02.

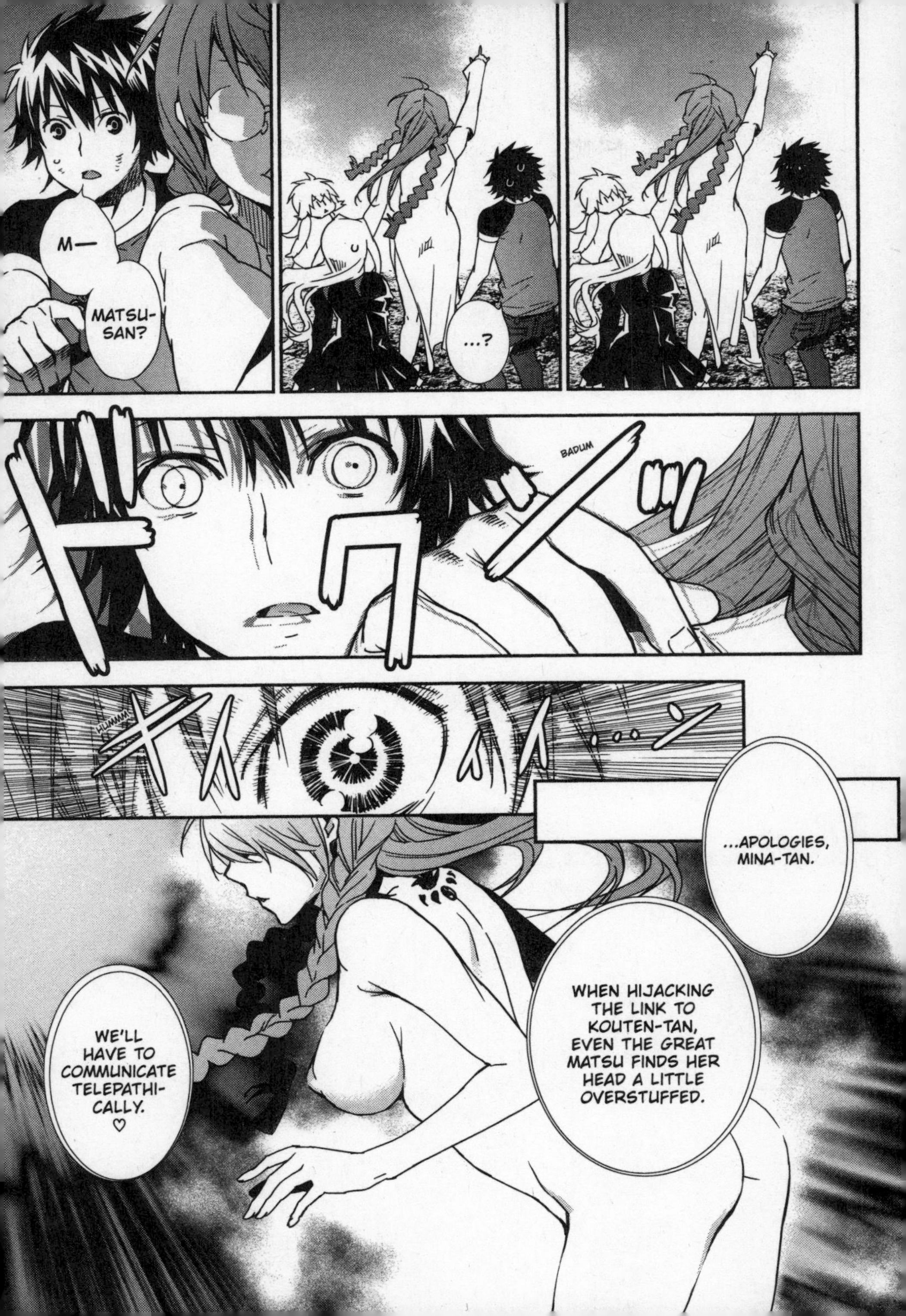
...?
M—
MATSU-SAN?
BADUM
HUMMM
...APOLOGIES, MINA-TAN.
WHEN HIJACKING THE LINK TO KOUTEN-TAN, EVEN THE GREAT MATSU FINDS HER HEAD A LITTLE OVERSTUFFED.
WE'LL HAVE TO COMMUNICATE TELEPATHI-CALLY. ♡

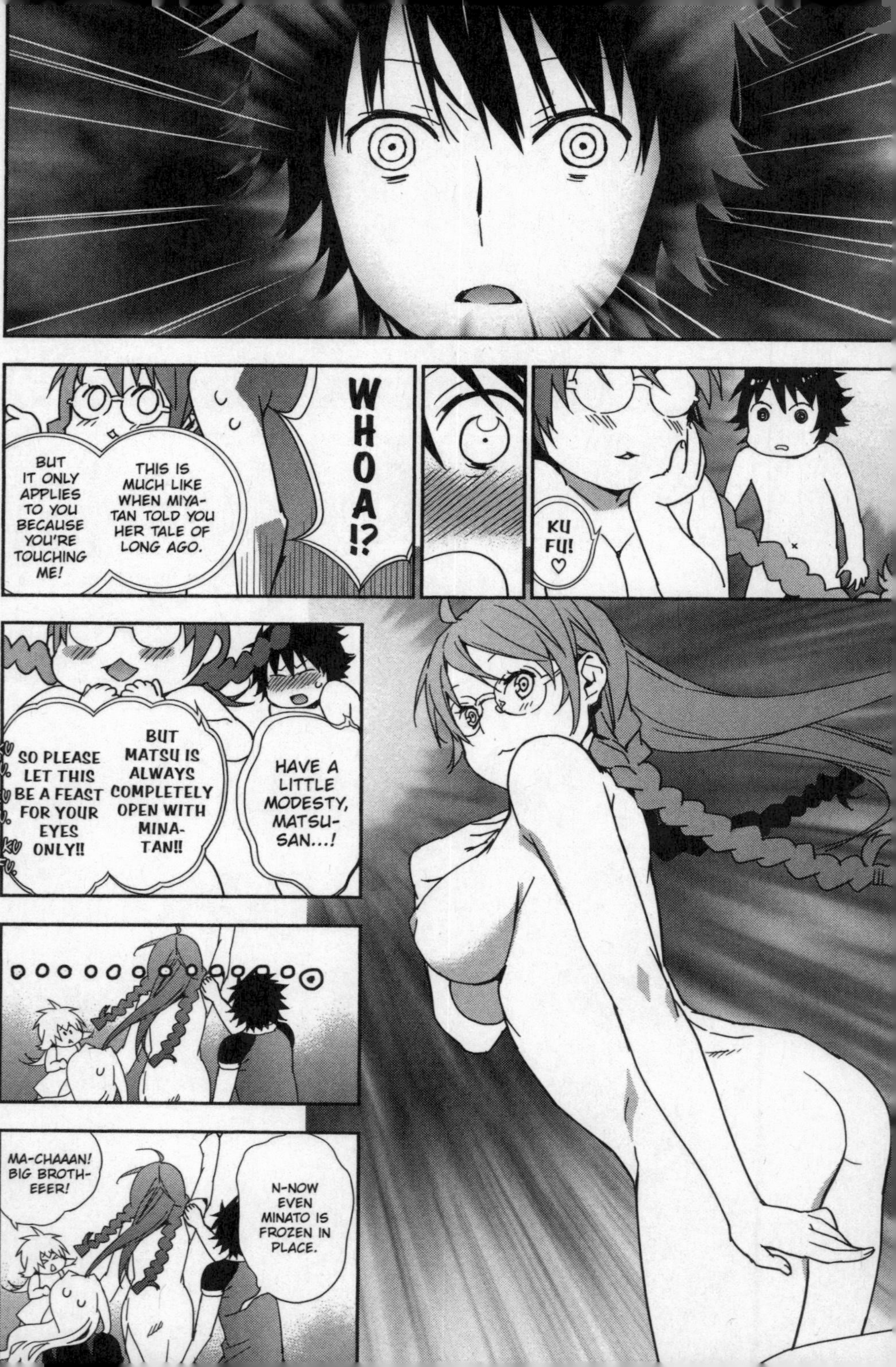
KU FU! ♥
WHOA!?
THIS IS MUCH LIKE WHEN MIYA-TAN TOLD YOU HER TALE OF LONG AGO.
BUT IT ONLY APPLIES TO YOU BECAUSE YOU'RE TOUCHING ME!
HAVE A LITTLE MODESTY, MATSU-SAN...!
BUT MATSU IS ALWAYS COMPLETELY OPEN WITH MINA-TAN!!
SO PLEASE LET THIS BE A FEAST FOR YOUR EYES ONLY!!
KU FU. KU FU. KU FU.
N-NOW EVEN MINATO IS FROZEN IN PLACE.
MA-CHAAAN! BIG BROTHEEER!

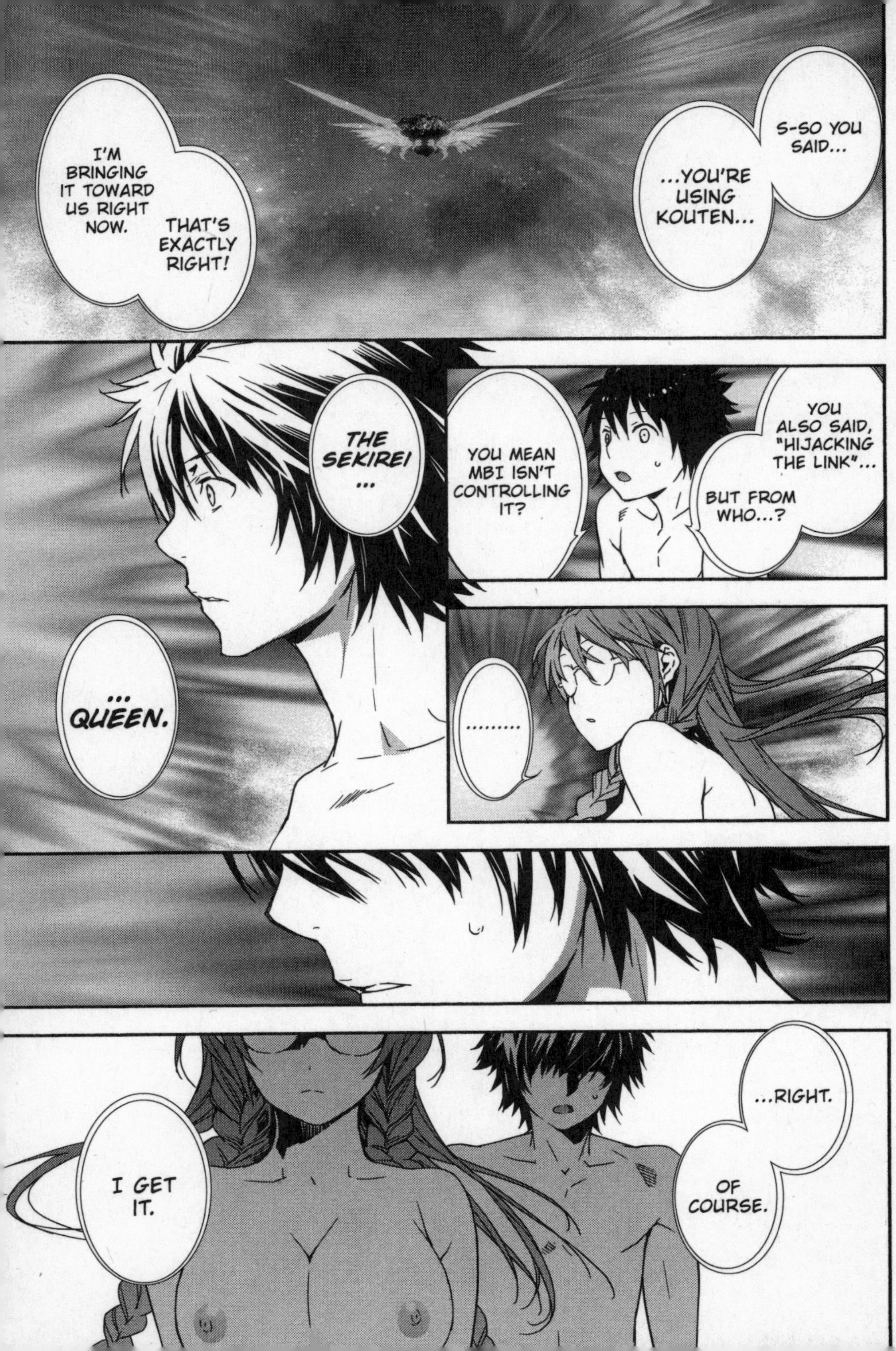
S-SO YOU SAID...
...YOU'RE USING KOUTEN...
THAT'S EXACTLY RIGHT!
I'M BRINGING IT TOWARD US RIGHT NOW.
YOU ALSO SAID, "HIJACKING THE LINK"...
BUT FROM WHO...?
YOU MEAN MBI ISN'T CONTROLLING IT?
....
THE SEKIREI ...
... QUEEN.
...RIGHT.
OF COURSE.
I GET IT.

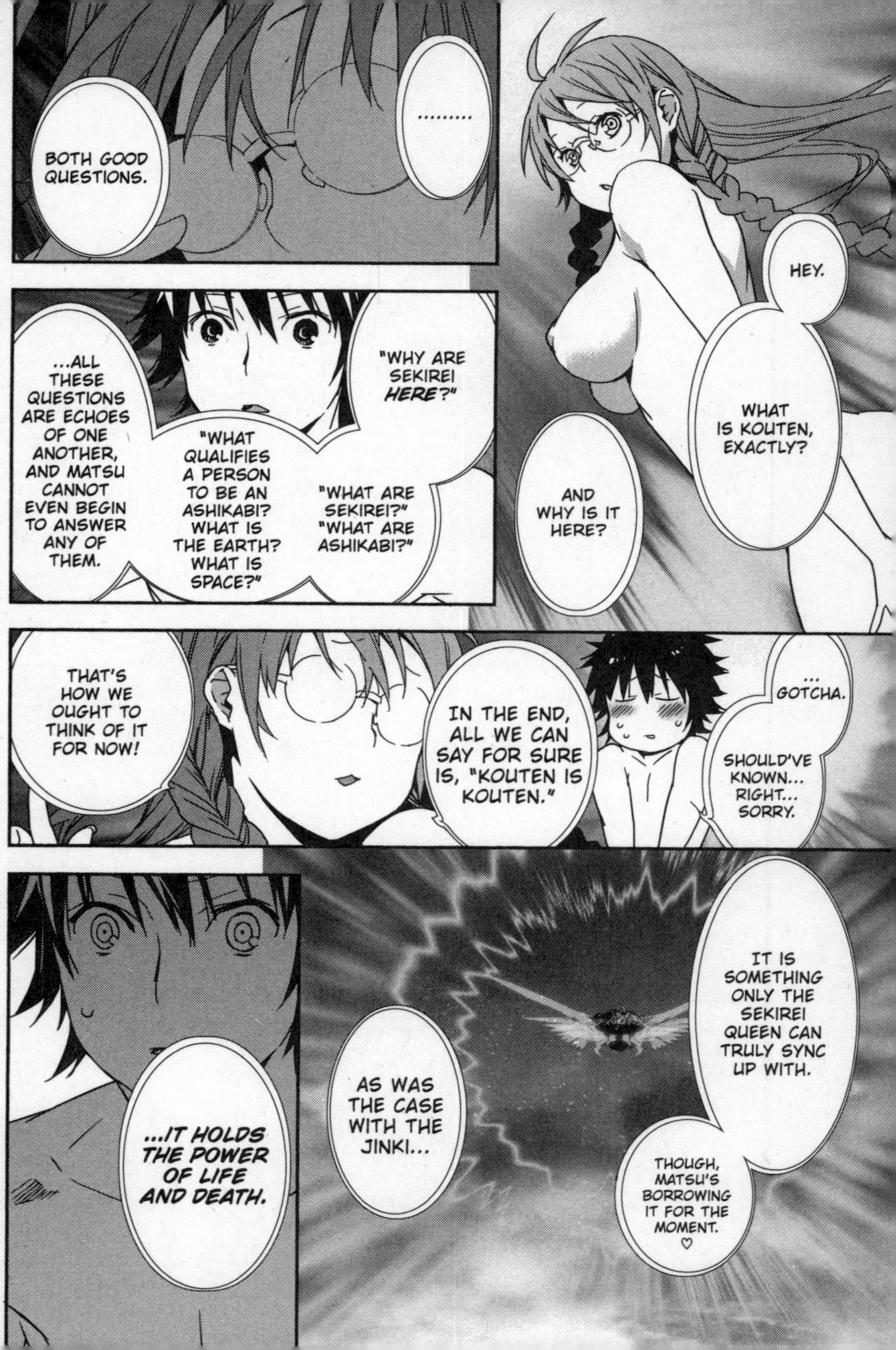
HEY.
WHAT IS KOUTEN, EXACTLY?
AND WHY IS IT HERE?
....
BOTH GOOD QUESTIONS.
"WHY ARE SEKIREI *HERE*?"
"WHAT ARE SEKIREI?" "WHAT ARE ASHIKABI?"
"WHAT QUALIFIES A PERSON TO BE AN ASHIKABI? WHAT IS THE EARTH? WHAT IS SPACE?"
...ALL THESE QUESTIONS ARE ECHOES OF ONE ANOTHER, AND MATSU CANNOT EVEN BEGIN TO ANSWER ANY OF THEM.
... GOTCHA.
SHOULD'VE KNOWN... RIGHT... SORRY.
IN THE END, ALL WE CAN SAY FOR SURE IS, "KOUTEN IS KOUTEN."
THAT'S HOW WE OUGHT TO THINK OF IT FOR NOW!
IT IS SOMETHING ONLY THE SEKIREI QUEEN CAN TRULY SYNC UP WITH.
THOUGH, MATSU'S BORROWING IT FOR THE MOMENT. ♡
AS WAS THE CASE WITH THE JINKI...
...IT HOLDS THE POWER OF LIFE AND DEATH.

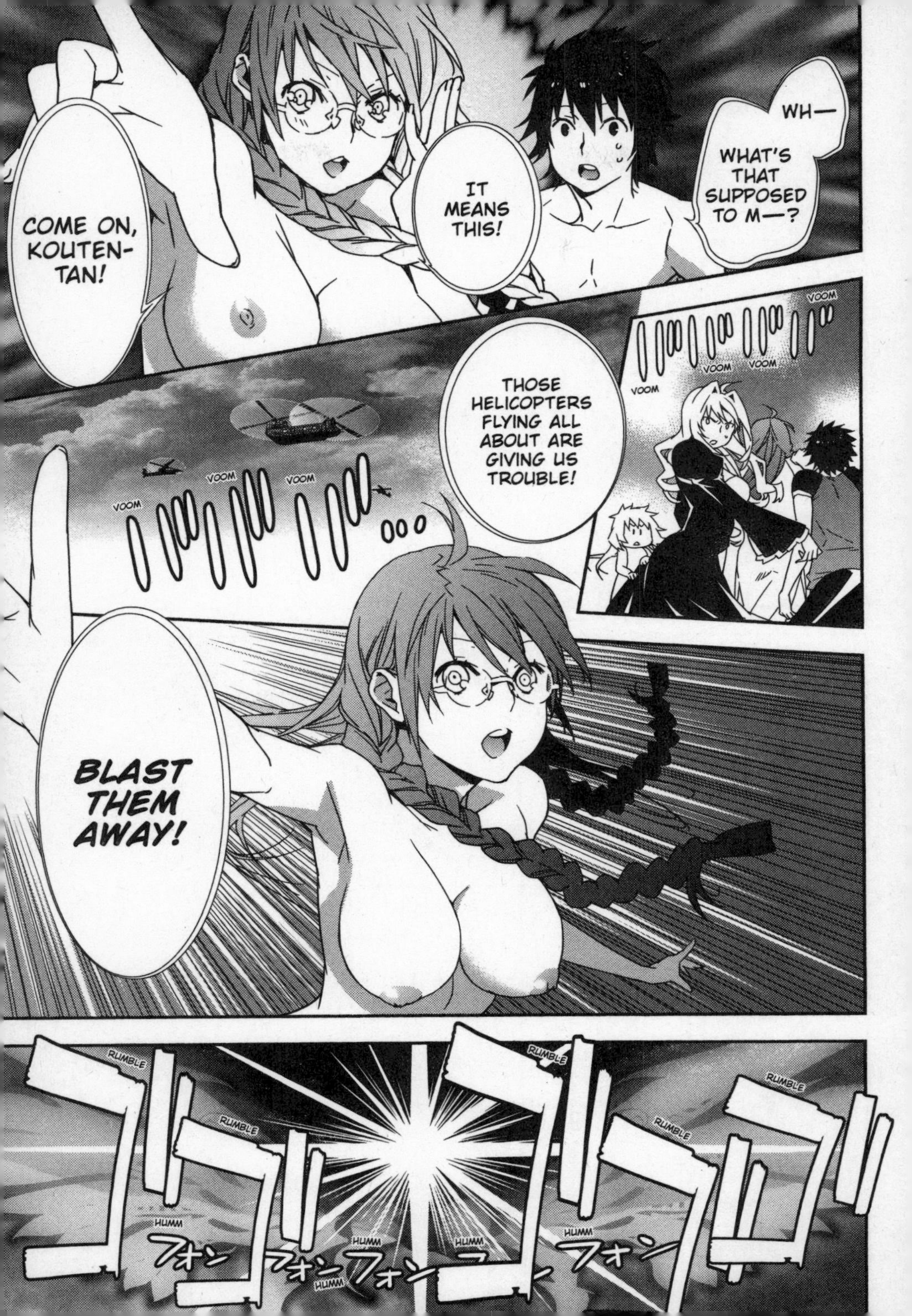
WH—
WHAT'S THAT SUPPOSED TO M—?
IT MEANS THIS!
COME ON, KOUTEN-TAN!
VOOM
VOOM VOOM
VOOM
THOSE HELICOPTERS FLYING ALL ABOUT ARE GIVING US TROUBLE!
VOOM
VOOM
VOOM
BLAST THEM AWAY!
RUMBLE
RUMBLE
RUMBLE
RUMBLE
RUMBLE
HUMM
フォン
HUMM
フォン
HUMM
フォン
HUMM
フォン
HUMM

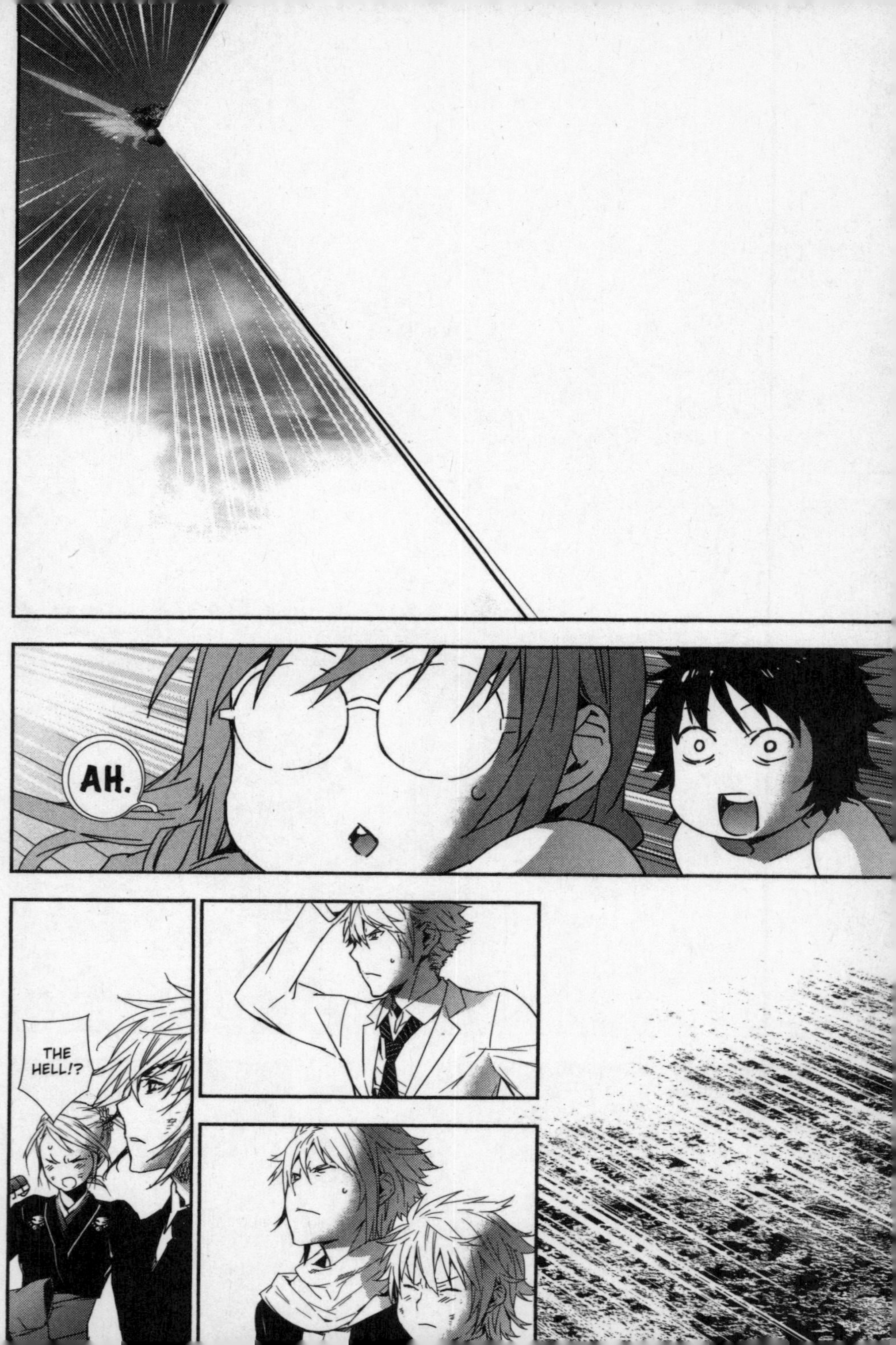
AH.
THE HELL!?

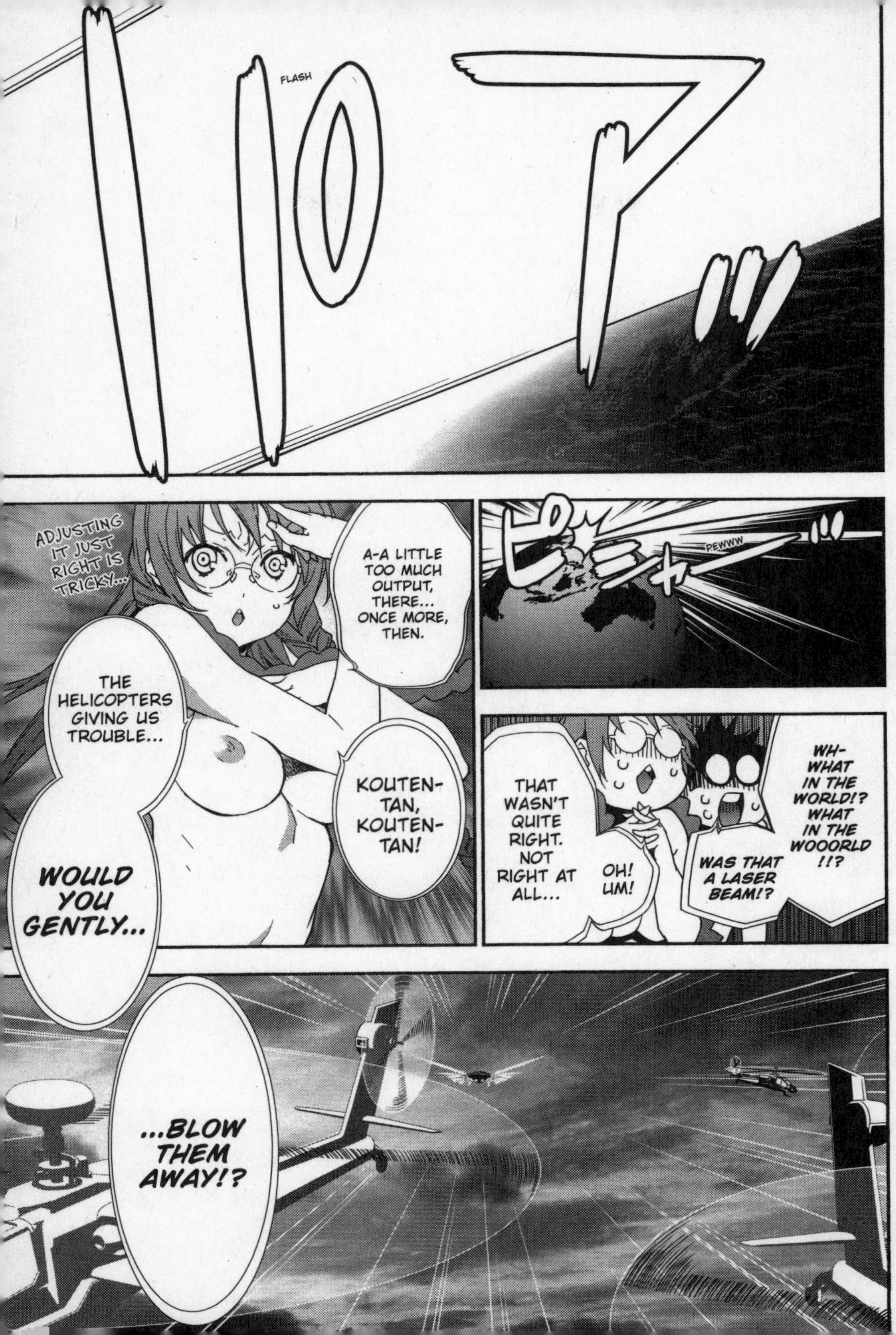
FLASH
PEWWW
WH-WHAT IN THE WORLD!? WHAT IN THE WOOORLD!!?
WAS THAT A LASER BEAM!?
THAT WASN'T QUITE RIGHT. NOT RIGHT AT ALL...
OH! UM!
A-A LITTLE TOO MUCH OUTPUT, THERE... ONCE MORE, THEN.
ADJUSTING IT JUST RIGHT IS TRICKY...
KOUTEN-TAN, KOUTEN-TAN!
THE HELICOPTERS GIVING US TROUBLE...
WOULD YOU GENTLY...
...BLOW THEM AWAY!?

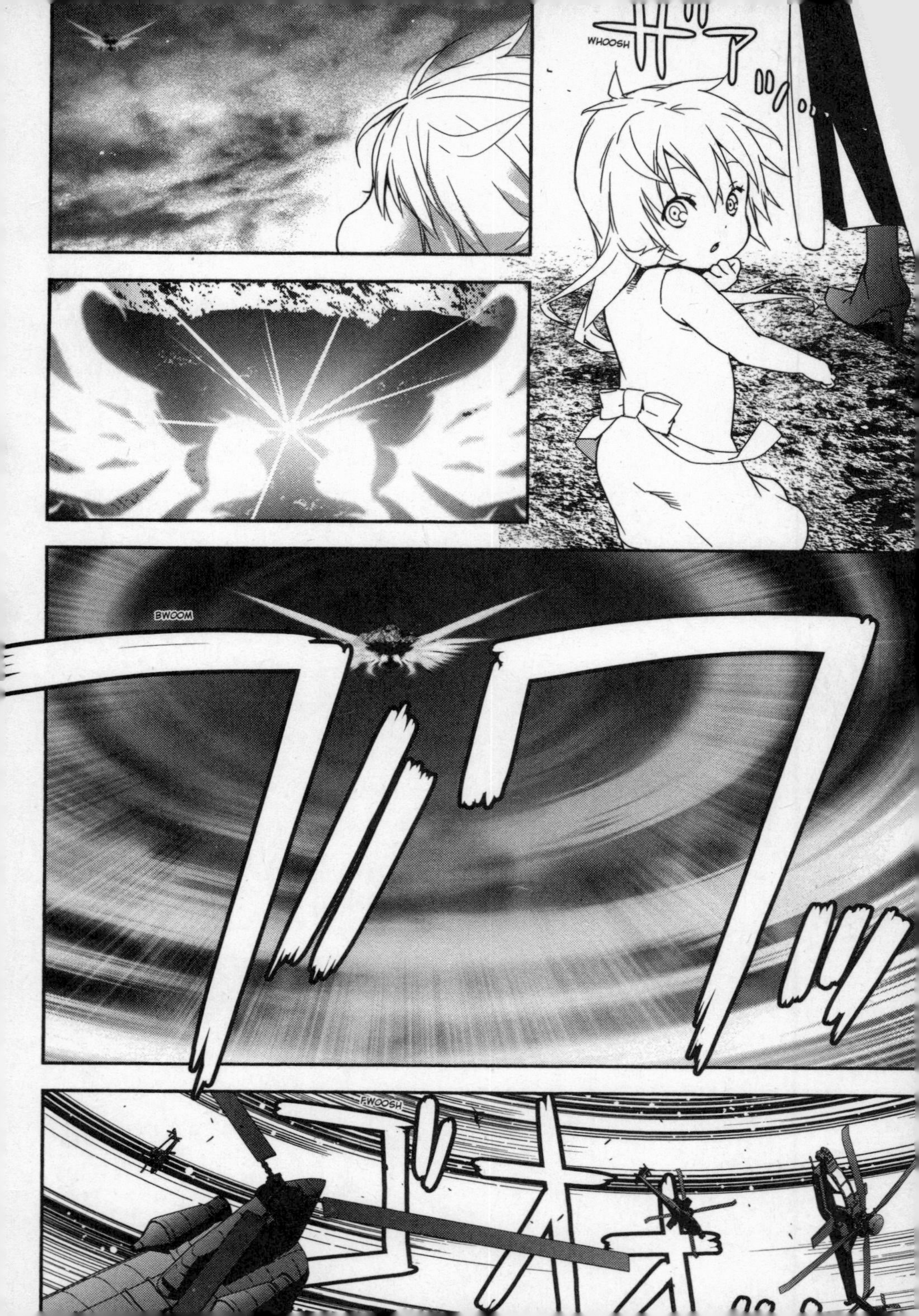
WHOOSH
BWOOM
FWOOSH

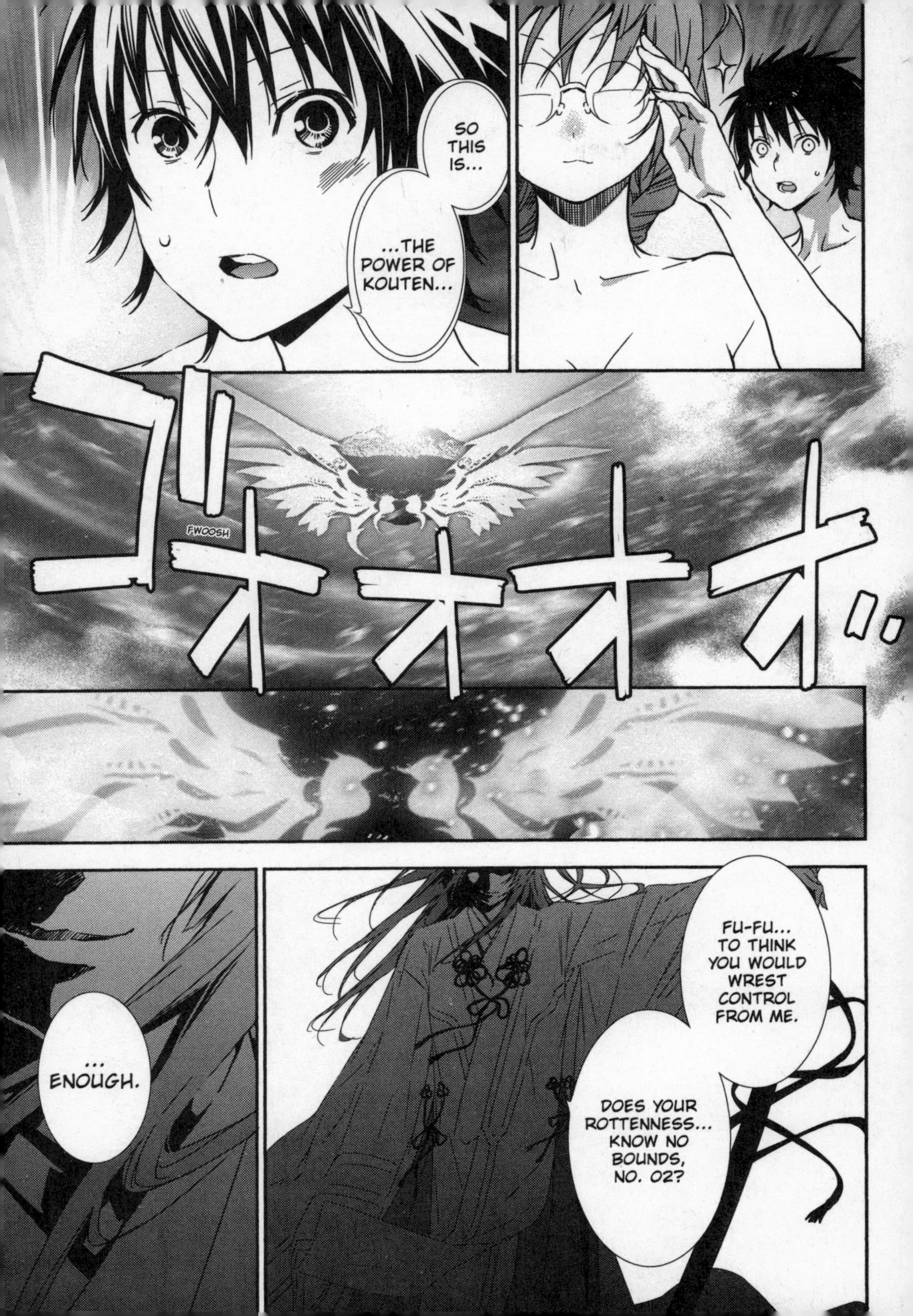
SO THIS IS...
...THE POWER OF KOUTEN...
ゴオオオ
FWOOSH
FU-FU... TO THINK YOU WOULD WREST CONTROL FROM ME.
DOES YOUR ROTTENNESS... KNOW NO BOUNDS, NO. 02?
...ENOUGH.

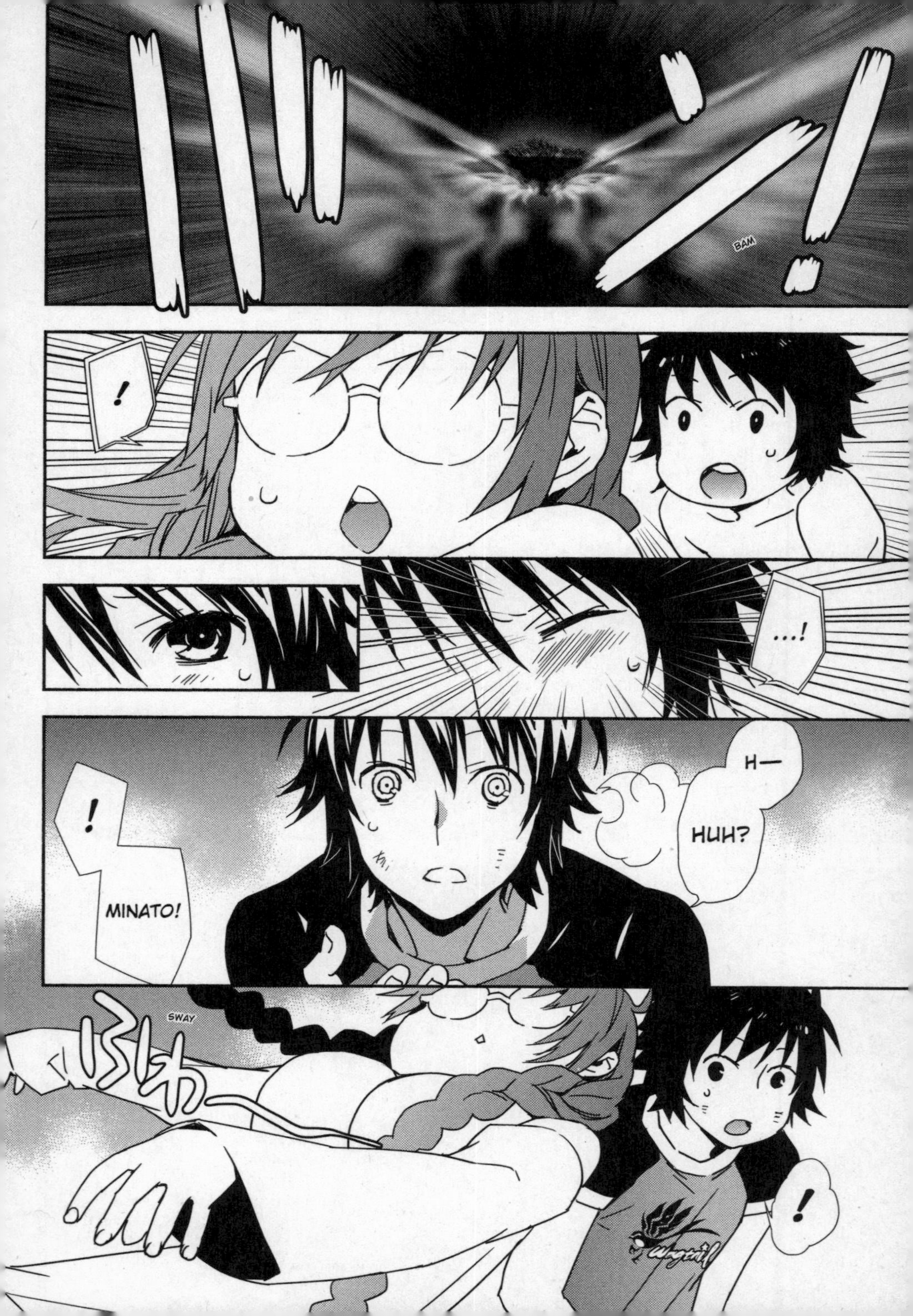
BAM
!
...!
H—
HUH?
!
MINATO!
SWAY
!

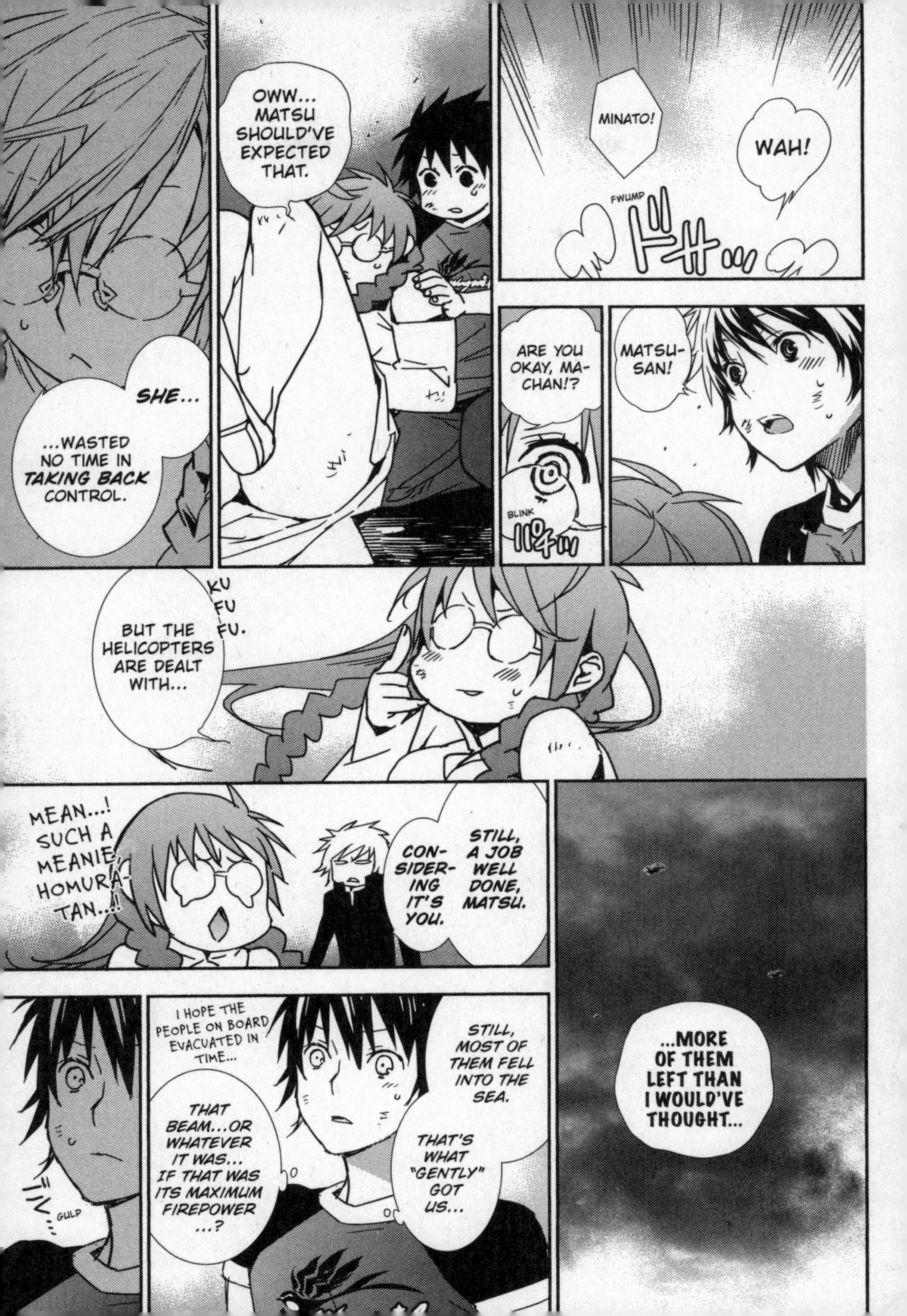
MINATO!
WAH!
FWUMP
MATSU-SAN!
ARE YOU OKAY, MA-CHAN!?
BLINK
OWW... MATSU SHOULD'VE EXPECTED THAT.
SHE...
...WASTED NO TIME IN TAKING BACK CONTROL.
KU FU FU.
BUT THE HELICOPTERS ARE DEALT WITH...
...MORE OF THEM LEFT THAN I WOULD'VE THOUGHT...
STILL, A JOB WELL DONE, MATSU.
CON-SIDER-ING IT'S YOU.
MEAN...! SUCH A MEANIE, HOMURA-TAN...!
STILL, MOST OF THEM FELL INTO THE SEA.
I HOPE THE PEOPLE ON BOARD EVACUATED IN TIME...
THAT'S WHAT "GENTLY" GOT US...
THAT BEAM...OR WHATEVER IT WAS... IF THAT WAS ITS MAXIMUM FIREPOWER ...?
GULP

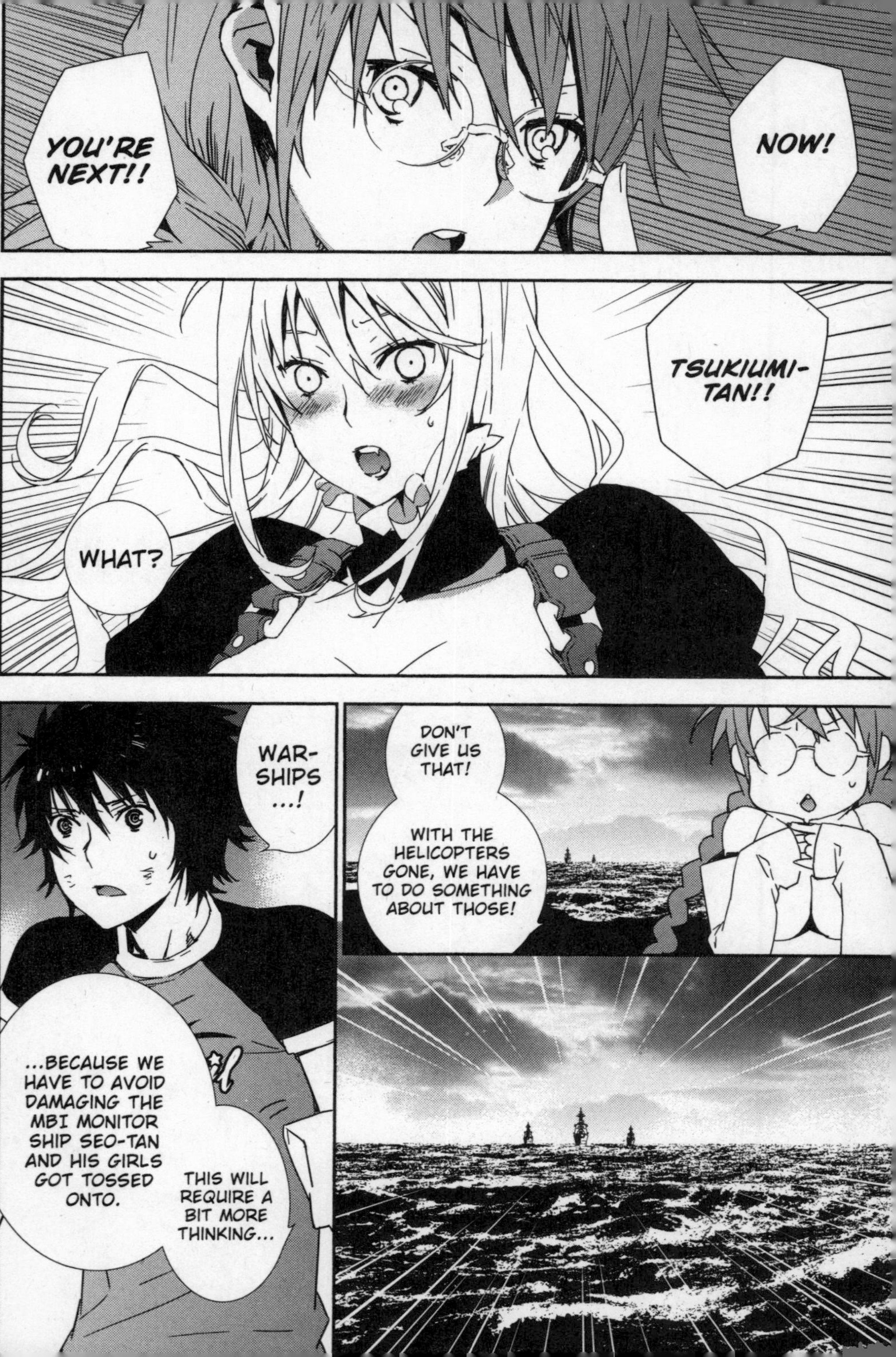
NOW!
YOU'RE NEXT!!
TSUKIUMI-TAN!!
WHAT?
DON'T GIVE US THAT!
WITH THE HELICOPTERS GONE, WE HAVE TO DO SOMETHING ABOUT THOSE!
WAR-SHIPS ...!
THIS WILL REQUIRE A BIT MORE THINKING...
...BECAUSE WE HAVE TO AVOID DAMAGING THE MBI MONITOR SHIP SEO-TAN AND HIS GIRLS GOT TOSSED ONTO.

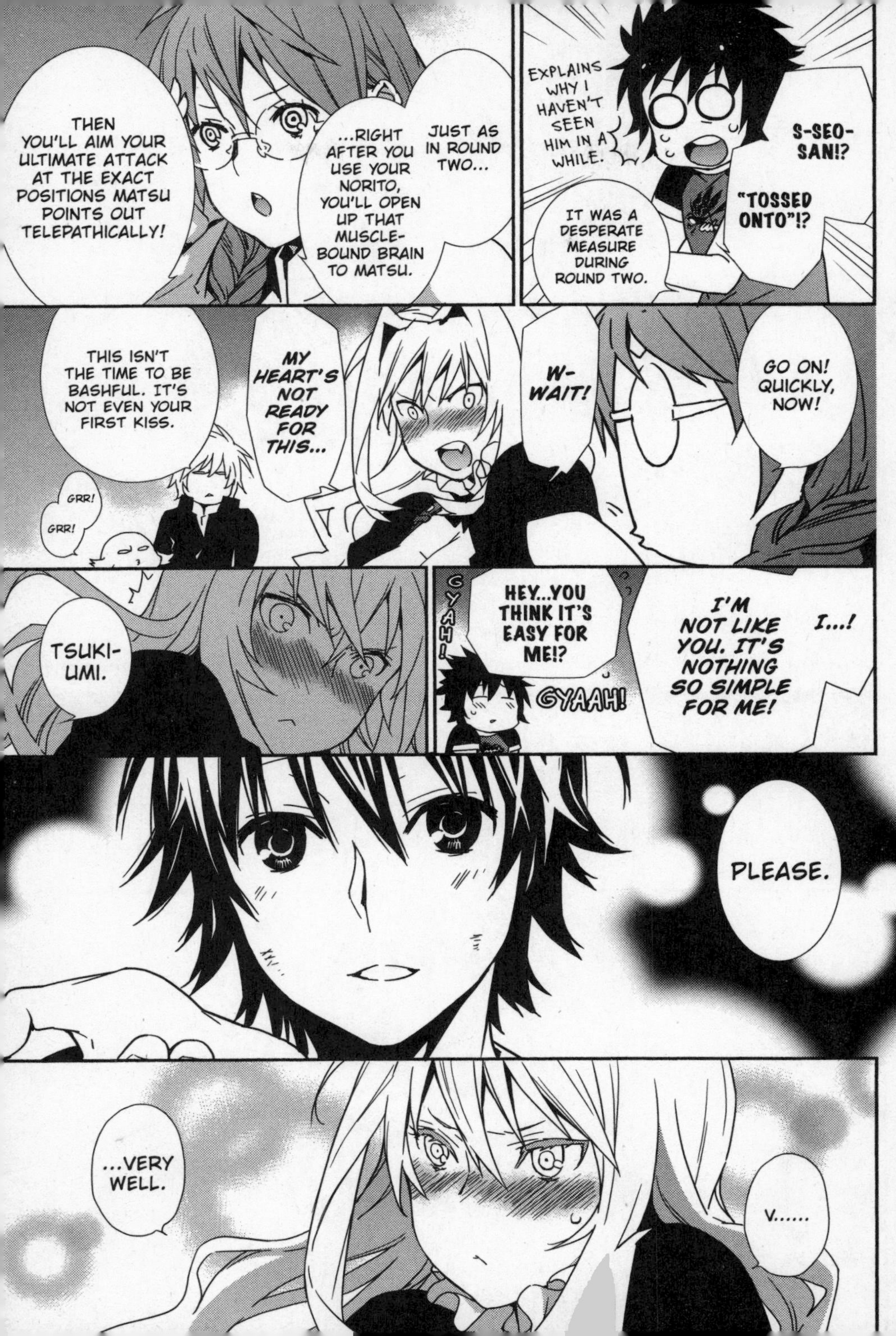
S-SEO-SAN!?
"TOSSED ONTO"!?
EXPLAINS WHY I HAVEN'T SEEN HIM IN A WHILE.
IT WAS A DESPERATE MEASURE DURING ROUND TWO.
JUST AS IN ROUND TWO...
...RIGHT AFTER YOU USE YOUR NORITO, YOU'LL OPEN UP THAT MUSCLE-BOUND BRAIN TO MATSU.
THEN YOU'LL AIM YOUR ULTIMATE ATTACK AT THE EXACT POSITIONS MATSU POINTS OUT TELEPATHICALLY!
GO ON! QUICKLY, NOW!
W-WAIT!
MY HEART'S NOT READY FOR THIS...
THIS ISN'T THE TIME TO BE BASHFUL. IT'S NOT EVEN YOUR FIRST KISS.
GRR!
GRR!
I...!
I'M NOT LIKE YOU. IT'S NOTHING SO SIMPLE FOR ME!
HEY...YOU THINK IT'S EASY FOR ME!?
GYAAH!
GYAAH!
TSUKI-UMI.
PLEASE.
V......
...VERY WELL.

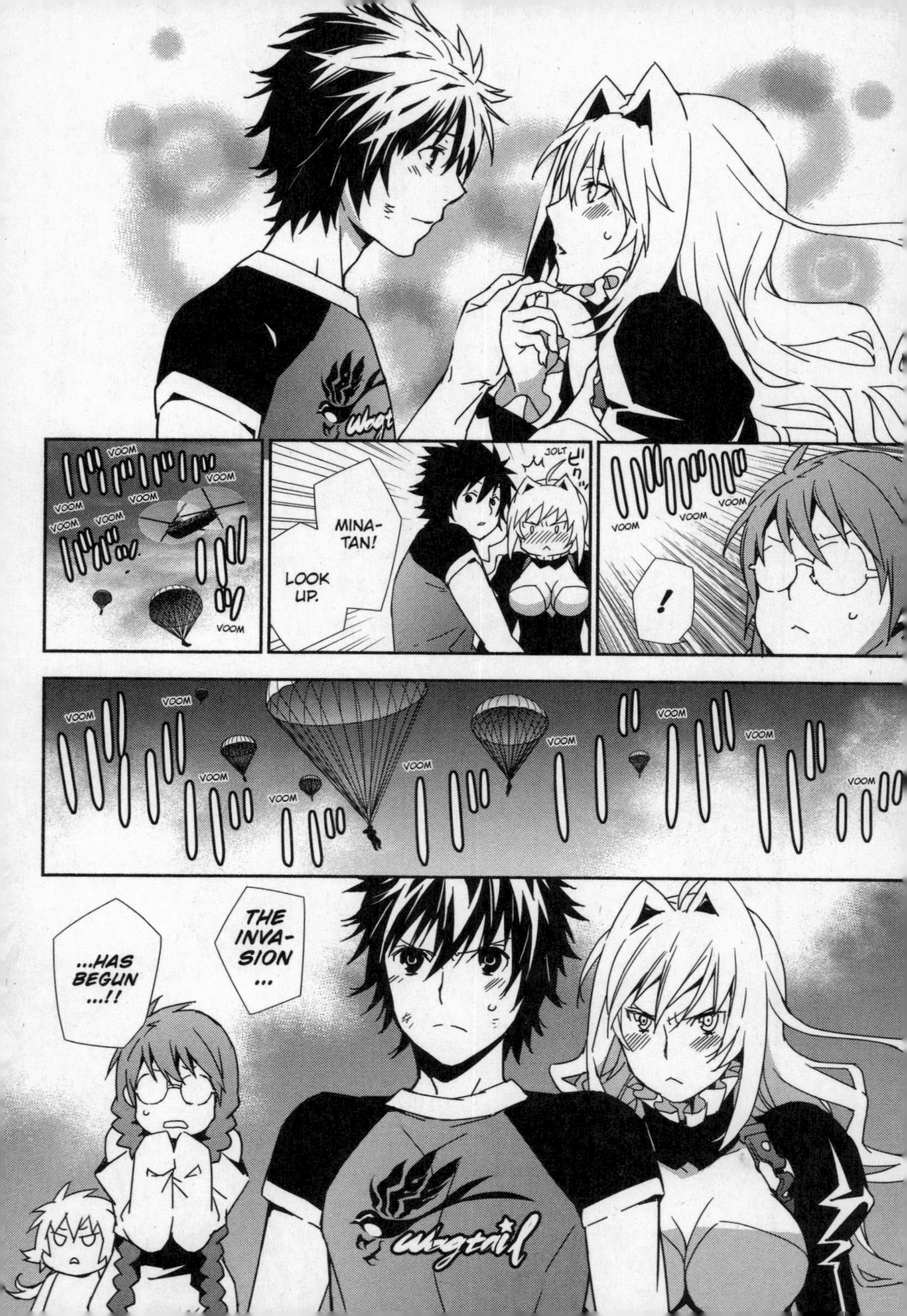
VOOM
VOOM
VOOM
!
JOLT
ビクッ
MINA-TAN!
LOOK UP.
VOOM
VOOM
VOOM
VOOM
VOOM
VOOM
VOOM
VOOM
VOOM
VOOM
VOOM
VOOM
VOOM
VOOM
VOOM
THE INVA-SION...
...HAS BEGUN...!!
Wagtail

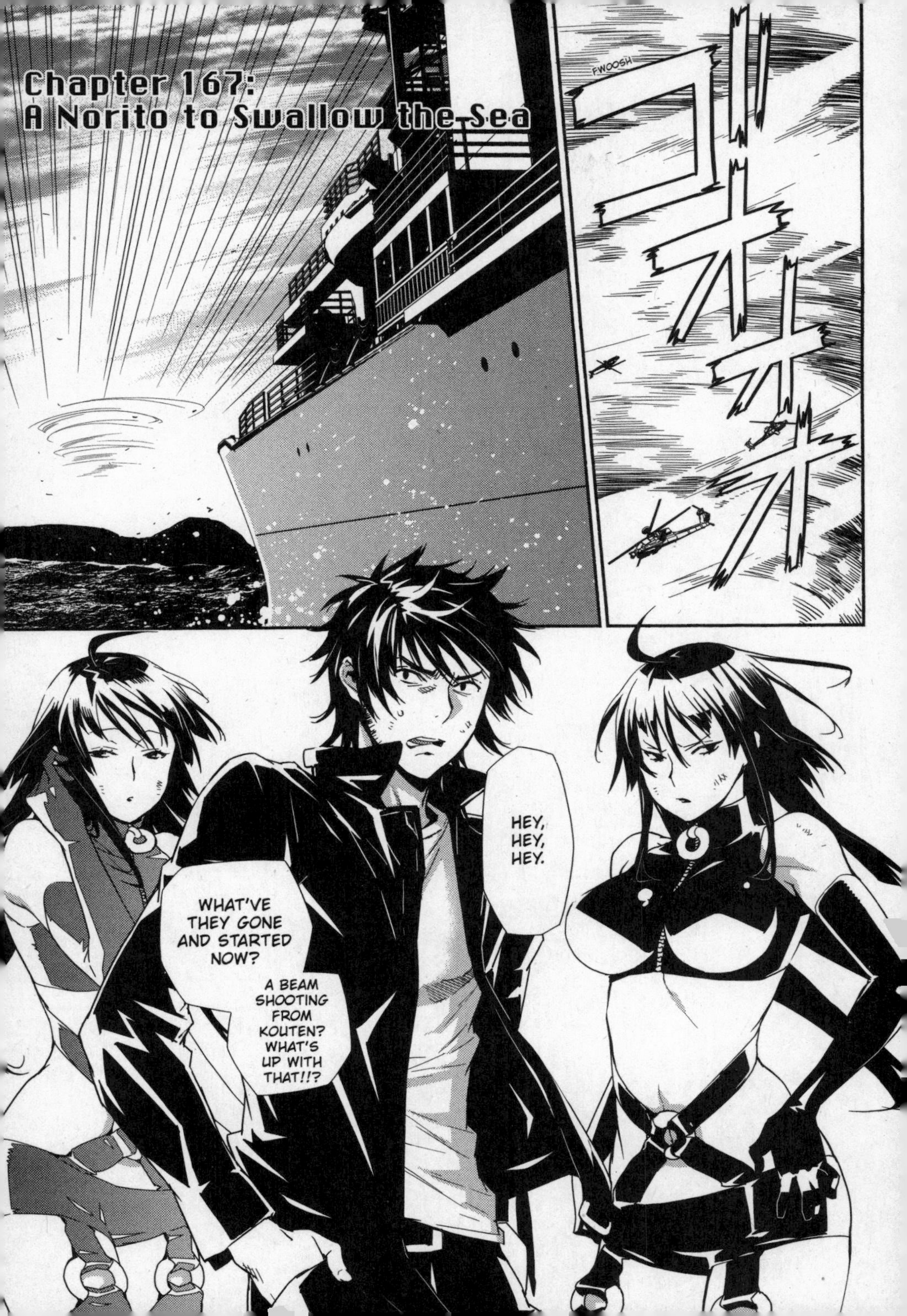
ゴオオオ
FWOOSH
Chapter 167:
A Norito to Swallow the Sea
HEY, HEY, HEY.
WHAT'VE THEY GONE AND STARTED NOW?
A BEAM SHOOTING FROM KOUTEN? WHAT'S UP WITH THAT!!?

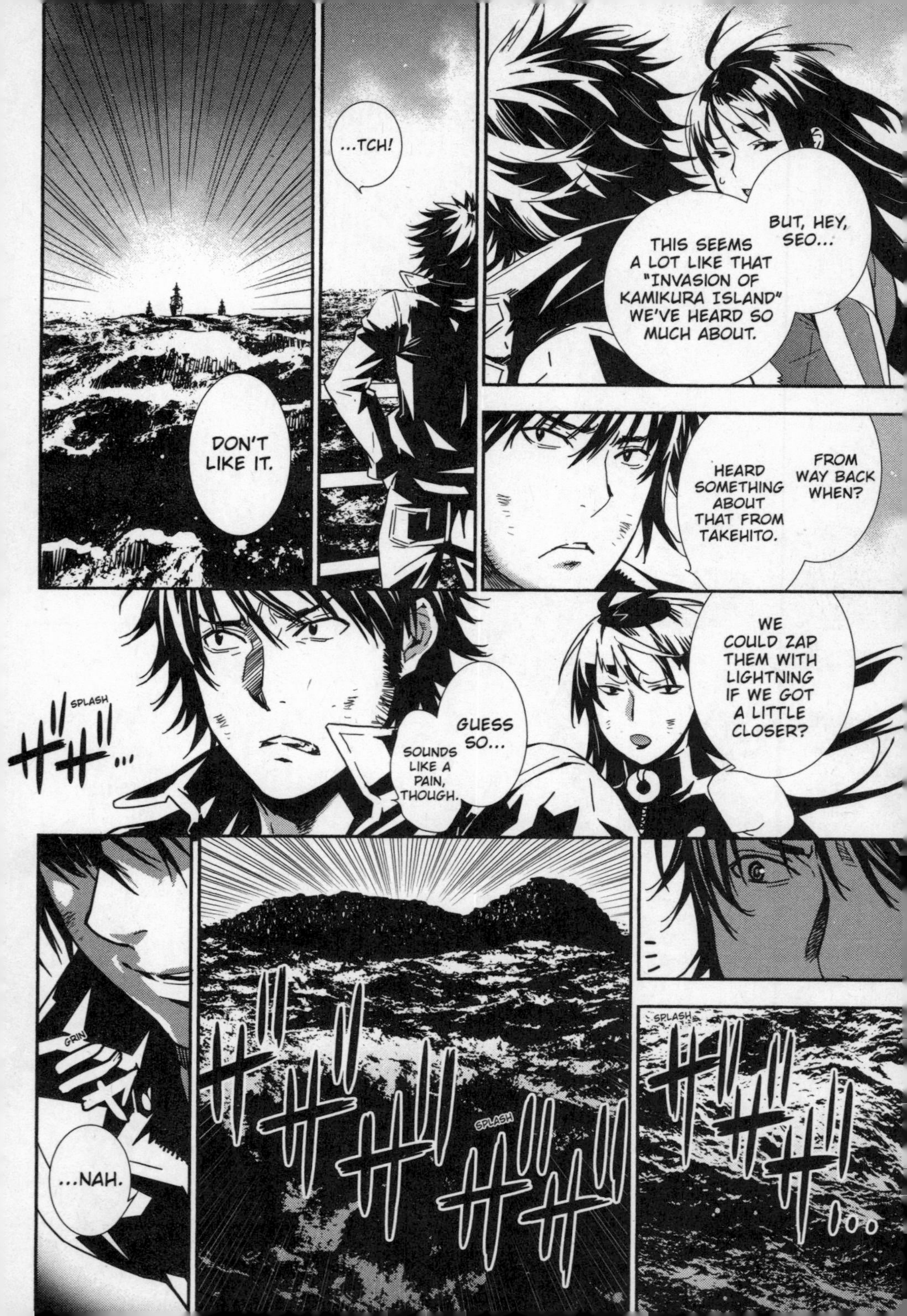
BUT, HEY, SEO...
THIS SEEMS A LOT LIKE THAT "INVASION OF KAMIKURA ISLAND" WE'VE HEARD SO MUCH ABOUT.
FROM WAY BACK WHEN?
HEARD SOMETHING ABOUT THAT FROM TAKEHITO.
...TCH!
DON'T LIKE IT.
WE COULD ZAP THEM WITH LIGHTNING IF WE GOT A LITTLE CLOSER?
GUESS SO...
SOUNDS LIKE A PAIN, THOUGH.
SPLASH
SPLASH
SPLASH
GRIN
...NAH.

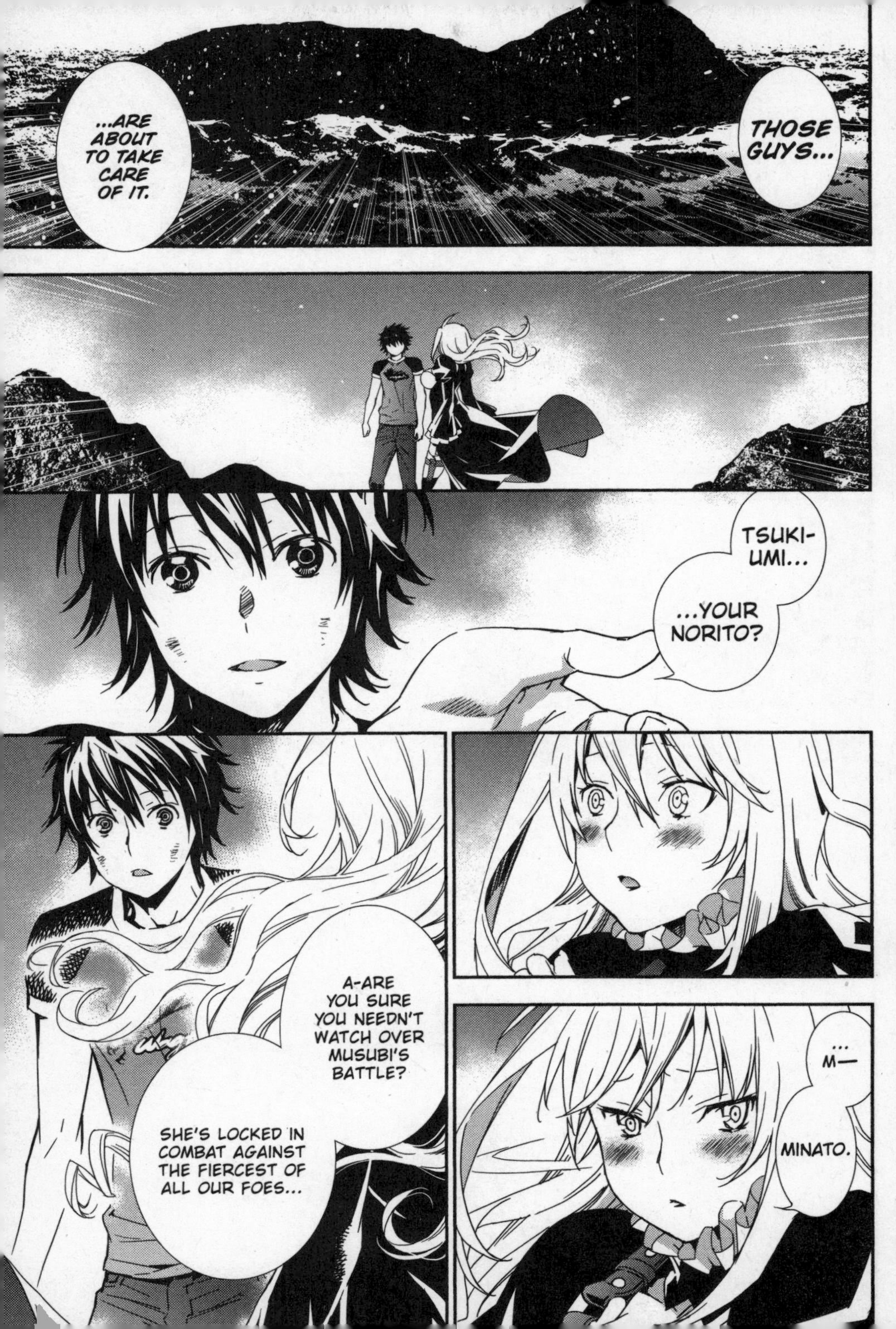
THOSE GUYS...
...ARE ABOUT TO TAKE CARE OF IT.
TSUKI-UMI...
...YOUR NORITO?
... M—
MINATO.
A-ARE YOU SURE YOU NEEDN'T WATCH OVER MUSUBI'S BATTLE?
SHE'S LOCKED IN COMBAT AGAINST THE FIERCEST OF ALL OUR FOES...

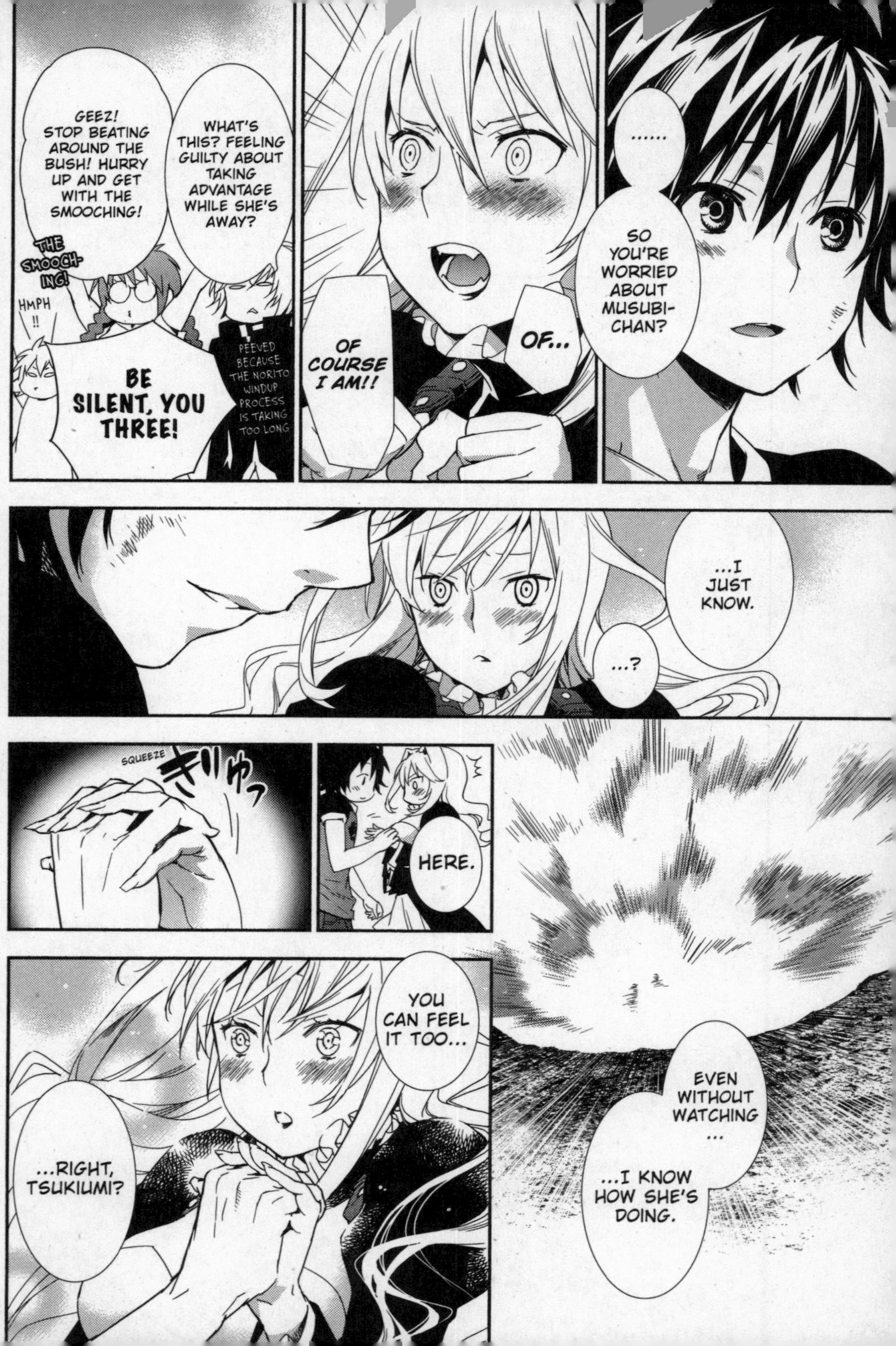
......
SO YOU'RE WORRIED ABOUT MUSUBI-CHAN?
OF...
OF COURSE I AM!!
WHAT'S THIS? FEELING GUILTY ABOUT TAKING ADVANTAGE WHILE SHE'S AWAY?
GEEZ! STOP BEATING AROUND THE BUSH! HURRY UP AND GET WITH THE SMOOCHING!
THE SMOOCH-ING!
HMPH !!
PEEVED BECAUSE THE NORITO WINDUP PROCESS IS TAKING TOO LONG
BE SILENT, YOU THREE!
...I JUST KNOW.
...?
EVEN WITHOUT WATCHING ...
...I KNOW HOW SHE'S DOING.
HERE.
SQUEEZE
YOU CAN FEEL IT TOO...
...RIGHT, TSUKIUMI?

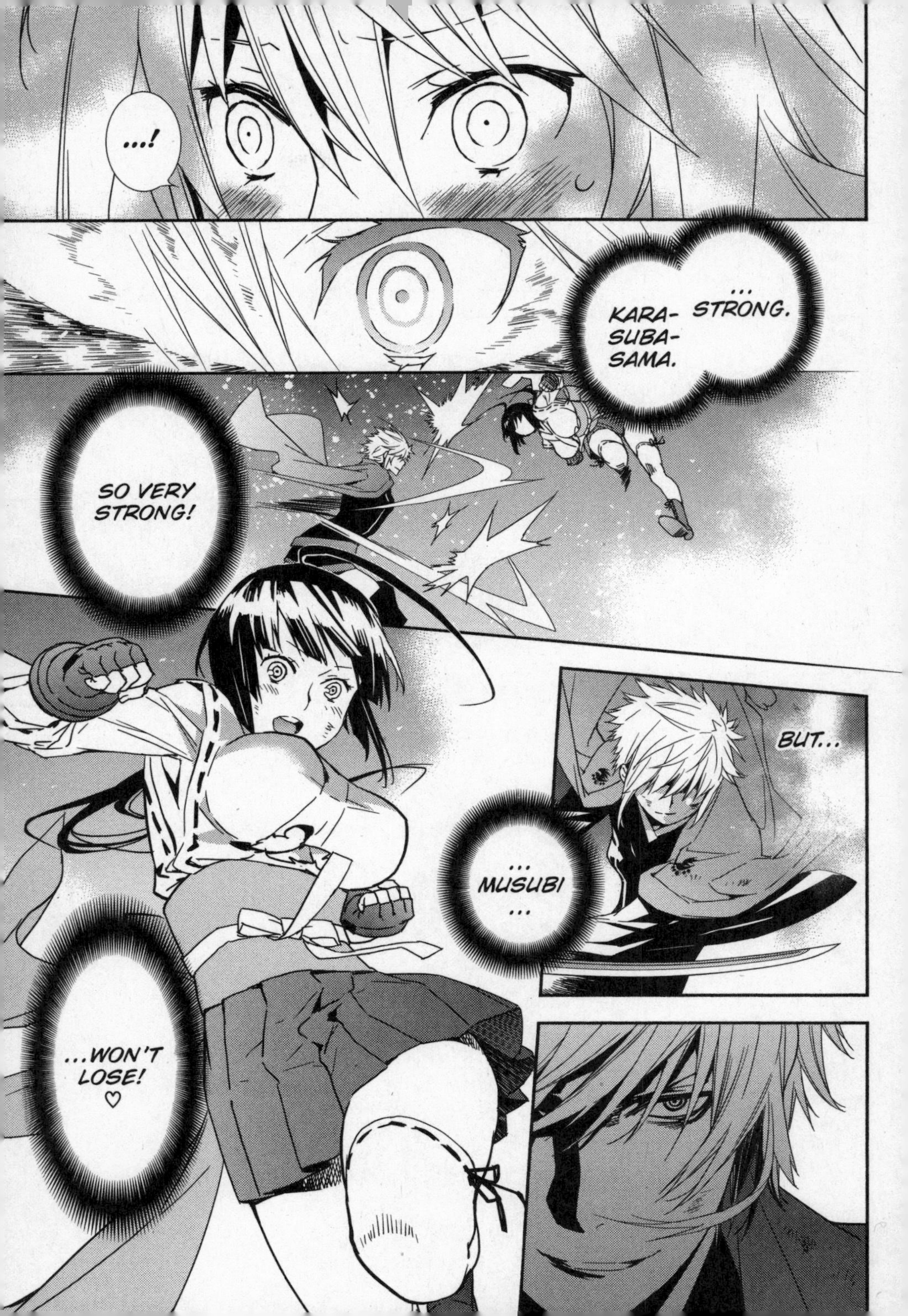
...!
KARA-SUBA-SAMA. ...STRONG.
SO VERY STRONG!
BUT...
...MUSUBI...
...WON'T LOSE! ♡

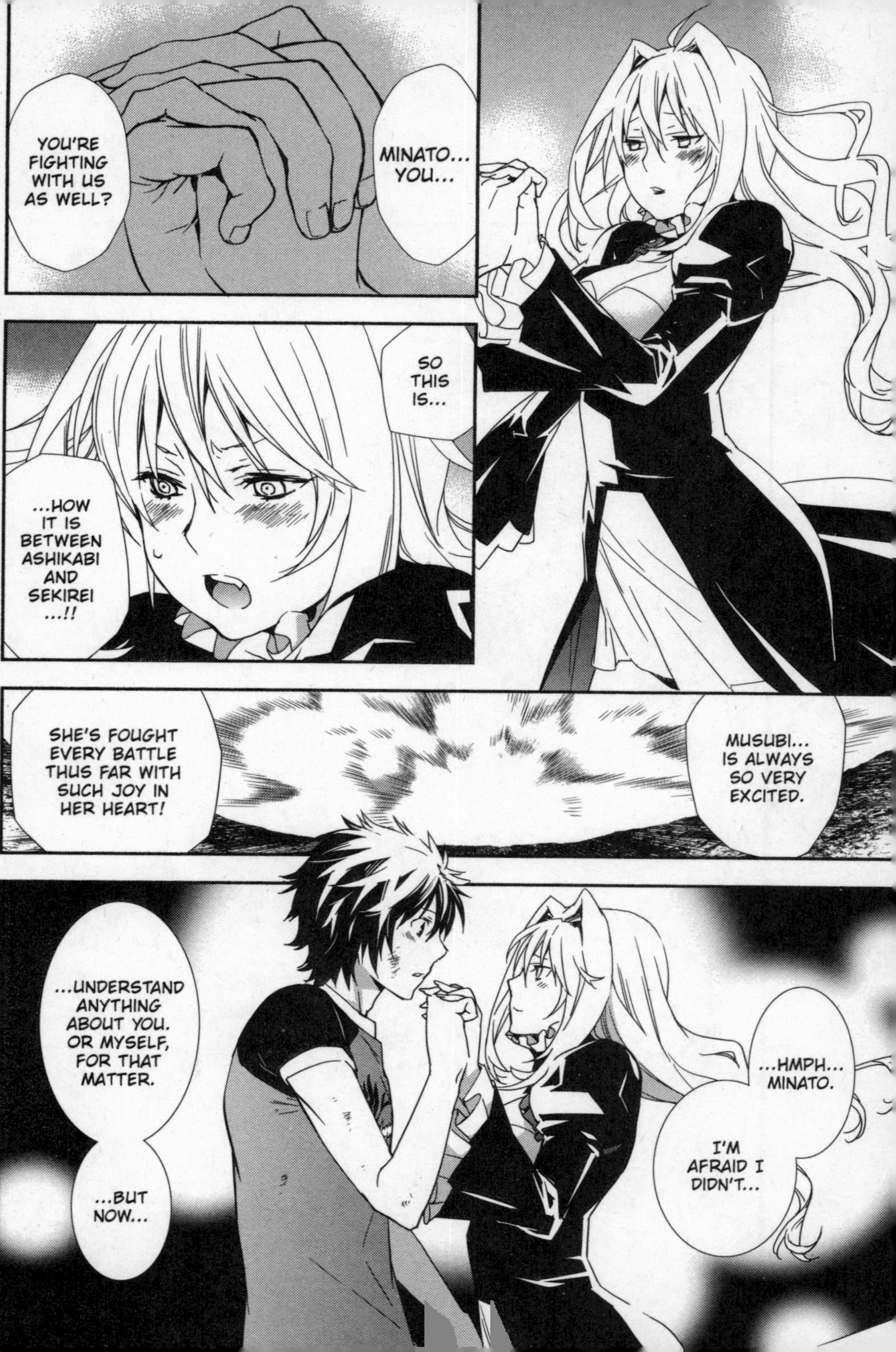
MINATO... YOU...
YOU'RE FIGHTING WITH US AS WELL?
SO THIS IS...
...HOW IT IS BETWEEN ASHIKABI AND SEKIREI ...!!
MUSUBI... IS ALWAYS SO VERY EXCITED.
SHE'S FOUGHT EVERY BATTLE THUS FAR WITH SUCH JOY IN HER HEART!
...HMPH... MINATO.
I'M AFRAID I DIDN'T...
...UNDERSTAND ANYTHING ABOUT YOU. OR MYSELF, FOR THAT MATTER.
...BUT NOW...

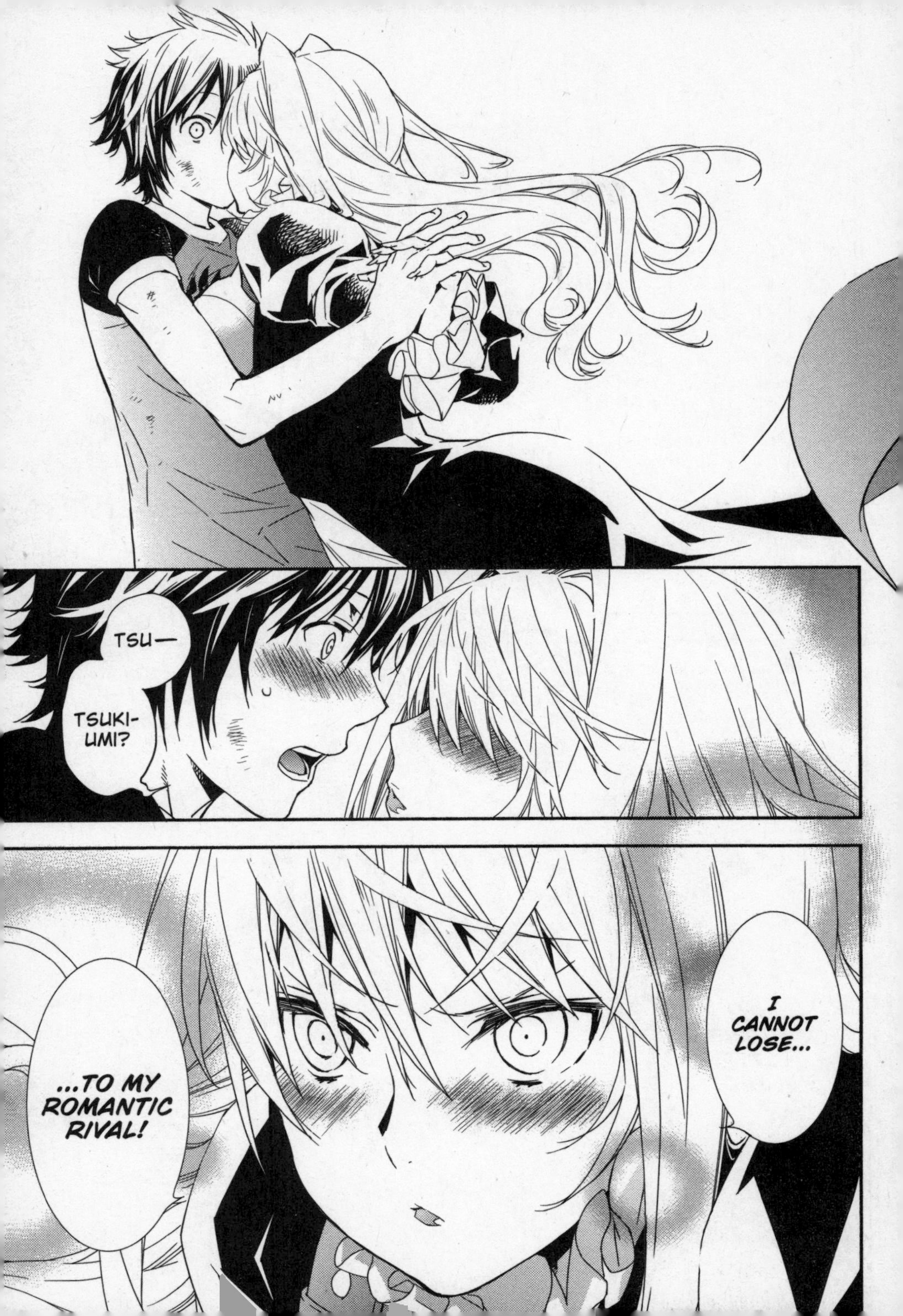
TSU—
TSUKI-UMI?
I CANNOT LOSE...
...TO MY ROMANTIC RIVAL!

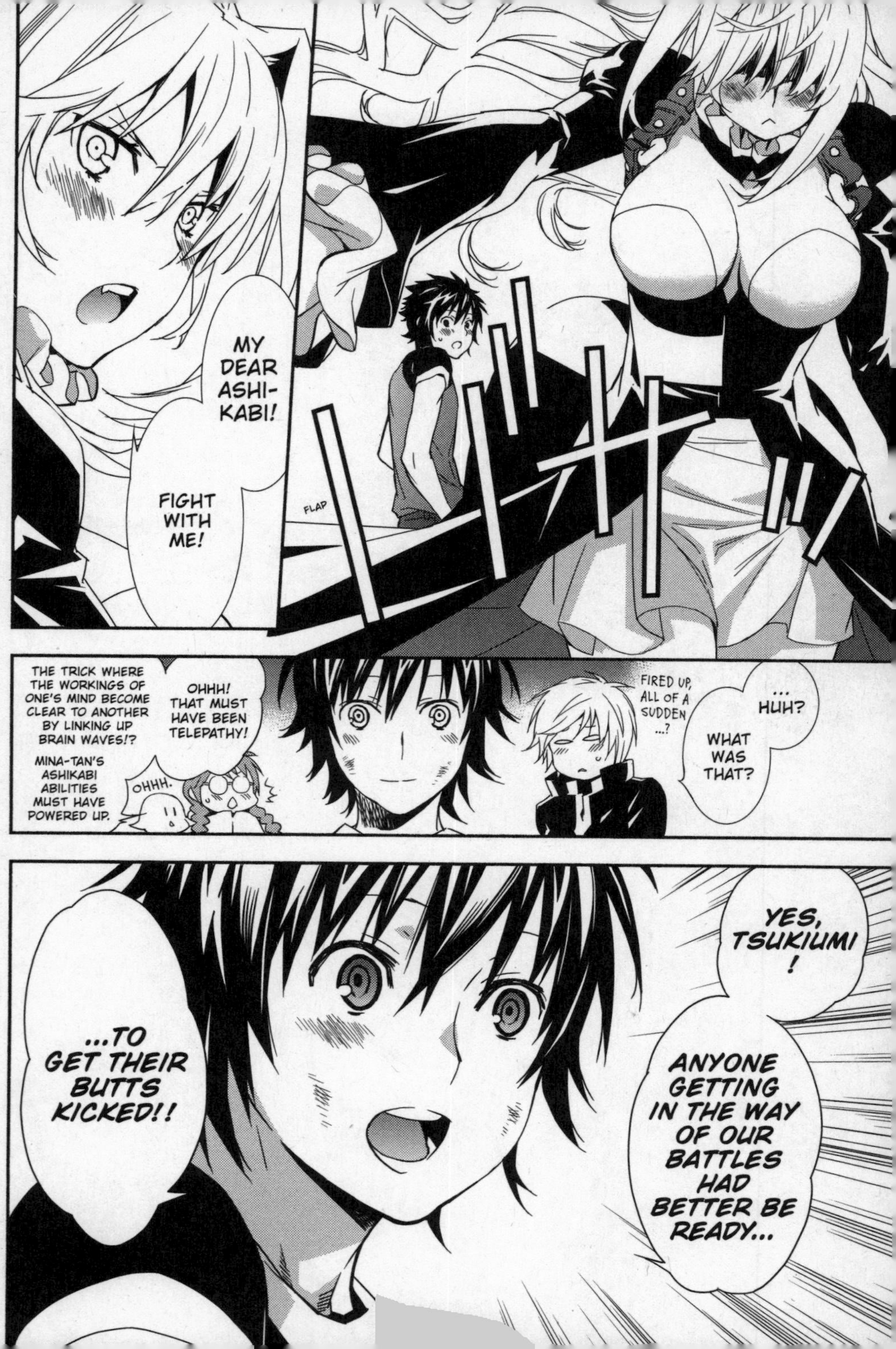
FLAP
MY DEAR ASHIKABI!
FIGHT WITH ME!
...HUH?
WHAT WAS THAT?
FIRED UP, ALL OF A SUDDEN ...?
OHHH! THAT MUST HAVE BEEN TELEPATHY!
THE TRICK WHERE THE WORKINGS OF ONE'S MIND BECOME CLEAR TO ANOTHER BY LINKING UP BRAIN WAVES!?
MINA-TAN'S ASHIKABI ABILITIES MUST HAVE POWERED UP.
OHHH.
YES, TSUKIUMI!
ANYONE GETTING IN THE WAY OF OUR BATTLES HAD BETTER BE READY...
...TO GET THEIR BUTTS KICKED!!

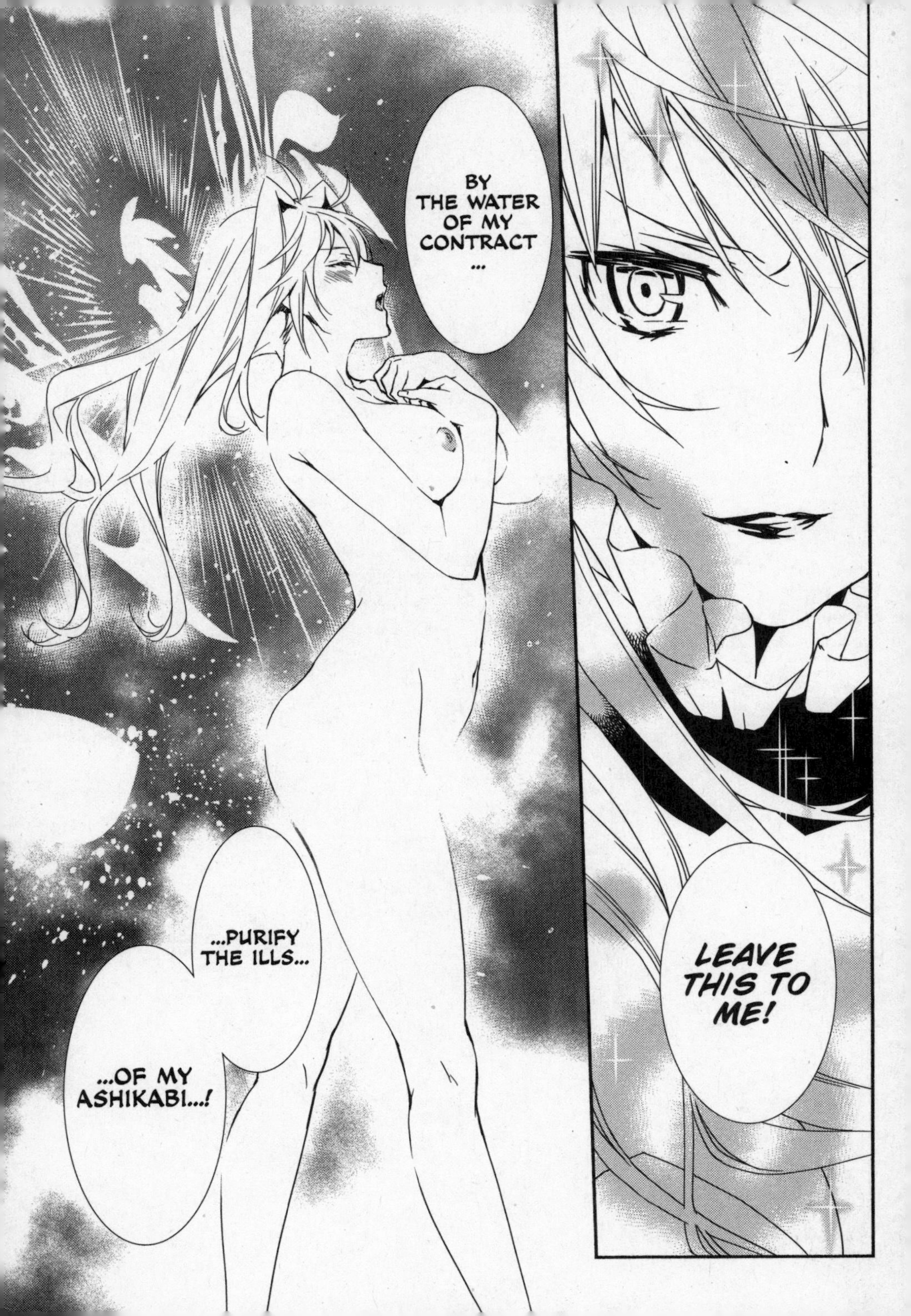
LEAVE THIS TO ME!
BY THE WATER OF MY CONTRACT ...
...PURIFY THE ILLS...
...OF MY ASHIKABI...!

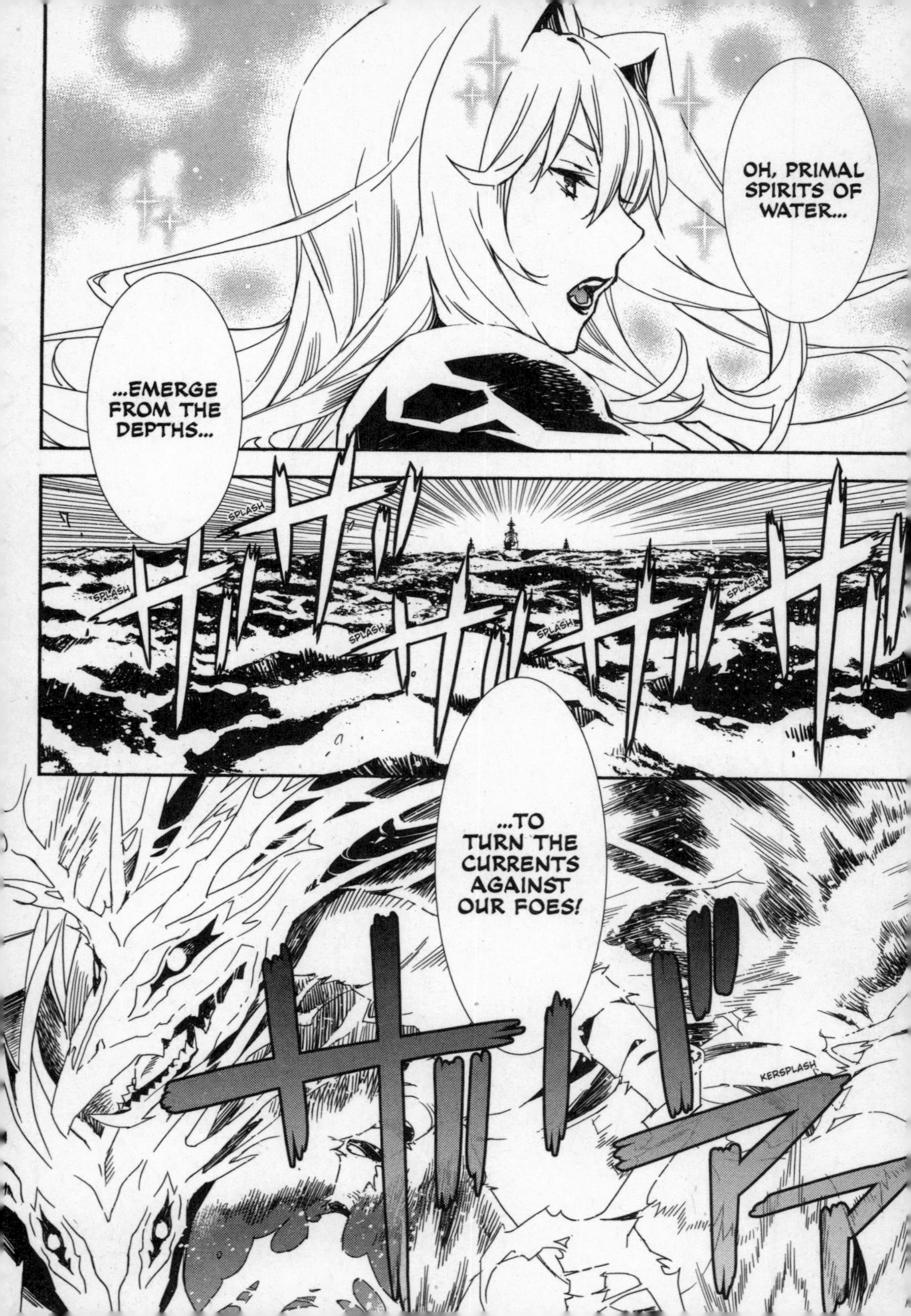
OH, PRIMAL SPIRITS OF WATER...
...EMERGE FROM THE DEPTHS...
SPLASH
SPLASH
SPLASH
SPLASH
SPLASH
...TO TURN THE CURRENTS AGAINST OUR FOES!
KERSPLASH

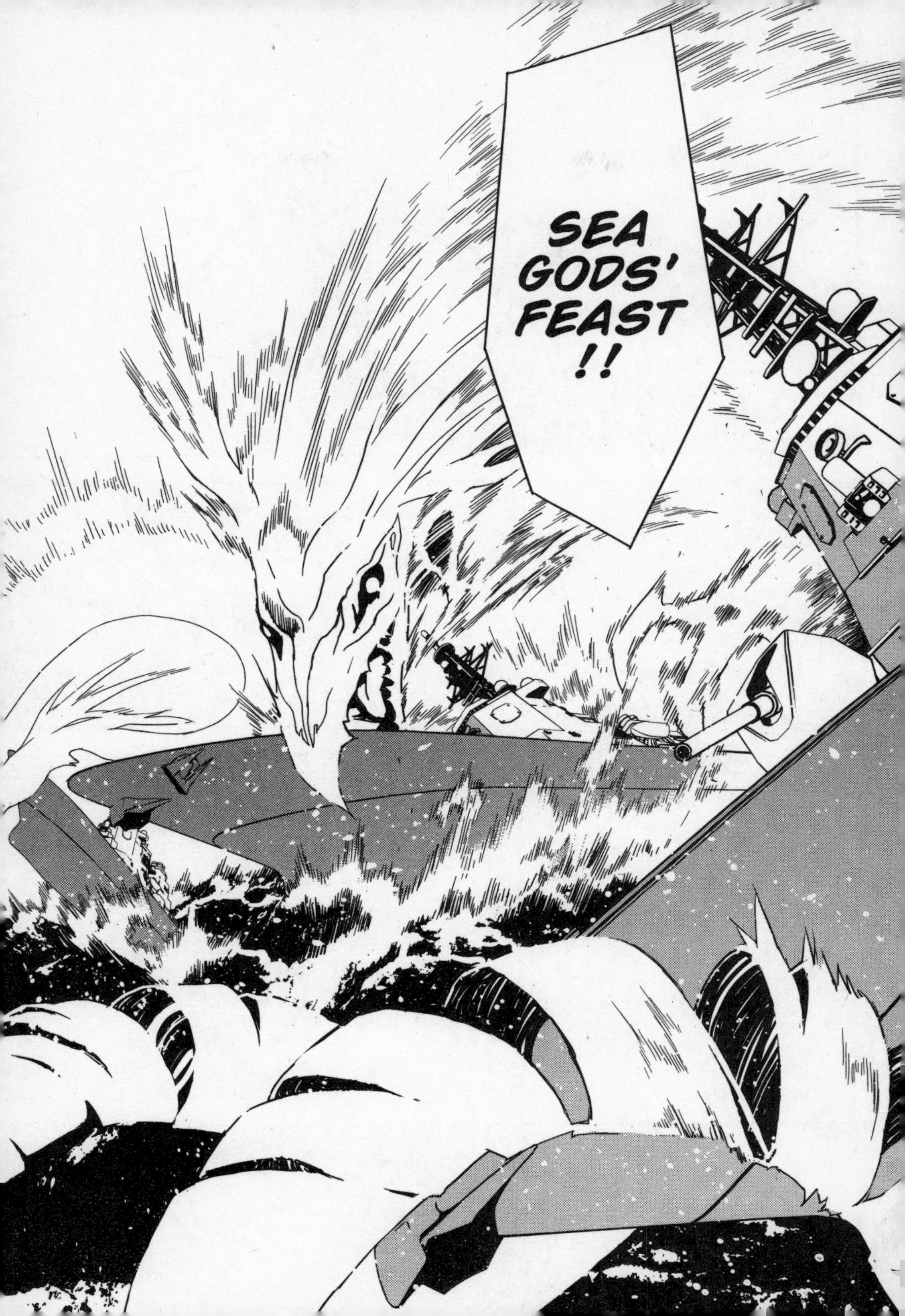
SEA GODS' FEAST !!

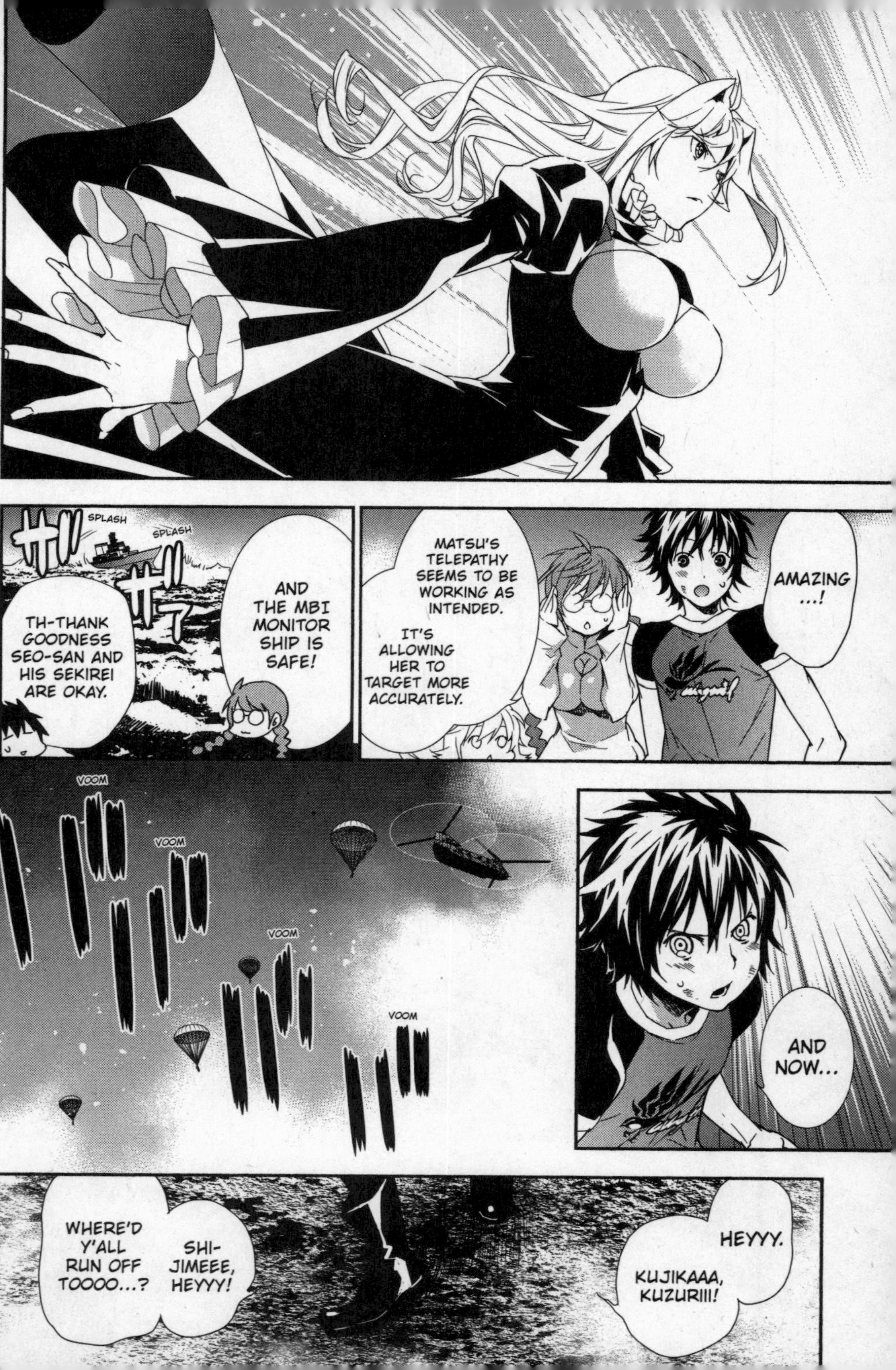
AMAZING ...!
MATSU'S TELEPATHY SEEMS TO BE WORKING AS INTENDED.
IT'S ALLOWING HER TO TARGET MORE ACCURATELY.
SPLASH
SPLASH
AND THE MBI MONITOR SHIP IS SAFE!
TH-THANK GOODNESS SEO-SAN AND HIS SEKIREI ARE OKAY.
AND NOW...
VOOM
VOOM
VOOM
VOOM
HEYYY.
KUJIKAAA, KUZURIII!
SHI-JIMEEE, HEYYY!
WHERE'D Y'ALL RUN OFF TOOOO...?

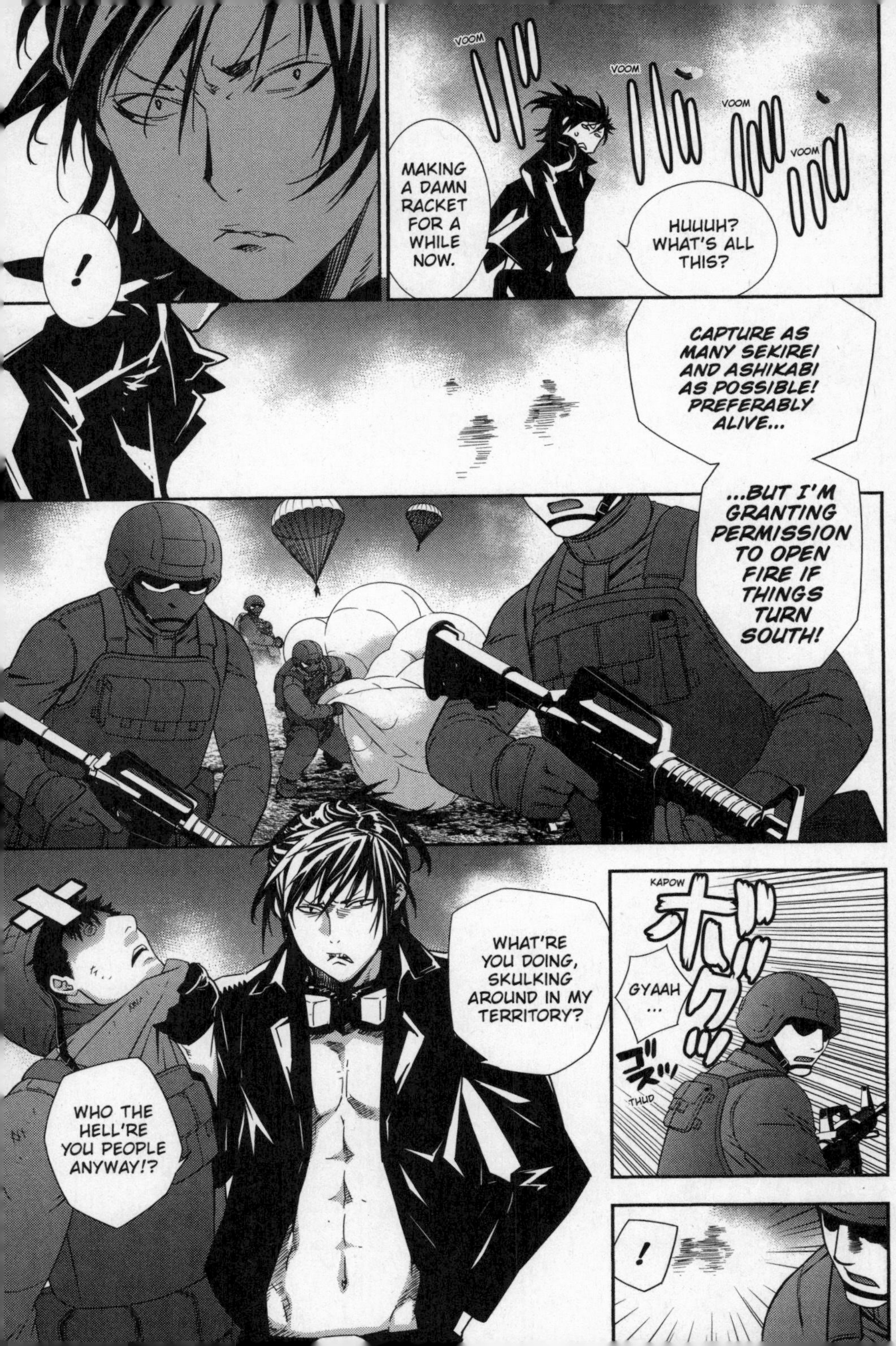
VOOM
VOOM
VOOM
VOOM
HUUUH? WHAT'S ALL THIS?
MAKING A DAMN RACKET FOR A WHILE NOW.
!
CAPTURE AS MANY SEKIREI AND ASHIKABI AS POSSIBLE! PREFERABLY ALIVE...
...BUT I'M GRANTING PERMISSION TO OPEN FIRE IF THINGS TURN SOUTH!
KAPOW
GYAAH ...
THUD
!
WHAT'RE YOU DOING, SKULKING AROUND IN MY TERRITORY?
WHO THE HELL'RE YOU PEOPLE ANYWAY!?

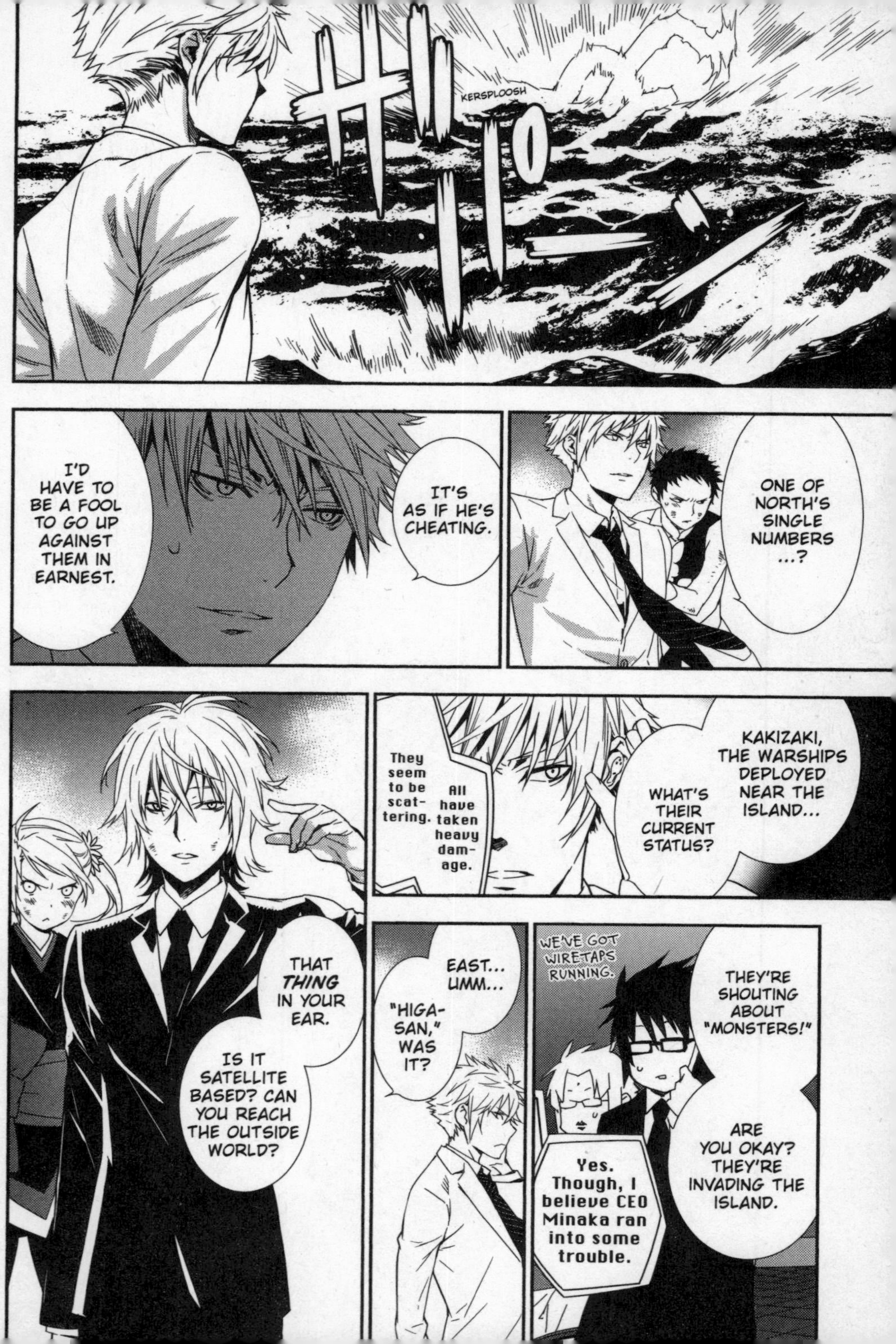
KERSPLOOSH
ONE OF NORTH'S SINGLE NUMBERS ...?
IT'S AS IF HE'S CHEATING.
I'D HAVE TO BE A FOOL TO GO UP AGAINST THEM IN EARNEST.
KAKIZAKI, THE WARSHIPS DEPLOYED NEAR THE ISLAND...
WHAT'S THEIR CURRENT STATUS?
All have taken heavy dam-age.
They seem to be scat-tering.
THEY'RE SHOUTING ABOUT "MONSTERS!"
WE'VE GOT WIRETAPS RUNNING.
ARE YOU OKAY? THEY'RE INVADING THE ISLAND.
Yes. Though, I believe CEO Minaka ran into some trouble.
EAST... UMM...
"HIGA-SAN," WAS IT?
THAT *THING* IN YOUR EAR.
IS IT SATELLITE BASED? CAN YOU REACH THE OUTSIDE WORLD?

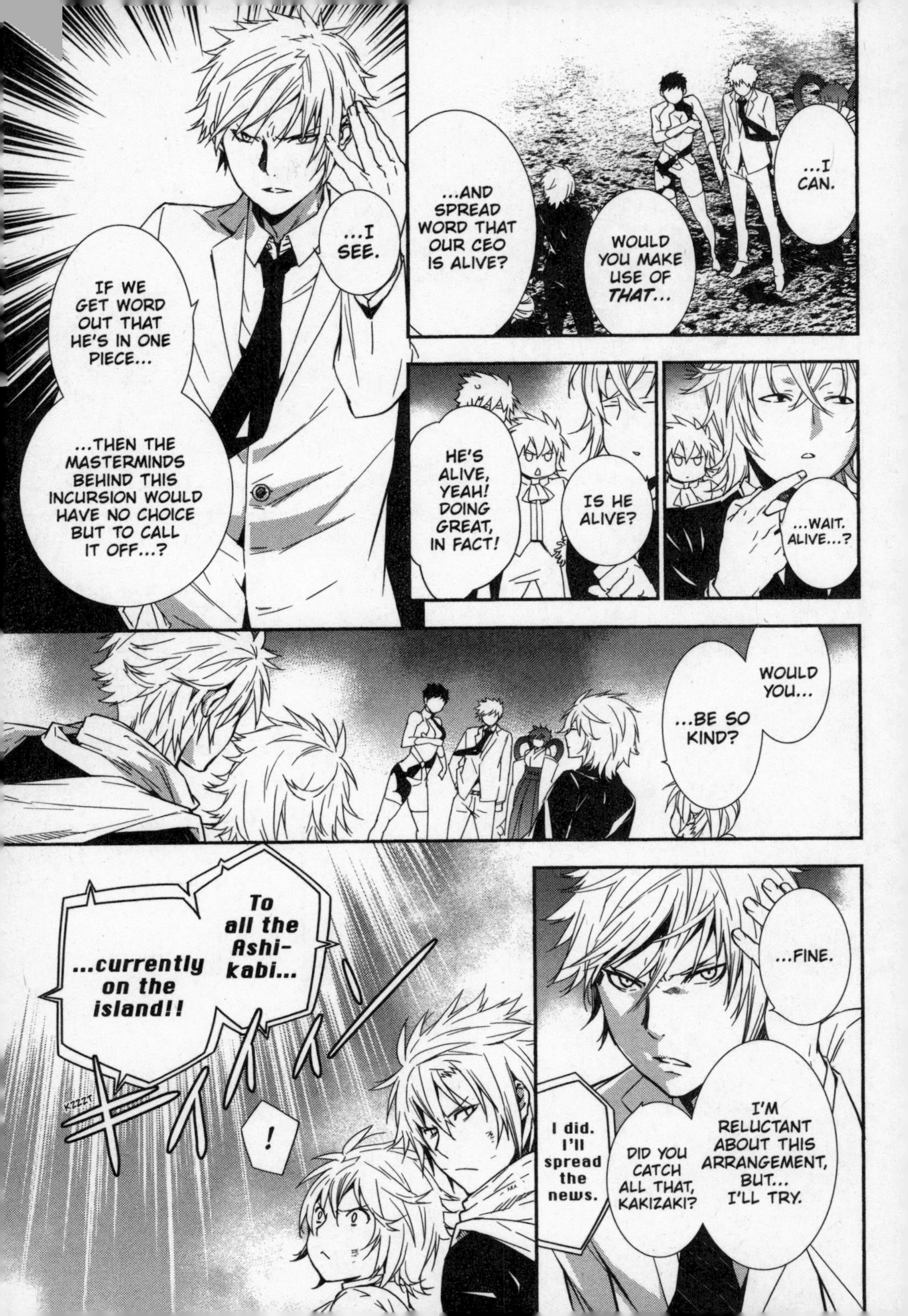
...I CAN.
WOULD YOU MAKE USE OF THAT...
...AND SPREAD WORD THAT OUR CEO IS ALIVE?
...WAIT. ALIVE...?
IS HE ALIVE?
HE'S ALIVE, YEAH! DOING GREAT, IN FACT!
...I SEE.
IF WE GET WORD OUT THAT HE'S IN ONE PIECE...
...THEN THE MASTERMINDS BEHIND THIS INCURSION WOULD HAVE NO CHOICE BUT TO CALL IT OFF...?
WOULD YOU...
...BE SO KIND?
...FINE.
I'M RELUCTANT ABOUT THIS ARRANGEMENT, BUT... I'LL TRY.
DID YOU CATCH ALL THAT, KAKIZAKI?
I did. I'll spread the news.
!
To all the Ashi-kabi...
...currently on the island!!
KZZZT

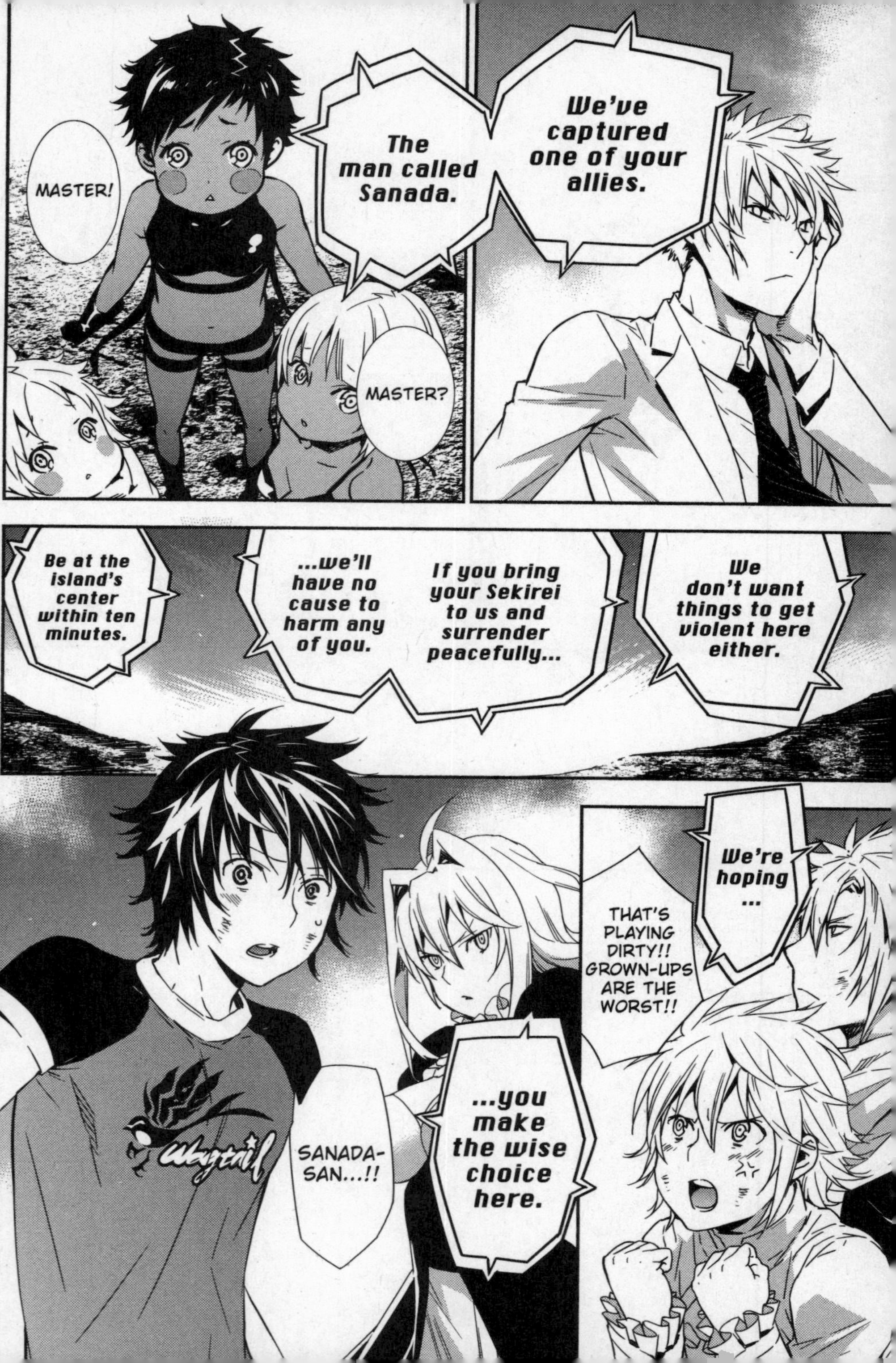

We've captured one of your allies.
The man called Sanada.
MASTER!
MASTER?
We don't want things to get violent here either.
If you bring your Sekirei to us and surrender peacefully...
...we'll have no cause to harm any of you.
Be at the island's center within ten minutes.
We're hoping...
THAT'S PLAYING DIRTY!! GROWN-UPS ARE THE WORST!!
...you make the wise choice here.
SANADA-SAN...!!

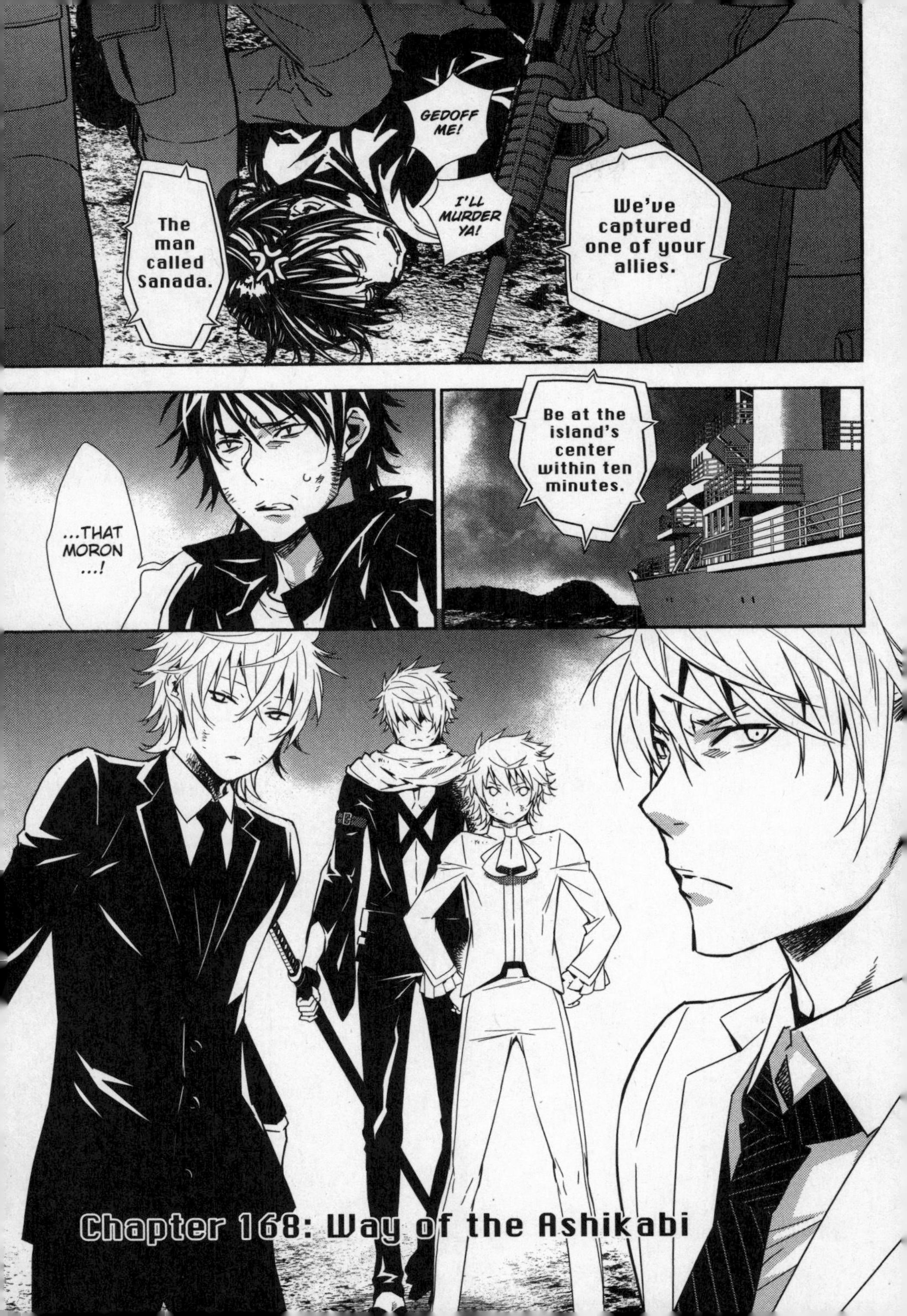
We've captured one of your allies.
GEDOFF ME!
I'LL MURDER YA!
The man called Sanada.
Be at the island's center within ten minutes.
...THAT MORON ...!
Chapter 168: Way of the Ashikabi

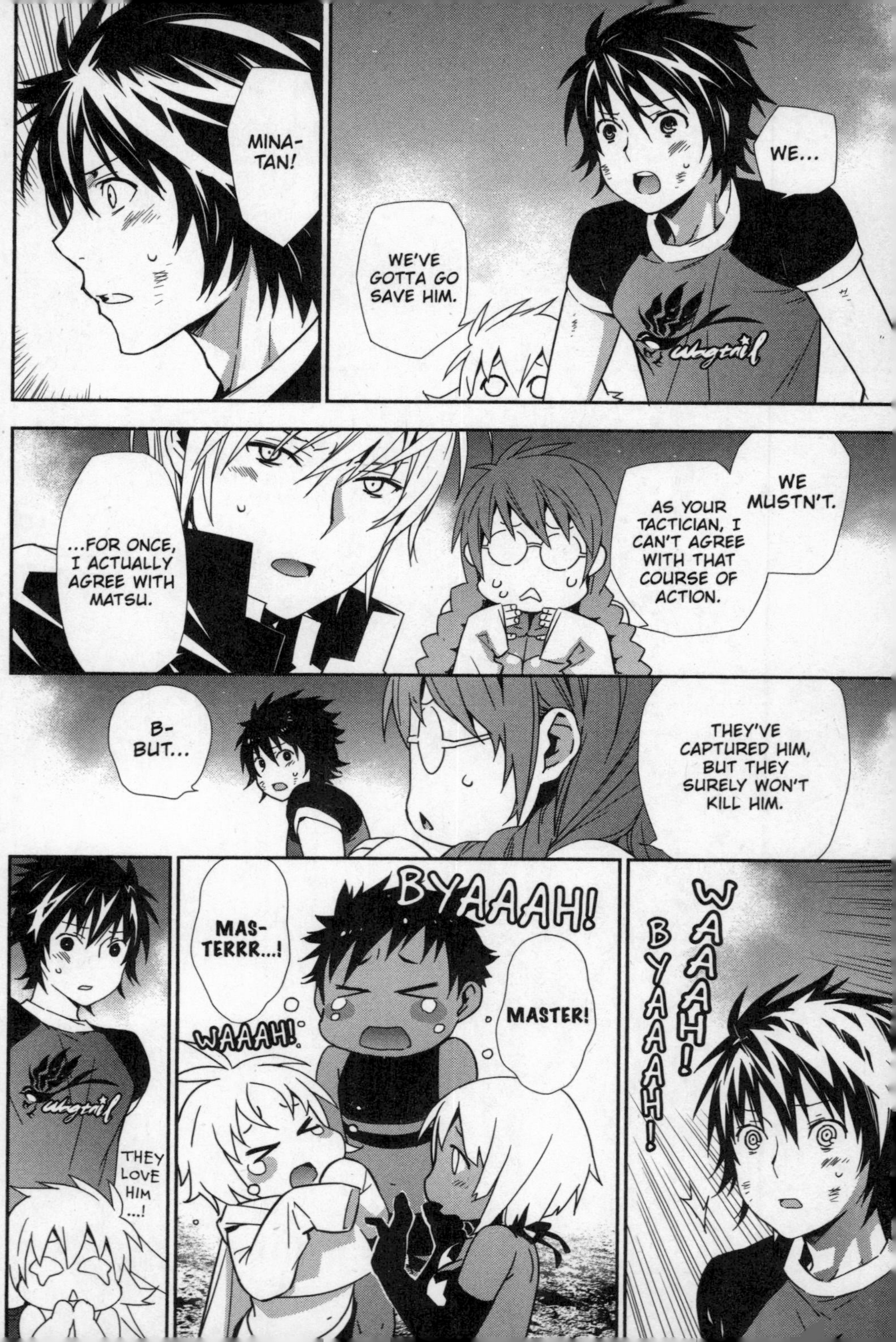
WE...
WE'VE GOTTA GO SAVE HIM.
MINA-TAN!
WE MUSTN'T.
AS YOUR TACTICIAN, I CAN'T AGREE WITH THAT COURSE OF ACTION.
...FOR ONCE, I ACTUALLY AGREE WITH MATSU.
THEY'VE CAPTURED HIM, BUT THEY SURELY WON'T KILL HIM.
B-BUT...
WAAAAH!
BYAAAAAH!
BYAAAH!
MASTER!
MAS-TERRR...!
WAAAH!
THEY LOVE HIM ...!

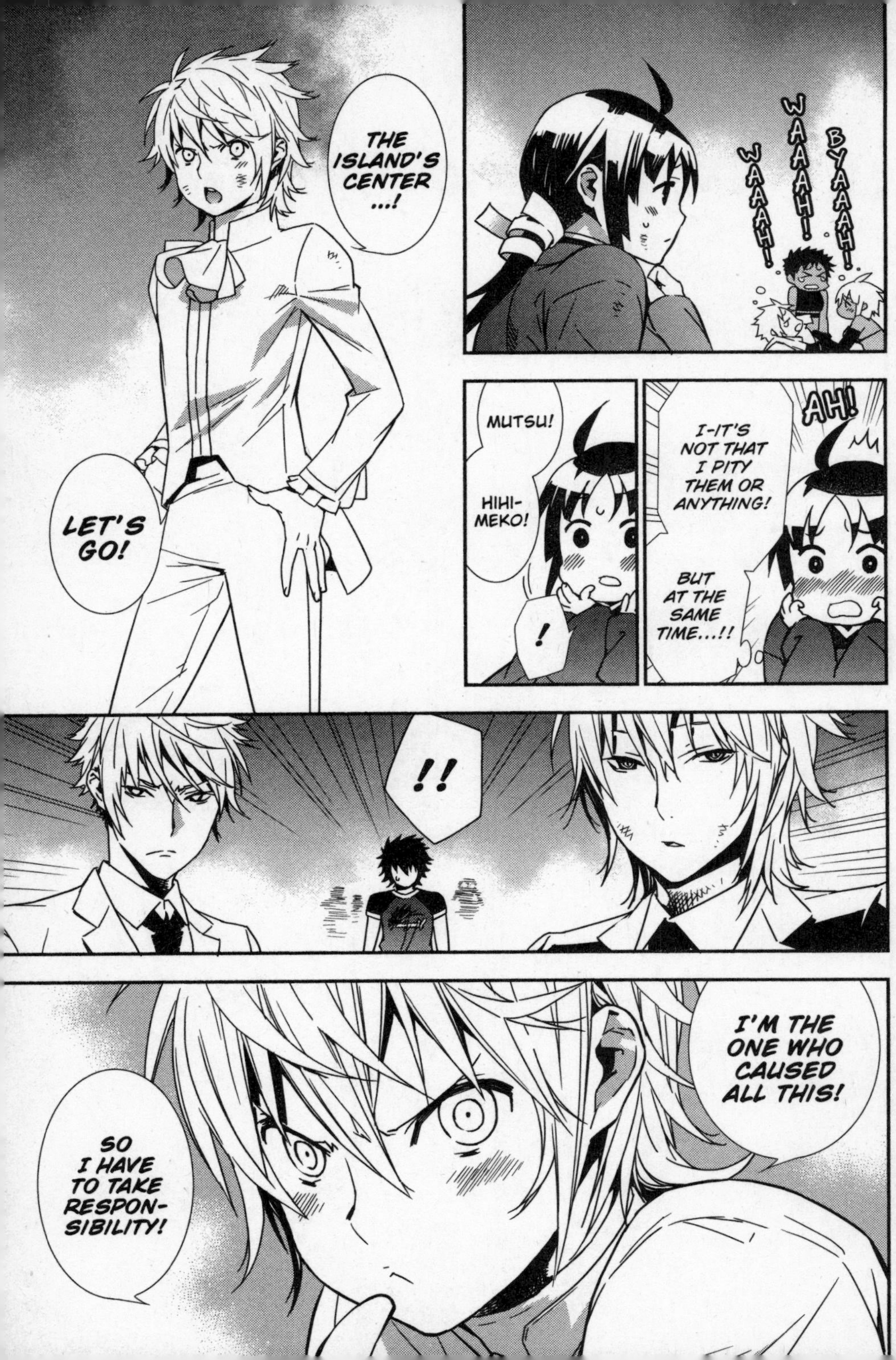
BYAAAAH!
WAAAAH!
WAAAAH!
AH!
I-IT'S NOT THAT I PITY THEM OR ANYTHING!
BUT AT THE SAME TIME...!!
MUTSU!
HIHI-MEKO!
!
THE ISLAND'S CENTER ...!
LET'S GO!
!!
I'M THE ONE WHO CAUSED ALL THIS!
SO I HAVE TO TAKE RESPON-SIBILITY!

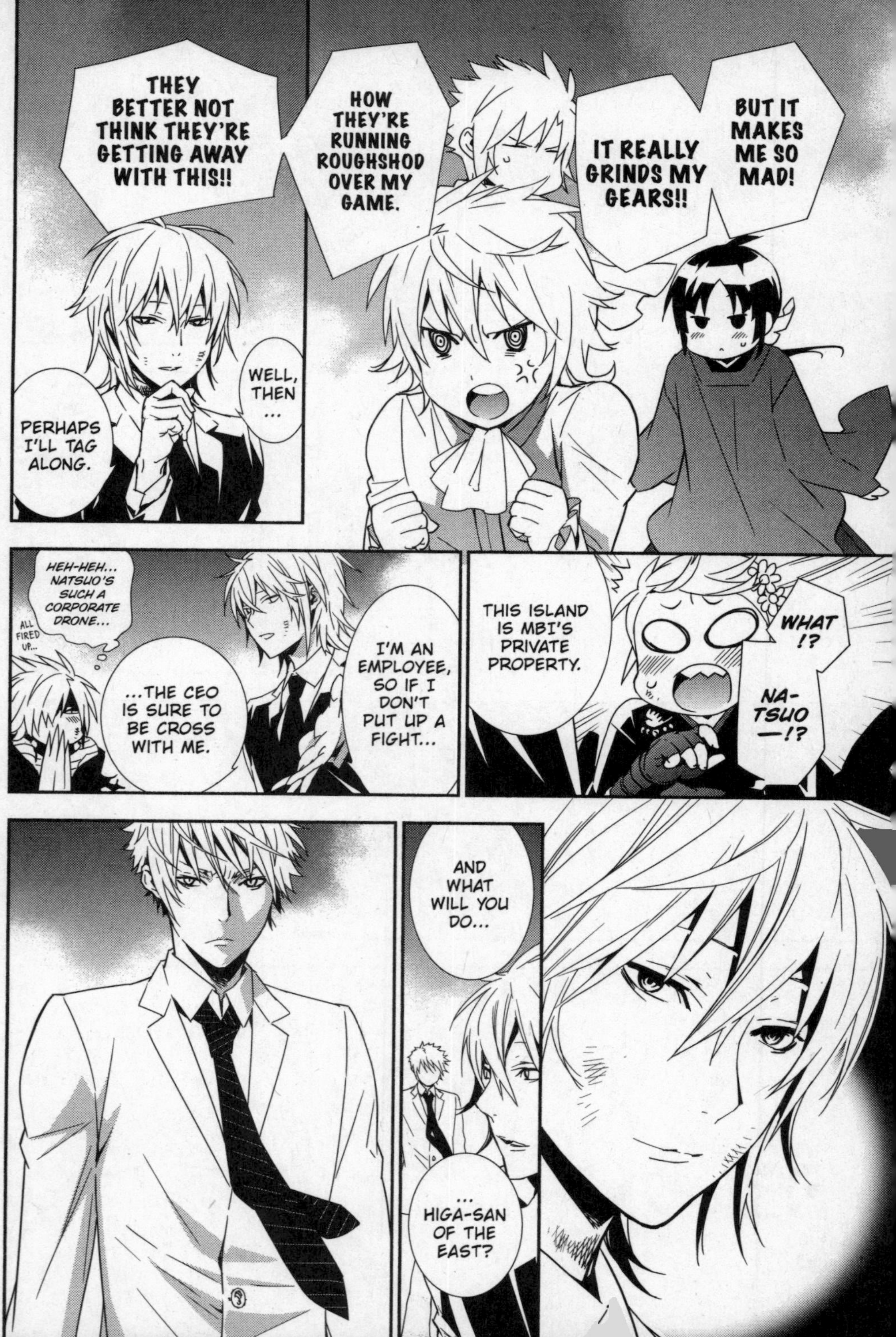
BUT IT MAKES ME SO MAD!
IT REALLY GRINDS MY GEARS!!
HOW THEY'RE RUNNING ROUGHSHOD OVER MY GAME.
THEY BETTER NOT THINK THEY'RE GETTING AWAY WITH THIS!!
WELL, THEN ...
PERHAPS I'LL TAG ALONG.
WHAT !?
THIS ISLAND IS MBI'S PRIVATE PROPERTY.
NA-TSUO—!?
I'M AN EMPLOYEE, SO IF I DON'T PUT UP A FIGHT...
HEH-HEH... NATSUO'S SUCH A CORPORATE DRONE...
...THE CEO IS SURE TO BE CROSS WITH ME.
ALL FIRED UP...
AND WHAT WILL YOU DO...
...HIGA-SAN OF THE EAST?

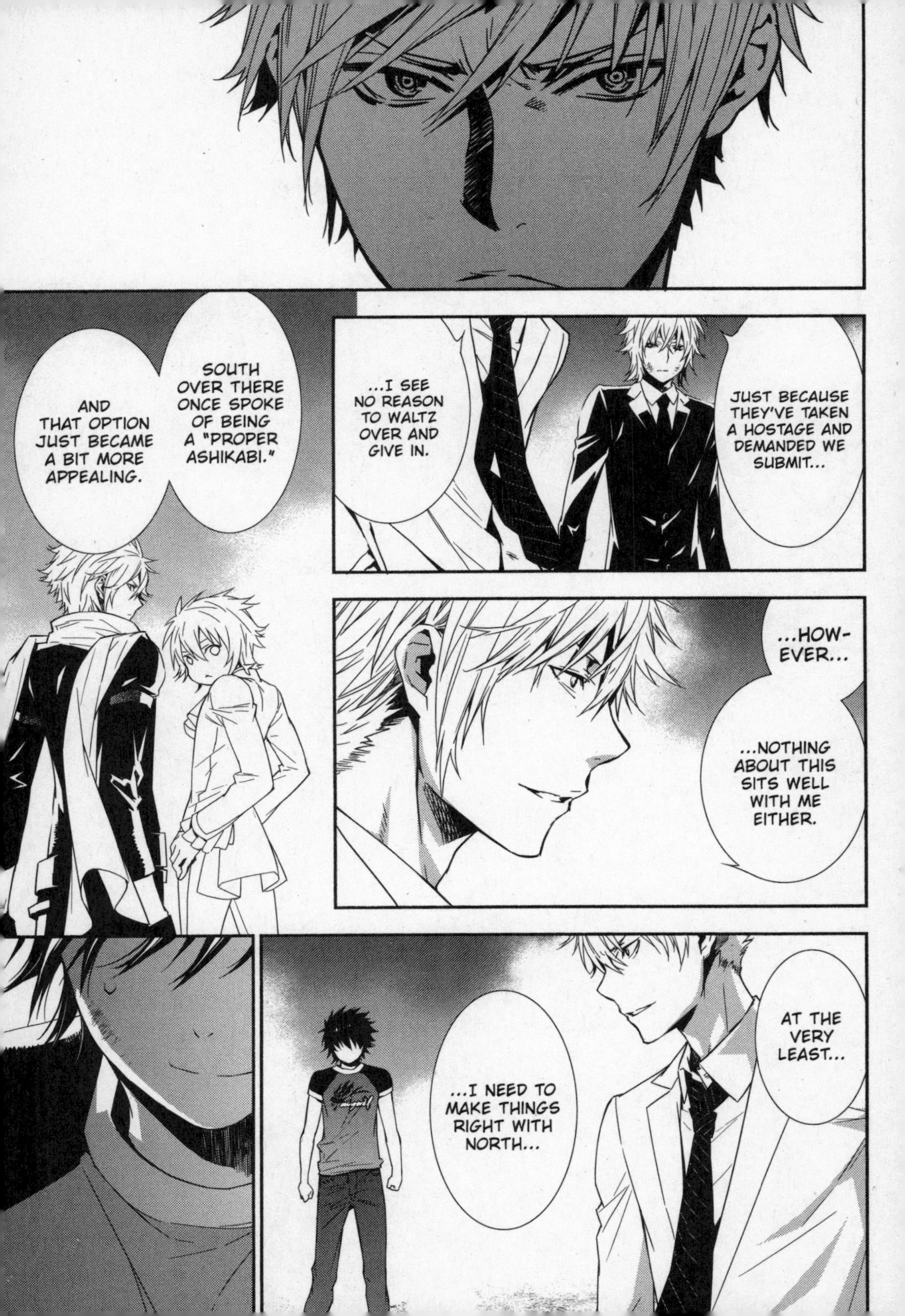
JUST BECAUSE THEY'VE TAKEN A HOSTAGE AND DEMANDED WE SUBMIT...
...I SEE NO REASON TO WALTZ OVER AND GIVE IN.
...HOW-EVER...
...NOTHING ABOUT THIS SITS WELL WITH ME EITHER.
SOUTH OVER THERE ONCE SPOKE OF BEING A "PROPER ASHIKABI."
AND THAT OPTION JUST BECAME A BIT MORE APPEALING.
AT THE VERY LEAST...
...I NEED TO MAKE THINGS RIGHT WITH NORTH...

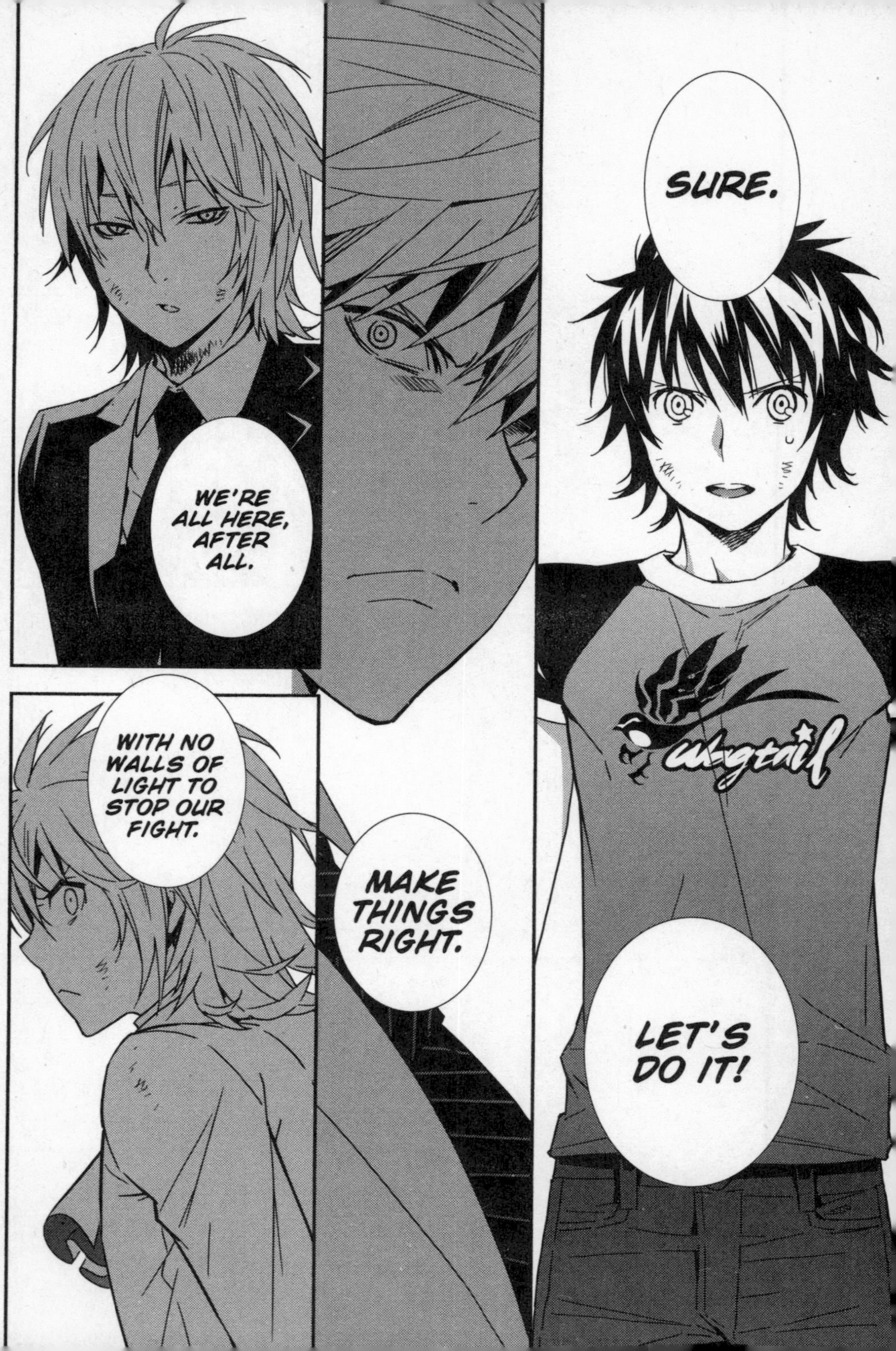
SURE.
LET'S DO IT!
MAKE THINGS RIGHT.
WE'RE ALL HERE, AFTER ALL.
WITH NO WALLS OF LIGHT TO STOP OUR FIGHT.

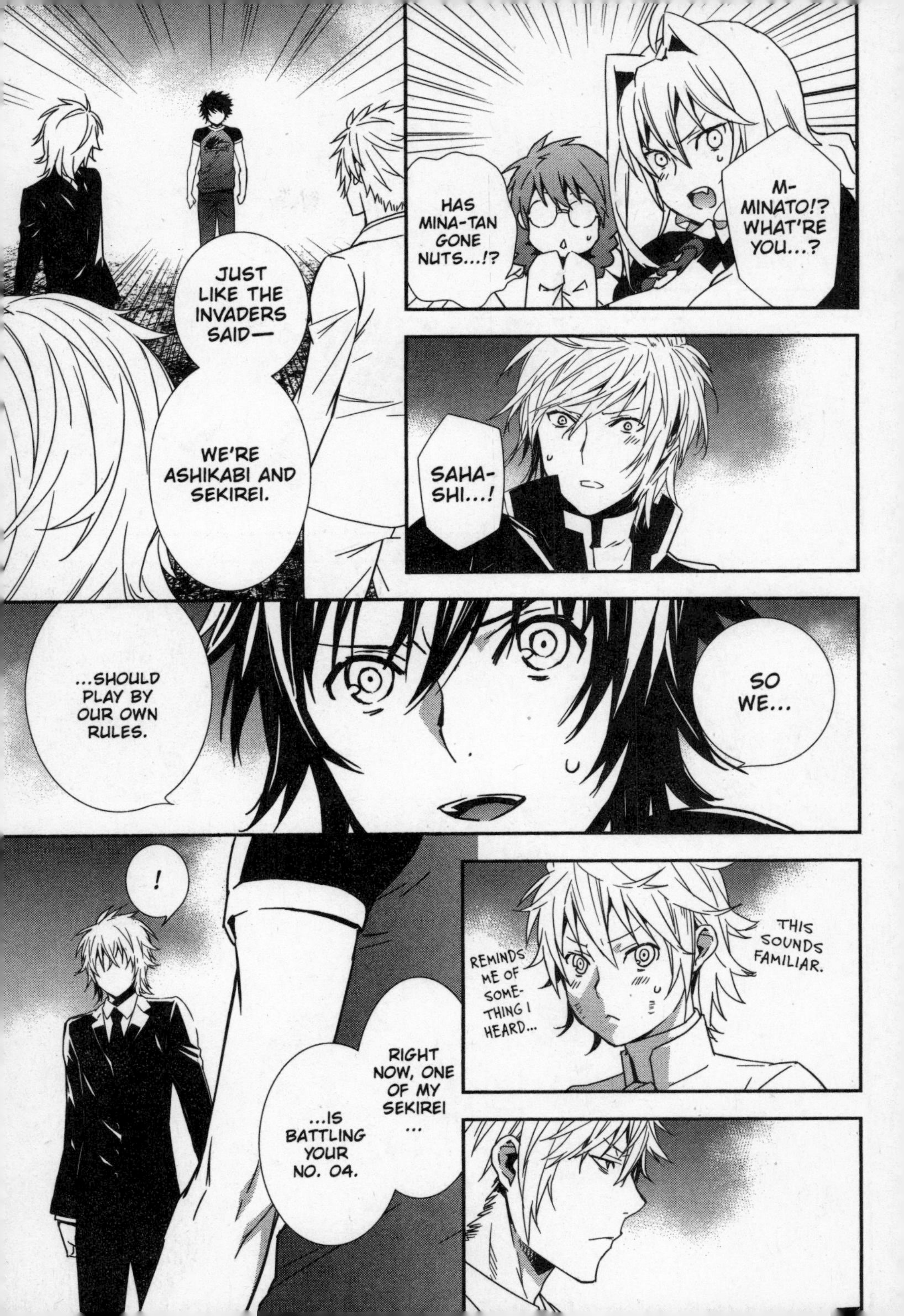
M-MINATO!? WHAT'RE YOU...?
HAS MINA-TAN GONE NUTS...!?
SAHA-SHI...!
JUST LIKE THE INVADERS SAID—
WE'RE ASHIKABI AND SEKIREI.
SO WE...
...SHOULD PLAY BY OUR OWN RULES.
THIS SOUNDS FAMILIAR.
REMINDS ME OF SOME-THING I HEARD...
!
RIGHT NOW, ONE OF MY SEKIREI...
...IS BATTLING YOUR NO. 04.

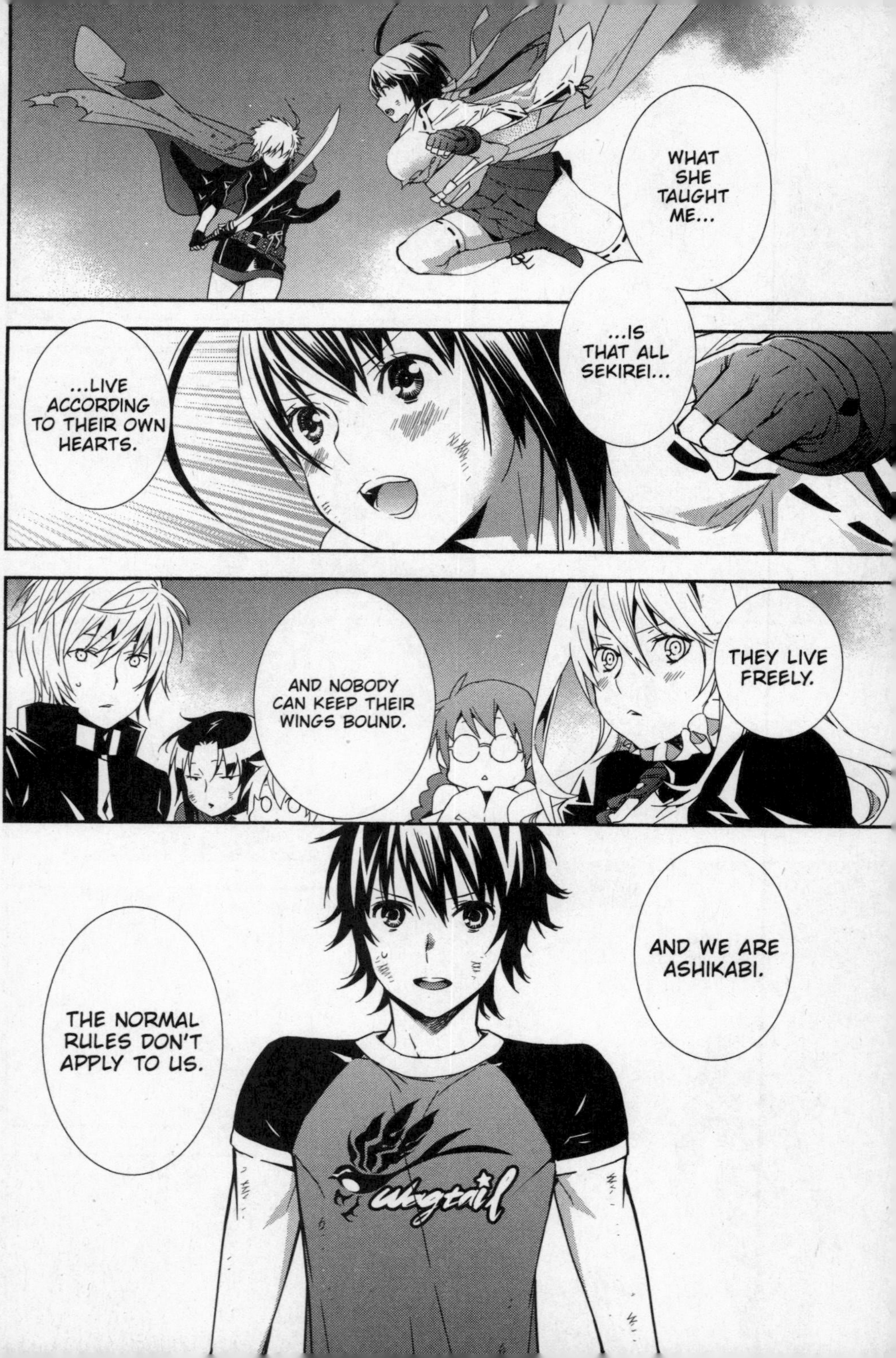
WHAT SHE TAUGHT ME...
...IS THAT ALL SEKIREI...
...LIVE ACCORDING TO THEIR OWN HEARTS.
THEY LIVE FREELY.
AND NOBODY CAN KEEP THEIR WINGS BOUND.
AND WE ARE ASHIKABI.
THE NORMAL RULES DON'T APPLY TO US.
wagtail

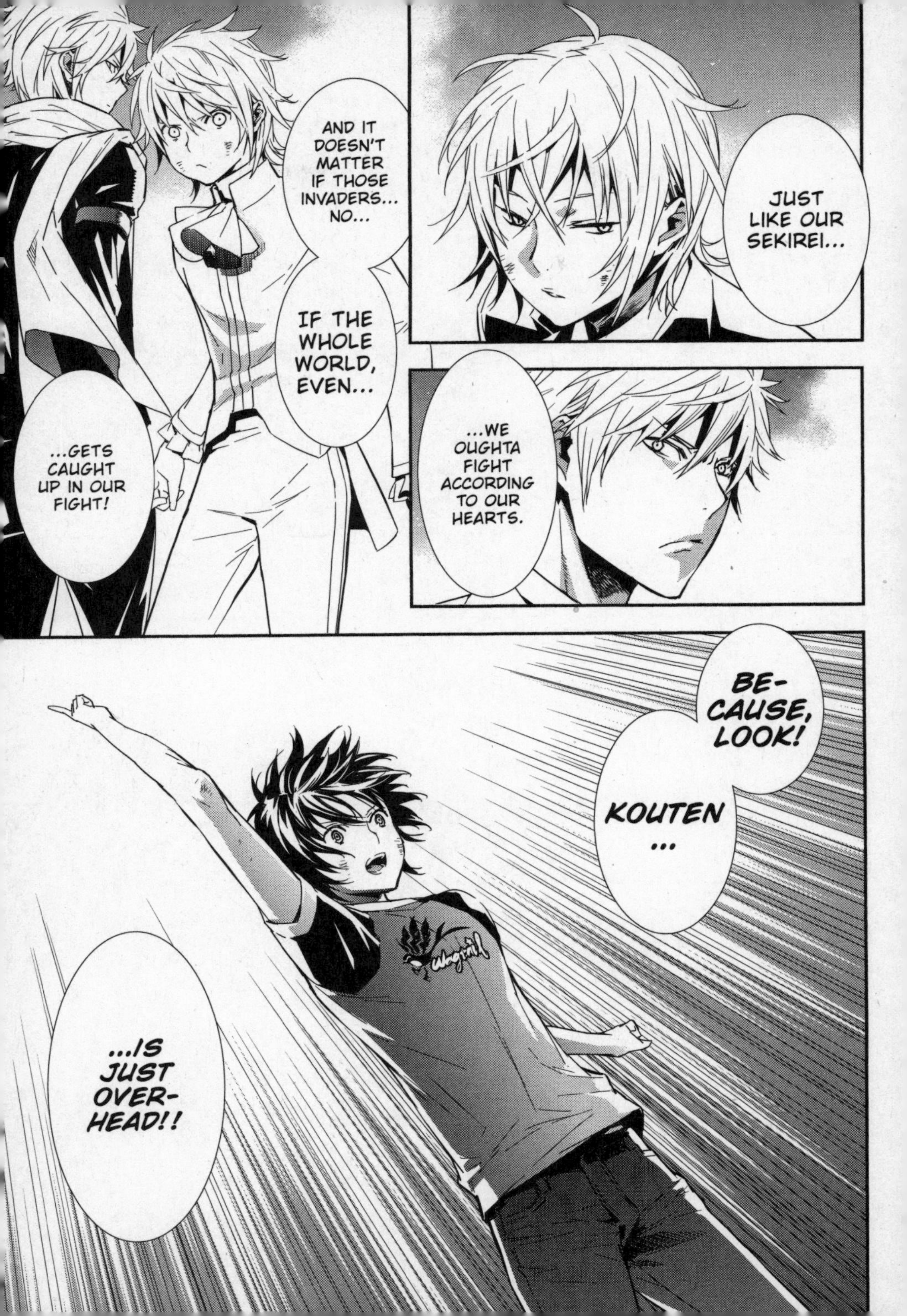
JUST LIKE OUR SEKIREI...
...WE OUGHTA FIGHT ACCORDING TO OUR HEARTS.
AND IT DOESN'T MATTER IF THOSE INVADERS... NO...
IF THE WHOLE WORLD, EVEN...
...GETS CAUGHT UP IN OUR FIGHT!
BE-CAUSE, LOOK!
KOUTEN ...
...IS JUST OVER-HEAD!!

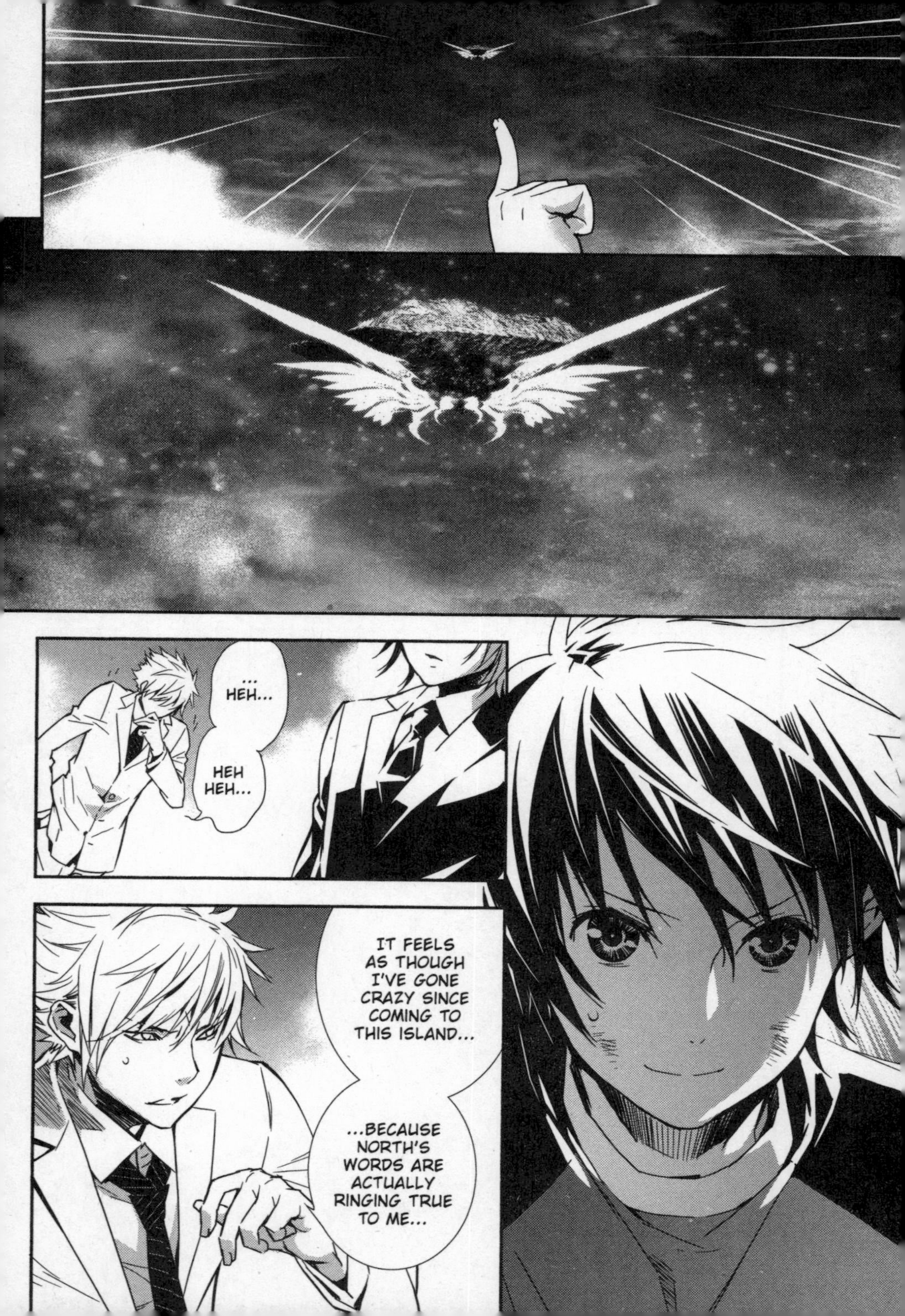
... HEH...
HEH HEH...
IT FEELS AS THOUGH I'VE GONE CRAZY SINCE COMING TO THIS ISLAND...
...BECAUSE NORTH'S WORDS ARE ACTUALLY RINGING TRUE TO ME...

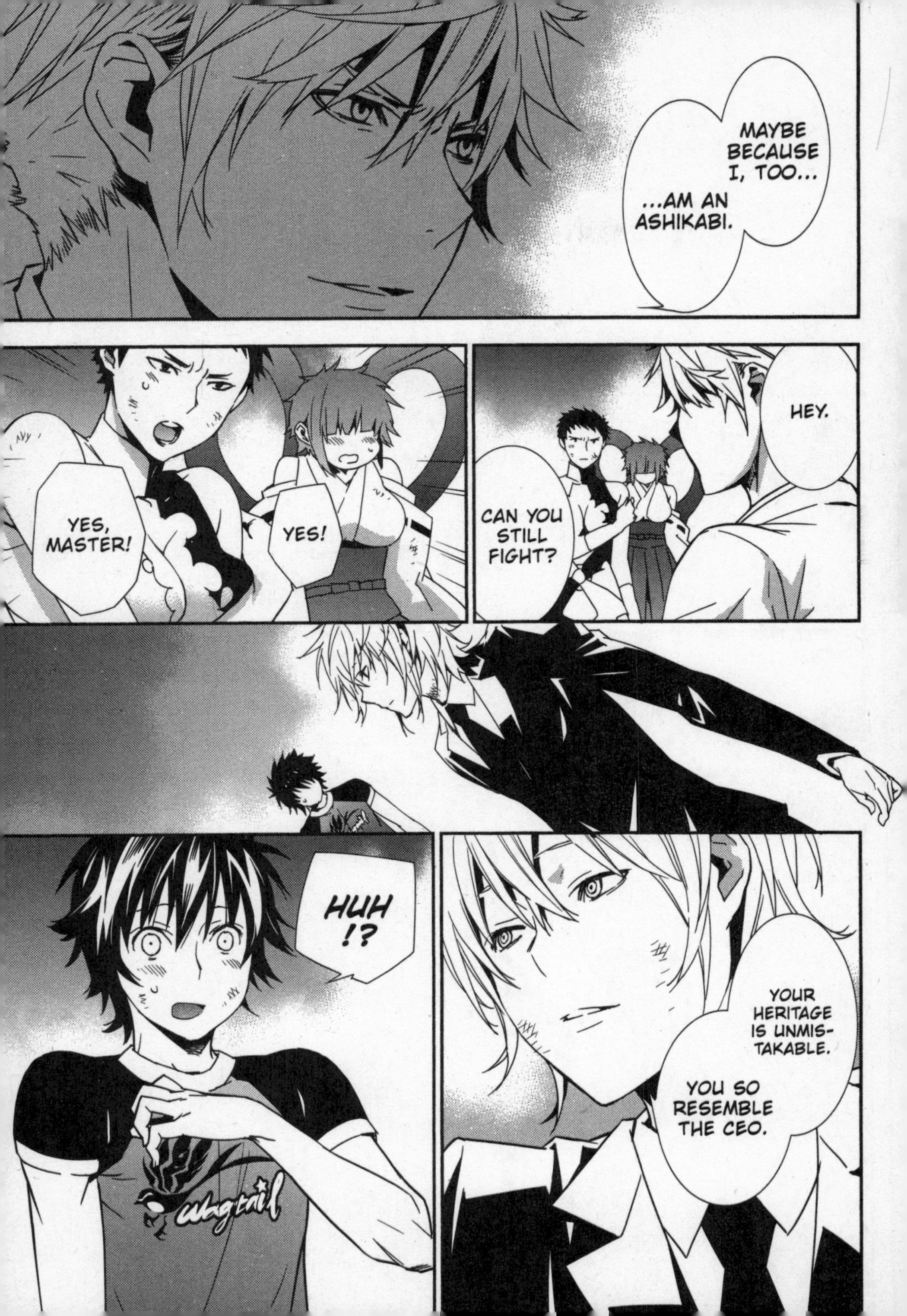
MAYBE BECAUSE I, TOO...
...AM AN ASHIKABI.
HEY.
CAN YOU STILL FIGHT?
YES!
YES, MASTER!
YOUR HERITAGE IS UNMIS-TAKABLE.
YOU SO RESEMBLE THE CEO.
HUH!?
Wagtail

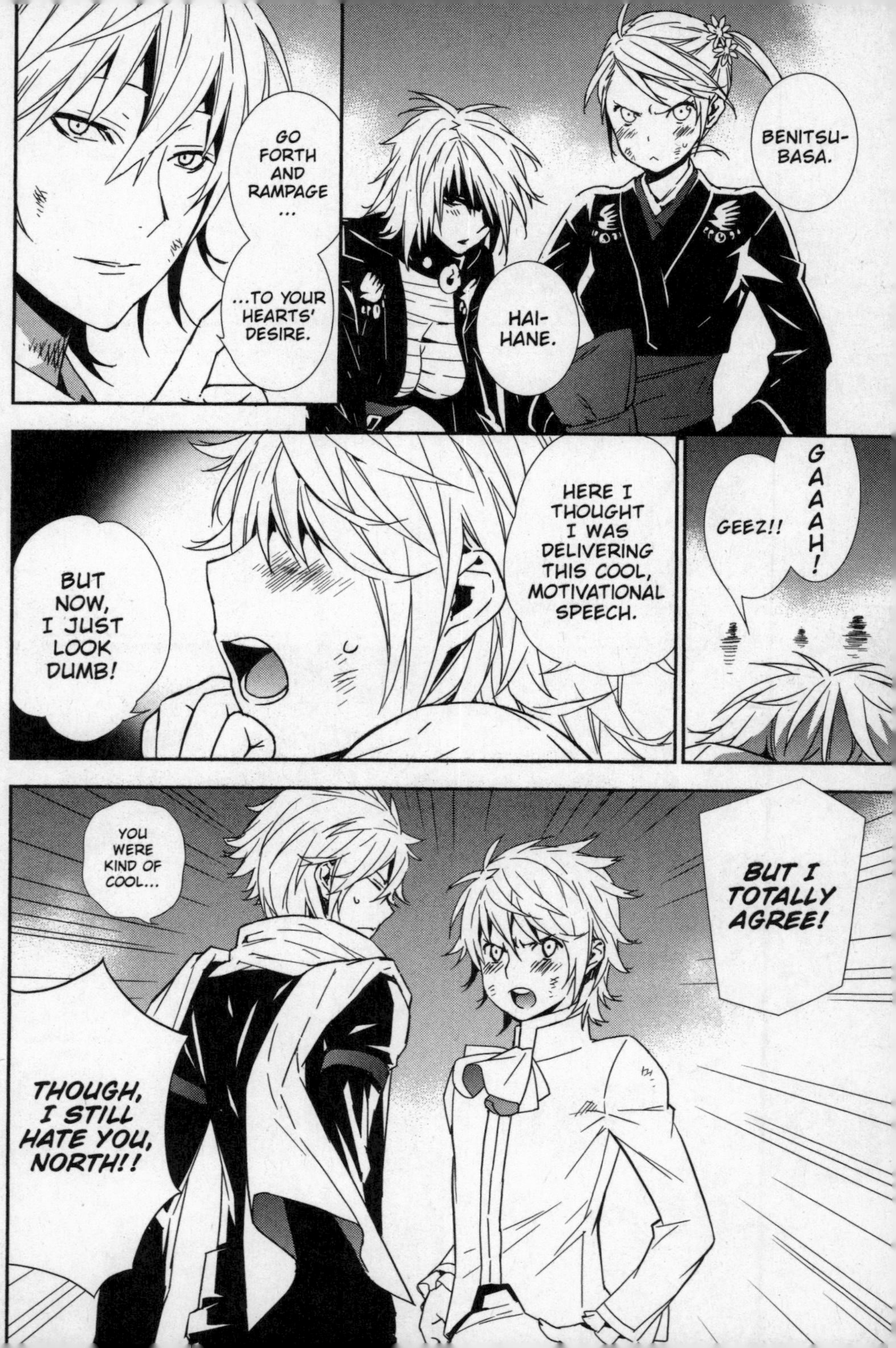
BENITSU-BASA.
HAI-HANE.
GO FORTH AND RAMPAGE...
...TO YOUR HEARTS' DESIRE.
GAAAH!
GEEZ!!
HERE I THOUGHT I WAS DELIVERING THIS COOL, MOTIVATIONAL SPEECH.
BUT NOW, I JUST LOOK DUMB!
BUT I TOTALLY AGREE!
YOU WERE KIND OF COOL...
THOUGH, I STILL HATE YOU, NORTH!!

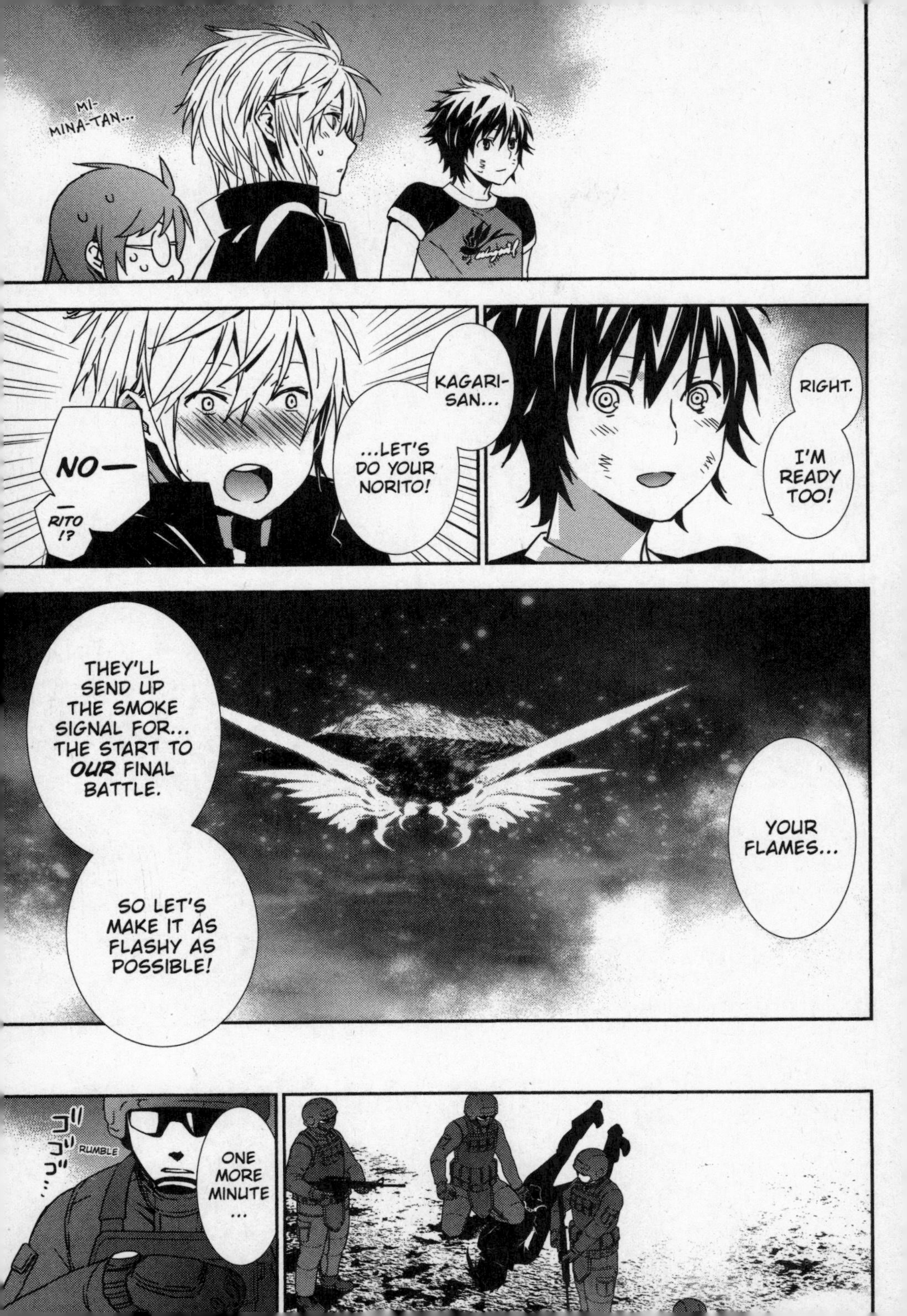
MI-
MINA-TAN...
RIGHT.
I'M READY TOO!
KAGARI-SAN...
...LET'S DO YOUR NORITO!
NO—
—RITO!?
YOUR FLAMES...
THEY'LL SEND UP THE SMOKE SIGNAL FOR... THE START TO OUR FINAL BATTLE.
SO LET'S MAKE IT AS FLASHY AS POSSIBLE!
ONE MORE MINUTE...
ゴゴゴ…
RUMBLE

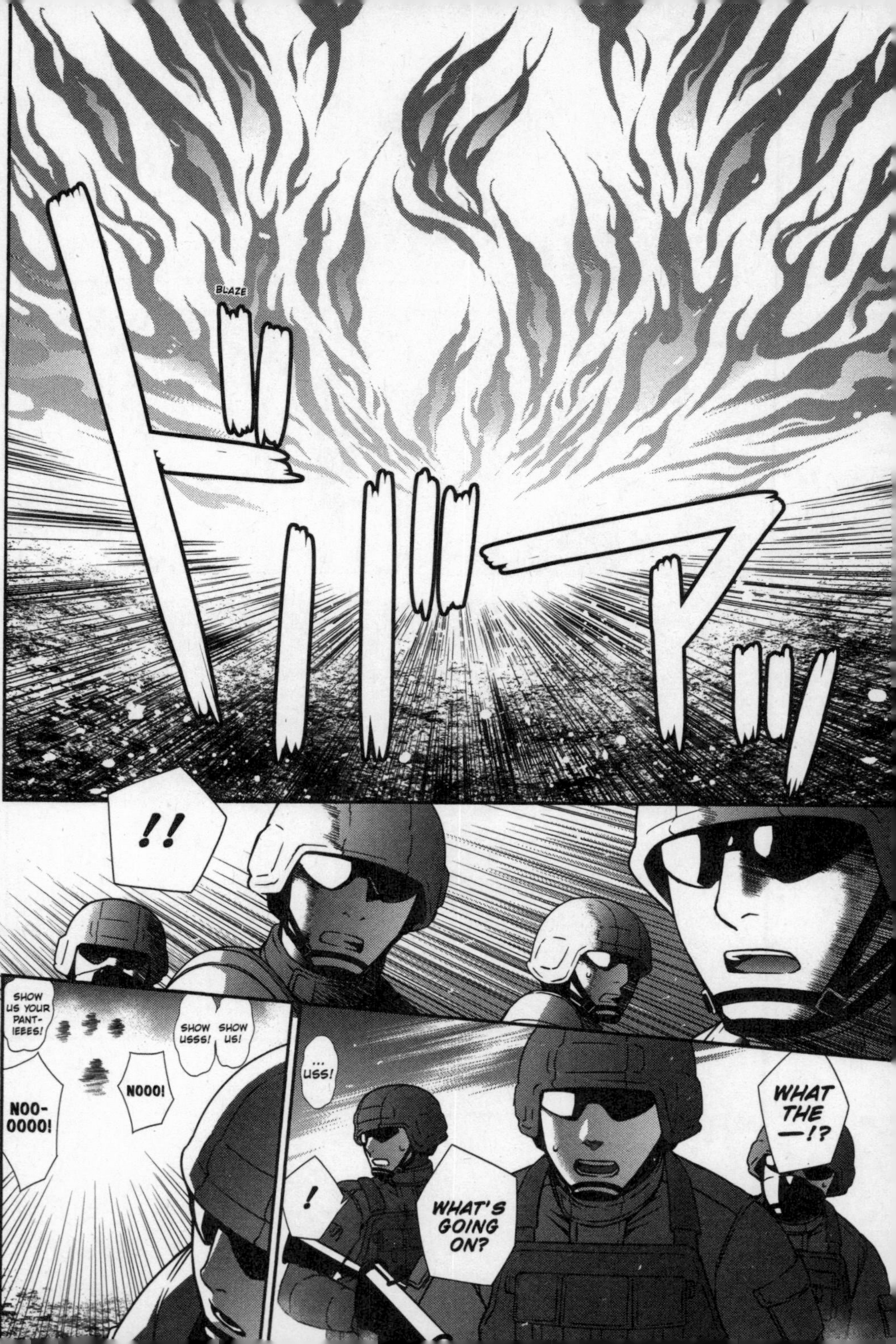
BLAZE
!!
WHAT THE—!?
WHAT'S GOING ON?
!
...USS!
SHOW US!
SHOW USSS!
NOOO!
SHOW US YOUR PANTIEEES!
NOO-OOOO!

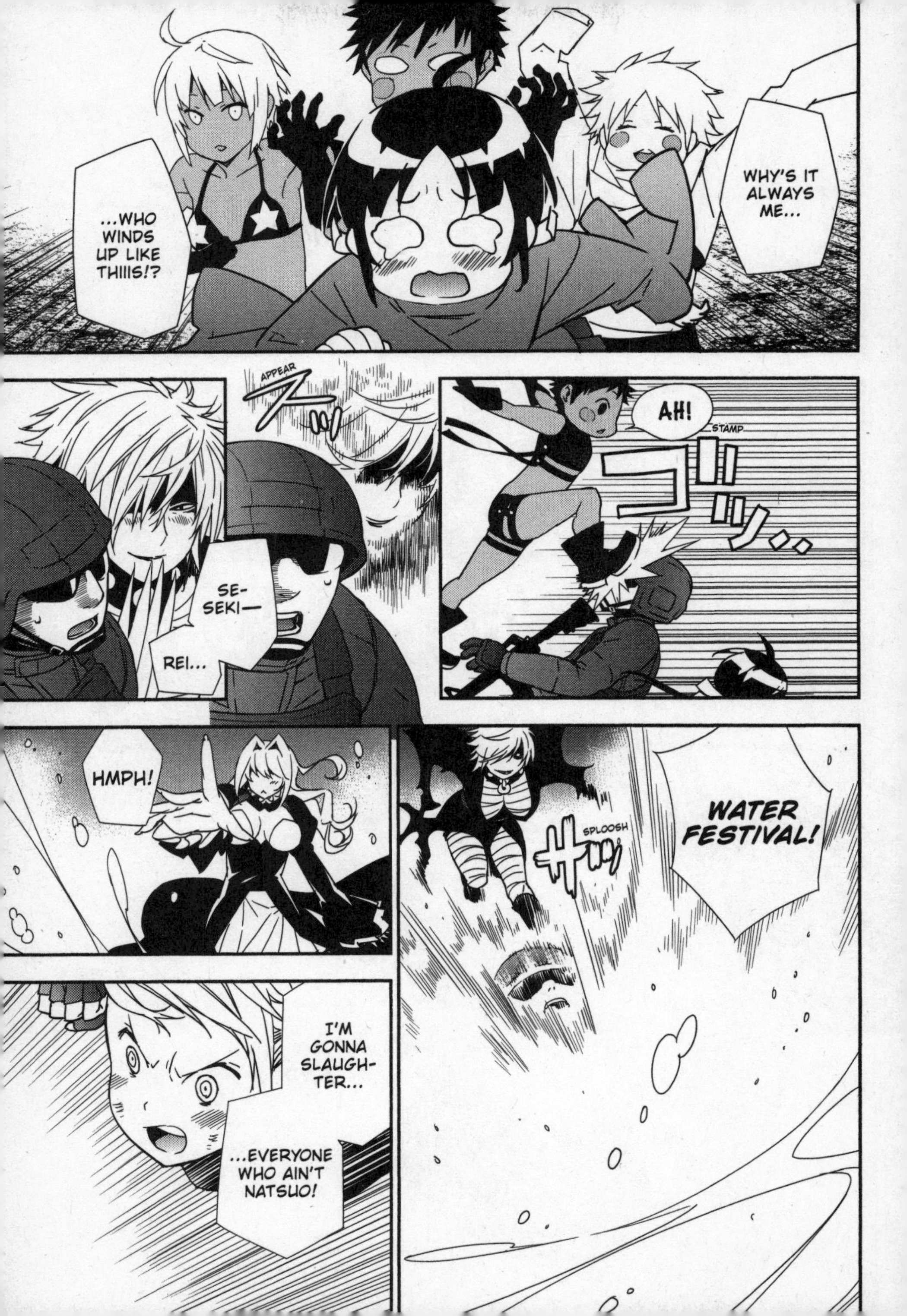
WHY'S IT ALWAYS ME...
...WHO WINDS UP LIKE THIIIS!?
AH!
STAMP
APPEAR
SE-SEKI—
REI...
SPLOOSH
WATER FESTIVAL!
HMPH!
I'M GONNA SLAUGHTER...
...EVERYONE WHO AIN'T NATSUO!

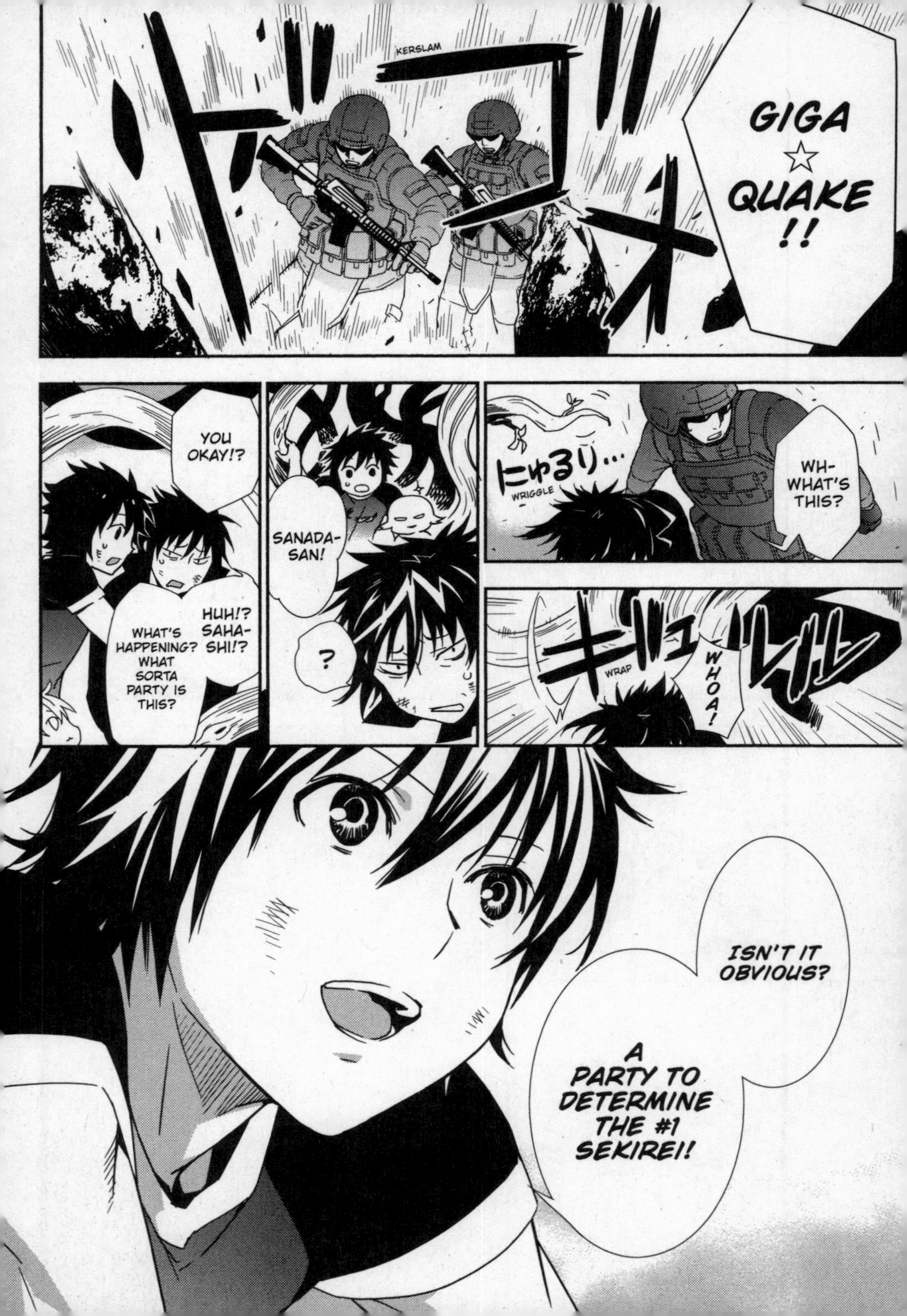
KERSLAM
GIGA ☆ QUAKE !!
にゅるり…
WRIGGLE
WH-WHAT'S THIS?
WRAP
WHOA!
SANADA-SAN!
?
YOU OKAY!?
HUH!? SAHASHI!?
WHAT'S HAPPENING? WHAT SORTA PARTY IS THIS?
ISN'T IT OBVIOUS?
A PARTY TO DETERMINE THE #1 SEKIREI!

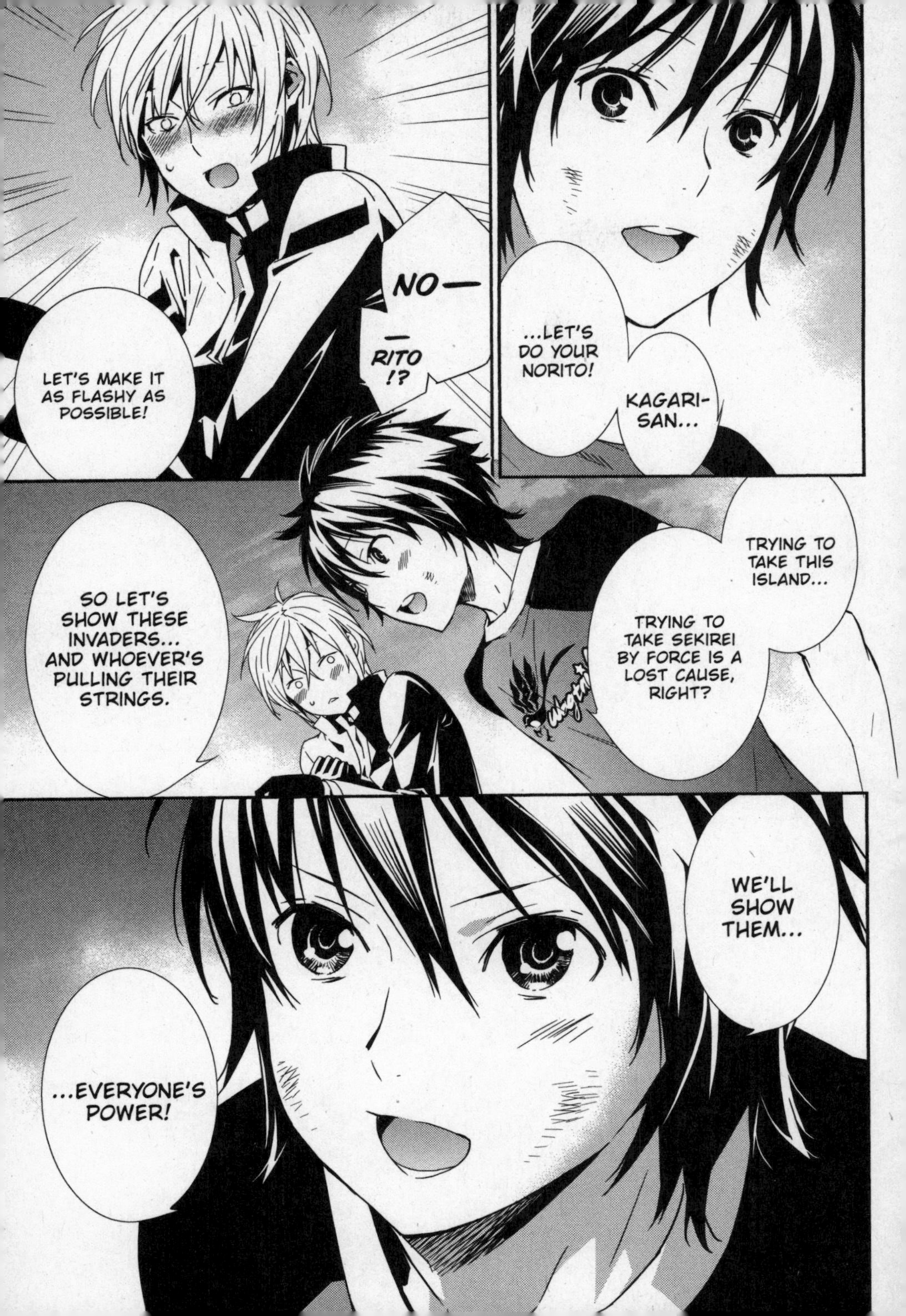
KAGARI-SAN...
...LET'S DO YOUR NORITO!
NO—
—RITO !?
LET'S MAKE IT AS FLASHY AS POSSIBLE!
TRYING TO TAKE THIS ISLAND...
TRYING TO TAKE SEKIREI BY FORCE IS A LOST CAUSE, RIGHT?
SO LET'S SHOW THESE INVADERS... AND WHOEVER'S PULLING THEIR STRINGS.
WE'LL SHOW THEM...
...EVERYONE'S POWER!

Chapter 169: Those With Wings of Light

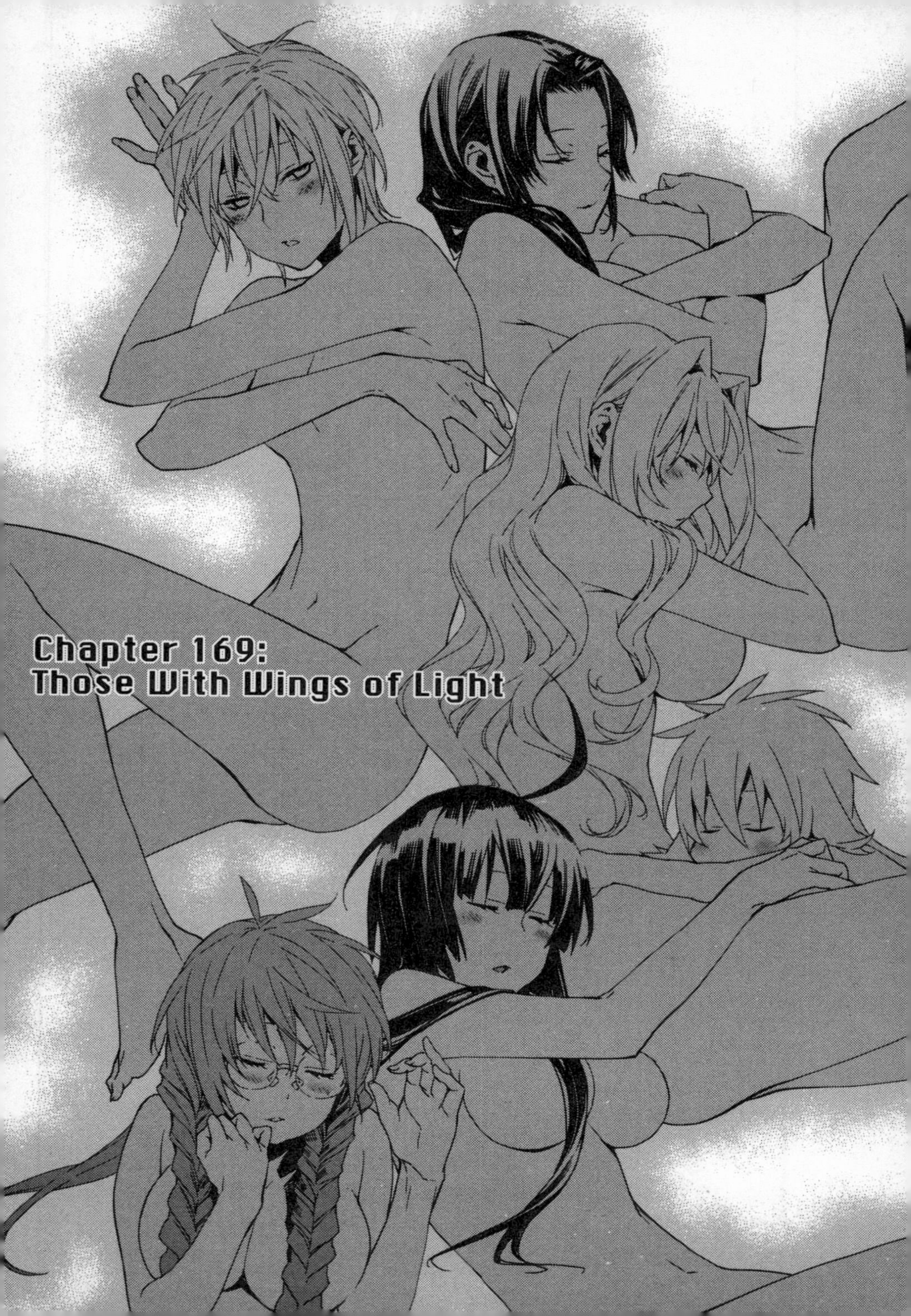

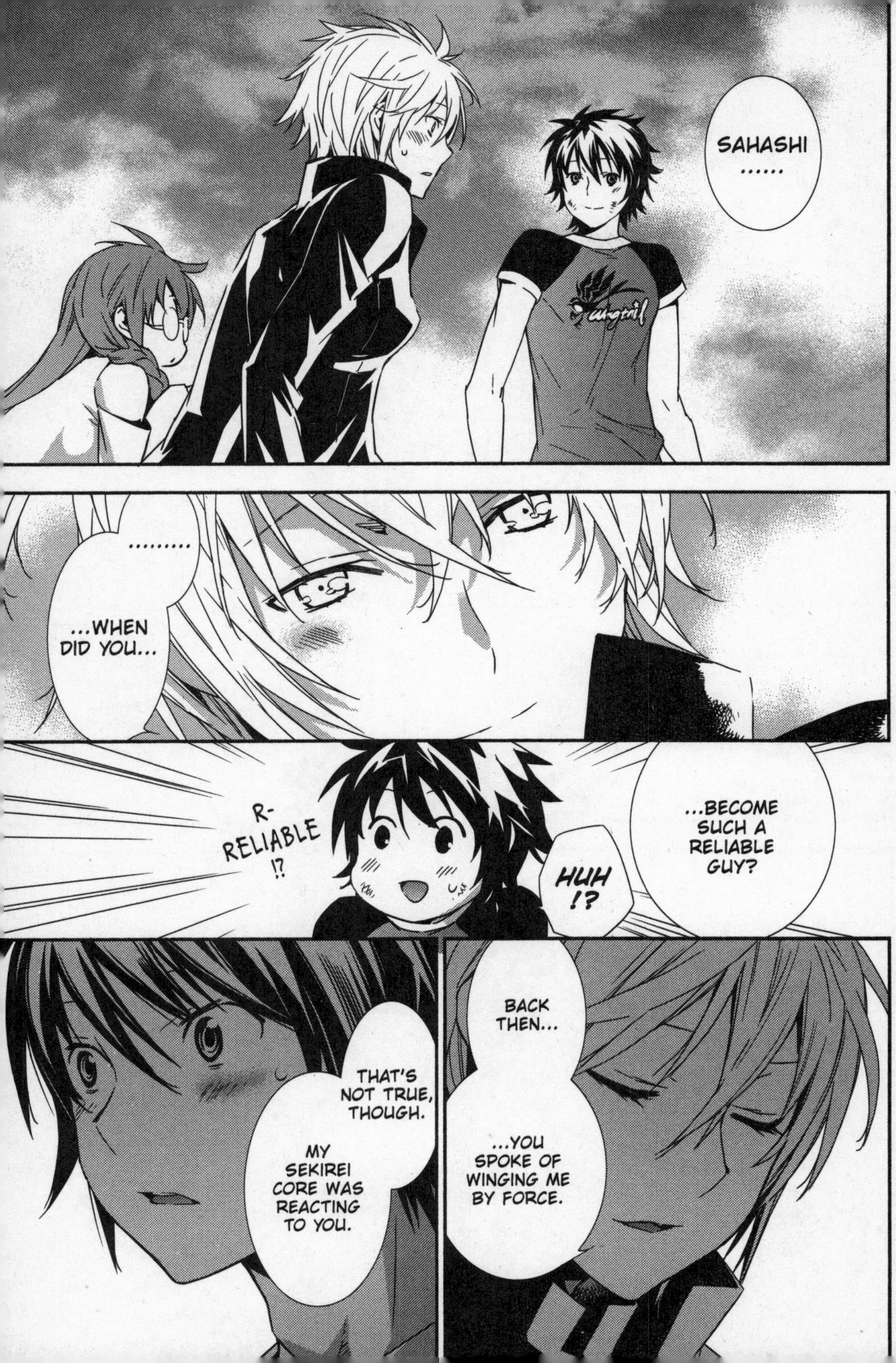
SAHASHI ......
....
...WHEN DID YOU...
...BECOME SUCH A RELIABLE GUY?
HUH !?
R-RELIABLE !?
BACK THEN...
...YOU SPOKE OF WINGING ME BY FORCE.
THAT'S NOT TRUE, THOUGH.
MY SEKIREI CORE WAS REACTING TO YOU.

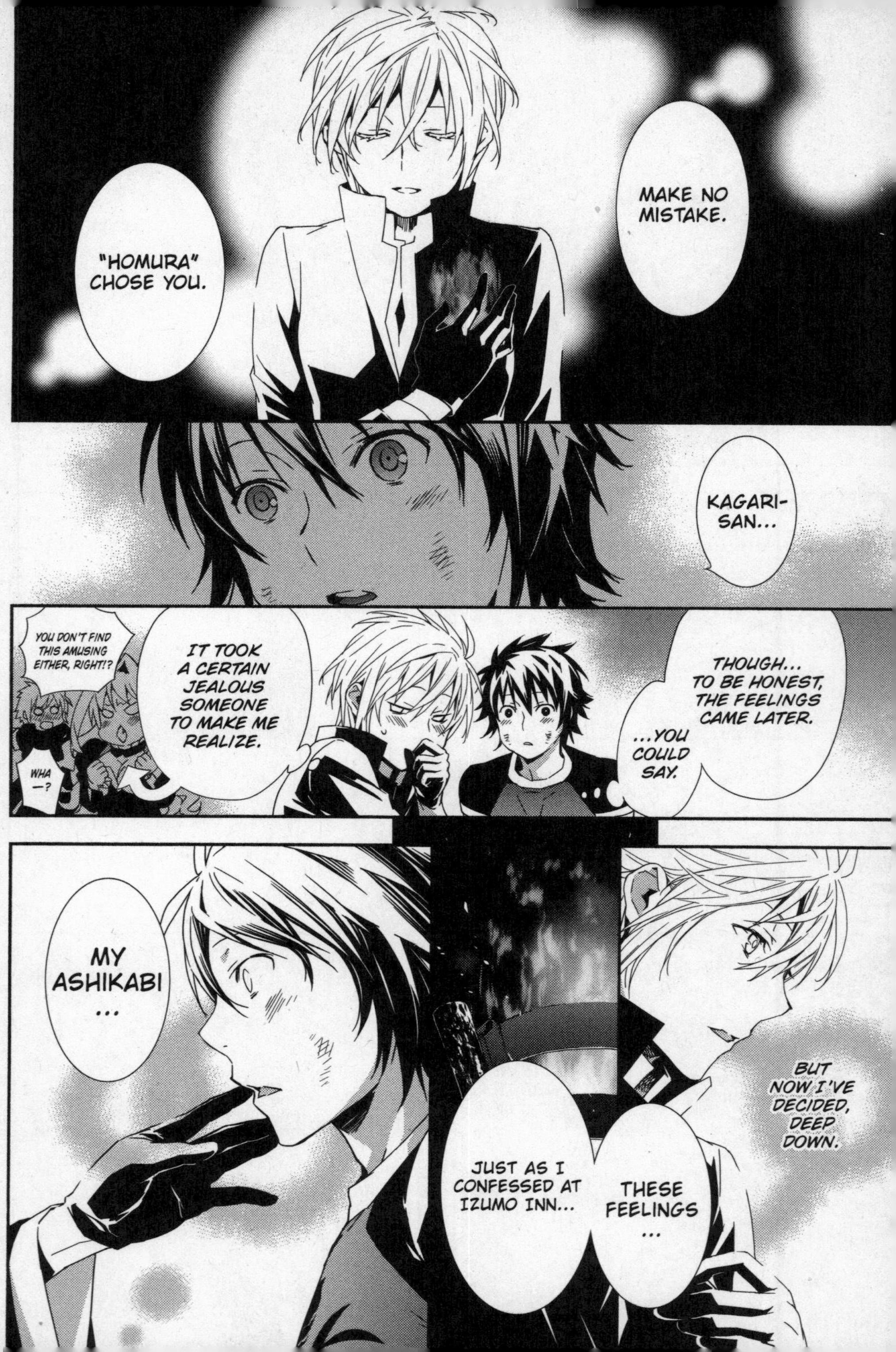
MAKE NO MISTAKE.
"HOMURA" CHOSE YOU.
KAGARI-SAN...
THOUGH... TO BE HONEST, THE FEELINGS CAME LATER.
...YOU COULD SAY.
IT TOOK A CERTAIN JEALOUS SOMEONE TO MAKE ME REALIZE.
YOU DON'T FIND THIS AMUSING EITHER, RIGHT!?
WHA—?
BUT NOW I'VE DECIDED, DEEP DOWN.
THESE FEELINGS...
JUST AS I CONFESSED AT IZUMO INN...
MY ASHIKABI...

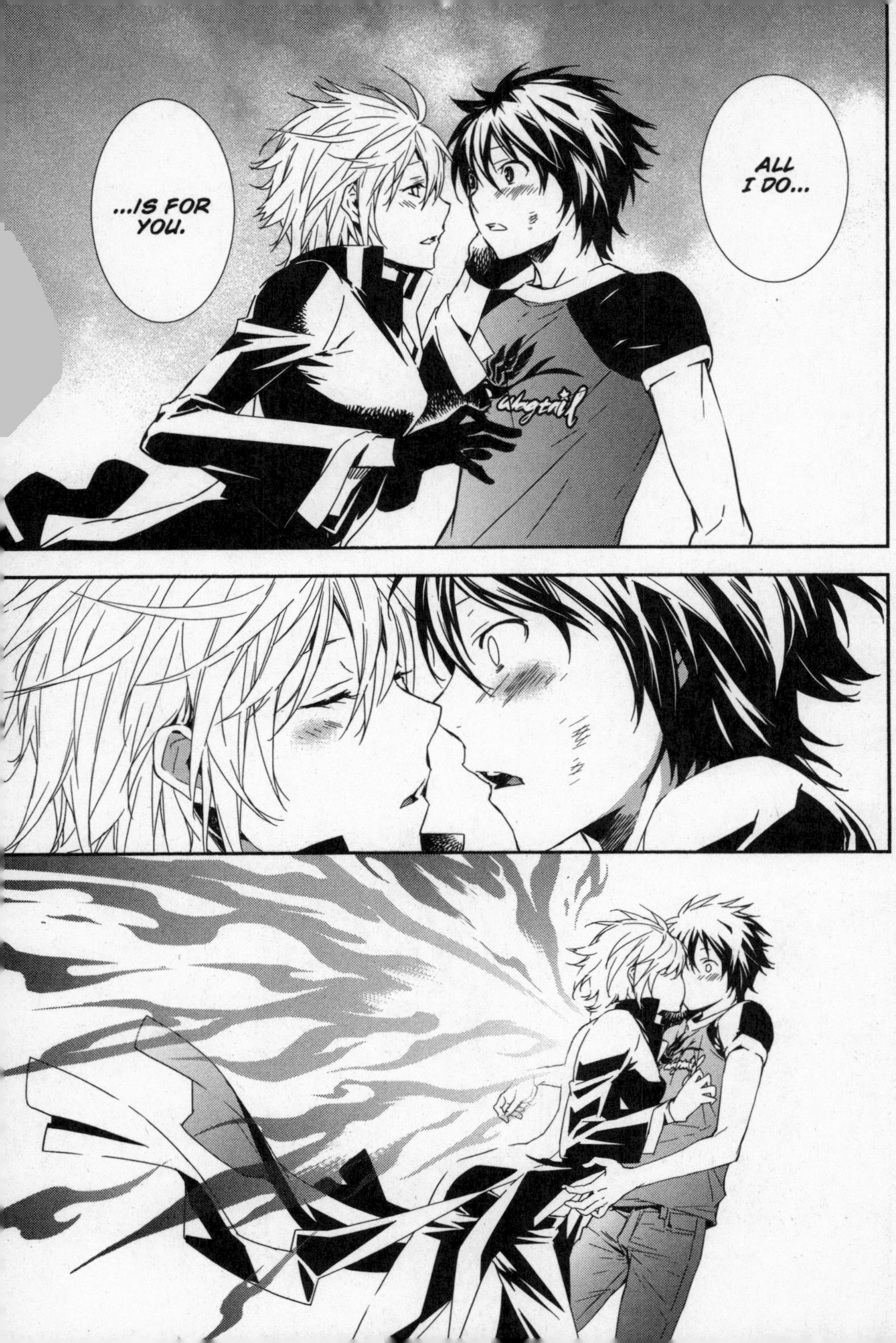
ALL I DO...
...IS FOR YOU.

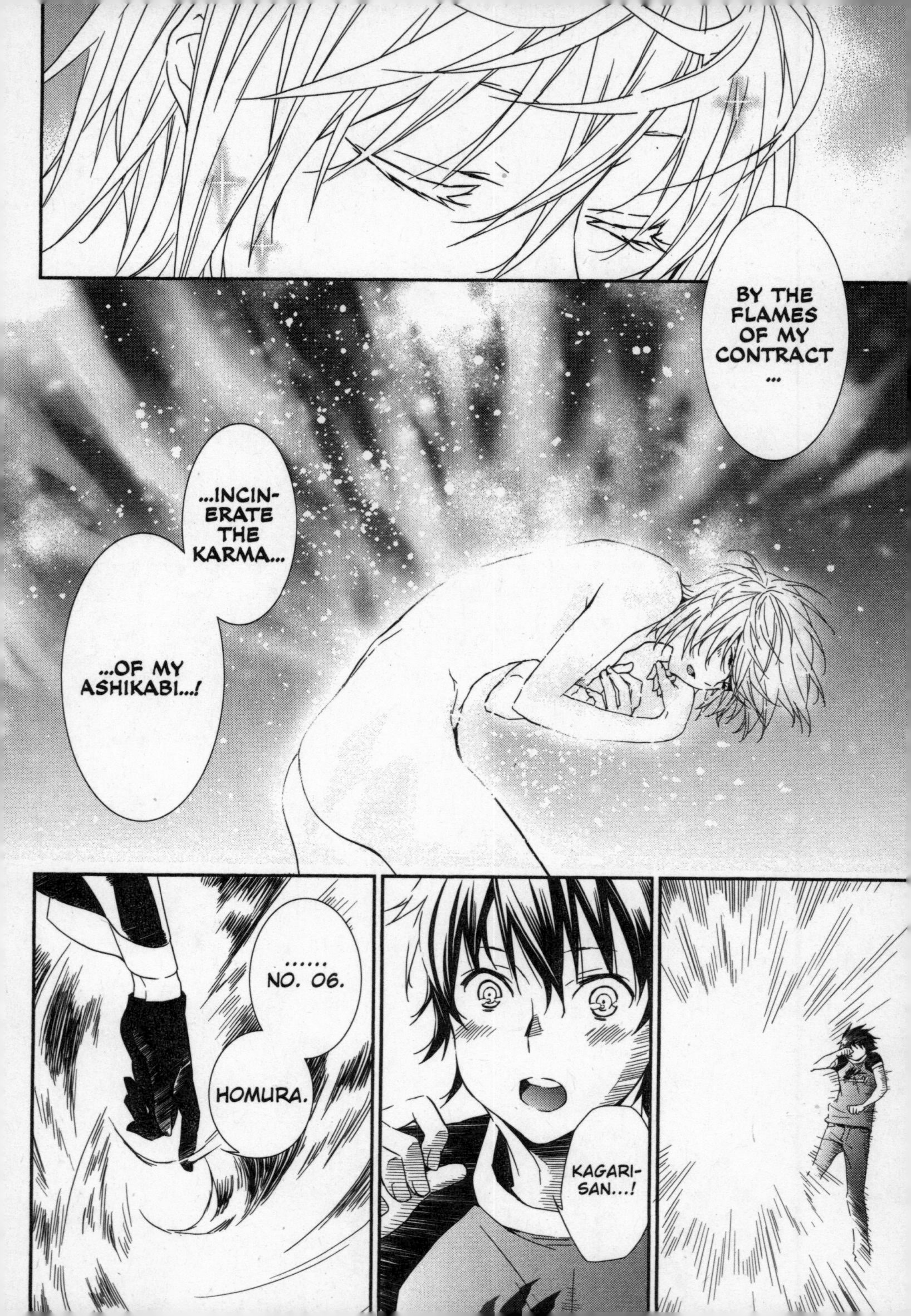
BY THE FLAMES OF MY CONTRACT ...
...INCIN-ERATE THE KARMA...
...OF MY ASHIKABI...!
KAGARI-SAN...!
...... NO. 06.
HOMURA.

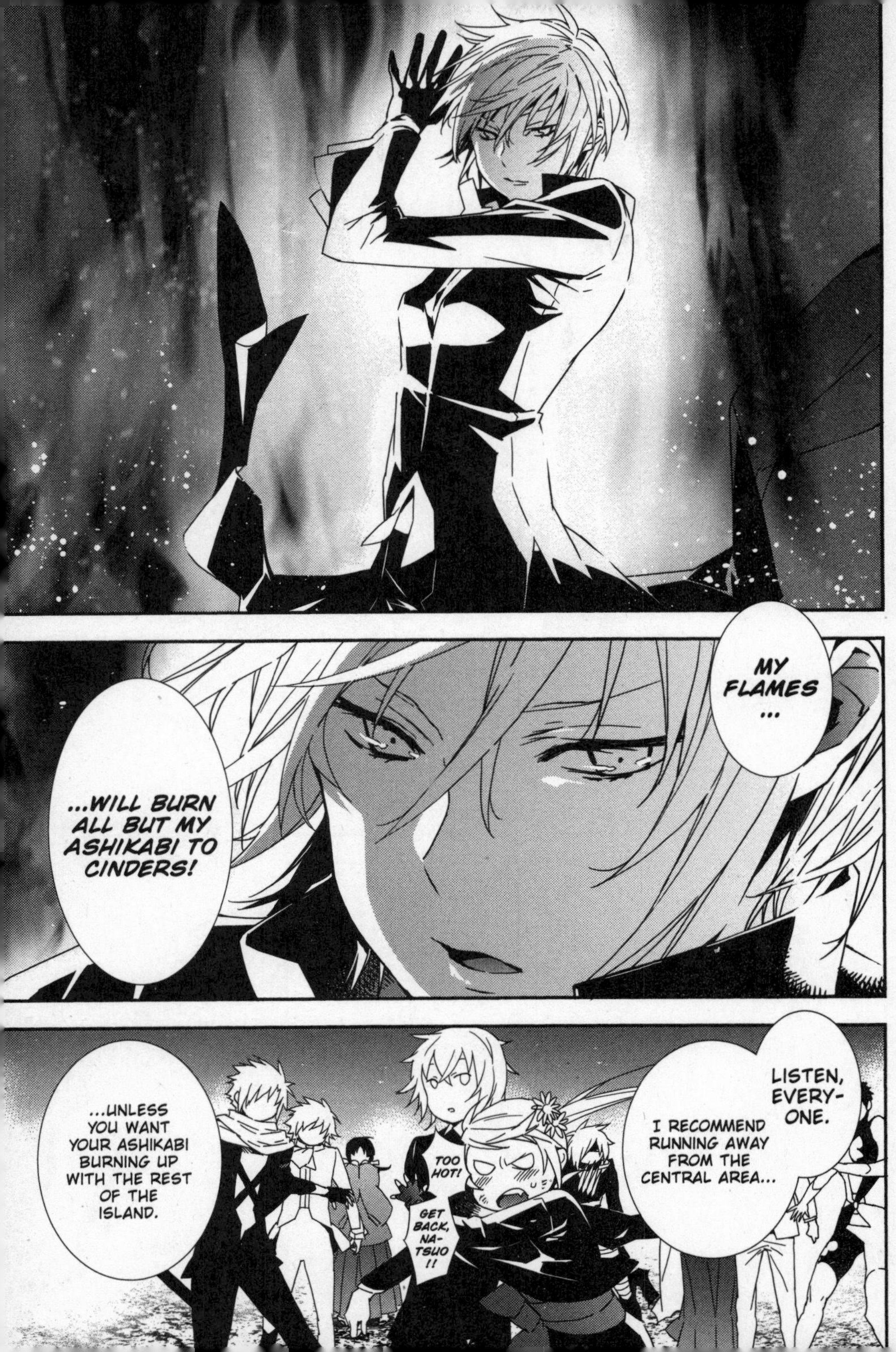
MY FLAMES ...
...WILL BURN ALL BUT MY ASHIKABI TO CINDERS!
LISTEN, EVERY-ONE.
I RECOMMEND RUNNING AWAY FROM THE CENTRAL AREA...
TOO HOT!
GET BACK, NA-TSUO!!
...UNLESS YOU WANT YOUR ASHIKABI BURNING UP WITH THE REST OF THE ISLAND.

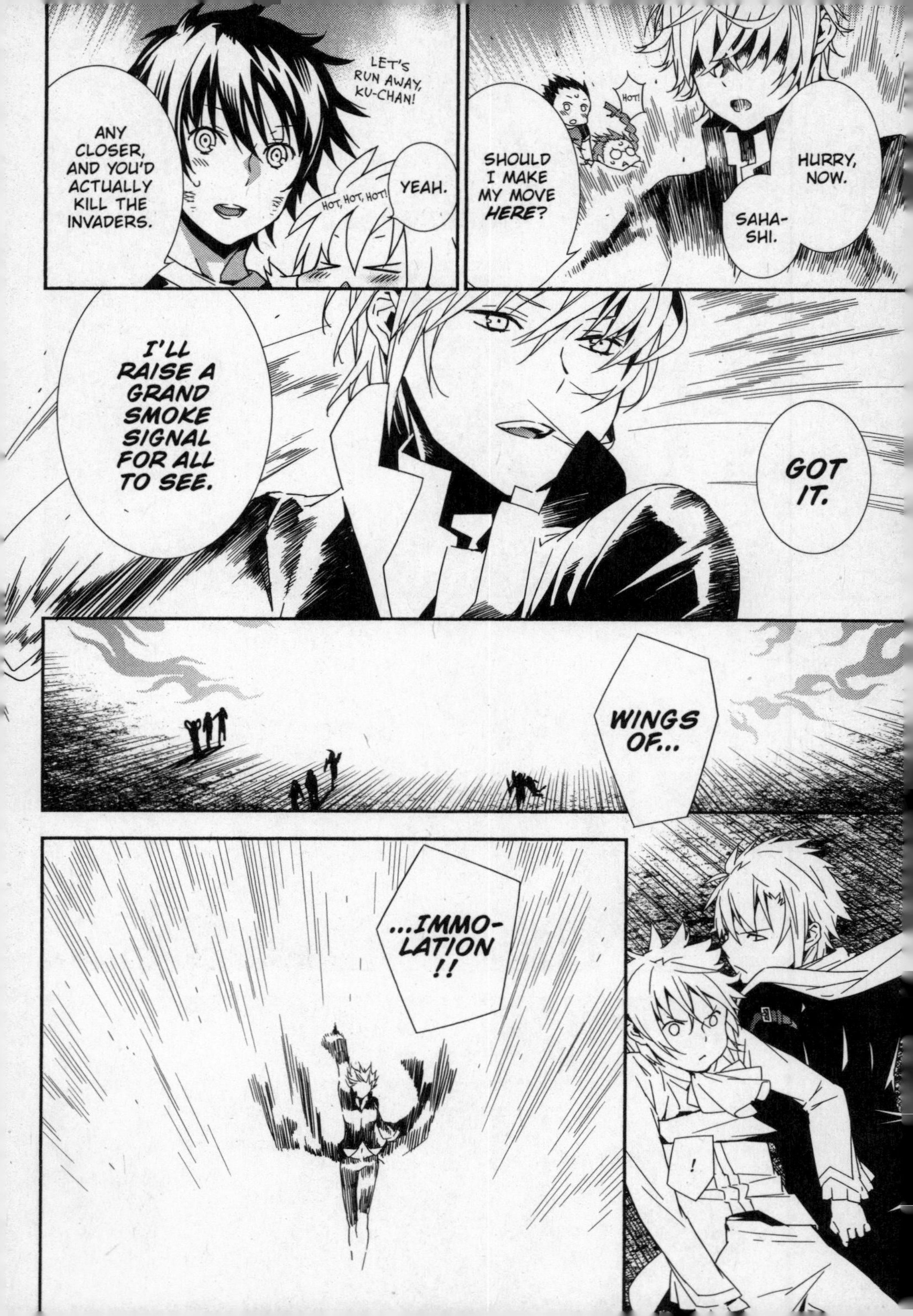
HURRY, NOW.
SAHA-SHI.
HOT!
SHOULD I MAKE MY MOVE HERE?
LET'S RUN AWAY, KU-CHAN!
YEAH.
HOT, HOT, HOT!
ANY CLOSER, AND YOU'D ACTUALLY KILL THE INVADERS.
GOT IT.
I'LL RAISE A GRAND SMOKE SIGNAL FOR ALL TO SEE.
WINGS OF...
...IMMOLATION!!
!

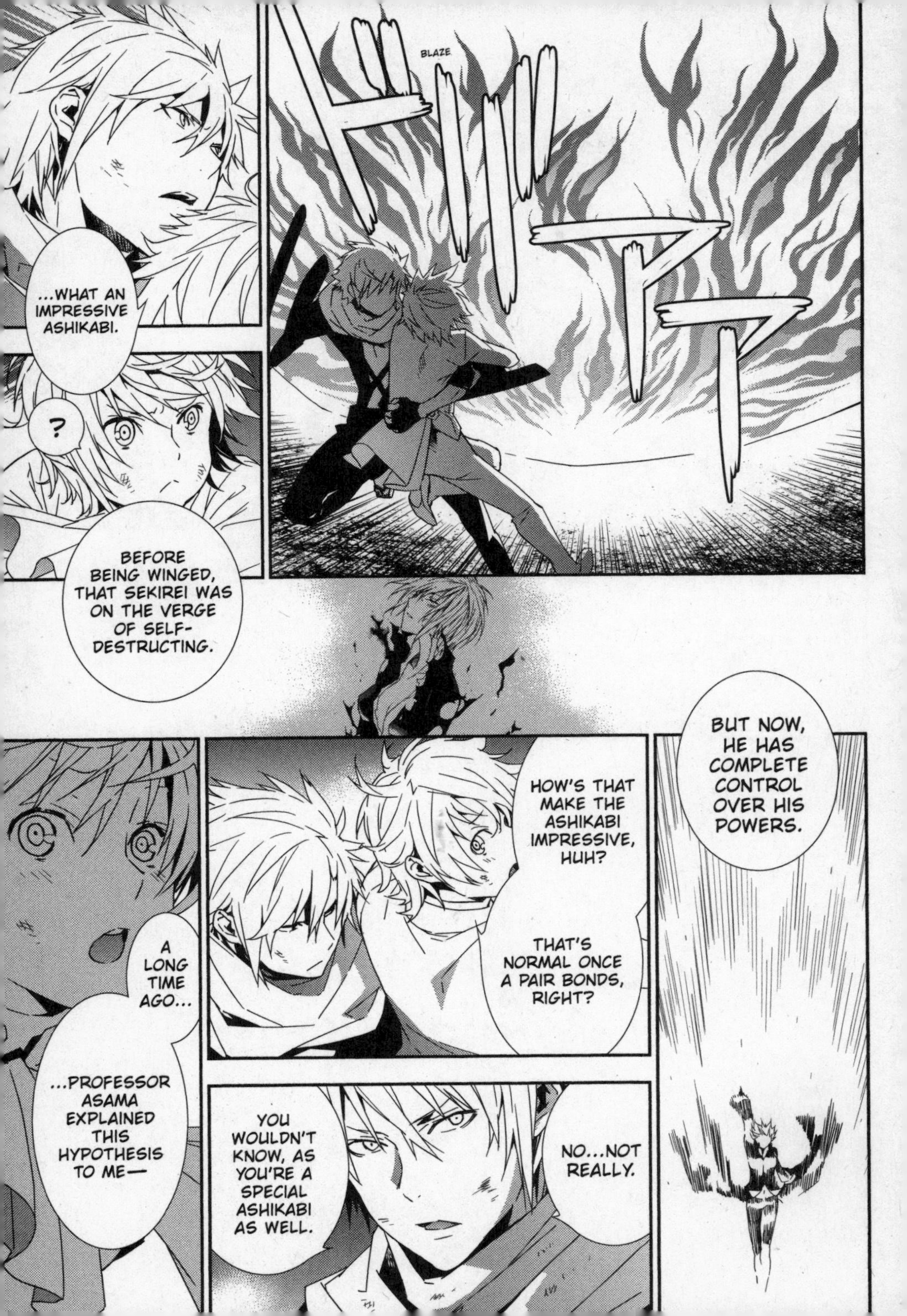
BLAZE
...WHAT AN IMPRESSIVE ASHIKABI.
?
BEFORE BEING WINGED, THAT SEKIREI WAS ON THE VERGE OF SELF-DESTRUCTING.
BUT NOW, HE HAS COMPLETE CONTROL OVER HIS POWERS.
HOW'S THAT MAKE THE ASHIKABI IMPRESSIVE, HUH?
THAT'S NORMAL ONCE A PAIR BONDS, RIGHT?
NO...NOT REALLY.
YOU WOULDN'T KNOW, AS YOU'RE A SPECIAL ASHIKABI AS WELL.
A LONG TIME AGO...
...PROFESSOR ASAMA EXPLAINED THIS HYPOTHESIS TO ME—

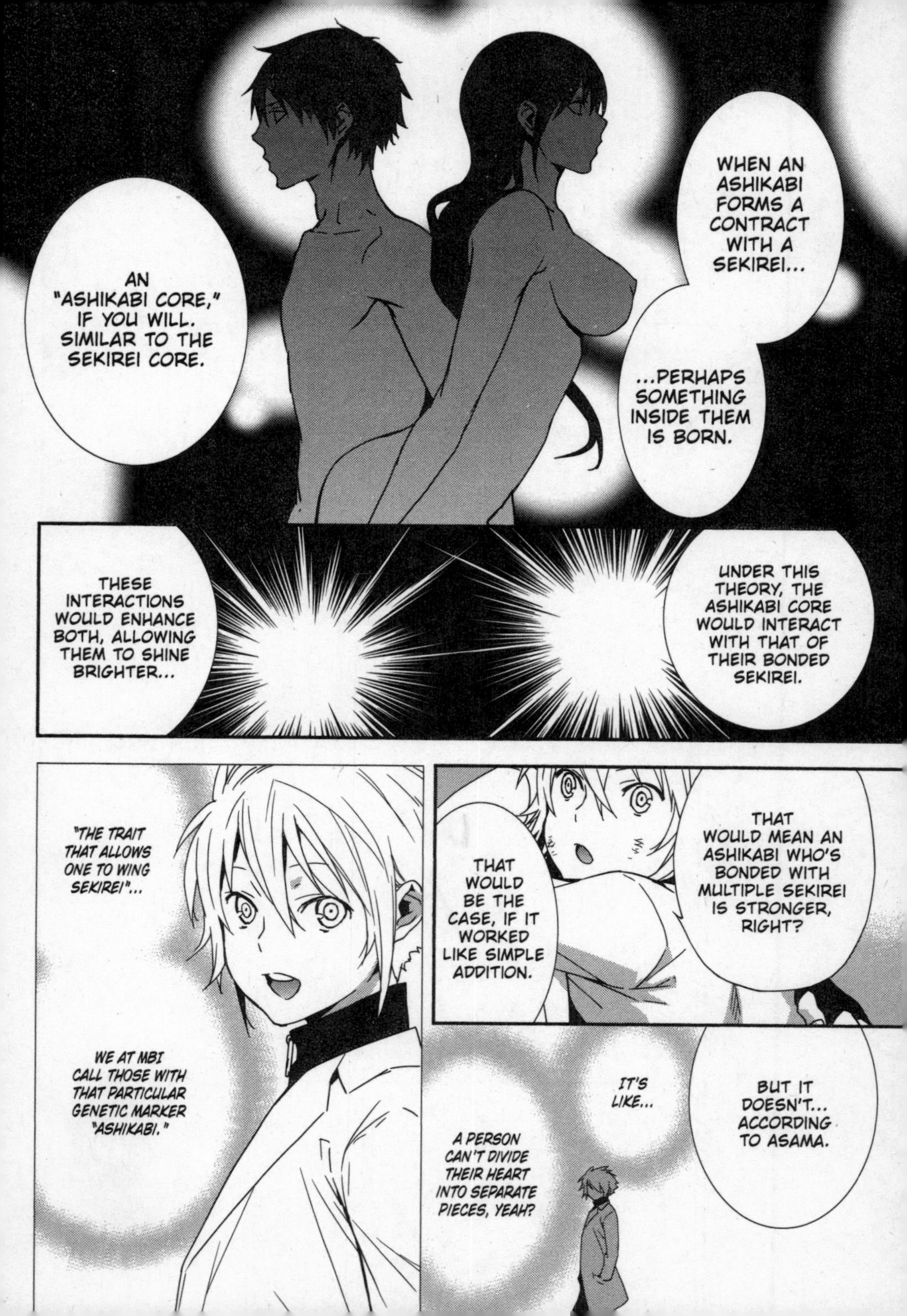
WHEN AN ASHIKABI FORMS A CONTRACT WITH A SEKIREI...
...PERHAPS SOMETHING INSIDE THEM IS BORN.
AN "ASHIKABI CORE," IF YOU WILL. SIMILAR TO THE SEKIREI CORE.
UNDER THIS THEORY, THE ASHIKABI CORE WOULD INTERACT WITH THAT OF THEIR BONDED SEKIREI.
THESE INTERACTIONS WOULD ENHANCE BOTH, ALLOWING THEM TO SHINE BRIGHTER...
THAT WOULD MEAN AN ASHIKABI WHO'S BONDED WITH MULTIPLE SEKIREI IS STRONGER, RIGHT?
THAT WOULD BE THE CASE, IF IT WORKED LIKE SIMPLE ADDITION.
BUT IT DOESN'T... ACCORDING TO ASAMA.
IT'S LIKE...
A PERSON CAN'T DIVIDE THEIR HEART INTO SEPARATE PIECES, YEAH?
"THE TRAIT THAT ALLOWS ONE TO WING SEKIREI"...
WE AT MBI CALL THOSE WITH THAT PARTICULAR GENETIC MARKER "ASHIKABI."

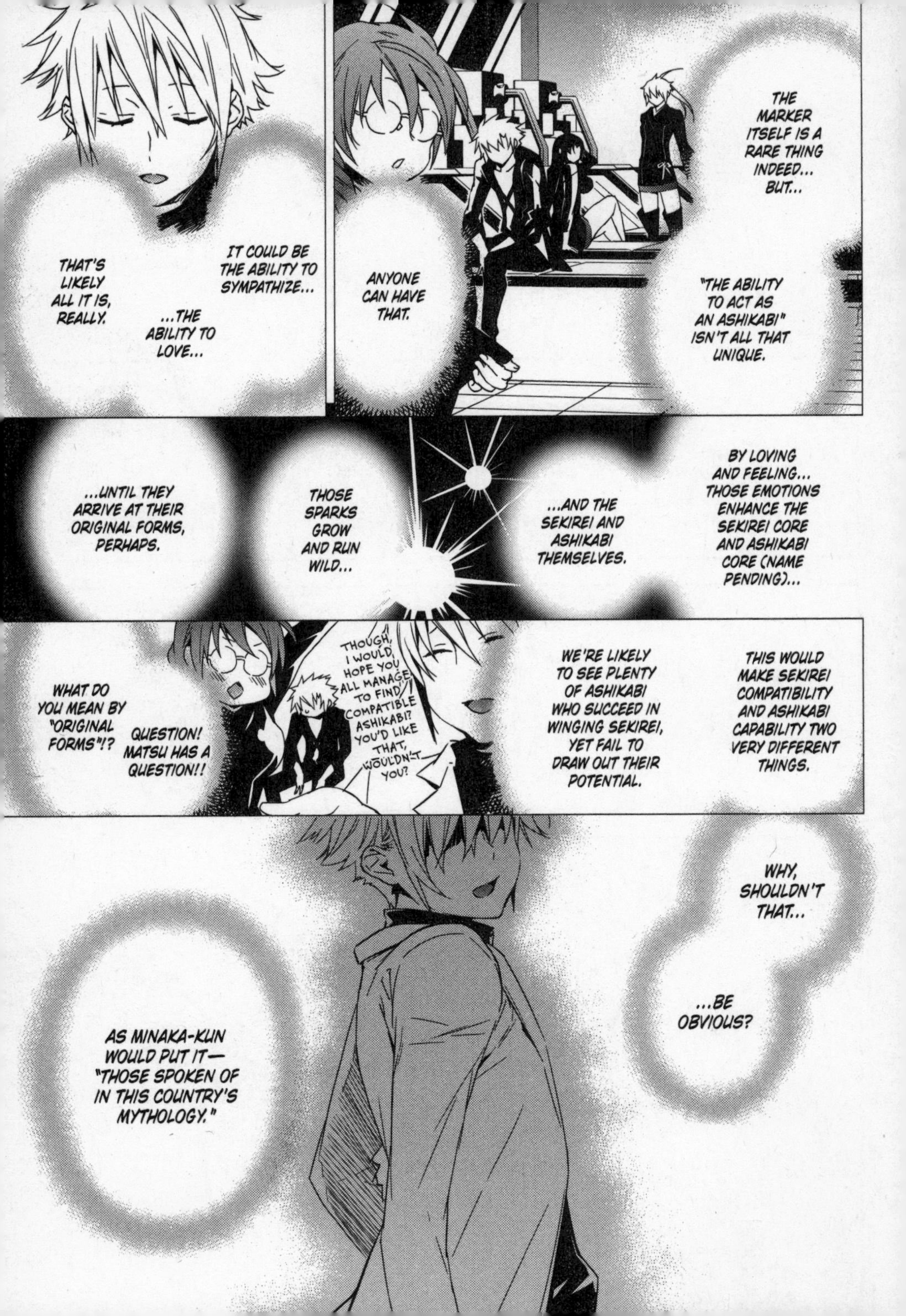
THE MARKER ITSELF IS A RARE THING INDEED... BUT...
"THE ABILITY TO ACT AS AN ASHIKABI" ISN'T ALL THAT UNIQUE.
ANYONE CAN HAVE THAT.
IT COULD BE THE ABILITY TO SYMPATHIZE...
...THE ABILITY TO LOVE...
THAT'S LIKELY ALL IT IS, REALLY.
BY LOVING AND FEELING... THOSE EMOTIONS ENHANCE THE SEKIREI CORE AND ASHIKABI CORE (NAME PENDING)...
...AND THE SEKIREI AND ASHIKABI THEMSELVES.
THOSE SPARKS GROW AND RUN WILD...
...UNTIL THEY ARRIVE AT THEIR ORIGINAL FORMS, PERHAPS.
THIS WOULD MAKE SEKIREI COMPATIBILITY AND ASHIKABI CAPABILITY TWO VERY DIFFERENT THINGS.
WE'RE LIKELY TO SEE PLENTY OF ASHIKABI WHO SUCCEED IN WINGING SEKIREI, YET FAIL TO DRAW OUT THEIR POTENTIAL.
THOUGH, I WOULD HOPE YOU ALL MANAGE TO FIND COMPATIBLE ASHIKABI? YOU'D LIKE THAT, WOULDN'T YOU?
QUESTION! MATSU HAS A QUESTION!!
WHAT DO YOU MEAN BY "ORIGINAL FORMS"!?
WHY, SHOULDN'T THAT...
...BE OBVIOUS?
AS MINAKA-KUN WOULD PUT IT— "THOSE SPOKEN OF IN THIS COUNTRY'S MYTHOLOGY."

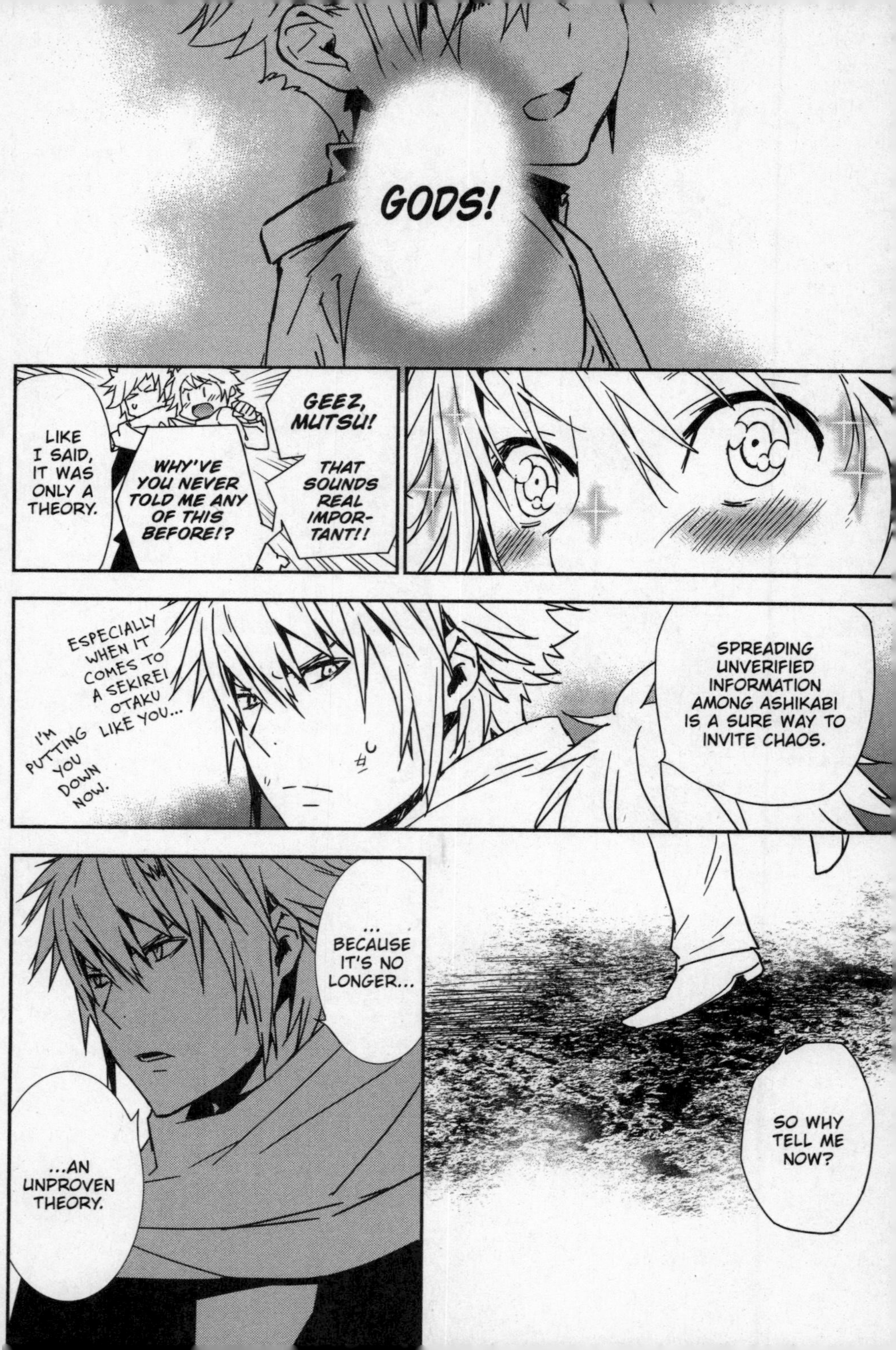
GODS!
GEEZ, MUTSU!
THAT SOUNDS REAL IMPORTANT!!
WHY'VE YOU NEVER TOLD ME ANY OF THIS BEFORE!?
LIKE I SAID, IT WAS ONLY A THEORY.
SPREADING UNVERIFIED INFORMATION AMONG ASHIKABI IS A SURE WAY TO INVITE CHAOS.
ESPECIALLY WHEN IT COMES TO A SEKIREI OTAKU LIKE YOU...
I'M PUTTING YOU DOWN NOW.
SO WHY TELL ME NOW?
...BECAUSE IT'S NO LONGER...
...AN UNPROVEN THEORY.

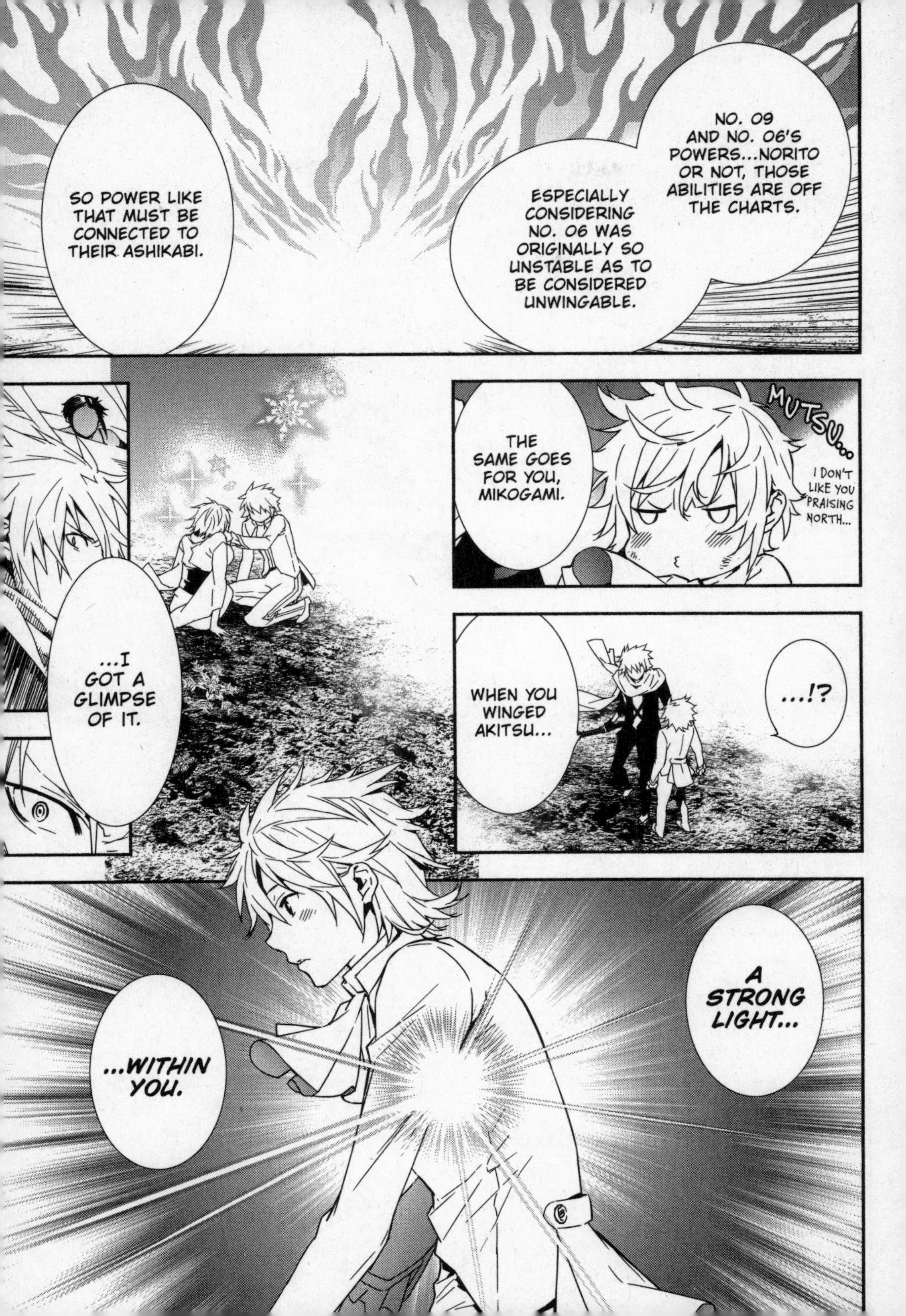
NO. 09 AND NO. 06'S POWERS...NORITO OR NOT, THOSE ABILITIES ARE OFF THE CHARTS.
ESPECIALLY CONSIDERING NO. 06 WAS ORIGINALLY SO UNSTABLE AS TO BE CONSIDERED UNWINGABLE.
SO POWER LIKE THAT MUST BE CONNECTED TO THEIR ASHIKABI.
MUTSU...
I DON'T LIKE YOU PRAISING NORTH...
THE SAME GOES FOR YOU, MIKOGAMI.
...!?
WHEN YOU WINGED AKITSU...
...I GOT A GLIMPSE OF IT.
A STRONG LIGHT...
...WITHIN YOU.

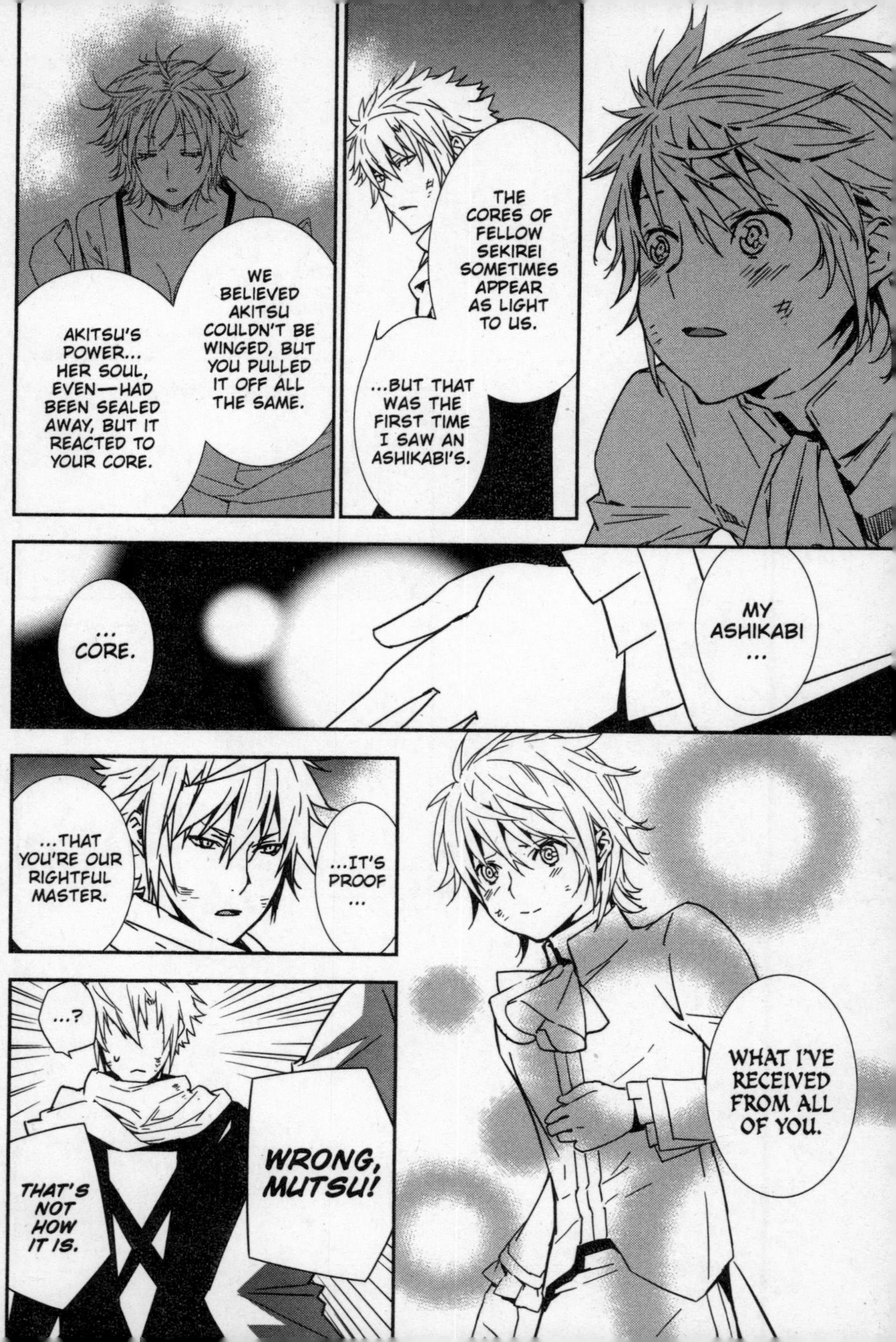
THE CORES OF FELLOW SEKIREI SOMETIMES APPEAR AS LIGHT TO US.
...BUT THAT WAS THE FIRST TIME I SAW AN ASHIKABI'S.
WE BELIEVED AKITSU COULDN'T BE WINGED, BUT YOU PULLED IT OFF ALL THE SAME.
AKITSU'S POWER... HER SOUL, EVEN—HAD BEEN SEALED AWAY, BUT IT REACTED TO YOUR CORE.
MY ASHIKABI...
...CORE.
WHAT I'VE RECEIVED FROM ALL OF YOU.
...IT'S PROOF...
...THAT YOU'RE OUR RIGHTFUL MASTER.
WRONG, MUTSU!
...?
THAT'S NOT HOW IT IS.

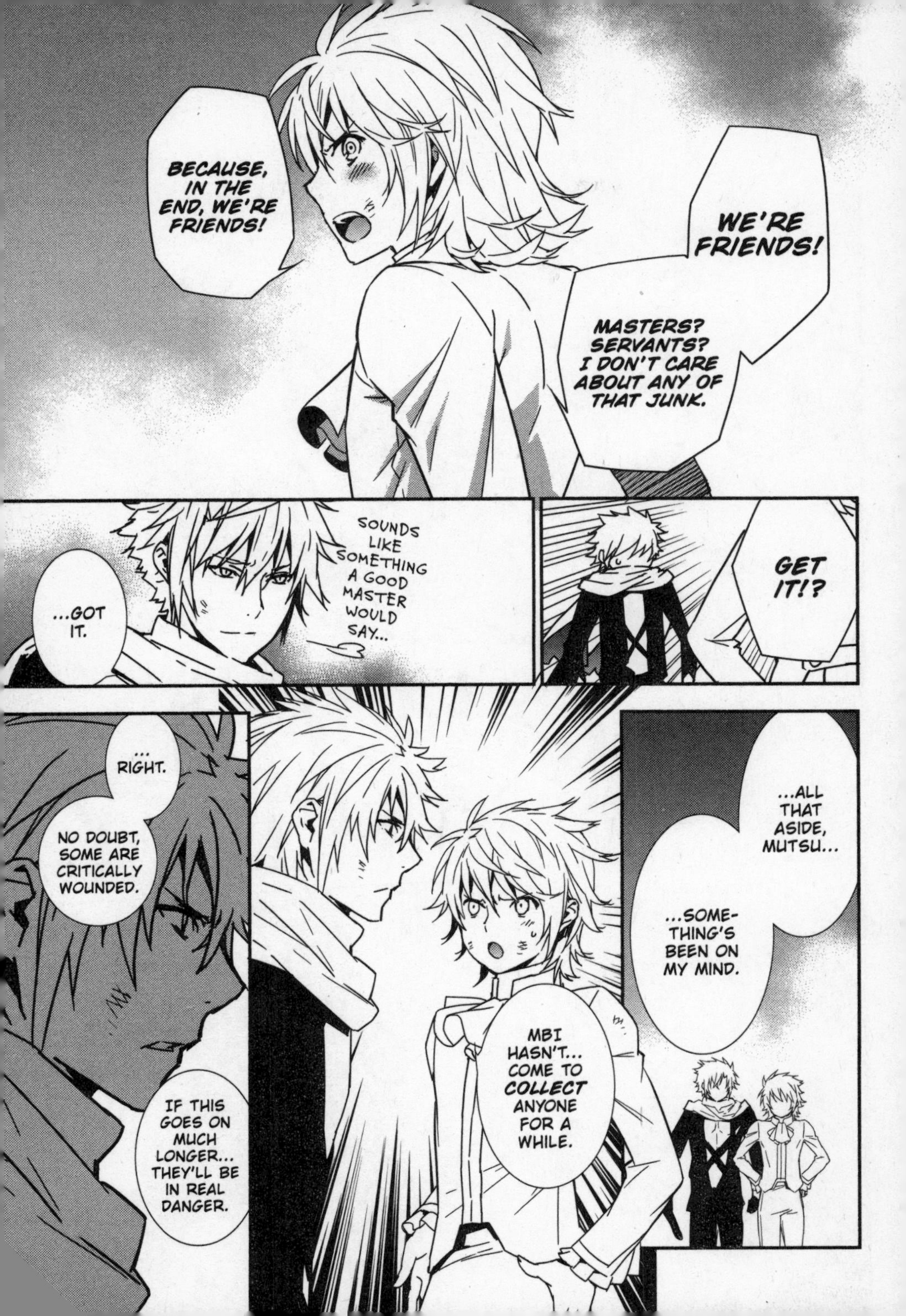
WE'RE FRIENDS!
MASTERS? SERVANTS? I DON'T CARE ABOUT ANY OF THAT JUNK.
BECAUSE, IN THE END, WE'RE FRIENDS!
GET IT!?
SOUNDS LIKE SOMETHING A GOOD MASTER WOULD SAY...
...GOT IT.
...ALL THAT ASIDE, MUTSU...
...SOME-THING'S BEEN ON MY MIND.
MBI HASN'T... COME TO COLLECT ANYONE FOR A WHILE.
... RIGHT.
NO DOUBT, SOME ARE CRITICALLY WOUNDED.
IF THIS GOES ON MUCH LONGER... THEY'LL BE IN REAL DANGER.

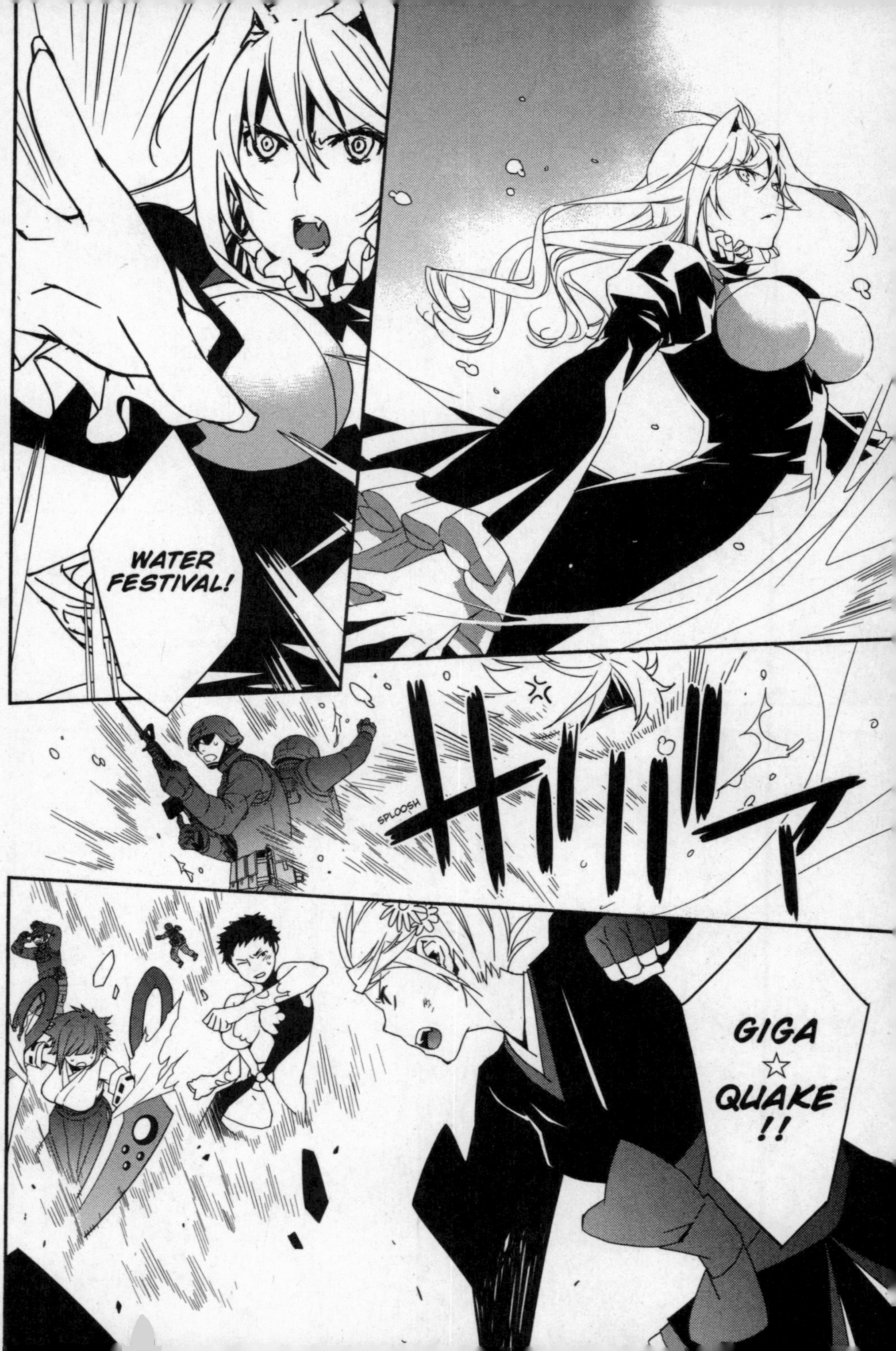
WATER FESTIVAL!
SPLOOSH
GIGA ☆ QUAKE !!

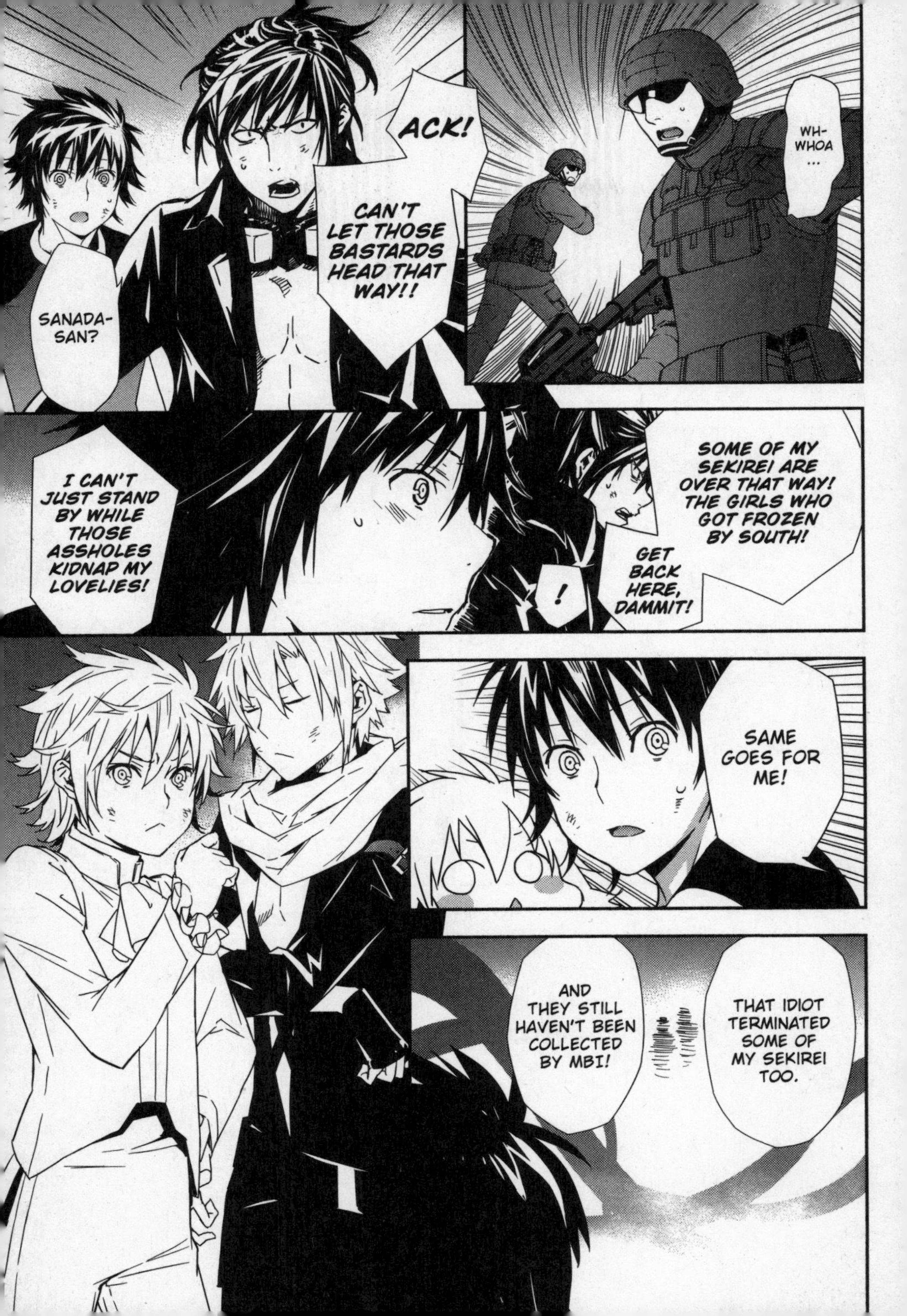
WH-WHOA ...
ACK!
CAN'T LET THOSE BASTARDS HEAD THAT WAY!!
SANADA-SAN?
SOME OF MY SEKIREI ARE OVER THAT WAY! THE GIRLS WHO GOT FROZEN BY SOUTH!
GET BACK HERE, DAMMIT!
!
I CAN'T JUST STAND BY WHILE THOSE ASSHOLES KIDNAP MY LOVELIES!
SAME GOES FOR ME!
THAT IDIOT TERMINATED SOME OF MY SEKIREI TOO.
AND THEY STILL HAVEN'T BEEN COLLECTED BY MBI!

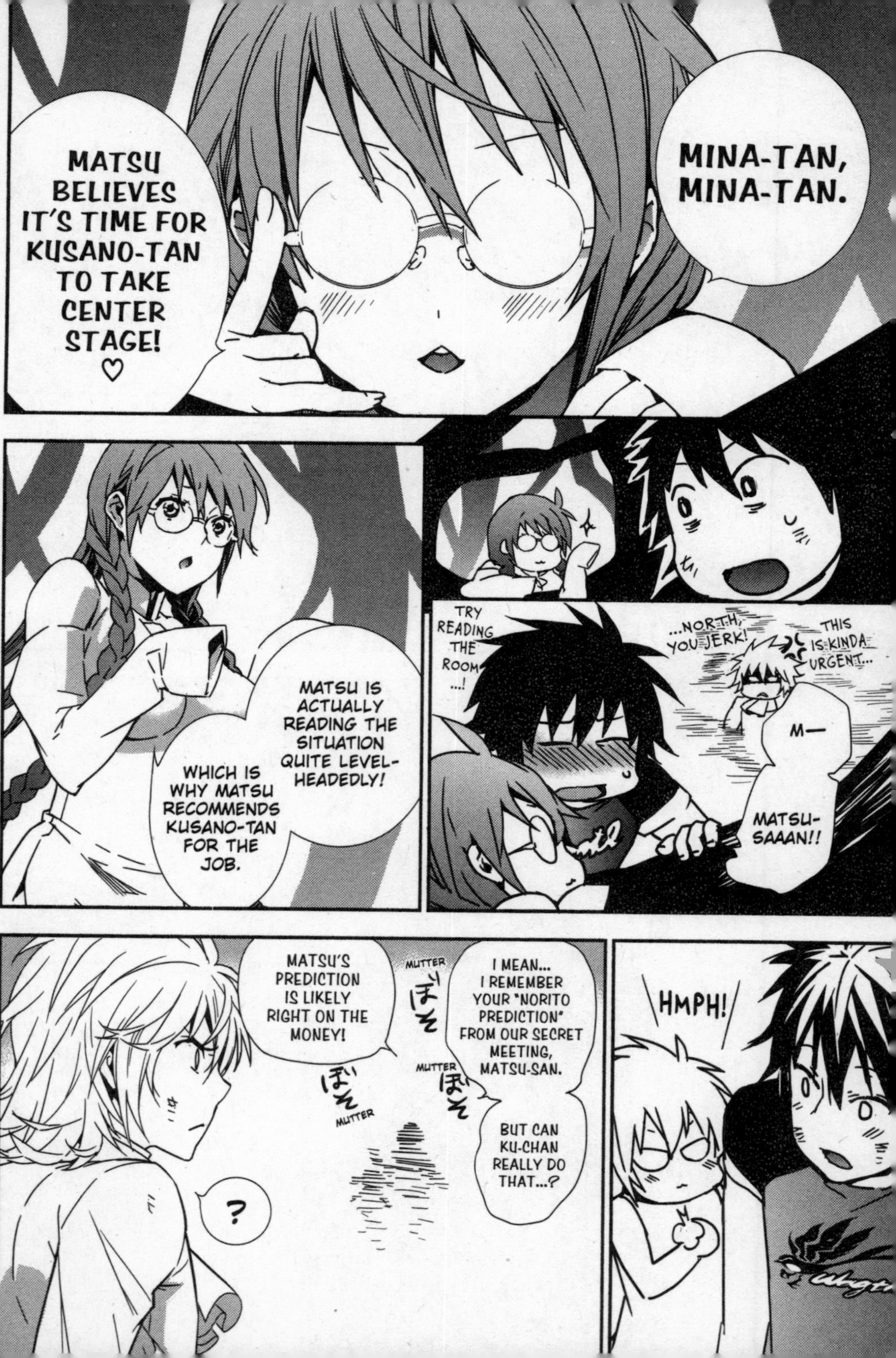
MINA-TAN, MINA-TAN.
MATSU BELIEVES IT'S TIME FOR KUSANO-TAN TO TAKE CENTER STAGE! ♡
THIS IS KINDA URGENT...
...NORTH, YOU JERK!
TRY READING THE ROOM...!
M—
MATSU-SAAAN!!
MATSU IS ACTUALLY READING THE SITUATION QUITE LEVEL-HEADEDLY!
WHICH IS WHY MATSU RECOMMENDS KUSANO-TAN FOR THE JOB.
HMPH!
I MEAN... I REMEMBER YOUR "NORITO PREDICTION" FROM OUR SECRET MEETING, MATSU-SAN.
MUTTER
MATSU'S PREDICTION IS LIKELY RIGHT ON THE MONEY!
MUTTER
MUTTER
BUT CAN KU-CHAN REALLY DO THAT...?
?

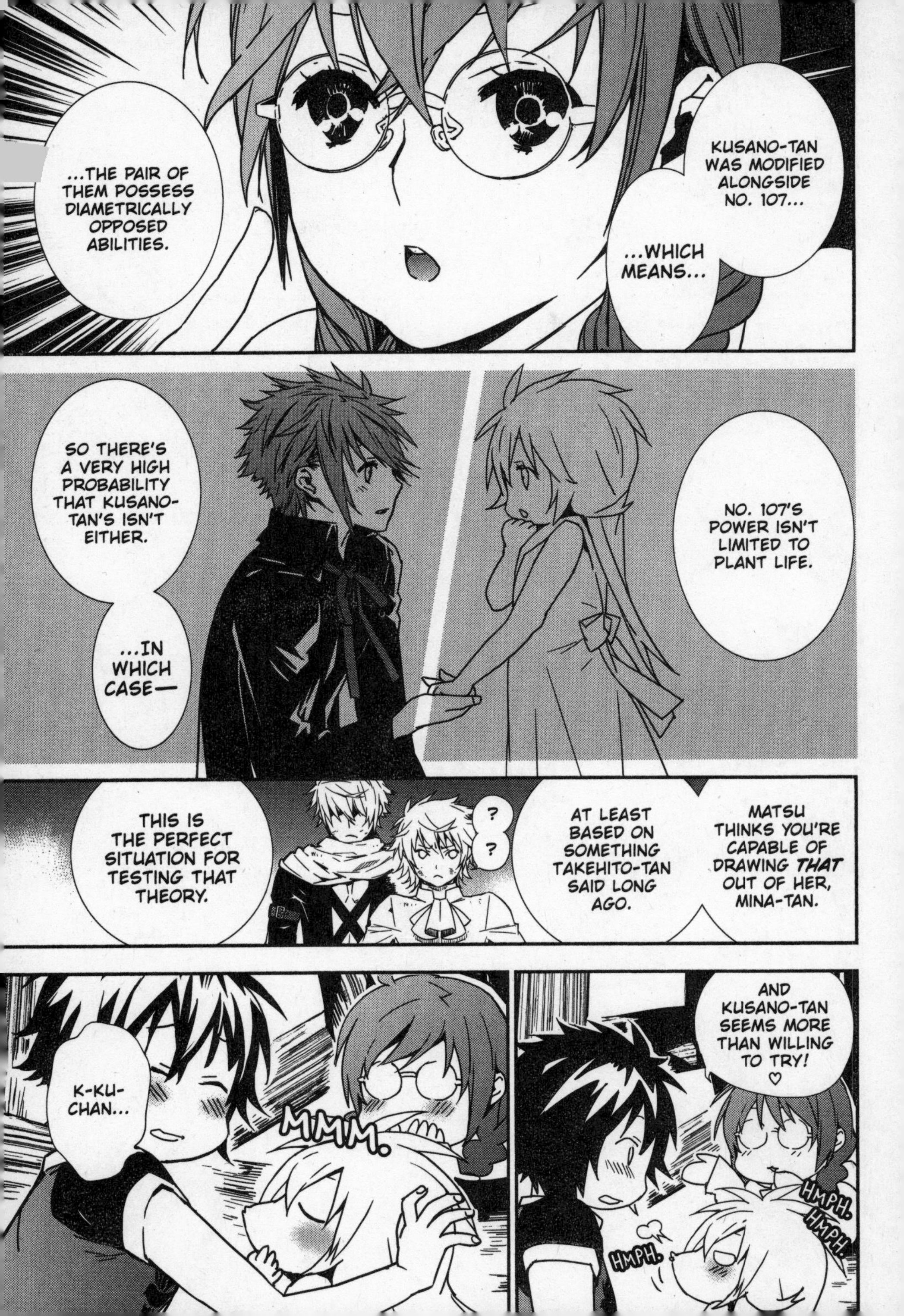
KUSANO-TAN WAS MODIFIED ALONGSIDE NO. 107...
...WHICH MEANS...
...THE PAIR OF THEM POSSESS DIAMETRICALLY OPPOSED ABILITIES.
NO. 107'S POWER ISN'T LIMITED TO PLANT LIFE.
SO THERE'S A VERY HIGH PROBABILITY THAT KUSANO-TAN'S ISN'T EITHER.
...IN WHICH CASE—
MATSU THINKS YOU'RE CAPABLE OF DRAWING *THAT* OUT OF HER, MINA-TAN.
AT LEAST BASED ON SOMETHING TAKEHITO-TAN SAID LONG AGO.
? ?
THIS IS THE PERFECT SITUATION FOR TESTING THAT THEORY.
AND KUSANO-TAN SEEMS MORE THAN WILLING TO TRY! ♡
HMPH. HMPH.
HMPH.
MMM.
K-KU-CHAN...

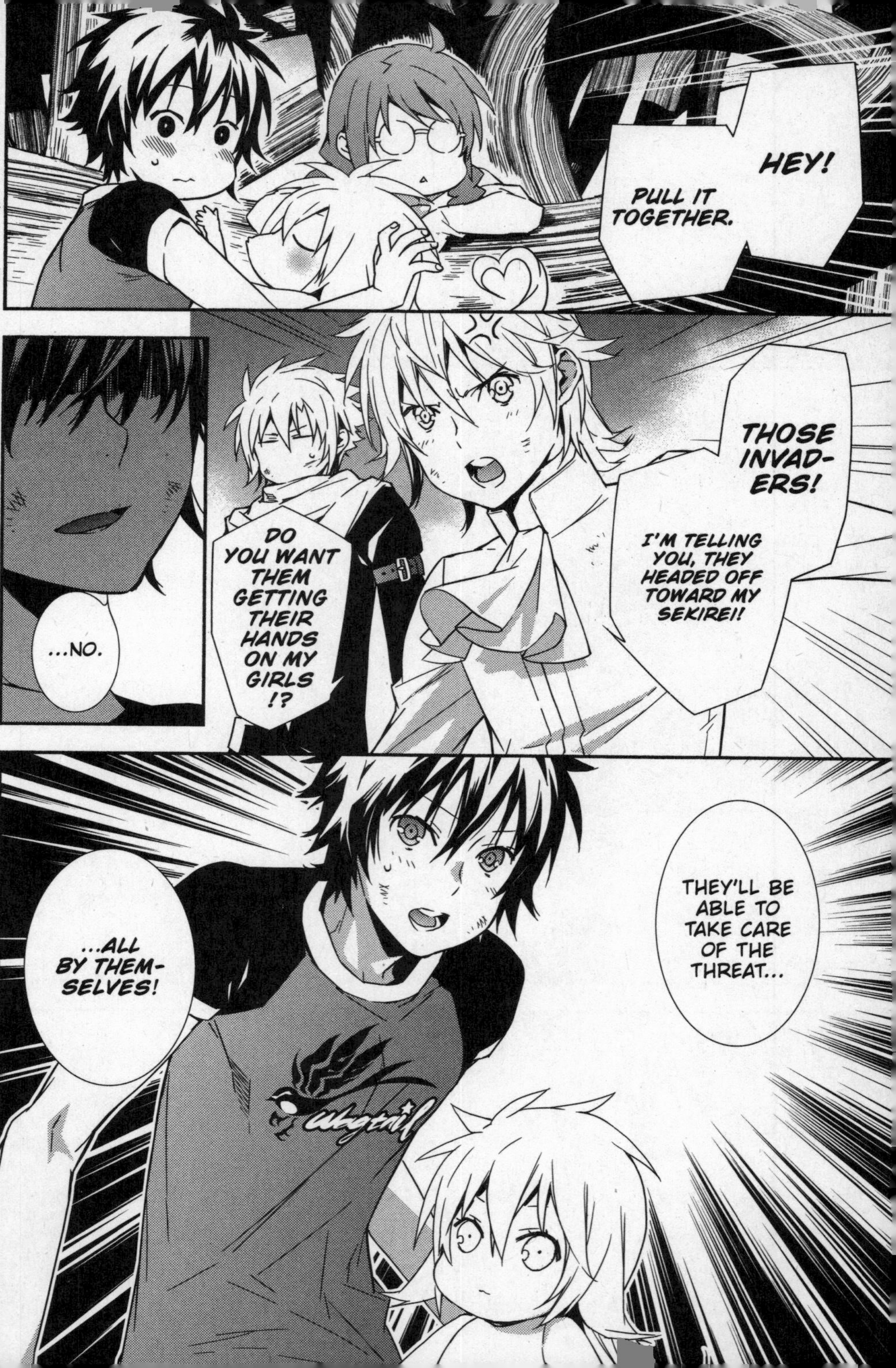
HEY!
PULL IT TOGETHER.
THOSE INVADERS!
I'M TELLING YOU, THEY HEADED OFF TOWARD MY SEKIREI!
DO YOU WANT THEM GETTING THEIR HANDS ON MY GIRLS!?
...NO.
THEY'LL BE ABLE TO TAKE CARE OF THE THREAT...
...ALL BY THEMSELVES!

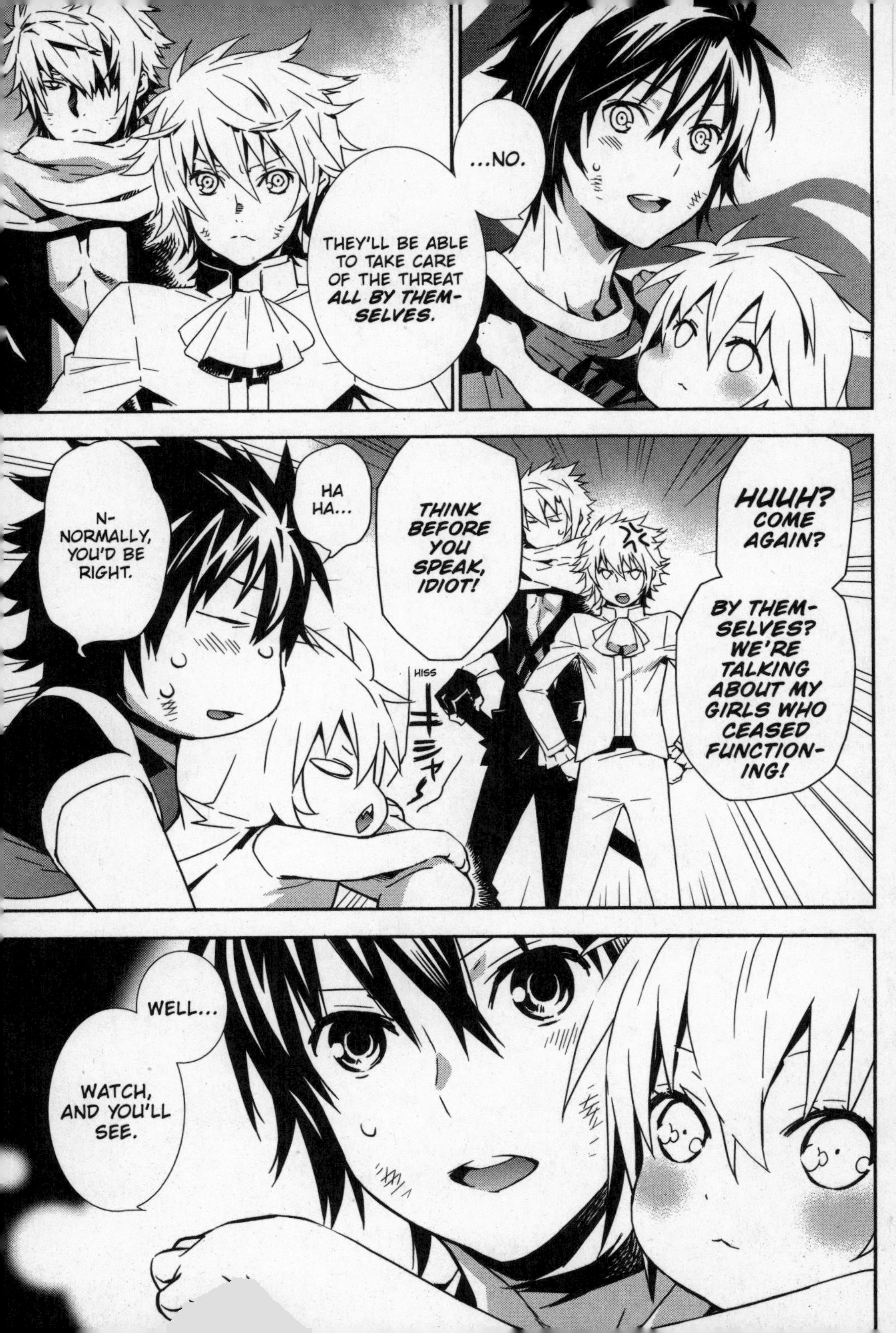
...NO.
THEY'LL BE ABLE TO TAKE CARE OF THE THREAT ALL BY THEM-SELVES.
HUUH? COME AGAIN?
BY THEM-SELVES? WE'RE TALKING ABOUT MY GIRLS WHO CEASED FUNCTION-ING!
THINK BEFORE YOU SPEAK, IDIOT!
HISS
HA HA...
N-NORMALLY, YOU'D BE RIGHT.
WELL...
WATCH, AND YOU'LL SEE.

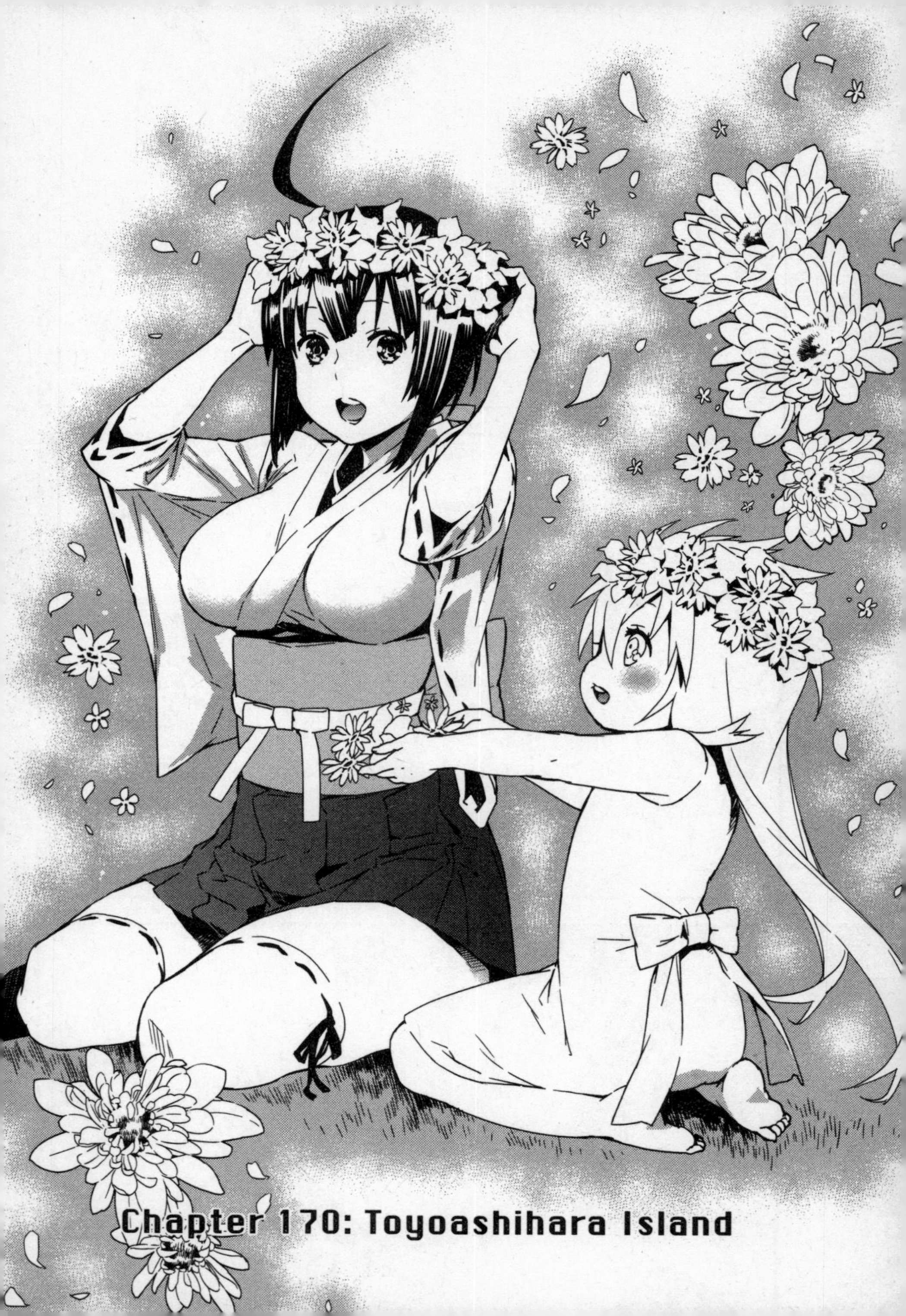

Chapter 170: Toyoashihara Island

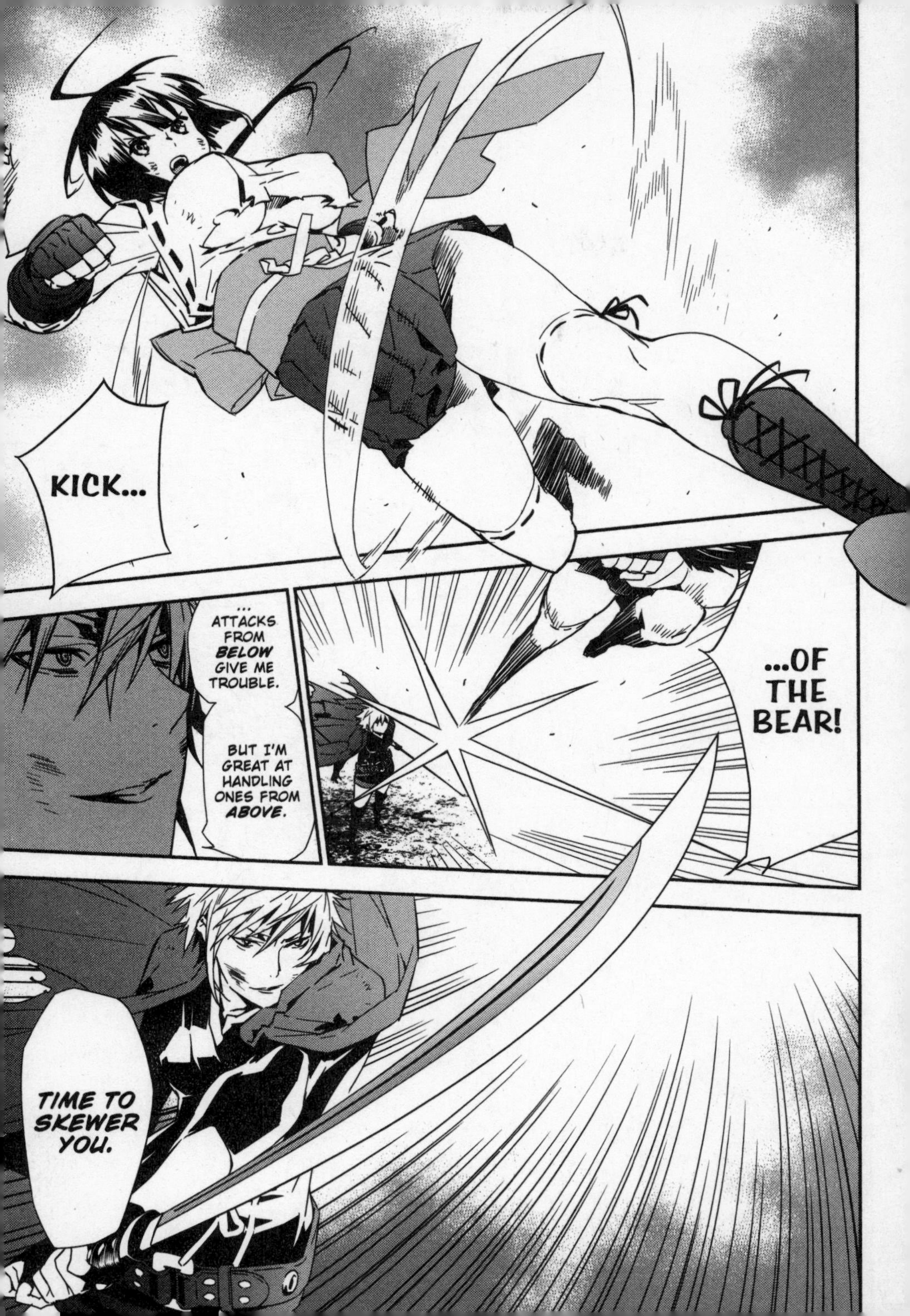
KICK...
...OF THE BEAR!
...ATTACKS FROM BELOW GIVE ME TROUBLE.
BUT I'M GREAT AT HANDLING ONES FROM ABOVE.
TIME TO SKEWER YOU.

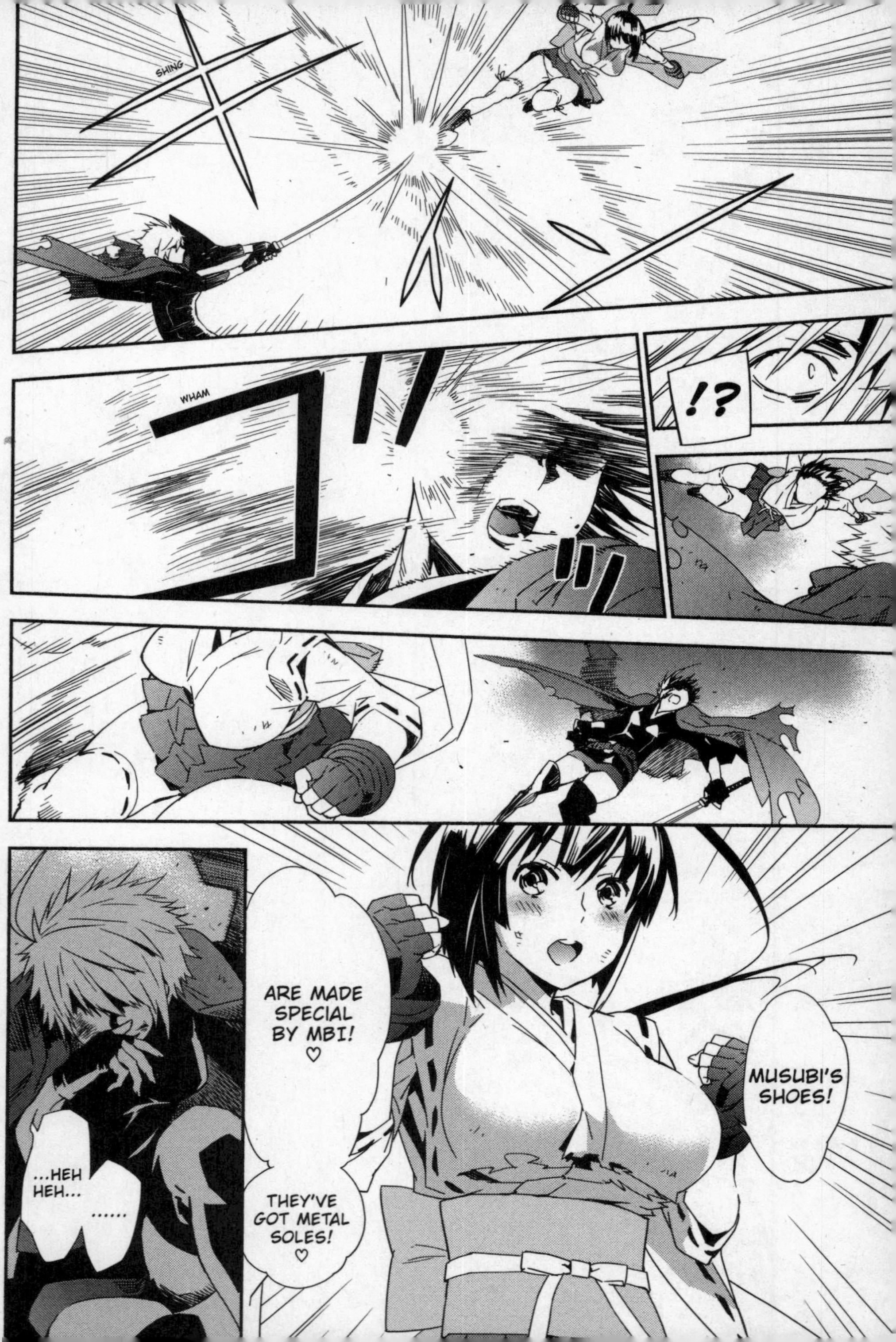
SHING
!?
WHAM
ゴッ
MUSUBI'S SHOES!
ARE MADE SPECIAL BY MBI! ♡
THEY'VE GOT METAL SOLES! ♡
...HEH HEH...
......

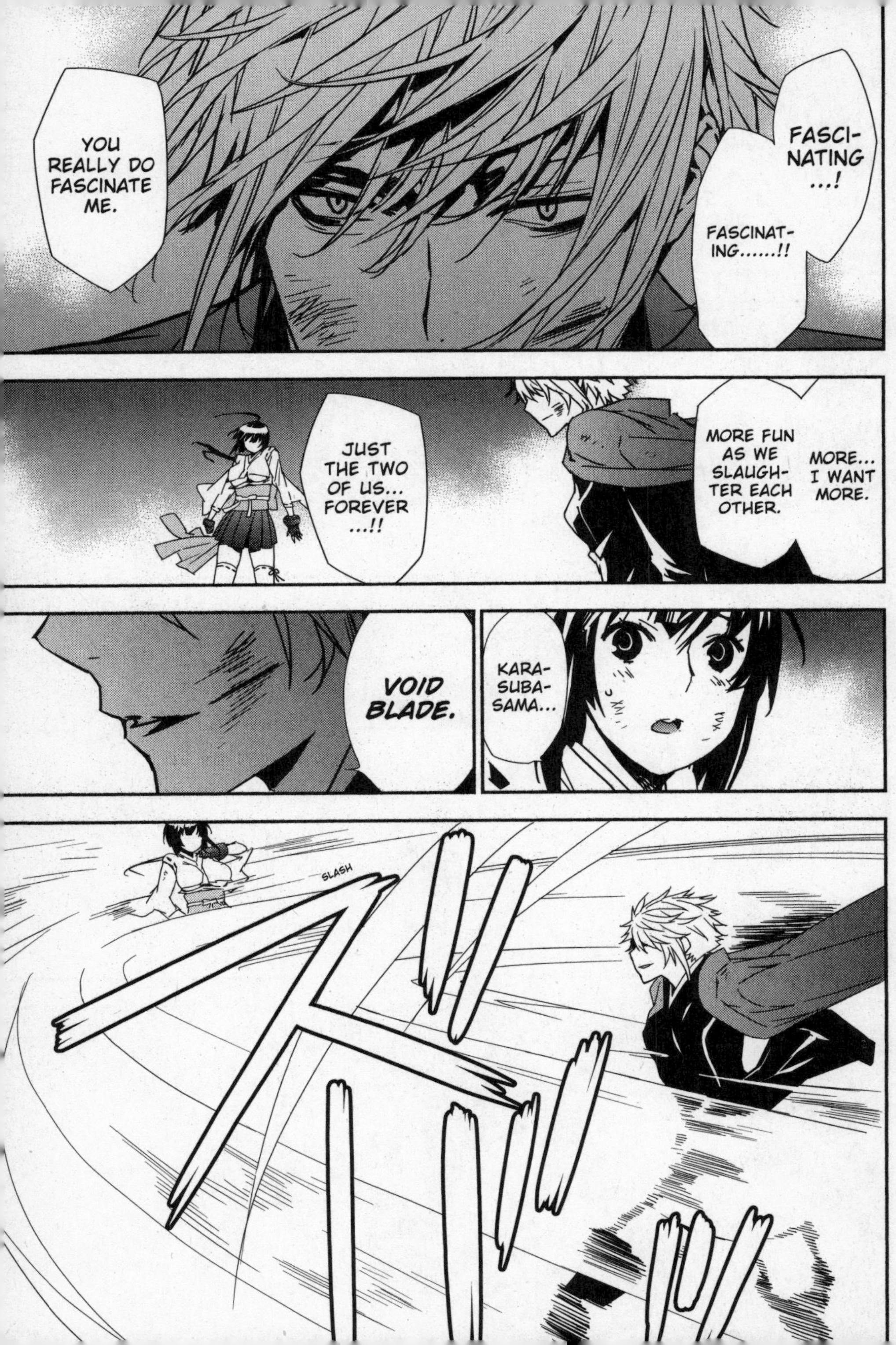
FASCINATING...!
FASCINATING......!!
YOU REALLY DO FASCINATE ME.
MORE... I WANT MORE.
MORE FUN AS WE SLAUGHTER EACH OTHER.
JUST THE TWO OF US... FOREVER...!!
KARASUBA-SAMA...
VOID BLADE.
SLASH

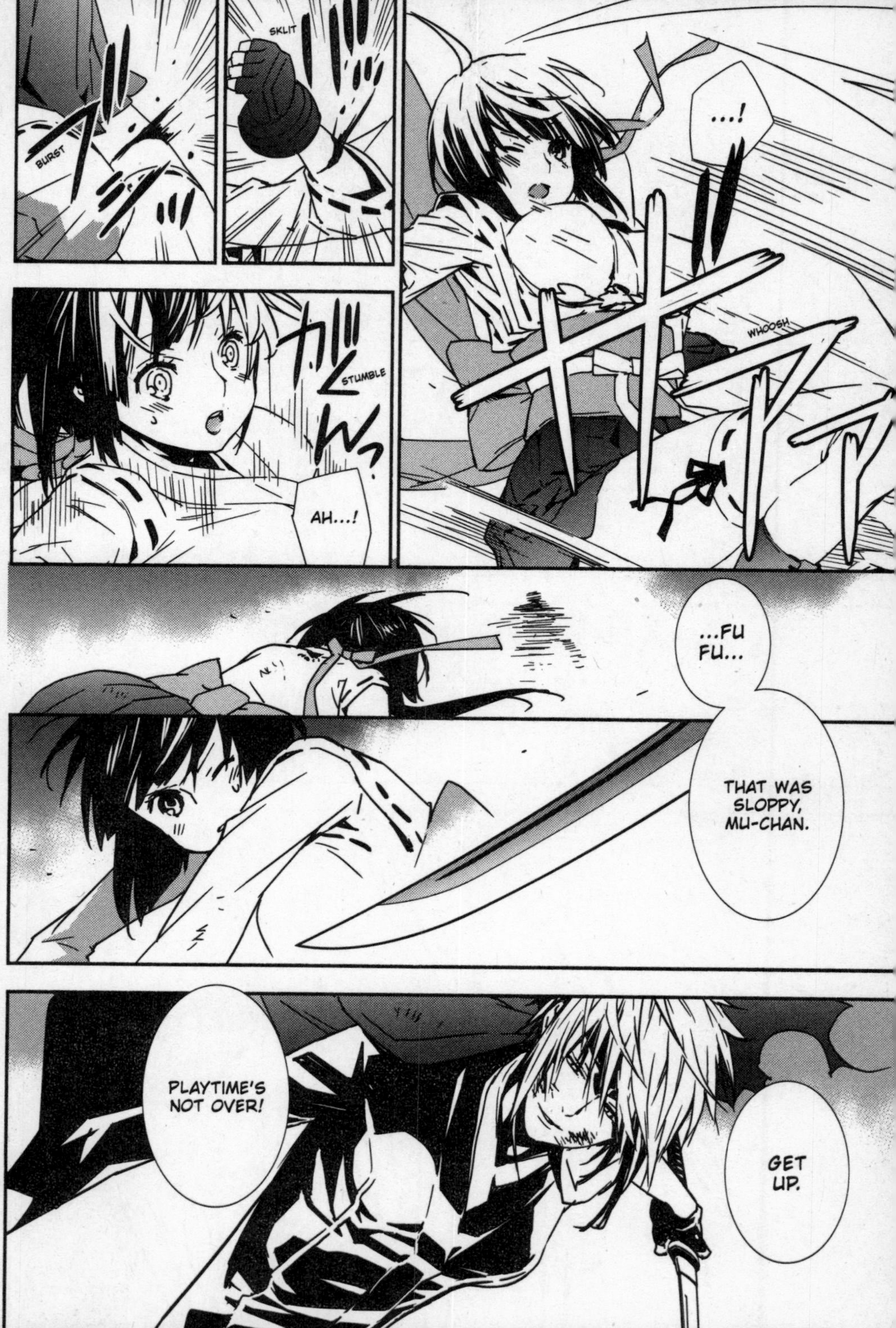
...!
WHOOSH
SKLIT
BURST
STUMBLE
AH...!
...FU FU...
THAT WAS SLOPPY, MU-CHAN.
GET UP.
PLAYTIME'S NOT OVER!

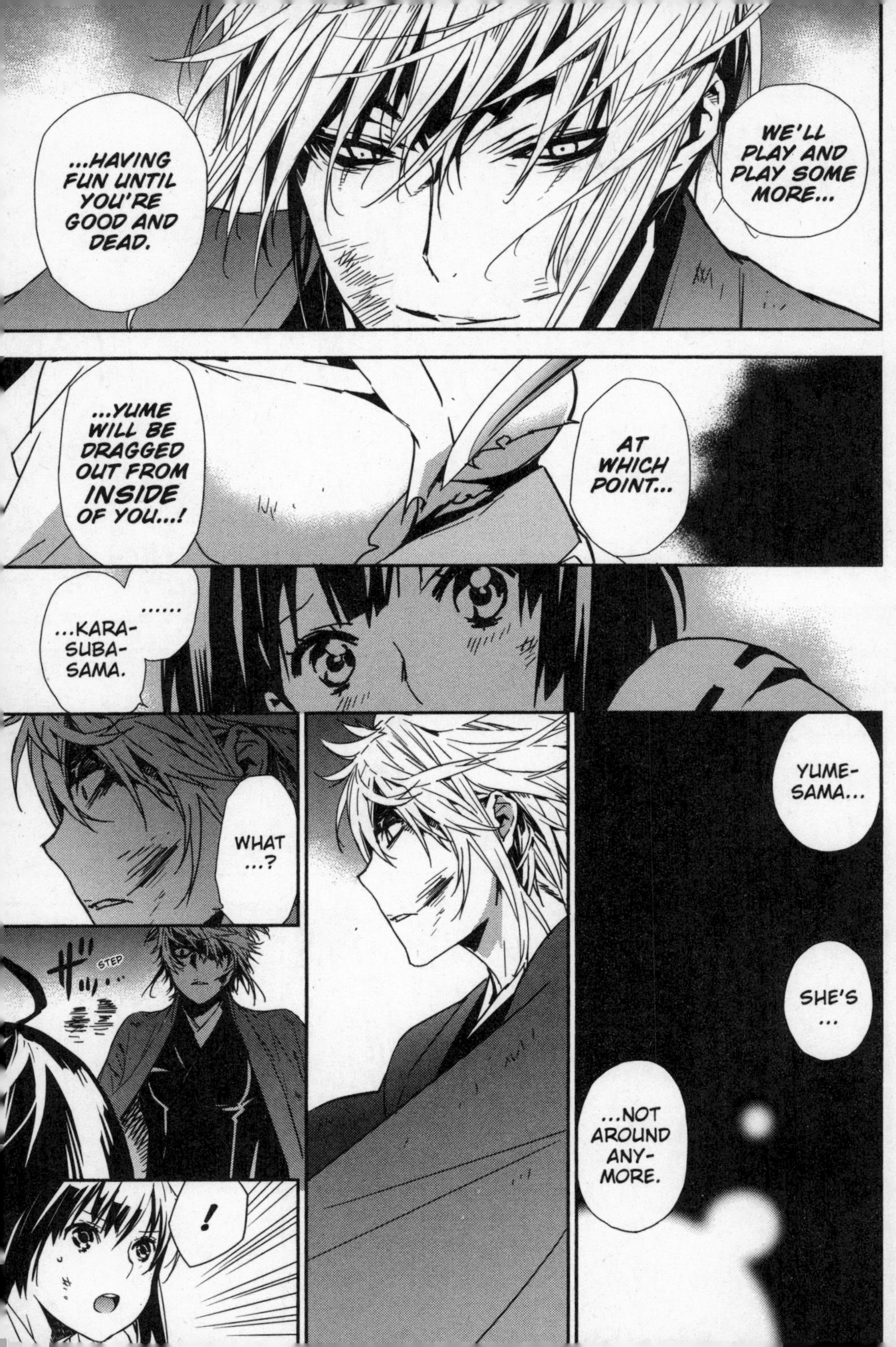
WE'LL PLAY AND PLAY SOME MORE...
...HAVING FUN UNTIL YOU'RE GOOD AND DEAD.
AT WHICH POINT...
...YUME WILL BE DRAGGED OUT FROM INSIDE OF YOU...!
......
...KARASUBA-SAMA.
YUME-SAMA...
SHE'S...
...NOT AROUND ANYMORE.
WHAT...?
STEP
!

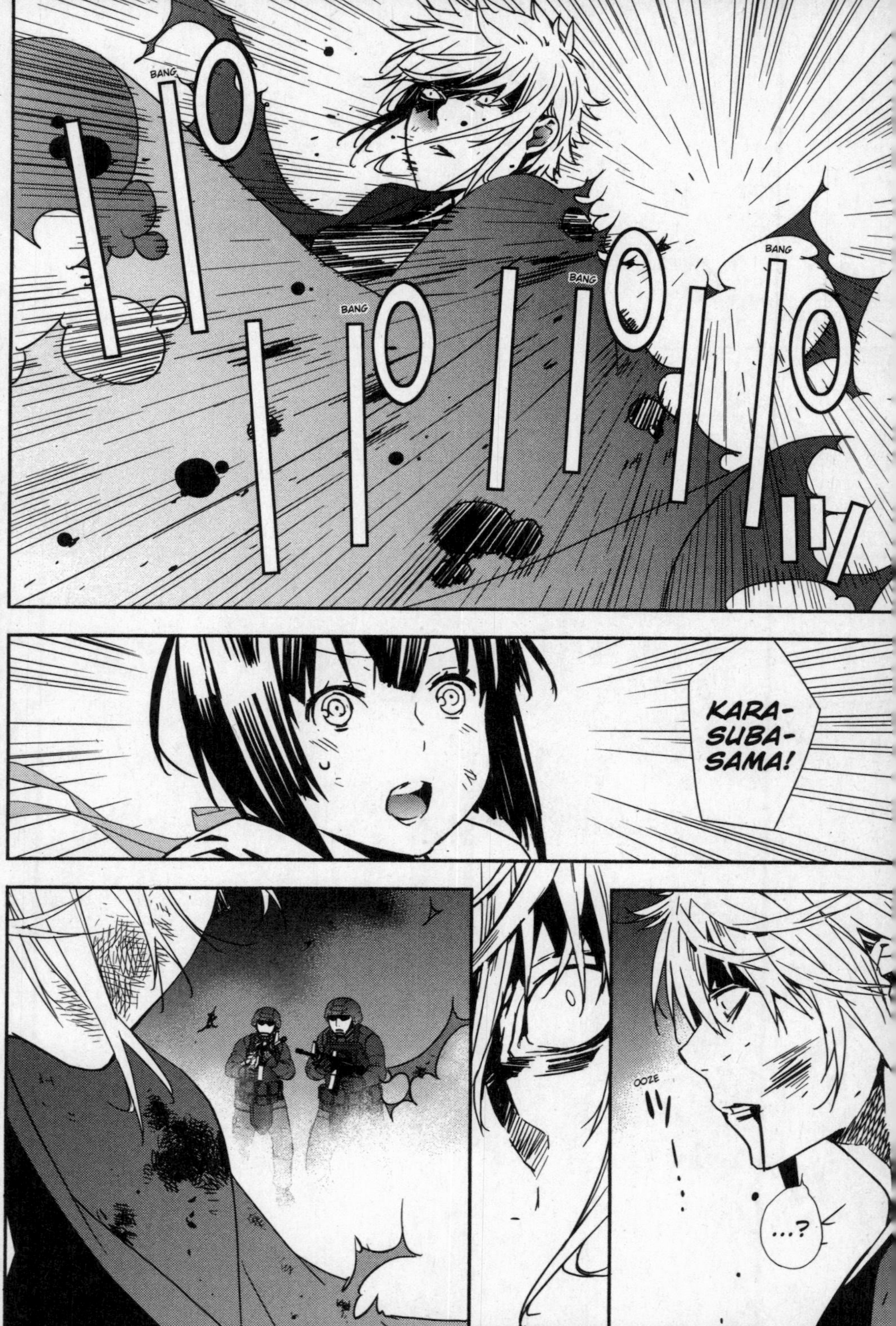
BANG
BANG
BANG
BANG
KARA-SUBA-SAMA!
OOZE
...?

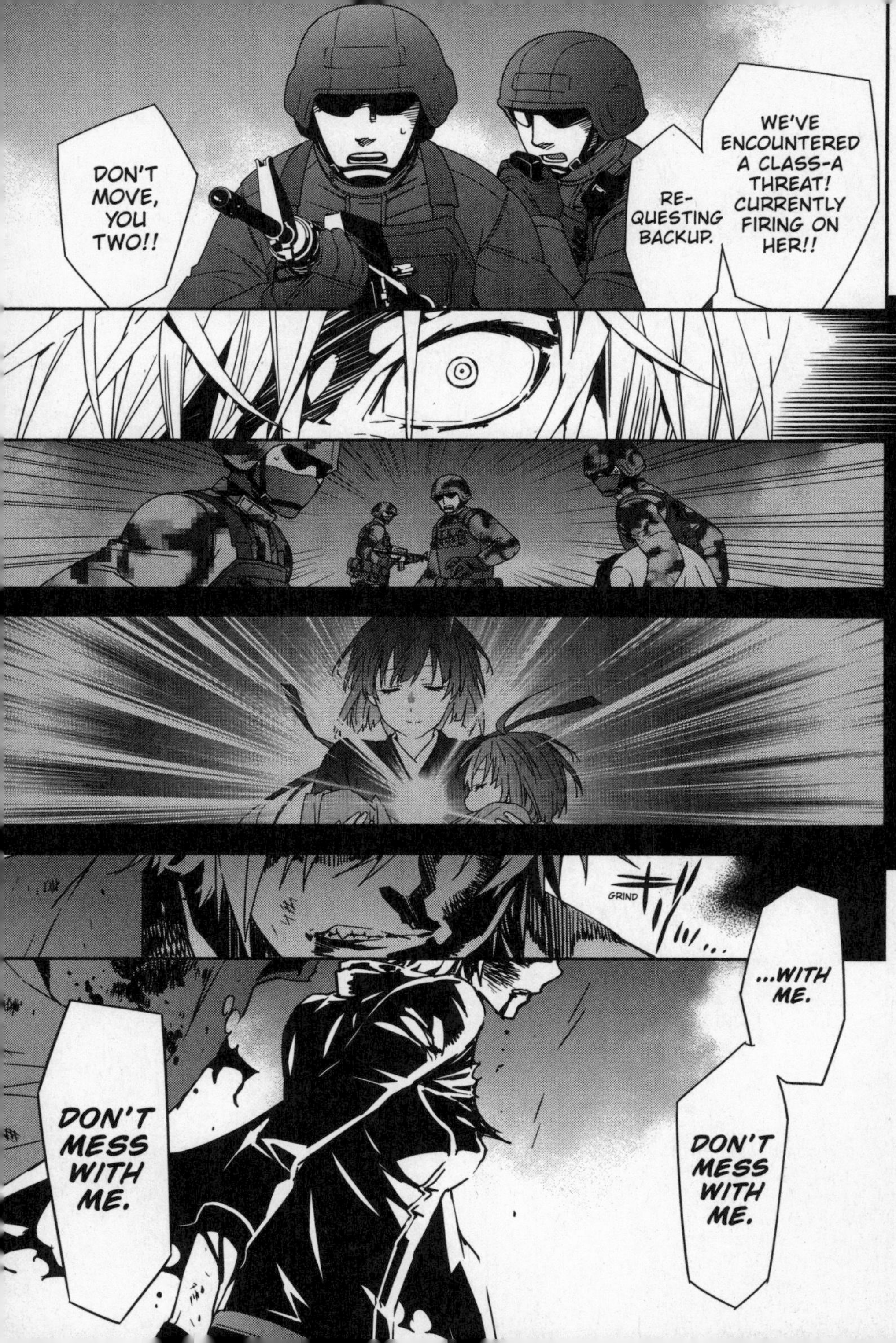
WE'VE ENCOUNTERED A CLASS-A THREAT! CURRENTLY FIRING ON HER!!
RE-QUESTING BACKUP.
DON'T MOVE, YOU TWO!!
GRIND
...WITH ME.
DON'T MESS WITH ME.
DON'T MESS WITH ME.

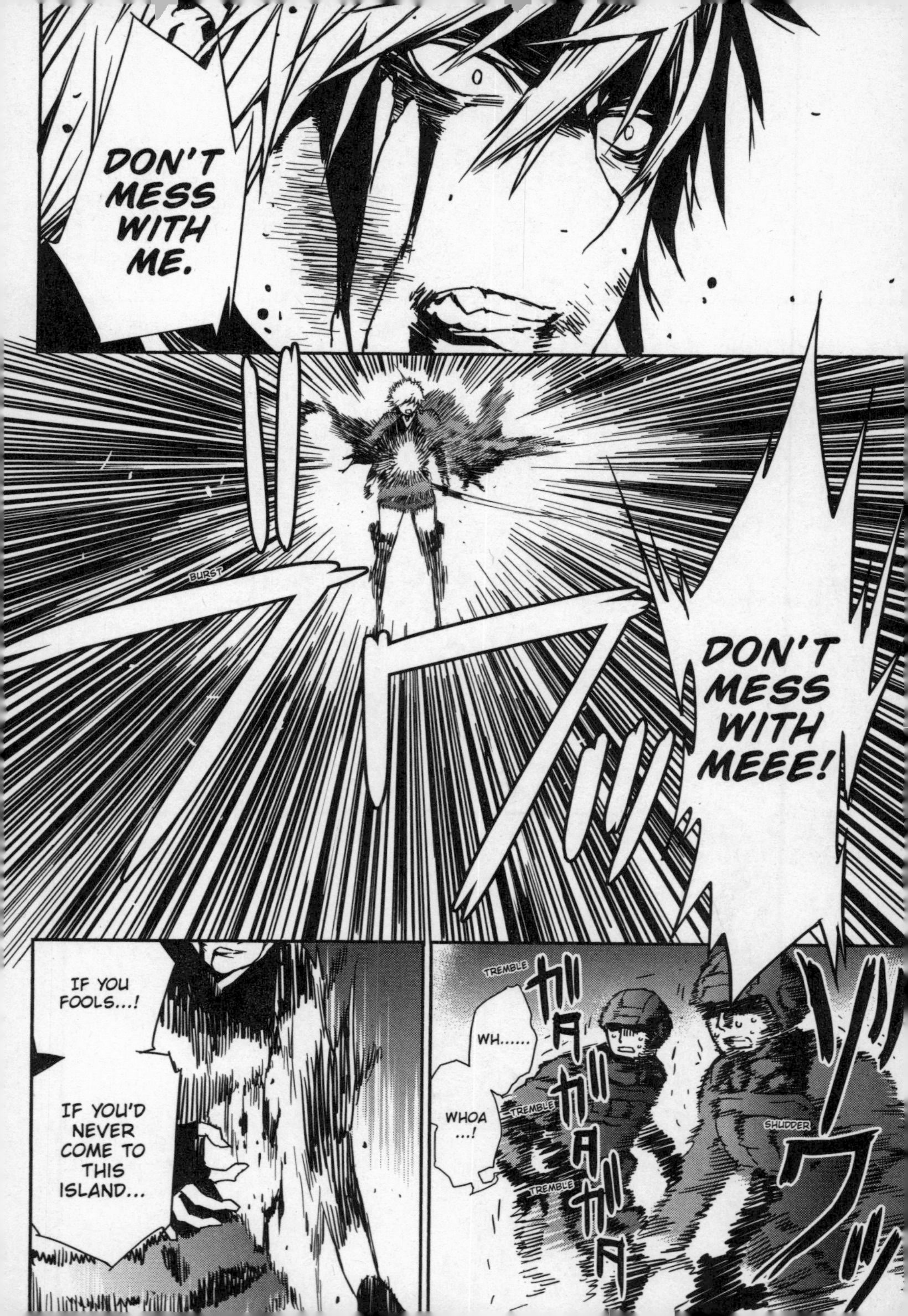
DON'T MESS WITH ME.
BURST
DON'T MESS WITH MEEE!
TREMBLE
WH......
SHUDDER
TREMBLE
WHOA ...!
TREMBLE
IF YOU FOOLS...!
IF YOU'D NEVER COME TO THIS ISLAND...

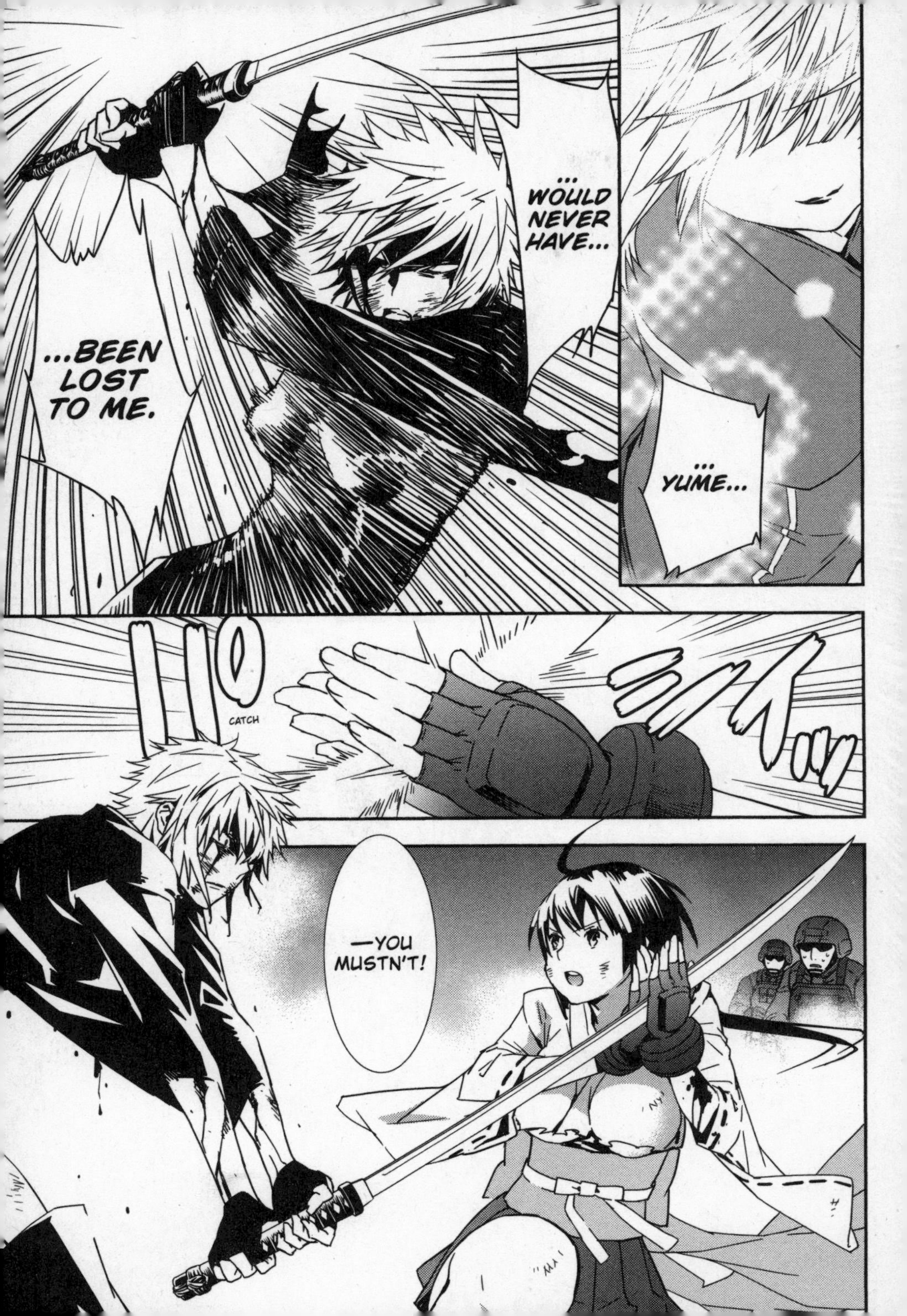
...YUME...
...WOULD NEVER HAVE...
...BEEN LOST TO ME.
CATCH
—YOU MUSTN'T!

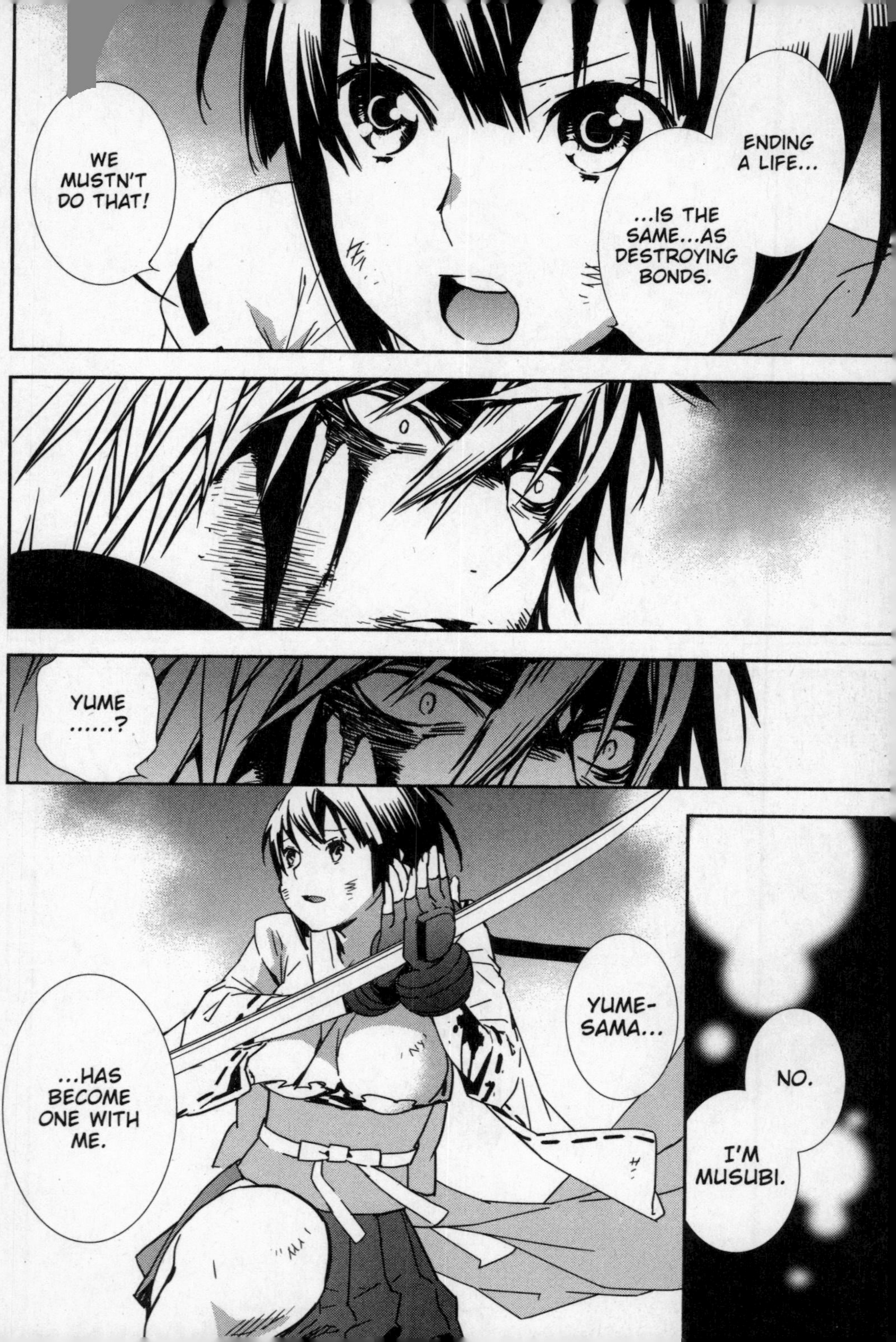
ENDING A LIFE...
...IS THE SAME...AS DESTROYING BONDS.
WE MUSTN'T DO THAT!
YUME ......?
NO.
I'M MUSUBI.
YUME-SAMA...
...HAS BECOME ONE WITH ME.

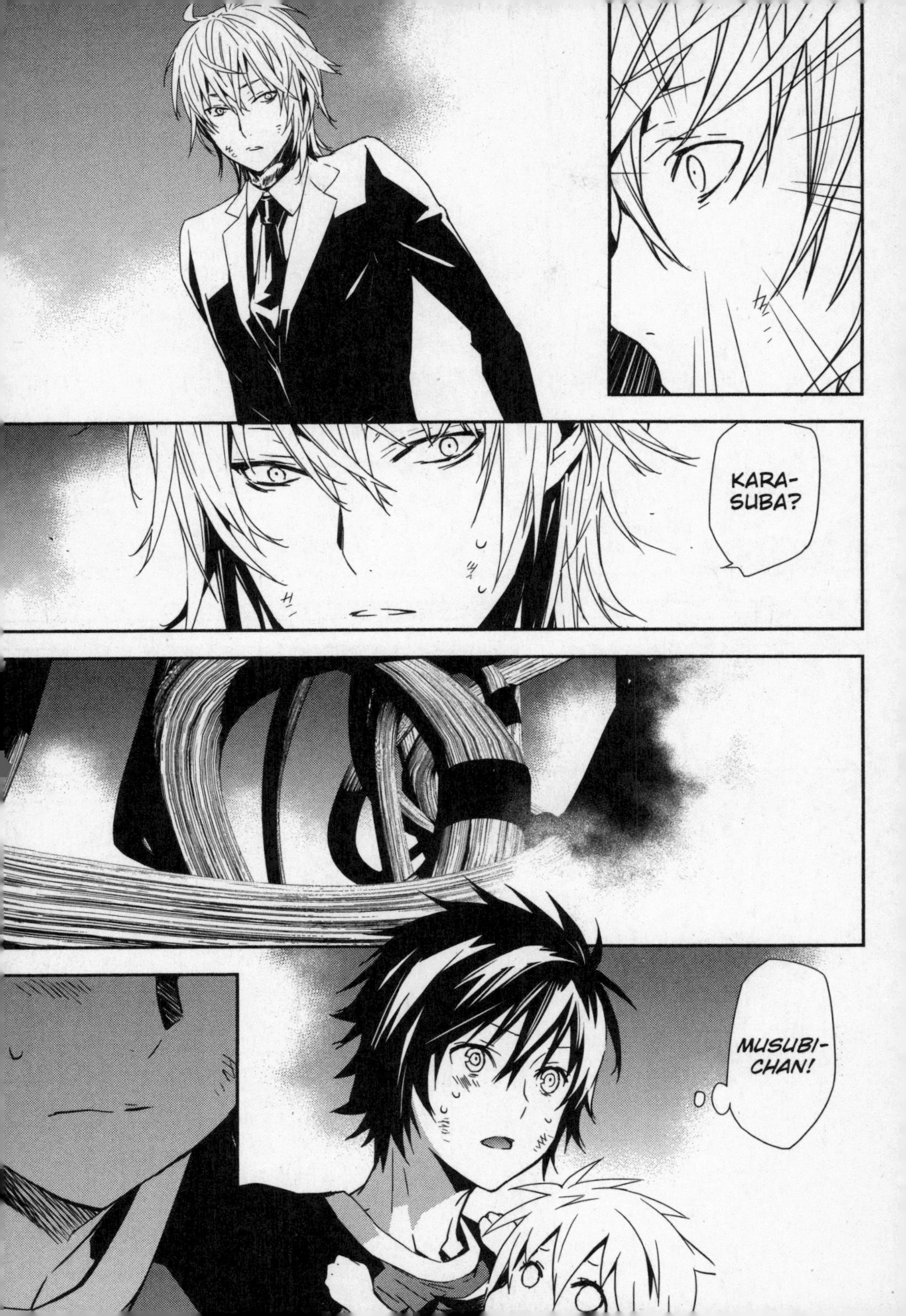
KARA-SUBA?
MUSUBI-CHAN!

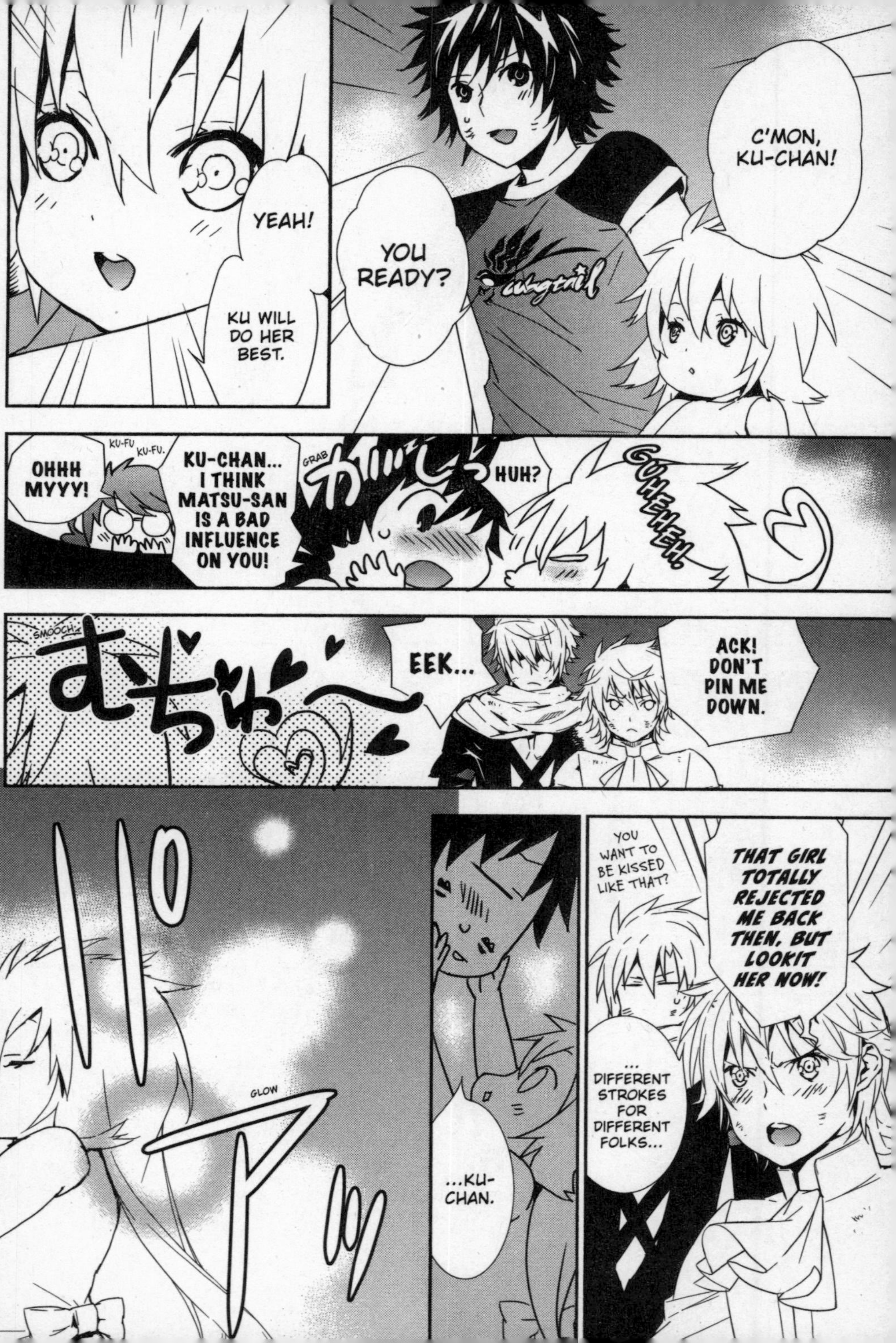
C'MON, KU-CHAN!
YOU READY?
YEAH!
KU WILL DO HER BEST.
GUHEHEH.
HUH?
GRAB
KU-CHAN... I THINK MATSU-SAN IS A BAD INFLUENCE ON YOU!
KU-FU KU-FU.
OHHH MYYY!
ACK! DON'T PIN ME DOWN.
EEK...
SMOOCH
THAT GIRL TOTALLY REJECTED ME BACK THEN, BUT LOOKIT HER NOW!
YOU WANT TO BE KISSED LIKE THAT?
...DIFFERENT STROKES FOR DIFFERENT FOLKS...
...KU-CHAN.
GLOW

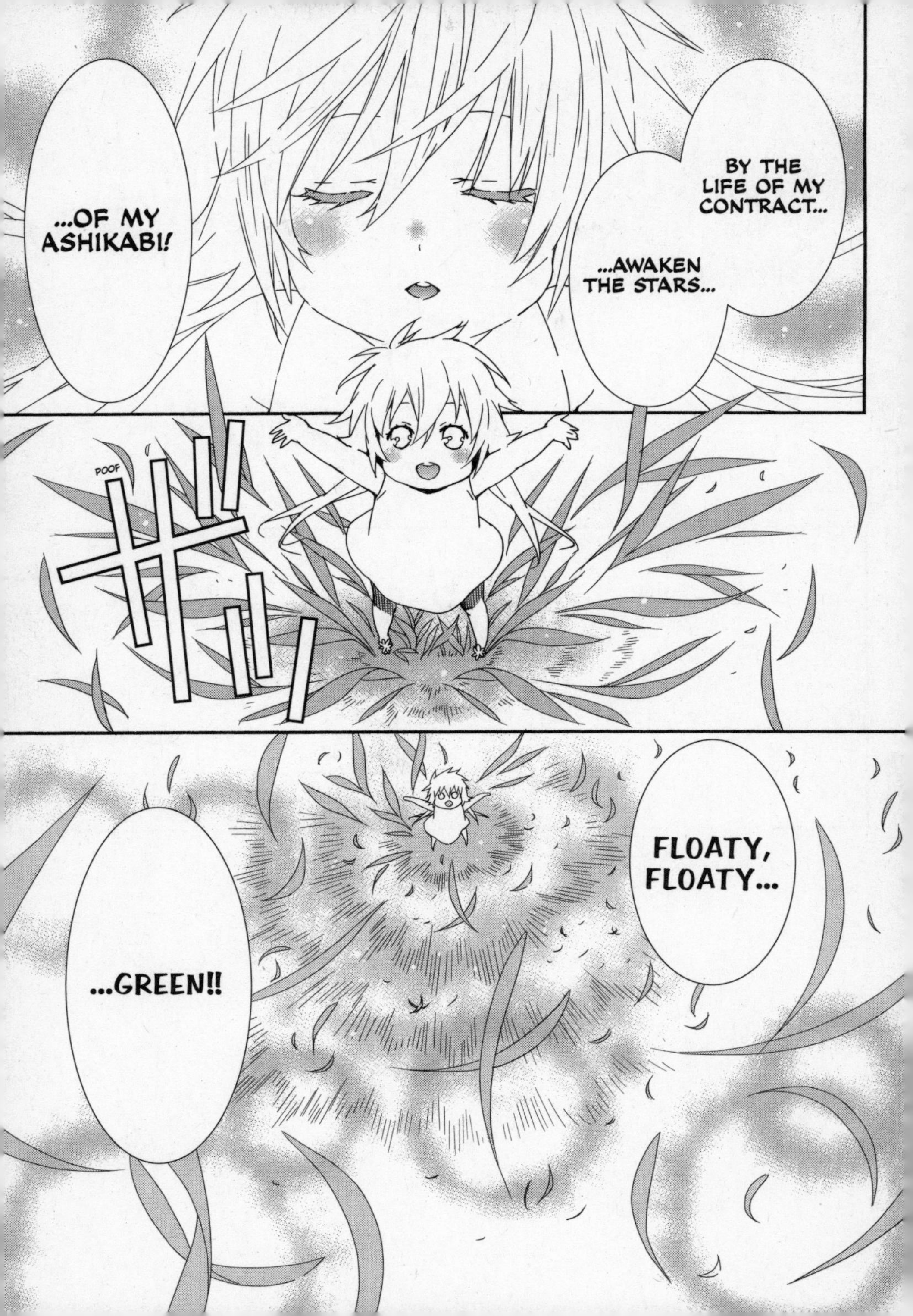
BY THE LIFE OF MY CONTRACT...
...AWAKEN THE STARS...
...OF MY ASHIKABI!
POOF
FLOATY, FLOATY...
...GREEN!!

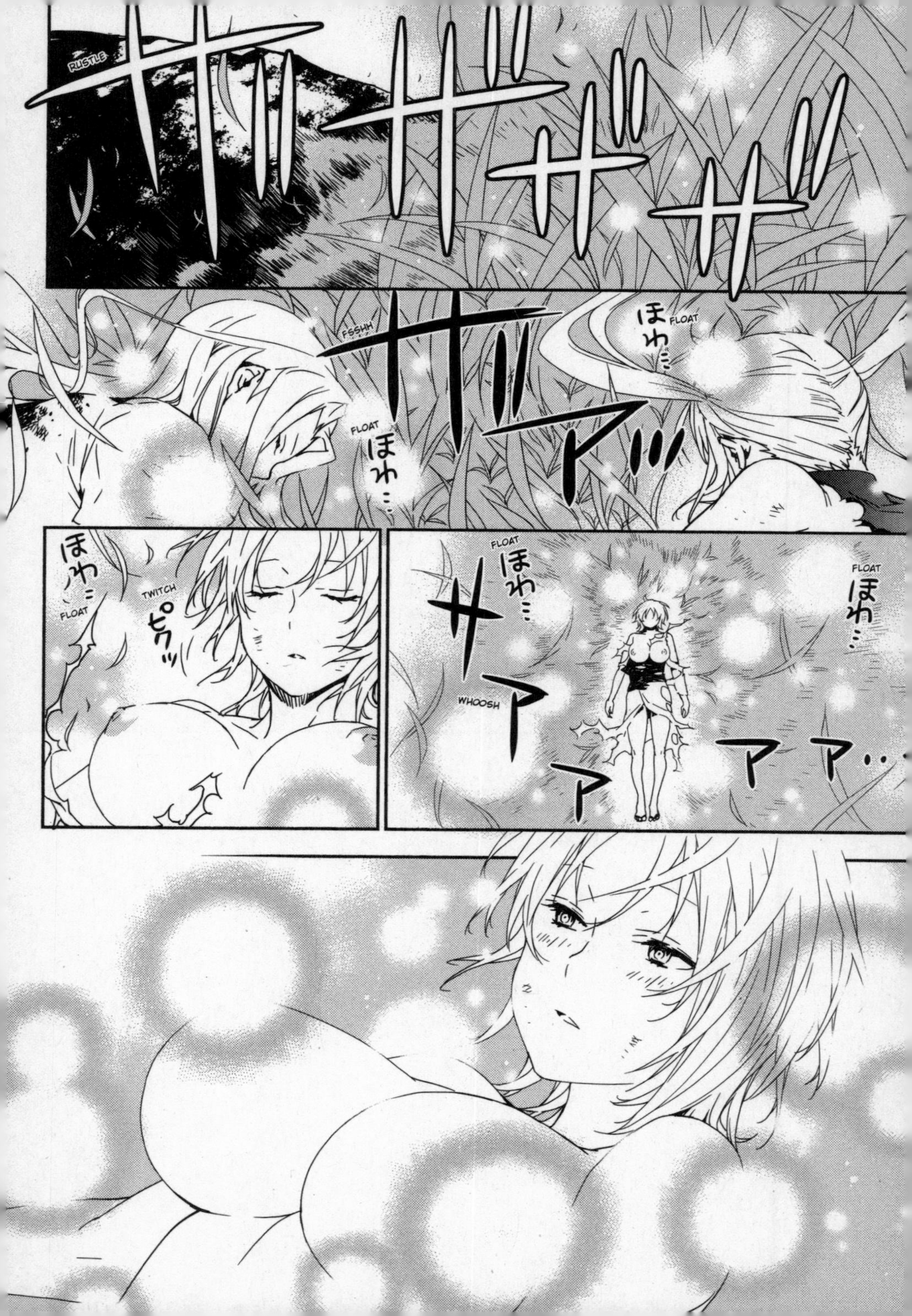
ザワザワザワ
RUSTLE
ほわ…
FLOAT
ザアッ
FSSHH
ほわ…
FLOAT
ほわ…
FLOAT
サアアアアア…
WHOOSH
ほわ…
FLOAT
ピクッ
TWITCH
ほわ…
FLOAT

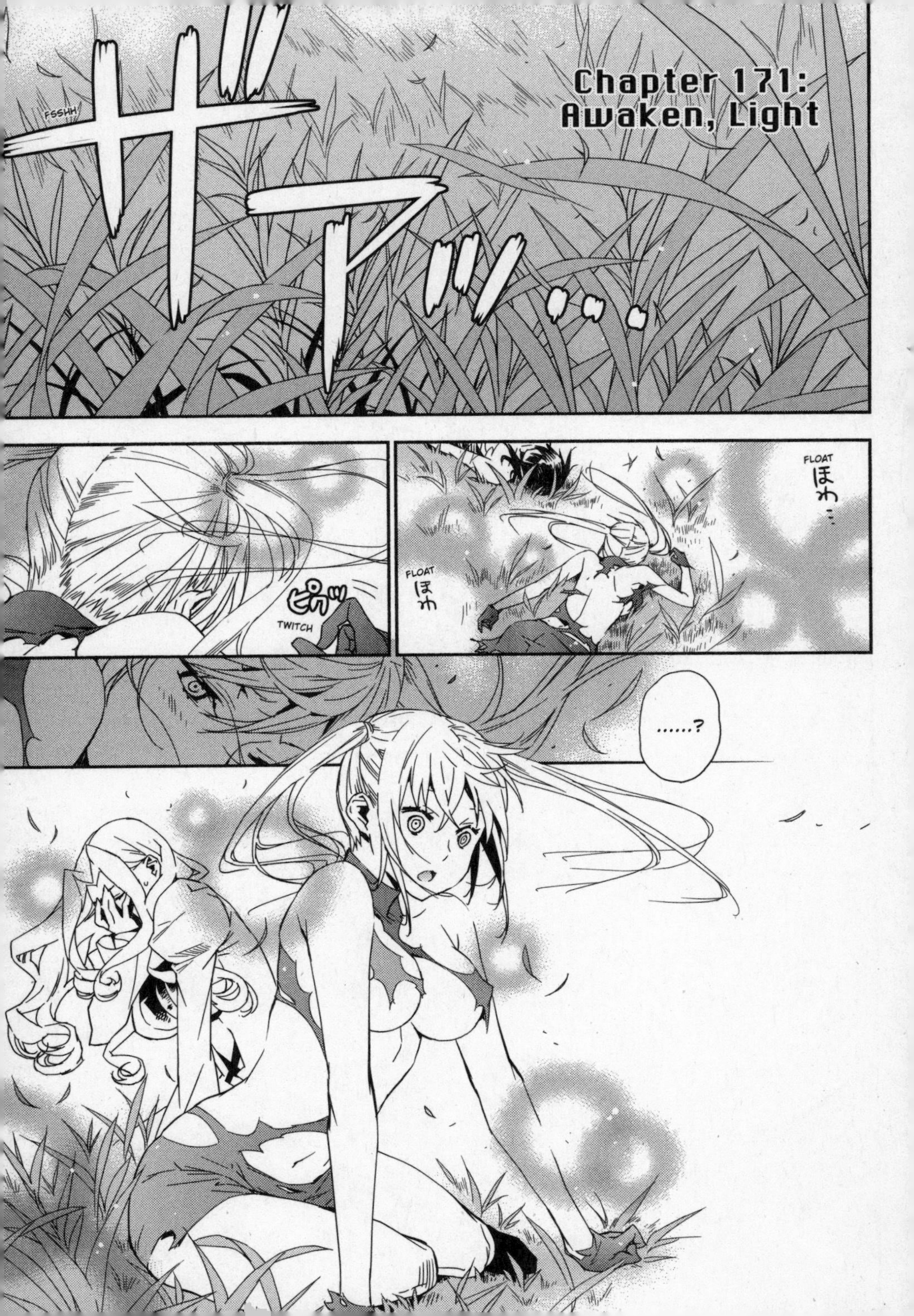
Chapter 171: Awaken, Light
FSSHH
ザアッ...
FLOAT
ほわ
FLOAT
ほわ
ピクッ
TWITCH
......?

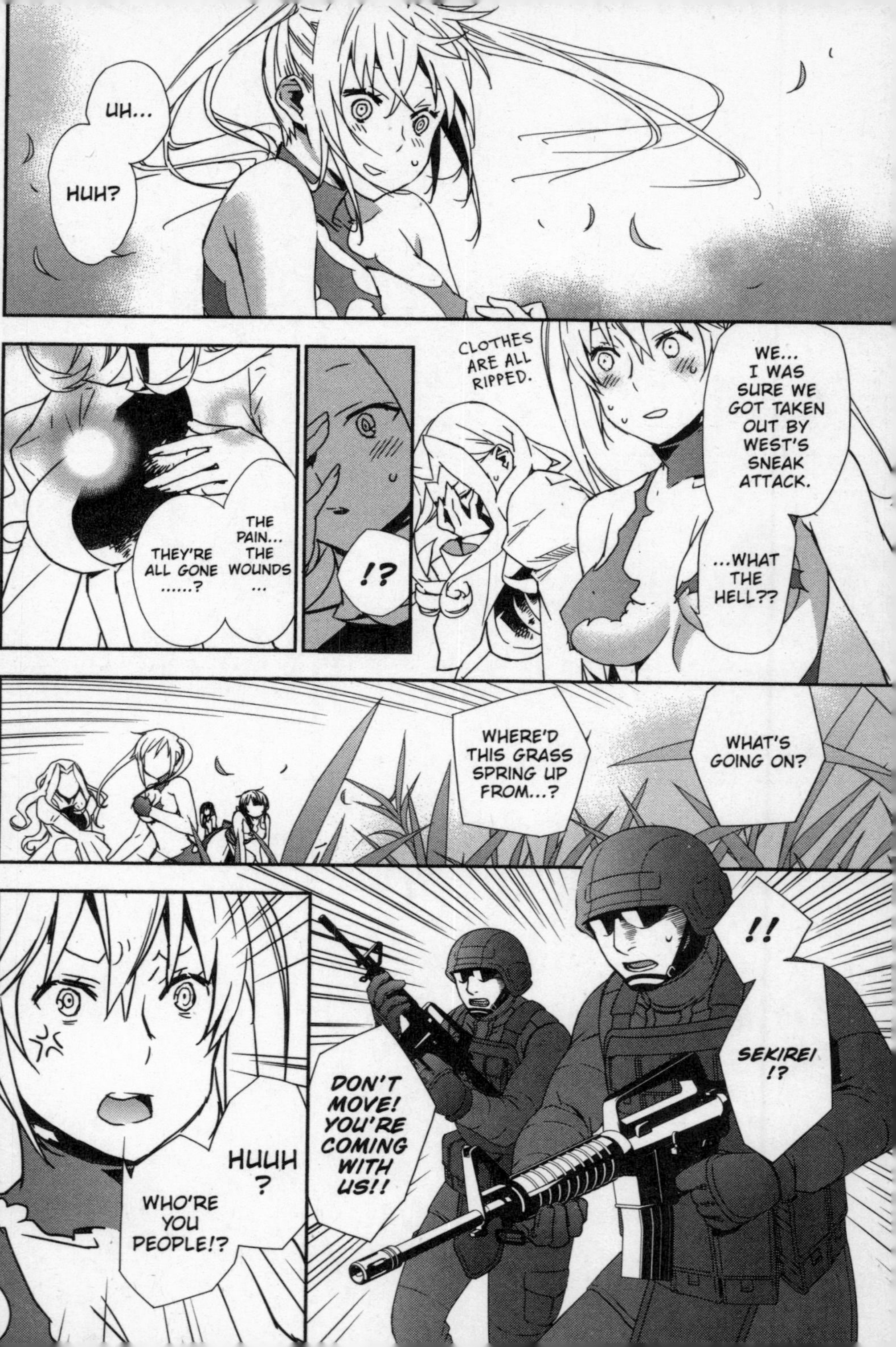
UH...
HUH?
WE... I WAS SURE WE GOT TAKEN OUT BY WEST'S SNEAK ATTACK.
CLOTHES ARE ALL RIPPED.
...WHAT THE HELL??
!?
THE PAIN... THE WOUNDS ...
THEY'RE ALL GONE ......?
WHAT'S GOING ON?
WHERE'D THIS GRASS SPRING UP FROM...?
!!
SEKIREI !?
DON'T MOVE! YOU'RE COMING WITH US!!
HUUH ?
WHO'RE YOU PEOPLE!?

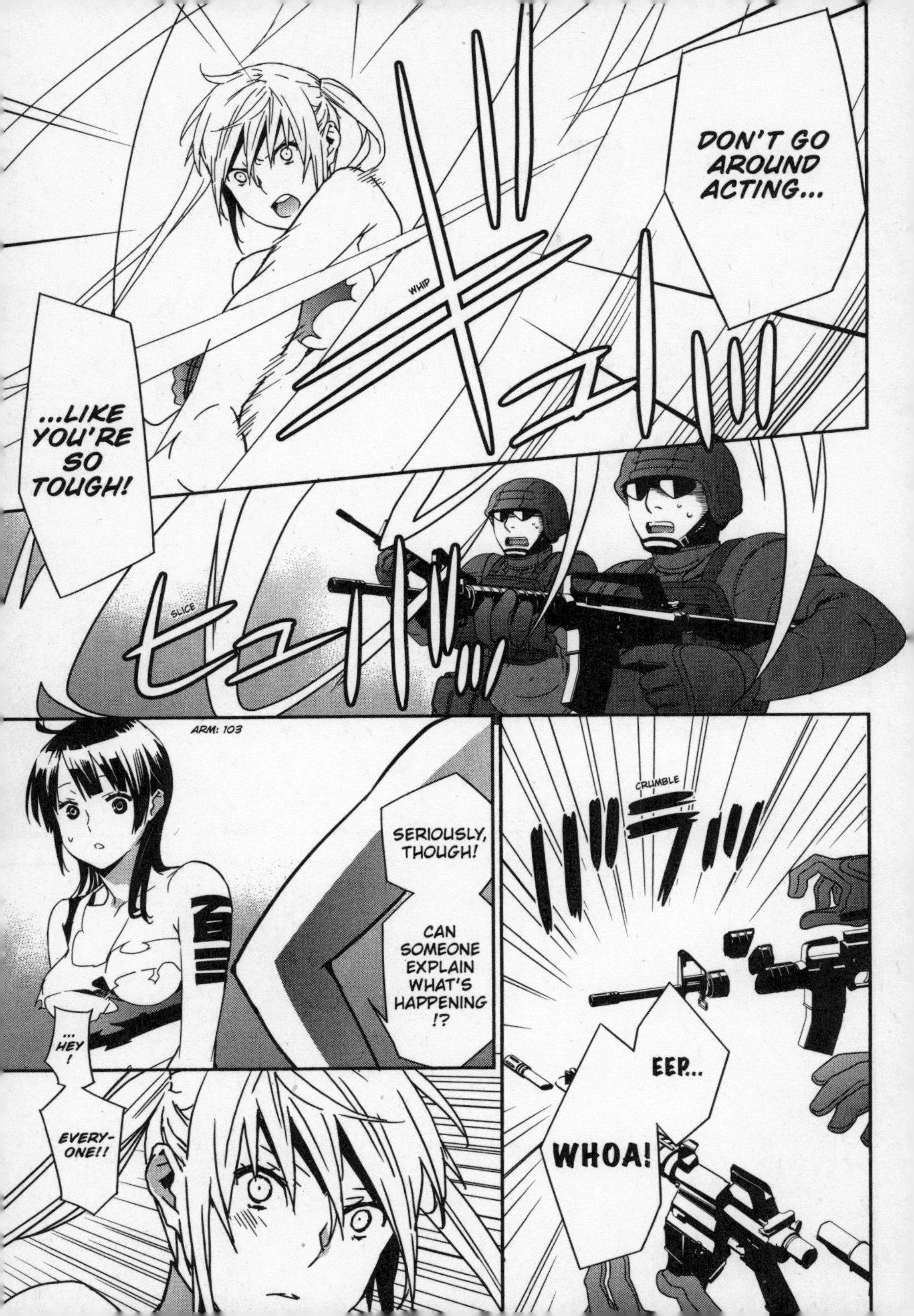
DON'T GO AROUND ACTING...
WHIP
...LIKE YOU'RE SO TOUGH!
SLICE
CRUMBLE
EEP...
WHOA!
ARM: 103
SERIOUSLY, THOUGH!
CAN SOMEONE EXPLAIN WHAT'S HAPPENING!?
...HEY!
EVERYONE!!

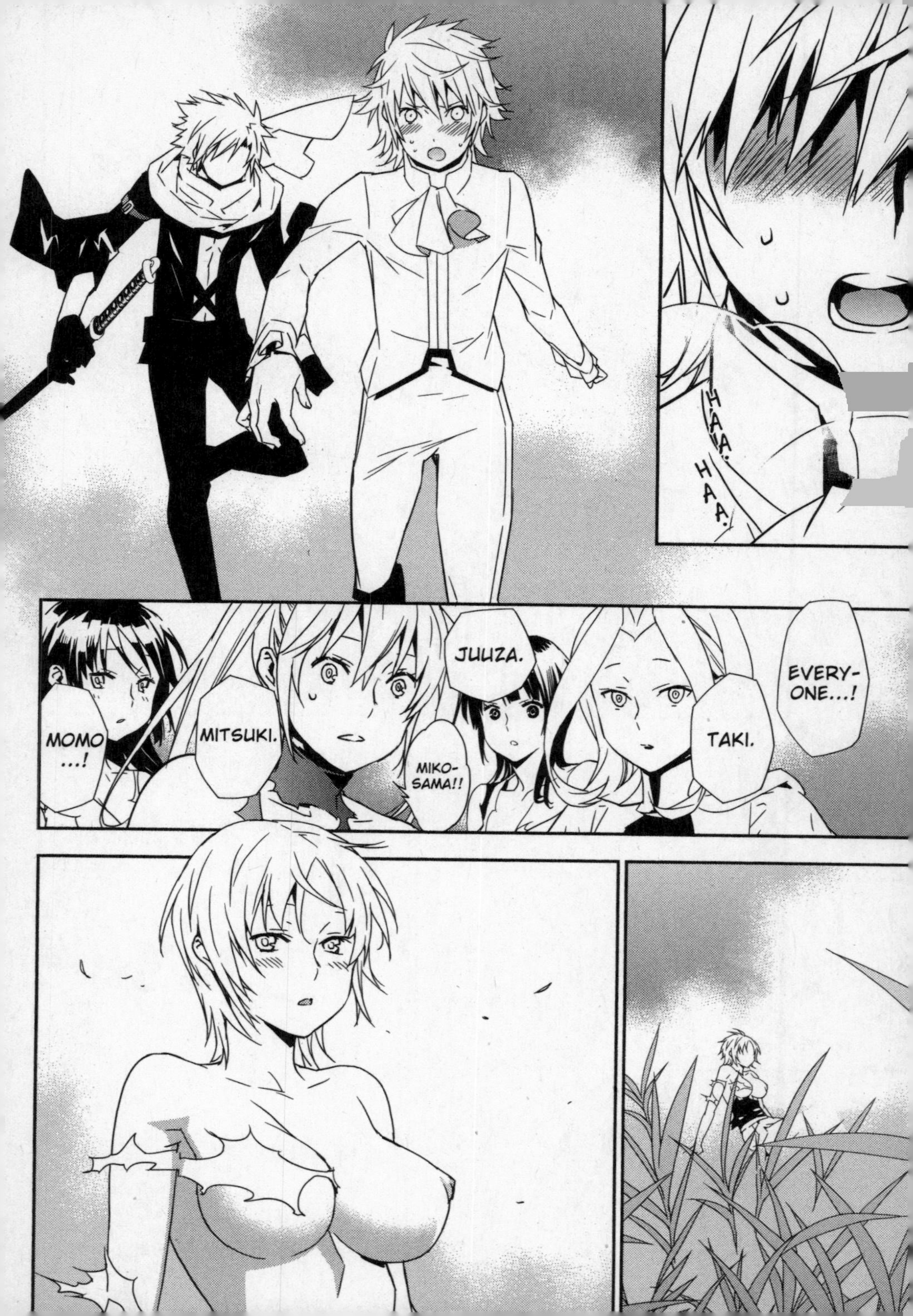
HAA. HAA.
EVERY- ONE...!
TAKI.
JUUZA.
MIKO- SAMA!!
MITSUKI.
MOMO ...!

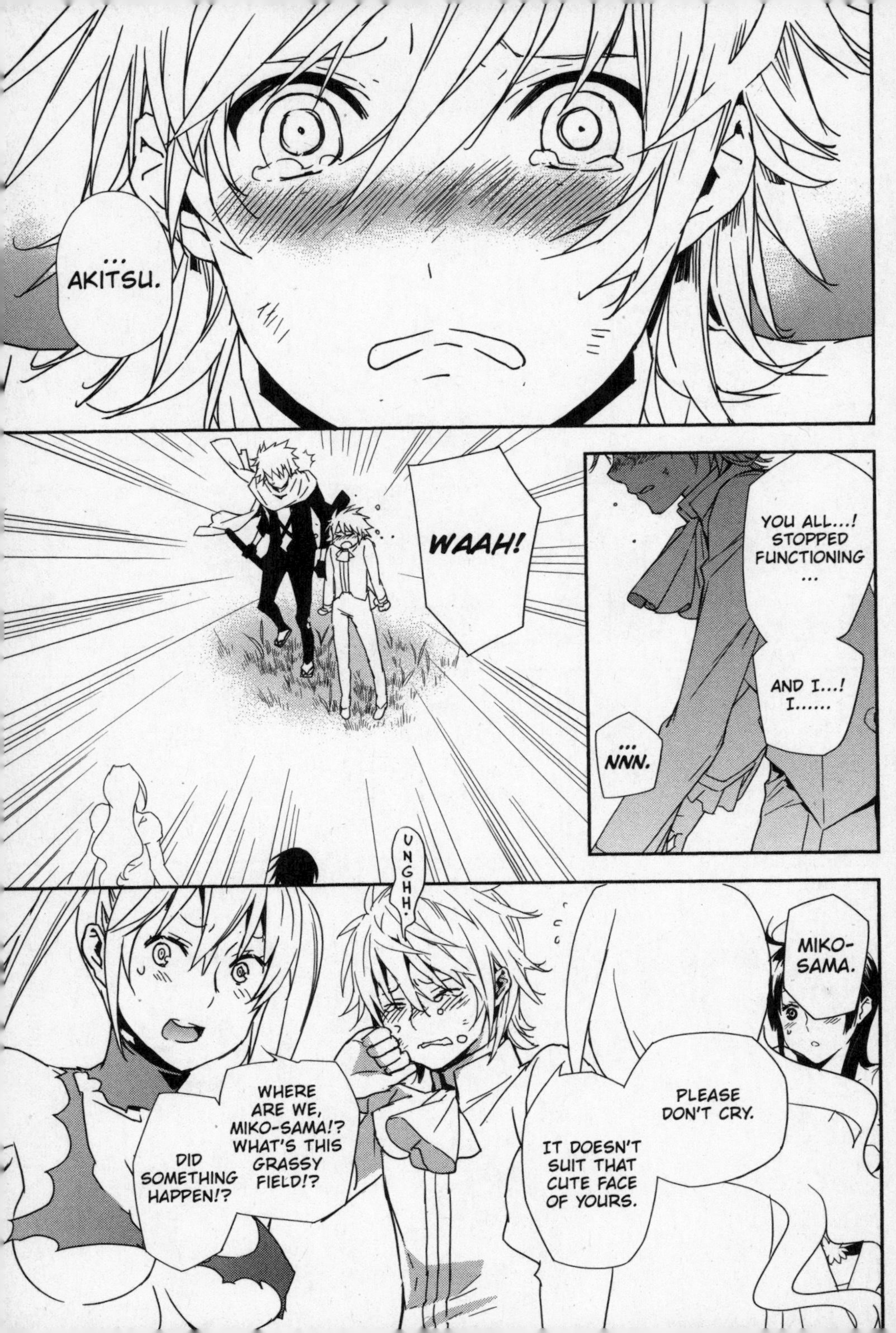
...AKITSU.
YOU ALL...! STOPPED FUNCTIONING...
AND I...! I......
...NNN.
WAAH!
MIKO-SAMA.
PLEASE DON'T CRY.
IT DOESN'T SUIT THAT CUTE FACE OF YOURS.
UNGHH.
WHERE ARE WE, MIKO-SAMA!? WHAT'S THIS GRASSY FIELD!?
DID SOMETHING HAPPEN!?

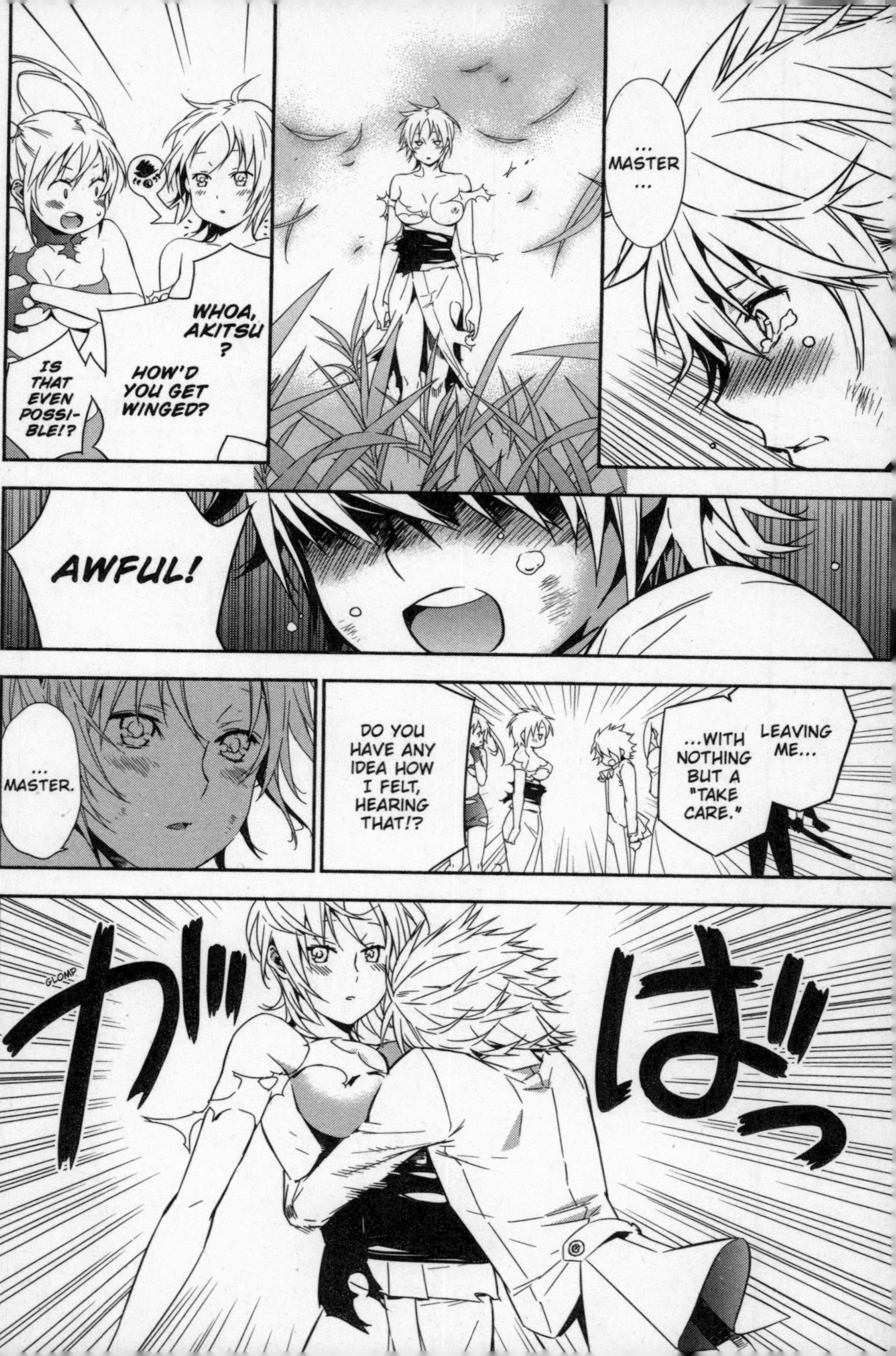
... MASTER ...
WHOA, AKITSU?
HOW'D YOU GET WINGED?
IS THAT EVEN POSSIBLE!?
AWFUL!
LEAVING ME...
...WITH NOTHING BUT A "TAKE CARE."
DO YOU HAVE ANY IDEA HOW I FELT, HEARING THAT!?
... MASTER.
GLOMP
がばっ

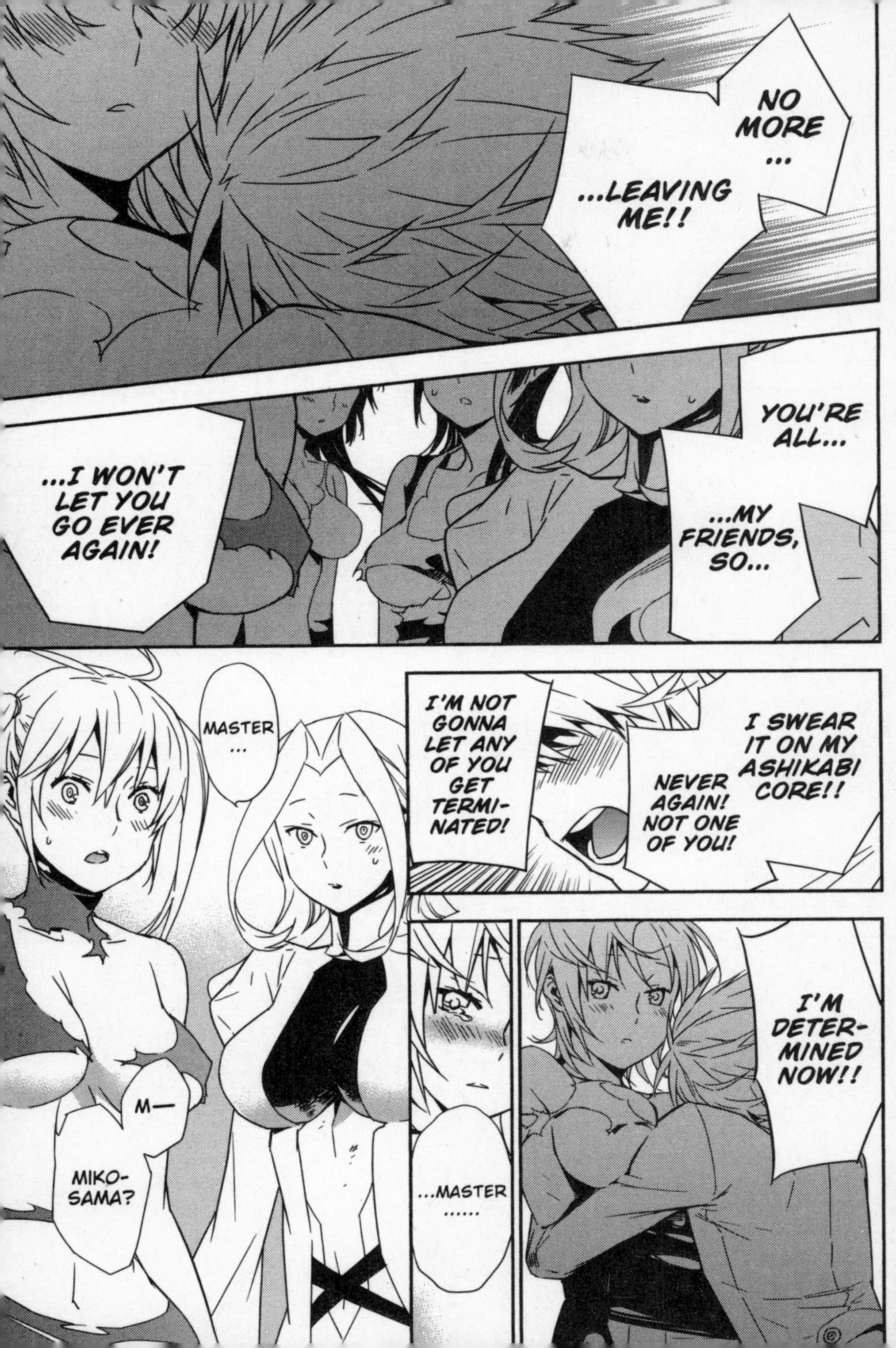
NO MORE ...
...LEAVING ME!!
YOU'RE ALL...
...MY FRIENDS, SO...
...I WON'T LET YOU GO EVER AGAIN!
I SWEAR IT ON MY ASHIKABI CORE!!
NEVER AGAIN! NOT ONE OF YOU!
I'M NOT GONNA LET ANY OF YOU GET TERMI-NATED!
I'M DETER-MINED NOW!!
...MASTER ......
MASTER ...
M—
MIKO-SAMA?

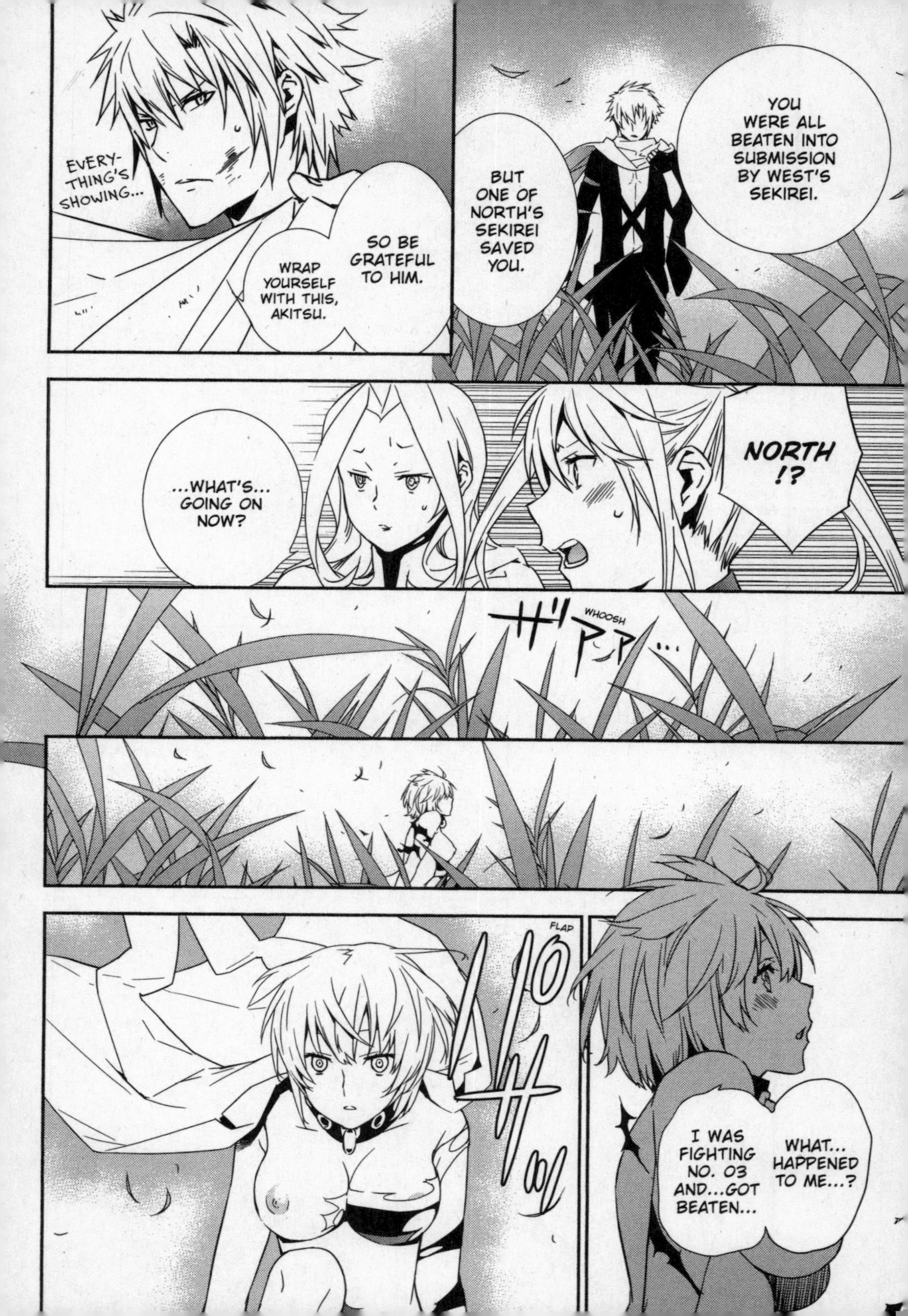
YOU WERE ALL BEATEN INTO SUBMISSION BY WEST'S SEKIREI.
BUT ONE OF NORTH'S SEKIREI SAVED YOU.
SO BE GRATEFUL TO HIM.
WRAP YOURSELF WITH THIS, AKITSU.
EVERY-THING'S SHOWING...
NORTH!?
...WHAT'S... GOING ON NOW?
WHOOSH
WHAT... HAPPENED TO ME...?
I WAS FIGHTING NO. 03 AND...GOT BEATEN...
FLAP

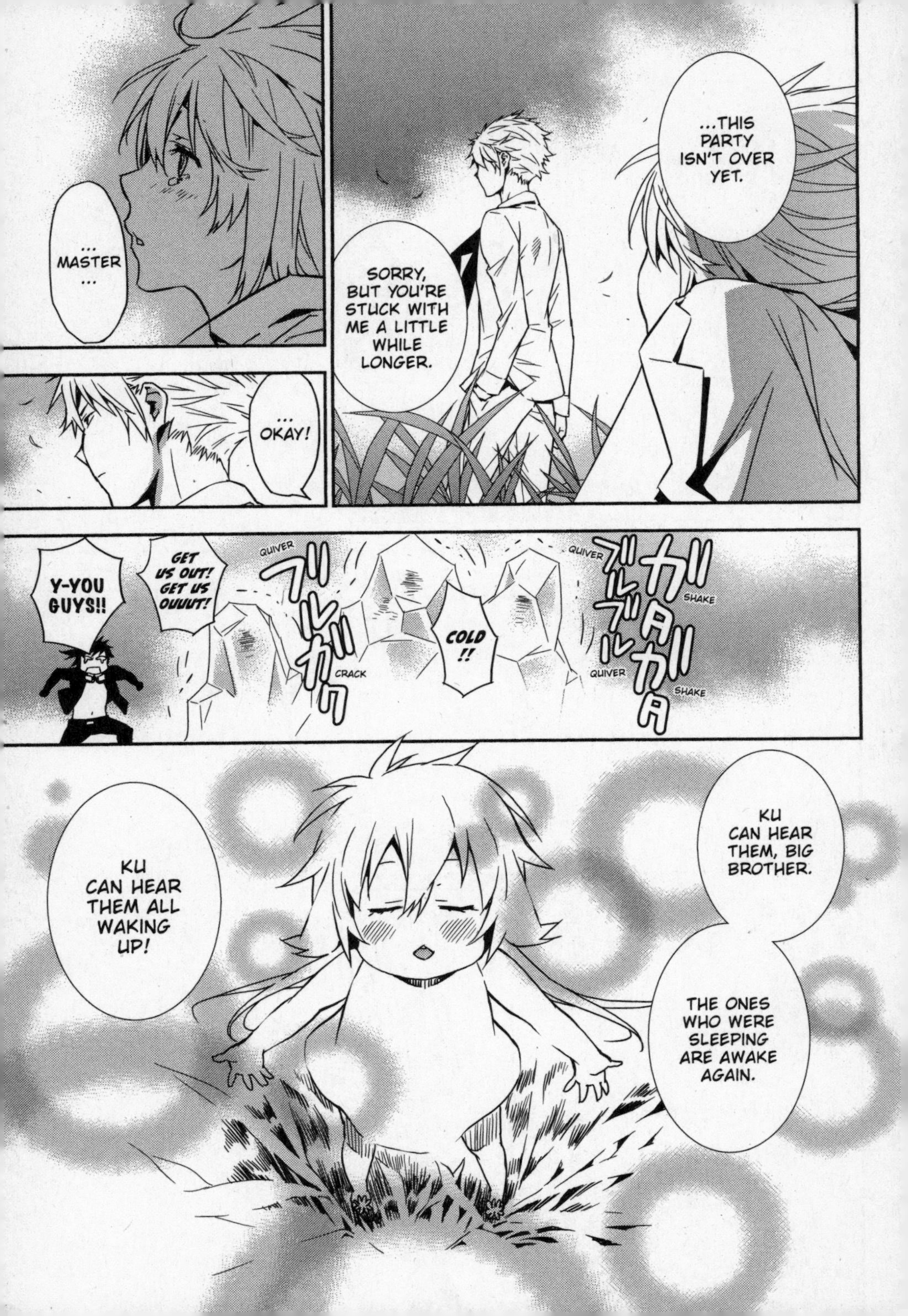
...THIS PARTY ISN'T OVER YET.
SORRY, BUT YOU'RE STUCK WITH ME A LITTLE WHILE LONGER.
...MASTER...
...OKAY!
ガタガタ SHAKE SHAKE
ブルブル QUIVER QUIVER
COLD!!
ブルガク QUIVER CRACK
GET US OUT! GET US OUUUT!
Y-YOU GUYS!!
KU CAN HEAR THEM, BIG BROTHER.
THE ONES WHO WERE SLEEPING ARE AWAKE AGAIN.
KU CAN HEAR THEM ALL WAKING UP!

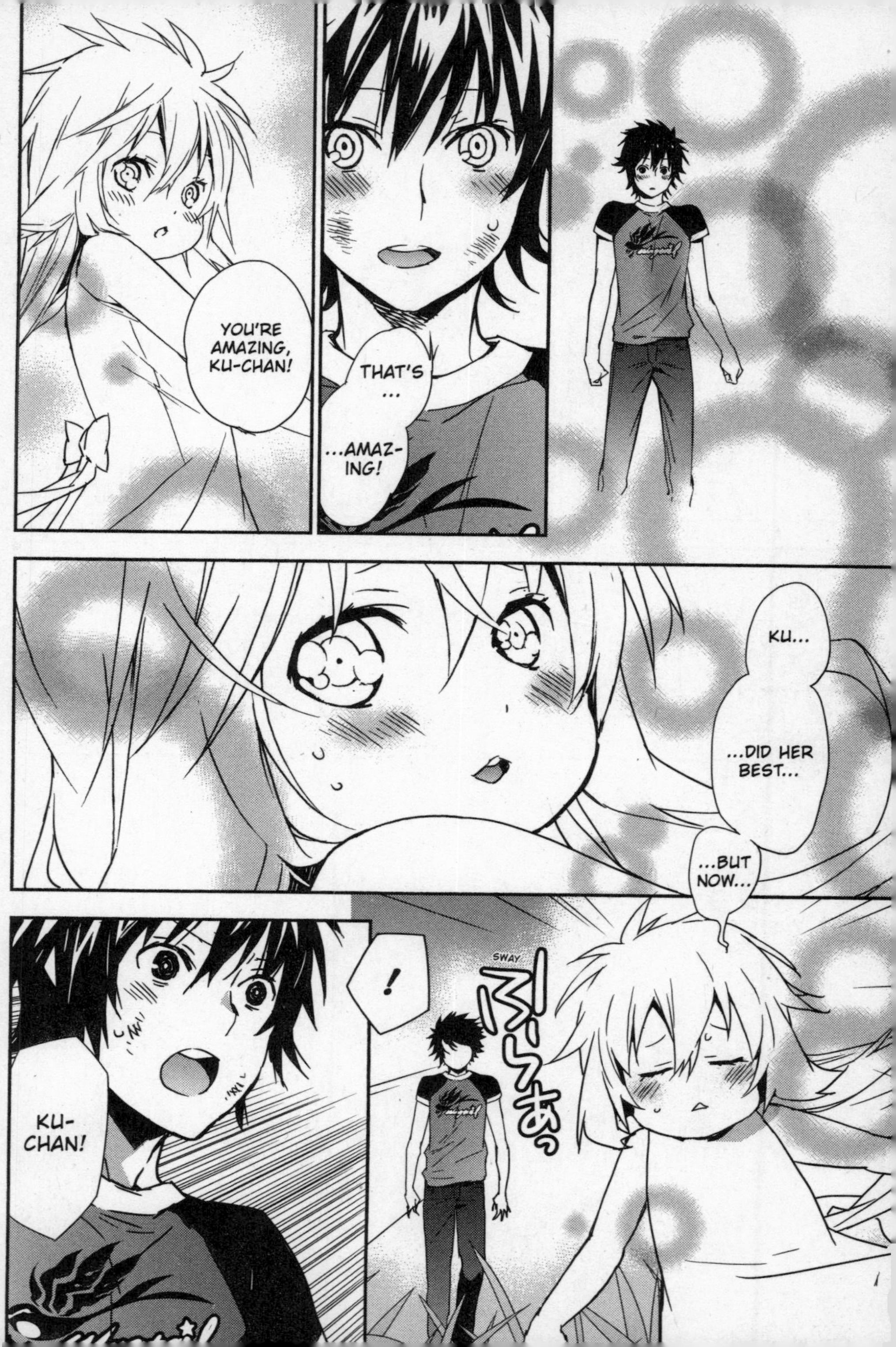
THAT'S ...
...AMAZ-ING!
YOU'RE AMAZING, KU-CHAN!
KU...
...DID HER BEST...
...BUT NOW...
SWAY
ふらぁっ
!
KU-CHAN!

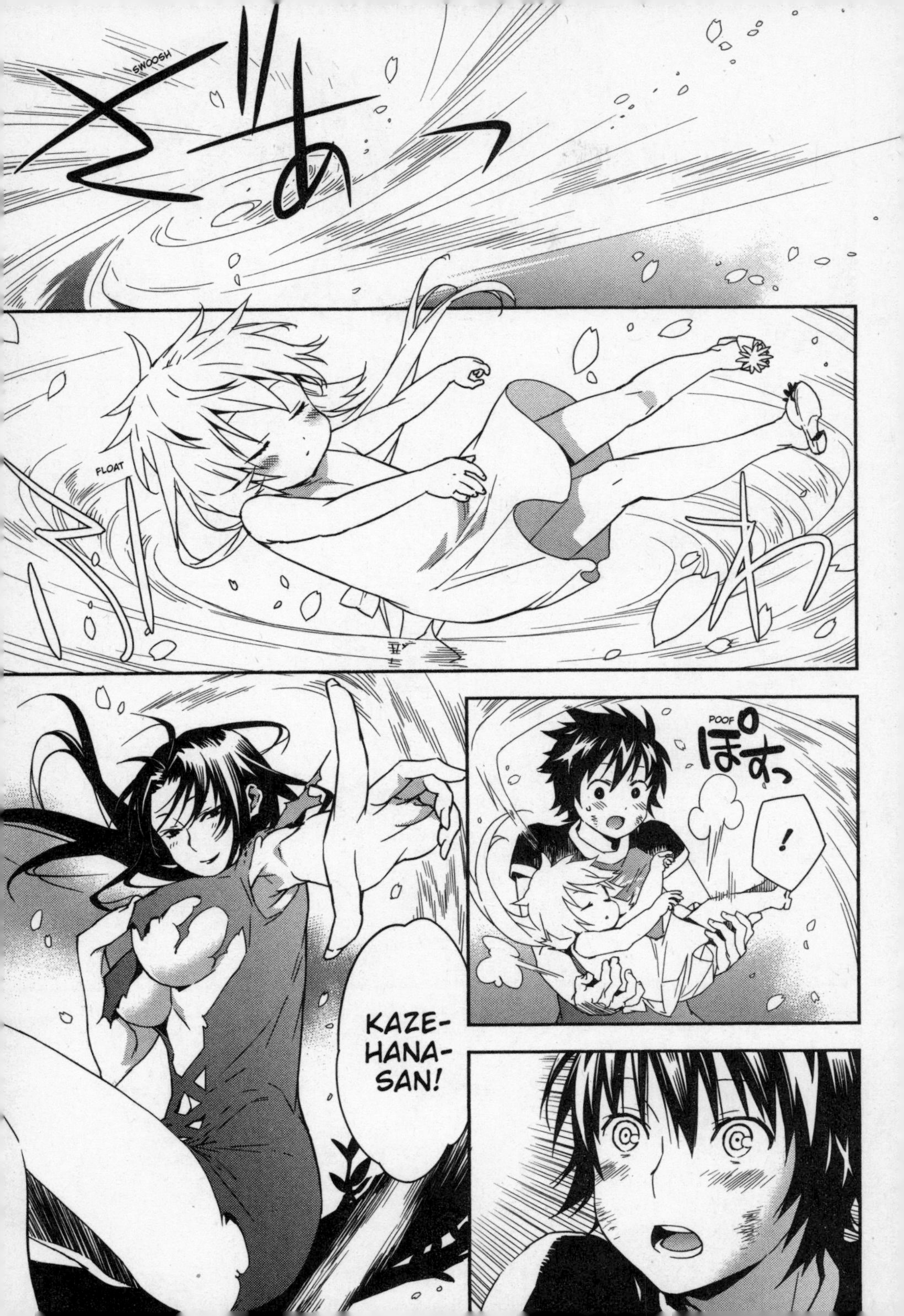
SWOOSH
FLOAT
POOF
ぽすっ
!
KAZE-HANA-SAN!

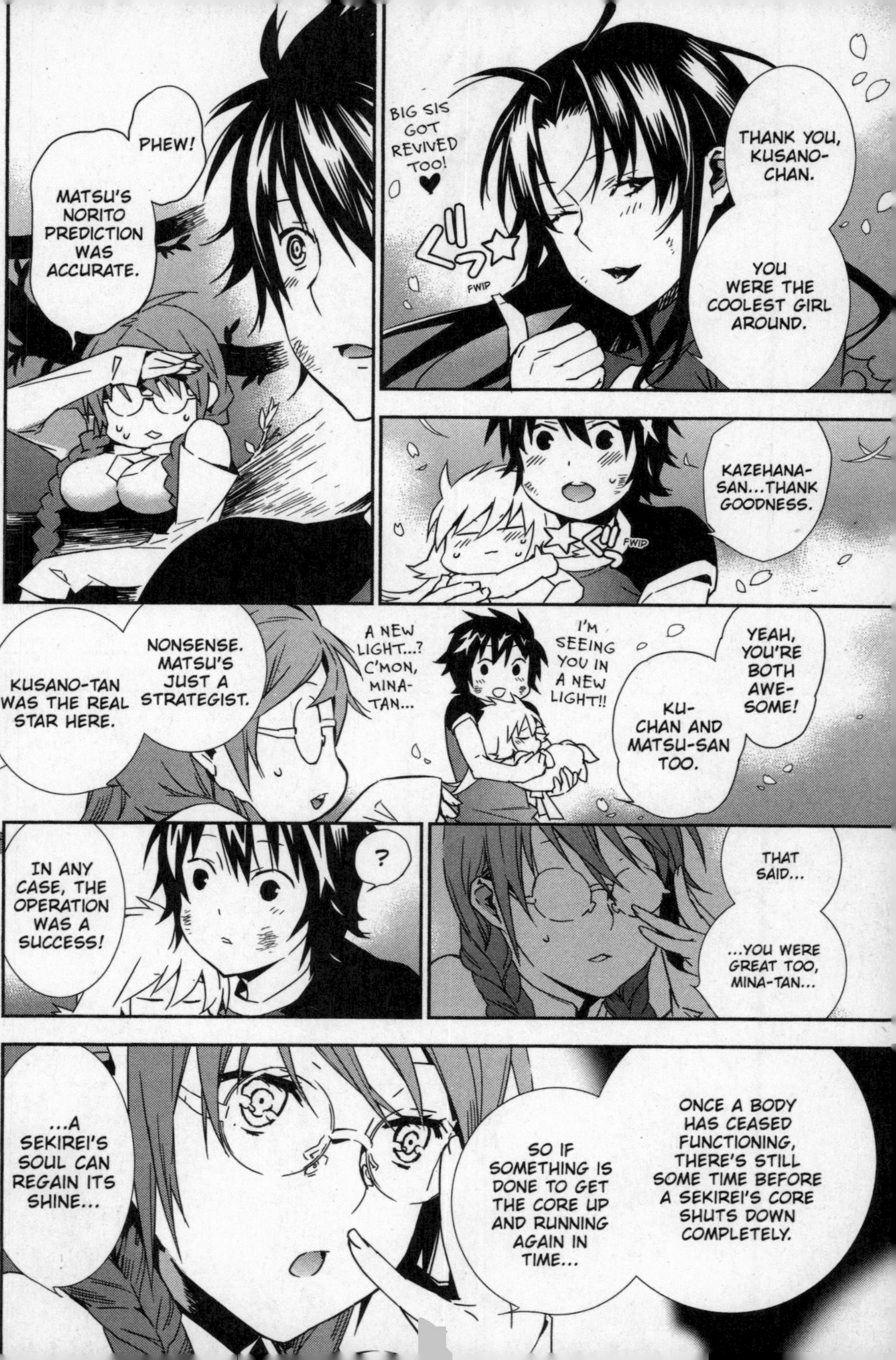
THANK YOU, KUSANO-CHAN.
YOU WERE THE COOLEST GIRL AROUND.
BIG SIS GOT REVIVED TOO! ♥
FWIP
KAZEHANA-SAN...THANK GOODNESS.
FWIP
PHEW!
MATSU'S NORITO PREDICTION WAS ACCURATE.
YEAH, YOU'RE BOTH AWESOME!
KU-CHAN AND MATSU-SAN TOO.
I'M SEEING YOU IN A NEW LIGHT!!
A NEW LIGHT...? C'MON, MINA-TAN...
NONSENSE. MATSU'S JUST A STRATEGIST.
KUSANO-TAN WAS THE REAL STAR HERE.
THAT SAID...
...YOU WERE GREAT TOO, MINA-TAN...
?
IN ANY CASE, THE OPERATION WAS A SUCCESS!
ONCE A BODY HAS CEASED FUNCTIONING, THERE'S STILL SOME TIME BEFORE A SEKIREI'S CORE SHUTS DOWN COMPLETELY.
SO IF SOMETHING IS DONE TO GET THE CORE UP AND RUNNING AGAIN IN TIME...
...A SEKIREI'S SOUL CAN REGAIN ITS SHINE...

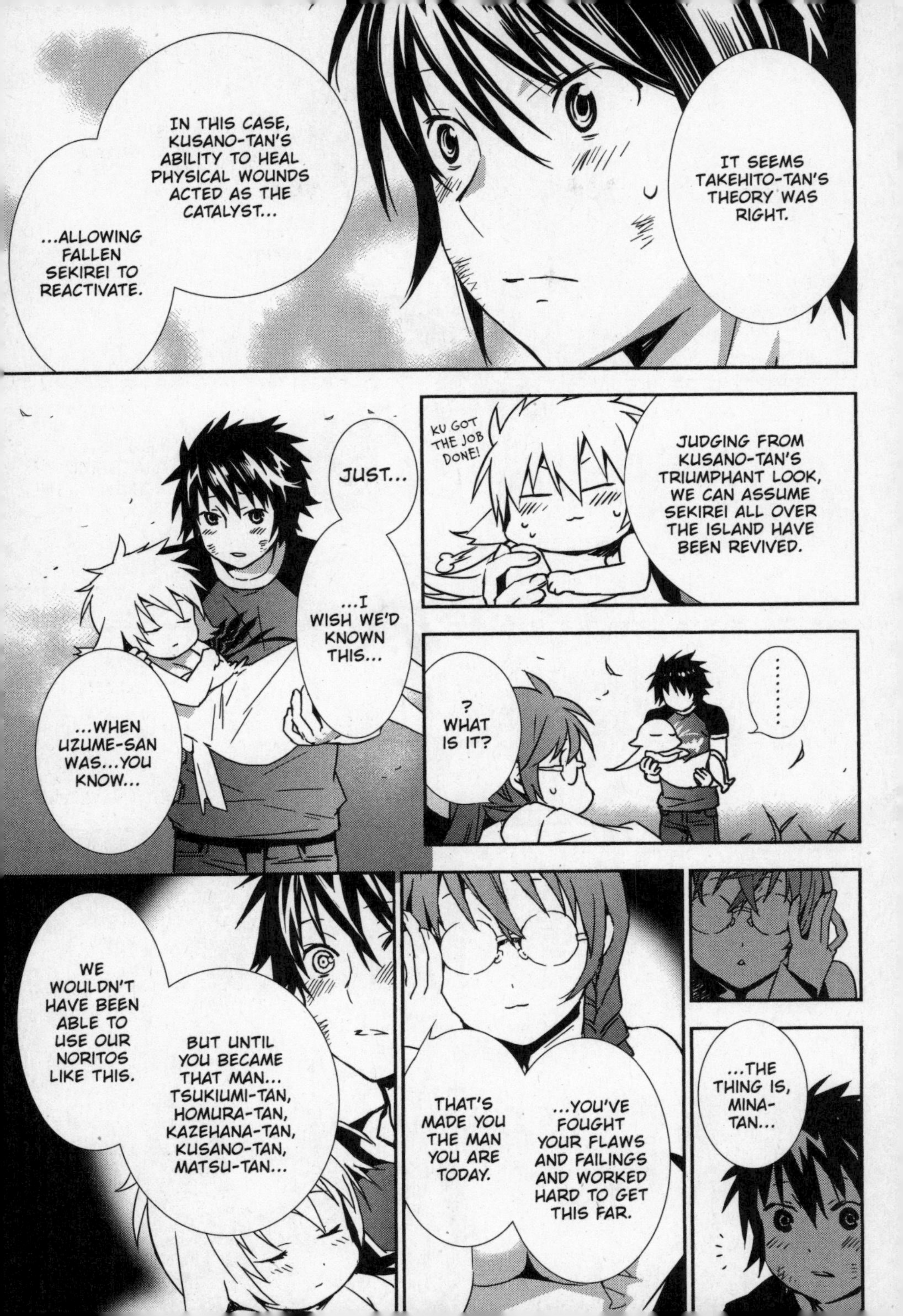
IT SEEMS TAKEHITO-TAN'S THEORY WAS RIGHT.
IN THIS CASE, KUSANO-TAN'S ABILITY TO HEAL PHYSICAL WOUNDS ACTED AS THE CATALYST...
...ALLOWING FALLEN SEKIREI TO REACTIVATE.
JUDGING FROM KUSANO-TAN'S TRIUMPHANT LOOK, WE CAN ASSUME SEKIREI ALL OVER THE ISLAND HAVE BEEN REVIVED.
KU GOT THE JOB DONE!
......
? WHAT IS IT?
JUST...
...I WISH WE'D KNOWN THIS...
...WHEN UZUME-SAN WAS...YOU KNOW...
...THE THING IS, MINA-TAN...
...YOU'VE FOUGHT YOUR FLAWS AND FAILINGS AND WORKED HARD TO GET THIS FAR.
THAT'S MADE YOU THE MAN YOU ARE TODAY.
BUT UNTIL YOU BECAME THAT MAN... TSUKIUMI-TAN, HOMURA-TAN, KAZEHANA-TAN, KUSANO-TAN, MATSU-TAN...
WE WOULDN'T HAVE BEEN ABLE TO USE OUR NORITOS LIKE THIS.

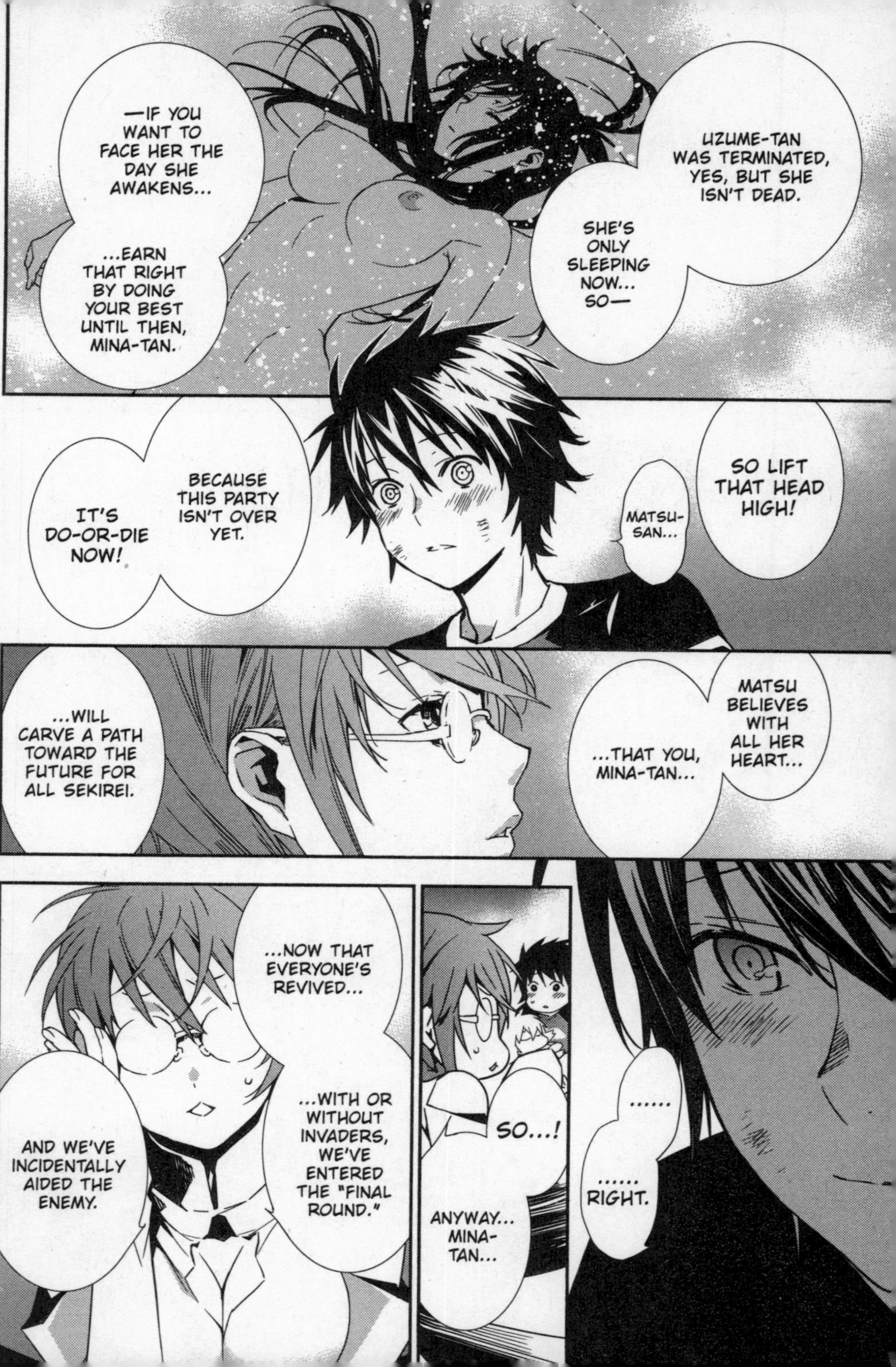
UZUME-TAN WAS TERMINATED, YES, BUT SHE ISN'T DEAD.
SHE'S ONLY SLEEPING NOW... SO—
—IF YOU WANT TO FACE HER THE DAY SHE AWAKENS...
...EARN THAT RIGHT BY DOING YOUR BEST UNTIL THEN, MINA-TAN.
SO LIFT THAT HEAD HIGH!
MATSU-SAN...
BECAUSE THIS PARTY ISN'T OVER YET.
IT'S DO-OR-DIE NOW!
MATSU BELIEVES WITH ALL HER HEART...
...THAT YOU, MINA-TAN...
...WILL CARVE A PATH TOWARD THE FUTURE FOR ALL SEKIREI.
......
......RIGHT.
SO...!
ANYWAY... MINA-TAN...
...NOW THAT EVERYONE'S REVIVED...
...WITH OR WITHOUT INVADERS, WE'VE ENTERED THE "FINAL ROUND."
AND WE'VE INCIDENTALLY AIDED THE ENEMY.

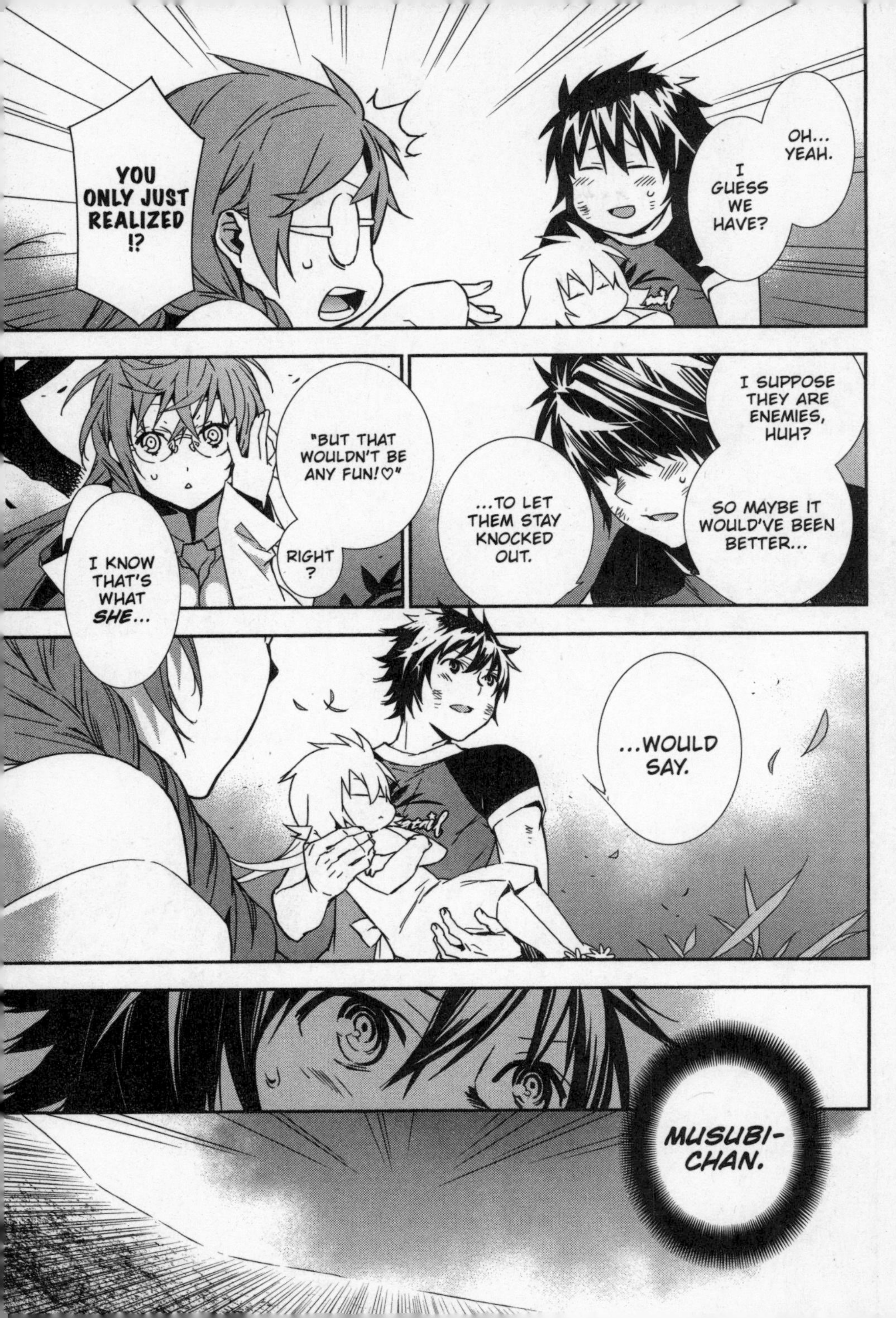
OH... YEAH.
I GUESS WE HAVE?
YOU ONLY JUST REALIZED!?
I SUPPOSE THEY ARE ENEMIES, HUH?
SO MAYBE IT WOULD'VE BEEN BETTER...
...TO LET THEM STAY KNOCKED OUT.
"BUT THAT WOULDN'T BE ANY FUN!♡"
RIGHT?
I KNOW THAT'S WHAT *SHE*...
...WOULD SAY.
MUSUBI-CHAN.

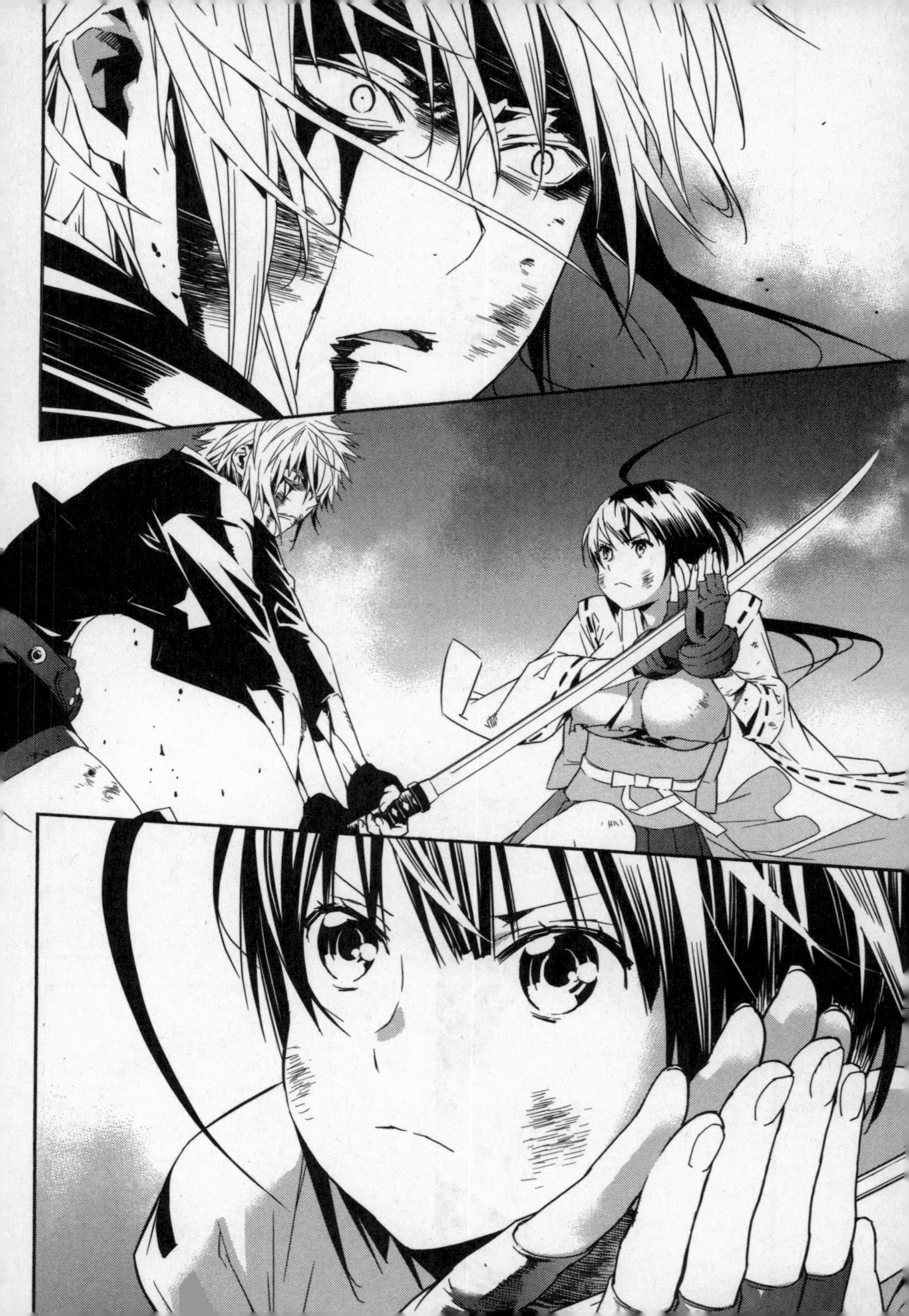

Chapter 172: Hollow Land, Birth of Bonds

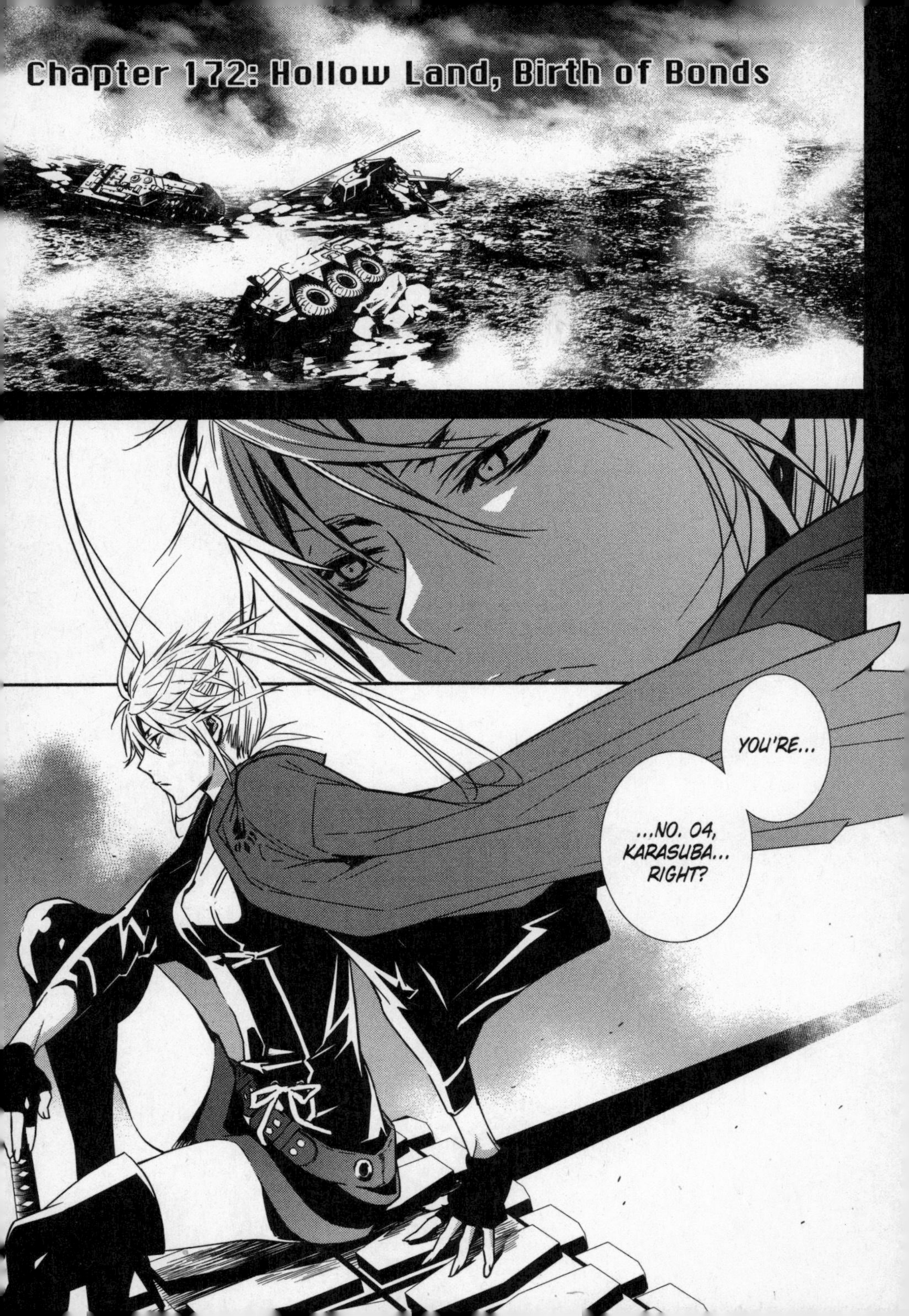
YOU'RE...
...NO. 04, KARASUBA... RIGHT?

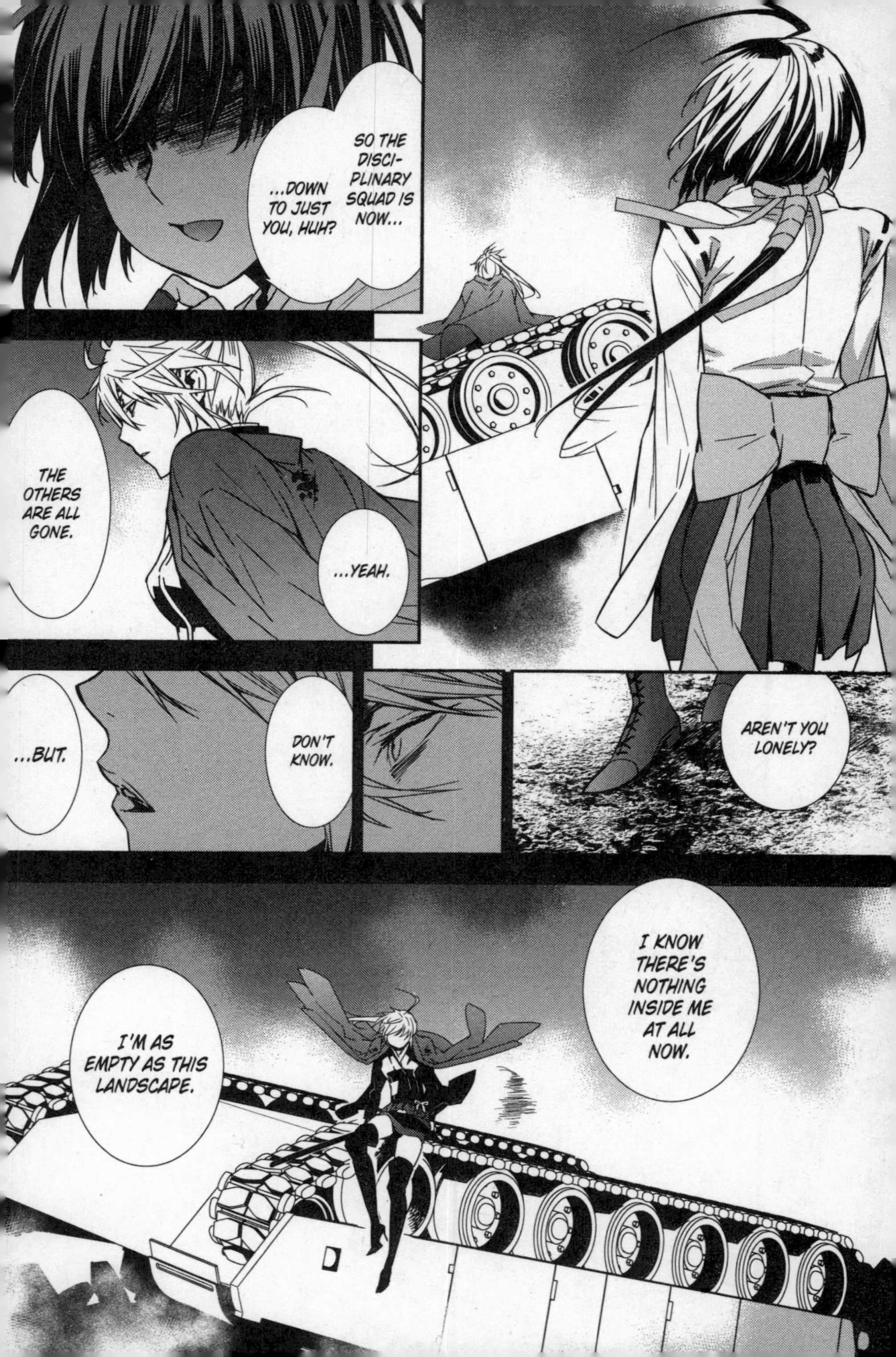
SO THE DISCI-PLINARY SQUAD IS NOW...
...DOWN TO JUST YOU, HUH?
...YEAH.
THE OTHERS ARE ALL GONE.
AREN'T YOU LONELY?
DON'T KNOW.
...BUT.
I KNOW THERE'S NOTHING INSIDE ME AT ALL NOW.
I'M AS EMPTY AS THIS LANDSCAPE.

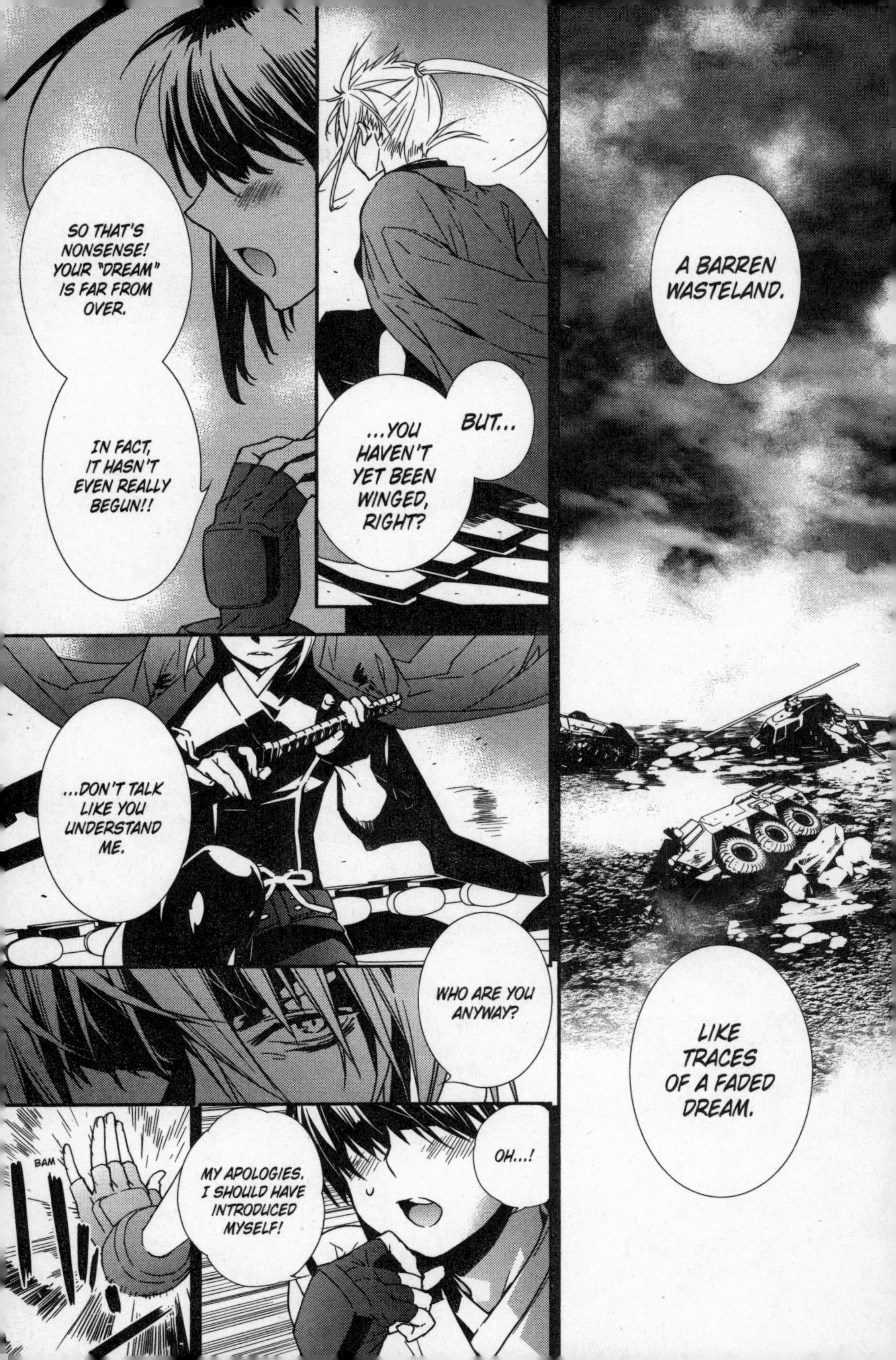
A BARREN WASTELAND.
LIKE TRACES OF A FADED DREAM.
BUT...
...YOU HAVEN'T YET BEEN WINGED, RIGHT?
SO THAT'S NONSENSE! YOUR "DREAM" IS FAR FROM OVER.
IN FACT, IT HASN'T EVEN REALLY BEGUN!!
...DON'T TALK LIKE YOU UNDERSTAND ME.
WHO ARE YOU ANYWAY?
OH...!
MY APOLOGIES. I SHOULD HAVE INTRODUCED MYSELF!
BAM

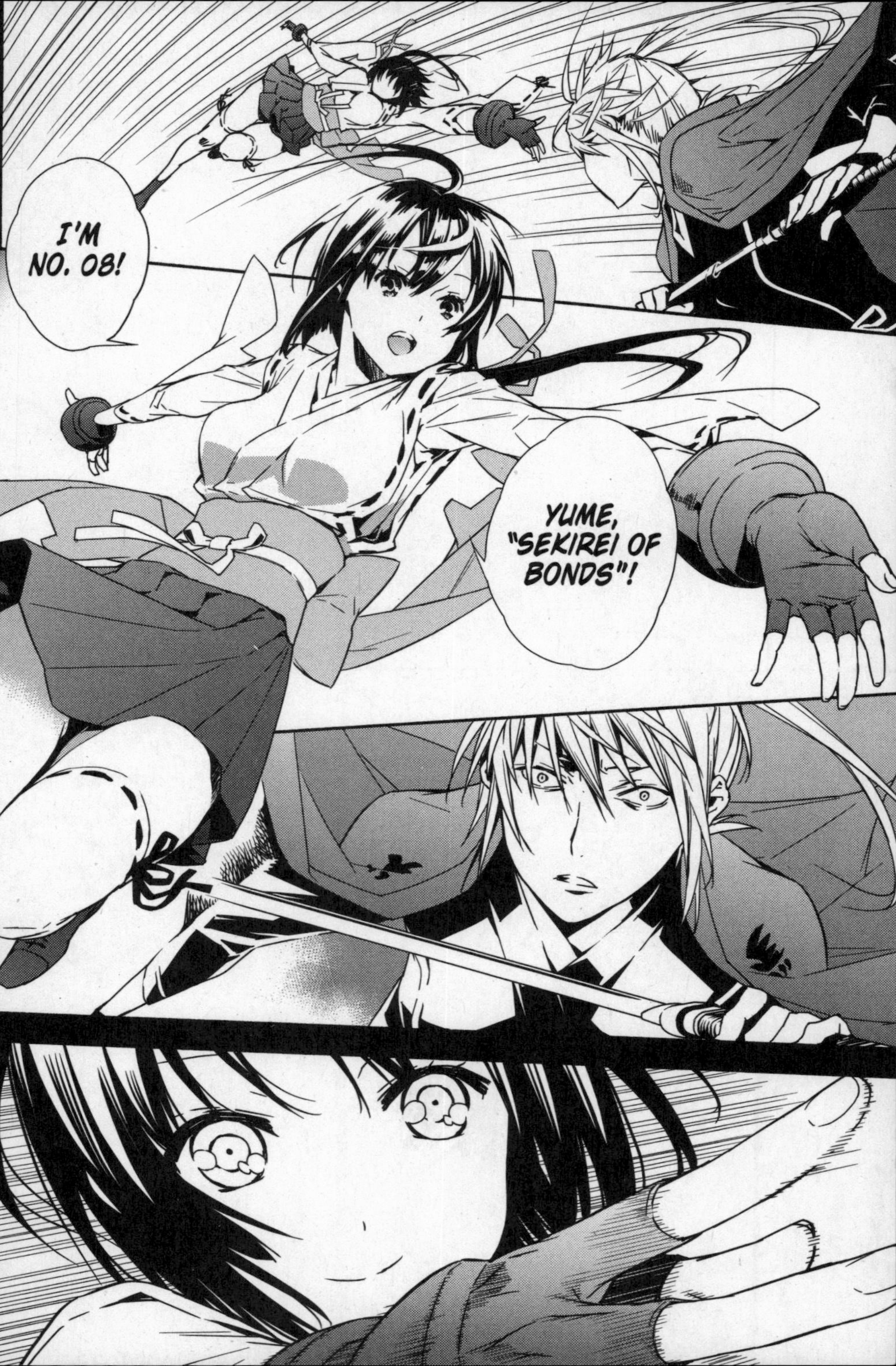
I'M NO. 08!
YUME, "SEKIREI OF BONDS"!

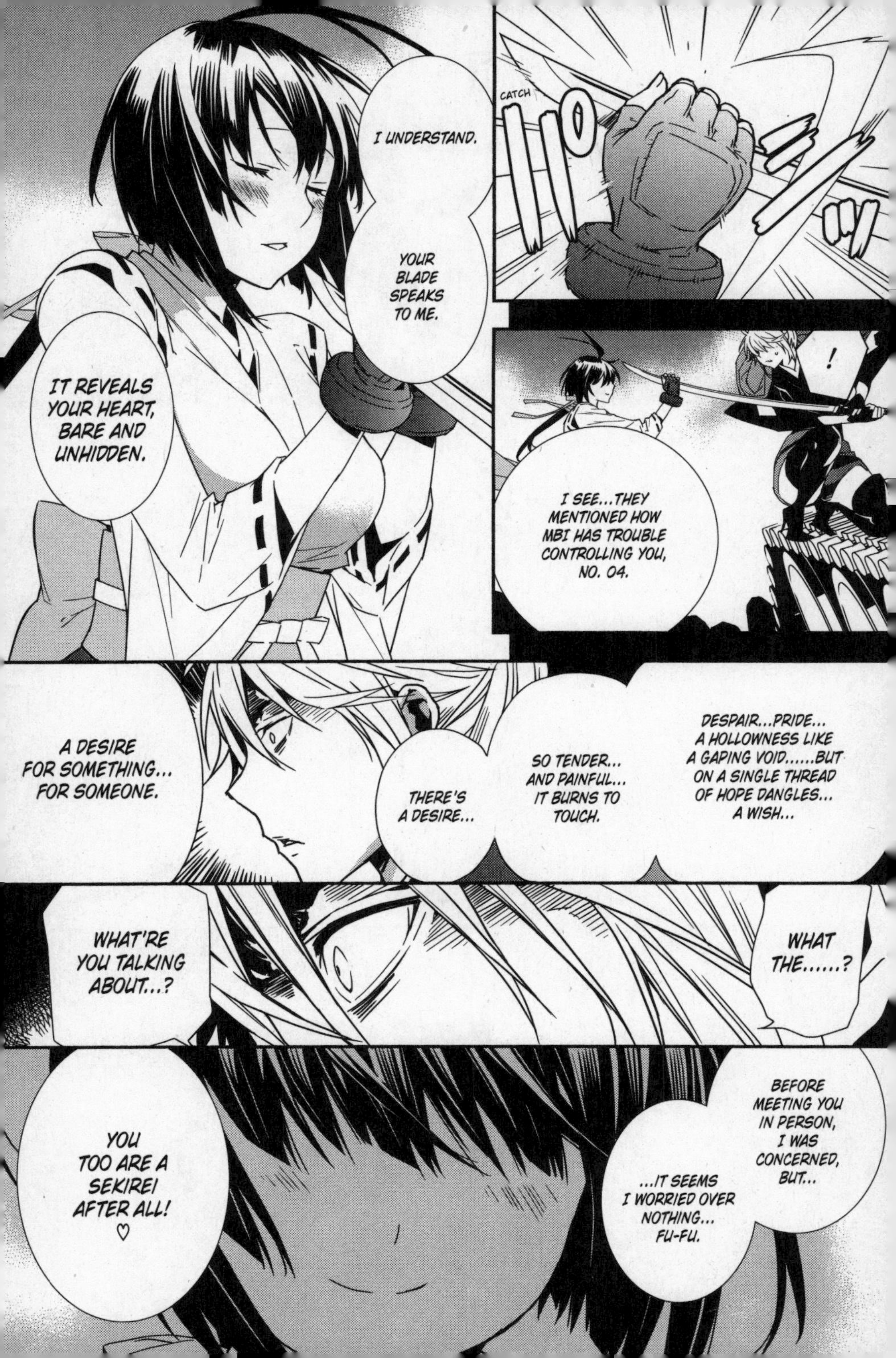
CATCH
!
I SEE...THEY MENTIONED HOW MBI HAS TROUBLE CONTROLLING YOU, NO. 04.
I UNDERSTAND.
YOUR BLADE SPEAKS TO ME.
IT REVEALS YOUR HEART, BARE AND UNHIDDEN.
DESPAIR...PRIDE... A HOLLOWNESS LIKE A GAPING VOID......BUT ON A SINGLE THREAD OF HOPE DANGLES... A WISH...
SO TENDER... AND PAINFUL... IT BURNS TO TOUCH.
THERE'S A DESIRE...
A DESIRE FOR SOMETHING... FOR SOMEONE.
WHAT THE......?
WHAT'RE YOU TALKING ABOUT...?
BEFORE MEETING YOU IN PERSON, I WAS CONCERNED, BUT...
...IT SEEMS I WORRIED OVER NOTHING... FU-FU.
YOU TOO ARE A SEKIREI AFTER ALL! ♡

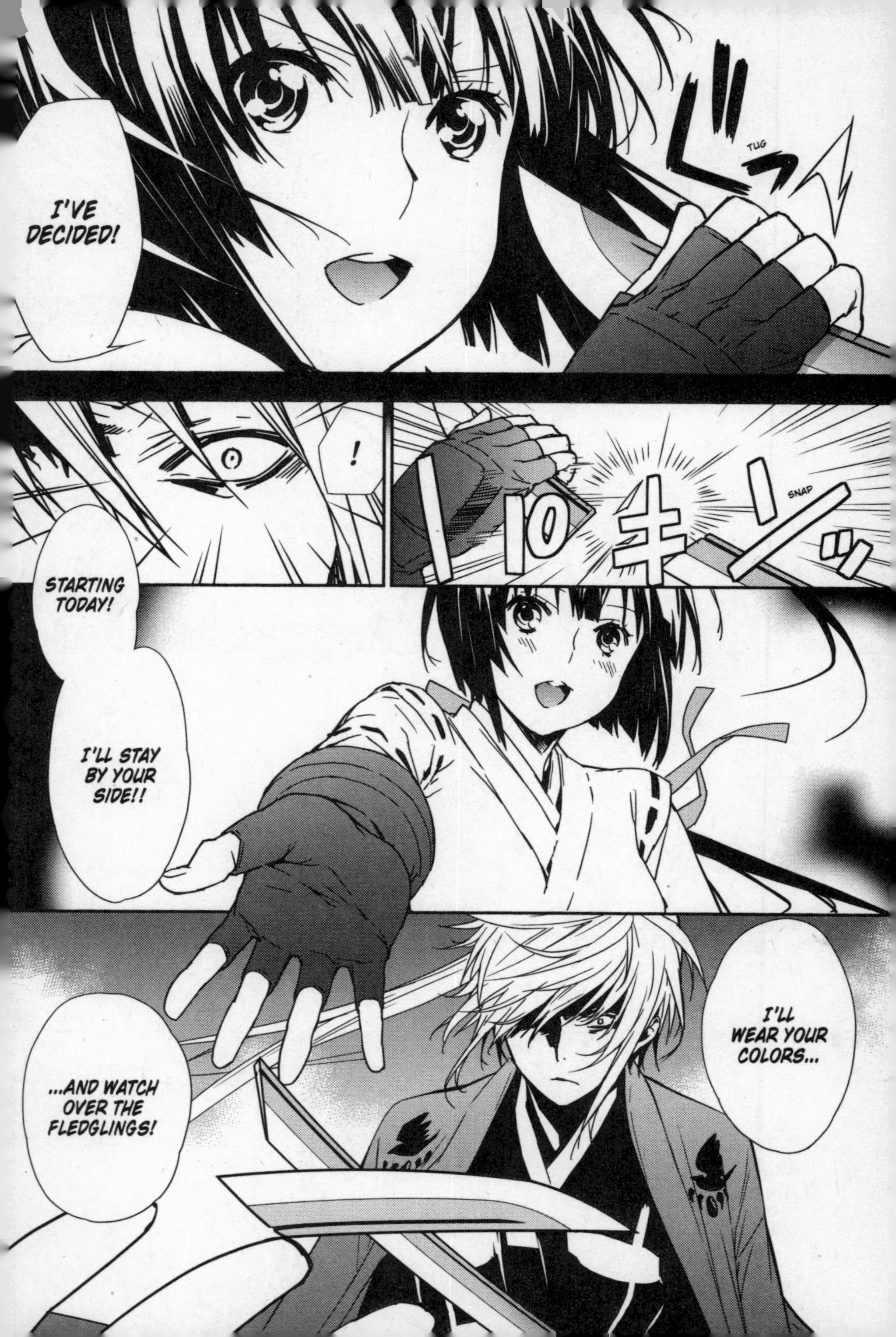
TUG
I'VE DECIDED!
SNAP
!
STARTING TODAY!
I'LL STAY BY YOUR SIDE!!
I'LL WEAR YOUR COLORS...
...AND WATCH OVER THE FLEDGLINGS!

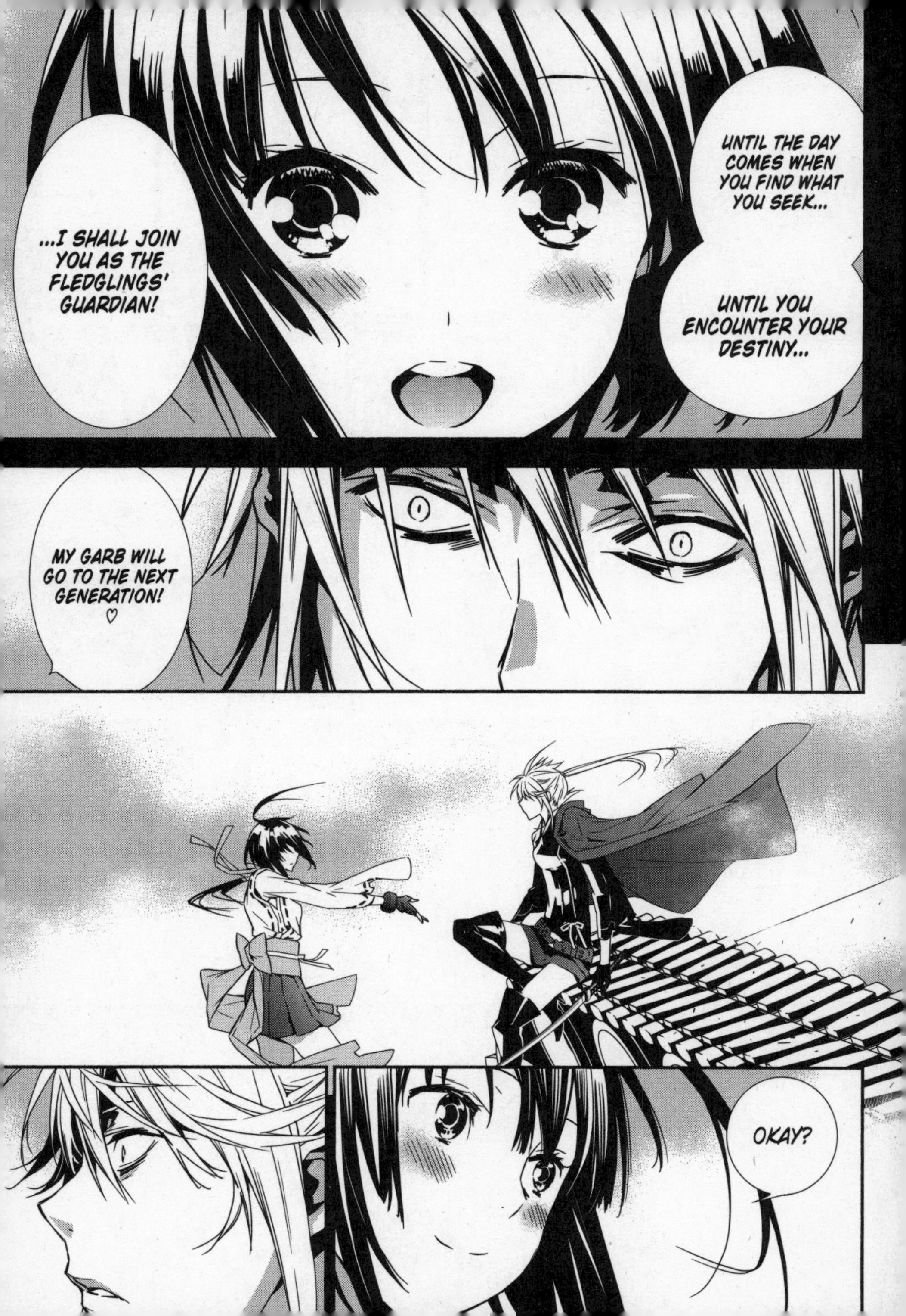
UNTIL THE DAY COMES WHEN YOU FIND WHAT YOU SEEK...
UNTIL YOU ENCOUNTER YOUR DESTINY...
...I SHALL JOIN YOU AS THE FLEDGLINGS' GUARDIAN!
MY GARB WILL GO TO THE NEXT GENERATION! ♡
OKAY?

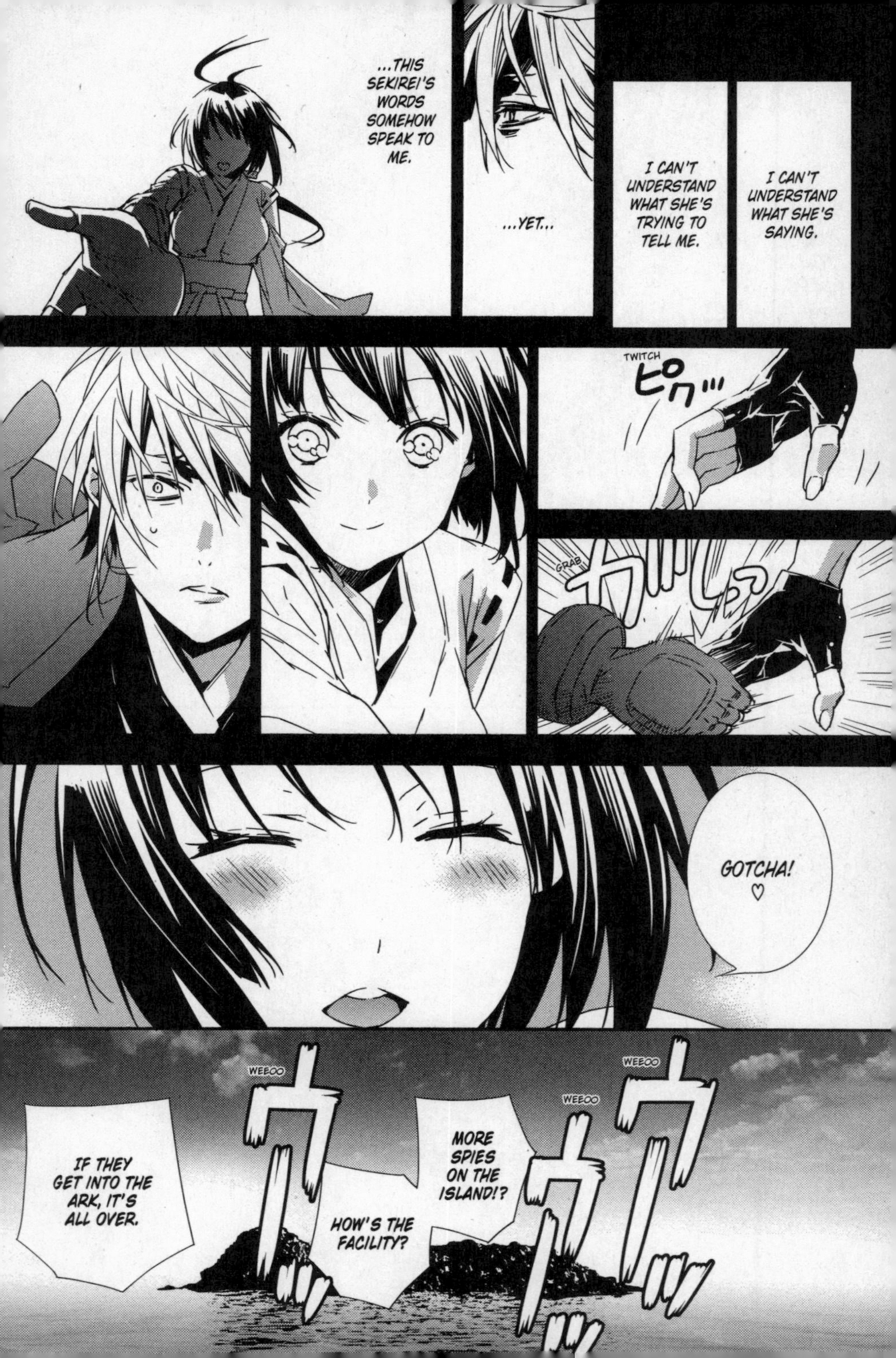
I CAN'T UNDERSTAND WHAT SHE'S SAYING.
I CAN'T UNDERSTAND WHAT SHE'S TRYING TO TELL ME.
...YET...
...THIS SEKIREI'S WORDS SOMEHOW SPEAK TO ME.
TWITCH
GRAB
GOTCHA! ♡
WEEOO
WEEOO
MORE SPIES ON THE ISLAND!?
HOW'S THE FACILITY?
WEEOO
IF THEY GET INTO THE ARK, IT'S ALL OVER.

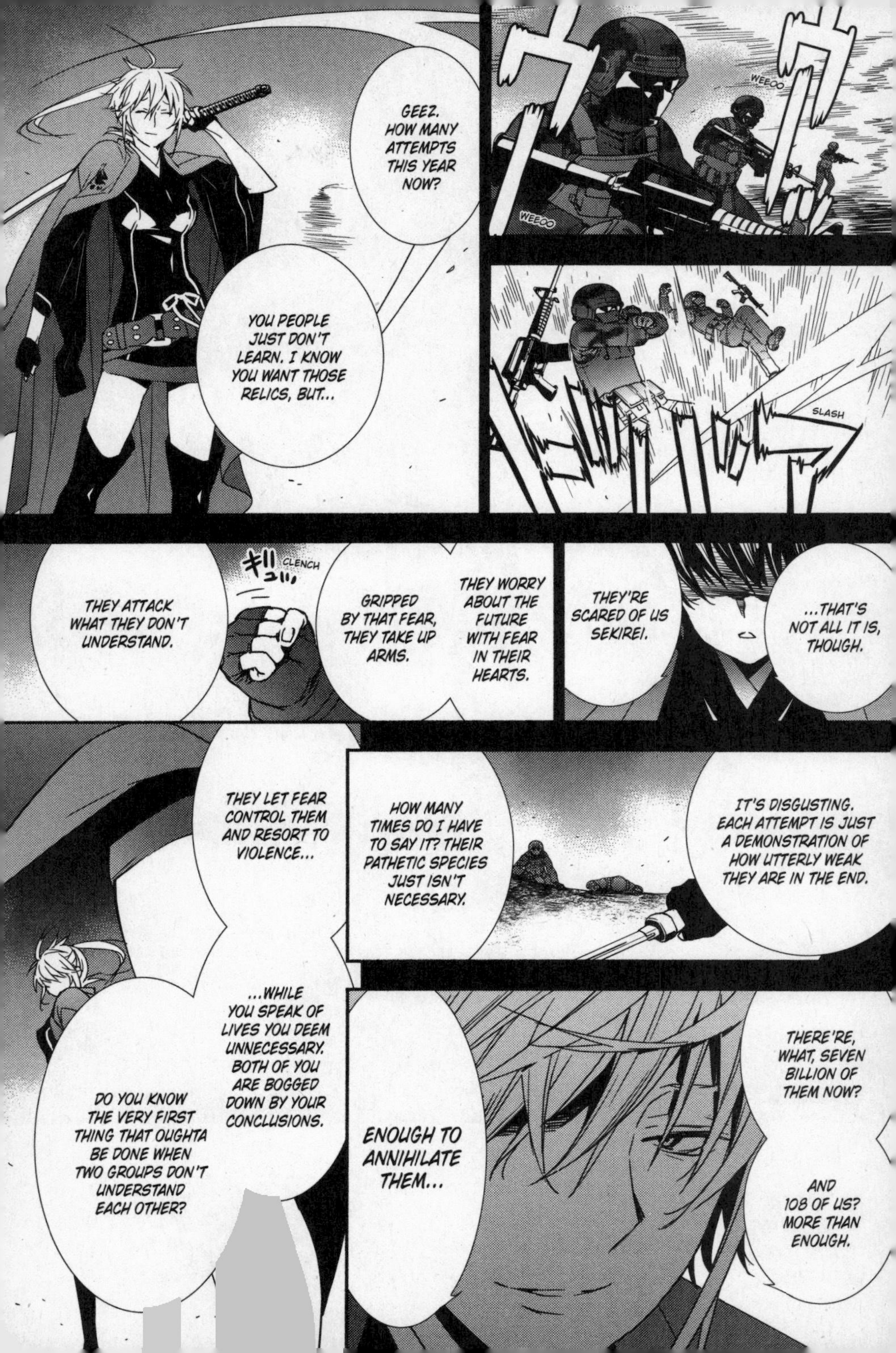
WEEOO
WEEOO
SLASH
GEEZ. HOW MANY ATTEMPTS THIS YEAR NOW?
YOU PEOPLE JUST DON'T LEARN. I KNOW YOU WANT THOSE RELICS, BUT...
...THAT'S NOT ALL IT IS, THOUGH.
THEY'RE SCARED OF US SEKIREI.
THEY WORRY ABOUT THE FUTURE WITH FEAR IN THEIR HEARTS.
GRIPPED BY THAT FEAR, THEY TAKE UP ARMS.
CLENCH
THEY ATTACK WHAT THEY DON'T UNDERSTAND.
IT'S DISGUSTING. EACH ATTEMPT IS JUST A DEMONSTRATION OF HOW UTTERLY WEAK THEY ARE IN THE END.
HOW MANY TIMES DO I HAVE TO SAY IT? THEIR PATHETIC SPECIES JUST ISN'T NECESSARY.
THERE'RE, WHAT, SEVEN BILLION OF THEM NOW?
AND 108 OF US? MORE THAN ENOUGH.
ENOUGH TO ANNIHILATE THEM...
THEY LET FEAR CONTROL THEM AND RESORT TO VIOLENCE...
...WHILE YOU SPEAK OF LIVES YOU DEEM UNNECESSARY. BOTH OF YOU ARE BOGGED DOWN BY YOUR CONCLUSIONS.
DO YOU KNOW THE VERY FIRST THING THAT OUGHTA BE DONE WHEN TWO GROUPS DON'T UNDERSTAND EACH OTHER?

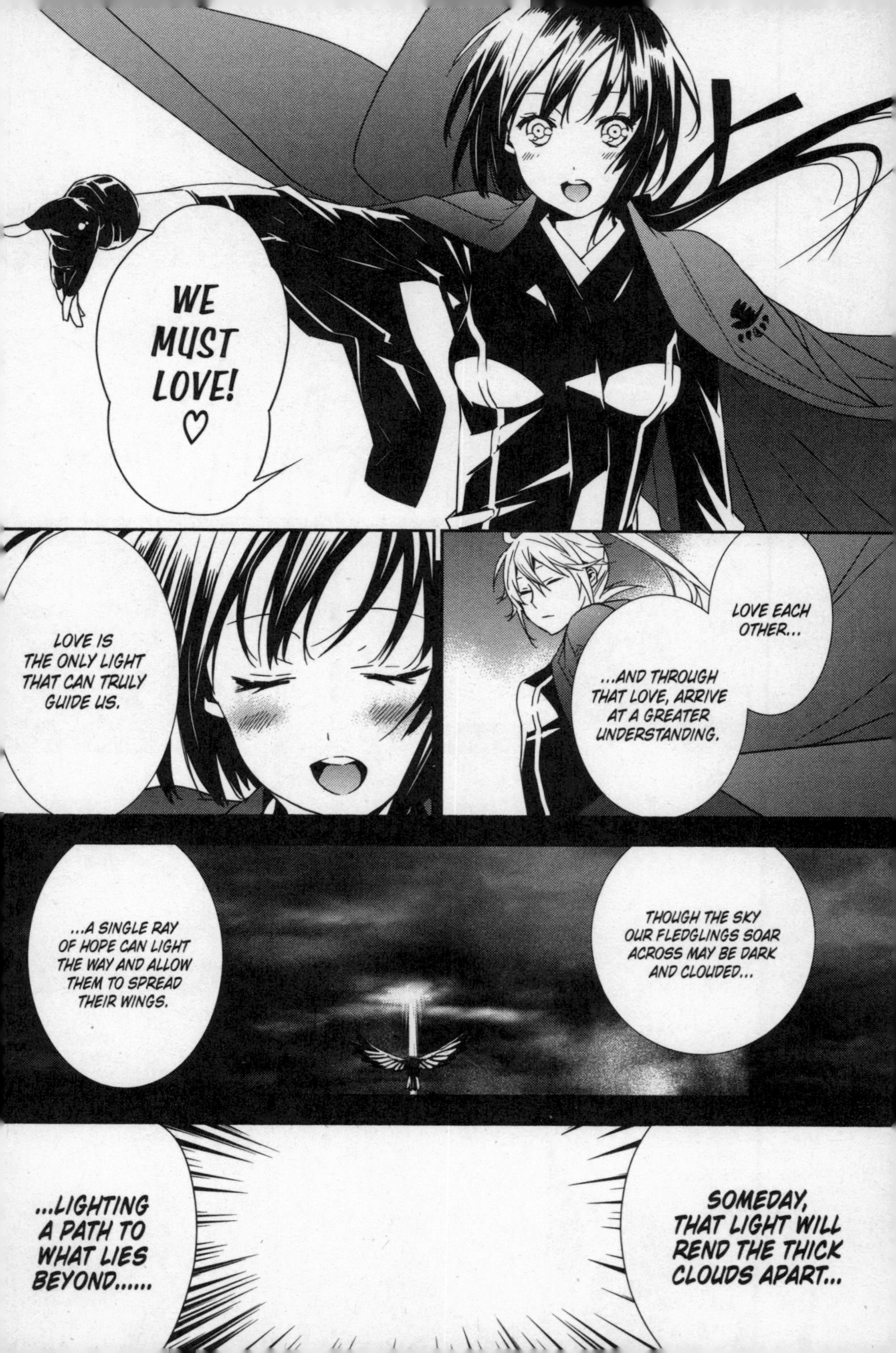
WE MUST LOVE! ♡
LOVE EACH OTHER...
...AND THROUGH THAT LOVE, ARRIVE AT A GREATER UNDERSTANDING.
LOVE IS THE ONLY LIGHT THAT CAN TRULY GUIDE US.
THOUGH THE SKY OUR FLEDGLINGS SOAR ACROSS MAY BE DARK AND CLOUDED...
...A SINGLE RAY OF HOPE CAN LIGHT THE WAY AND ALLOW THEM TO SPREAD THEIR WINGS.
SOMEDAY, THAT LIGHT WILL REND THE THICK CLOUDS APART...
...LIGHTING A PATH TO WHAT LIES BEYOND......

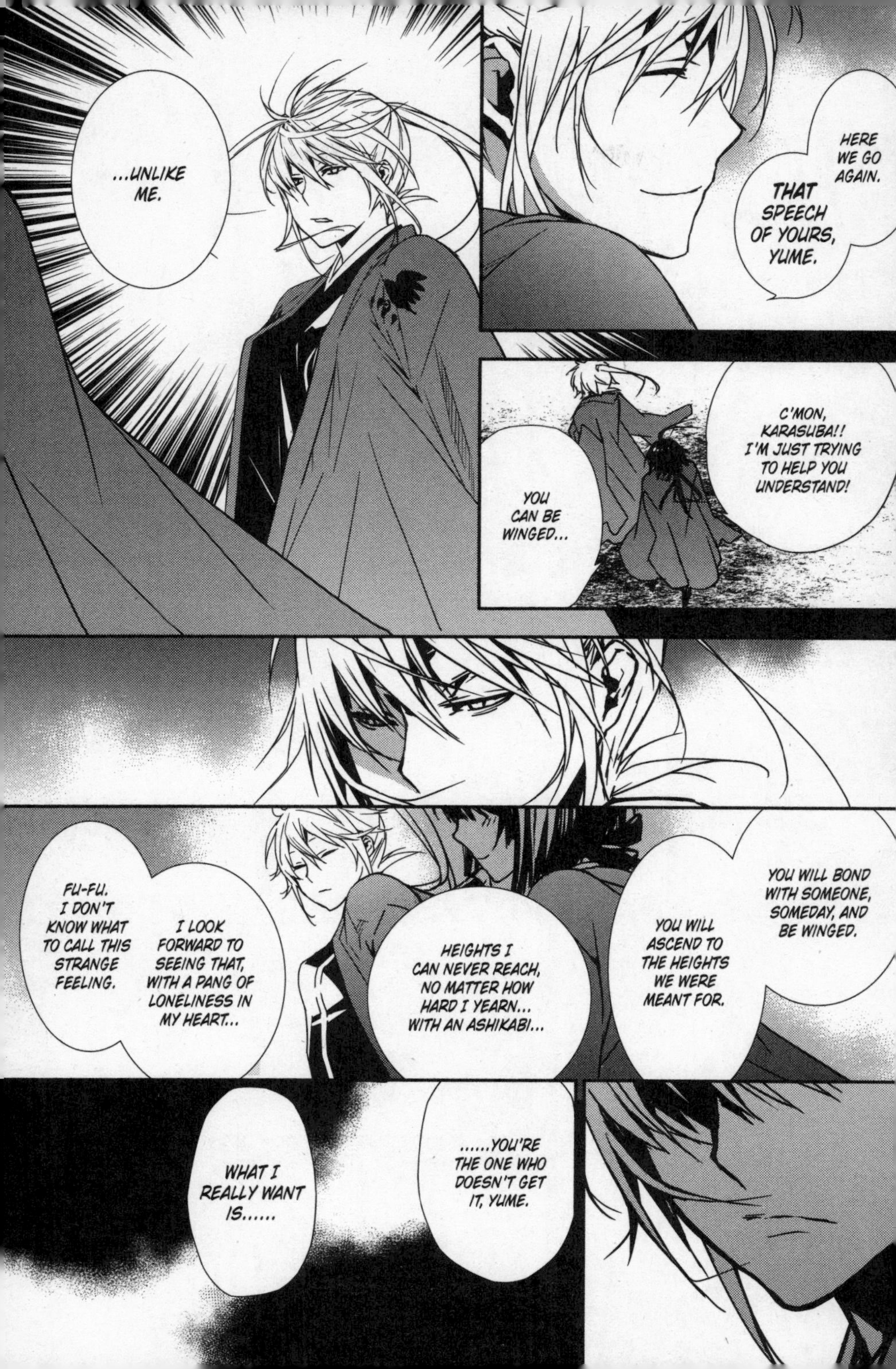
HERE WE GO AGAIN.
THAT SPEECH OF YOURS, YUME.
C'MON, KARASUBA!! I'M JUST TRYING TO HELP YOU UNDERSTAND!
YOU CAN BE WINGED...
...UNLIKE ME.
YOU WILL BOND WITH SOMEONE, SOMEDAY, AND BE WINGED.
YOU WILL ASCEND TO THE HEIGHTS WE WERE MEANT FOR.
HEIGHTS I CAN NEVER REACH, NO MATTER HOW HARD I YEARN... WITH AN ASHIKABI...
I LOOK FORWARD TO SEEING THAT, WITH A PANG OF LONELINESS IN MY HEART...
FU-FU. I DON'T KNOW WHAT TO CALL THIS STRANGE FEELING.
......YOU'RE THE ONE WHO DOESN'T GET IT, YUME.
WHAT I REALLY WANT IS......

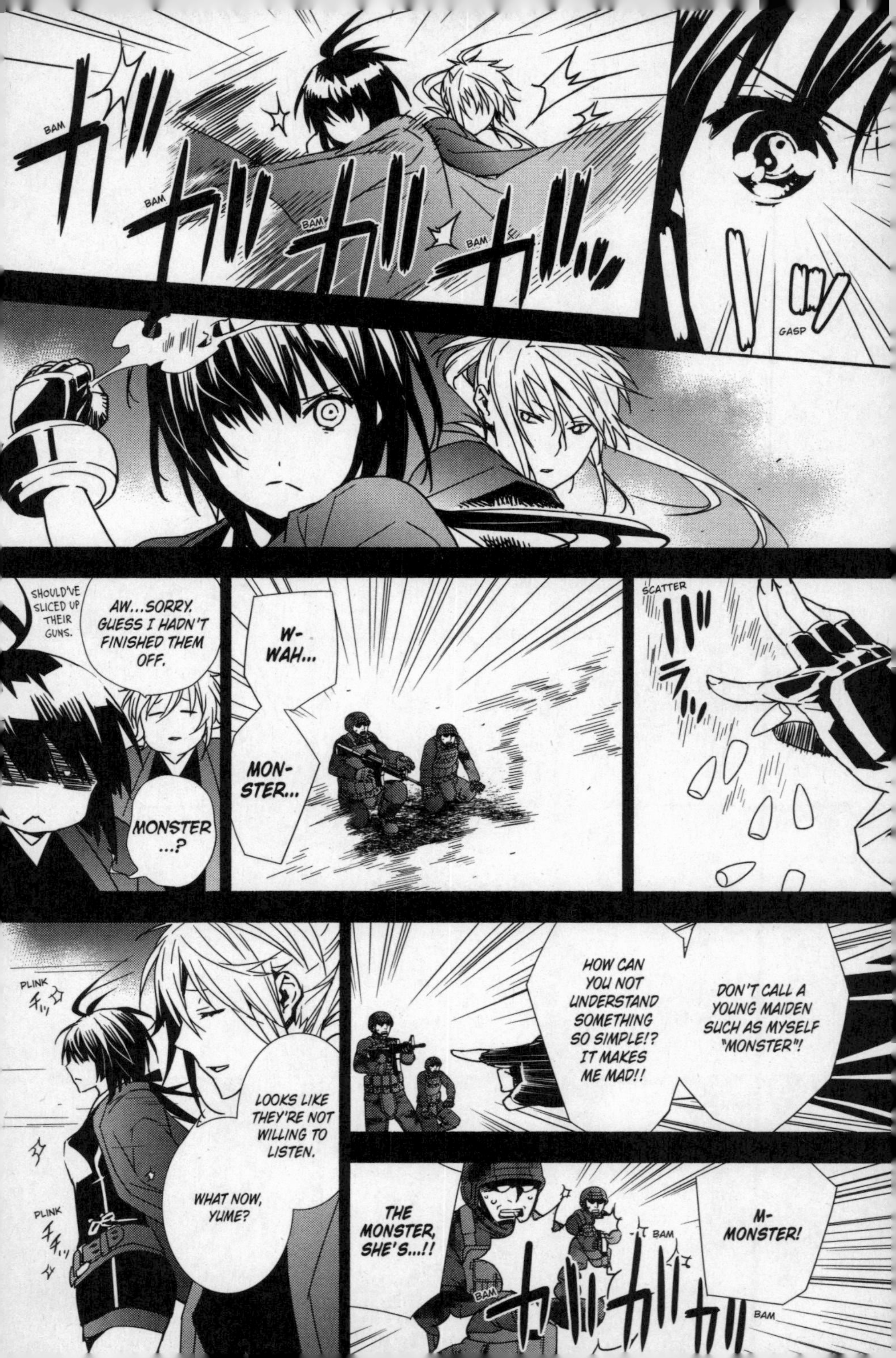
GASP
BAM
BAM
BAM
BAM
SCATTER
W-WAH...
MON-STER...
AW...SORRY. GUESS I HADN'T FINISHED THEM OFF.
SHOULD'VE SLICED UP THEIR GUNS.
MONSTER ...?
DON'T CALL A YOUNG MAIDEN SUCH AS MYSELF "MONSTER"!
HOW CAN YOU NOT UNDERSTAND SOMETHING SO SIMPLE!? IT MAKES ME MAD!!
M-MONSTER!
BAM
THE MONSTER, SHE'S...!!
BAM
BAM
PLINK
LOOKS LIKE THEY'RE NOT WILLING TO LISTEN.
WHAT NOW, YUME?
PLINK

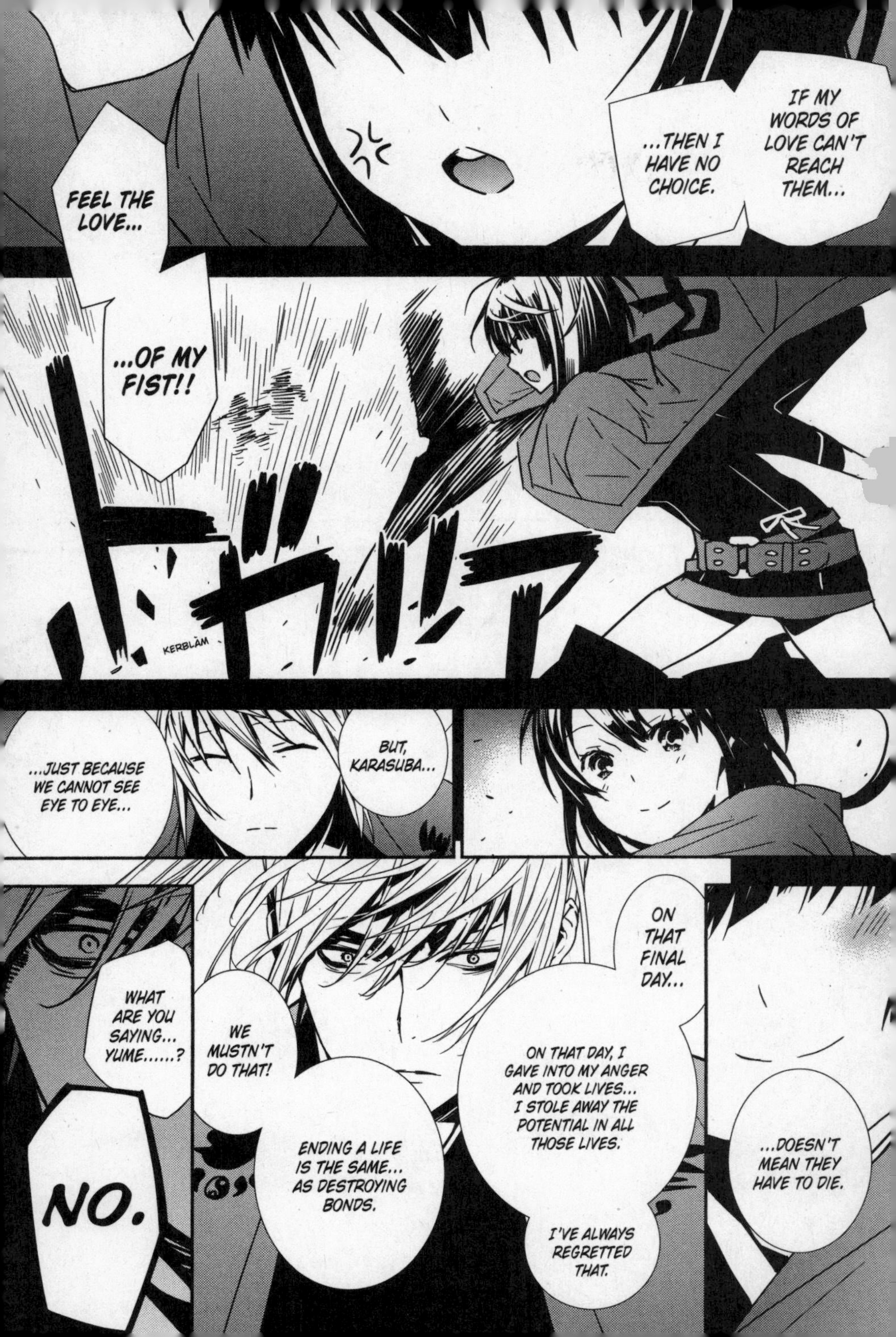
IF MY WORDS OF LOVE CAN'T REACH THEM...
...THEN I HAVE NO CHOICE.
FEEL THE LOVE...
...OF MY FIST!!
KERBLAM
BUT, KARASUBA...
...JUST BECAUSE WE CANNOT SEE EYE TO EYE...
...DOESN'T MEAN THEY HAVE TO DIE.
ON THAT FINAL DAY...
ON THAT DAY, I GAVE INTO MY ANGER AND TOOK LIVES... I STOLE AWAY THE POTENTIAL IN ALL THOSE LIVES.
I'VE ALWAYS REGRETTED THAT.
WE MUSTN'T DO THAT!
ENDING A LIFE IS THE SAME... AS DESTROYING BONDS.
WHAT ARE YOU SAYING... YUME......?
NO.

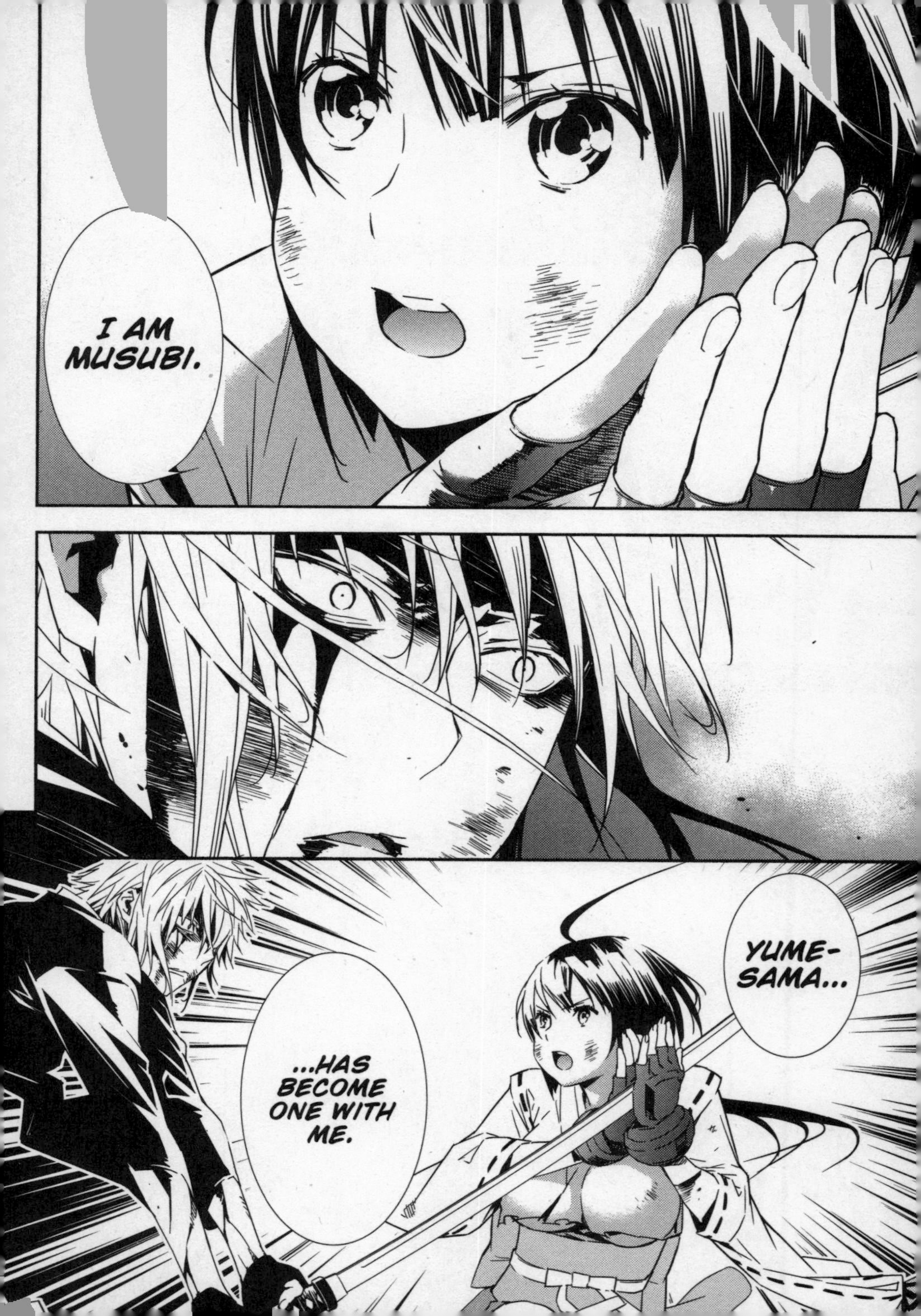
I AM MUSUBI.
YUME-SAMA...
...HAS BECOME ONE WITH ME.

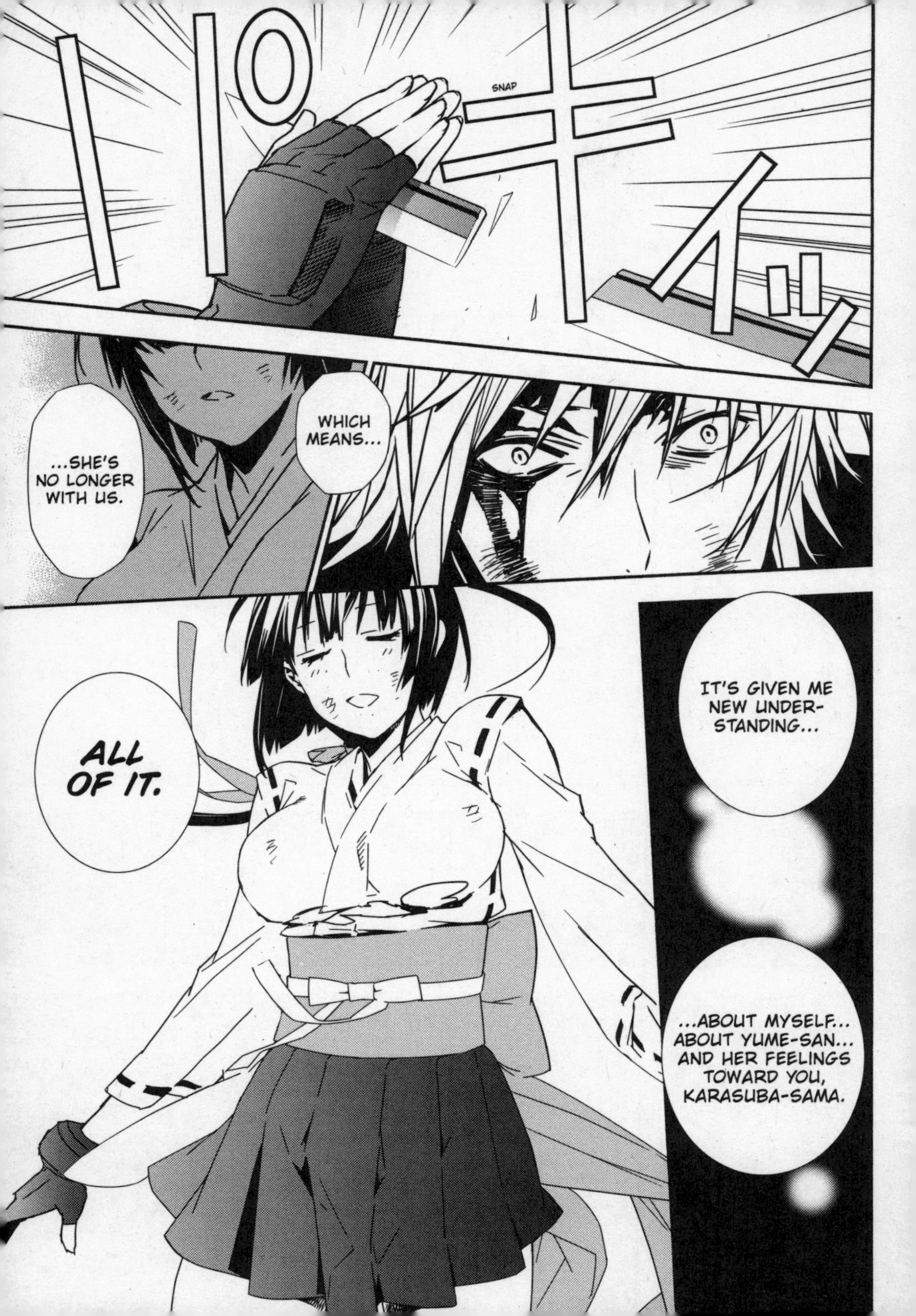
パキィッ
SNAP
WHICH MEANS...
...SHE'S NO LONGER WITH US.
IT'S GIVEN ME NEW UNDER-STANDING...
...ABOUT MYSELF... ABOUT YUME-SAN... AND HER FEELINGS TOWARD YOU, KARASUBA-SAMA.
ALL OF IT.

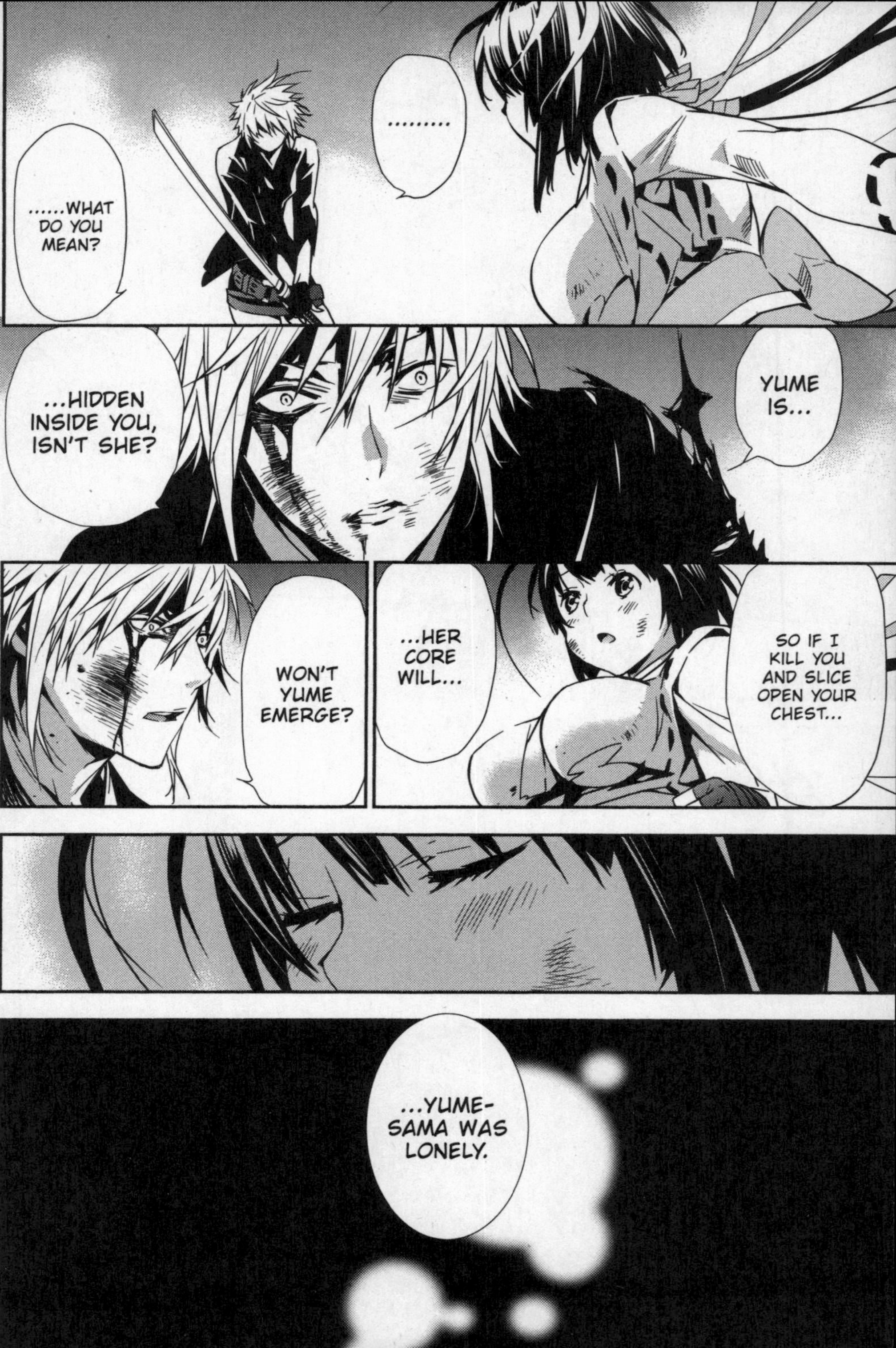
....
......WHAT DO YOU MEAN?
YUME IS...
...HIDDEN INSIDE YOU, ISN'T SHE?
SO IF I KILL YOU AND SLICE OPEN YOUR CHEST...
...HER CORE WILL...
WON'T YUME EMERGE?
...YUME-SAMA WAS LONELY.

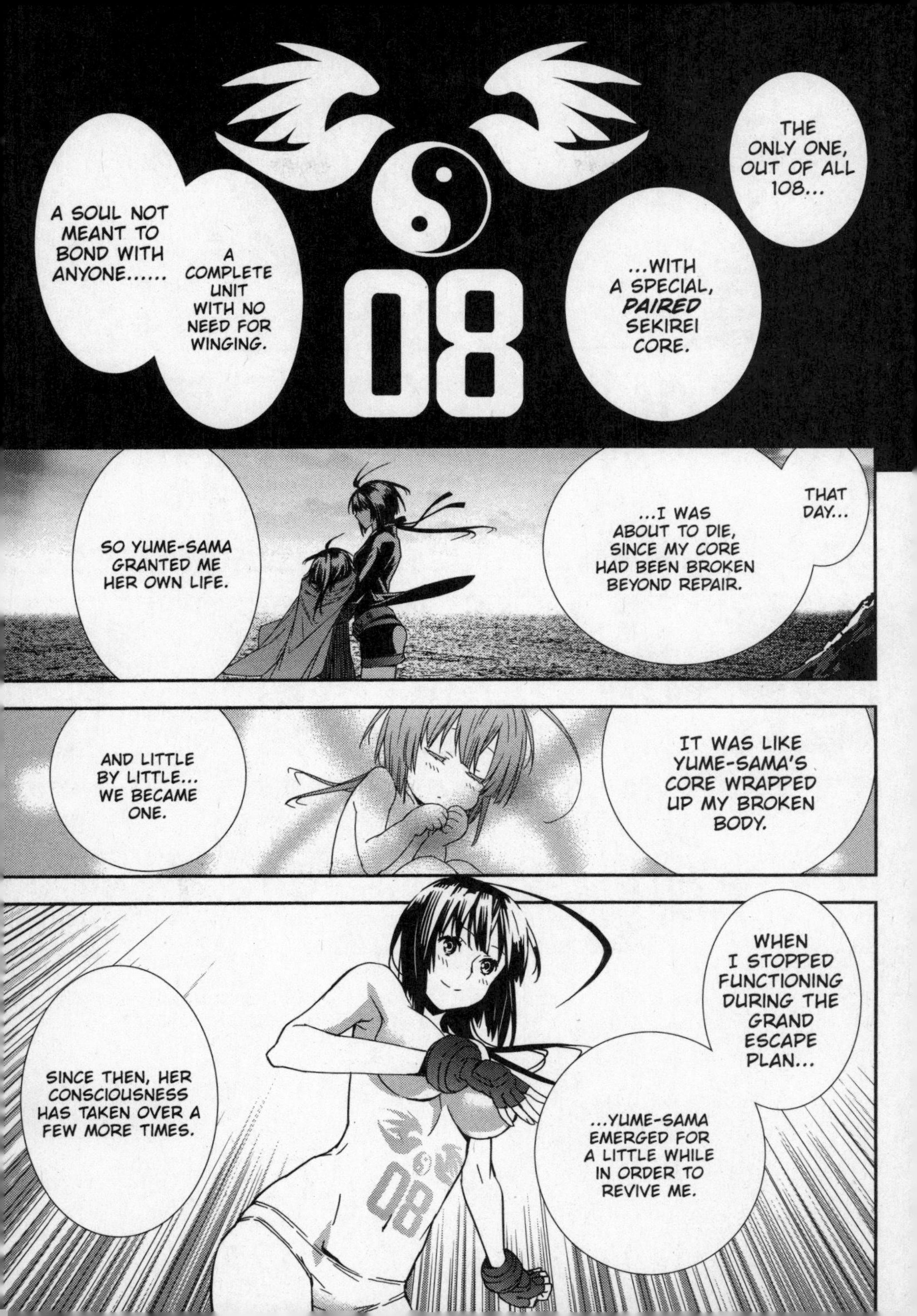
THE ONLY ONE, OUT OF ALL 108...
...WITH A SPECIAL, *PAIRED* SEKIREI CORE.
08
A COMPLETE UNIT WITH NO NEED FOR WINGING.
A SOUL NOT MEANT TO BOND WITH ANYONE......
THAT DAY...
...I WAS ABOUT TO DIE, SINCE MY CORE HAD BEEN BROKEN BEYOND REPAIR.
SO YUME-SAMA GRANTED ME HER OWN LIFE.
IT WAS LIKE YUME-SAMA'S CORE WRAPPED UP MY BROKEN BODY.
AND LITTLE BY LITTLE... WE BECAME ONE.
WHEN I STOPPED FUNCTIONING DURING THE GRAND ESCAPE PLAN...
...YUME-SAMA EMERGED FOR A LITTLE WHILE IN ORDER TO REVIVE ME.
SINCE THEN, HER CONSCIOUSNESS HAS TAKEN OVER A FEW MORE TIMES.

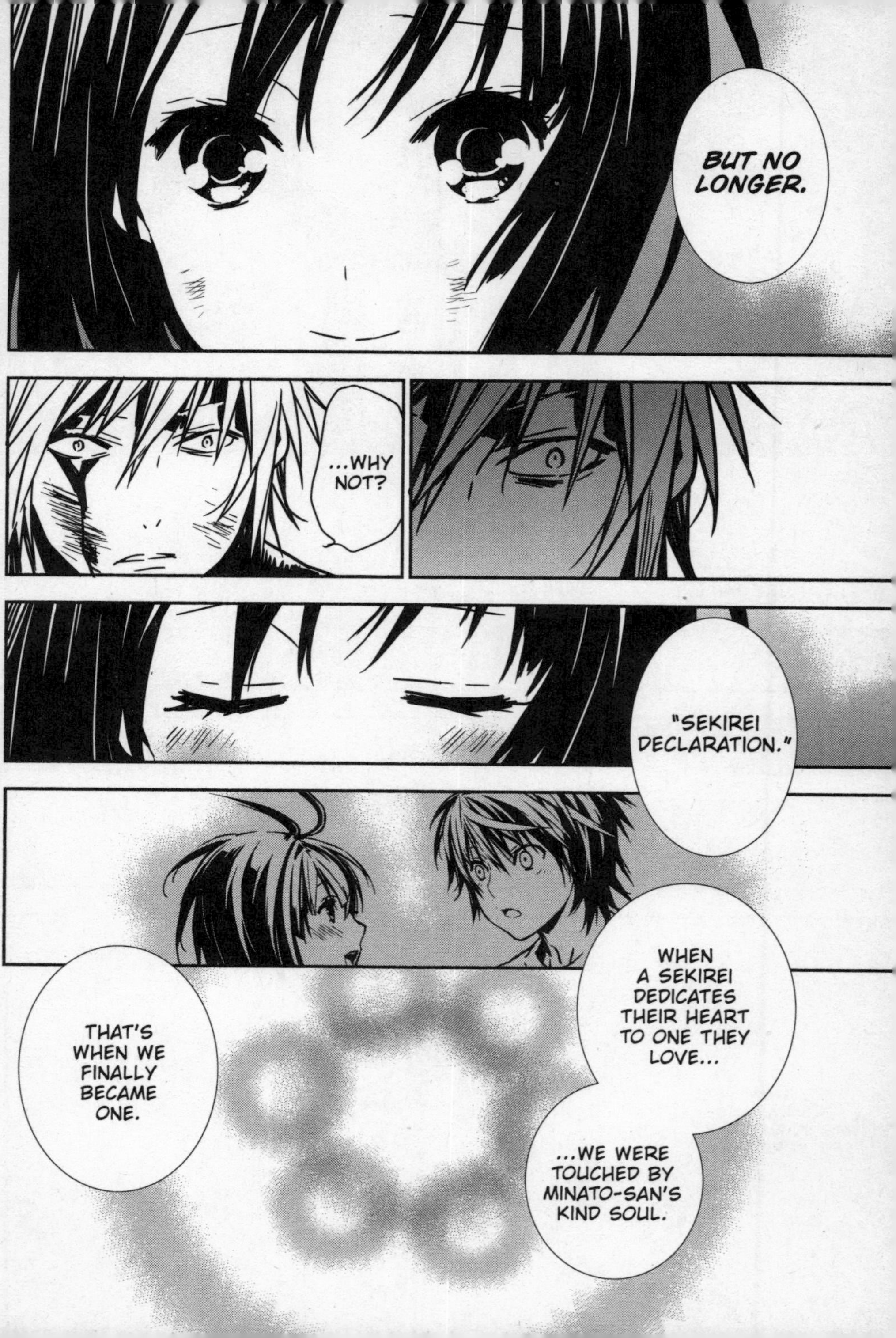
BUT NO LONGER.
...WHY NOT?
"SEKIREI DECLARATION."
WHEN A SEKIREI DEDICATES THEIR HEART TO ONE THEY LOVE...
...WE WERE TOUCHED BY MINATO-SAN'S KIND SOUL.
THAT'S WHEN WE FINALLY BECAME ONE.

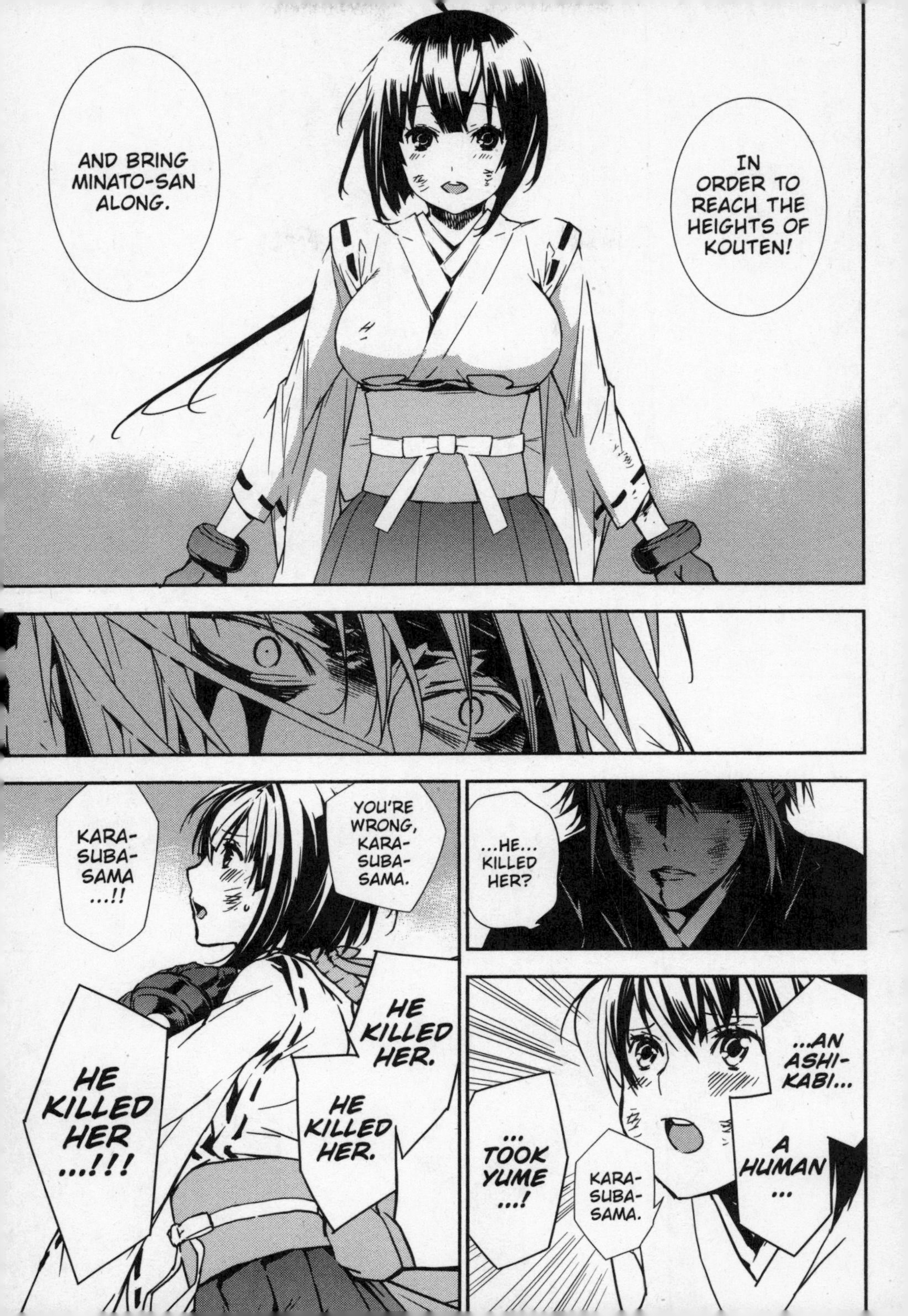
IN ORDER TO REACH THE HEIGHTS OF KOUTEN!
AND BRING MINATO-SAN ALONG.
...HE... KILLED HER?
...AN ASHI-KABI...
A HUMAN...
KARA-SUBA-SAMA.
...TOOK YUME...!
YOU'RE WRONG, KARA-SUBA-SAMA.
KARA-SUBA-SAMA...!!
HE KILLED HER.
HE KILLED HER.
HE KILLED HER...!!!

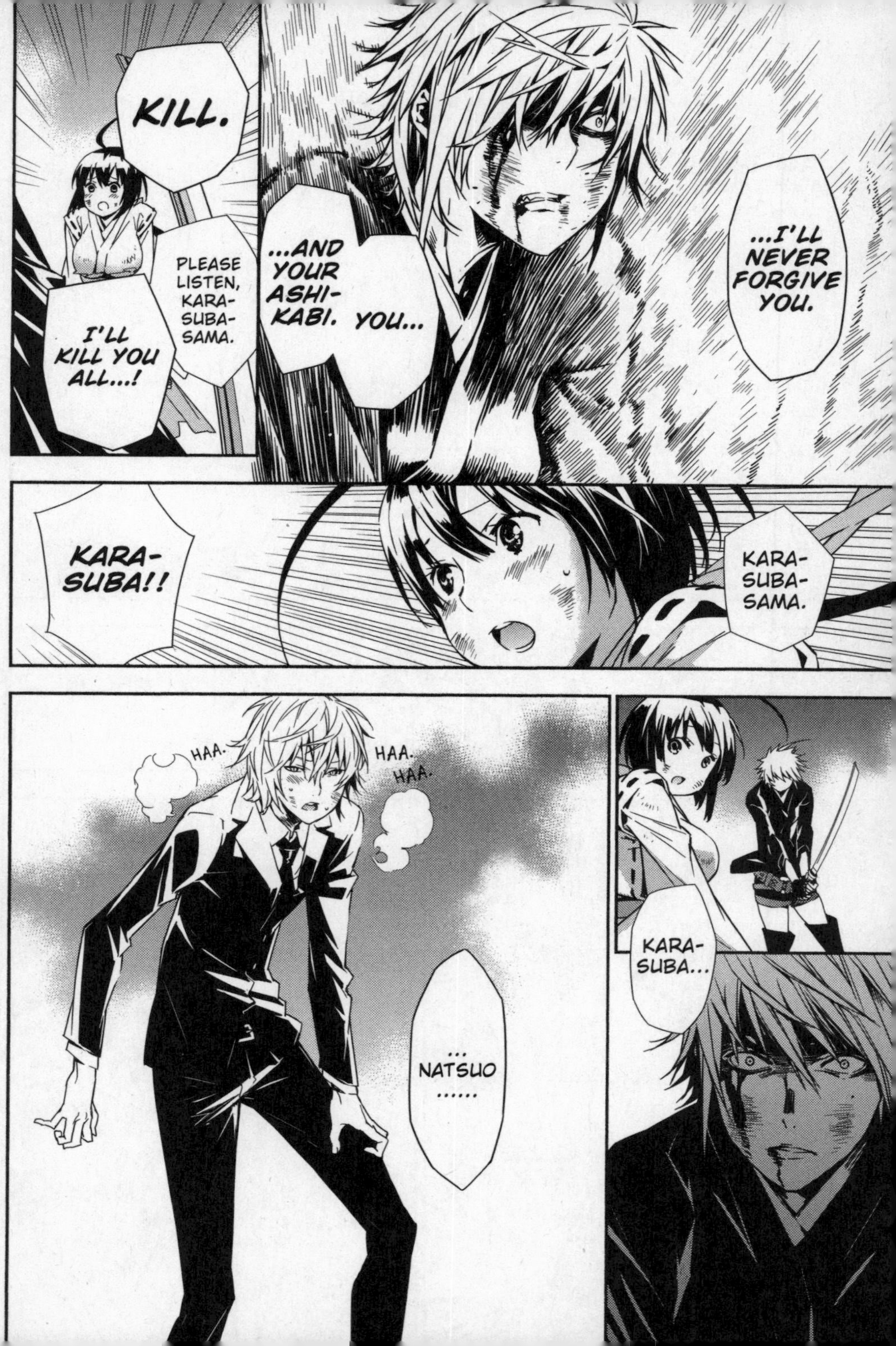
...I'LL NEVER FORGIVE YOU.
YOU...
...AND YOUR ASHIKABI.
KILL.
PLEASE LISTEN, KARA-SUBA-SAMA.
I'LL KILL YOU ALL...!
KARA-SUBA-SAMA.
KARA-SUBA!!
KARA-SUBA...
HAA.
HAA.
HAA.
... NATSUO ......

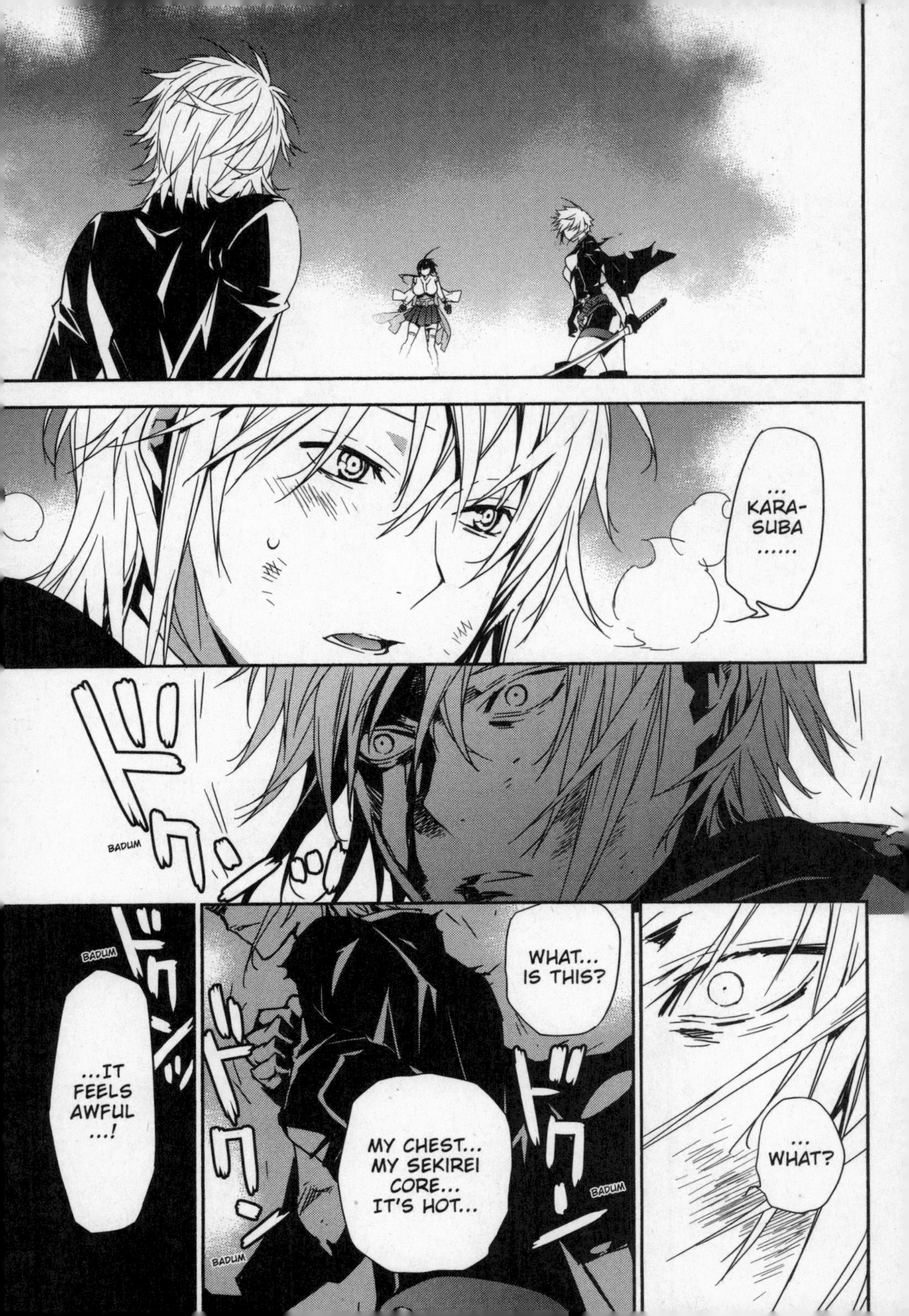

...KARA-SUBA......
BADUM
...WHAT?
BADUM
WHAT... IS THIS?
MY CHEST... MY SEKIREI CORE... IT'S HOT...
BADUM
BADUM
...IT FEELS AWFUL...!

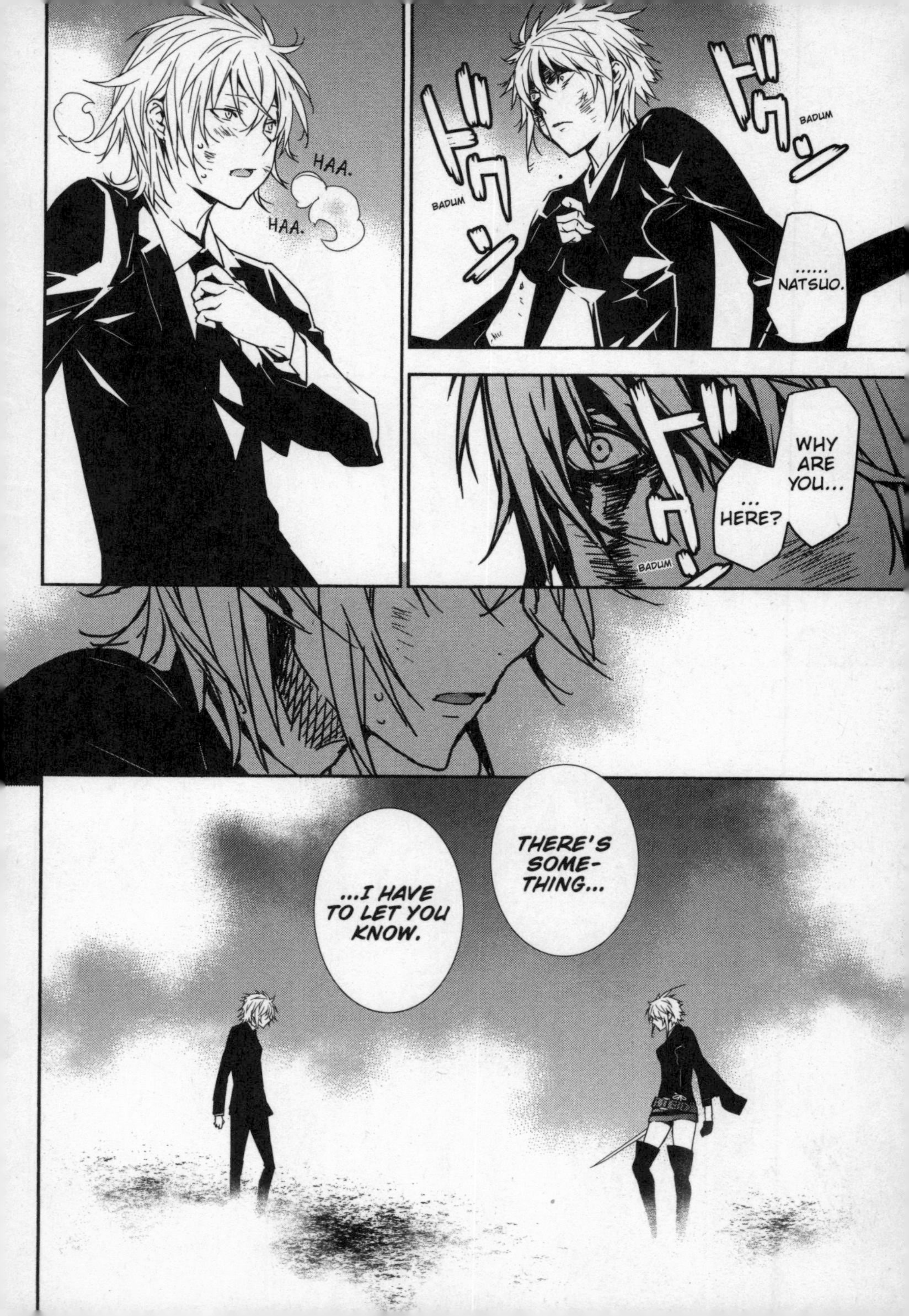
BADUM
BADUM
......NATSUO.
WHY ARE YOU...
...HERE?
BADUM
HAA.
HAA.
THERE'S SOMETHING...
...I HAVE TO LET YOU KNOW.

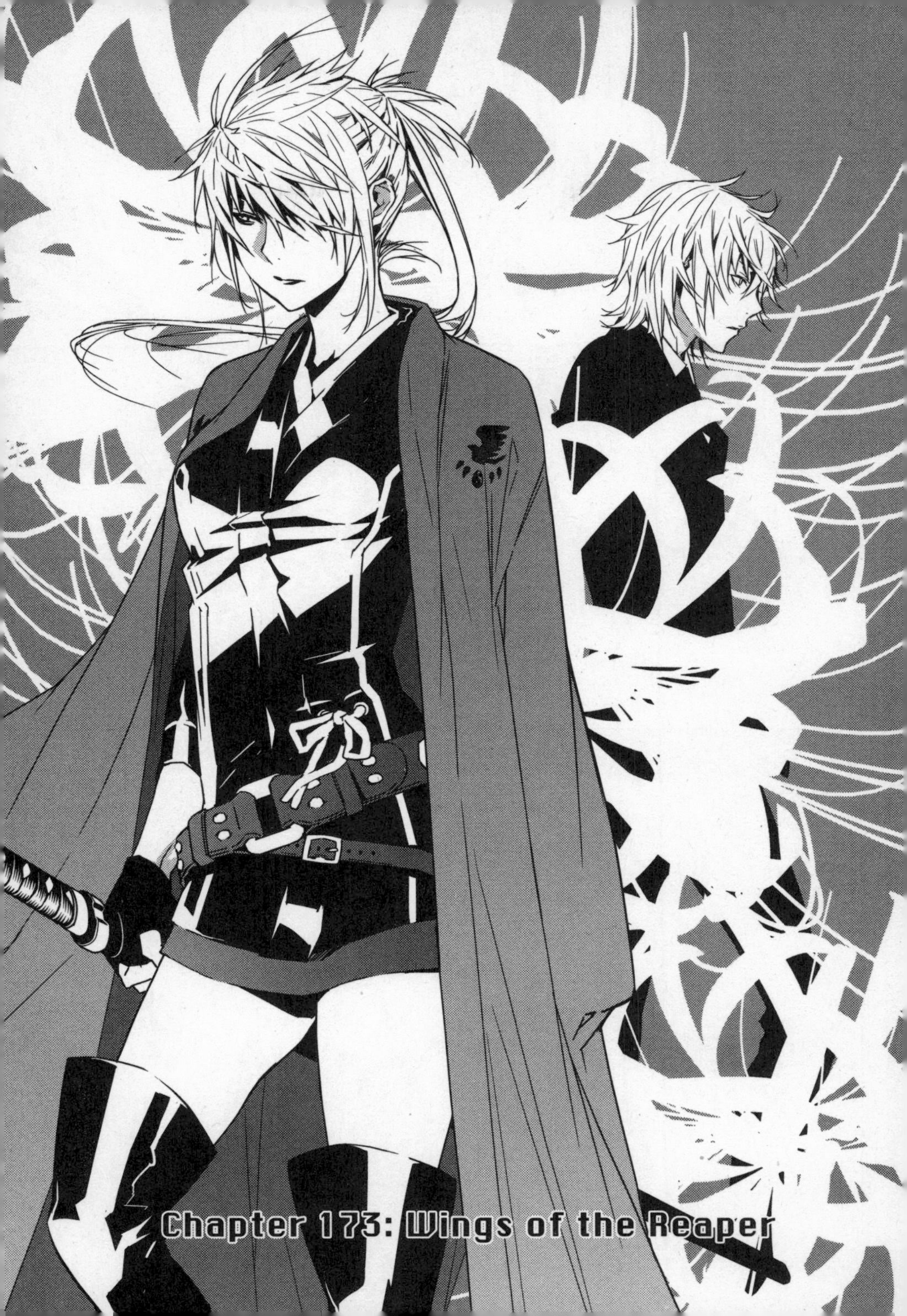
Chapter 173: Wings of the Reaper

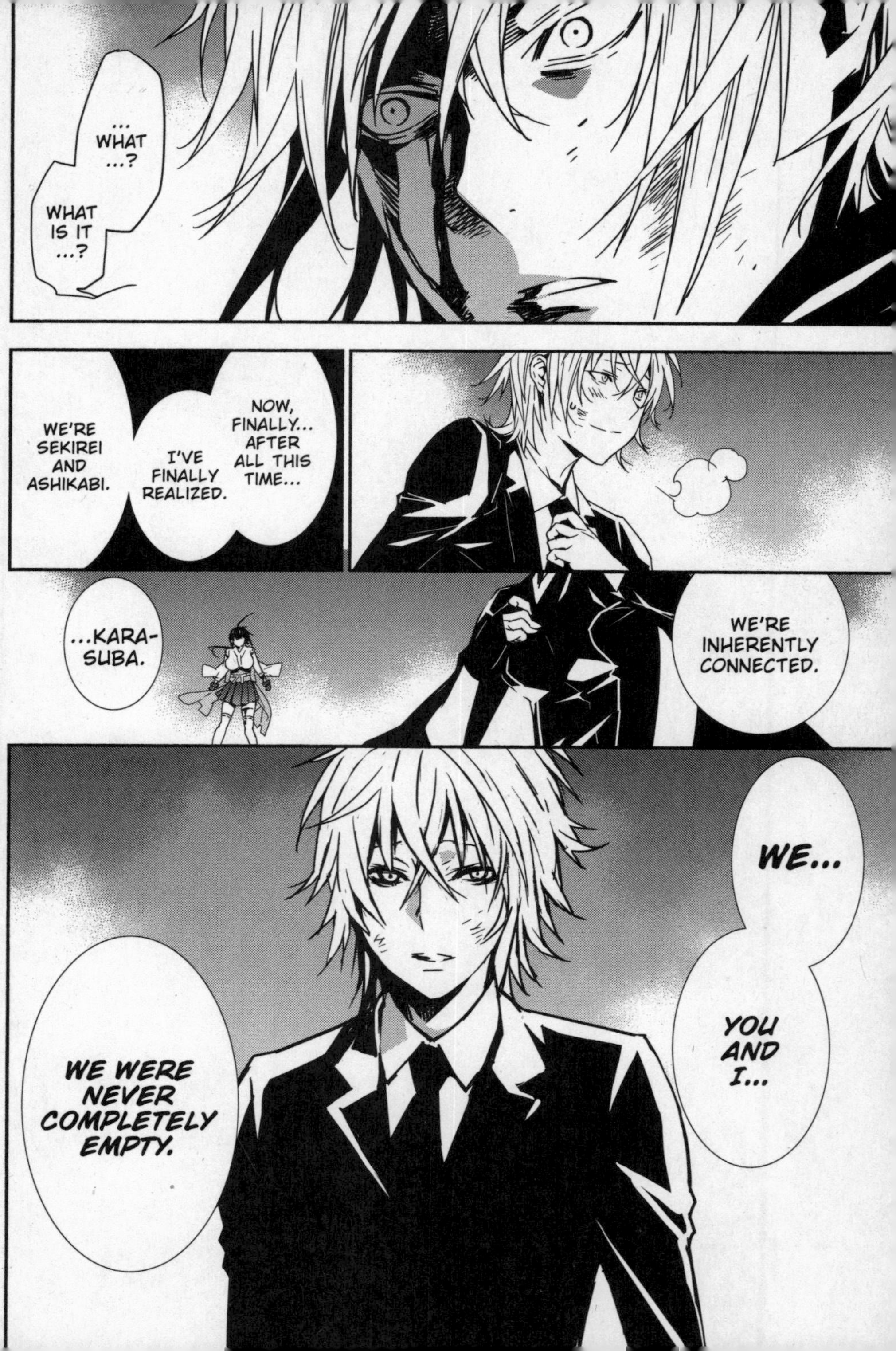

... WHAT ...?
WHAT IS IT ...?
NOW, FINALLY... AFTER ALL THIS TIME...
I'VE FINALLY REALIZED.
WE'RE SEKIREI AND ASHIKABI.
WE'RE INHERENTLY CONNECTED.
...KARA-SUBA.
WE...
YOU AND I...
WE WERE NEVER COMPLETELY EMPTY.

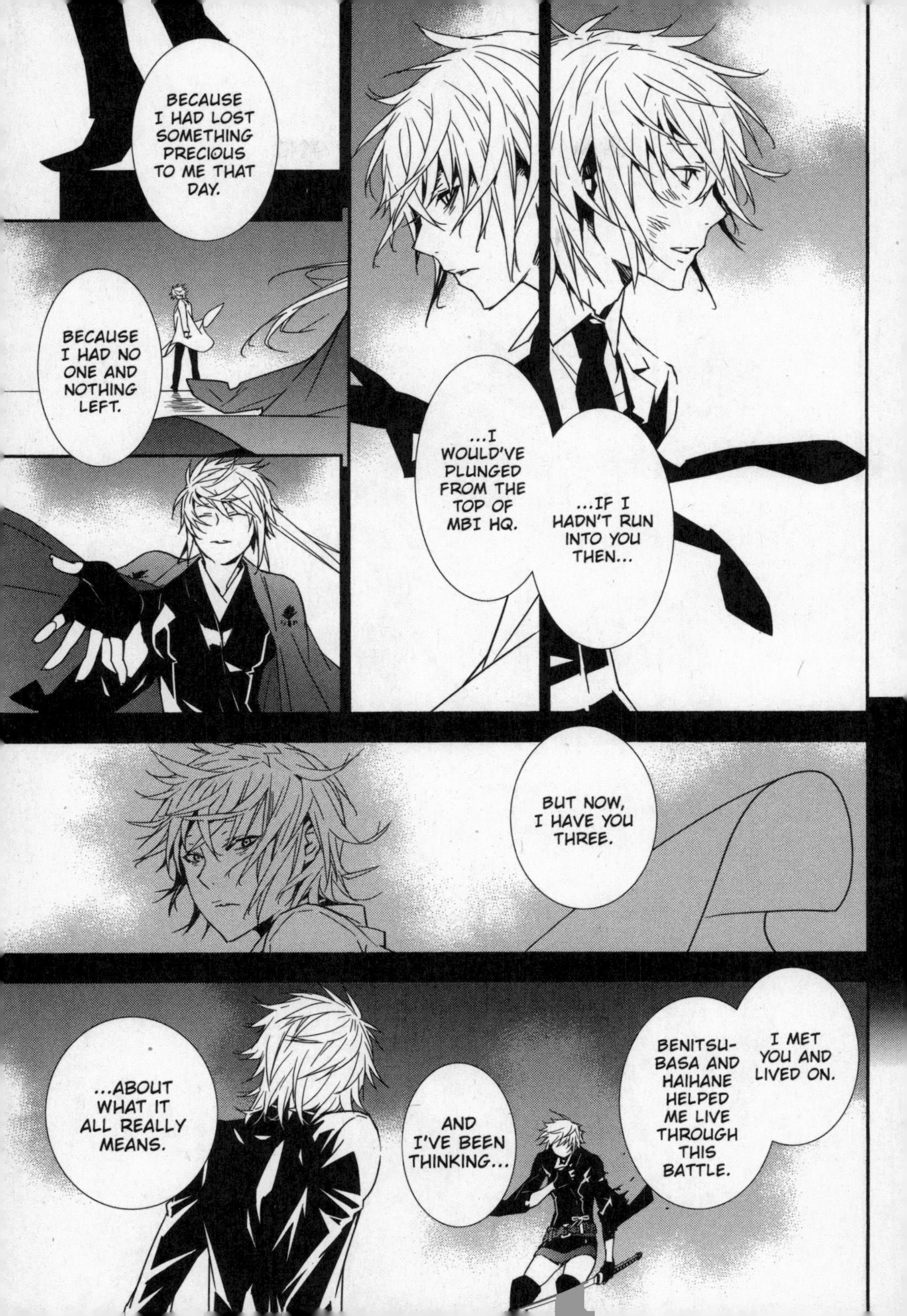
...IF I HADN'T RUN INTO YOU THEN...
...I WOULD'VE PLUNGED FROM THE TOP OF MBI HQ.
BECAUSE I HAD LOST SOMETHING PRECIOUS TO ME THAT DAY.
BECAUSE I HAD NO ONE AND NOTHING LEFT.
BUT NOW, I HAVE YOU THREE.
I MET YOU AND LIVED ON.
BENITSU-BASA AND HAIHANE HELPED ME LIVE THROUGH THIS BATTLE.
AND I'VE BEEN THINKING...
...ABOUT WHAT IT ALL REALLY MEANS.

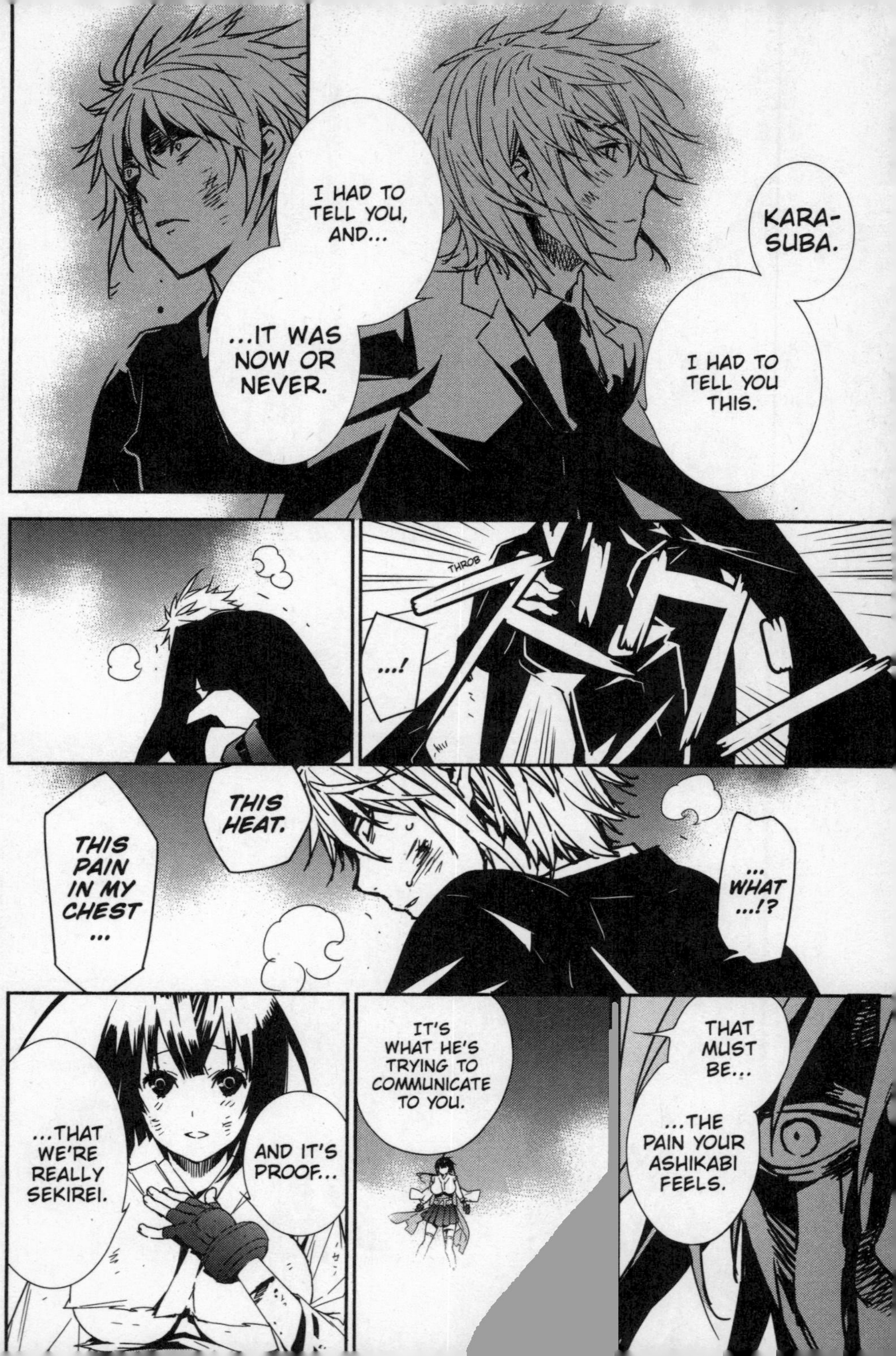
KARA-SUBA.
I HAD TO TELL YOU THIS.
I HAD TO TELL YOU, AND...
...IT WAS NOW OR NEVER.
THROB
...!
... WHAT ...!?
THIS HEAT.
THIS PAIN IN MY CHEST ...
THAT MUST BE...
...THE PAIN YOUR ASHIKABI FEELS.
IT'S WHAT HE'S TRYING TO COMMUNICATE TO YOU.
AND IT'S PROOF...
...THAT WE'RE REALLY SEKIREI.

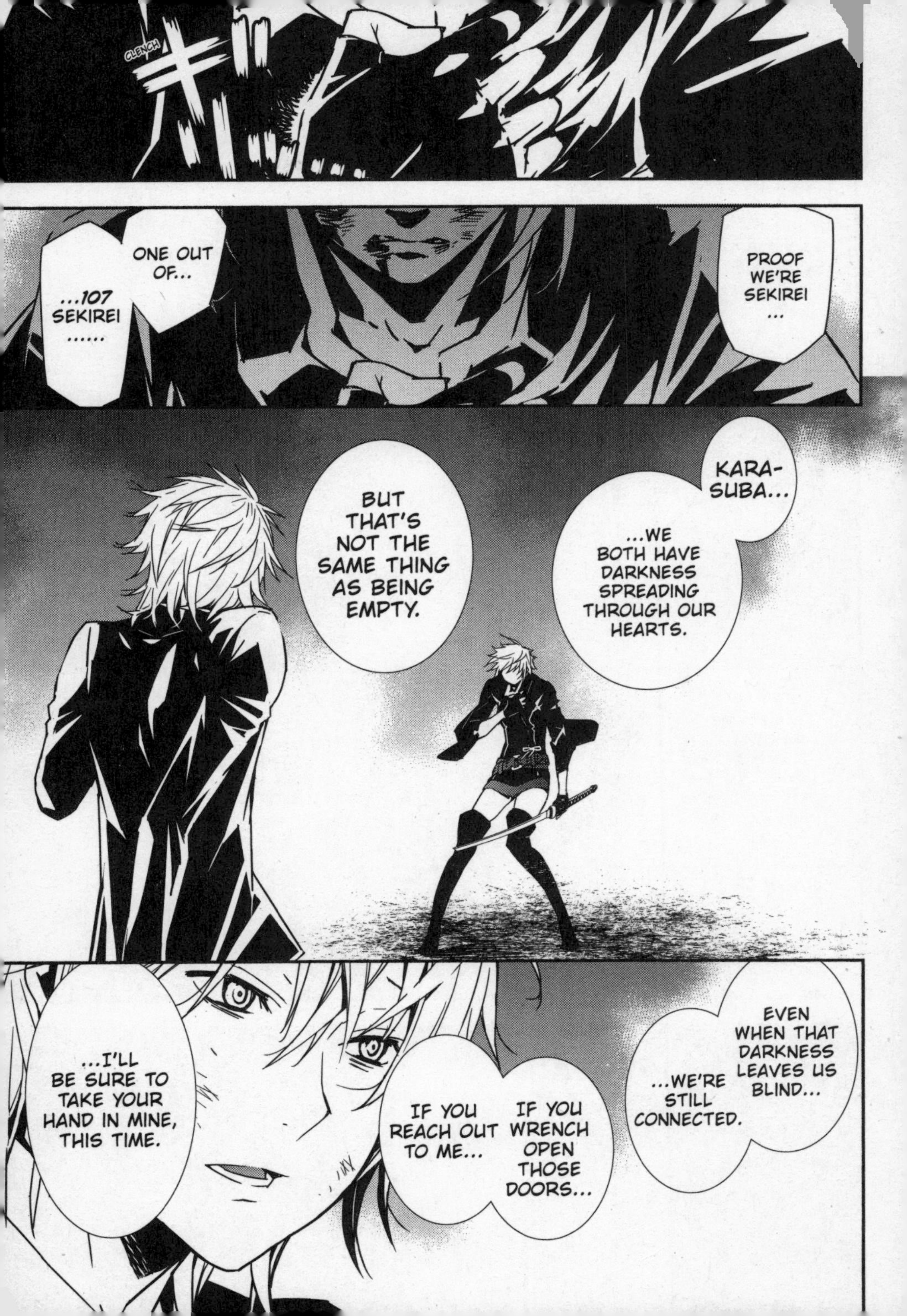
CLENCH
PROOF WE'RE SEKIREI ...
ONE OUT OF...
...107 SEKIREI ......
KARA-SUBA...
...WE BOTH HAVE DARKNESS SPREADING THROUGH OUR HEARTS.
BUT THAT'S NOT THE SAME THING AS BEING EMPTY.
EVEN WHEN THAT DARKNESS LEAVES US BLIND...
...WE'RE STILL CONNECTED.
IF YOU WRENCH OPEN THOSE DOORS...
IF YOU REACH OUT TO ME...
...I'LL BE SURE TO TAKE YOUR HAND IN MINE, THIS TIME.

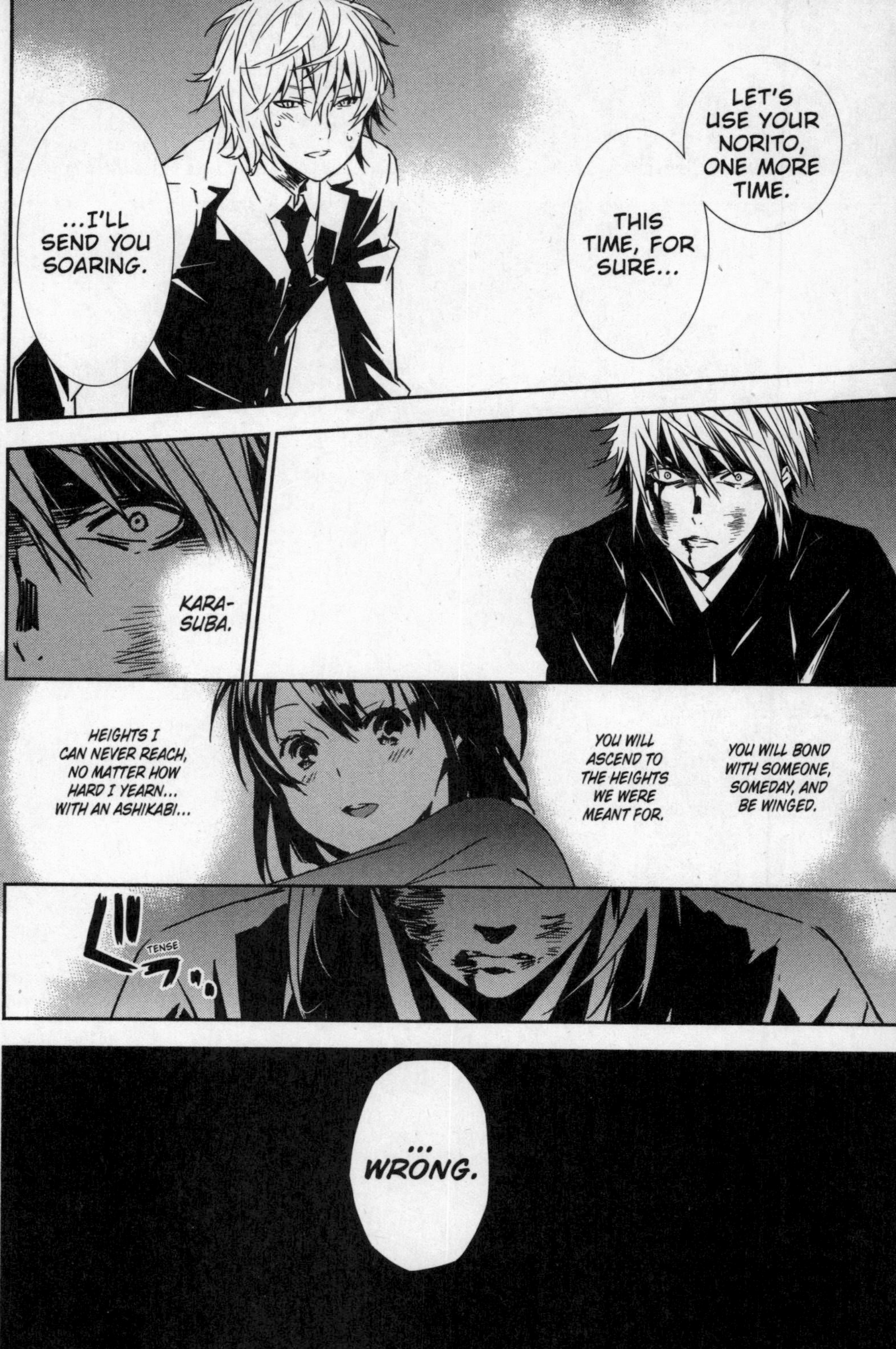
LET'S USE YOUR NORITO, ONE MORE TIME.
THIS TIME, FOR SURE...
...I'LL SEND YOU SOARING.
KARA-SUBA.
YOU WILL BOND WITH SOMEONE, SOMEDAY, AND BE WINGED.
YOU WILL ASCEND TO THE HEIGHTS WE WERE MEANT FOR.
HEIGHTS I CAN NEVER REACH, NO MATTER HOW HARD I YEARN... WITH AN ASHIKABI...
TENSE
... WRONG.

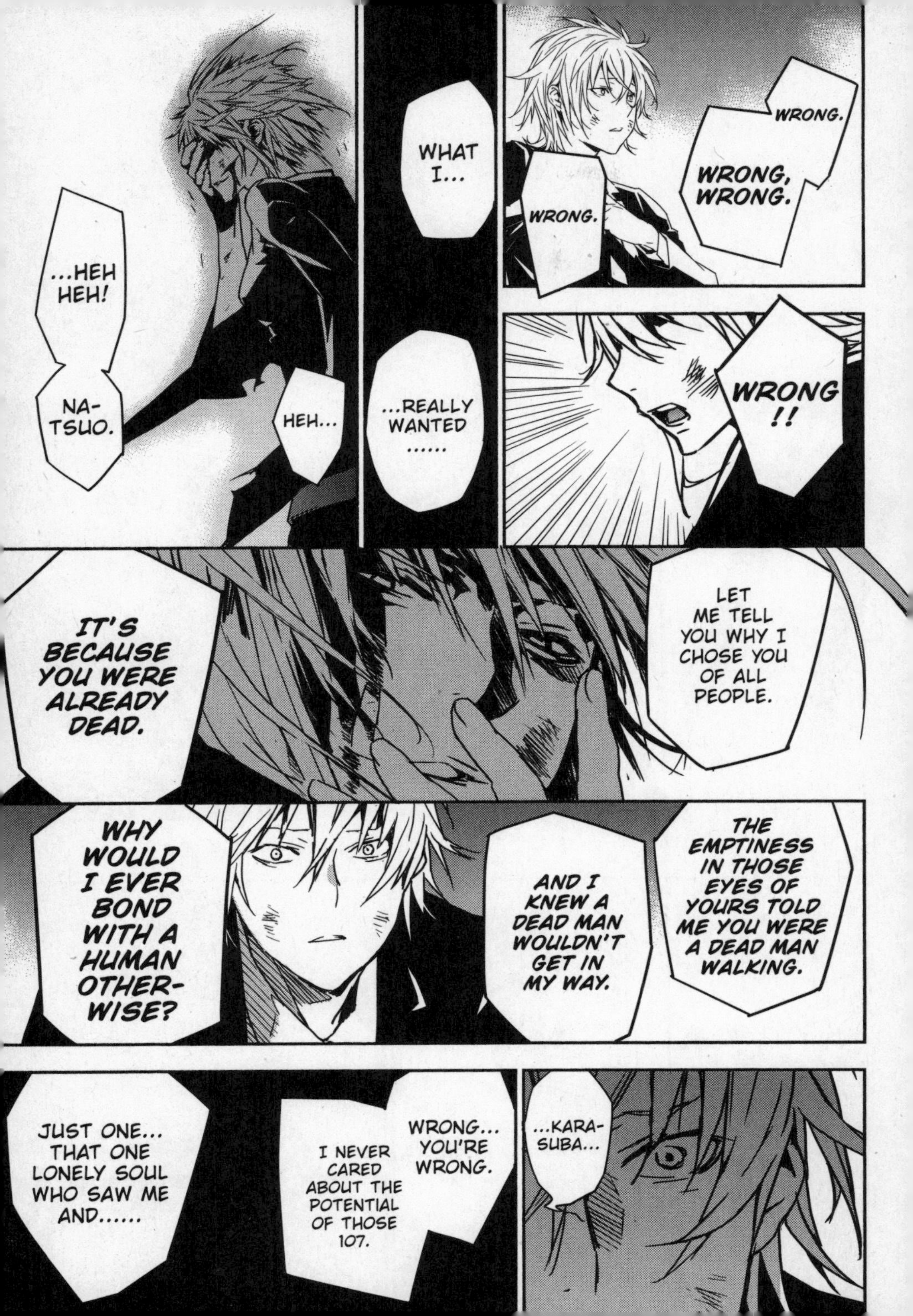
WRONG.
WRONG, WRONG.
WRONG.
WRONG !!
WHAT I...
...REALLY WANTED ......
...HEH HEH!
NA-TSUO.
HEH...
LET ME TELL YOU WHY I CHOSE YOU OF ALL PEOPLE.
IT'S BECAUSE YOU WERE ALREADY DEAD.
THE EMPTINESS IN THOSE EYES OF YOURS TOLD ME YOU WERE A DEAD MAN WALKING.
AND I KNEW A DEAD MAN WOULDN'T GET IN MY WAY.
WHY WOULD I EVER BOND WITH A HUMAN OTHER-WISE?
...KARA-SUBA...
WRONG... YOU'RE WRONG.
I NEVER CARED ABOUT THE POTENTIAL OF THOSE 107.
JUST ONE... THAT ONE LONELY SOUL WHO SAW ME AND......

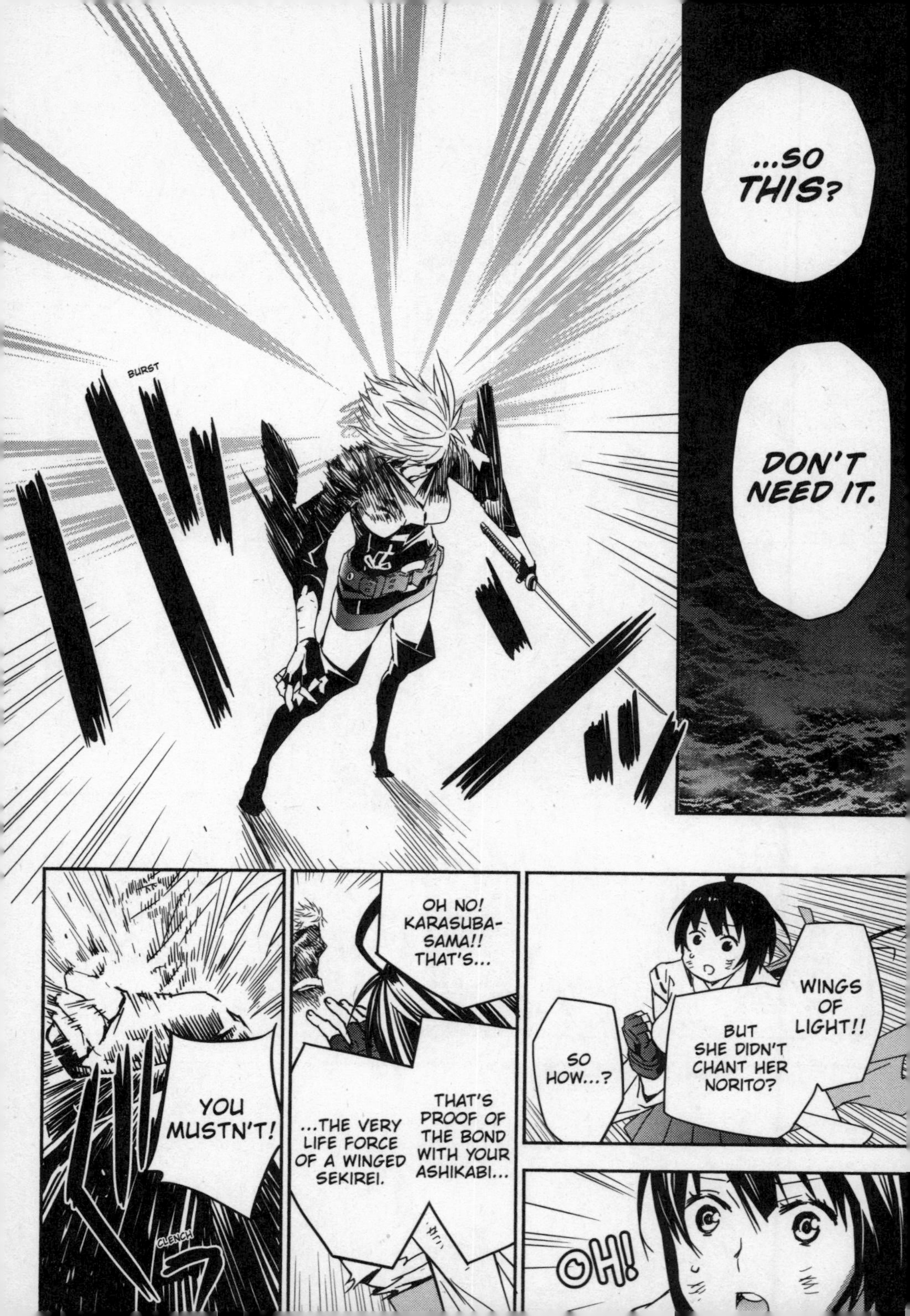
...SO THIS?
DON'T NEED IT.
BURST
WINGS OF LIGHT!!
BUT SHE DIDN'T CHANT HER NORITO?
SO HOW...?
OH!
OH NO! KARASUBA-SAMA!! THAT'S...
THAT'S PROOF OF THE BOND WITH YOUR ASHIKABI...
...THE VERY LIFE FORCE OF A WINGED SEKIREI.
YOU MUSTN'T!
CLENCH

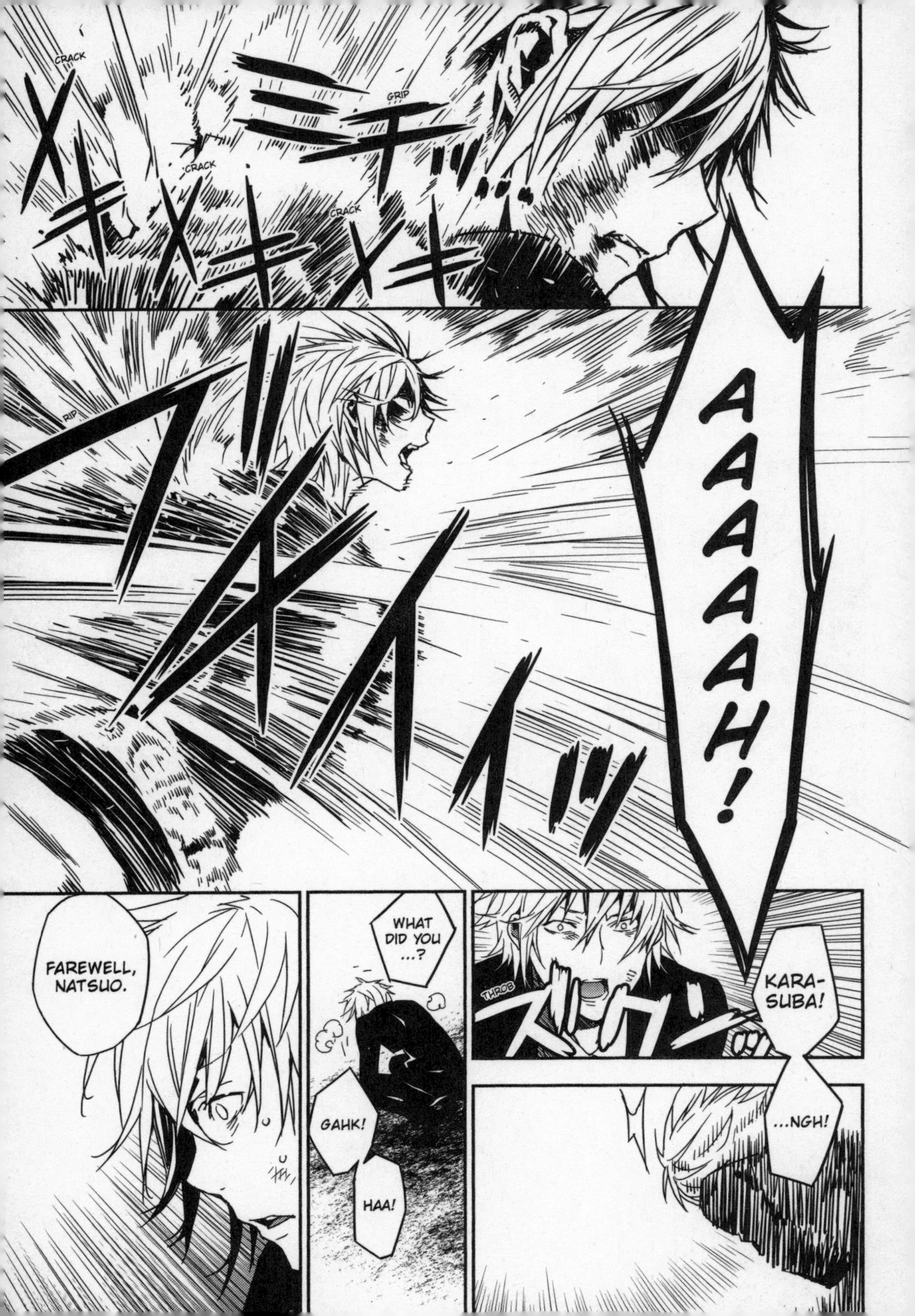
GRIP
CRACK
CRACK
CRACK
AAAAAH!
RIP
KARA-SUBA!
THROB
...NGH!
WHAT DID YOU ...?
GAHK!
HAA!
FAREWELL, NATSUO.

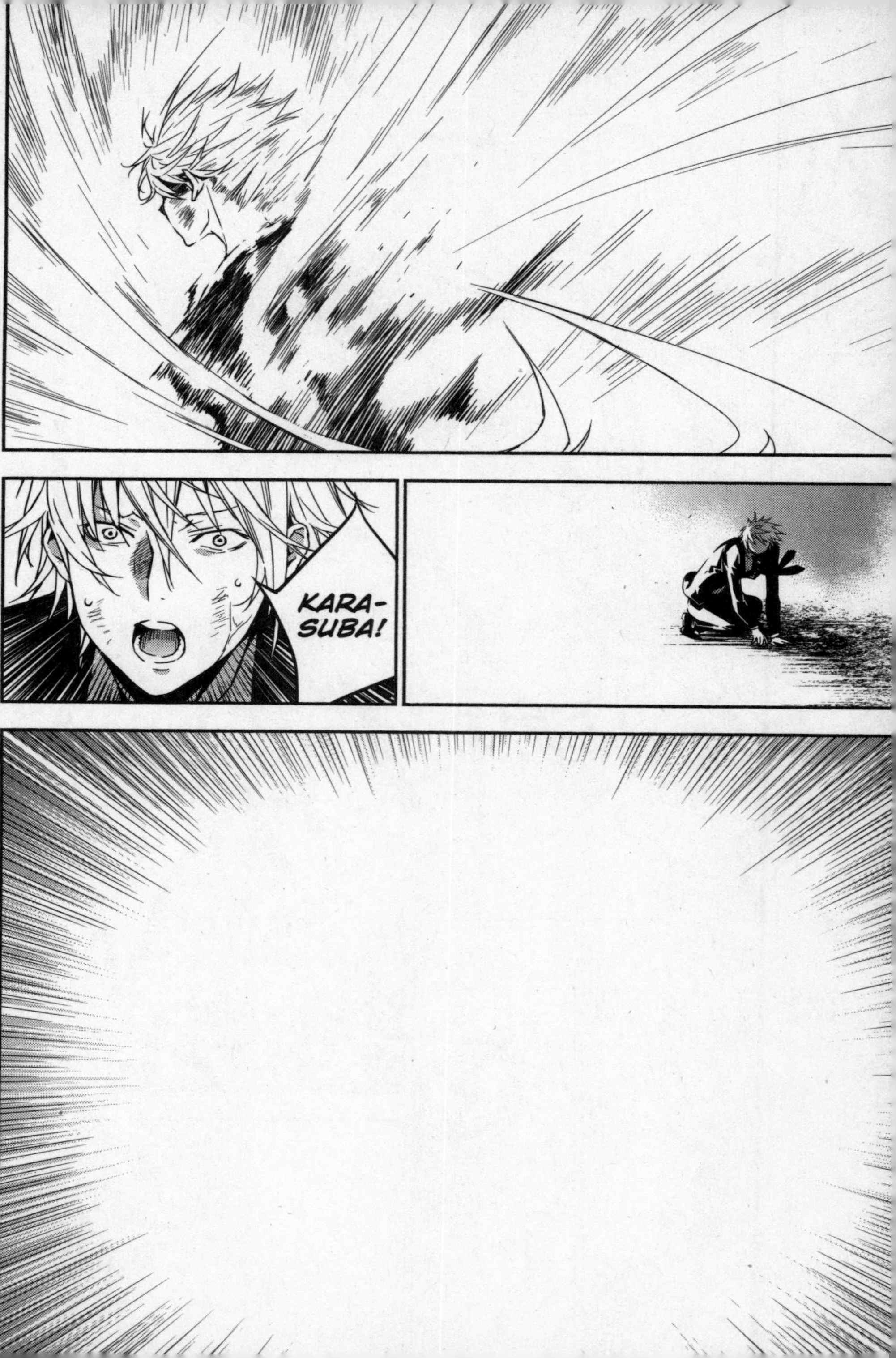
KARA-SUBA!

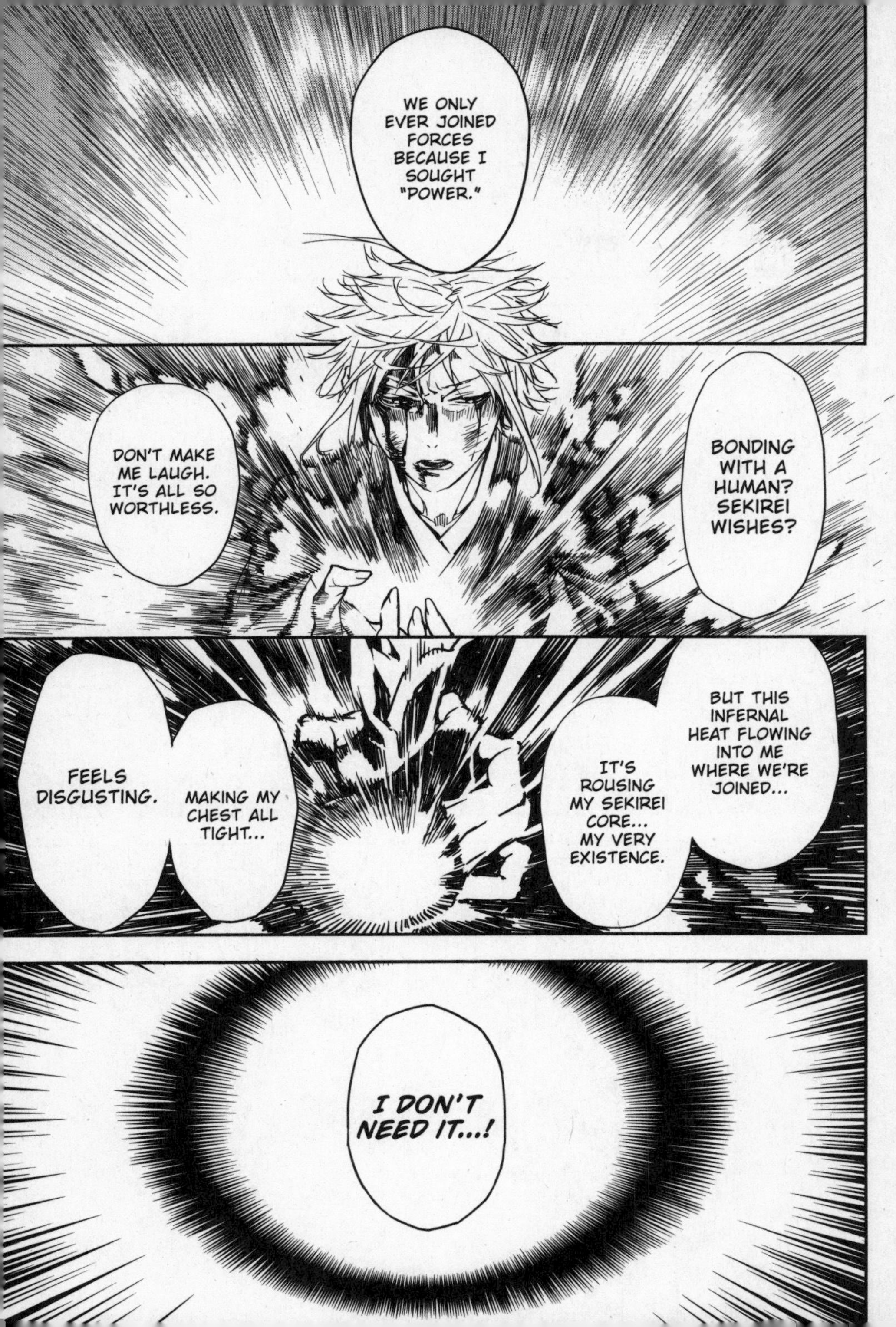
WE ONLY EVER JOINED FORCES BECAUSE I SOUGHT "POWER."
BONDING WITH A HUMAN? SEKIREI WISHES?
DON'T MAKE ME LAUGH. IT'S ALL SO WORTHLESS.
BUT THIS INFERNAL HEAT FLOWING INTO ME WHERE WE'RE JOINED...
IT'S ROUSING MY SEKIREI CORE... MY VERY EXISTENCE.
MAKING MY CHEST ALL TIGHT...
FEELS DISGUSTING.
I DON'T NEED IT...!

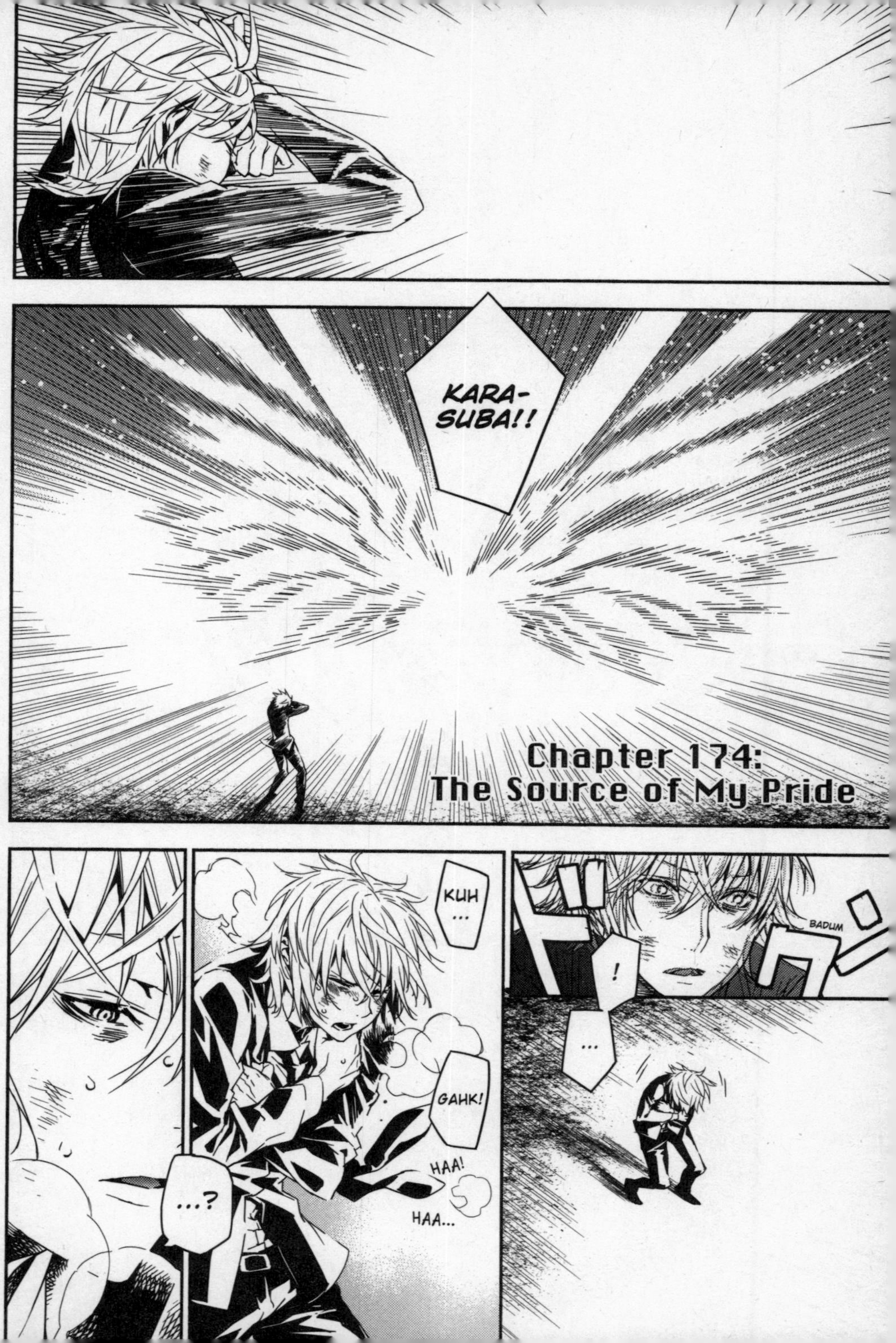
KARA-SUBA!!
Chapter 174:
The Source of My Pride
BADUM
!
...
KUH...
GAHK!
HAA!
HAA...
...?

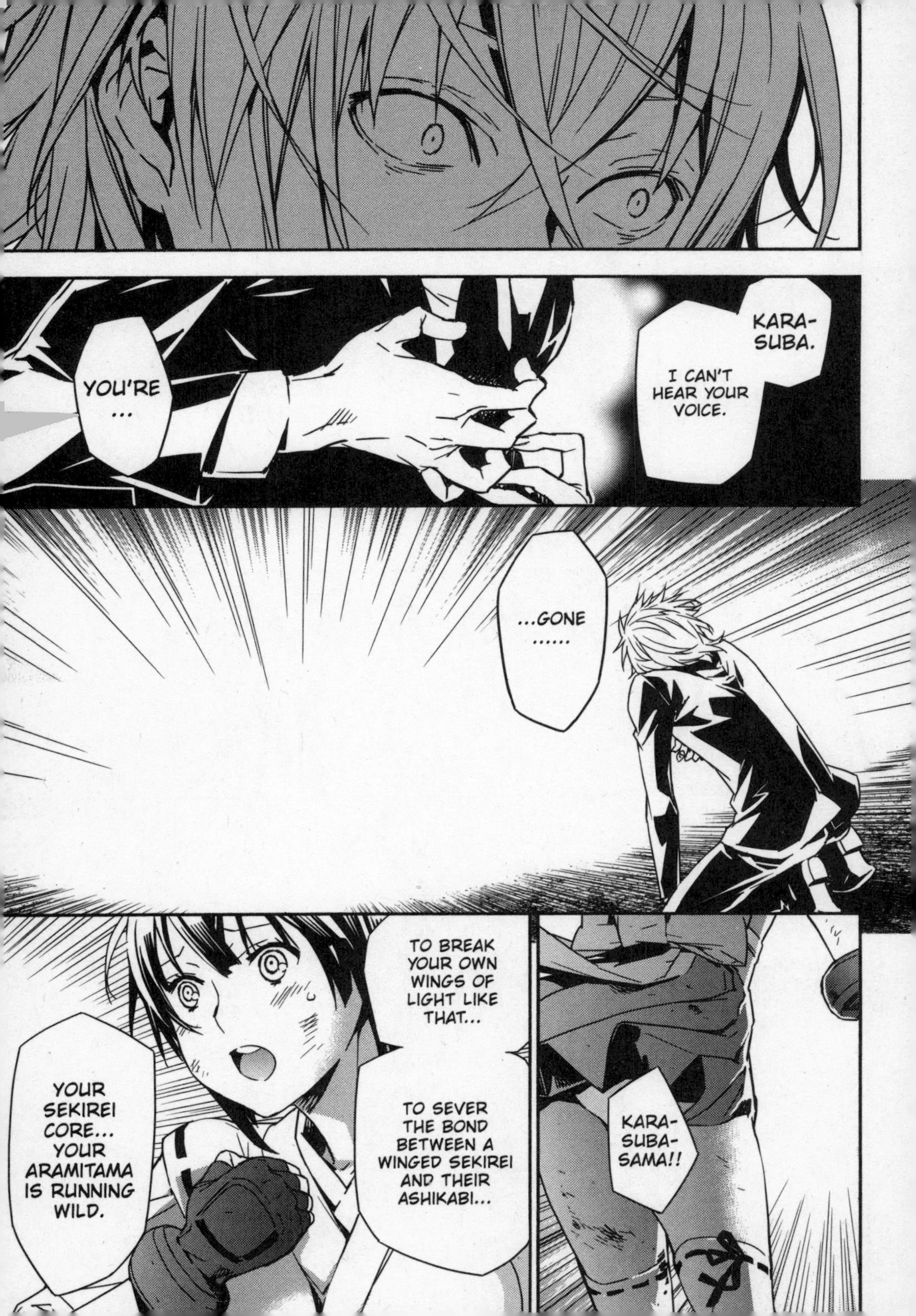
KARA-SUBA.
I CAN'T HEAR YOUR VOICE.
YOU'RE ...
...GONE ......
KARA-SUBA-SAMA!!
TO BREAK YOUR OWN WINGS OF LIGHT LIKE THAT...
TO SEVER THE BOND BETWEEN A WINGED SEKIREI AND THEIR ASHIKABI...
YOUR SEKIREI CORE... YOUR ARAMITAMA IS RUNNING WILD.

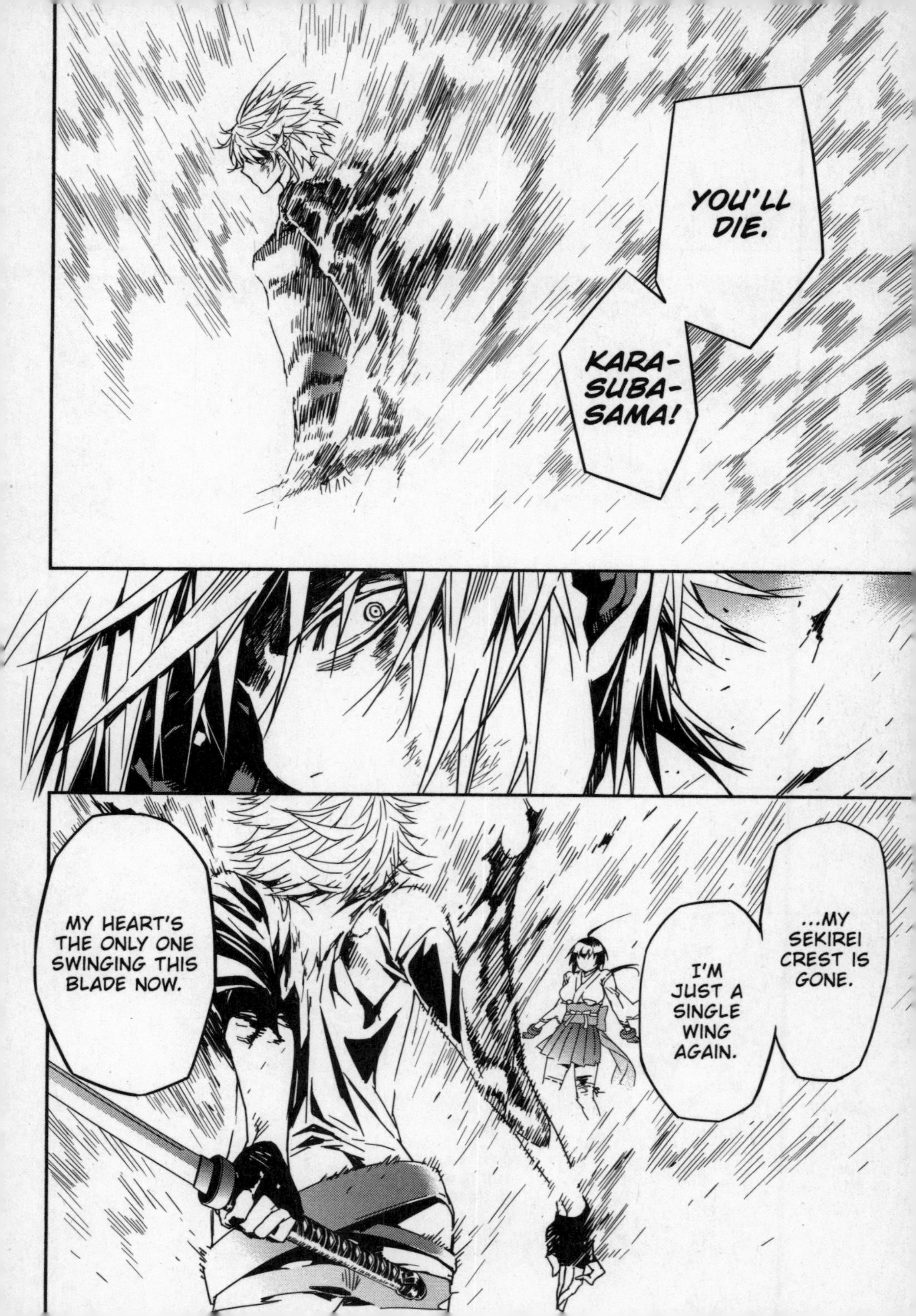
YOU'LL DIE.
KARA-SUBA-SAMA!
...MY SEKIREI CREST IS GONE.
I'M JUST A SINGLE WING AGAIN.
MY HEART'S THE ONLY ONE SWINGING THIS BLADE NOW.

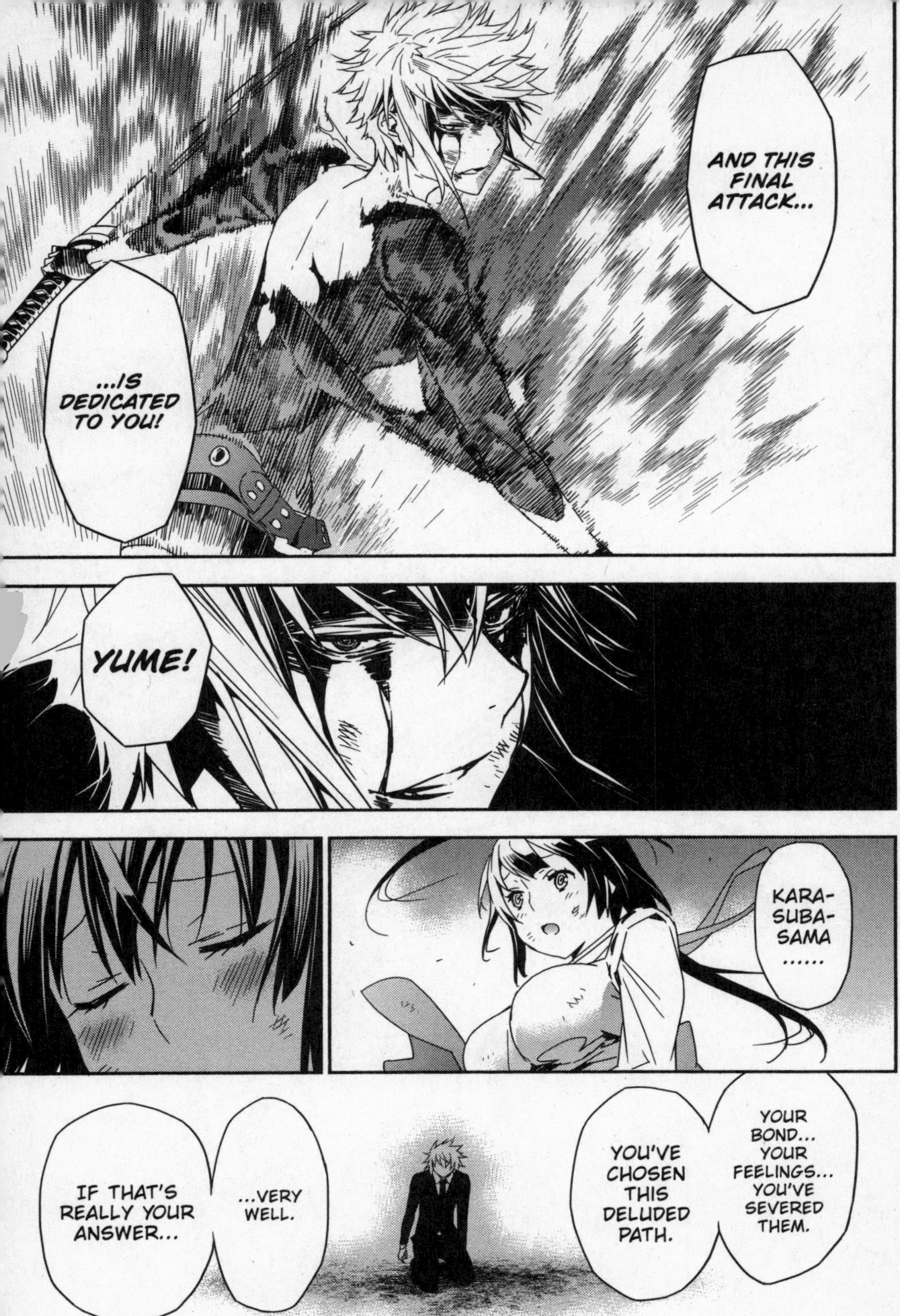
AND THIS FINAL ATTACK...
...IS DEDICATED TO YOU!
YUME!
KARA-SUBA-SAMA ......
YOUR BOND... YOUR FEELINGS... YOU'VE SEVERED THEM.
YOU'VE CHOSEN THIS DELUDED PATH.
...VERY WELL.
IF THAT'S REALLY YOUR ANSWER...

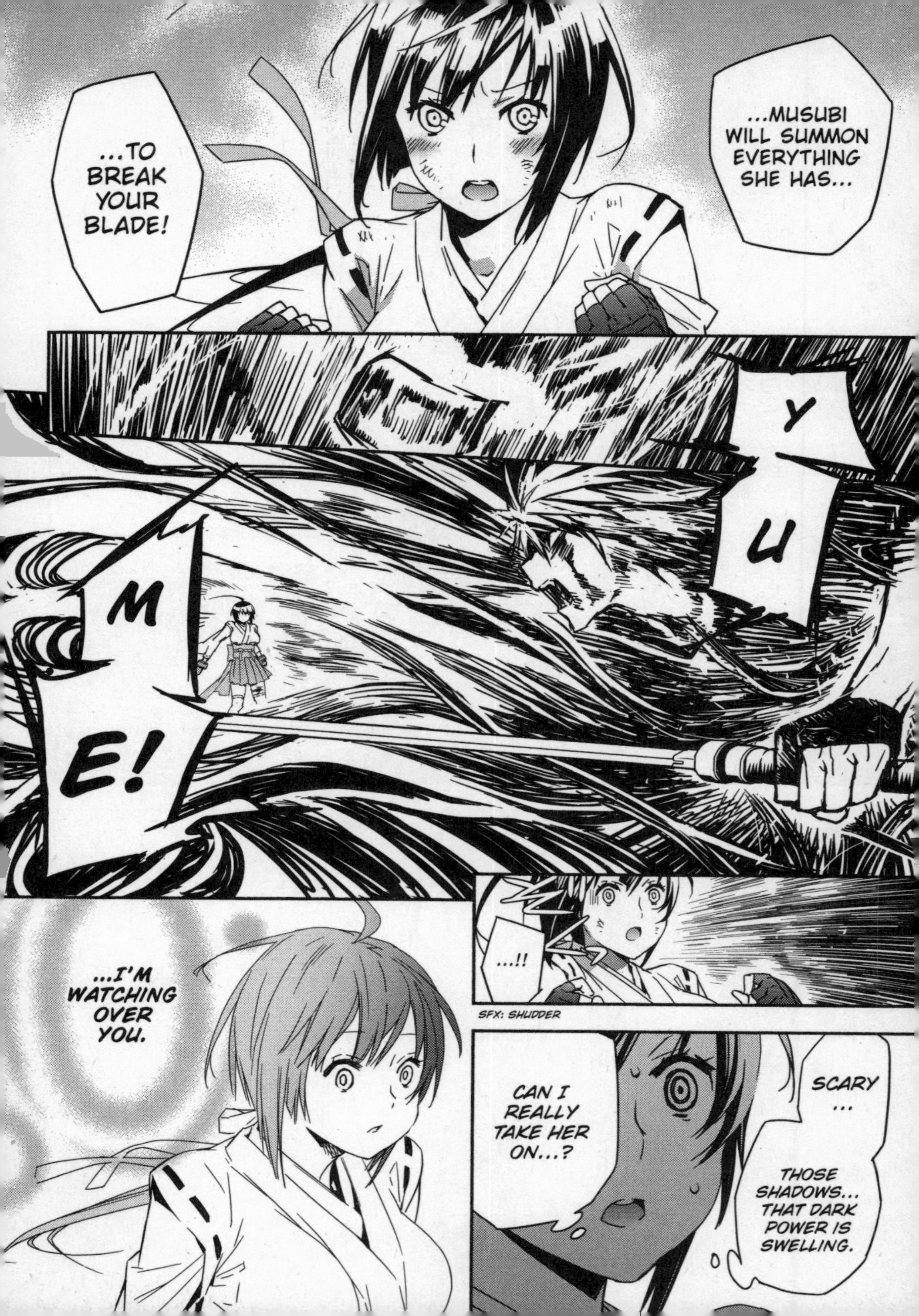
...MUSUBI WILL SUMMON EVERYTHING SHE HAS...
...TO BREAK YOUR BLADE!
Y U M E!
...!!
SFX: SHUDDER
SCARY ...
CAN I REALLY TAKE HER ON...?
THOSE SHADOWS... THAT DARK POWER IS SWELLING.
...I'M WATCHING OVER YOU.

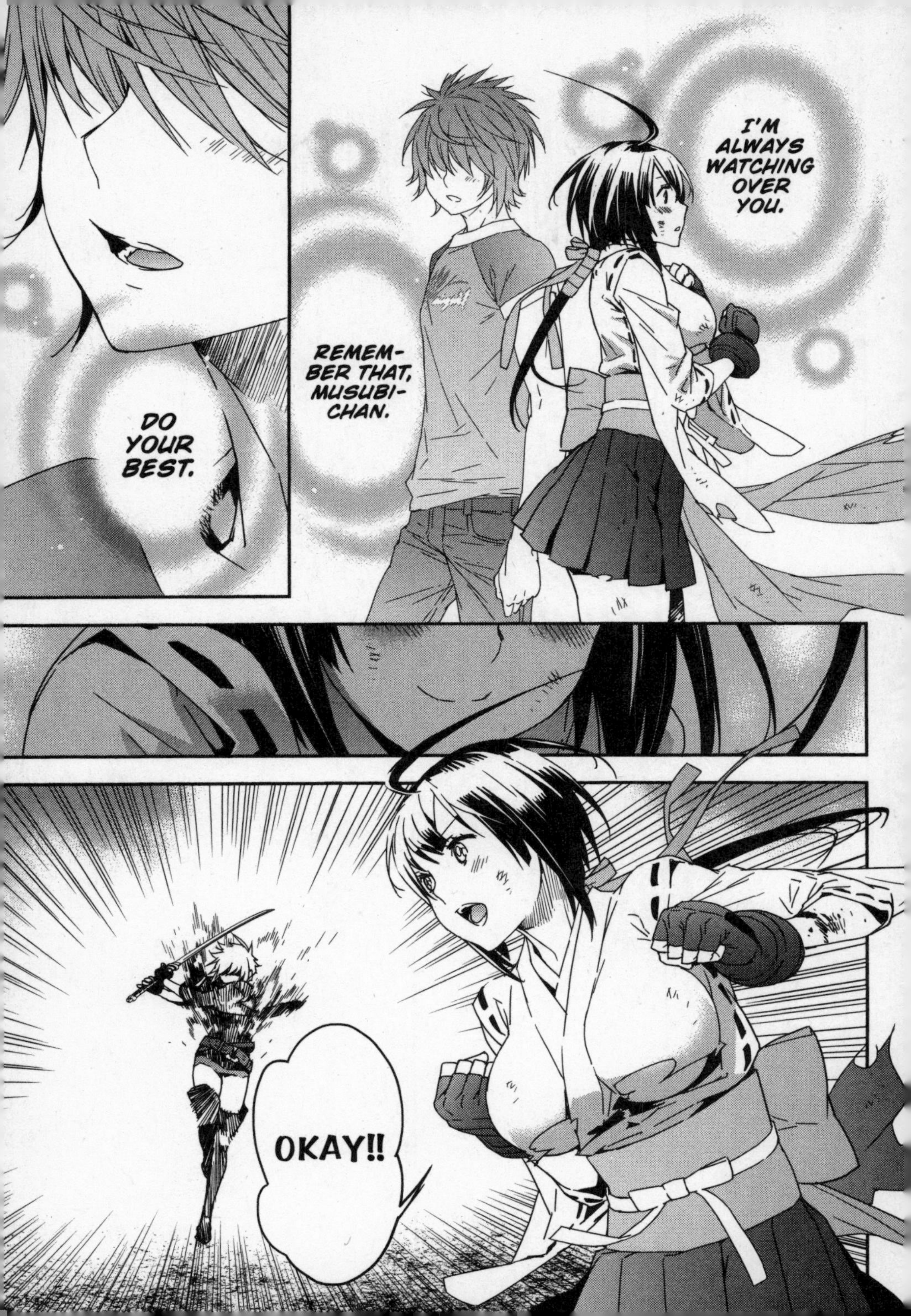
I'M ALWAYS WATCHING OVER YOU.
REMEMBER THAT, MUSUBI-CHAN.
DO YOUR BEST.
OKAY!!

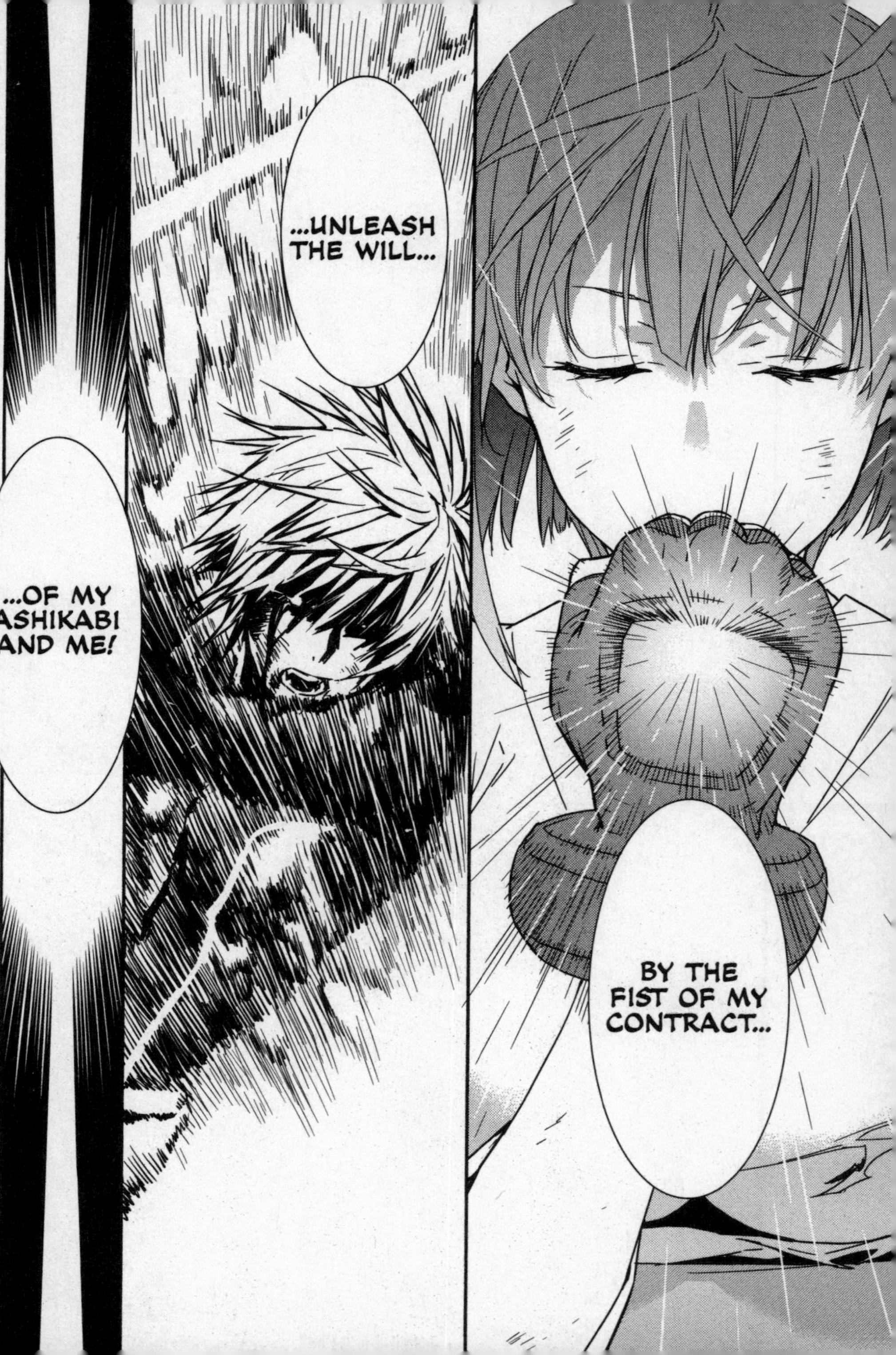
BY THE FIST OF MY CONTRACT...
...UNLEASH THE WILL...
...OF MY ASHIKABI AND ME!

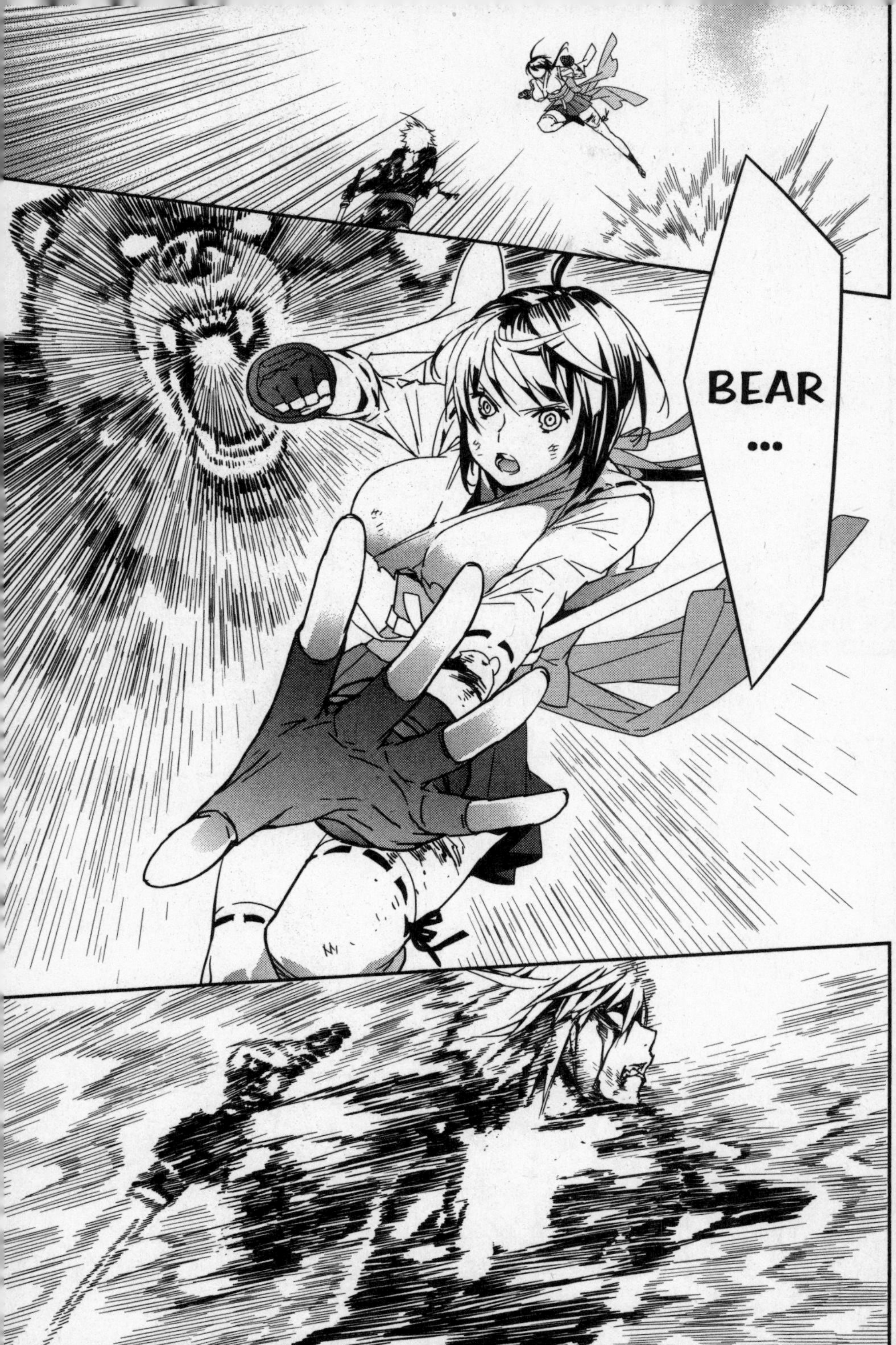
BEAR ...

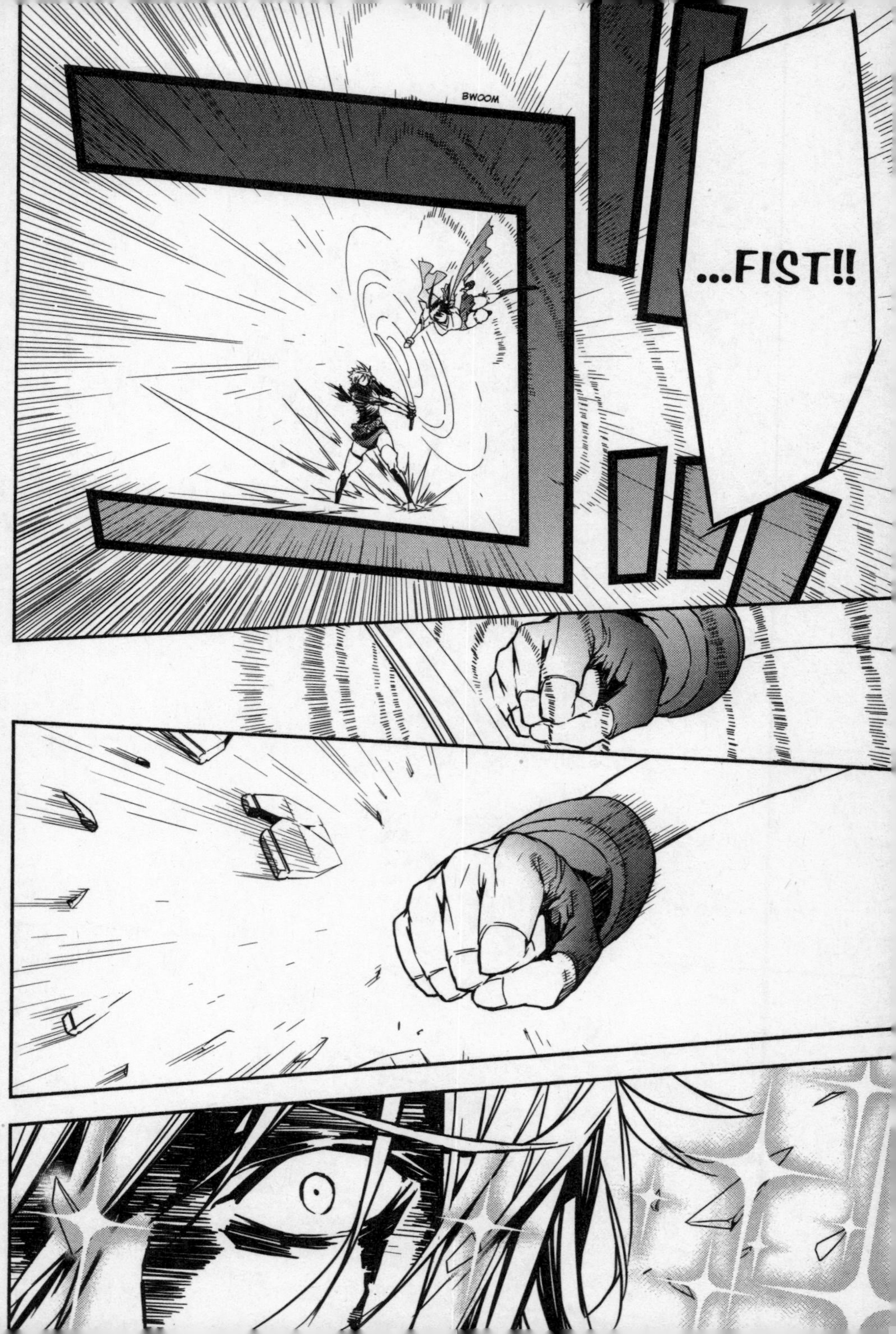

...FIST!!
BWOOM

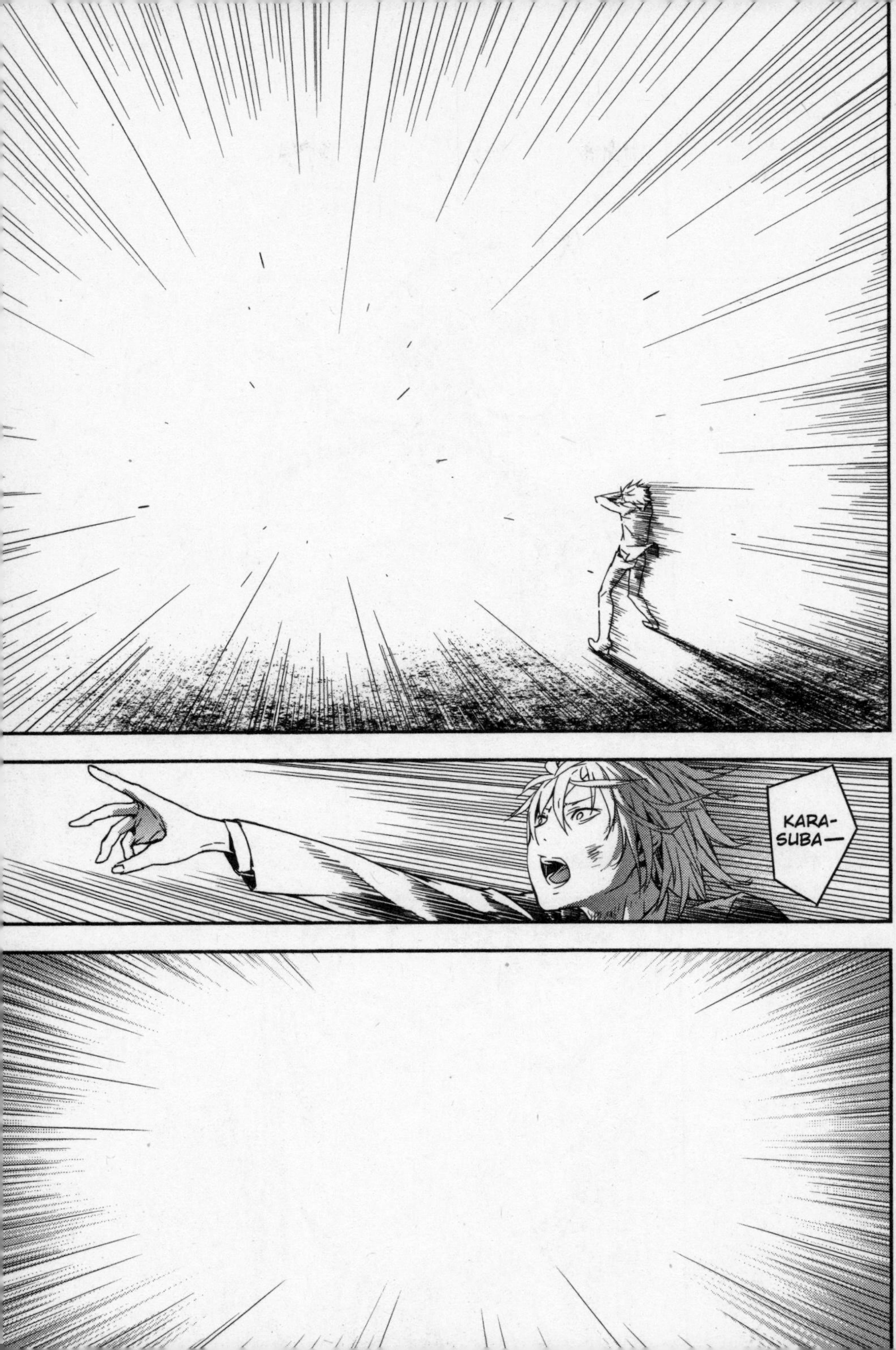
KARA-
SUBA—

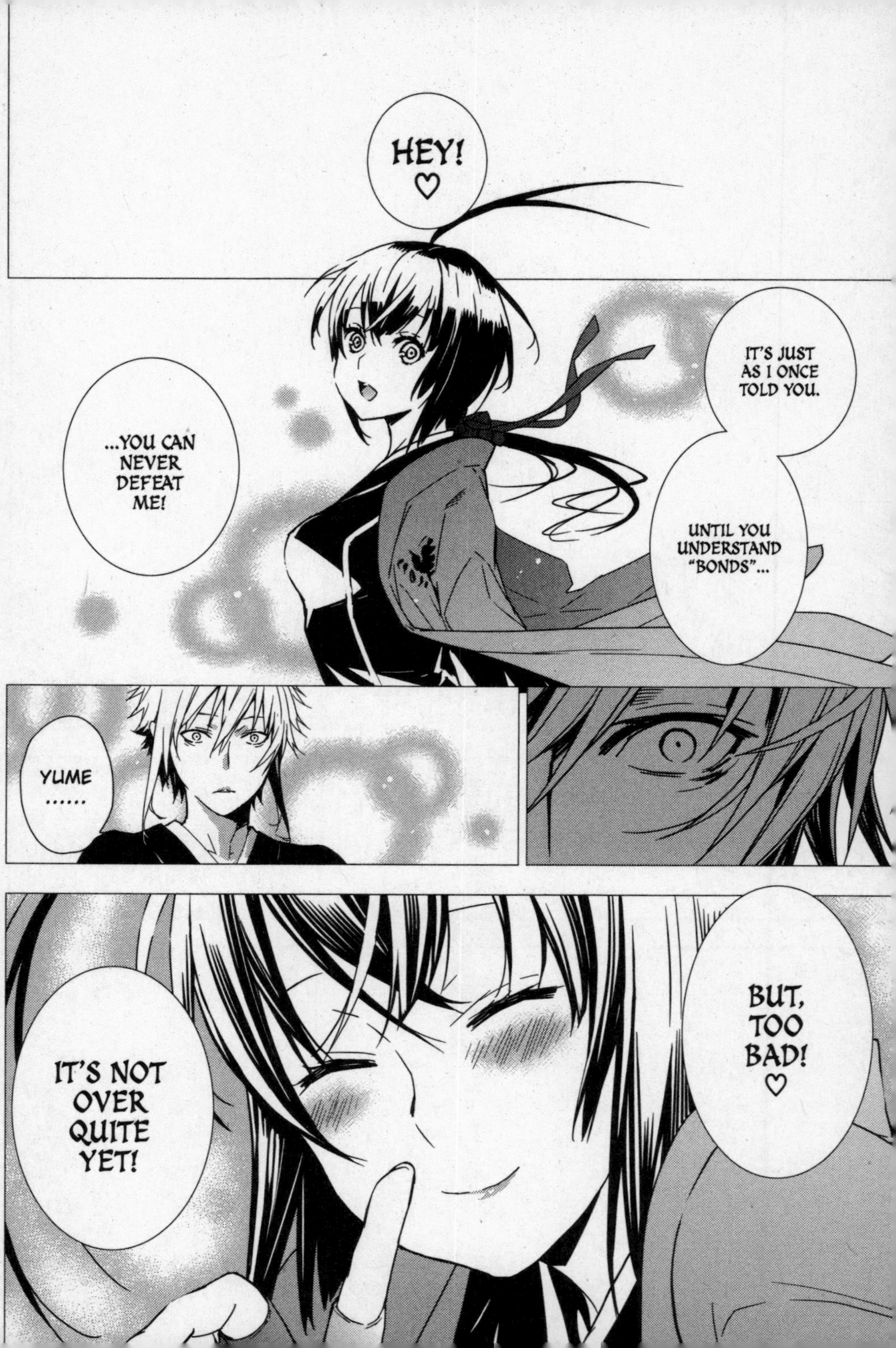
HEY! ♡
IT'S JUST AS I ONCE TOLD YOU.
UNTIL YOU UNDERSTAND "BONDS"...
...YOU CAN NEVER DEFEAT ME!
YUME ......
BUT, TOO BAD! ♡
IT'S NOT OVER QUITE YET!

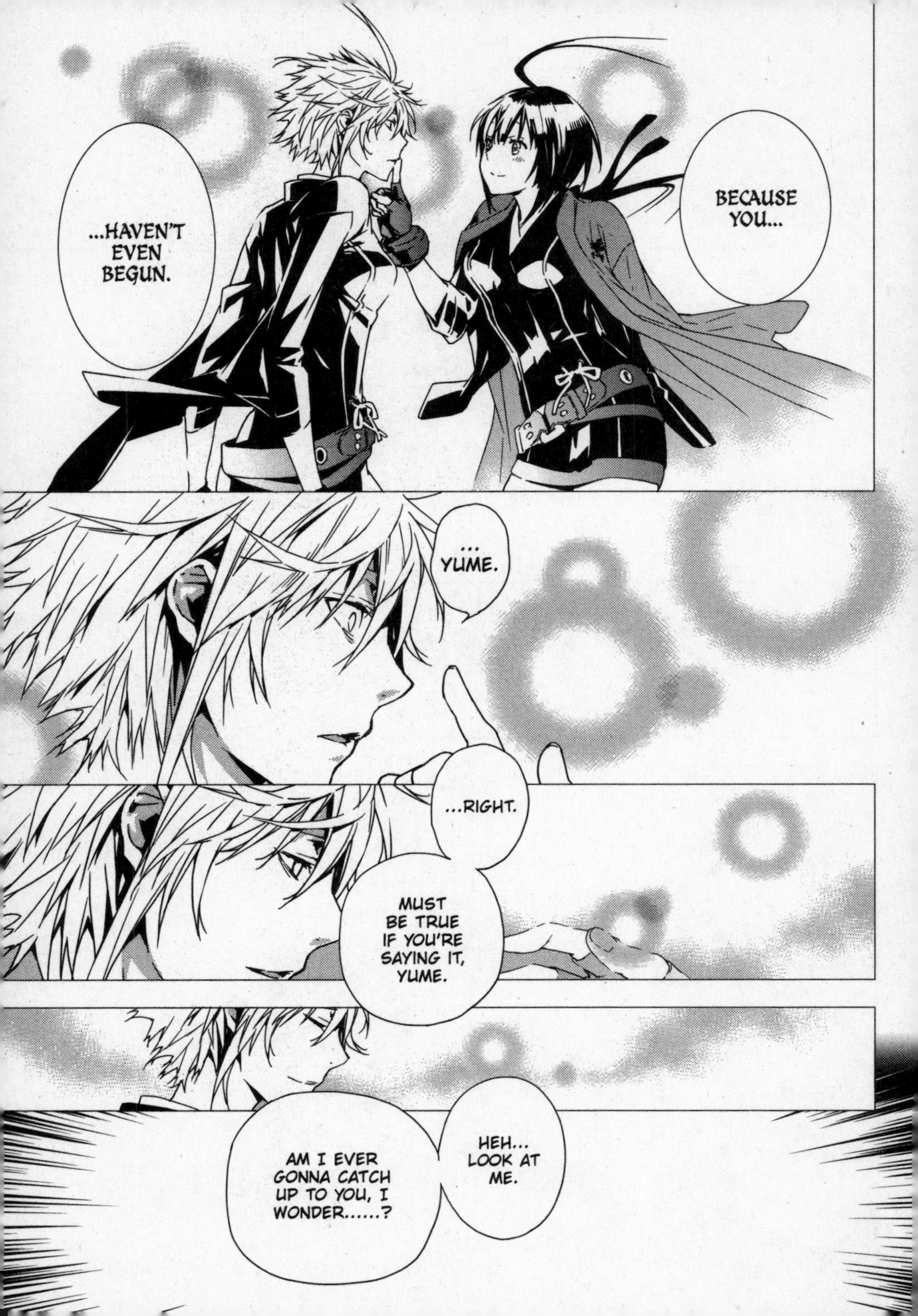
BECAUSE YOU...
...HAVEN'T EVEN BEGUN.
...YUME.
...RIGHT.
MUST BE TRUE IF YOU'RE SAYING IT, YUME.
HEH... LOOK AT ME.
AM I EVER GONNA CATCH UP TO YOU, I WONDER......?

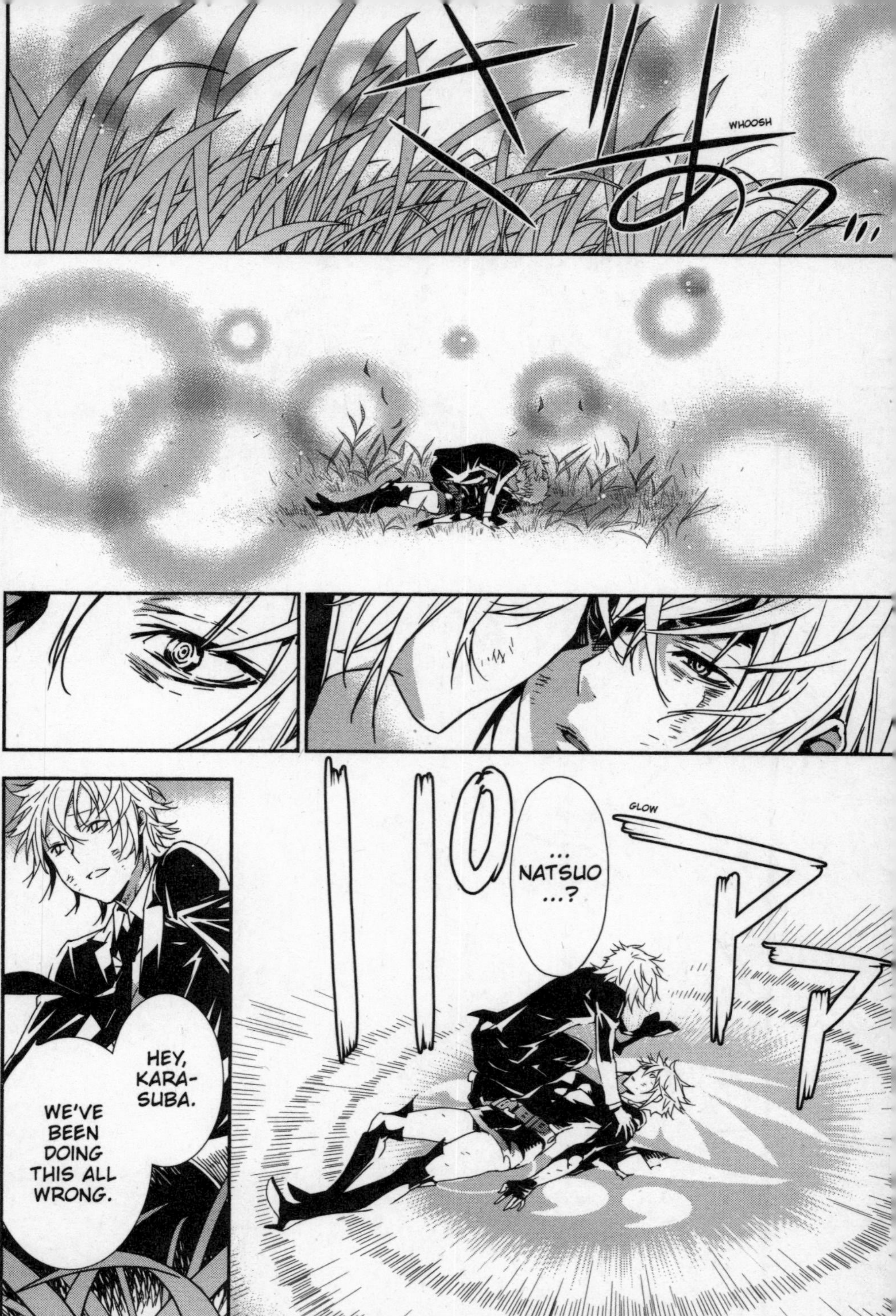
WHOOSH
GLOW
...NATSUO...?
HEY, KARA-SUBA.
WE'VE BEEN DOING THIS ALL WRONG.

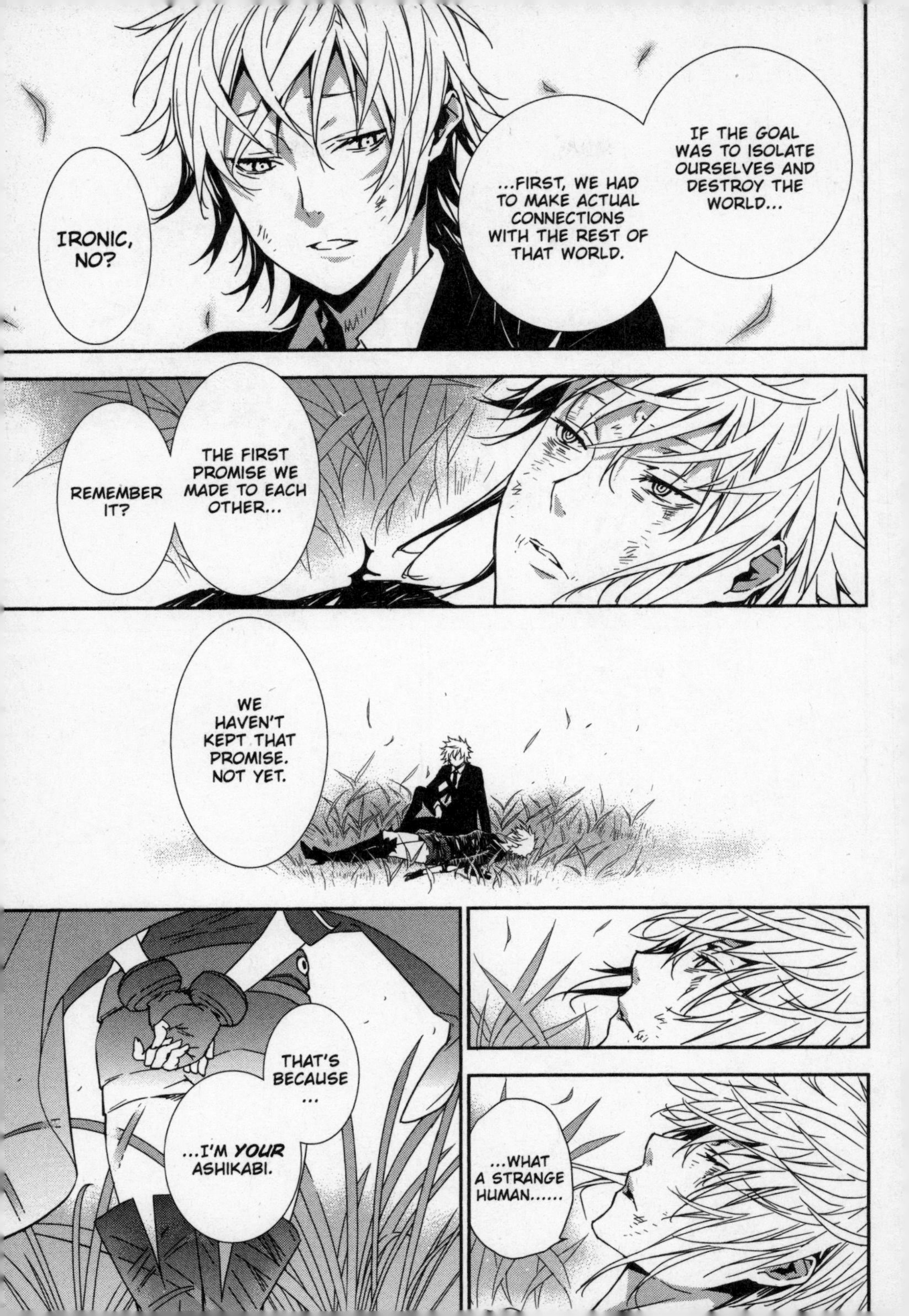
IF THE GOAL WAS TO ISOLATE OURSELVES AND DESTROY THE WORLD...
...FIRST, WE HAD TO MAKE ACTUAL CONNECTIONS WITH THE REST OF THAT WORLD.
IRONIC, NO?
THE FIRST PROMISE WE MADE TO EACH OTHER...
REMEMBER IT?
WE HAVEN'T KEPT THAT PROMISE. NOT YET.
...WHAT A STRANGE HUMAN......
THAT'S BECAUSE ...
...I'M *YOUR* ASHIKABI.

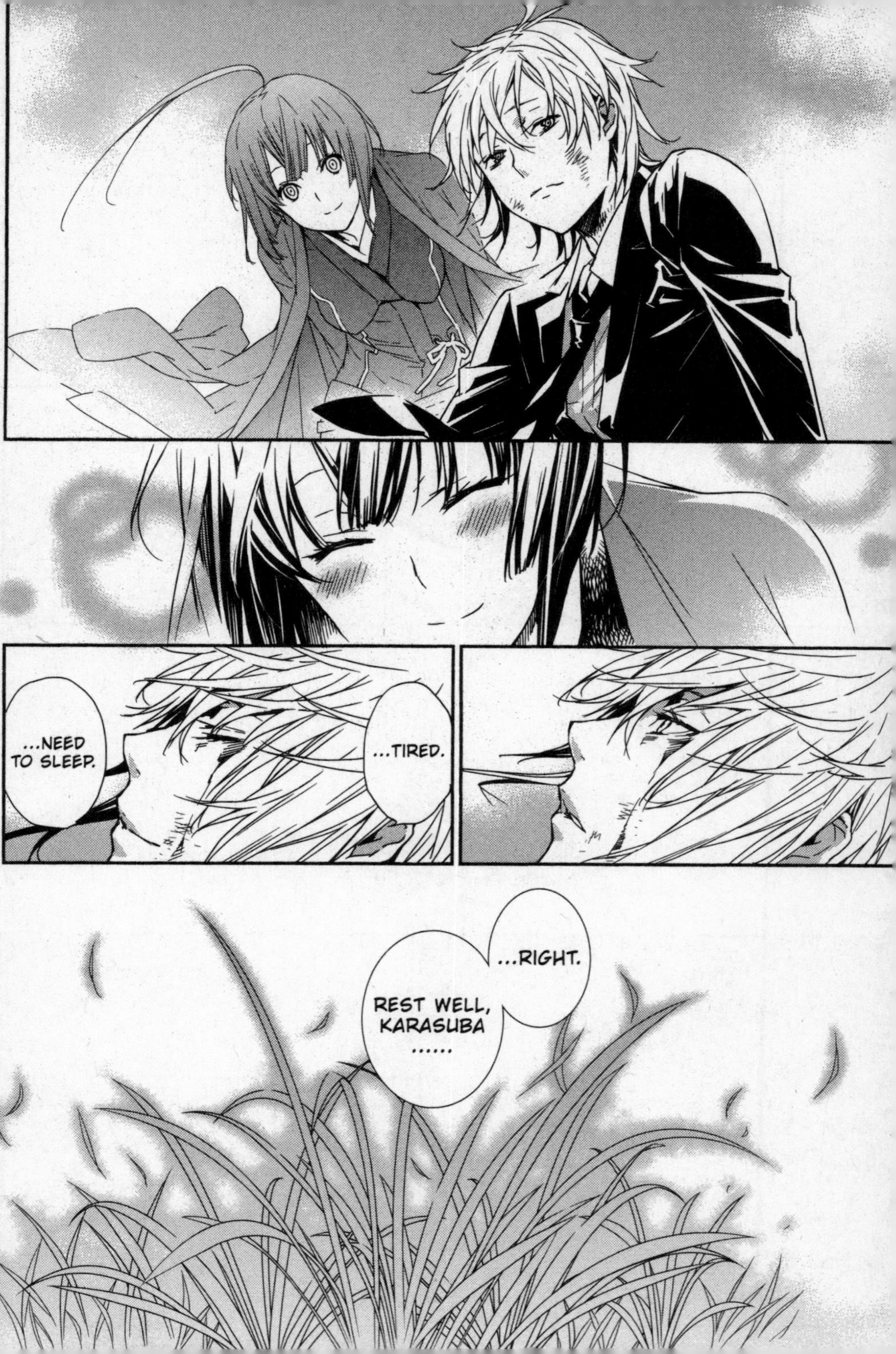
...TIRED.
...NEED TO SLEEP.
...RIGHT.
REST WELL, KARASUBA ......

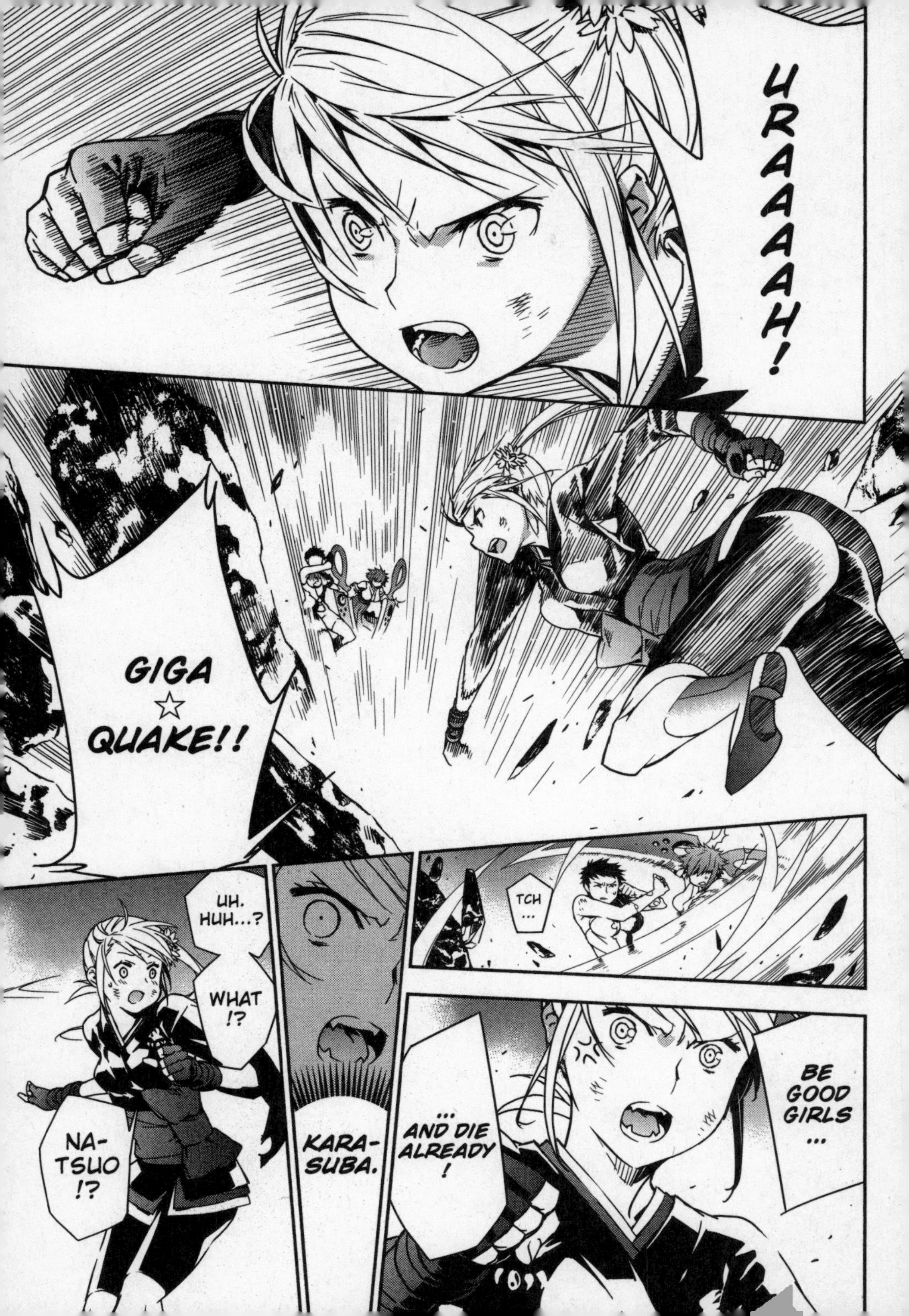
URAAAAAH!
GIGA ☆ QUAKE!!
TCH ...
BE GOOD GIRLS ...
... AND DIE ALREADY !
KARA-SUBA.
UH. HUH...?
WHAT !?
NA-TSUO !?

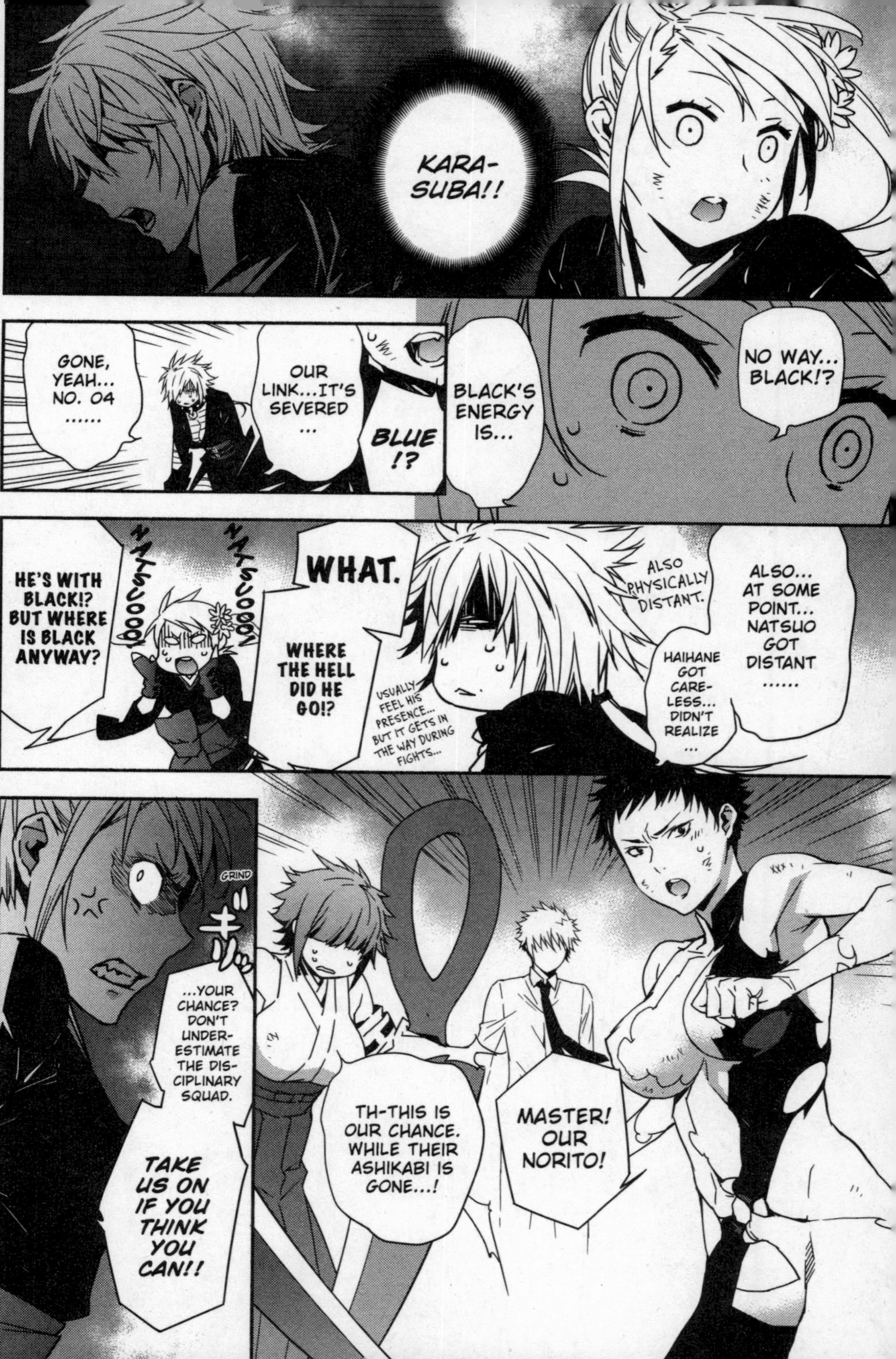
KARA-SUBA!!
NO WAY... BLACK!?
BLACK'S ENERGY IS...
BLUE!?
OUR LINK...IT'S SEVERED...
GONE, YEAH... NO. 04 ......
ALSO... AT SOME POINT... NATSUO GOT DISTANT ......
ALSO PHYSICALLY DISTANT.
HAIHANE GOT CARE-LESS... DIDN'T REALIZE ...
USUALLY FEEL HIS PRESENCE... BUT IT GETS IN THE WAY DURING FIGHTS...
WHAT.
WHERE THE HELL DID HE GO!?
NATSUOOO!
NATSUOOO!
HE'S WITH BLACK!? BUT WHERE IS BLACK ANYWAY?
MASTER! OUR NORITO!
TH-THIS IS OUR CHANCE. WHILE THEIR ASHIKABI IS GONE...!
GRIND
...YOUR CHANCE? DON'T UNDER-ESTIMATE THE DIS-CIPLINARY SQUAD.
TAKE US ON IF YOU THINK YOU CAN!!

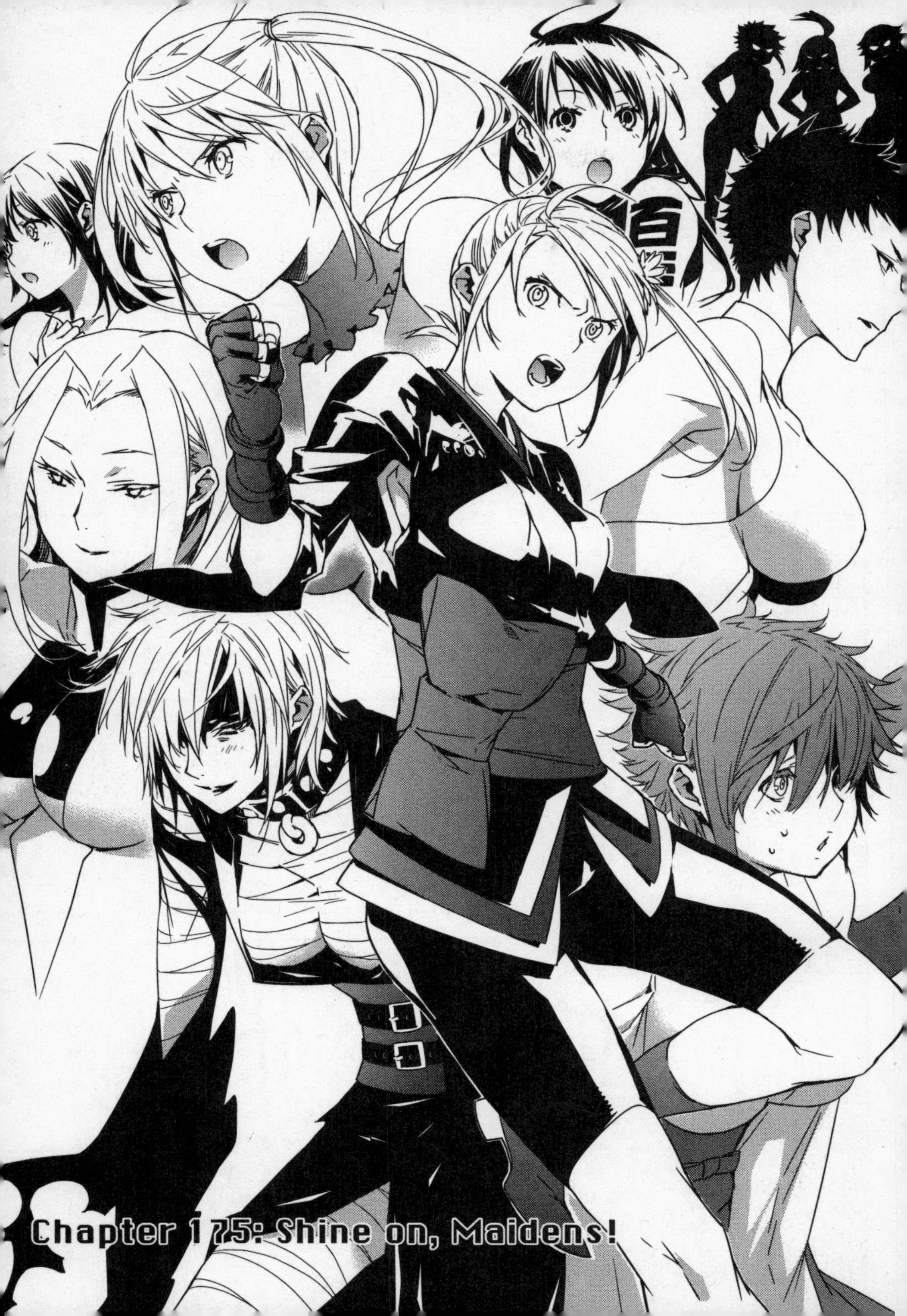

Chapter 175: Shine on, Maidens!

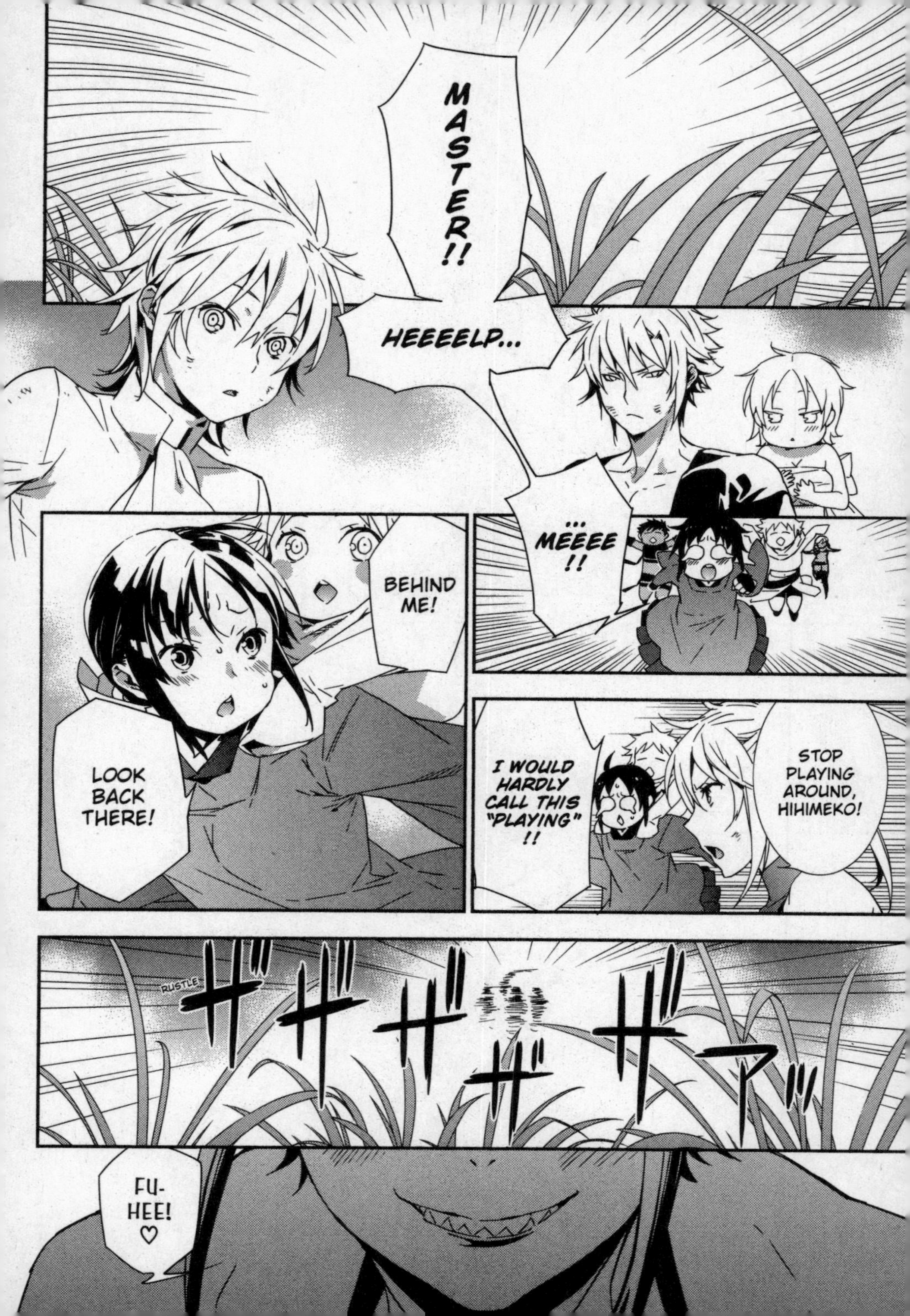
MASTER!!
HEEEELP...
... MËEEE !!
STOP PLAYING AROUND, HIHIMEKO!
I WOULD HARDLY CALL THIS "PLAYING" !!
BEHIND ME!
LOOK BACK THERE!
RUSTLE
ザザザザザァッ
FU-HEE! ♡

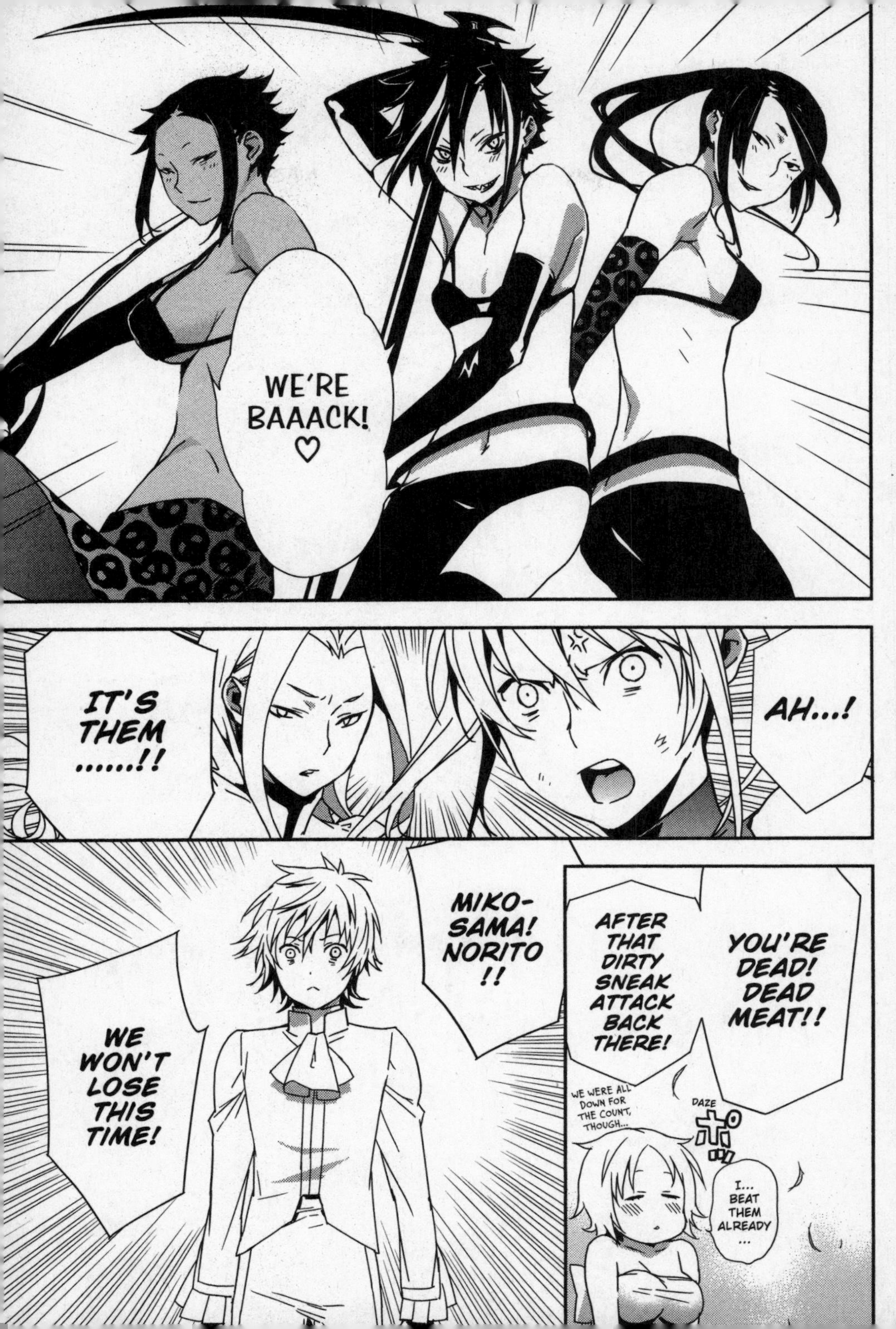
WE'RE BAAACK! ♡
AH...!
IT'S THEM ......!!
YOU'RE DEAD! DEAD MEAT!!
AFTER THAT DIRTY SNEAK ATTACK BACK THERE!
DAZE
WE WERE ALL DOWN FOR THE COUNT, THOUGH...
I... BEAT THEM ALREADY ...
MIKO-SAMA! NORITO!!
WE WON'T LOSE THIS TIME!

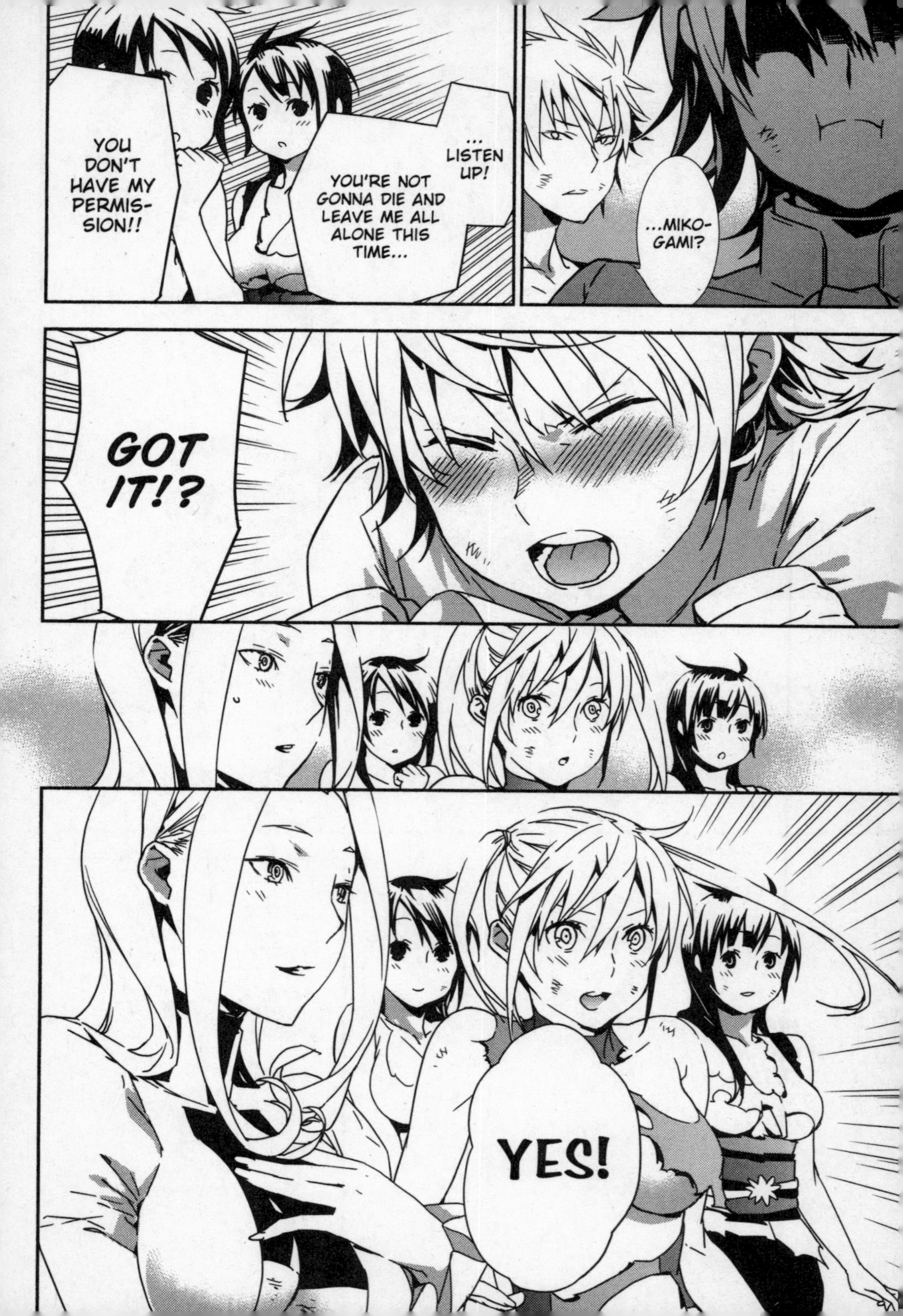
...MIKO-GAMI?
...LISTEN UP!
YOU'RE NOT GONNA DIE AND LEAVE ME ALL ALONE THIS TIME...
YOU DON'T HAVE MY PERMIS-SION!!
GOT IT!?
YES!

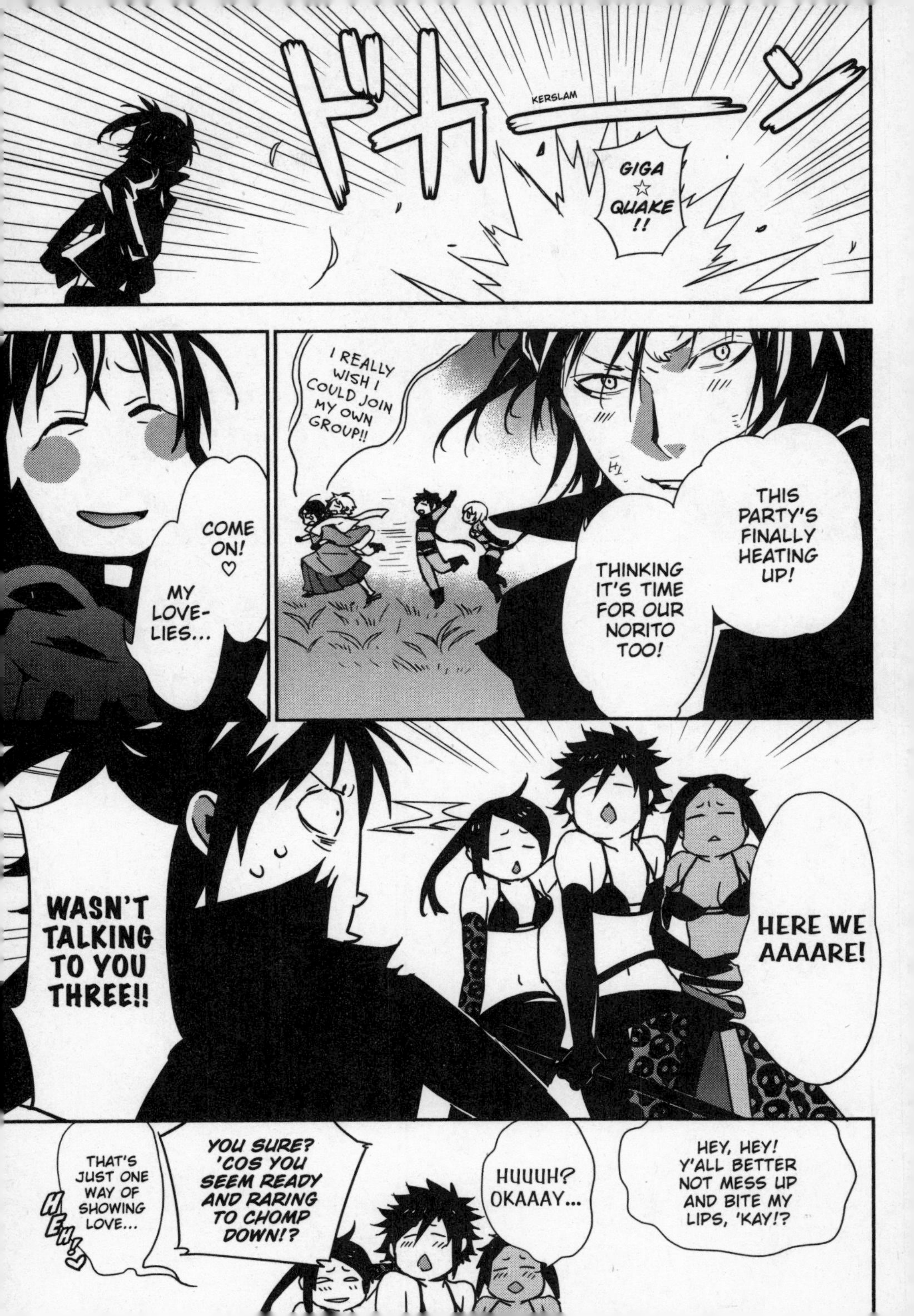
ドカーン
KERSLAM
GIGA ☆ QUAKE!!
THIS PARTY'S FINALLY HEATING UP!
THINKING IT'S TIME FOR OUR NORITO TOO!
I REALLY WISH I COULD JOIN MY OWN GROUP!!
COME ON! ♡
MY LOVE-LIES...
HERE WE AAAARE!
WASN'T TALKING TO YOU THREE!!
HEY, HEY! Y'ALL BETTER NOT MESS UP AND BITE MY LIPS, 'KAY!?
HUUUH? OKAAAY...
YOU SURE? 'COS YOU SEEM READY AND RARING TO CHOMP DOWN!?
THAT'S JUST ONE WAY OF SHOWING LOVE...
HEH!♡

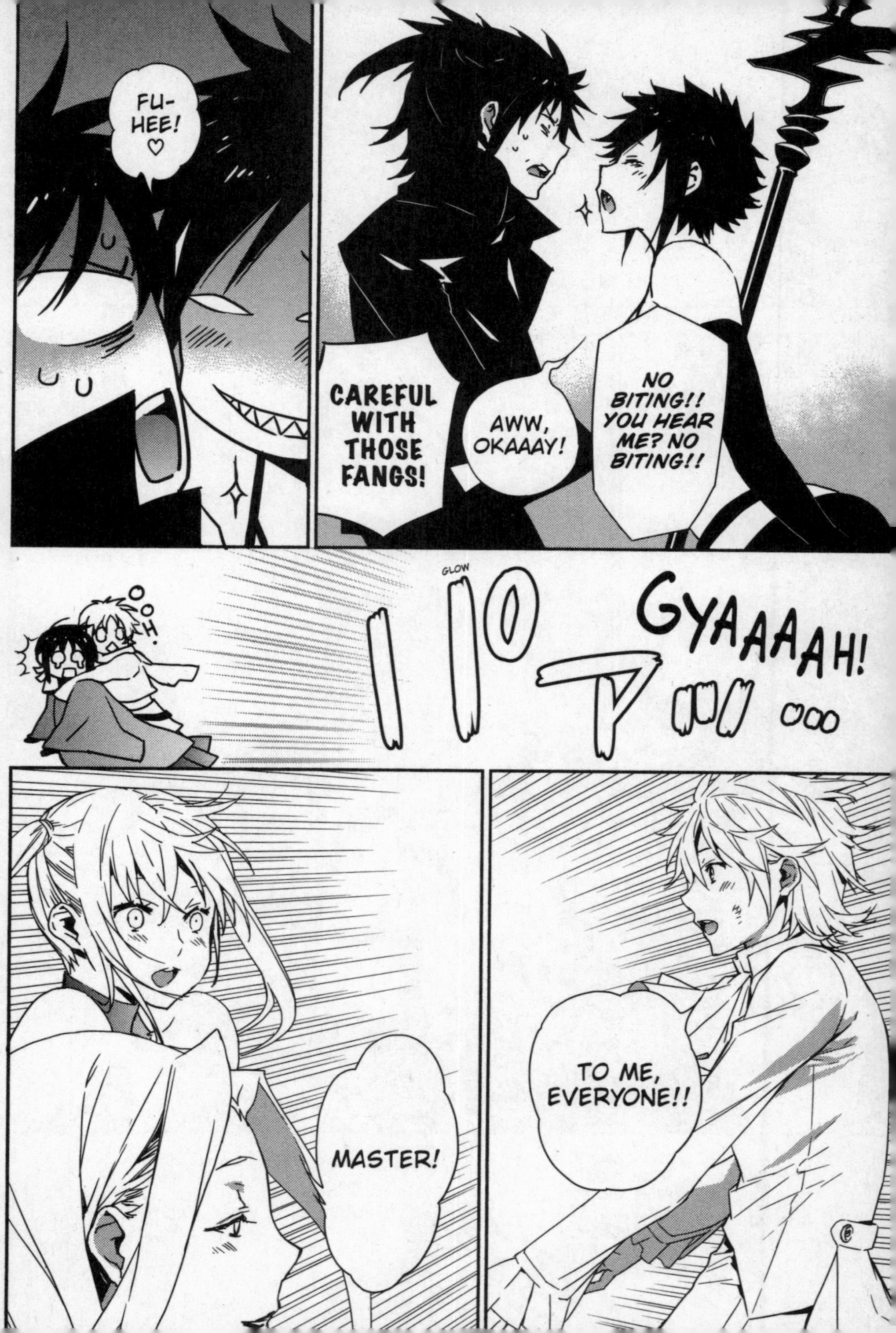
NO BITING!! YOU HEAR ME? NO BITING!!
AWW, OKAAAY!
CAREFUL WITH THOSE FANGS!
FU-HEE! ♡
GYAAAAH!
GLOW
OOH!
TO ME, EVERYONE!!
MASTER!

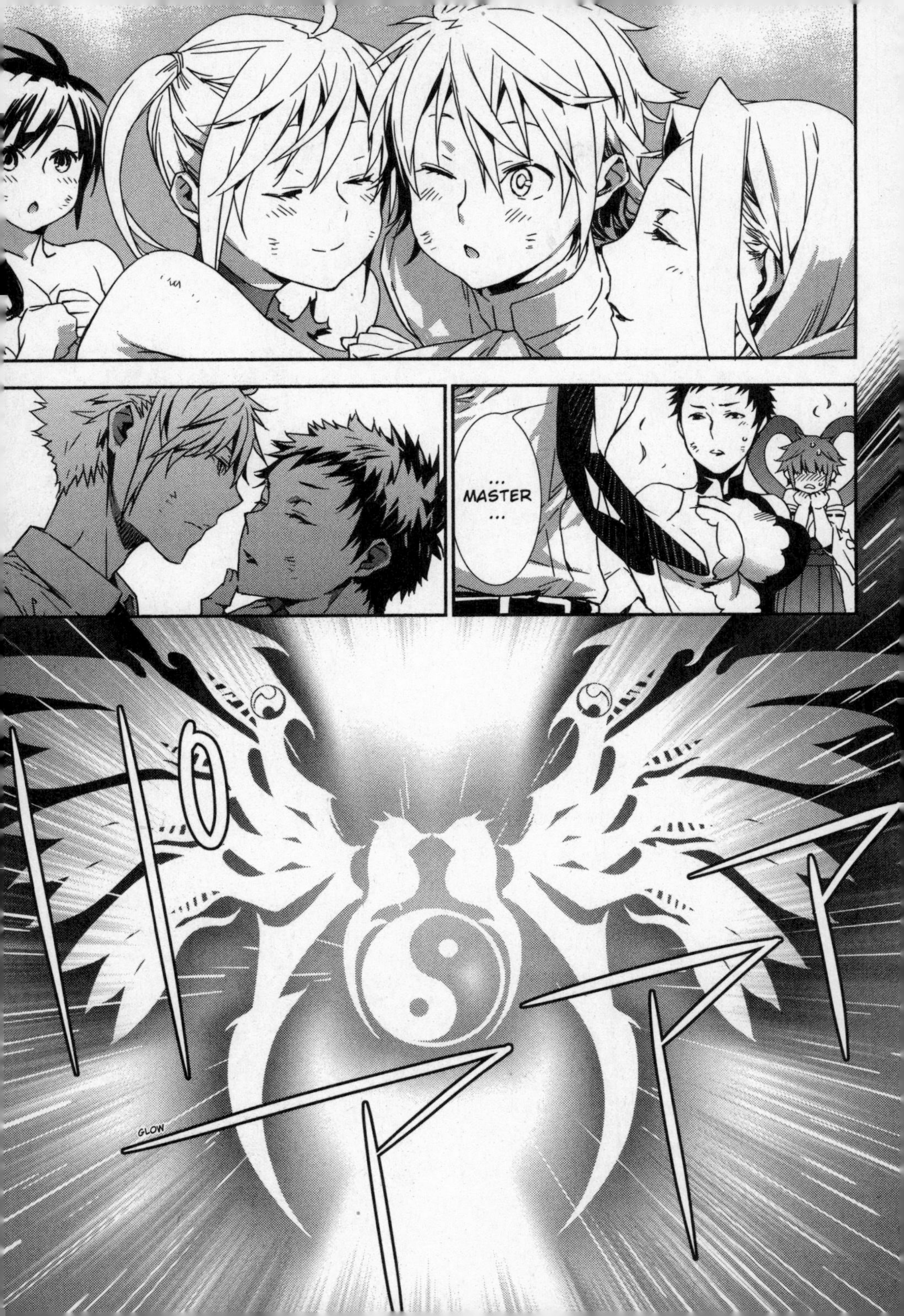
... MASTER ...
GLOW

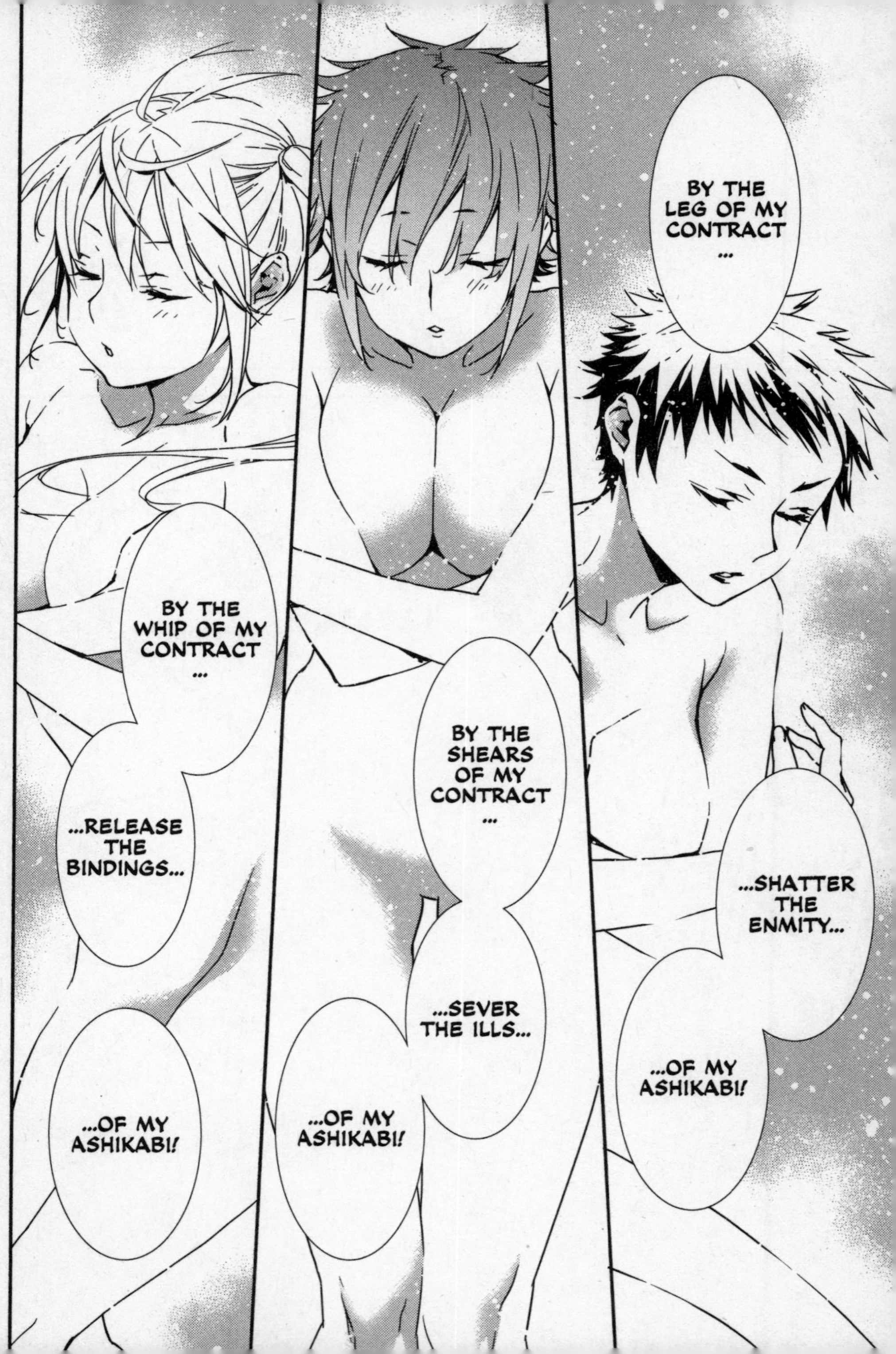
BY THE LEG OF MY CONTRACT ...
...SHATTER THE ENMITY...
...OF MY ASHIKABI!
BY THE SHEARS OF MY CONTRACT ...
...SEVER THE ILLS...
...OF MY ASHIKABI!
BY THE WHIP OF MY CONTRACT ...
...RELEASE THE BINDINGS...
...OF MY ASHIKABI!

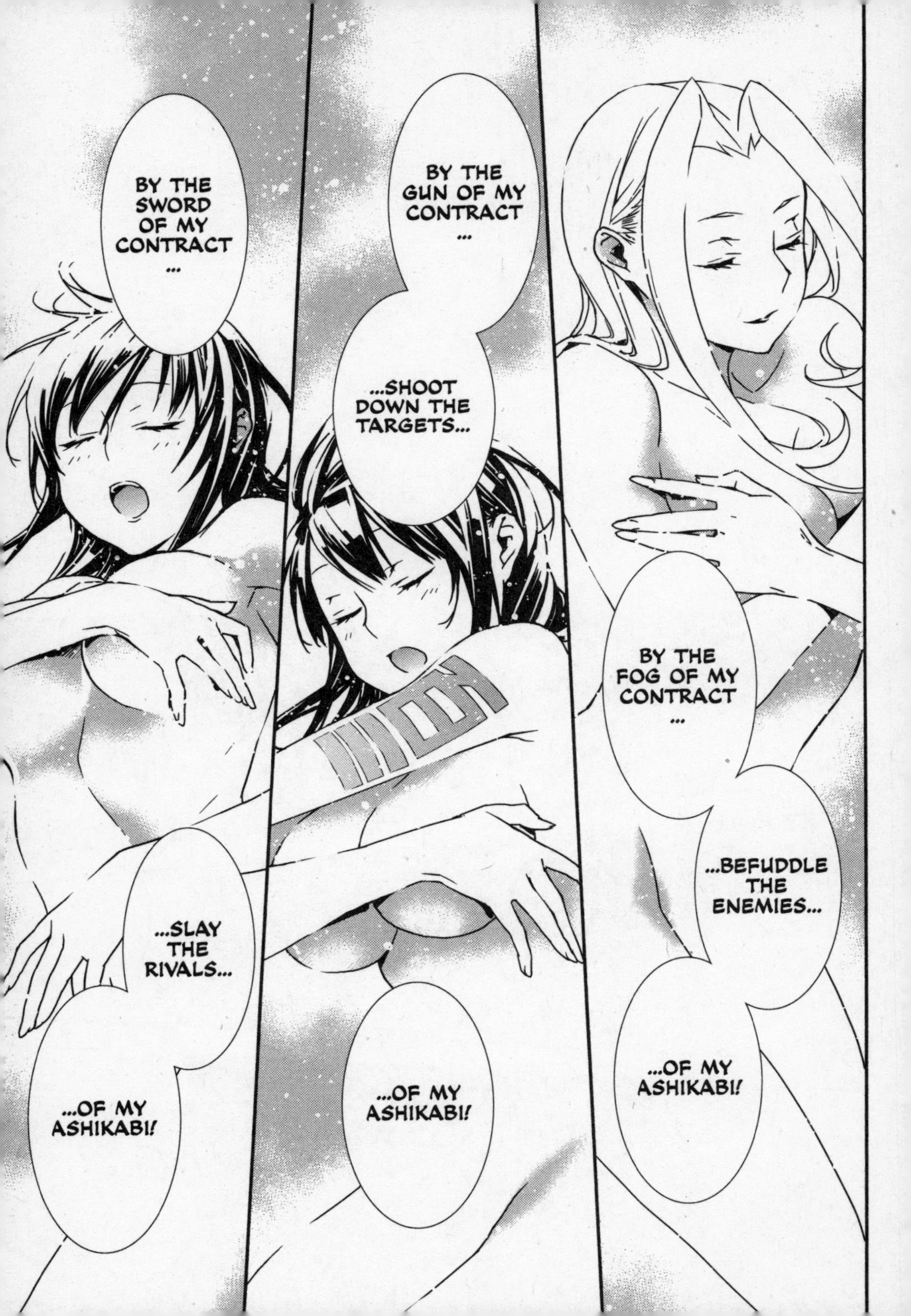
BY THE FOG OF MY CONTRACT ...
...BEFUDDLE THE ENEMIES...
...OF MY ASHIKABI!
BY THE GUN OF MY CONTRACT ...
...SHOOT DOWN THE TARGETS...
...OF MY ASHIKABI!
BY THE SWORD OF MY CONTRACT ...
...SLAY THE RIVALS...
...OF MY ASHIKABI!

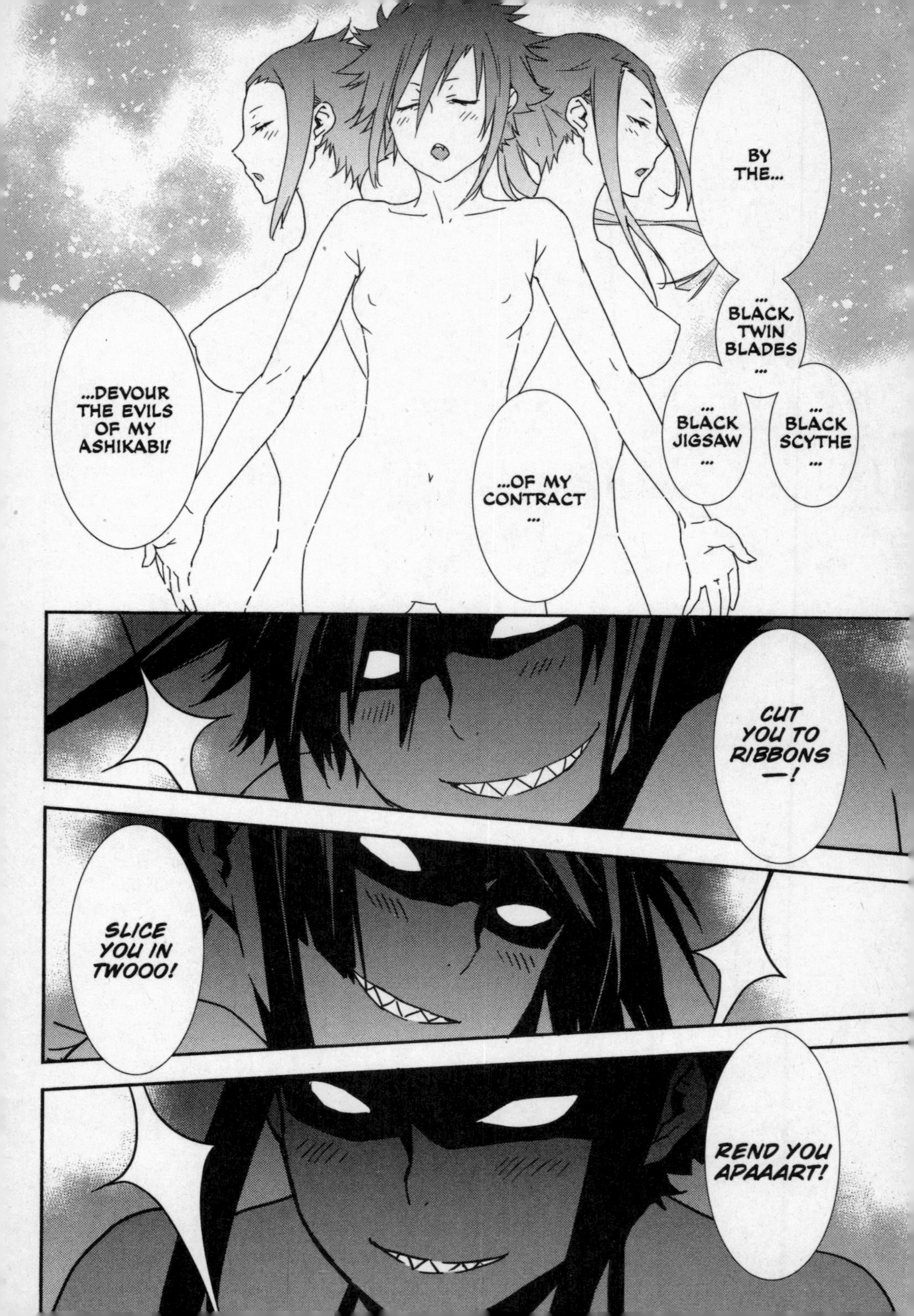
BY THE...
...BLACK, TWIN BLADES...
...BLACK SCYTHE...
...BLACK JIGSAW...
...OF MY CONTRACT...
...DEVOUR THE EVILS OF MY ASHIKABI!
CUT YOU TO RIBBONS—!
SLICE YOU IN TWOOO!
REND YOU APAAART!

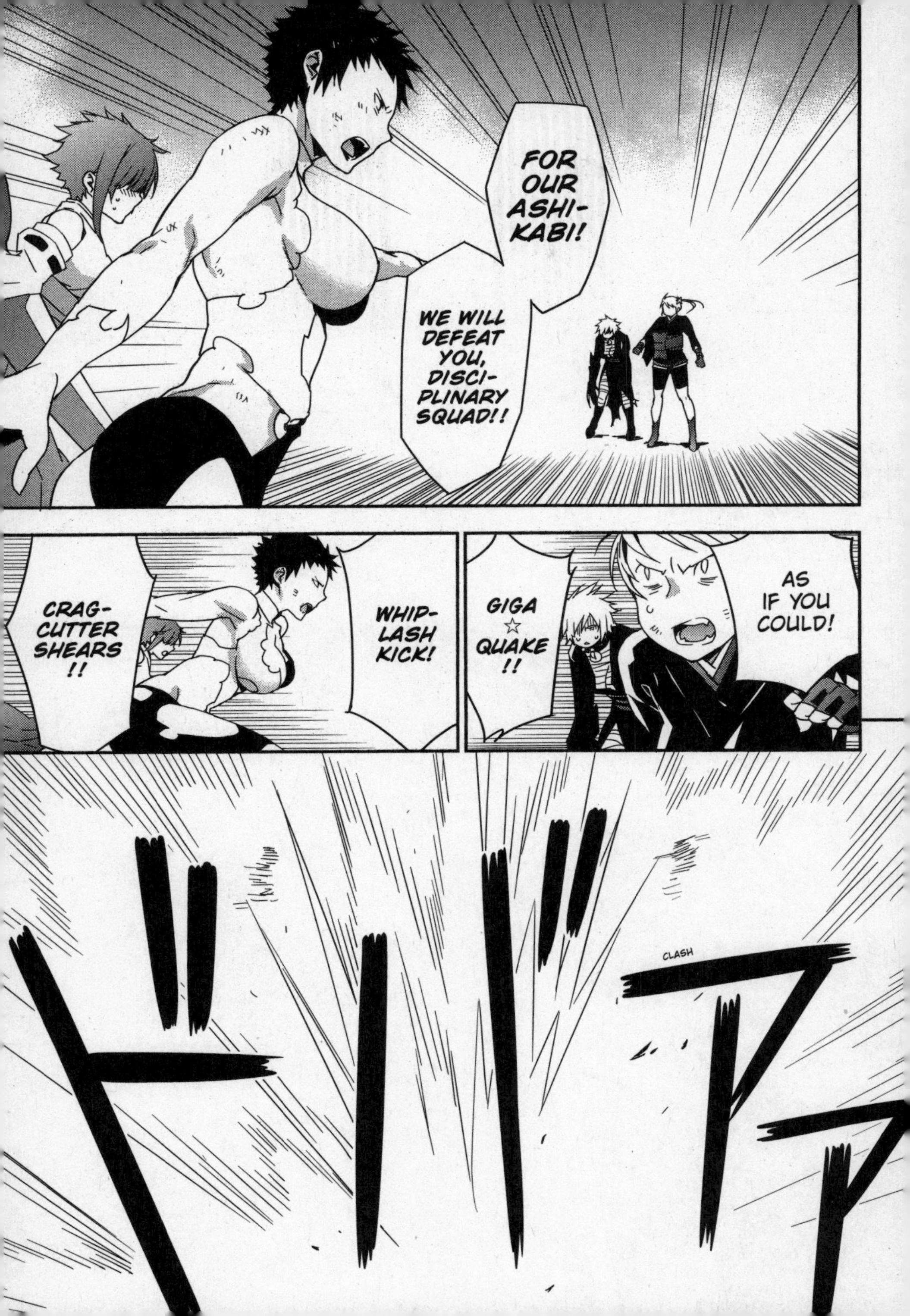
FOR OUR ASHI-KABI!
WE WILL DEFEAT YOU, DISCI-PLINARY SQUAD!!
AS IF YOU COULD!
GIGA ☆ QUAKE !!
WHIP-LASH KICK!
CRAG-CUTTER SHEARS !!
CLASH

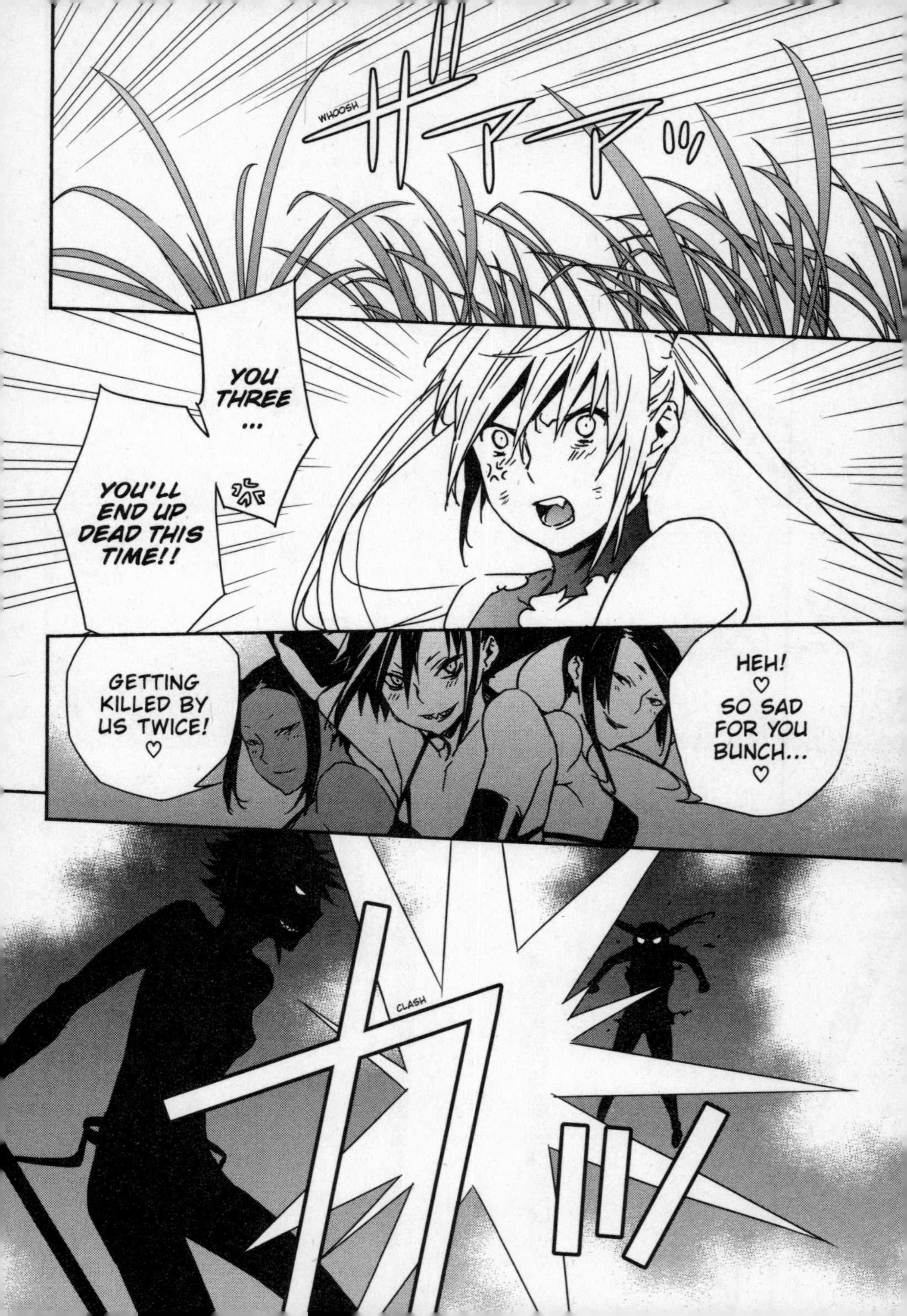
WHOOSH
ザアアッ
YOU THREE ...
YOU'LL END UP DEAD THIS TIME!!
HEH! ♡ SO SAD FOR YOU BUNCH... ♡
GETTING KILLED BY US TWICE! ♡
CLASH

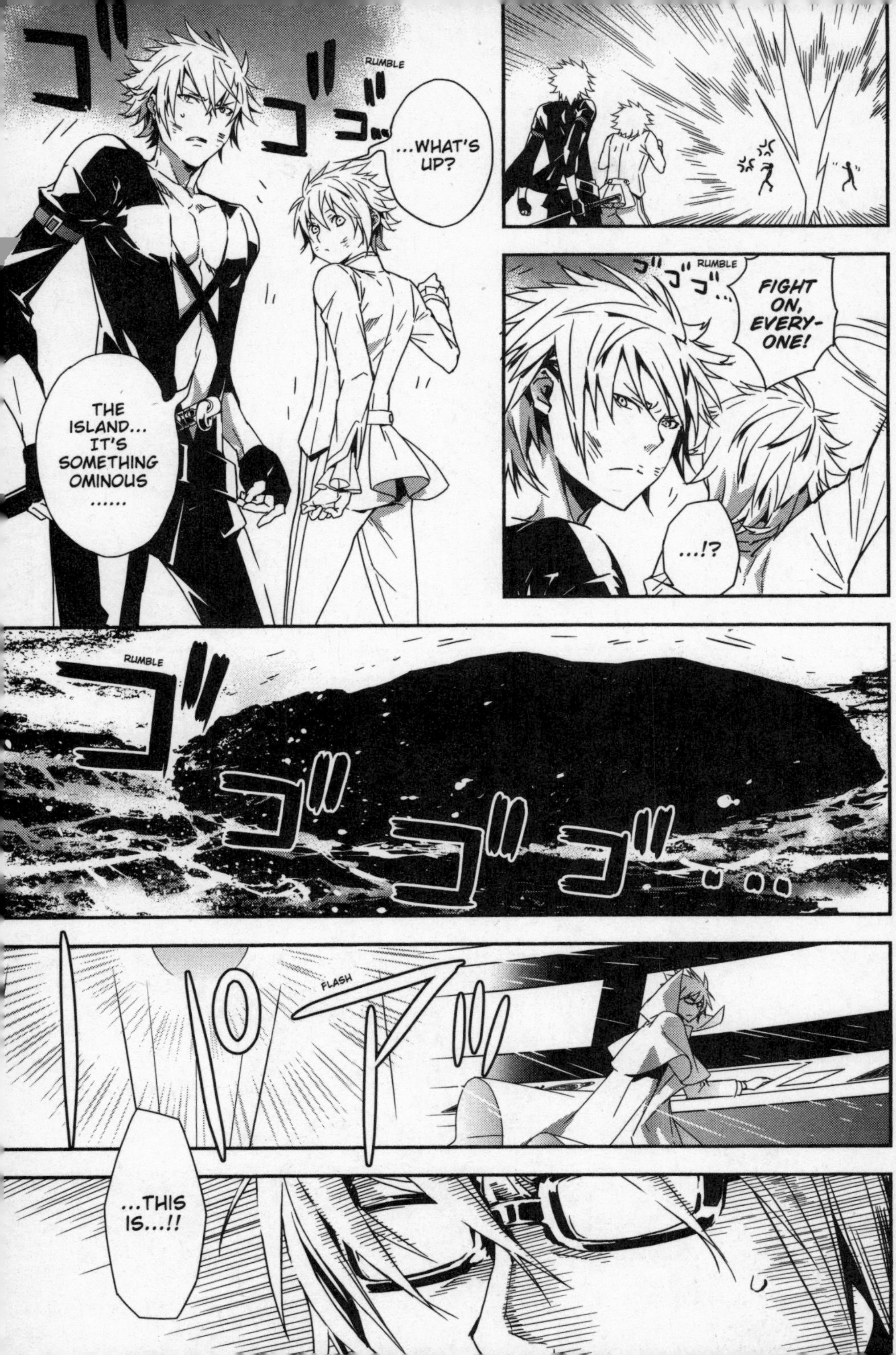
RUMBLE
FIGHT ON, EVERY-ONE!
...!?
RUMBLE
...WHAT'S UP?
THE ISLAND... IT'S SOMETHING OMINOUS ......
RUMBLE
FLASH
...THIS IS...!!

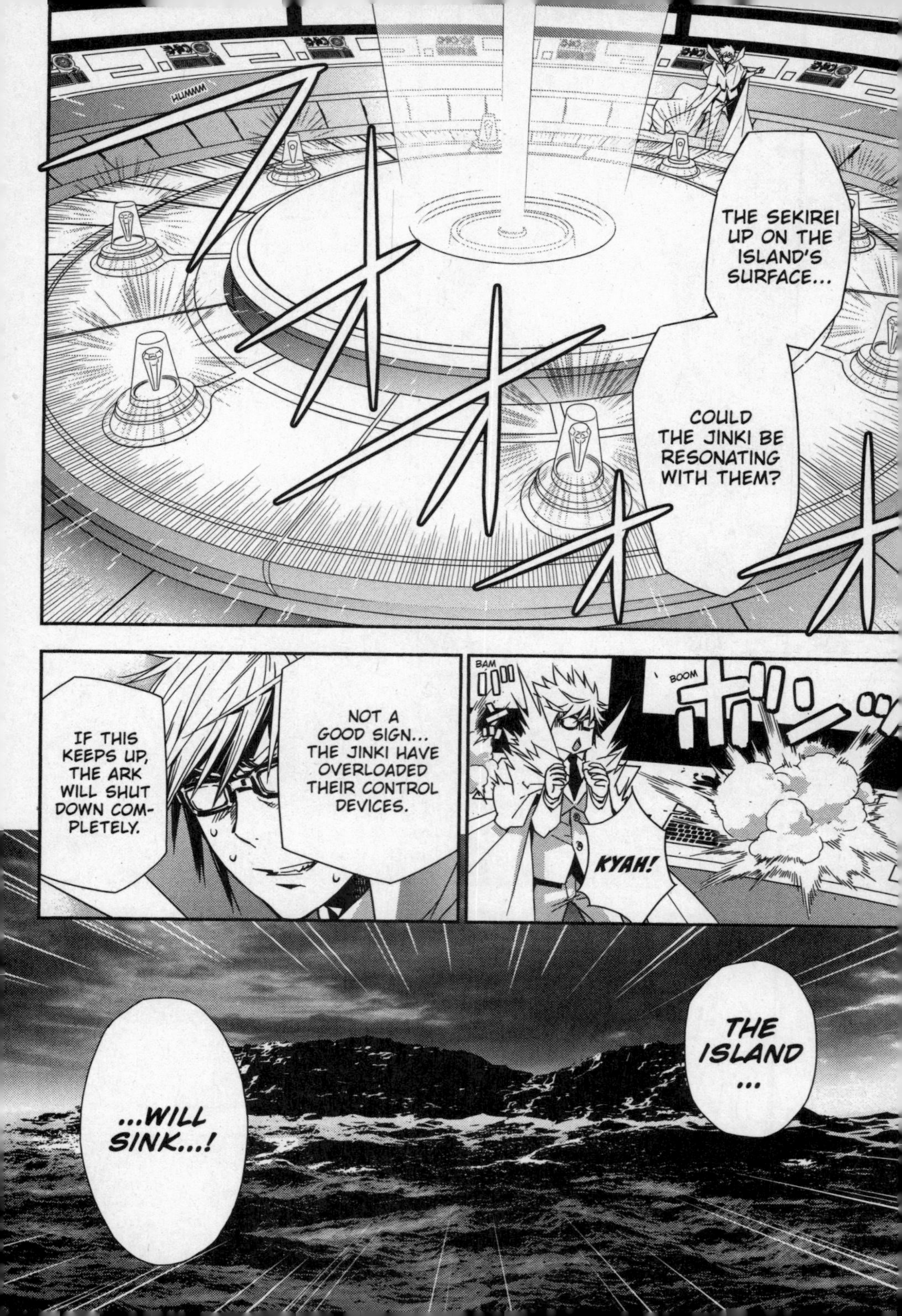
THE SEKIREI UP ON THE ISLAND'S SURFACE...
COULD THE JINKI BE RESONATING WITH THEM?
BAM
BOOM
KYAH!
NOT A GOOD SIGN... THE JINKI HAVE OVERLOADED THEIR CONTROL DEVICES.
IF THIS KEEPS UP, THE ARK WILL SHUT DOWN COM-PLETELY.
THE ISLAND...
...WILL SINK...!

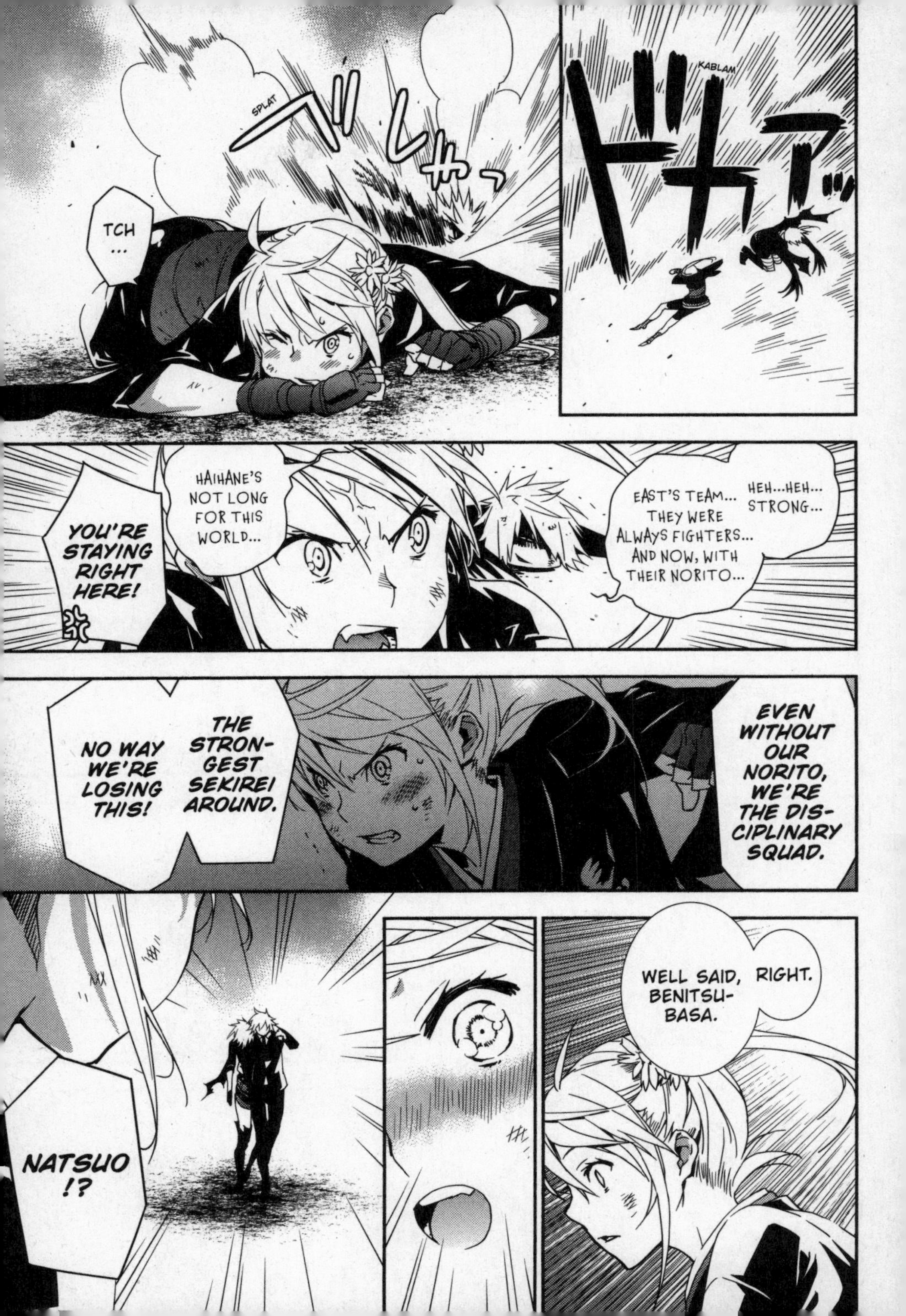
KABLAM
SPLAT
TCH...
HEH...HEH... STRONG...
EAST'S TEAM... THEY WERE ALWAYS FIGHTERS... AND NOW, WITH THEIR NORITO...
HAIHANE'S NOT LONG FOR THIS WORLD...
YOU'RE STAYING RIGHT HERE!
EVEN WITHOUT OUR NORITO, WE'RE THE DISCIPLINARY SQUAD.
THE STRONGEST SEKIREI AROUND.
NO WAY WE'RE LOSING THIS!
RIGHT.
WELL SAID, BENITSUBASA.
NATSUO !?

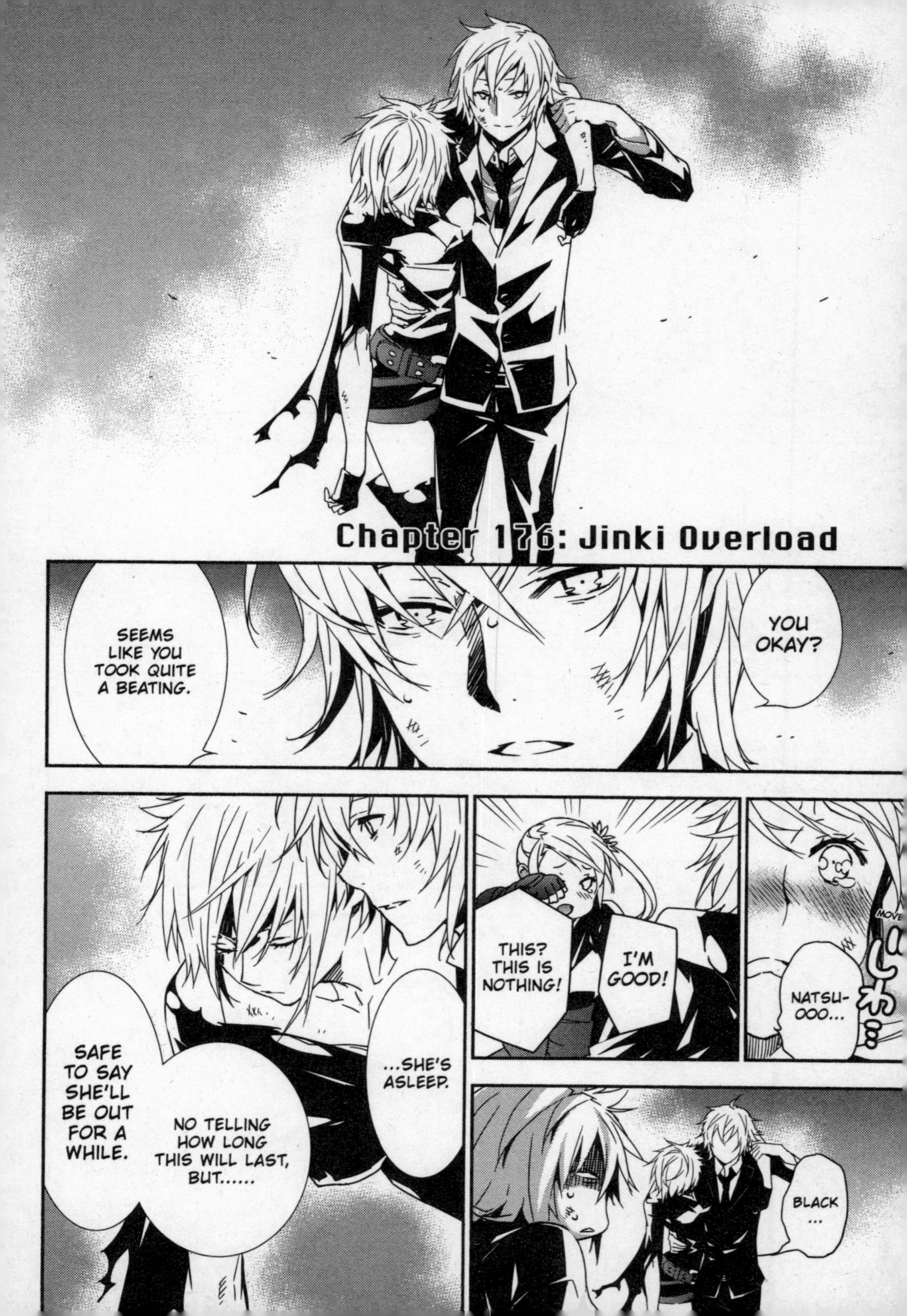
Chapter 176: Jinki Overload
YOU OKAY?
SEEMS LIKE YOU TOOK QUITE A BEATING.
MOVE
NATSU-OOO...
I'M GOOD!
THIS? THIS IS NOTHING!
...SHE'S ASLEEP.
NO TELLING HOW LONG THIS WILL LAST, BUT......
SAFE TO SAY SHE'LL BE OUT FOR A WHILE.
BLACK...

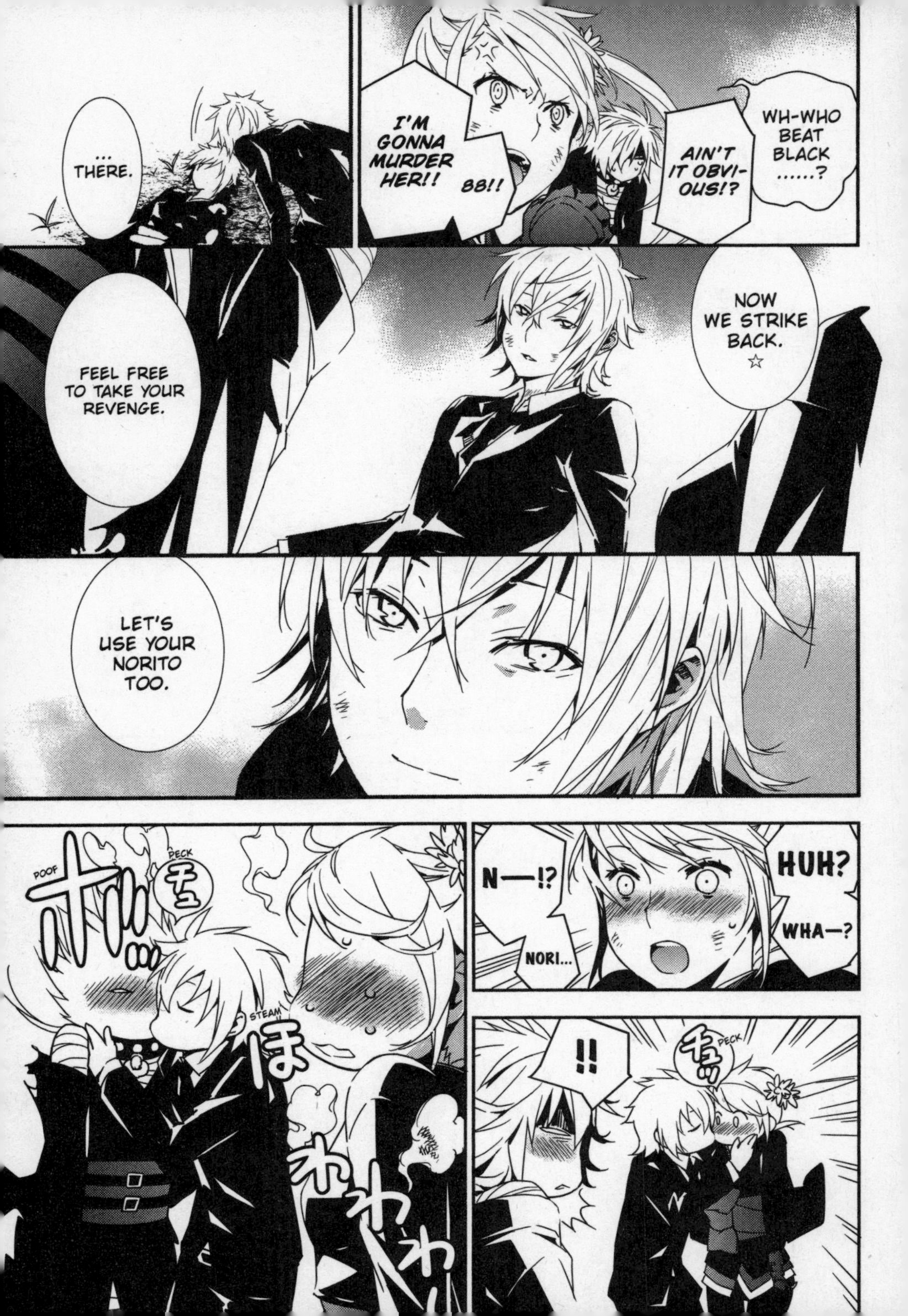
WH-WHO BEAT BLACK ......?
AIN'T IT OBVI-OUS!?
I'M GONNA MURDER HER!!
88!!
... THERE.
NOW WE STRIKE BACK. ☆
FEEL FREE TO TAKE YOUR REVENGE.
LET'S USE YOUR NORITO TOO.
HUH?
WHA—?
N—!?
NORI...
!!
チュ
PECK
PECK
チュ
POOF
STEAM

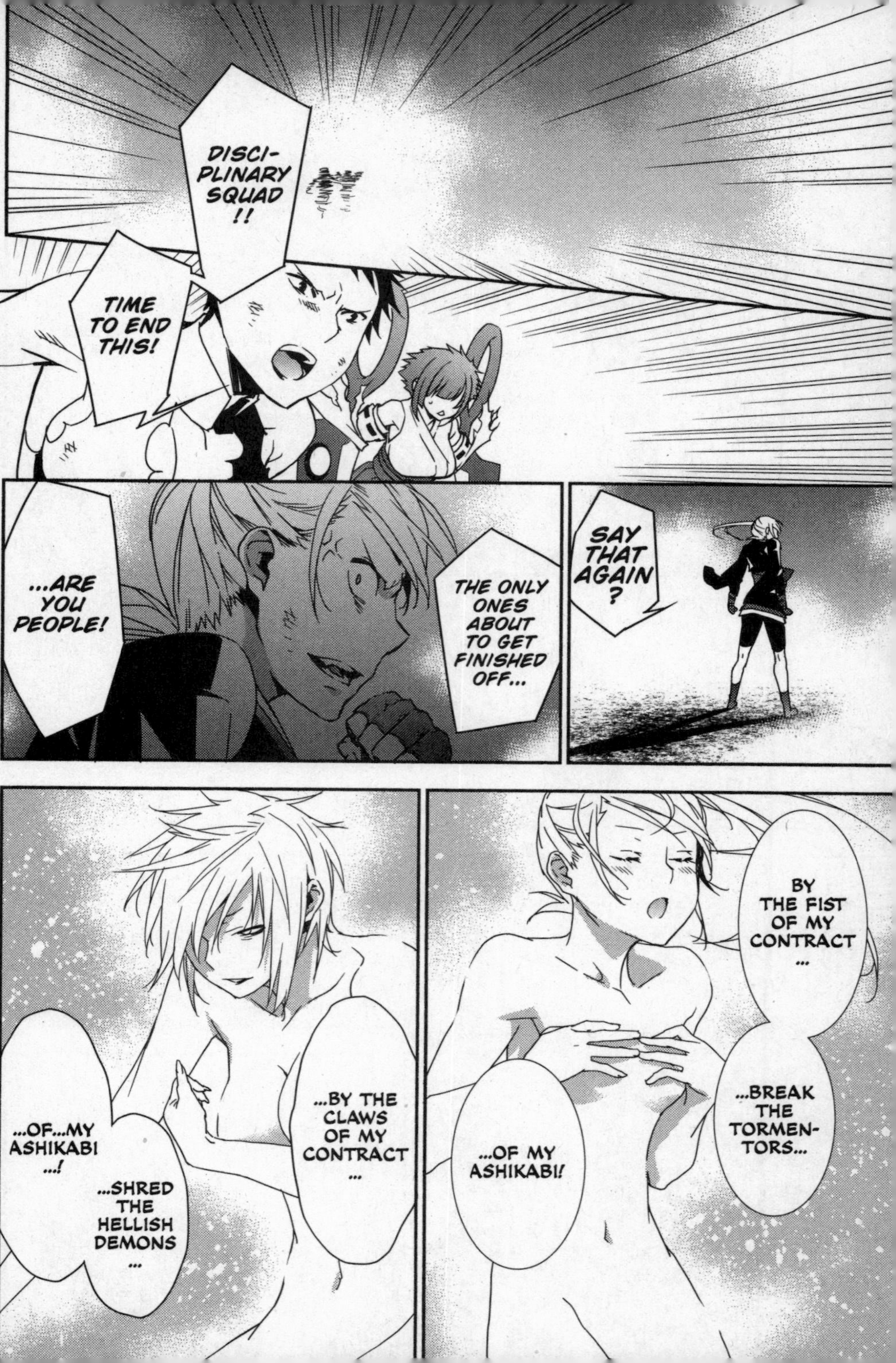
DISCI-PLINARY SQUAD !!
TIME TO END THIS!
SAY THAT AGAIN ?
THE ONLY ONES ABOUT TO GET FINISHED OFF...
...ARE YOU PEOPLE!
BY THE FIST OF MY CONTRACT ...
...BREAK THE TORMEN-TORS...
...OF MY ASHIKABI!
...BY THE CLAWS OF MY CONTRACT ...
...SHRED THE HELLISH DEMONS ...
...OF...MY ASHIKABI ...!

KAPOW

POINT
☆
EXPLO-
SION!!

FLASH
REND
CLAW
...!

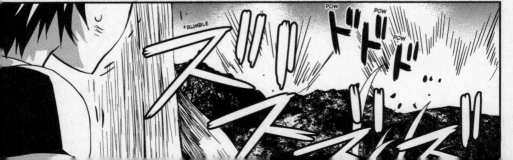

*RUMBLE

POW

POW

POW

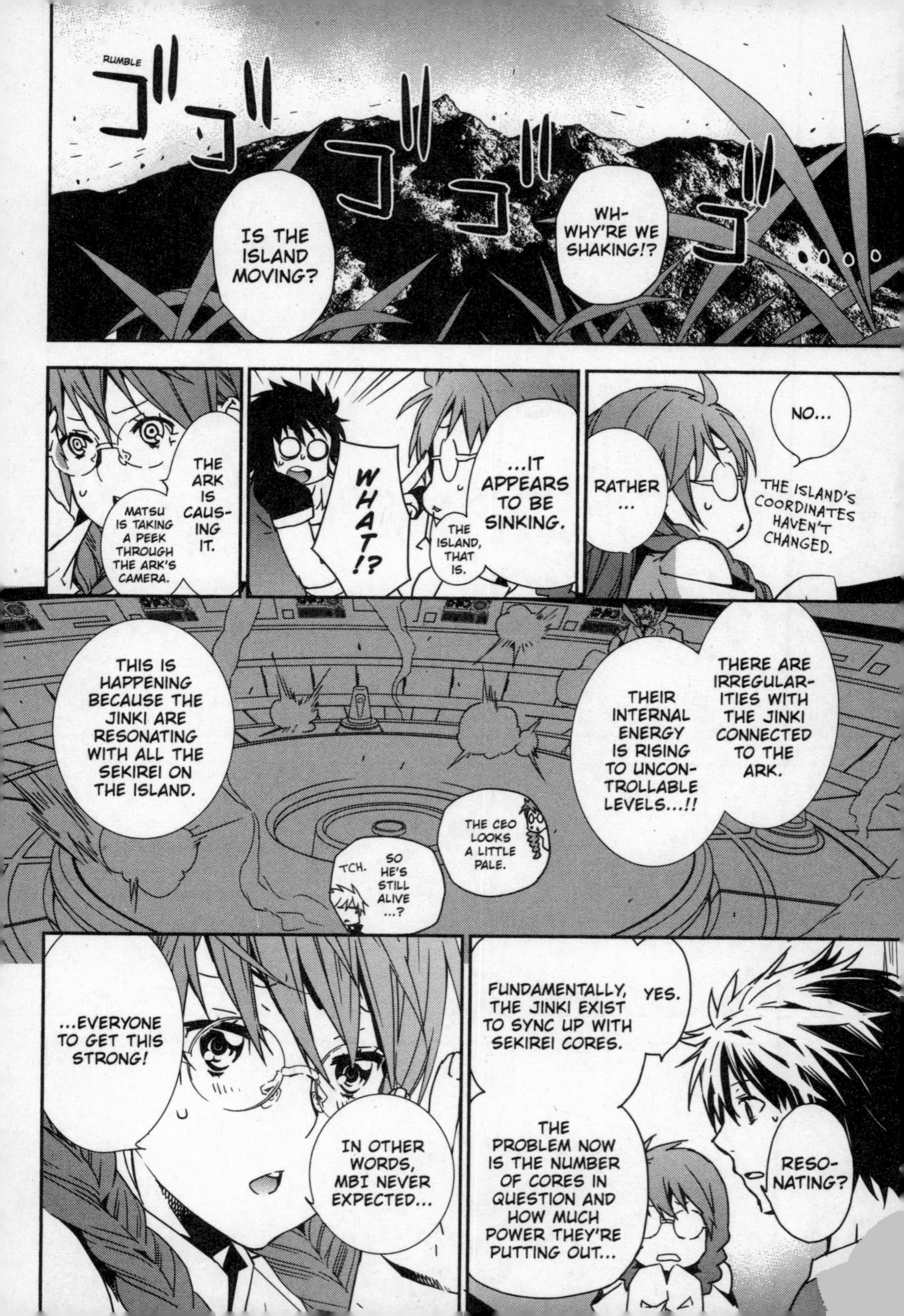
RUMBLE
WH- WHY'RE WE SHAKING!?
IS THE ISLAND MOVING?
NO...
THE ISLAND'S COORDINATES HAVEN'T CHANGED.
RATHER...
...IT APPEARS TO BE SINKING.
THE ISLAND, THAT IS.
WHAT!?
THE ARK IS CAUSING IT.
MATSU IS TAKING A PEEK THROUGH THE ARK'S CAMERA.
THERE ARE IRREGULARITIES WITH THE JINKI CONNECTED TO THE ARK.
THEIR INTERNAL ENERGY IS RISING TO UNCONTROLLABLE LEVELS...!!
THIS IS HAPPENING BECAUSE THE JINKI ARE RESONATING WITH ALL THE SEKIREI ON THE ISLAND.
THE CEO LOOKS A LITTLE PALE.
SO HE'S STILL ALIVE...?
TCH.
YES.
FUNDAMENTALLY, THE JINKI EXIST TO SYNC UP WITH SEKIREI CORES.
RESONATING?
THE PROBLEM NOW IS THE NUMBER OF CORES IN QUESTION AND HOW MUCH POWER THEY'RE PUTTING OUT...
IN OTHER WORDS, MBI NEVER EXPECTED...
...EVERYONE TO GET THIS STRONG!

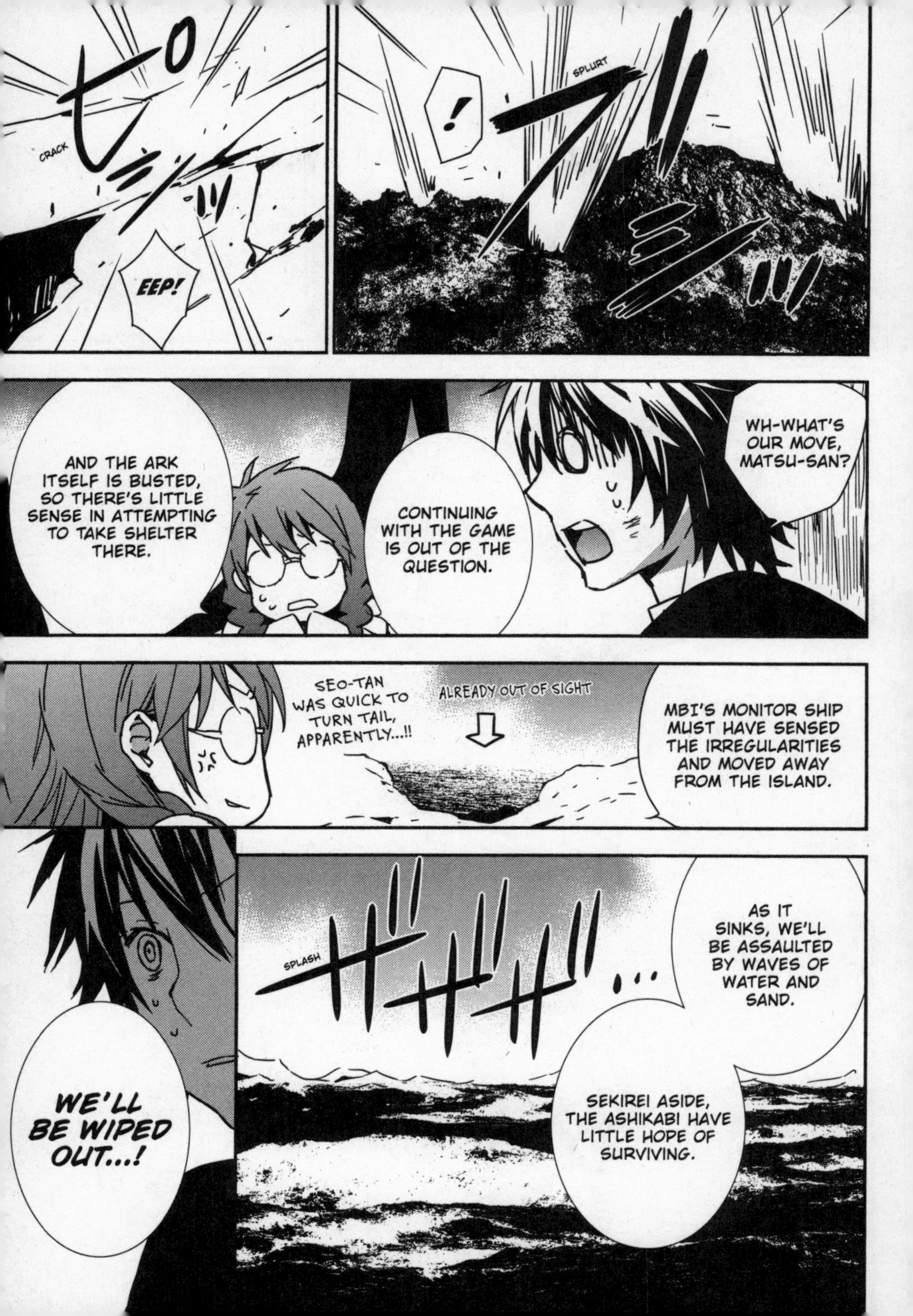
SPLURT
!
CRACK
EEP!
WH-WHAT'S OUR MOVE, MATSU-SAN?
CONTINUING WITH THE GAME IS OUT OF THE QUESTION.
AND THE ARK ITSELF IS BUSTED, SO THERE'S LITTLE SENSE IN ATTEMPTING TO TAKE SHELTER THERE.
MBI'S MONITOR SHIP MUST HAVE SENSED THE IRREGULARITIES AND MOVED AWAY FROM THE ISLAND.
ALREADY OUT OF SIGHT
SEO-TAN WAS QUICK TO TURN TAIL, APPARENTLY...!!
AS IT SINKS, WE'LL BE ASSAULTED BY WAVES OF WATER AND SAND.
SPLASH
SEKIREI ASIDE, THE ASHIKABI HAVE LITTLE HOPE OF SURVIVING.
WE'LL BE WIPED OUT...!

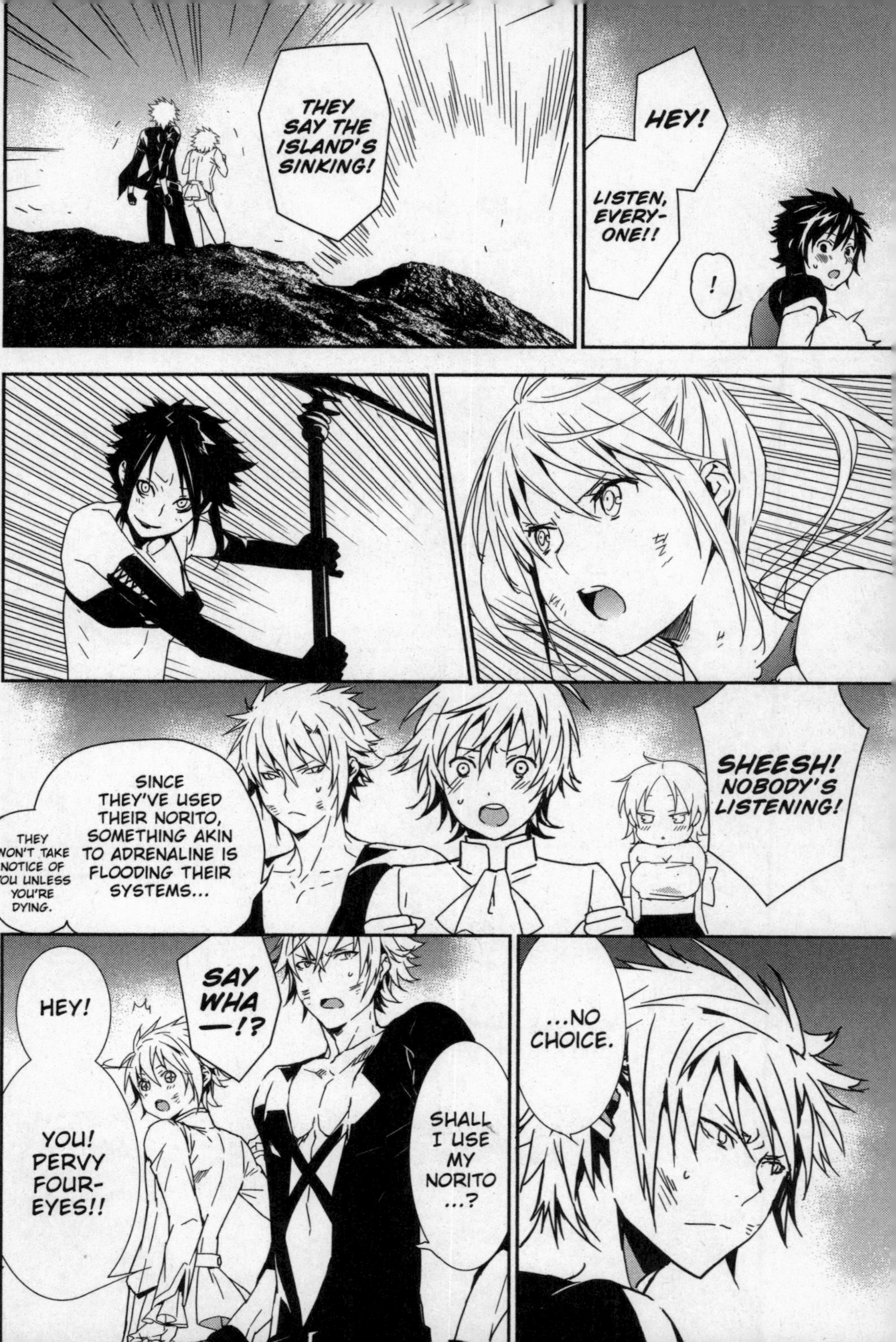
HEY!
LISTEN, EVERY-ONE!!
!
THEY SAY THE ISLAND'S SINKING!
SHEESH! NOBODY'S LISTENING!
SINCE THEY'VE USED THEIR NORITO, SOMETHING AKIN TO ADRENALINE IS FLOODING THEIR SYSTEMS...
THEY WON'T TAKE NOTICE OF YOU UNLESS YOU'RE DYING.
...NO CHOICE.
SHALL I USE MY NORITO...?
SAY WHA—!?
HEY!
YOU! PERVY FOUR-EYES!!

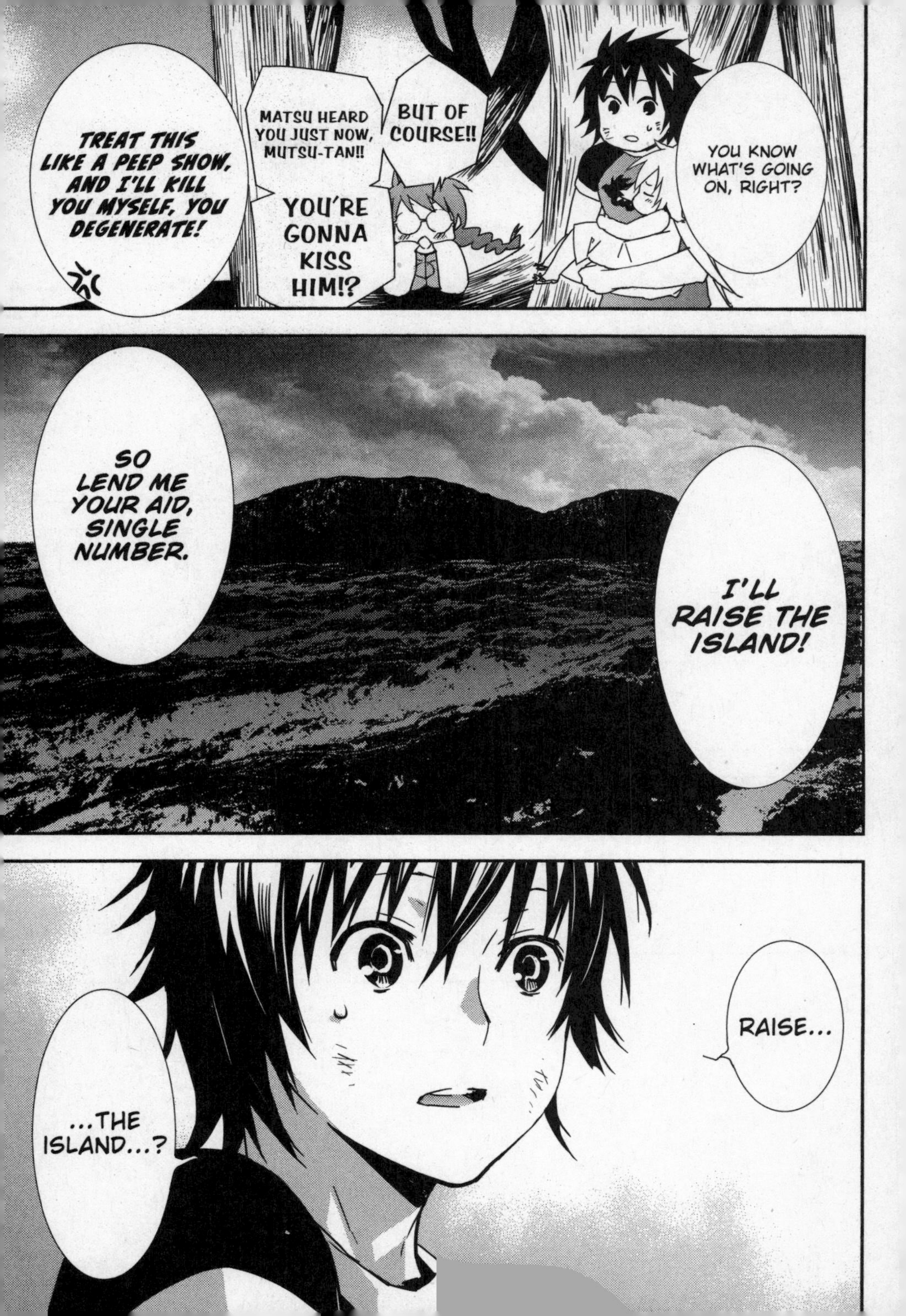
YOU KNOW WHAT'S GOING ON, RIGHT?
BUT OF COURSE!!
MATSU HEARD YOU JUST NOW, MUTSU-TAN!!
YOU'RE GONNA KISS HIM!?
TREAT THIS LIKE A PEEP SHOW, AND I'LL KILL YOU MYSELF, YOU DEGENERATE!
I'LL RAISE THE ISLAND!
SO LEND ME YOUR AID, SINGLE NUMBER.
RAISE...
...THE ISLAND...?

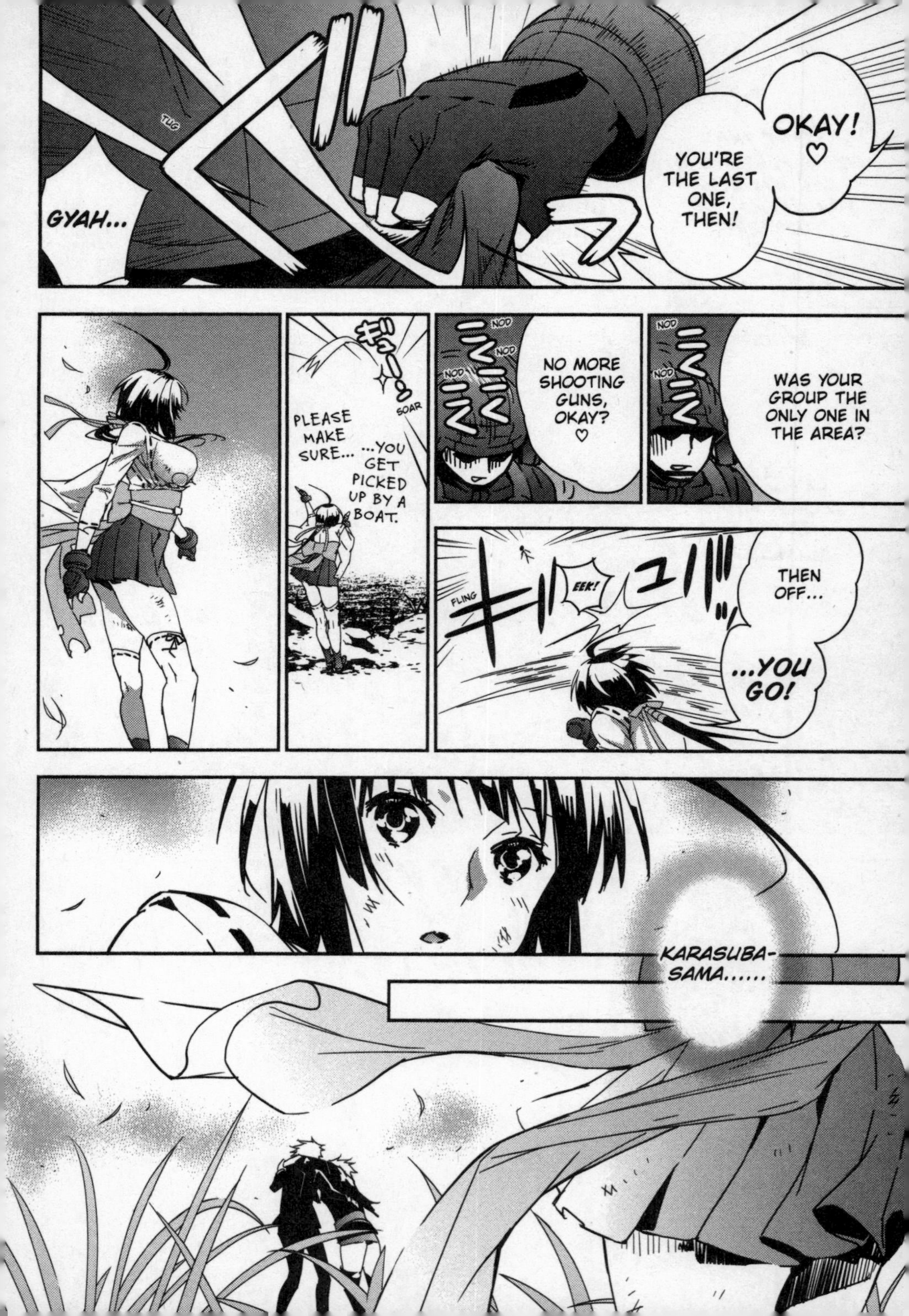
OKAY! ♡
YOU'RE THE LAST ONE, THEN!
TUG
GYAH...
NOD
NOD
WAS YOUR GROUP THE ONLY ONE IN THE AREA?
NOD
NOD
NOD
NO MORE SHOOTING GUNS, OKAY? ♡
THEN OFF...
...YOU GO!
EEK!
FLING
SOAR
PLEASE MAKE SURE... ...YOU GET PICKED UP BY A BOAT.
KARASUBA-SAMA......

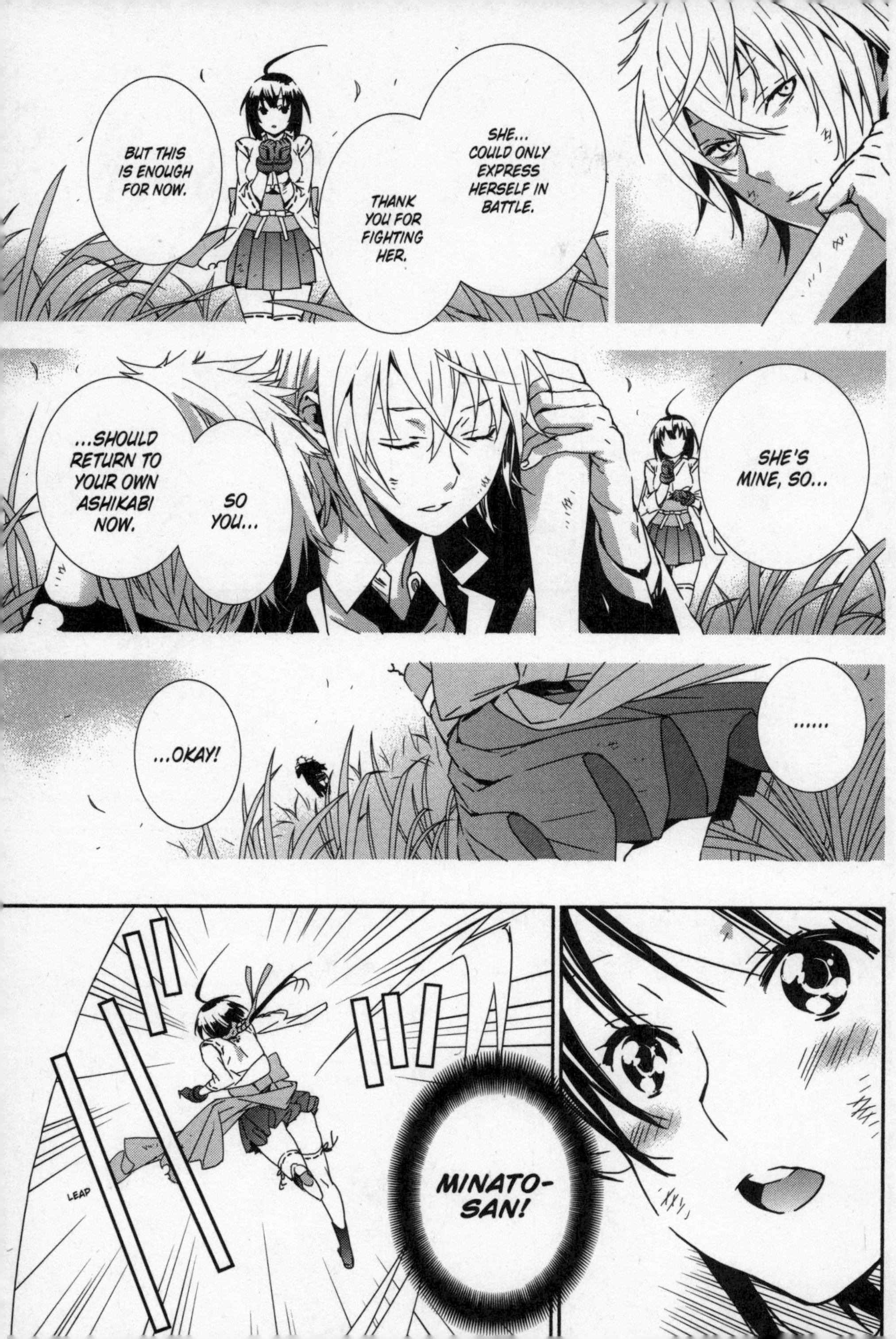
SHE... COULD ONLY EXPRESS HERSELF IN BATTLE.
THANK YOU FOR FIGHTING HER.
BUT THIS IS ENOUGH FOR NOW.
SHE'S MINE, SO...
SO YOU...
...SHOULD RETURN TO YOUR OWN ASHIKABI NOW.
......
...OKAY!
MINATO-SAN!
LEAP

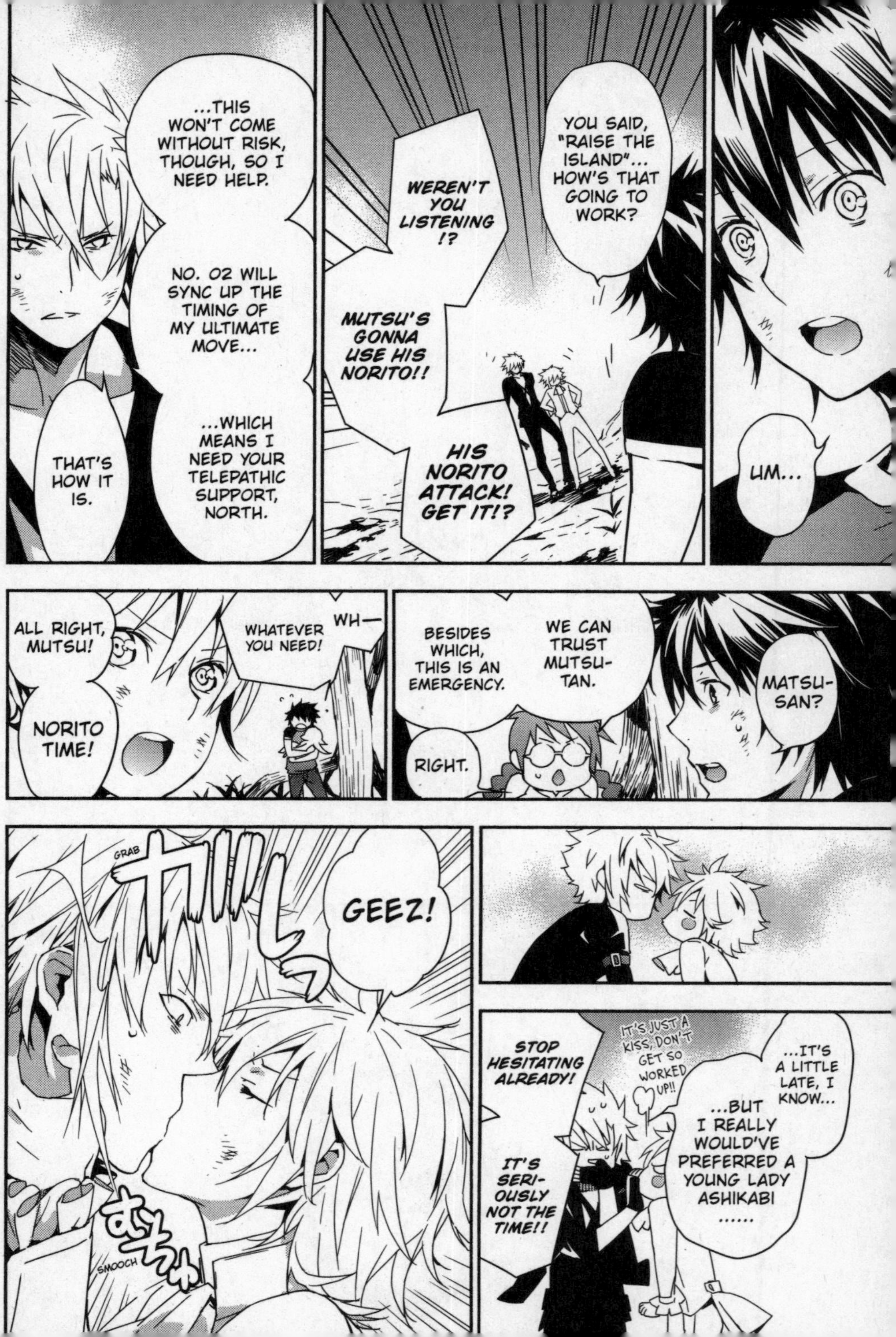
UM...
YOU SAID, "RAISE THE ISLAND"... HOW'S THAT GOING TO WORK?
WEREN'T YOU LISTENING !?
MUTSU'S GONNA USE HIS NORITO!!
HIS NORITO ATTACK! GET IT!?
...THIS WON'T COME WITHOUT RISK, THOUGH, SO I NEED HELP.
NO. 02 WILL SYNC UP THE TIMING OF MY ULTIMATE MOVE...
...WHICH MEANS I NEED YOUR TELEPATHIC SUPPORT, NORTH.
THAT'S HOW IT IS.
MATSU-SAN?
WE CAN TRUST MUTSU-TAN.
BESIDES WHICH, THIS IS AN EMERGENCY.
RIGHT.
WH—
WHATEVER YOU NEED!
ALL RIGHT, MUTSU!
NORITO TIME!
...IT'S A LITTLE LATE, I KNOW...
...BUT I REALLY WOULD'VE PREFERRED A YOUNG LADY ASHIKABI ......
IT'S JUST A KISS, DON'T GET SO WORKED UP!!
STOP HESITATING ALREADY!
IT'S SERI-OUSLY NOT THE TIME!!
GEEZ!
GRAB
SMOOCH

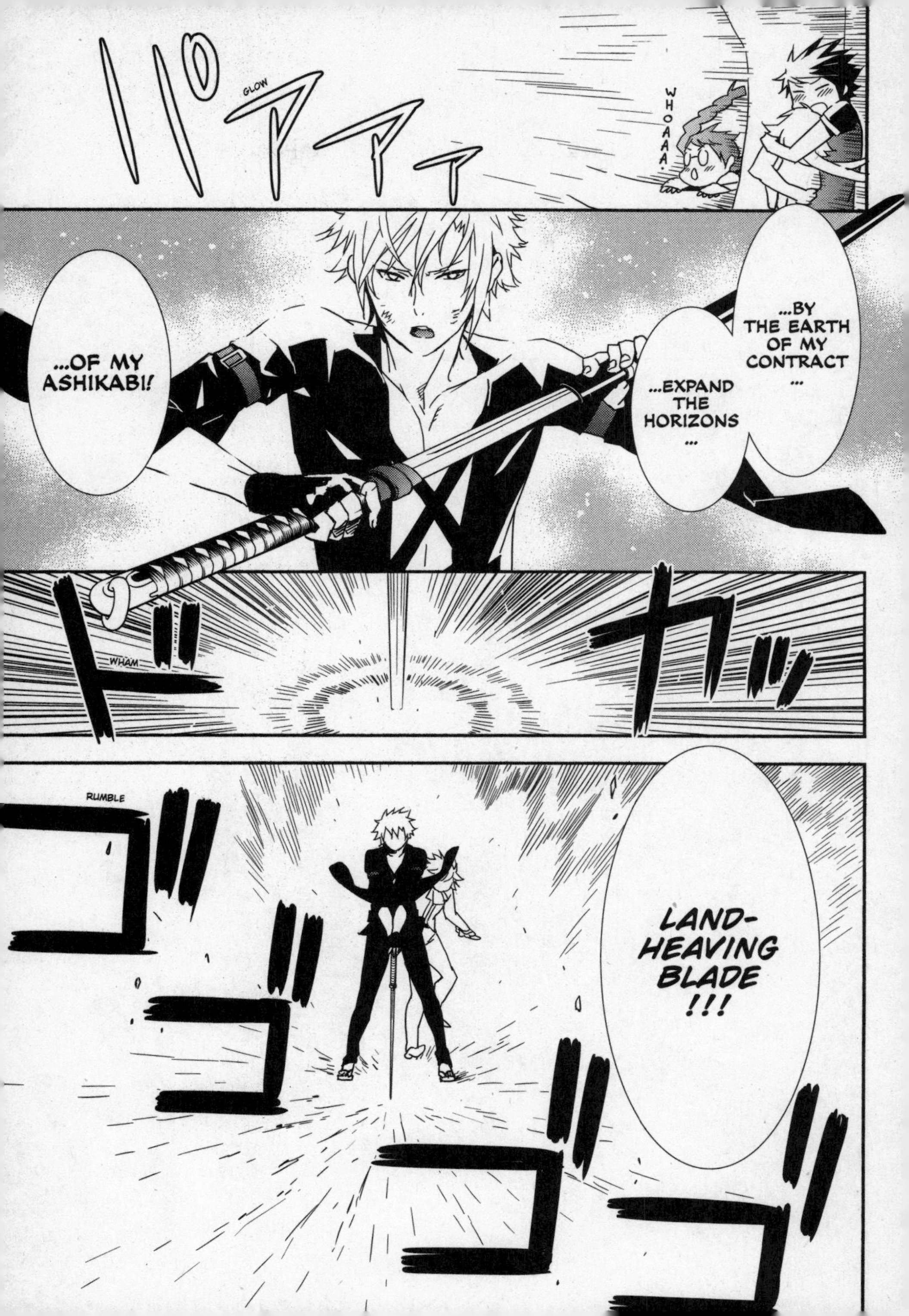
WHOAAA!
パァァァ
GLOW
...BY THE EARTH OF MY CONTRACT ...
...EXPAND THE HORIZONS ...
...OF MY ASHIKABI!
ガッ
ドッ
WHAM
LAND-HEAVING BLADE !!!
ゴゴゴゴ
RUMBLE

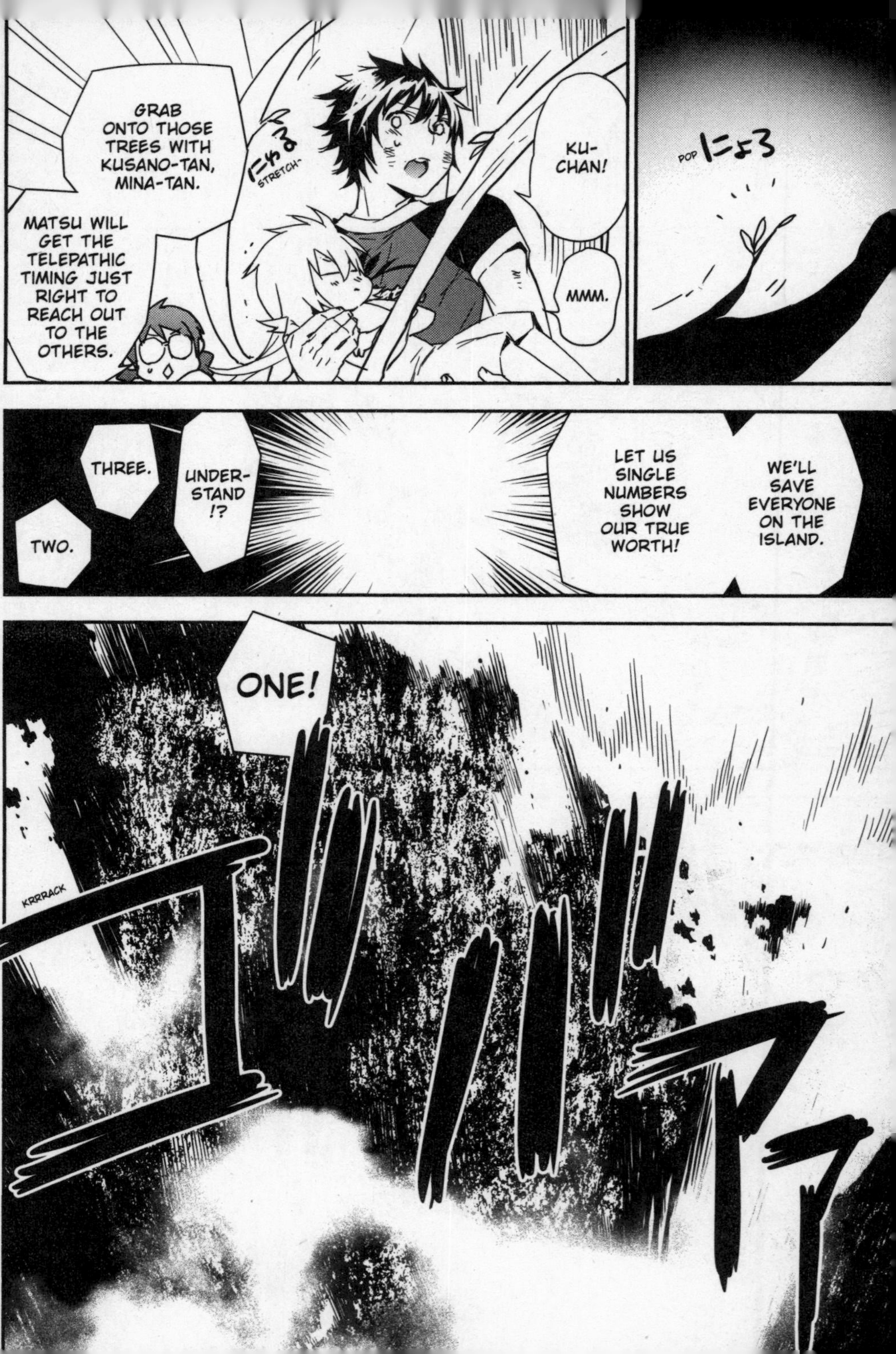
POP にょろ
KU-CHAN!
MMM.
にゅる STRETCH-
GRAB ONTO THOSE TREES WITH KUSANO-TAN, MINA-TAN.
MATSU WILL GET THE TELEPATHIC TIMING JUST RIGHT TO REACH OUT TO THE OTHERS.
WE'LL SAVE EVERYONE ON THE ISLAND.
LET US SINGLE NUMBERS SHOW OUR TRUE WORTH!
UNDER-STAND!?
THREE.
TWO.
ONE!
KRRRACK

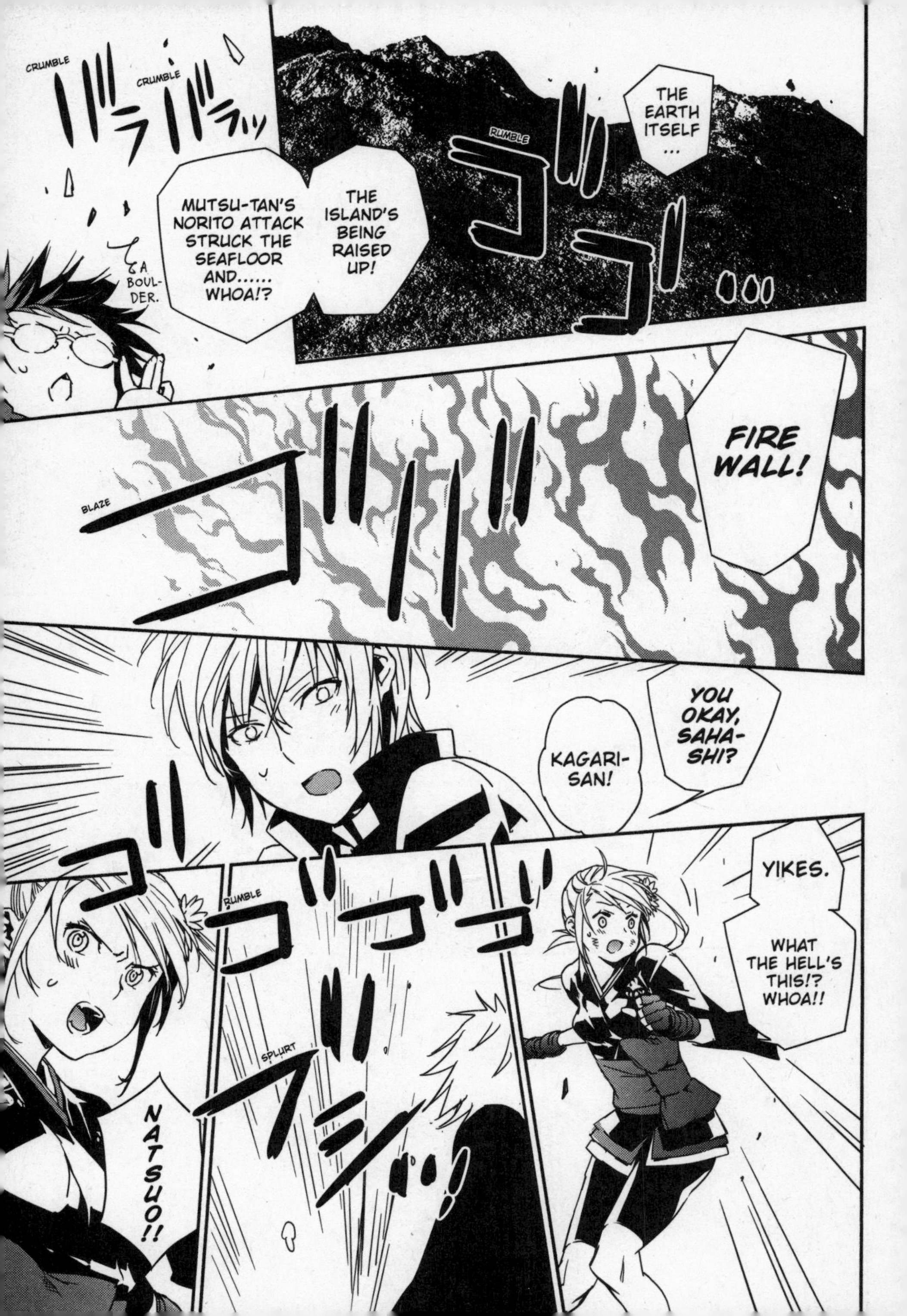
THE EARTH ITSELF ...
RUMBLE
THE ISLAND'S BEING RAISED UP!
MUTSU-TAN'S NORITO ATTACK STRUCK THE SEAFLOOR AND...... WHOA!?
CRUMBLE
CRUMBLE
A BOULDER.
FIRE WALL!
BLAZE
YOU OKAY, SAHASHI?
KAGARI-SAN!
YIKES.
WHAT THE HELL'S THIS!? WHOA!!
RUMBLE
SPLURT
NATSUO!!

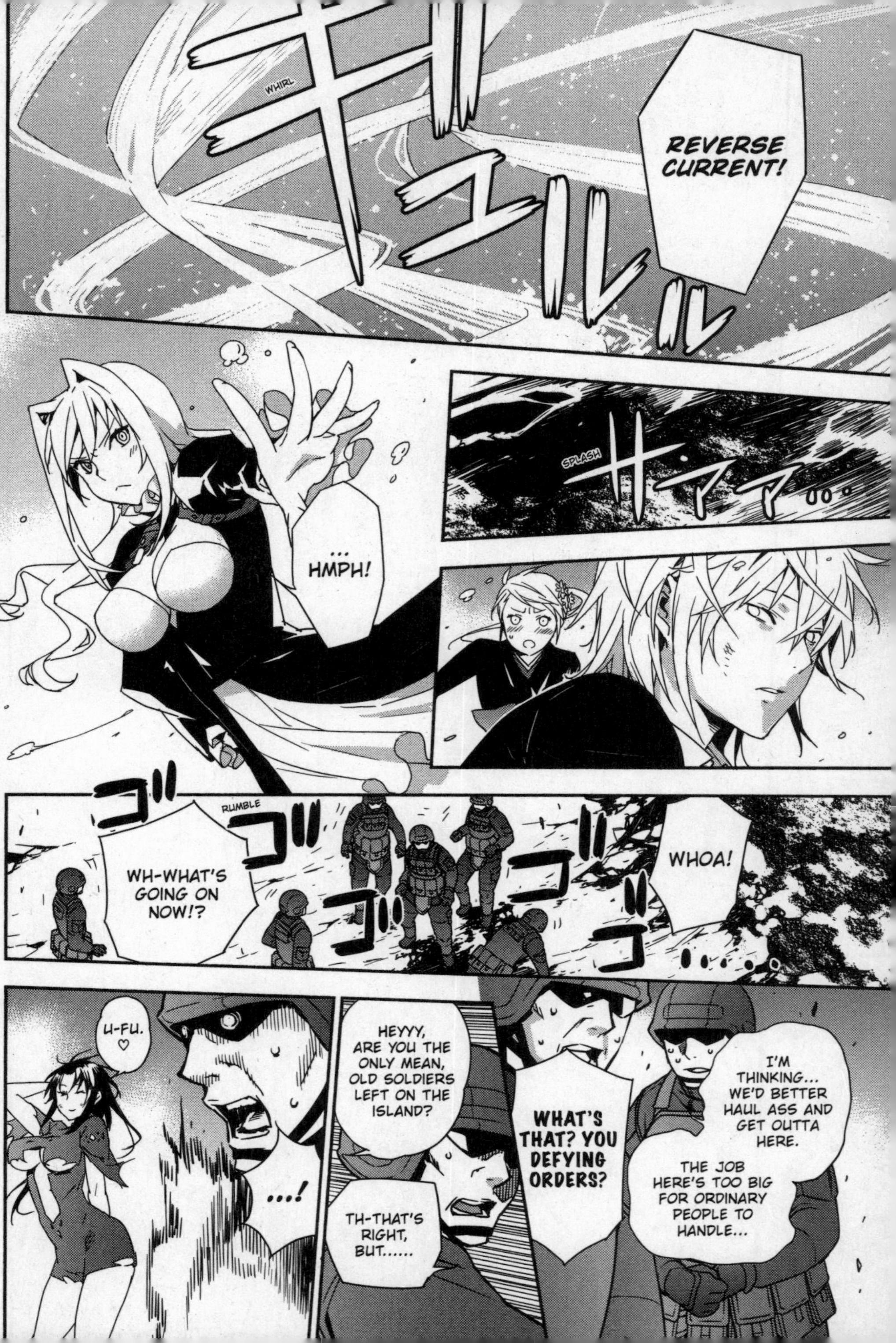
REVERSE CURRENT!
WHIRL
SPLASH
... HMPH!
WHOA!
RUMBLE
WH-WHAT'S GOING ON NOW!?
I'M THINKING... WE'D BETTER HAUL ASS AND GET OUTTA HERE.
THE JOB HERE'S TOO BIG FOR ORDINARY PEOPLE TO HANDLE...
WHAT'S THAT? YOU DEFYING ORDERS?
TH-THAT'S RIGHT, BUT......
HEYYY, ARE YOU THE ONLY MEAN, OLD SOLDIERS LEFT ON THE ISLAND?
U-FU. ♥
...!

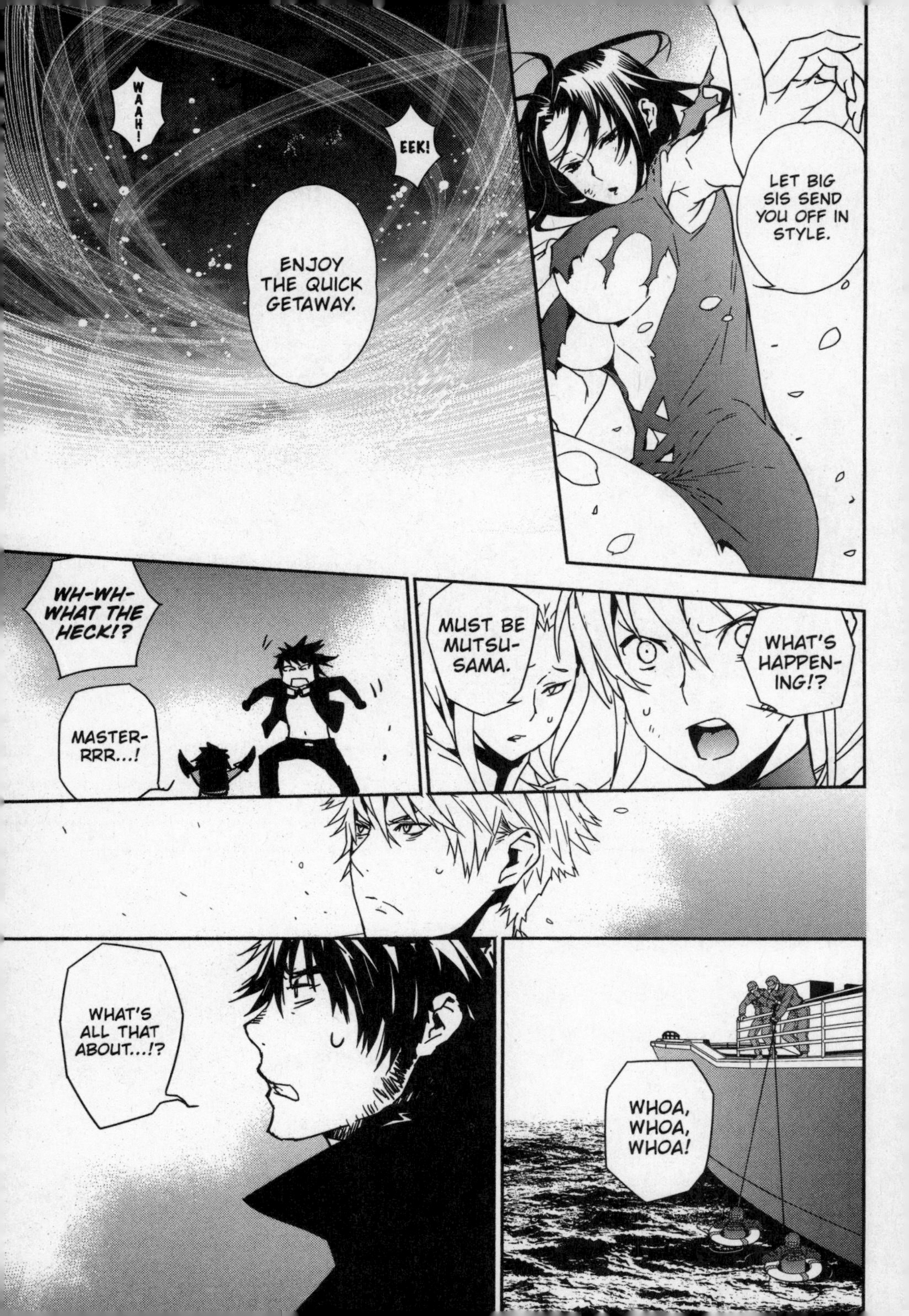
LET BIG SIS SEND YOU OFF IN STYLE.
EEK!
WAAH!
ENJOY THE QUICK GETAWAY.
WHAT'S HAPPEN-ING!?
MUST BE MUTSU-SAMA.
WH-WH-WHAT THE HECK!?
MASTER-RRR...!
WHOA, WHOA, WHOA!
WHAT'S ALL THAT ABOUT...!?

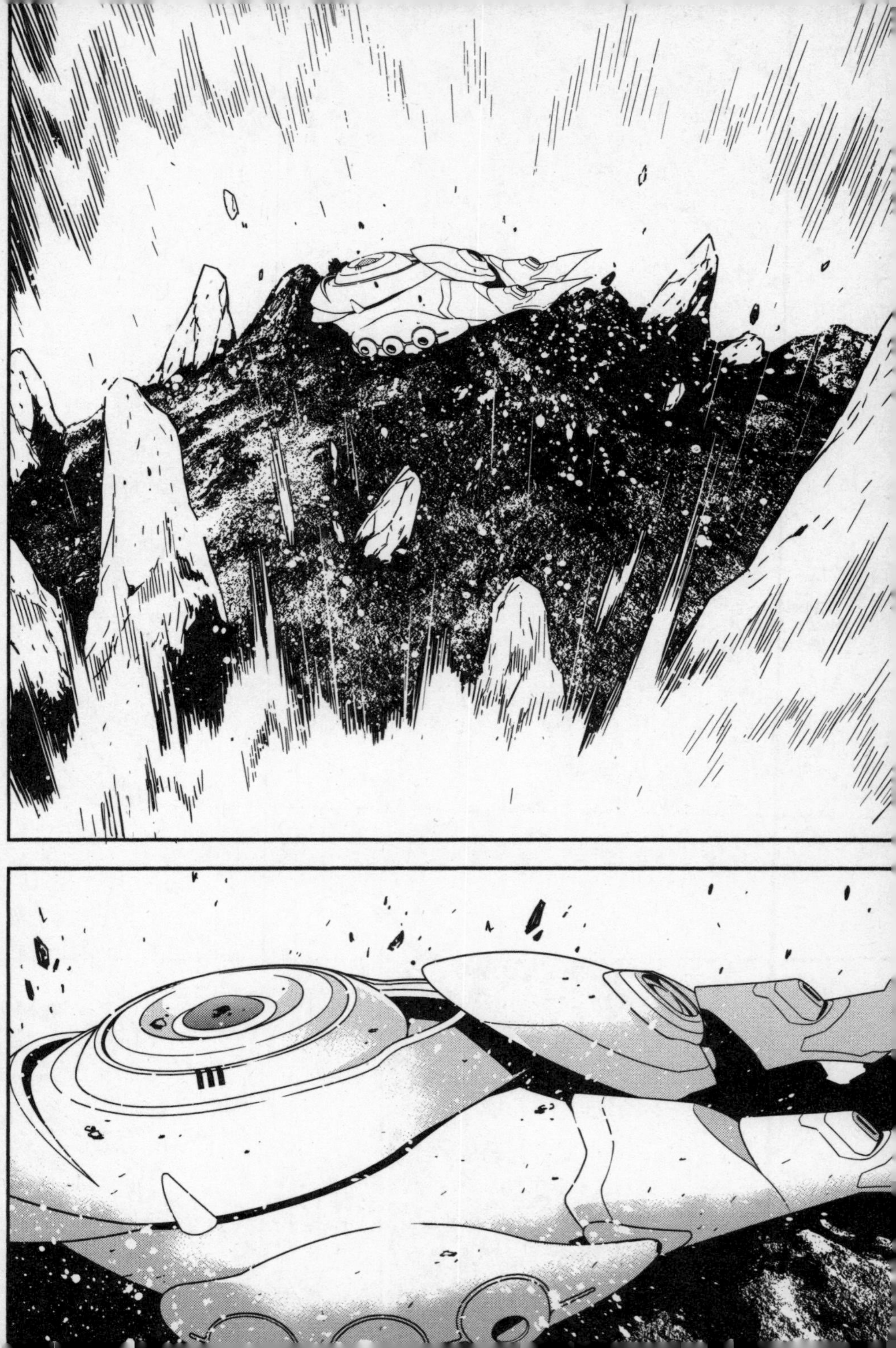

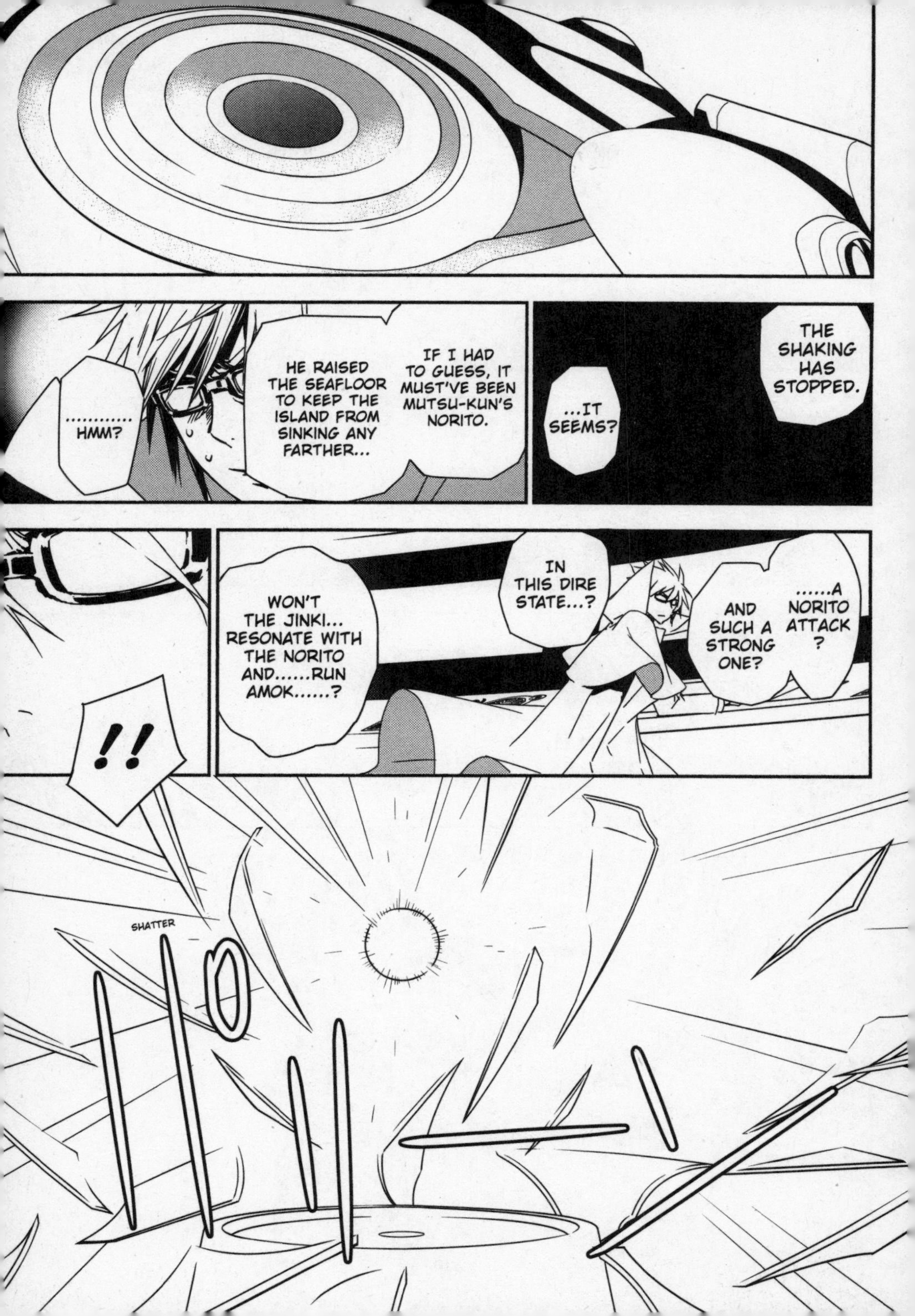
THE SHAKING HAS STOPPED.
...IT SEEMS?
IF I HAD TO GUESS, IT MUST'VE BEEN MUTSU-KUN'S NORITO.
HE RAISED THE SEAFLOOR TO KEEP THE ISLAND FROM SINKING ANY FARTHER...
............HMM?
......A NORITO ATTACK?
AND SUCH A STRONG ONE?
IN THIS DIRE STATE...?
WON'T THE JINKI... RESONATE WITH THE NORITO AND......RUN AMOK......?
!!
SHATTER

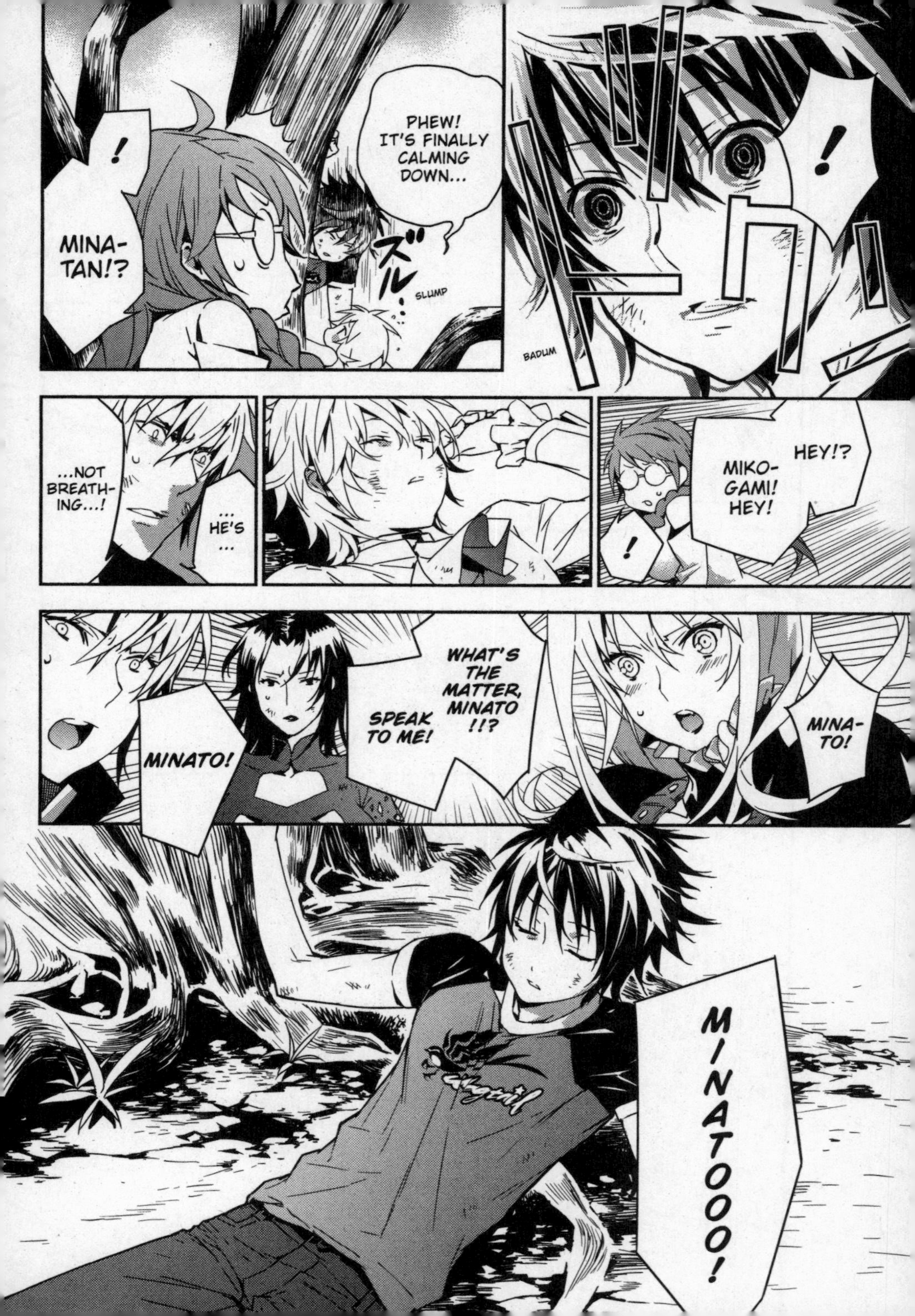
!
BADUM
PHEW! IT'S FINALLY CALMING DOWN...
ズル
SLUMP
!
MINA-TAN!?
HEY!?
MIKO-GAMI! HEY!
!
...HE'S...
...NOT BREATHING...!
MINA-TO!
WHAT'S THE MATTER, MINATO!!?
SPEAK TO ME!
MINATO!
MINATOOO!

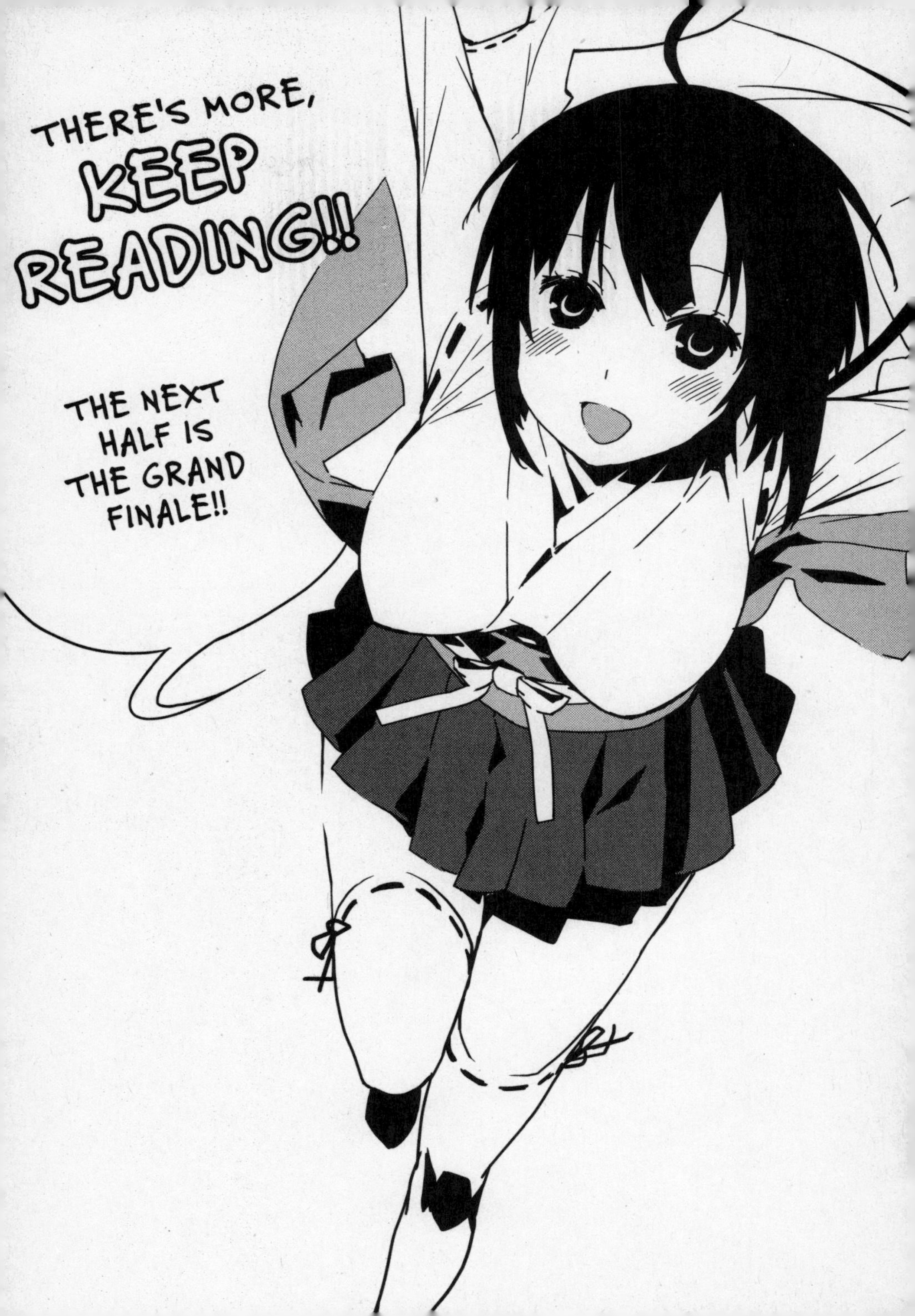
THERE'S MORE, KEEP READING!!
THE NEXT HALF IS THE GRAND FINALE!!

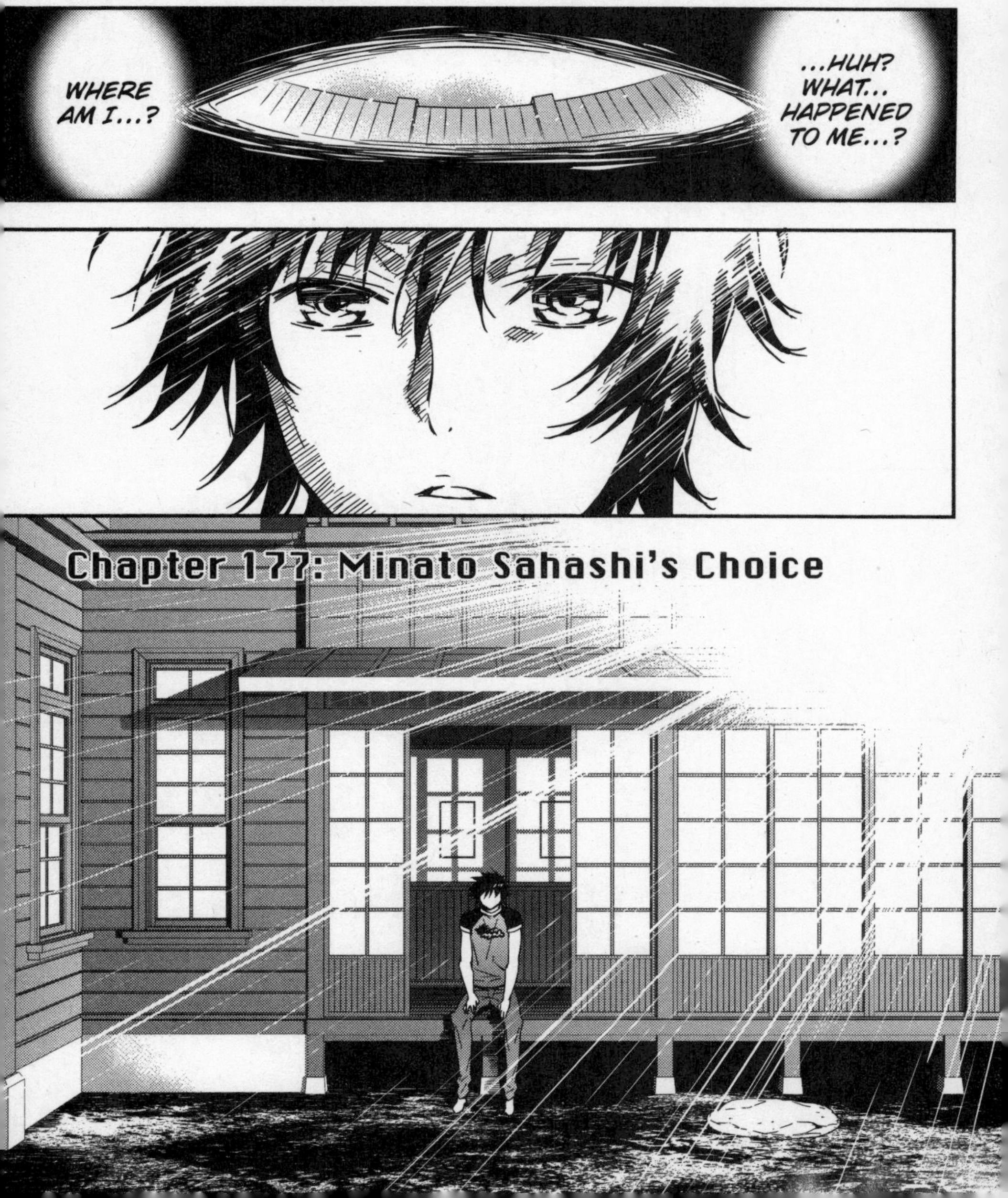
...HUH? WHAT... HAPPENED TO ME...?
WHERE AM I...?

Chapter 177: Minato Sahashi's Choice

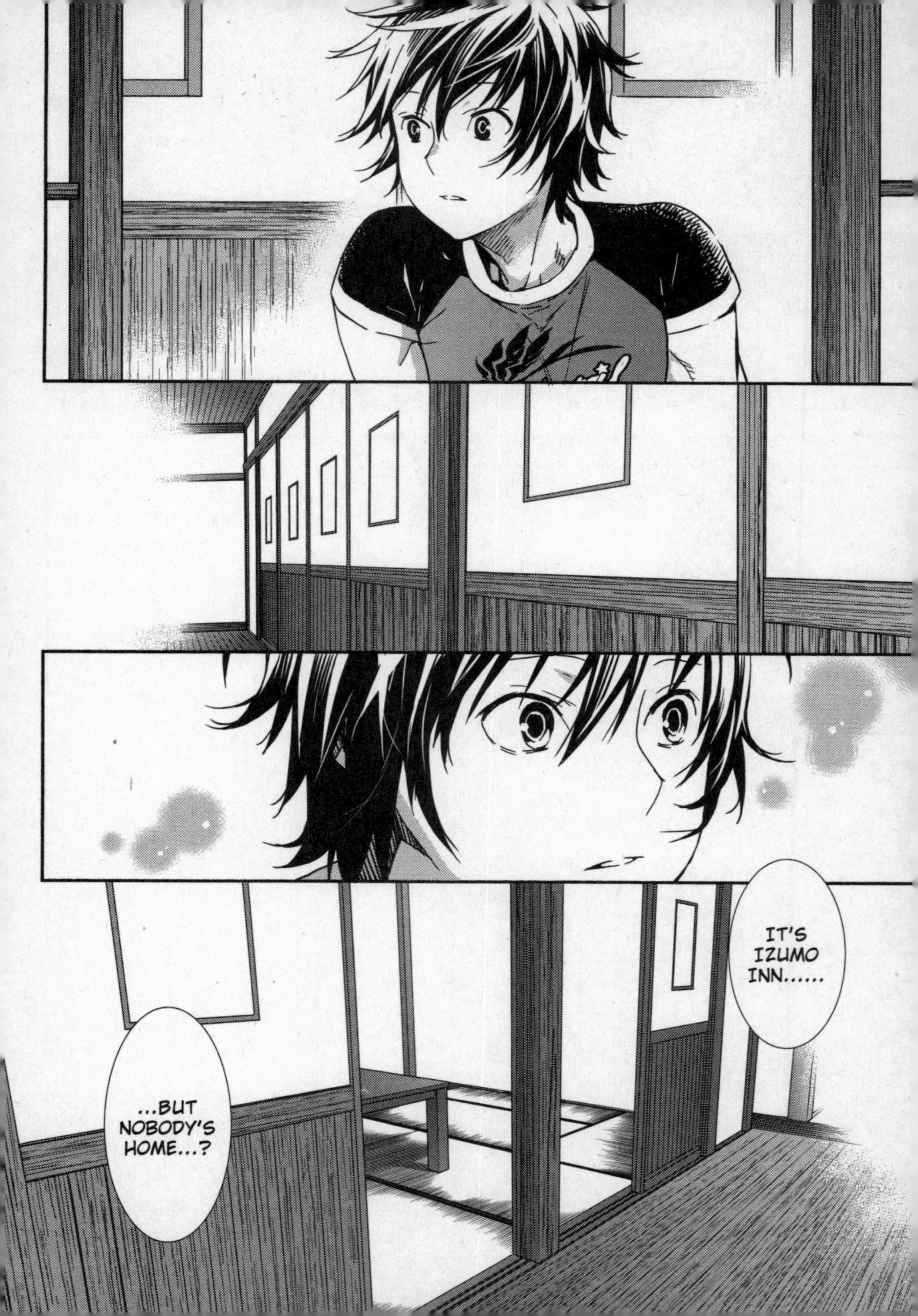
IT'S IZUMO INN......
...BUT NOBODY'S HOME...?

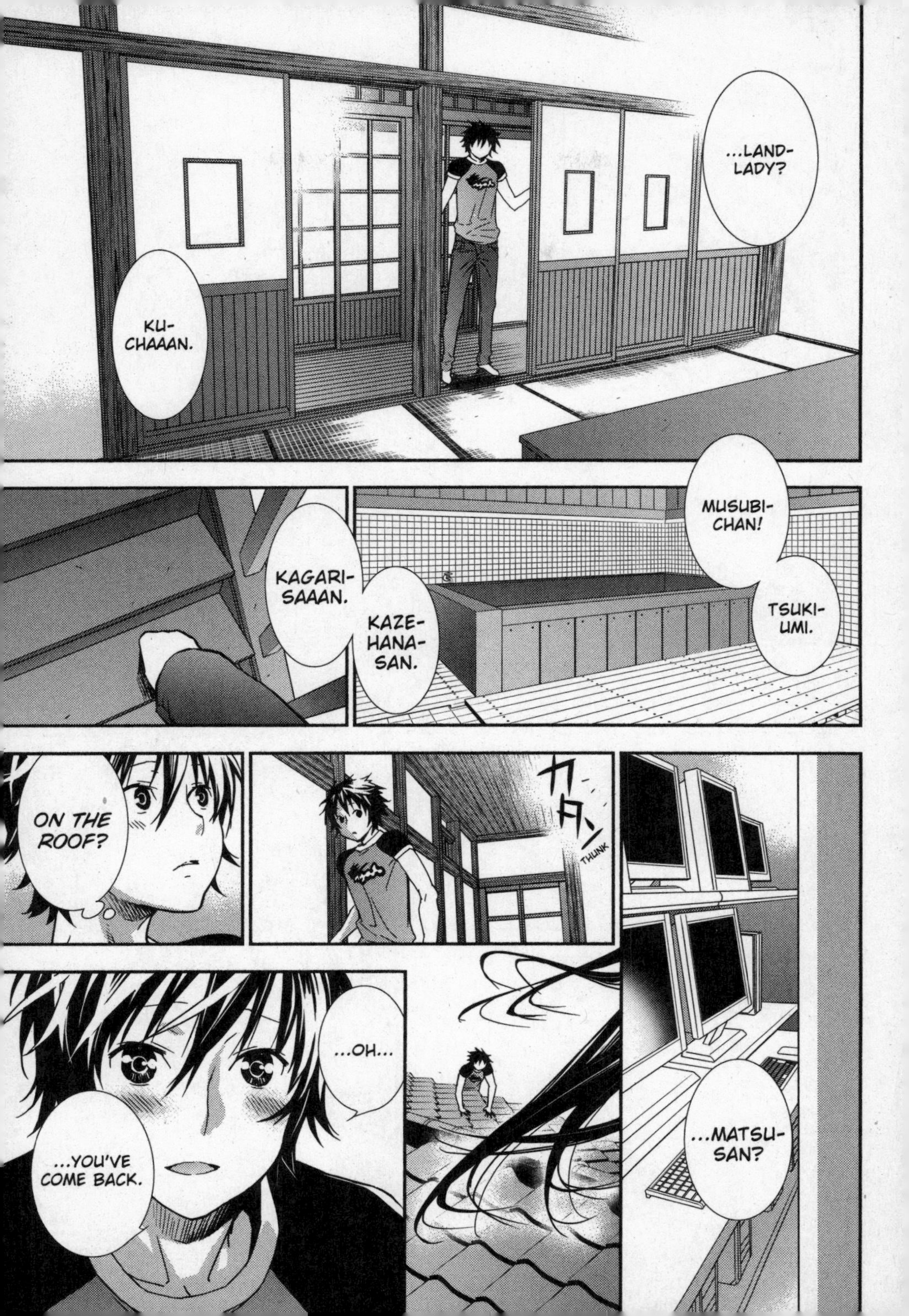

...LAND-LADY?
KU-CHAAAN.
MUSUBI-CHAN!
TSUKI-UMI.
KAGARI-SAAAN.
KAZE-HANA-SAN.
...MATSU-SAN?
カタン
THUNK
ON THE ROOF?
...OH...
...YOU'VE COME BACK.

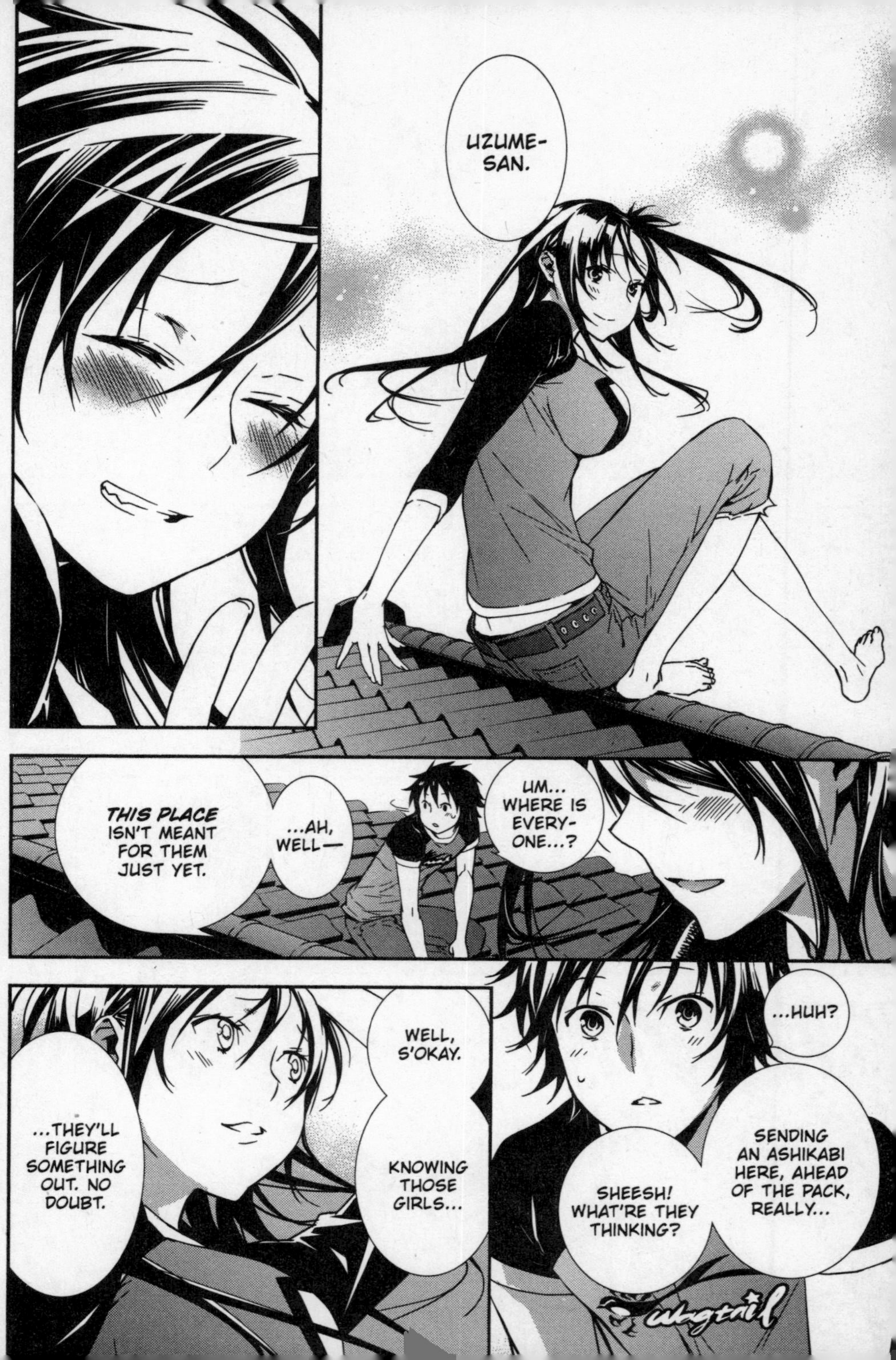
UZUME-SAN.
UM... WHERE IS EVERY-ONE...?
...AH, WELL—
THIS PLACE ISN'T MEANT FOR THEM JUST YET.
...HUH?
SENDING AN ASHIKABI HERE, AHEAD OF THE PACK, REALLY...
SHEESH! WHAT'RE THEY THINKING?
WELL, S'OKAY.
KNOWING THOSE GIRLS...
...THEY'LL FIGURE SOMETHING OUT. NO DOUBT.

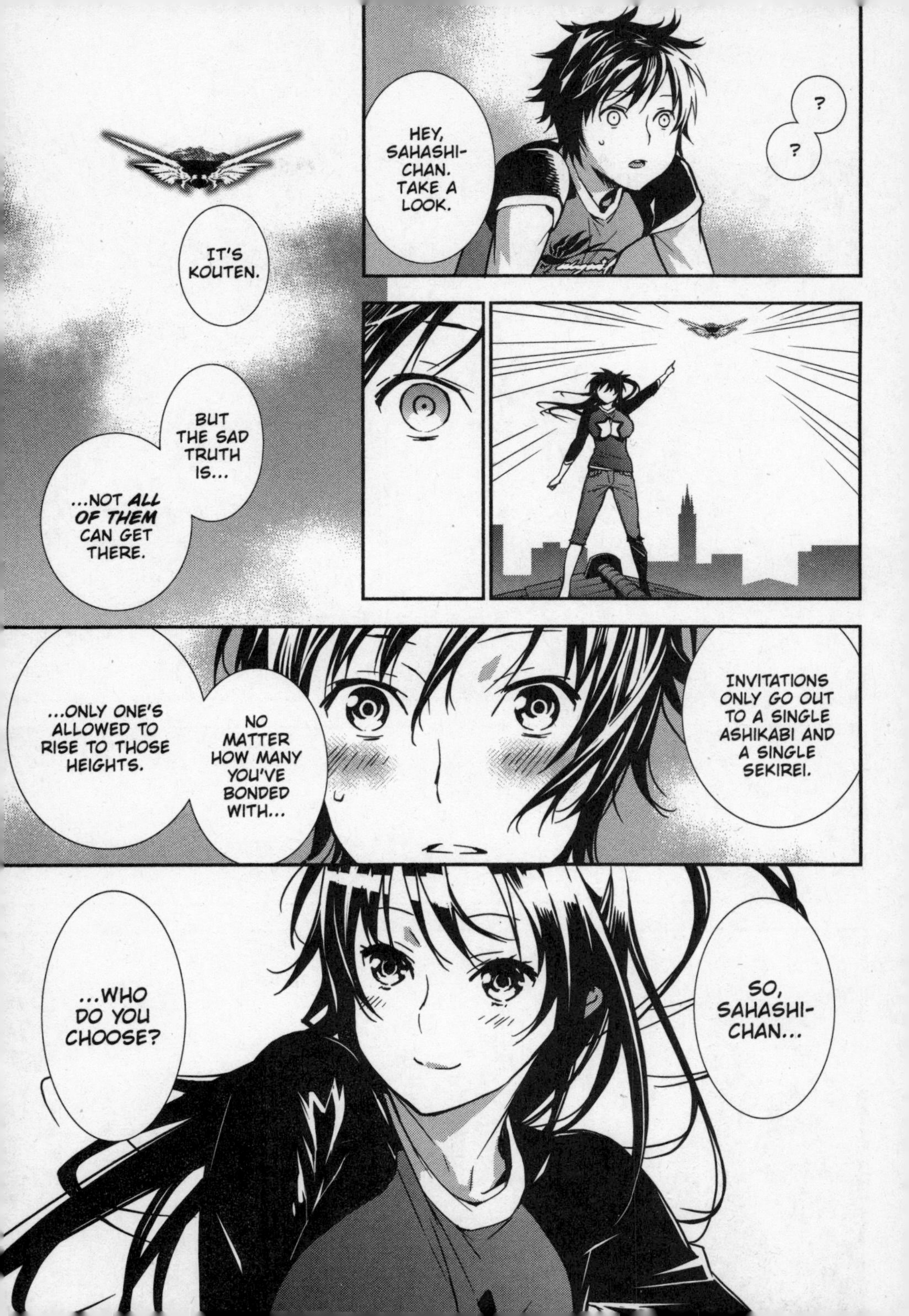
?
?
HEY, SAHASHI-CHAN. TAKE A LOOK.
IT'S KOUTEN.
BUT THE SAD TRUTH IS...
...NOT ***ALL OF THEM*** CAN GET THERE.
INVITATIONS ONLY GO OUT TO A SINGLE ASHIKABI AND A SINGLE SEKIREI.
NO MATTER HOW MANY YOU'VE BONDED WITH...
...ONLY ONE'S ALLOWED TO RISE TO THOSE HEIGHTS.
SO, SAHASHI-CHAN...
...WHO DO YOU CHOOSE?

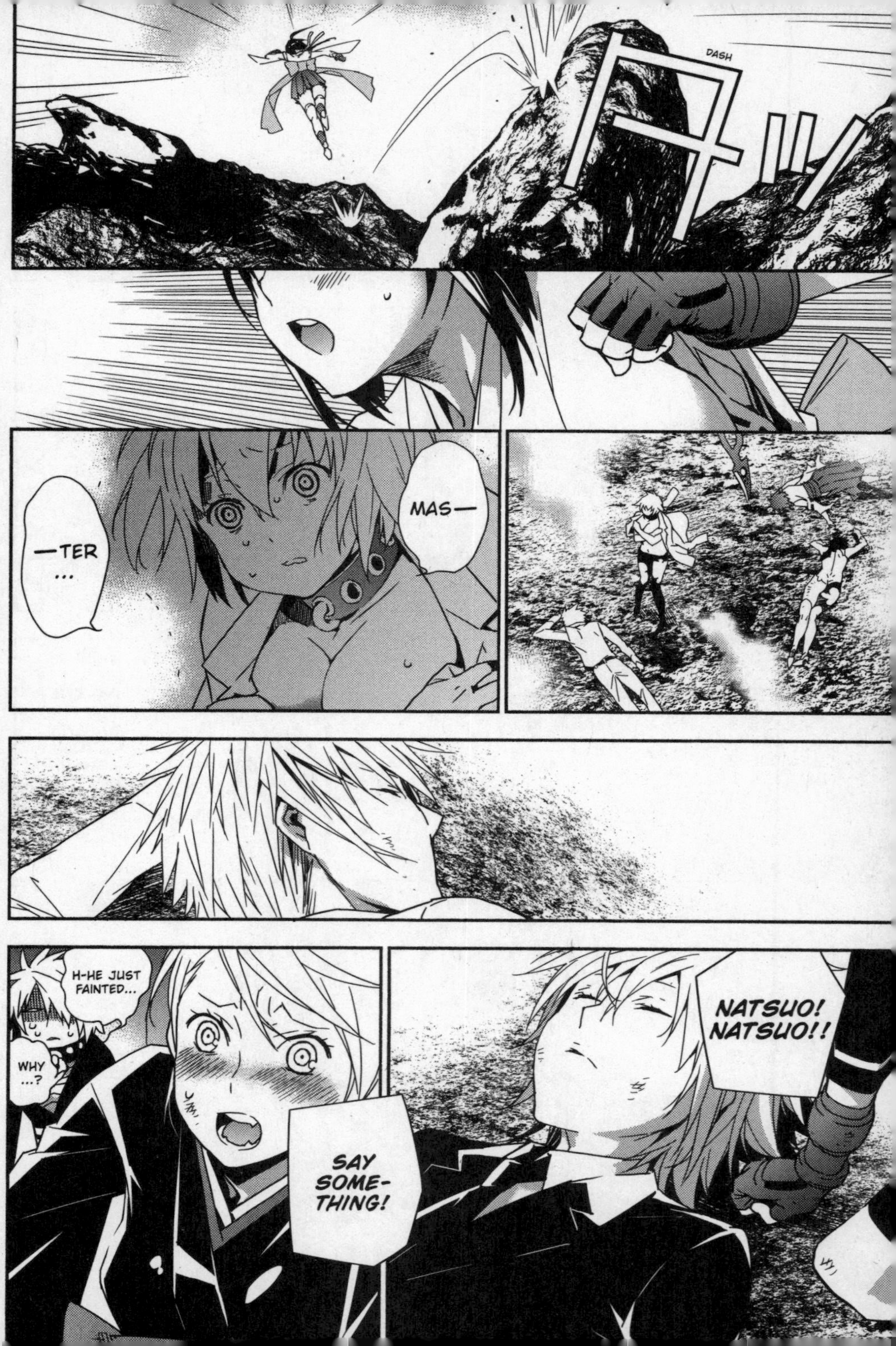
DASH
MAS—
—TER ...
NATSUO! NATSUO!!
SAY SOME-THING!
H-HE JUST FAINTED...
WHY ...?

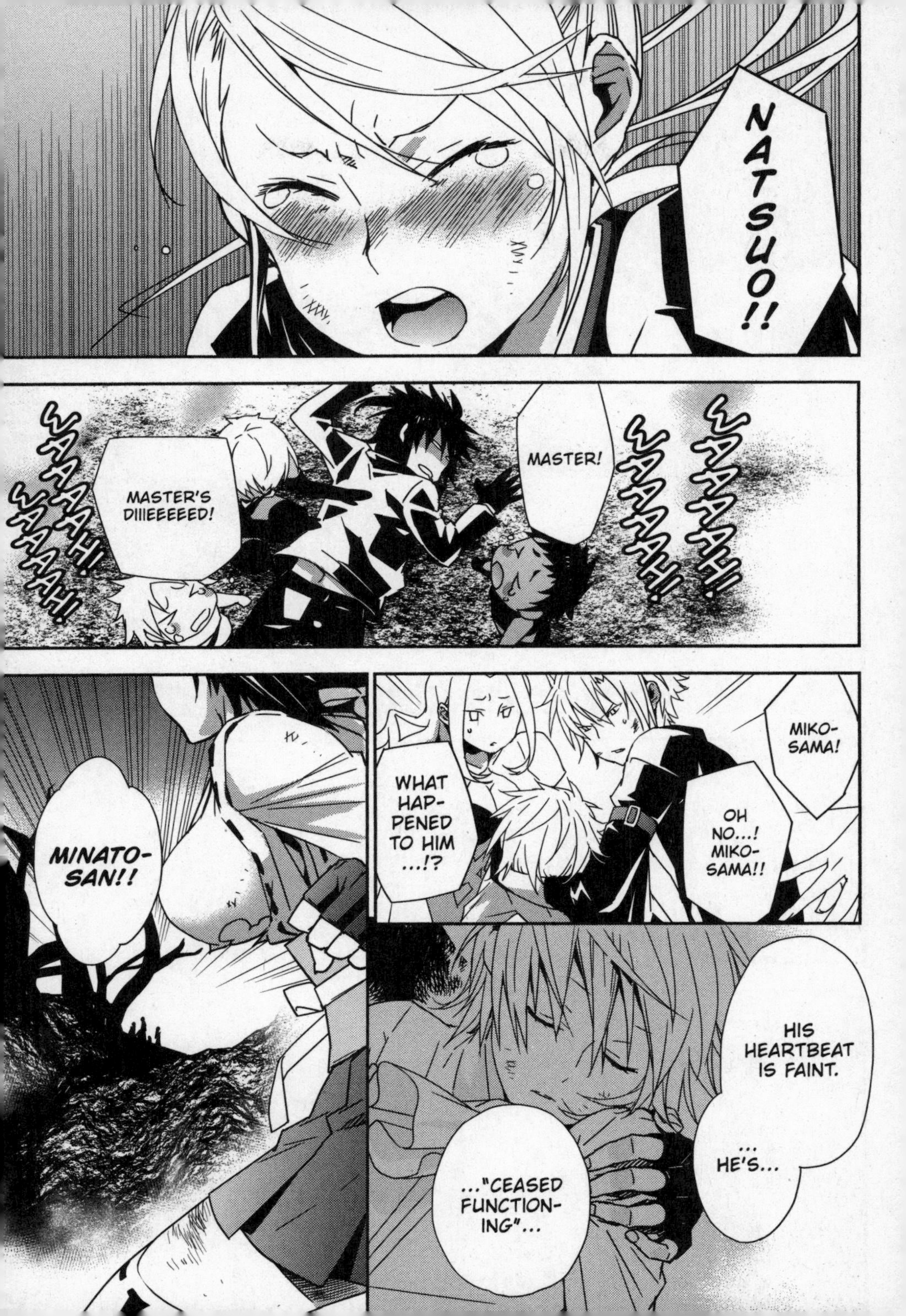
NATSUO!!
WAAAAAH!!
WAAAAAH!!
MASTER!
MASTER'S DIIIEEEEED!
WAAAAAH!
WAAAAAH!
MIKO-SAMA!
OH NO...! MIKO-SAMA!!
WHAT HAPPENED TO HIM ...!?
HIS HEARTBEAT IS FAINT.
...HE'S...
..."CEASED FUNCTIONING"...
MINATO-SAN!!

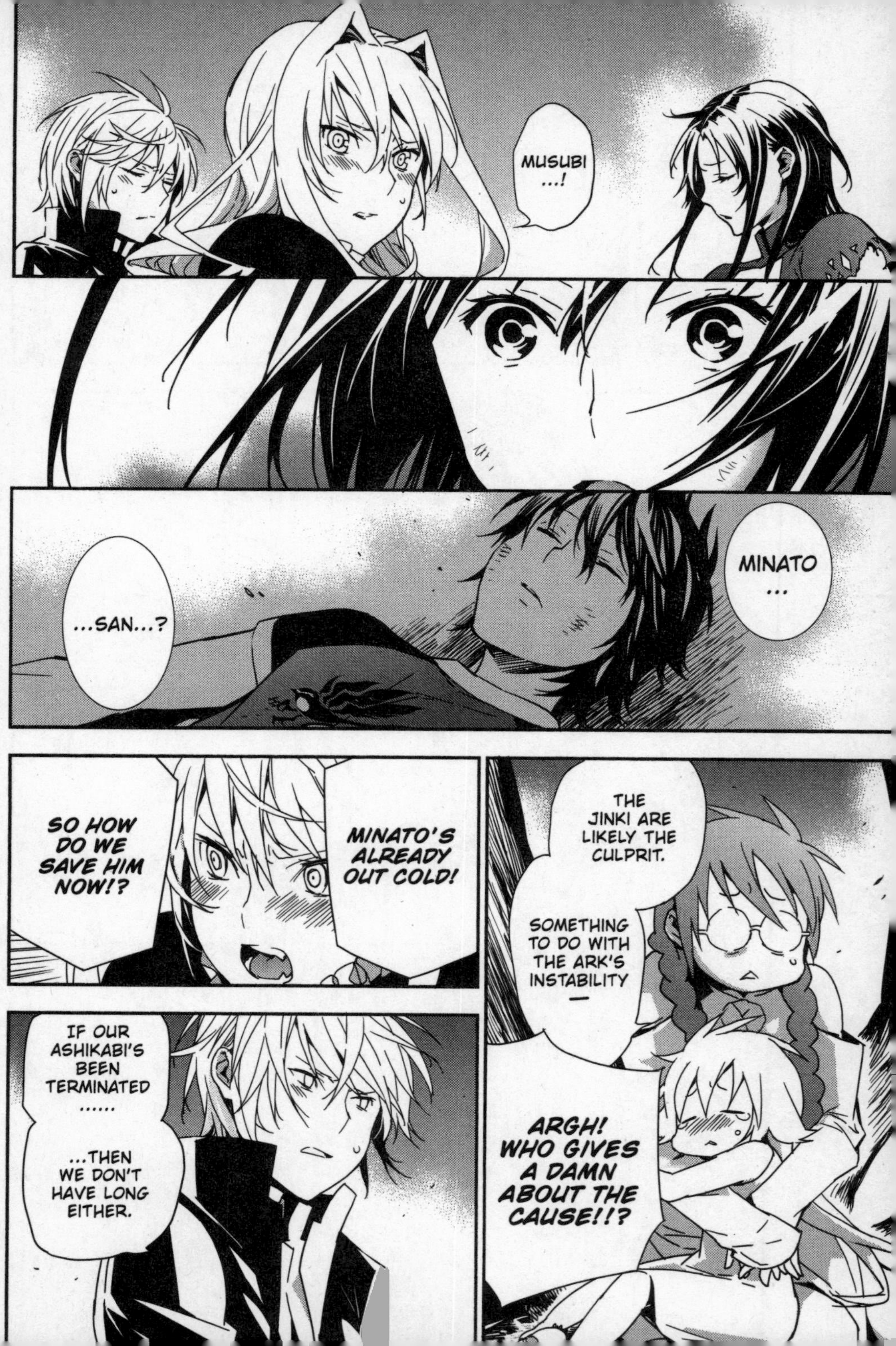
MUSUBI ...!
MINATO ...
...SAN...?
THE JINKI ARE LIKELY THE CULPRIT.
SOMETHING TO DO WITH THE ARK'S INSTABILITY —
ARGH! WHO GIVES A DAMN ABOUT THE CAUSE!!?
MINATO'S ALREADY OUT COLD!
SO HOW DO WE SAVE HIM NOW!?
IF OUR ASHIKABI'S BEEN TERMINATED ......
...THEN WE DON'T HAVE LONG EITHER.

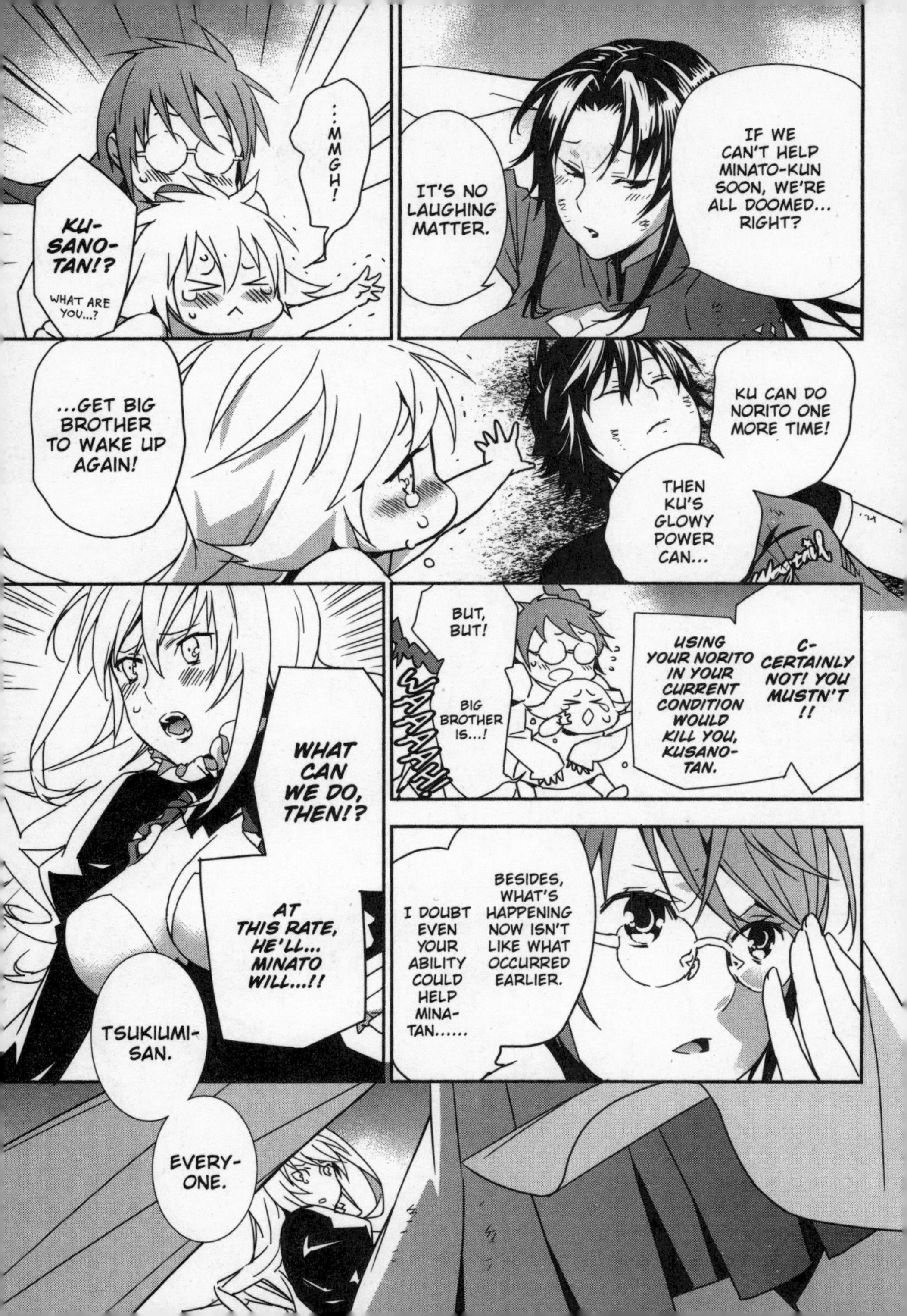
IF WE CAN'T HELP MINATO-KUN SOON, WE'RE ALL DOOMED... RIGHT?
IT'S NO LAUGHING MATTER.
...MMGH!
KU-SANO-TAN!?
WHAT ARE YOU...?
KU CAN DO NORITO ONE MORE TIME!
THEN KU'S GLOWY POWER CAN...
...GET BIG BROTHER TO WAKE UP AGAIN!
C-CERTAINLY NOT! YOU MUSTN'T!!
USING YOUR NORITO IN YOUR CURRENT CONDITION WOULD KILL YOU, KUSANO-TAN.
BUT, BUT!
BIG BROTHER IS...!
BESIDES, WHAT'S HAPPENING NOW ISN'T LIKE WHAT OCCURRED EARLIER.
I DOUBT EVEN YOUR ABILITY COULD HELP MINA-TAN......
WHAT CAN WE DO, THEN!?
AT THIS RATE, HE'LL... MINATO WILL...!!
TSUKIUMI-SAN.
EVERY-ONE.

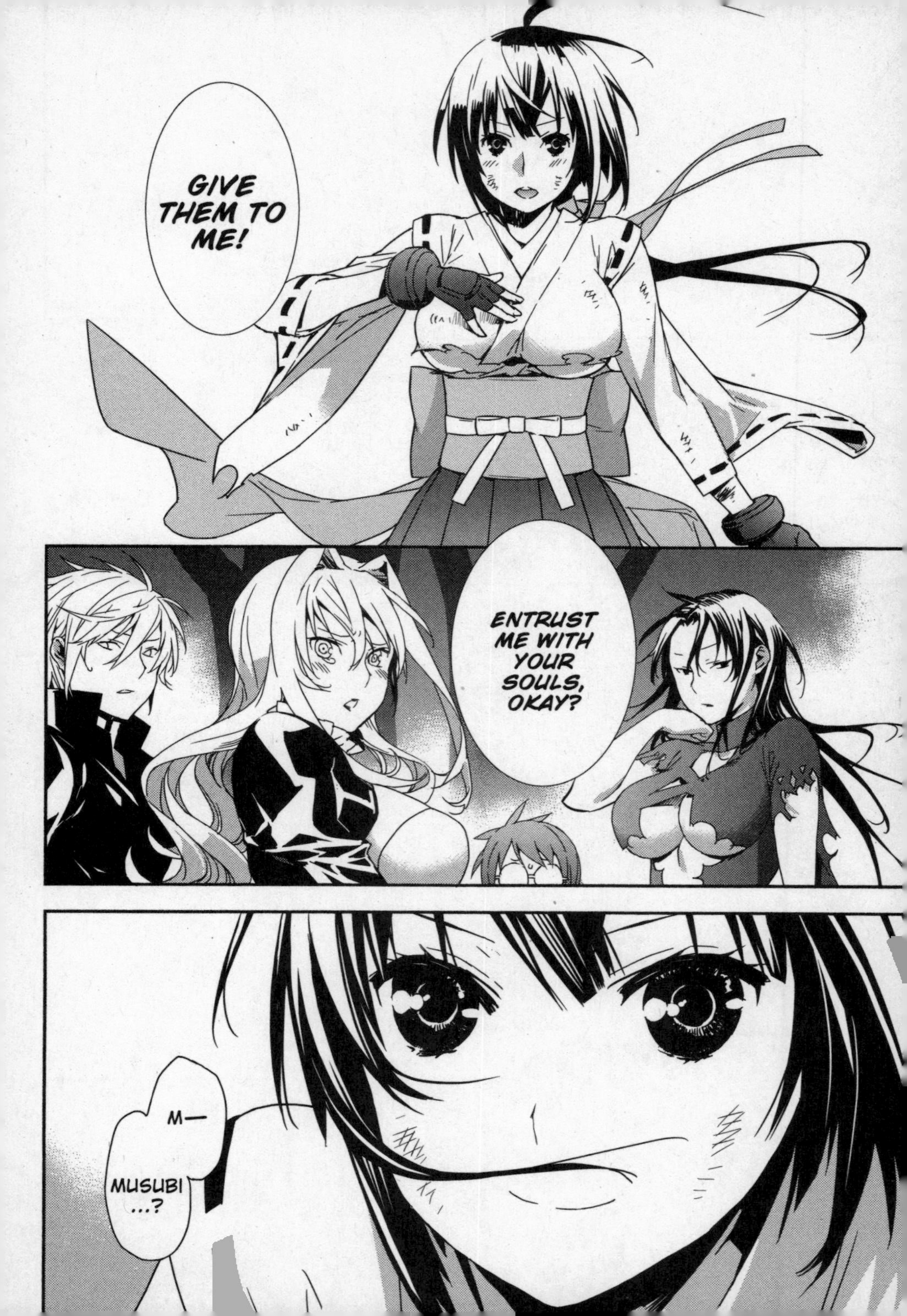
GIVE THEM TO ME!
ENTRUST ME WITH YOUR SOULS, OKAY?
M—
MUSUBI ...?

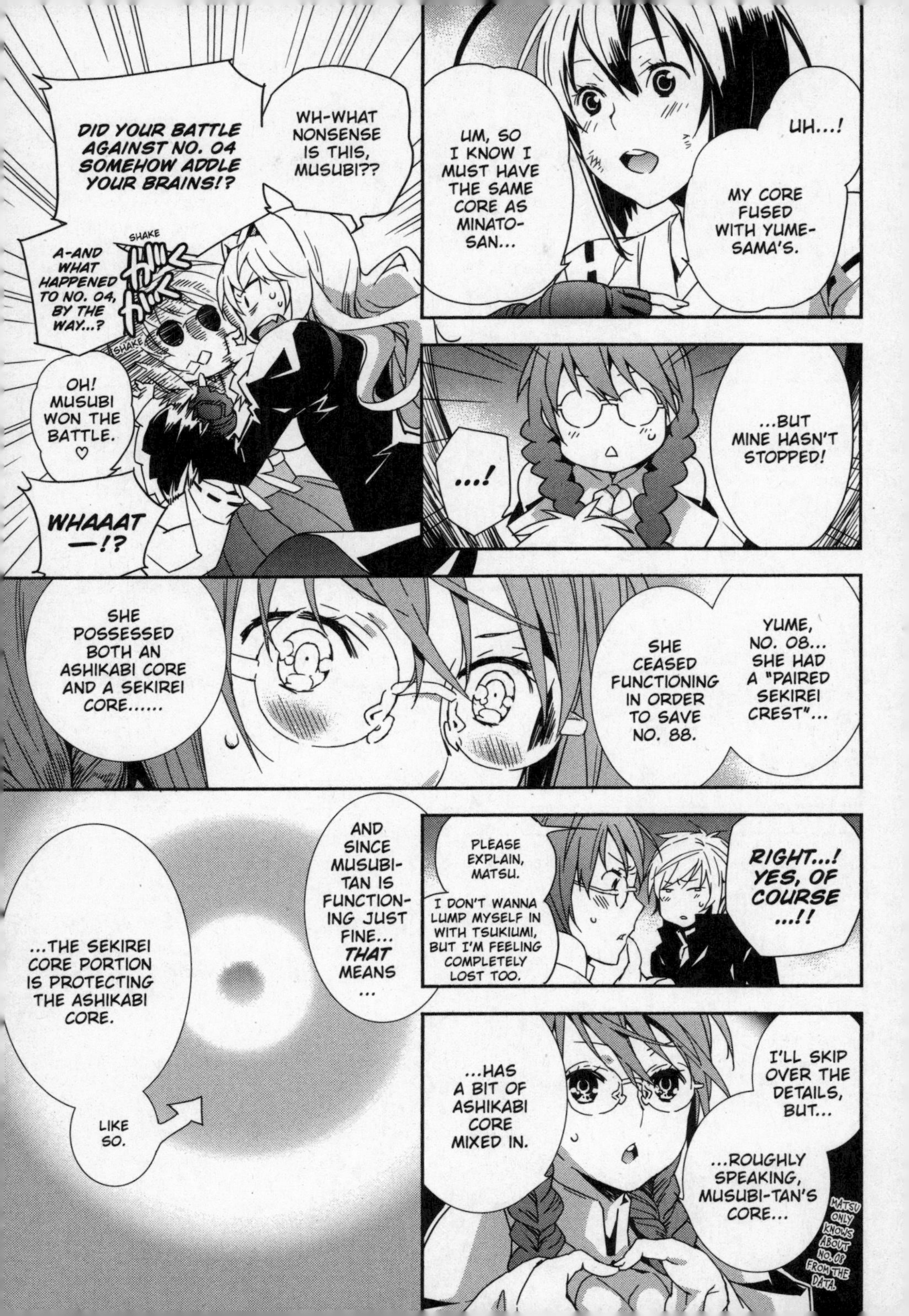
UH...!
MY CORE FUSED WITH YUME-SAMA'S.
UM, SO I KNOW I MUST HAVE THE SAME CORE AS MINATO-SAN...
...BUT MINE HASN'T STOPPED!
...!
WH-WHAT NONSENSE IS THIS, MUSUBI??
DID YOUR BATTLE AGAINST NO. 04 SOMEHOW ADDLE YOUR BRAINS!?
SHAKE
A-AND WHAT HAPPENED TO NO. 04, BY THE WAY...?
SHAKE
OH! MUSUBI WON THE BATTLE. ♡
WHAAAT—!?
YUME, NO. 08... SHE HAD A "PAIRED SEKIREI CREST"...
SHE CEASED FUNCTIONING IN ORDER TO SAVE NO. 88.
SHE POSSESSED BOTH AN ASHIKABI CORE AND A SEKIREI CORE......
RIGHT...! YES, OF COURSE ...!!
PLEASE EXPLAIN, MATSU.
I DON'T WANNA LUMP MYSELF IN WITH TSUKIUMI, BUT I'M FEELING COMPLETELY LOST TOO.
I'LL SKIP OVER THE DETAILS, BUT...
...ROUGHLY SPEAKING, MUSUBI-TAN'S CORE...
...HAS A BIT OF ASHIKABI CORE MIXED IN.
MATSU ONLY KNOWS ABOUT NO. 08 FROM THE DATA.
AND SINCE MUSUBI-TAN IS FUNCTIONING JUST FINE... THAT MEANS ...
...THE SEKIREI CORE PORTION IS PROTECTING THE ASHIKABI CORE.
LIKE SO.

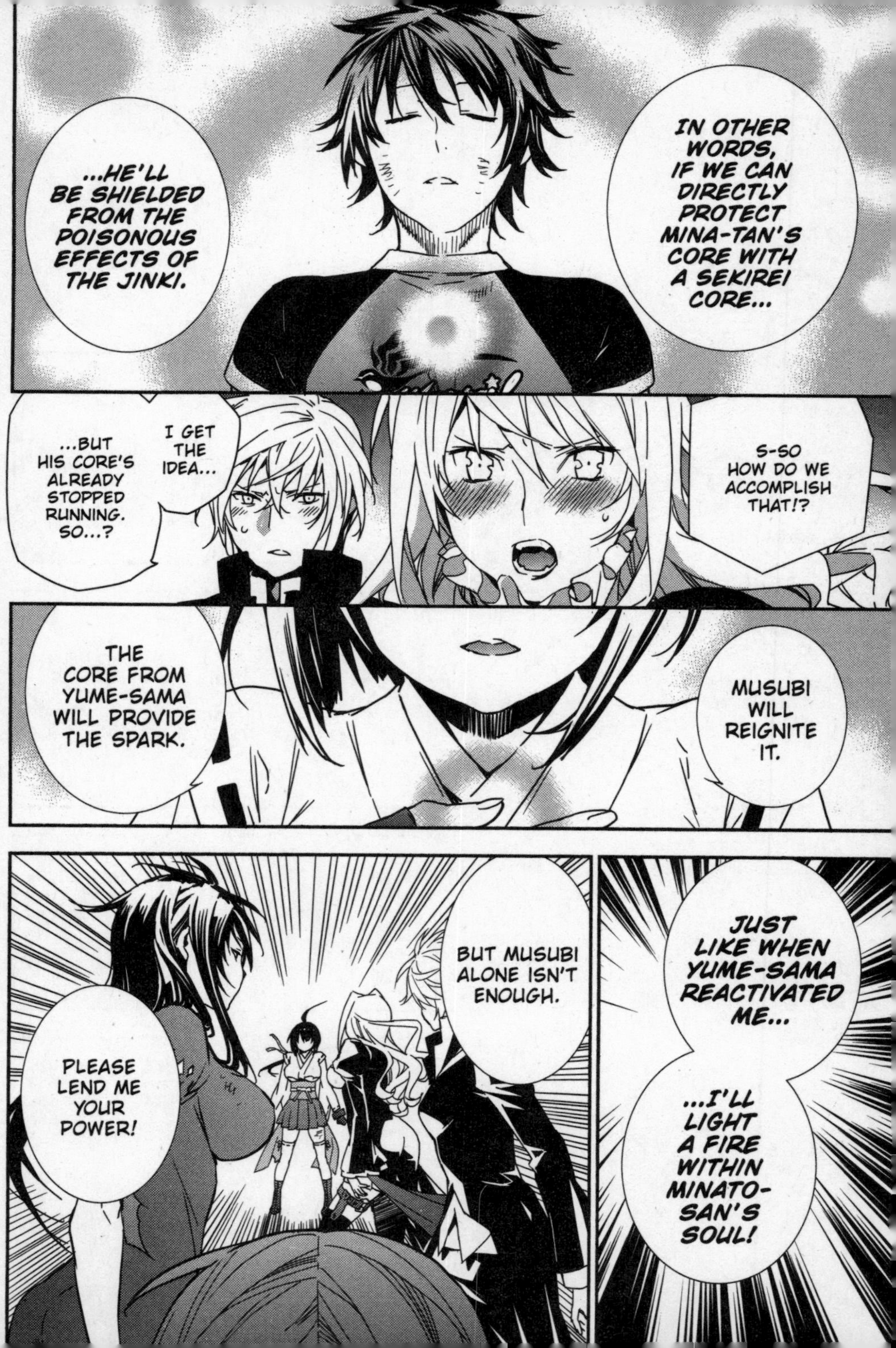
IN OTHER WORDS, IF WE CAN DIRECTLY PROTECT MINA-TAN'S CORE WITH A SEKIREI CORE...
...HE'LL BE SHIELDED FROM THE POISONOUS EFFECTS OF THE JINKI.
S-SO HOW DO WE ACCOMPLISH THAT!?
I GET THE IDEA...
...BUT HIS CORE'S ALREADY STOPPED RUNNING. SO...?
MUSUBI WILL REIGNITE IT.
THE CORE FROM YUME-SAMA WILL PROVIDE THE SPARK.
JUST LIKE WHEN YUME-SAMA REACTIVATED ME...
...I'LL LIGHT A FIRE WITHIN MINATO-SAN'S SOUL!
BUT MUSUBI ALONE ISN'T ENOUGH.
PLEASE LEND ME YOUR POWER!

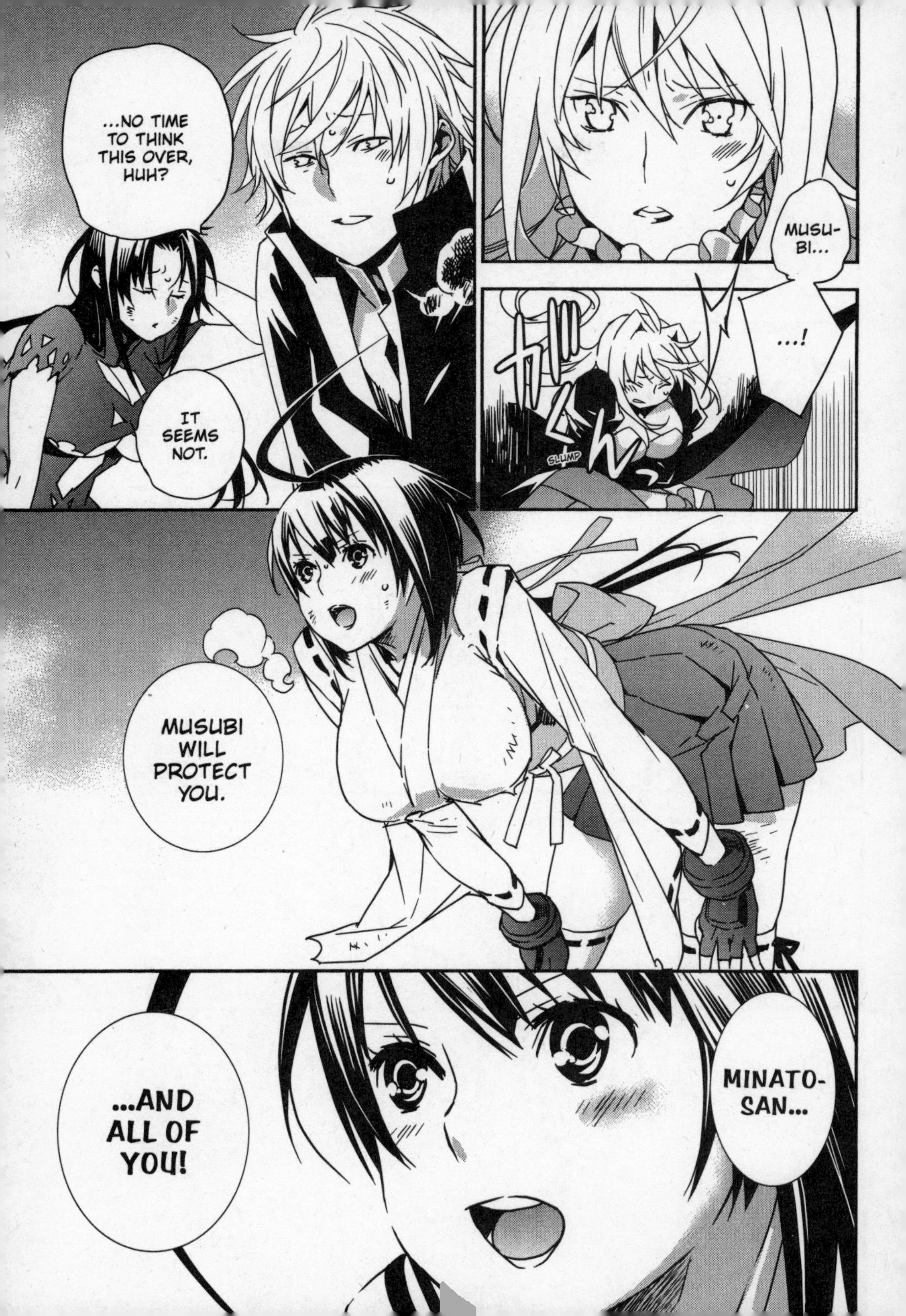
MUSU-BI...
...!
SLUMP
...NO TIME TO THINK THIS OVER, HUH?
IT SEEMS NOT.
MUSUBI WILL PROTECT YOU.
MINATO-SAN...
...AND ALL OF YOU!

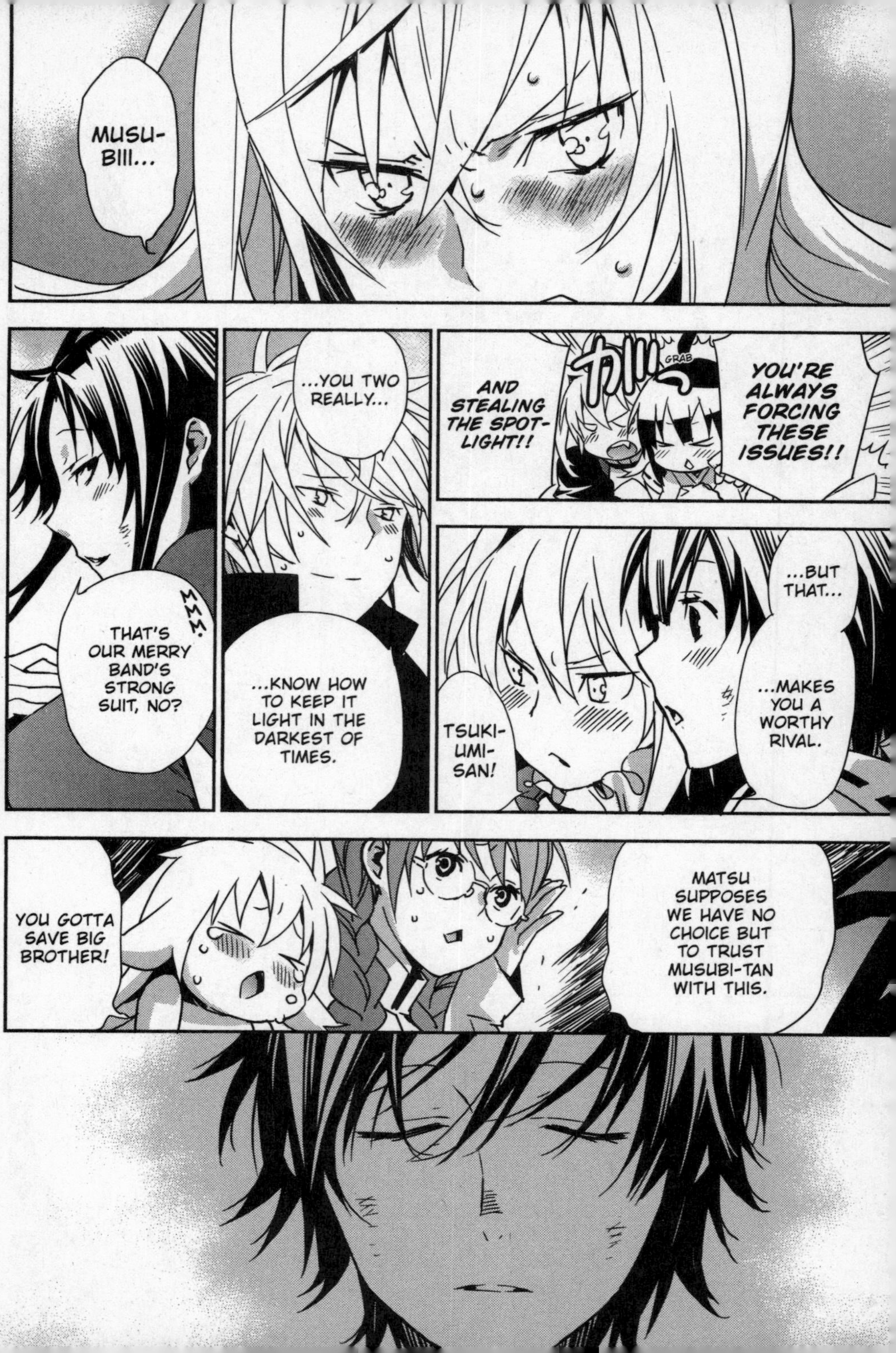
MUSU-BIII...
GRAB
YOU'RE ALWAYS FORCING THESE ISSUES!!
AND STEALING THE SPOT-LIGHT!!
...BUT THAT...
...MAKES YOU A WORTHY RIVAL.
TSUKI-UMI-SAN!
...YOU TWO REALLY...
...KNOW HOW TO KEEP IT LIGHT IN THE DARKEST OF TIMES.
MMM.
THAT'S OUR MERRY BAND'S STRONG SUIT, NO?
MATSU SUPPOSES WE HAVE NO CHOICE BUT TO TRUST MUSUBI-TAN WITH THIS.
YOU GOTTA SAVE BIG BROTHER!

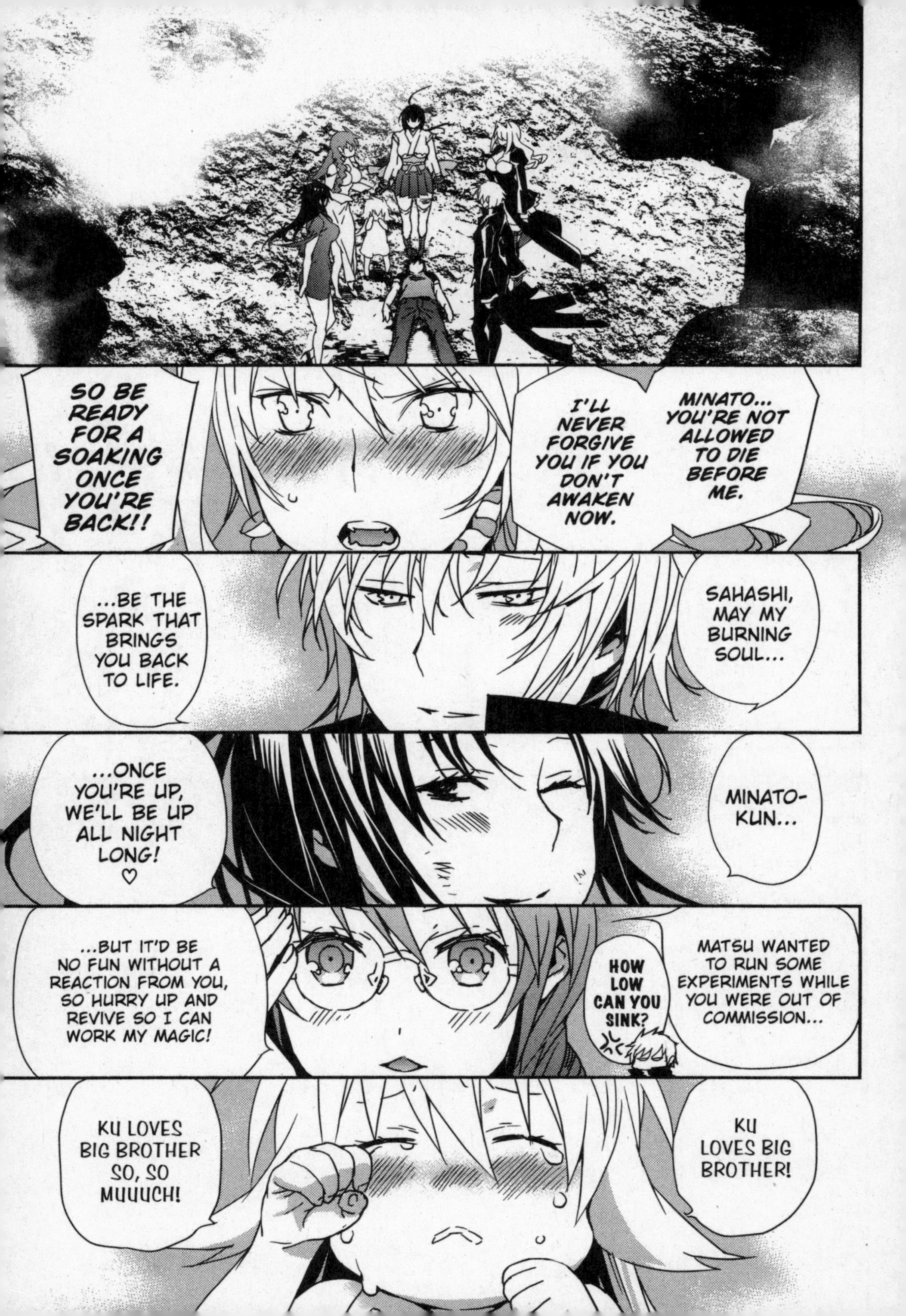
MINATO... YOU'RE NOT ALLOWED TO DIE BEFORE ME.
I'LL NEVER FORGIVE YOU IF YOU DON'T AWAKEN NOW.
SO BE READY FOR A SOAKING ONCE YOU'RE BACK!!
SAHASHI, MAY MY BURNING SOUL...
...BE THE SPARK THAT BRINGS YOU BACK TO LIFE.
MINATO-KUN...
...ONCE YOU'RE UP, WE'LL BE UP ALL NIGHT LONG! ♡
MATSU WANTED TO RUN SOME EXPERIMENTS WHILE YOU WERE OUT OF COMMISSION...
HOW LOW CAN YOU SINK?
...BUT IT'D BE NO FUN WITHOUT A REACTION FROM YOU, SO HURRY UP AND REVIVE SO I CAN WORK MY MAGIC!
KU LOVES BIG BROTHER!
KU LOVES BIG BROTHER SO, SO MUUUCH!

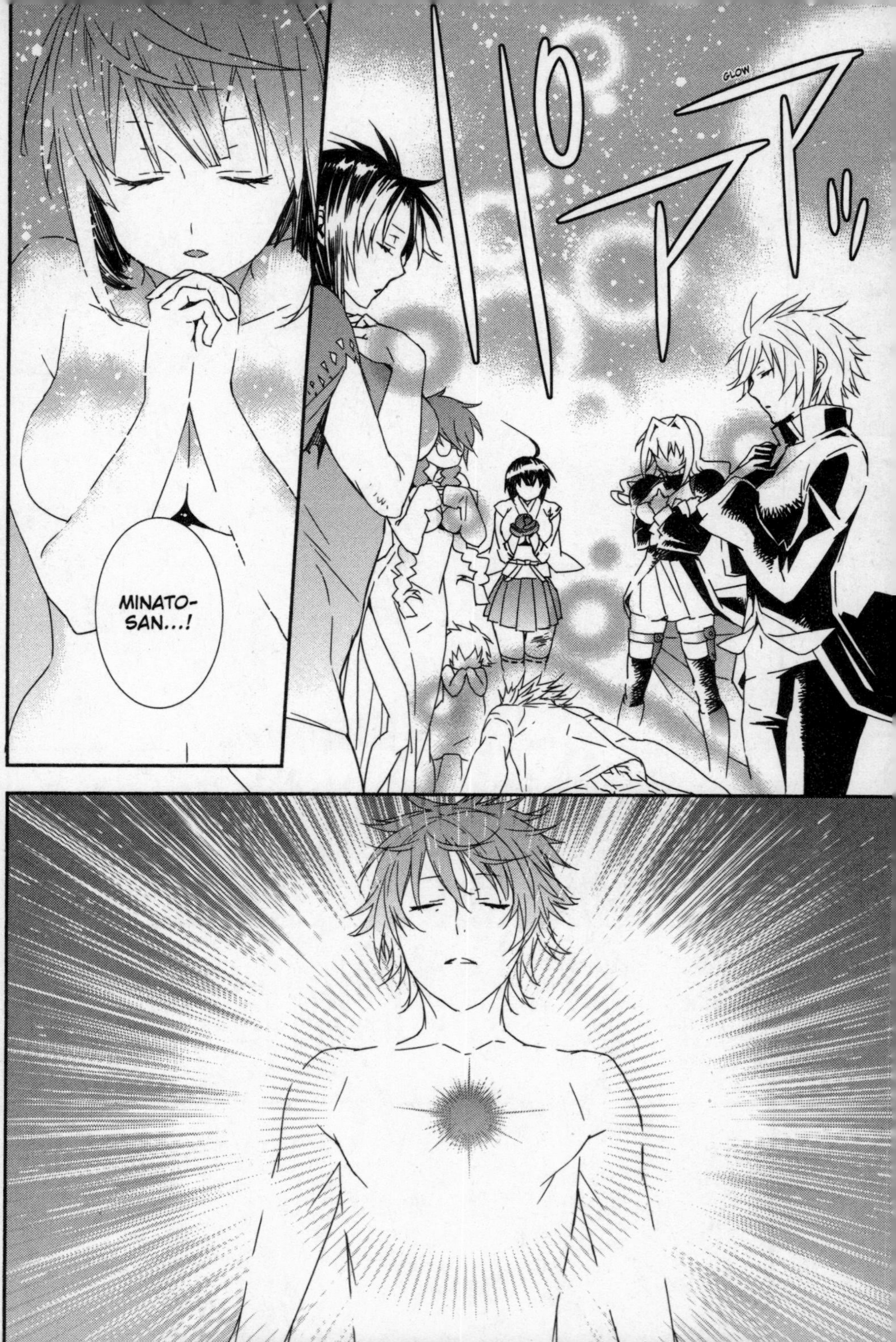
GLOW
MINATO-SAN...!

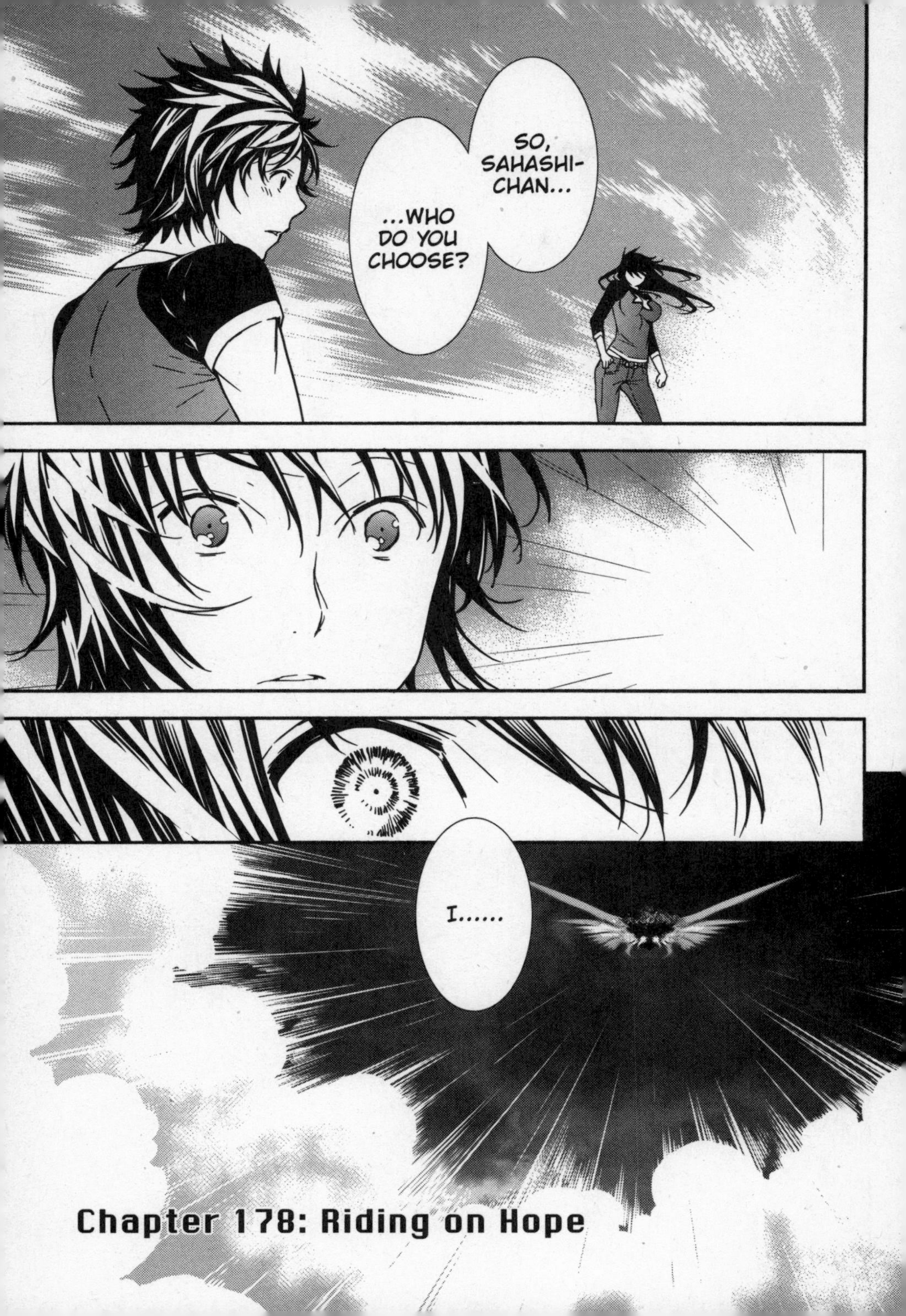
SO, SAHASHI-CHAN...
...WHO DO YOU CHOOSE?
I......

Chapter 178: Riding on Hope

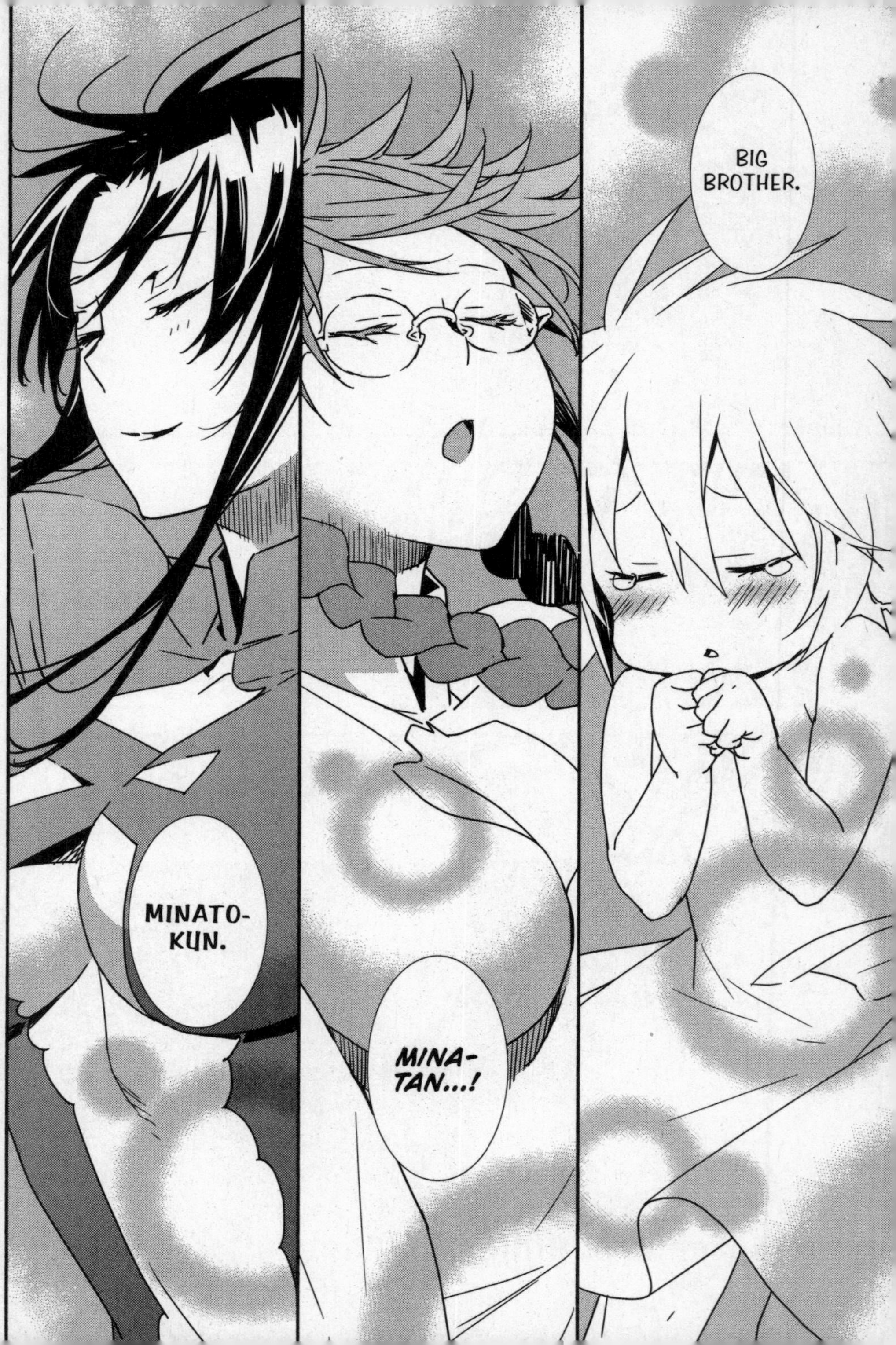
BIG BROTHER.
MINA-TAN...!
MINATO-KUN.

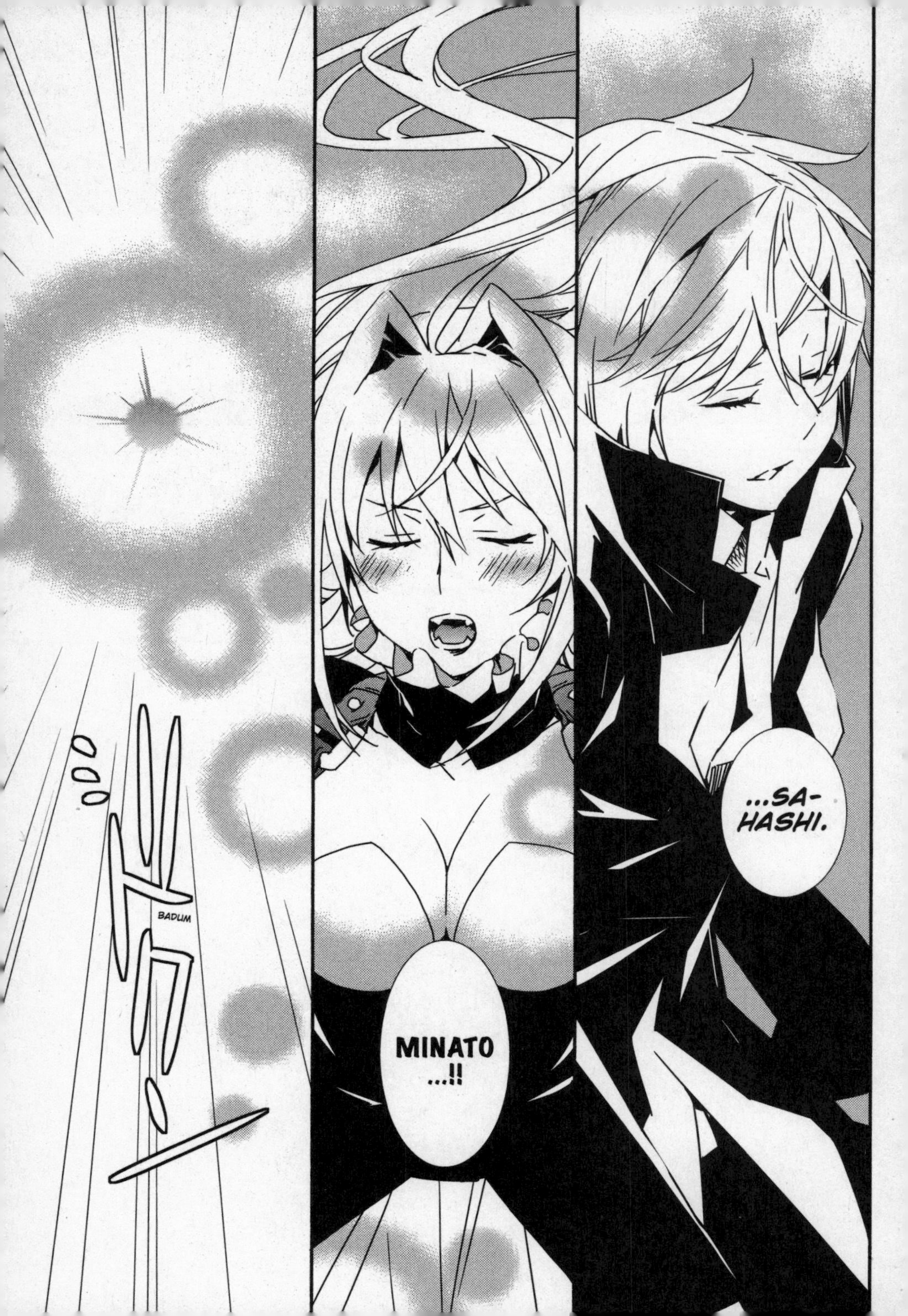
...SA-
HASHI.
MINATO
...!!
BADUM

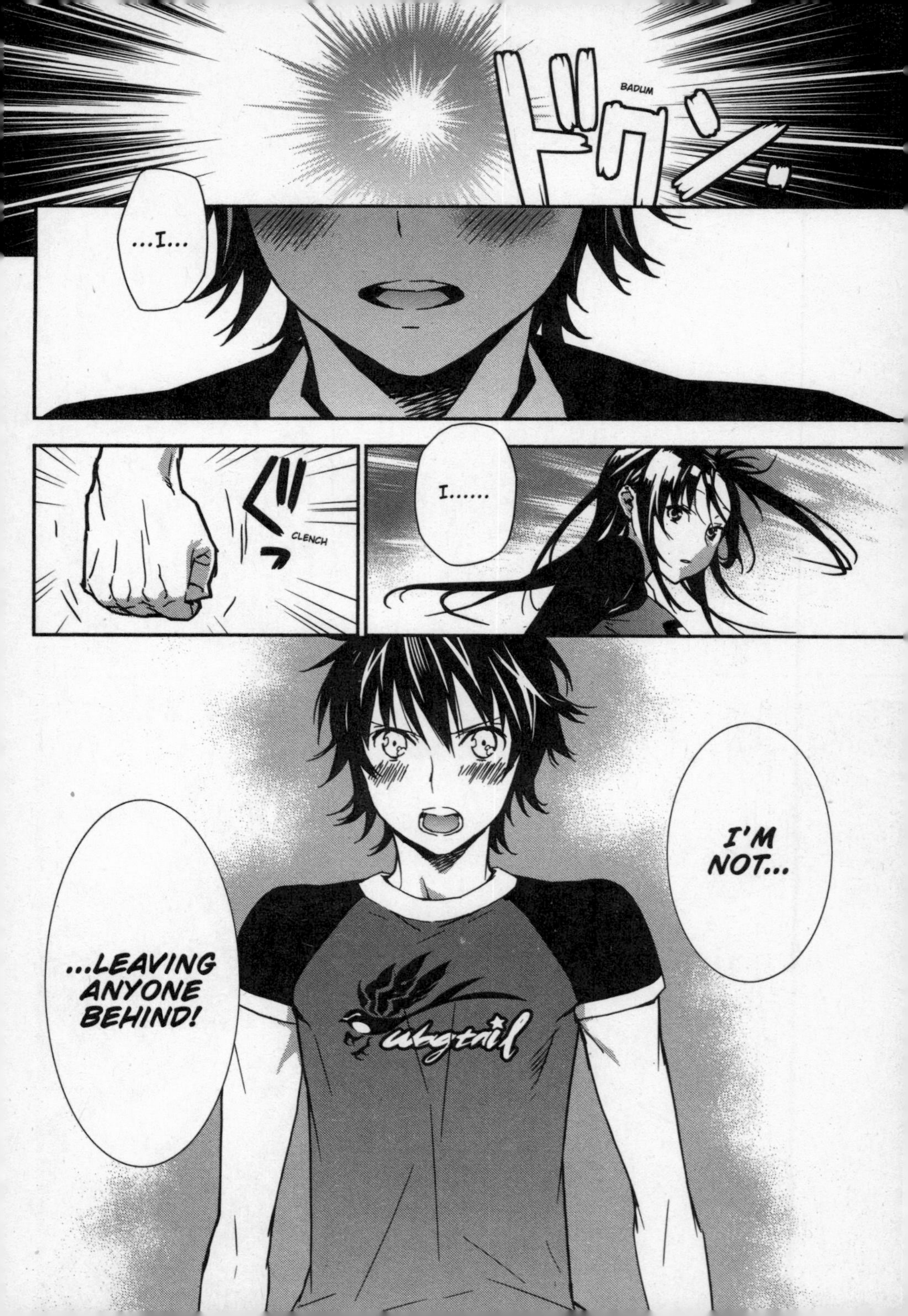
ドクン
BADUM
...I...
I......
ぐっ
CLENCH
I'M NOT...
...LEAVING ANYONE BEHIND!

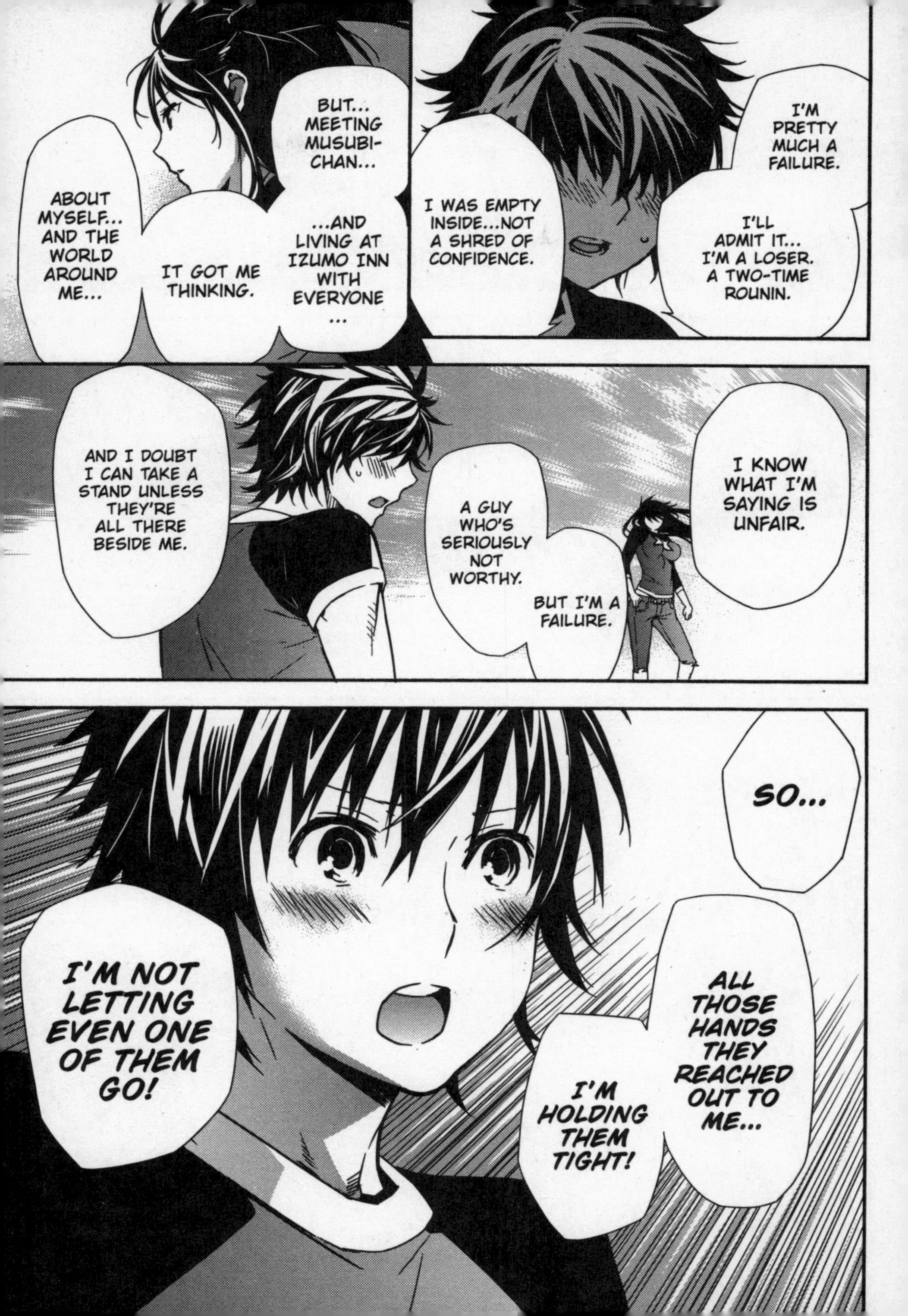
I'M PRETTY MUCH A FAILURE.
I'LL ADMIT IT... I'M A LOSER. A TWO-TIME ROUNIN.
I WAS EMPTY INSIDE...NOT A SHRED OF CONFIDENCE.
BUT... MEETING MUSUBI-CHAN...
...AND LIVING AT IZUMO INN WITH EVERYONE ...
IT GOT ME THINKING.
ABOUT MYSELF... AND THE WORLD AROUND ME...
I KNOW WHAT I'M SAYING IS UNFAIR.
BUT I'M A FAILURE.
A GUY WHO'S SERIOUSLY NOT WORTHY.
AND I DOUBT I CAN TAKE A STAND UNLESS THEY'RE ALL THERE BESIDE ME.
SO...
ALL THOSE HANDS THEY REACHED OUT TO ME...
I'M HOLDING THEM TIGHT!
I'M NOT LETTING EVEN ONE OF THEM GO!

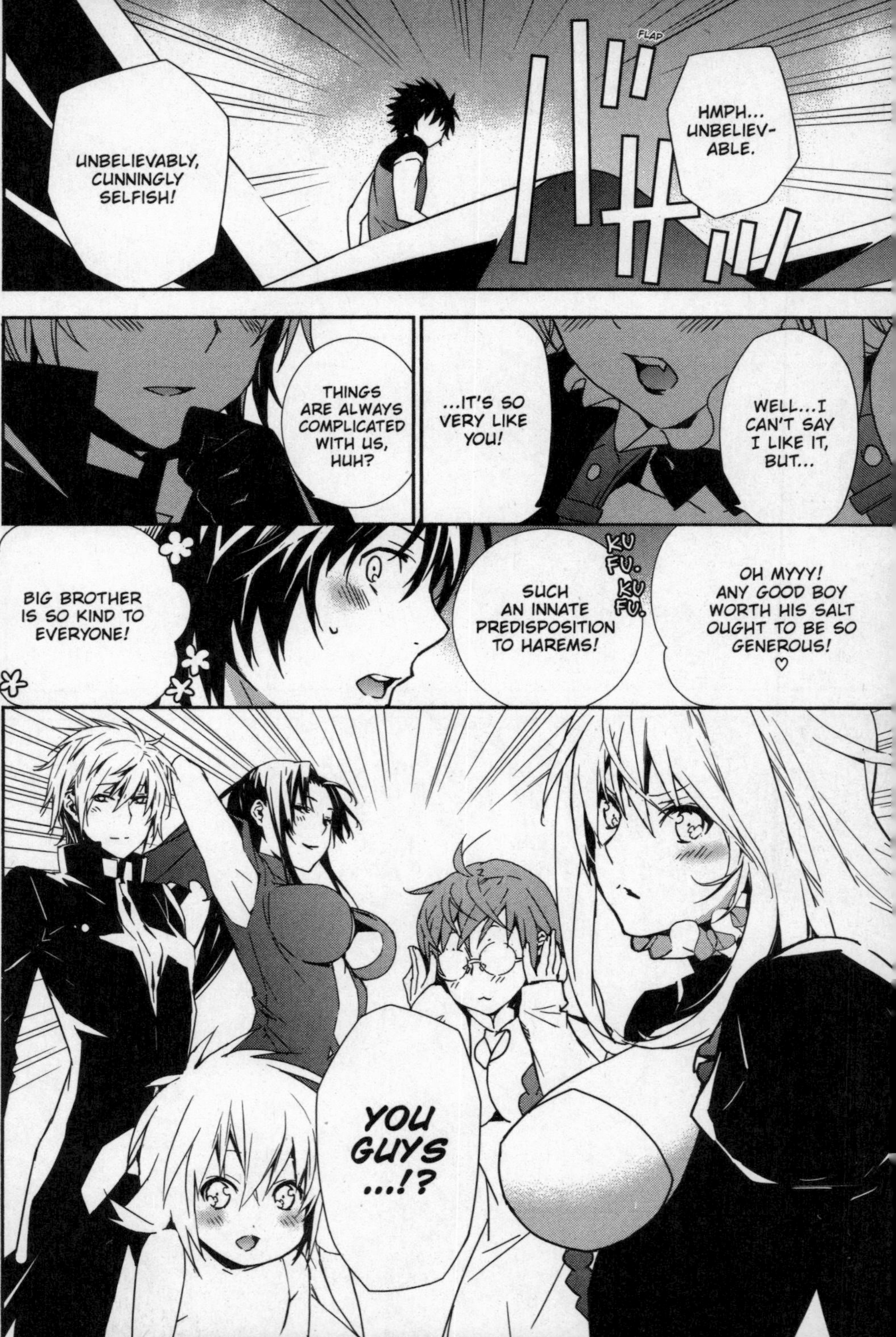
FLAP
HMPH... UNBELIEVABLE.
UNBELIEVABLY, CUNNINGLY SELFISH!
WELL...I CAN'T SAY I LIKE IT, BUT...
...IT'S SO VERY LIKE YOU!
THINGS ARE ALWAYS COMPLICATED WITH US, HUH?
OH MYYY! ANY GOOD BOY WORTH HIS SALT OUGHT TO BE SO GENEROUS! ♡
KU FU. KU FU.
SUCH AN INNATE PREDISPOSITION TO HAREMS!
BIG BROTHER IS SO KIND TO EVERYONE!
YOU GUYS ...!?

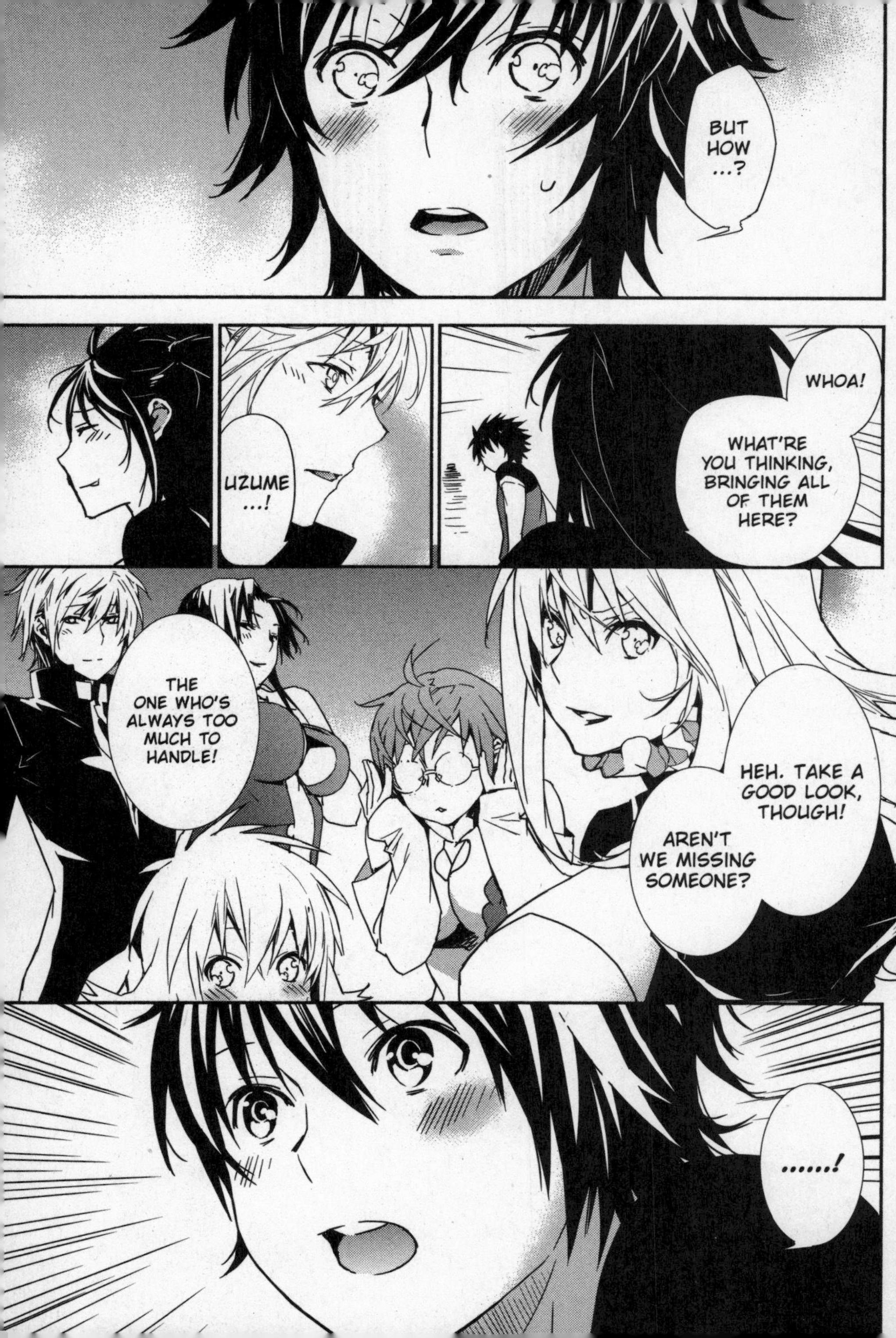
BUT HOW ...?
WHOA!
WHAT'RE YOU THINKING, BRINGING ALL OF THEM HERE?
UZUME ...!
HEH. TAKE A GOOD LOOK, THOUGH!
AREN'T WE MISSING SOMEONE?
THE ONE WHO'S ALWAYS TOO MUCH TO HANDLE!
......!

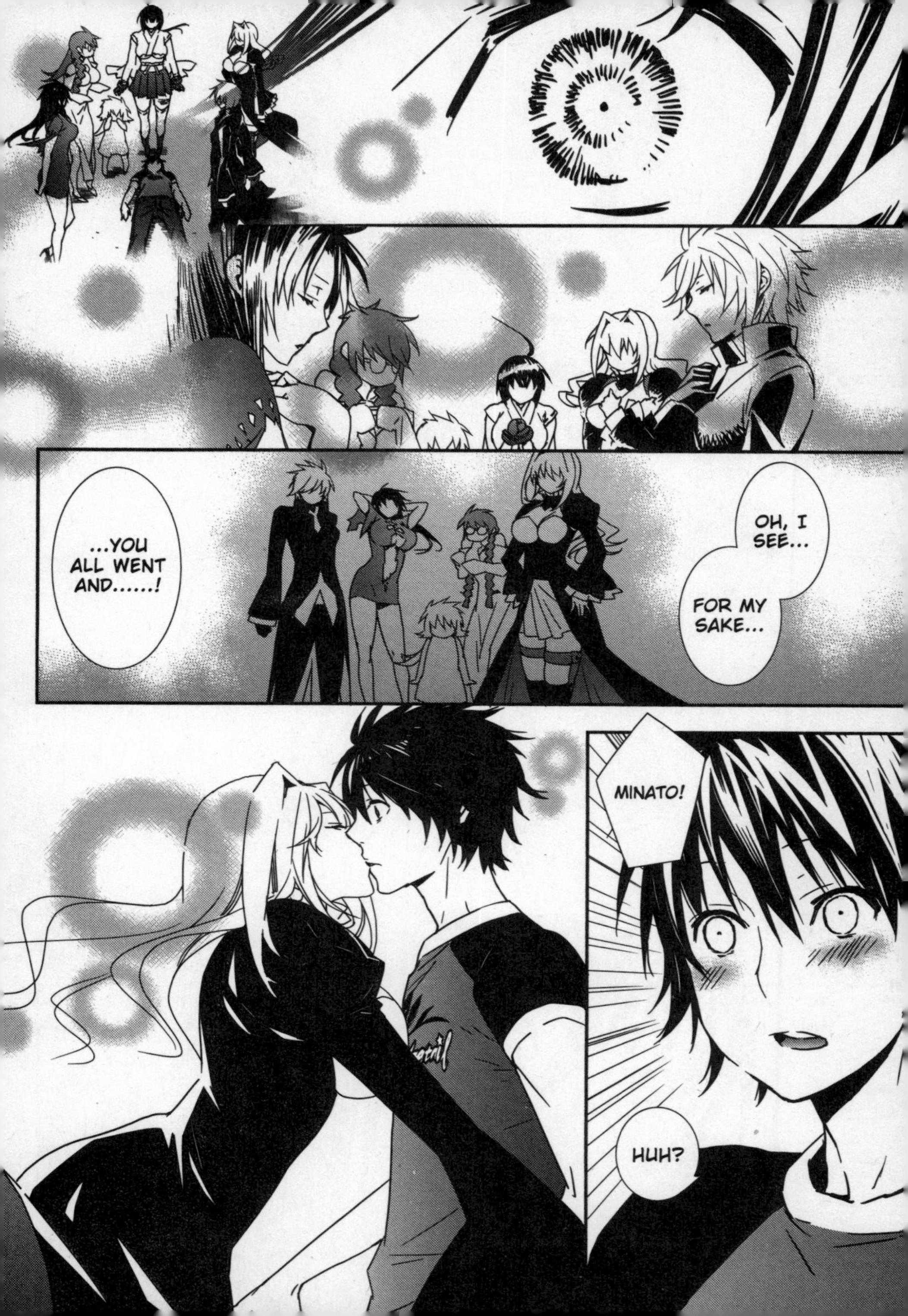
OH, I SEE...
FOR MY SAKE...
...YOU ALL WENT AND......!
MINATO!
HUH?

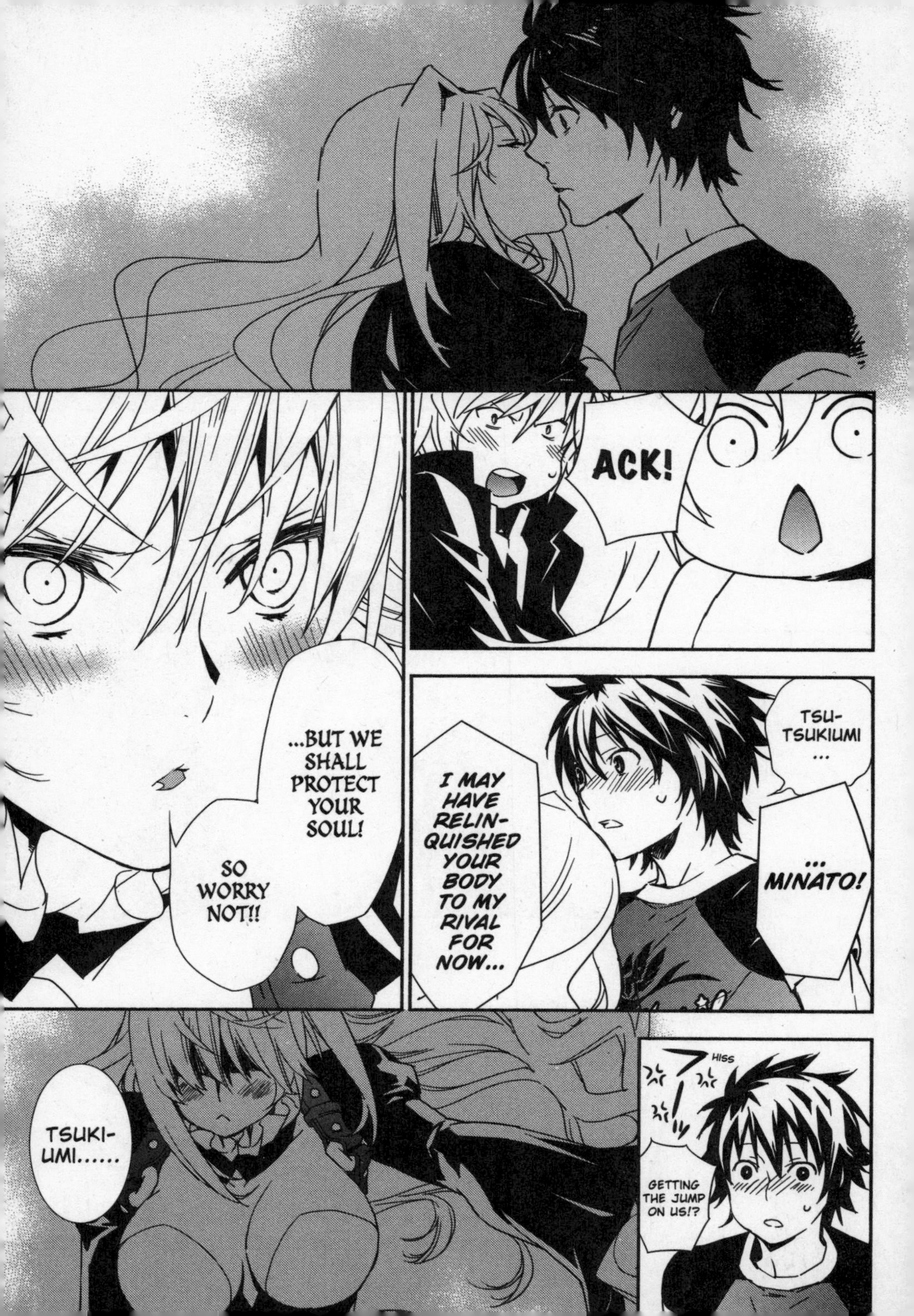
ACK!
TSU-TSUKIUMI...
...MINATO!
I MAY HAVE RELIN-QUISHED YOUR BODY TO MY RIVAL FOR NOW...
...BUT WE SHALL PROTECT YOUR SOUL!
SO WORRY NOT!!
HISS
GETTING THE JUMP ON US!?
TSUKI-UMI......

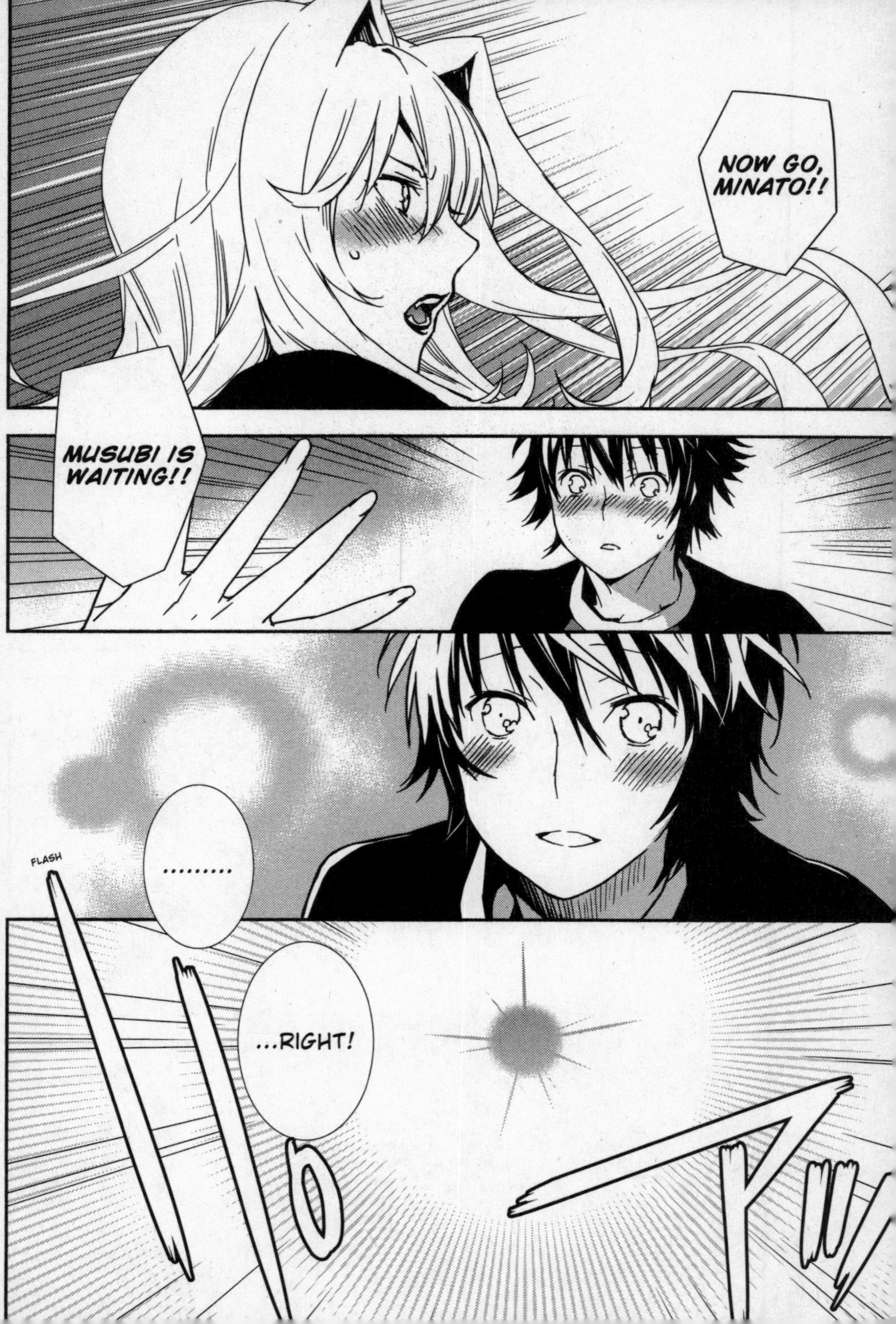
NOW GO, MINATO!!
MUSUBI IS WAITING!!
....
FLASH
...RIGHT!

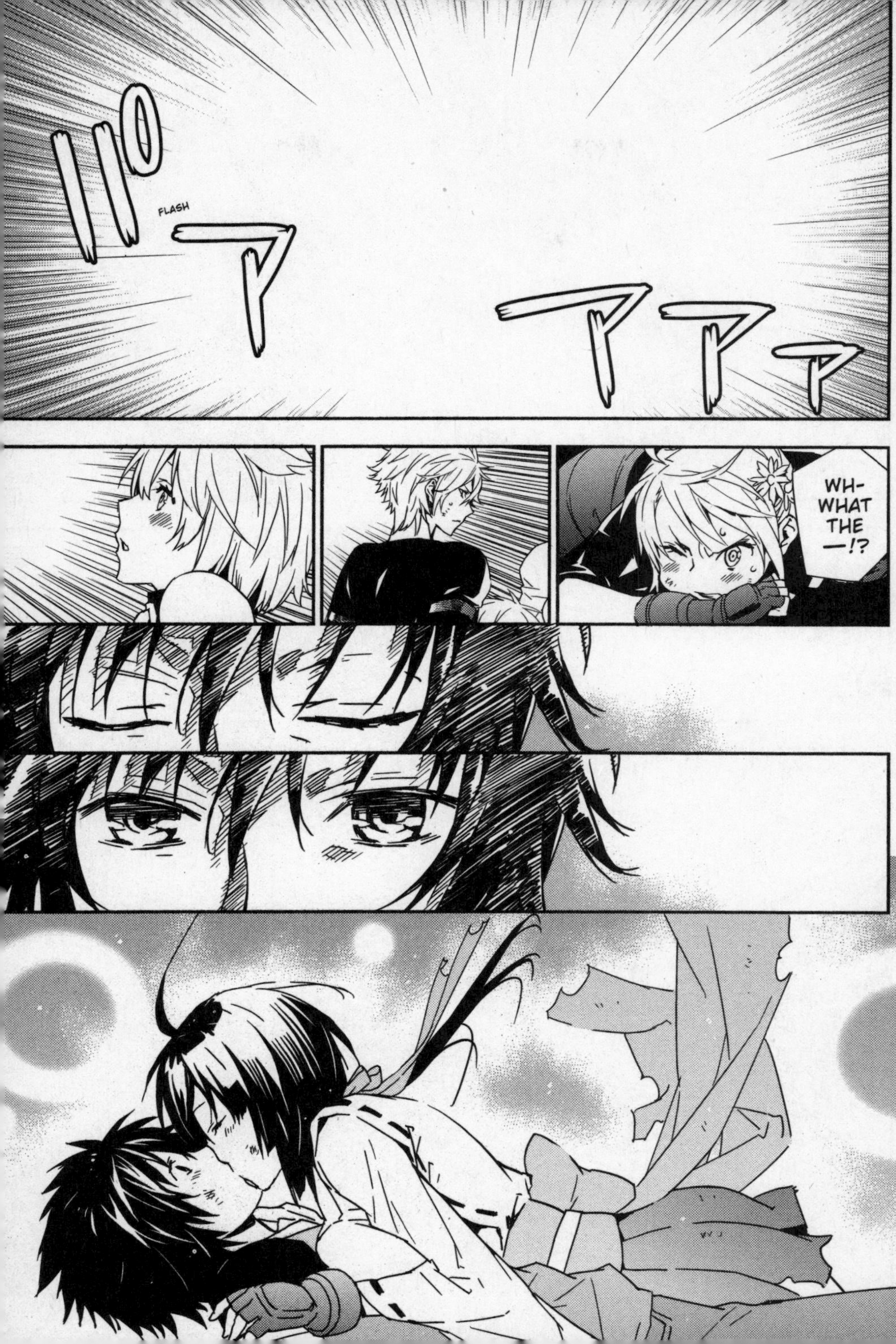
パアアアア
FLASH
WH-WHAT THE—!?

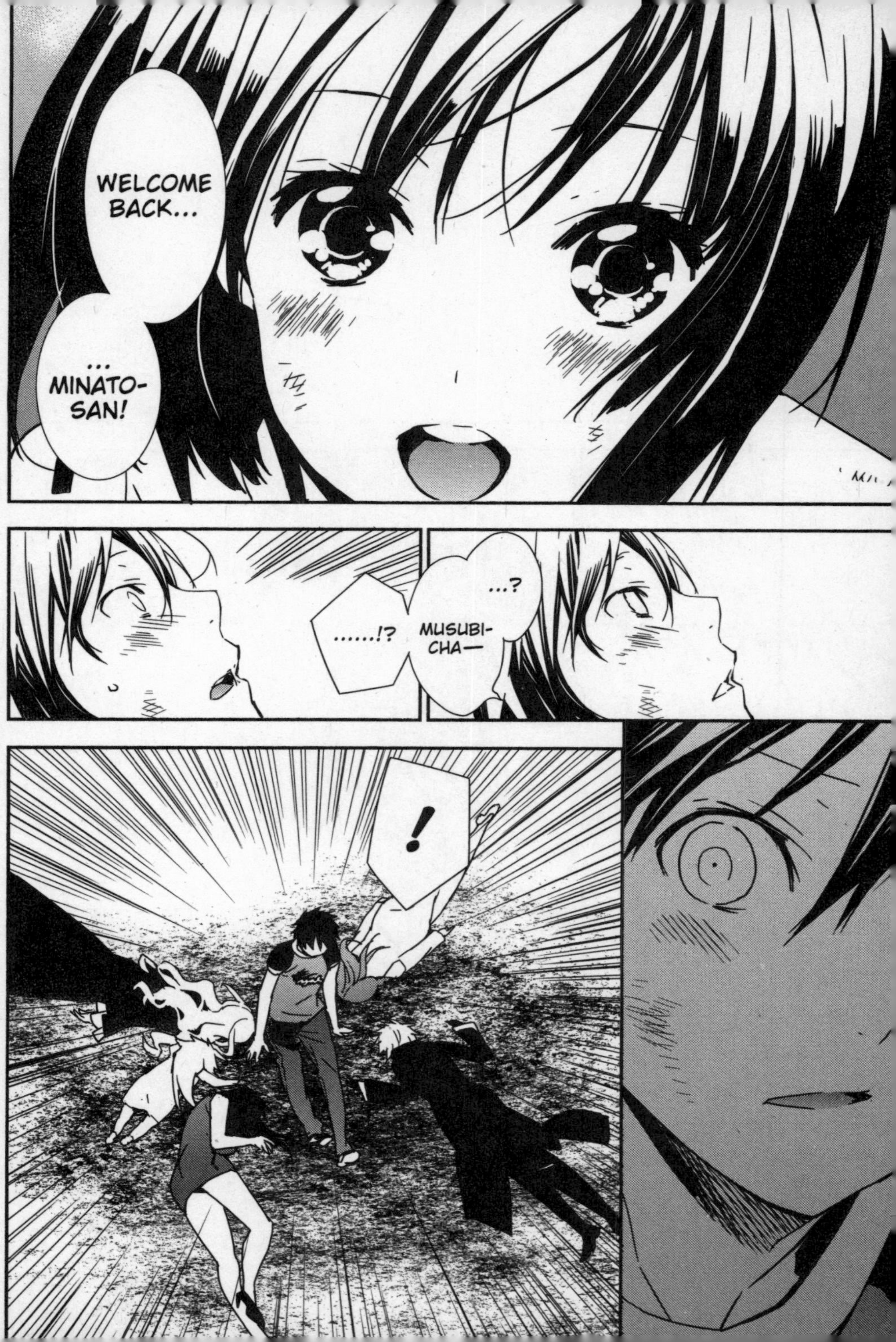
WELCOME BACK...
... MINATO-SAN!
...?
MUSUBI-CHA—
......!?
!

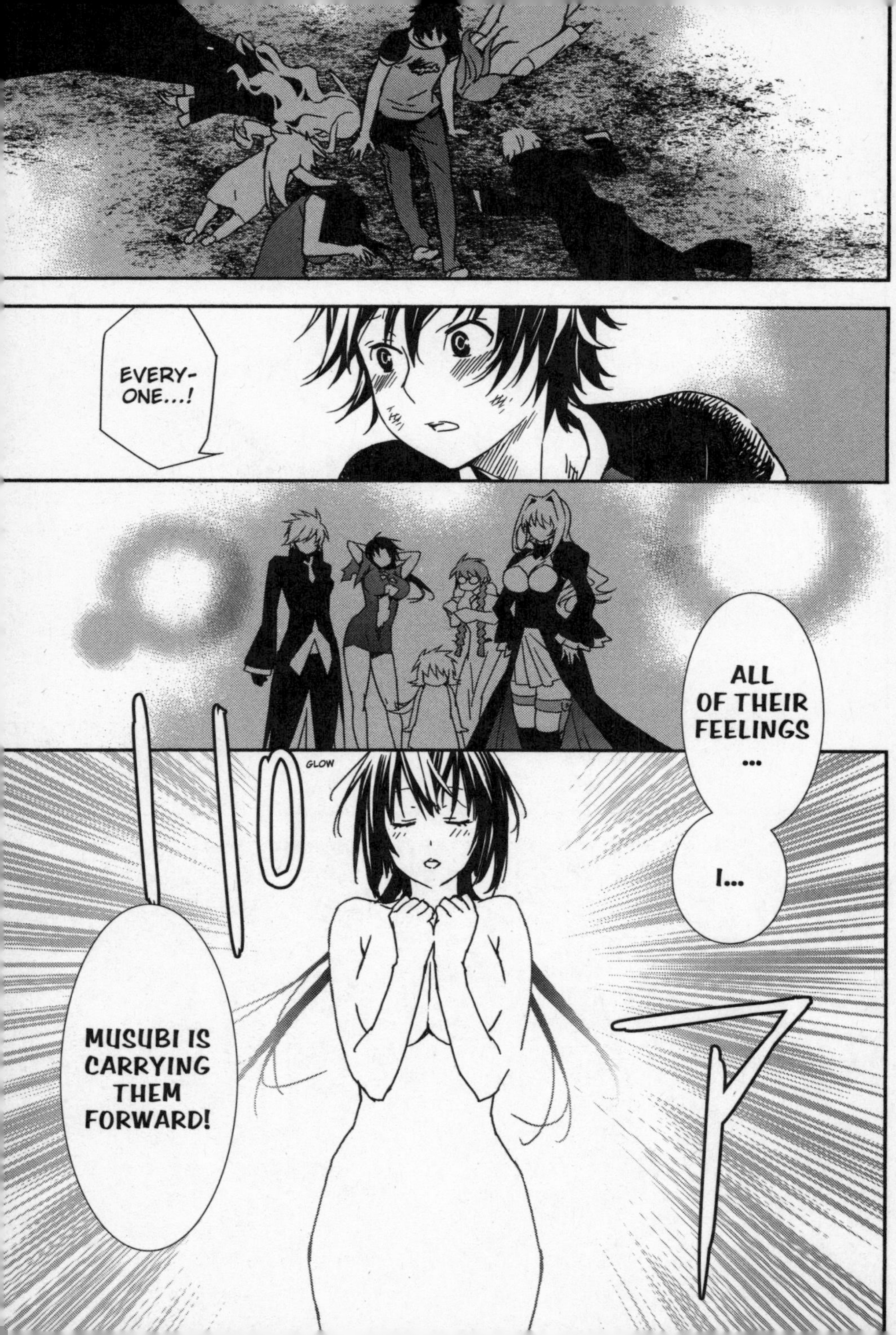
EVERY-ONE...!
ALL OF THEIR FEELINGS...
I...
GLOW
MUSUBI IS CARRYING THEM FORWARD!

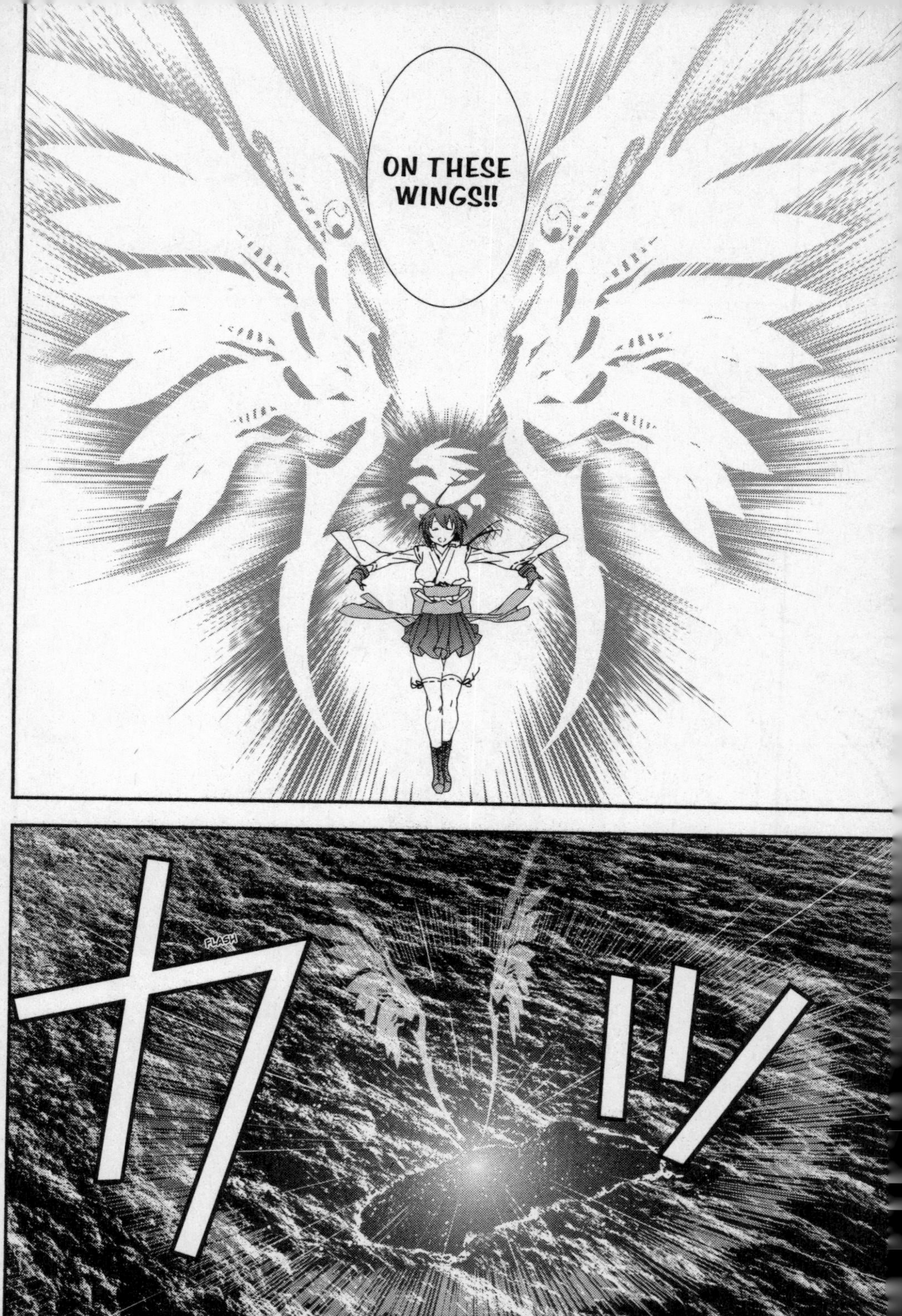
ON THESE WINGS!!
カッ
FLASH

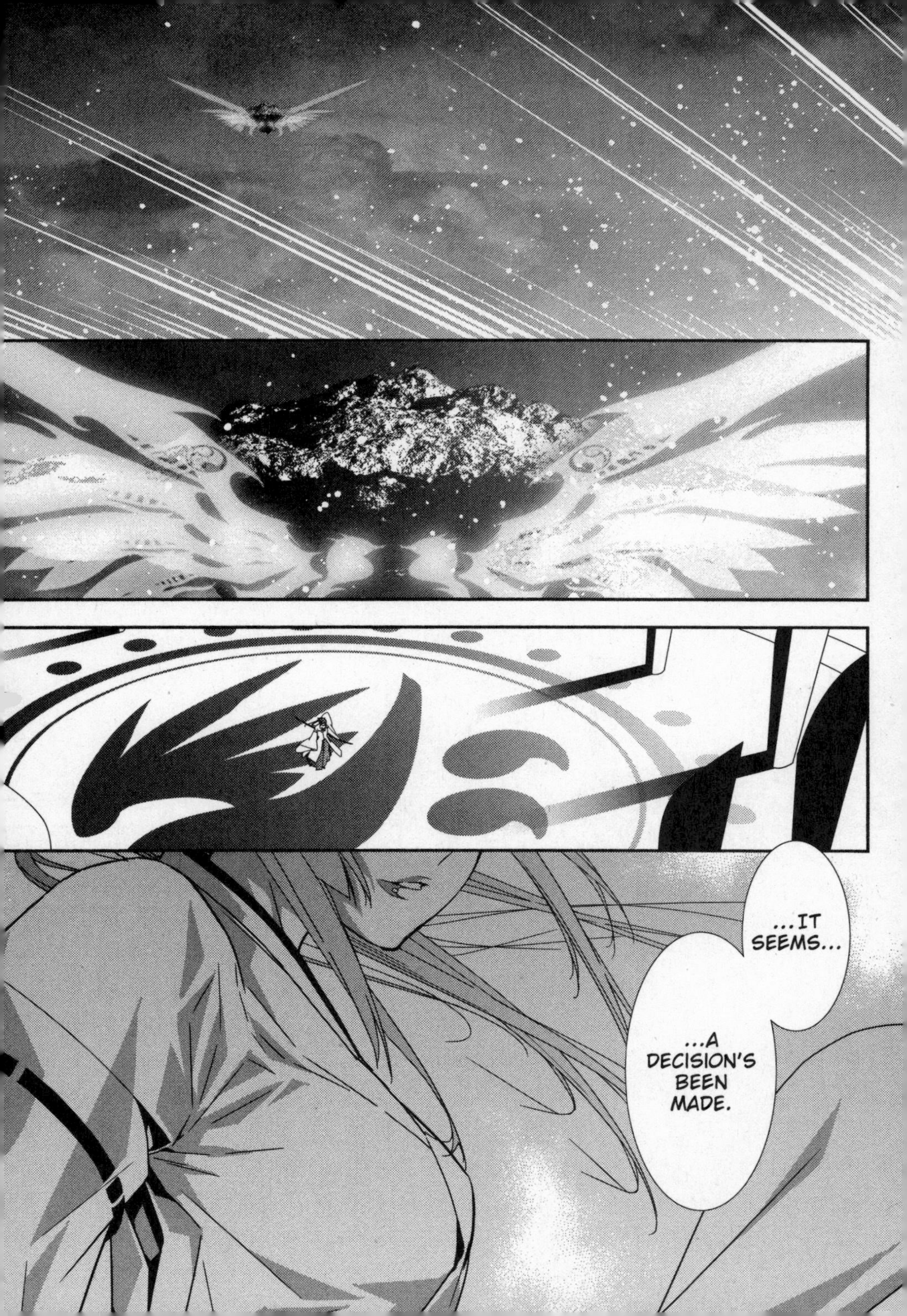
...IT SEEMS...
...A DECISION'S BEEN MADE.

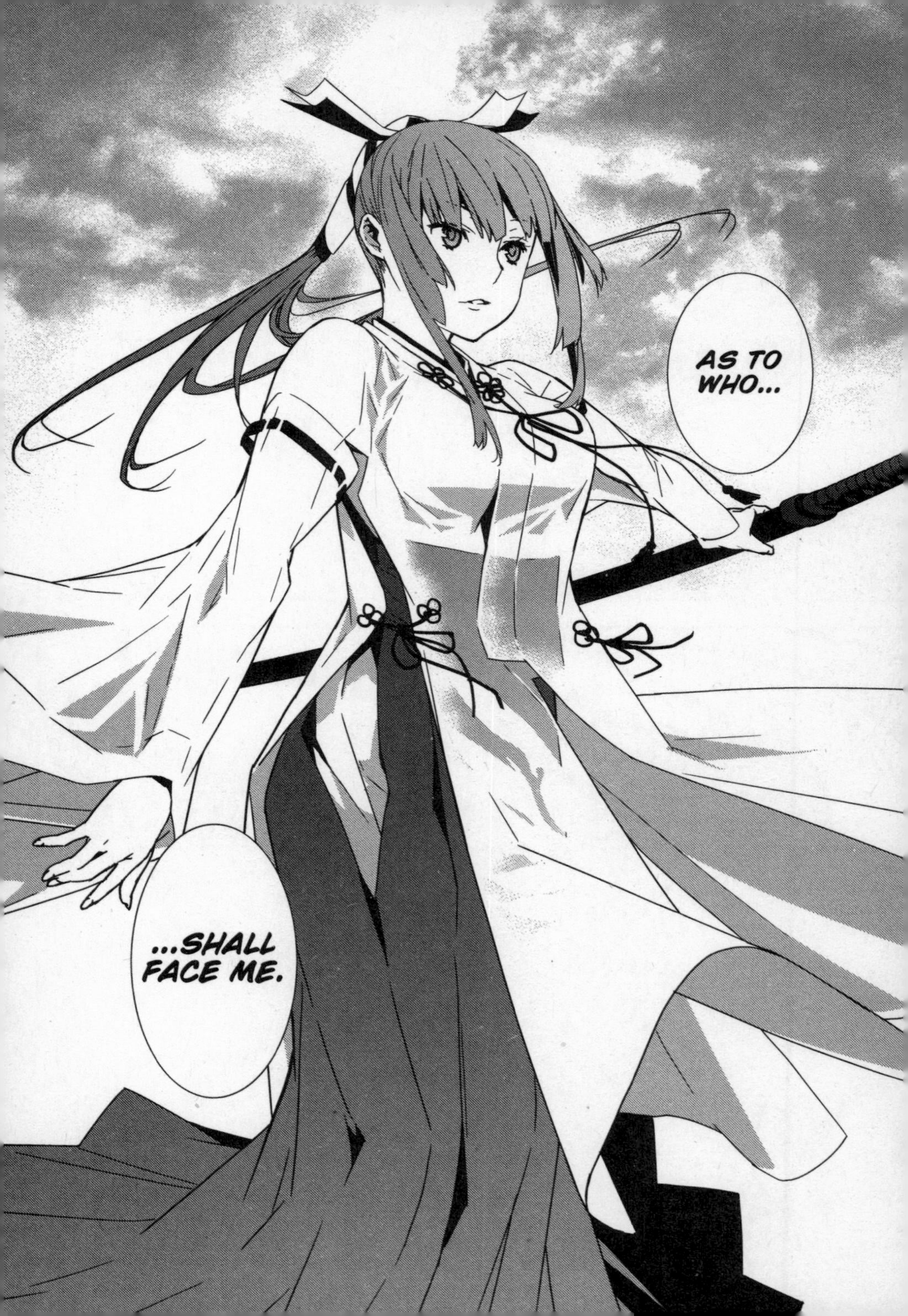
AS TO WHO...
...SHALL FACE ME.

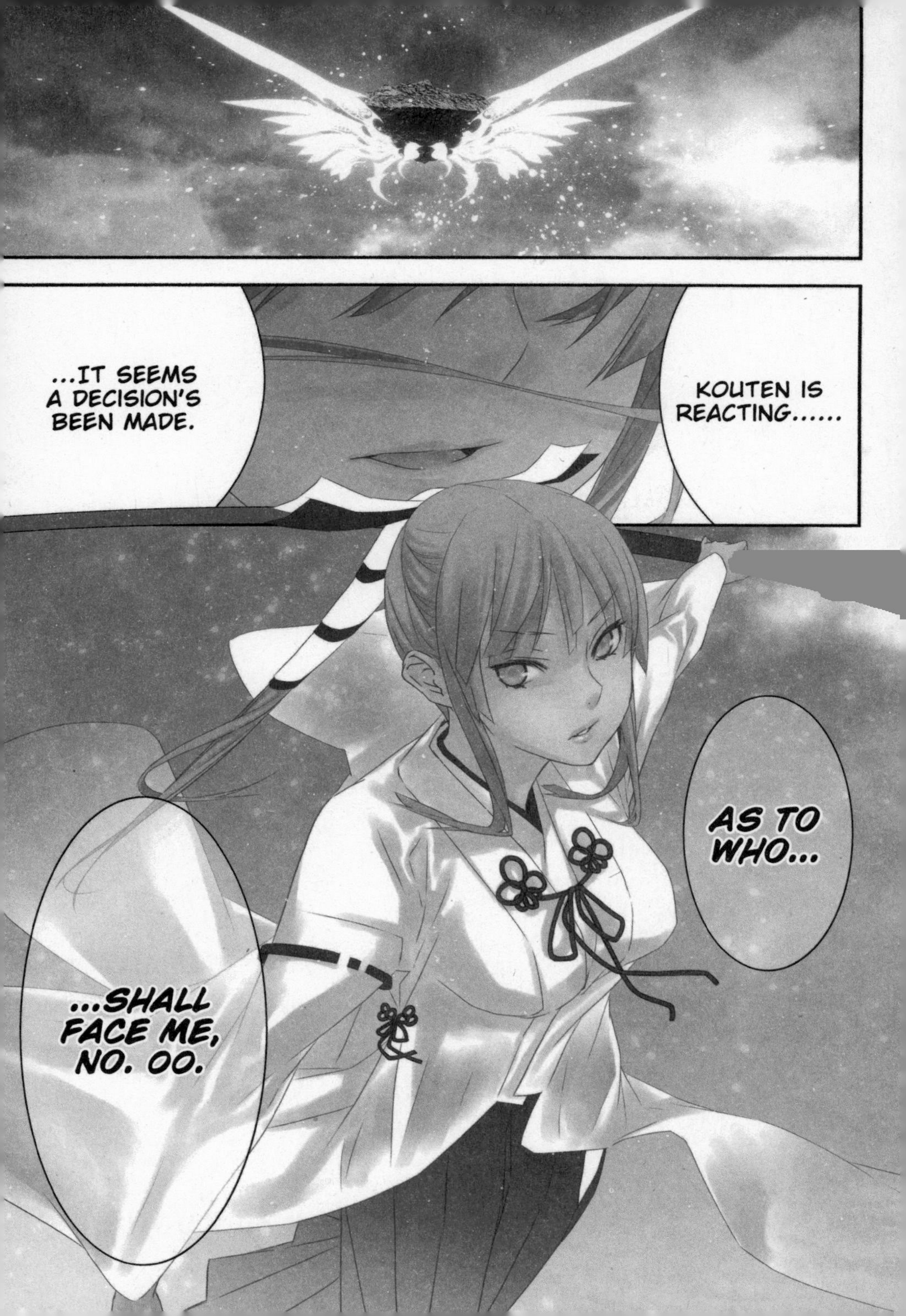
KOUTEN IS REACTING......
...IT SEEMS A DECISION'S BEEN MADE.
AS TO WHO...
...SHALL FACE ME, NO. 00.

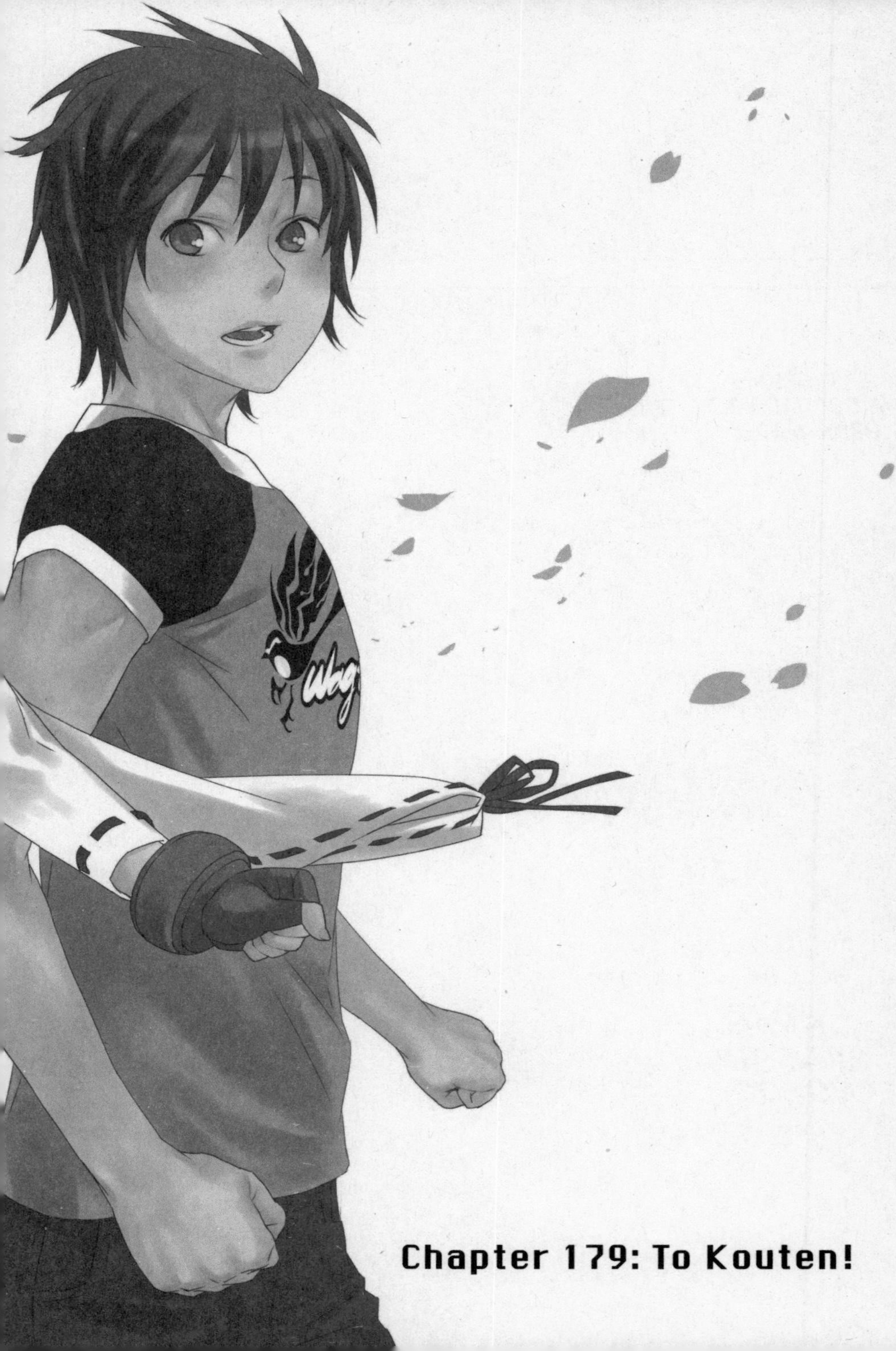

Chapter 179: To Kouten!

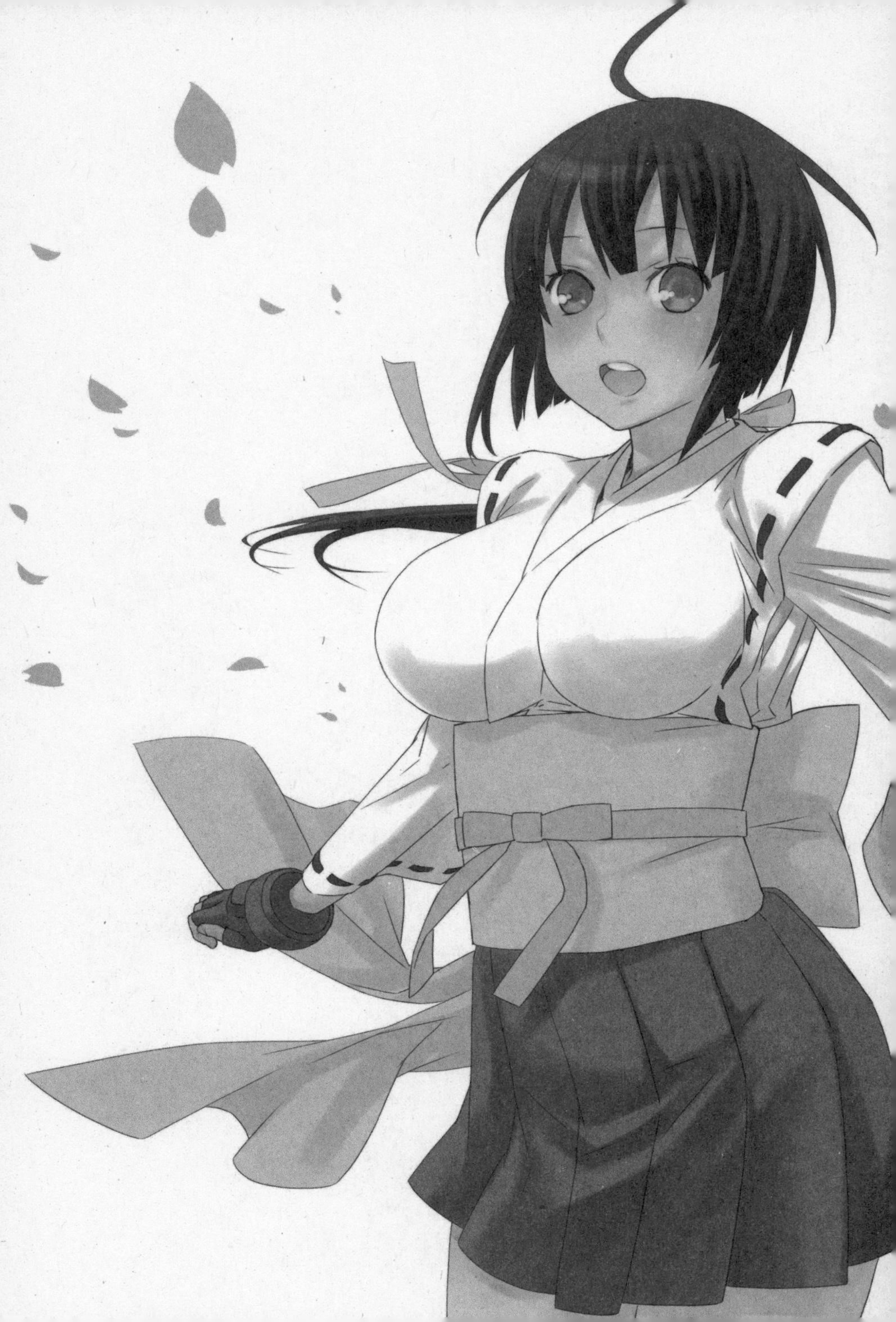

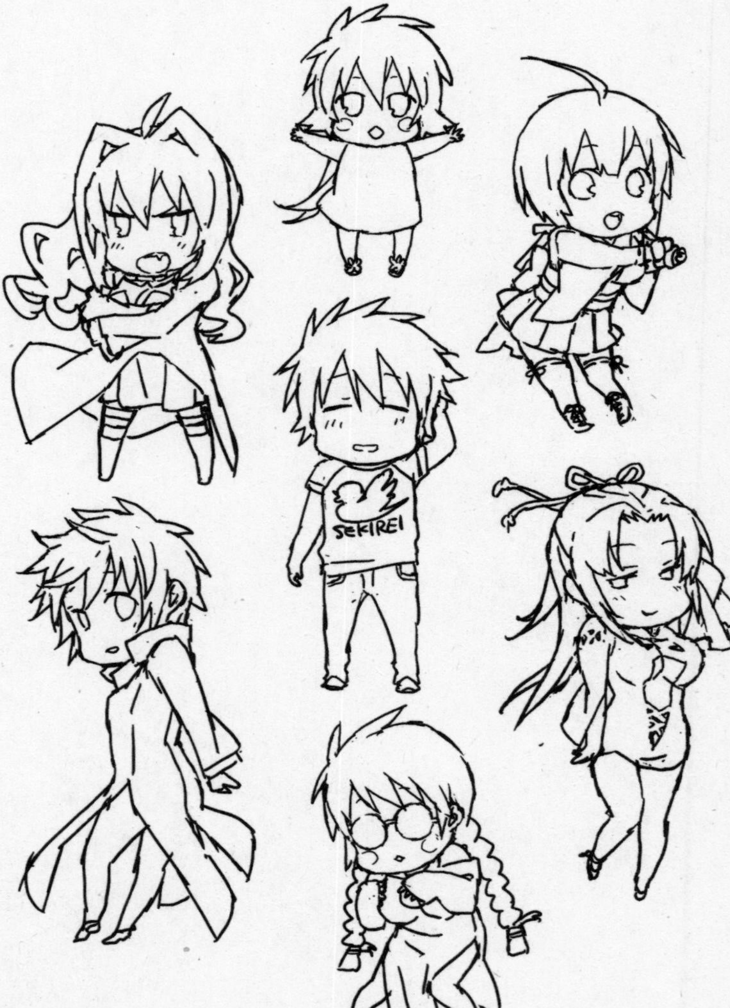
SEKIREI

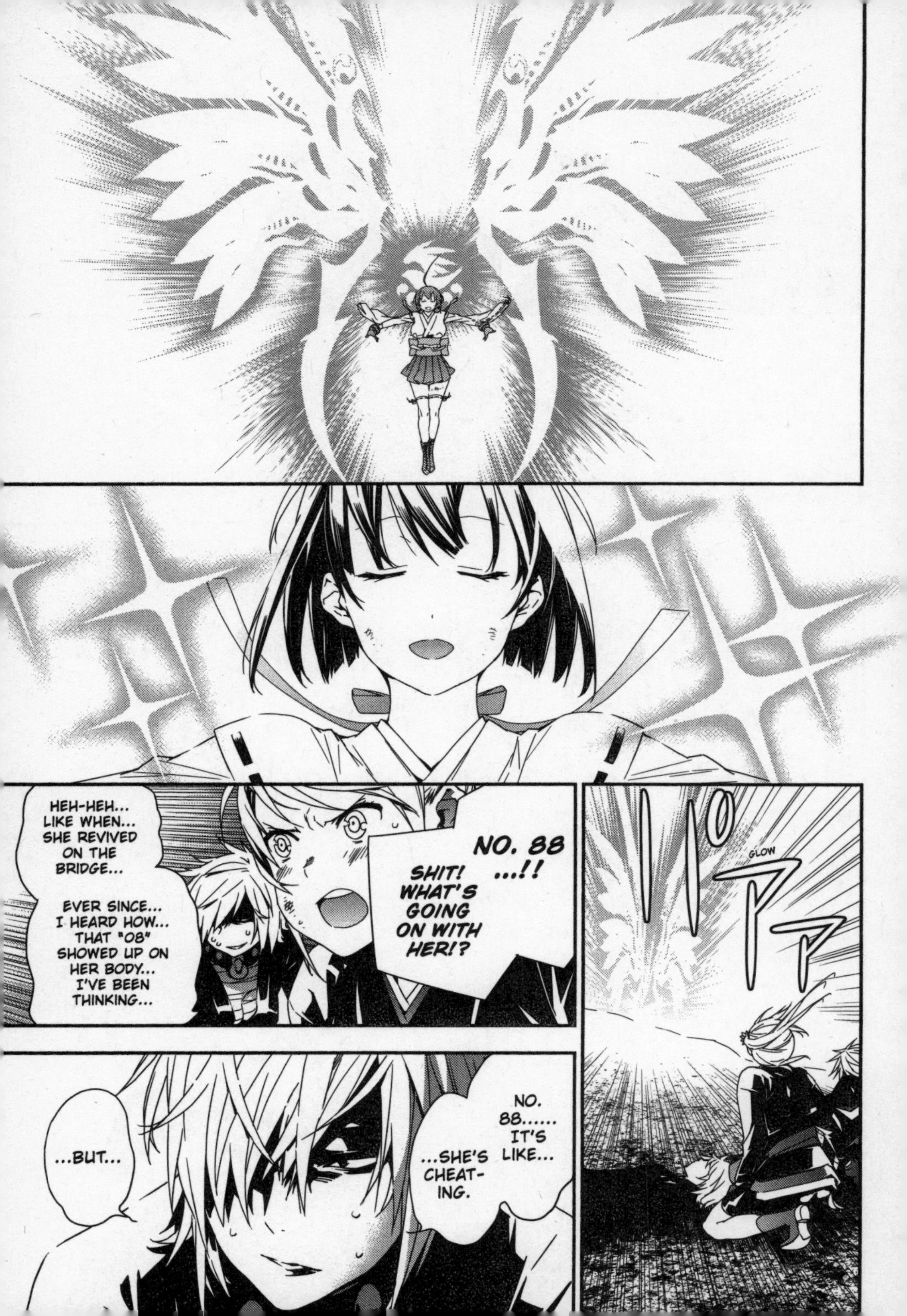
GLOW
NO. 88 ...!!
SHIT! WHAT'S GOING ON WITH HER!?
HEH-HEH... LIKE WHEN... SHE REVIVED ON THE BRIDGE...
EVER SINCE... I HEARD HOW... THAT "08" SHOWED UP ON HER BODY... I'VE BEEN THINKING...
NO. 88...... IT'S LIKE...
...SHE'S CHEAT-ING.
...BUT...

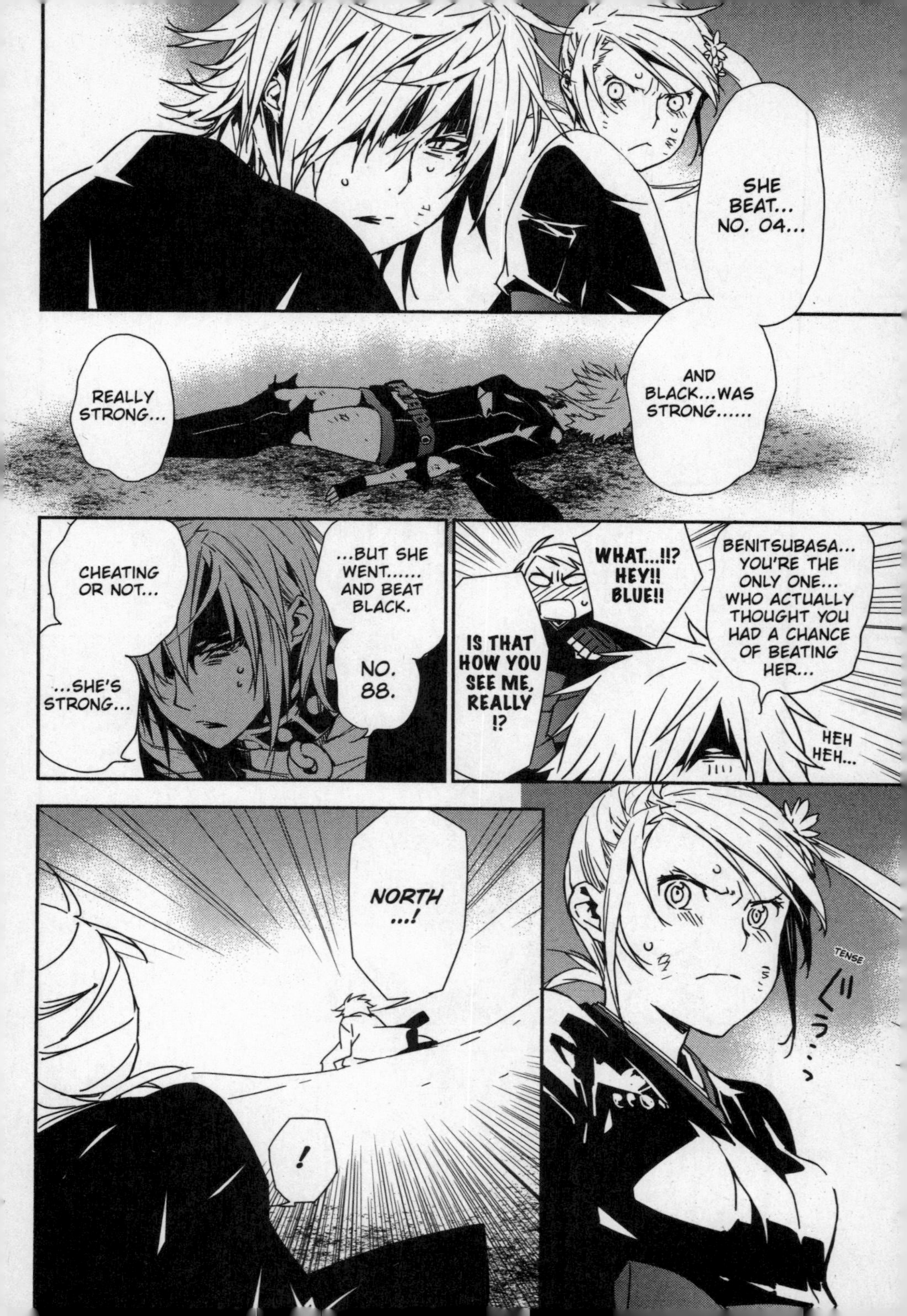
SHE BEAT... NO. 04...
AND BLACK...WAS STRONG......
REALLY STRONG...
BENITSUBASA... YOU'RE THE ONLY ONE... WHO ACTUALLY THOUGHT YOU HAD A CHANCE OF BEATING HER...
WHAT...!!? HEY!! BLUE!!
IS THAT HOW YOU SEE ME, REALLY !?
HEH HEH...
...BUT SHE WENT...... AND BEAT BLACK.
NO. 88.
CHEATING OR NOT...
...SHE'S STRONG...
TENSE
NORTH ...!
!

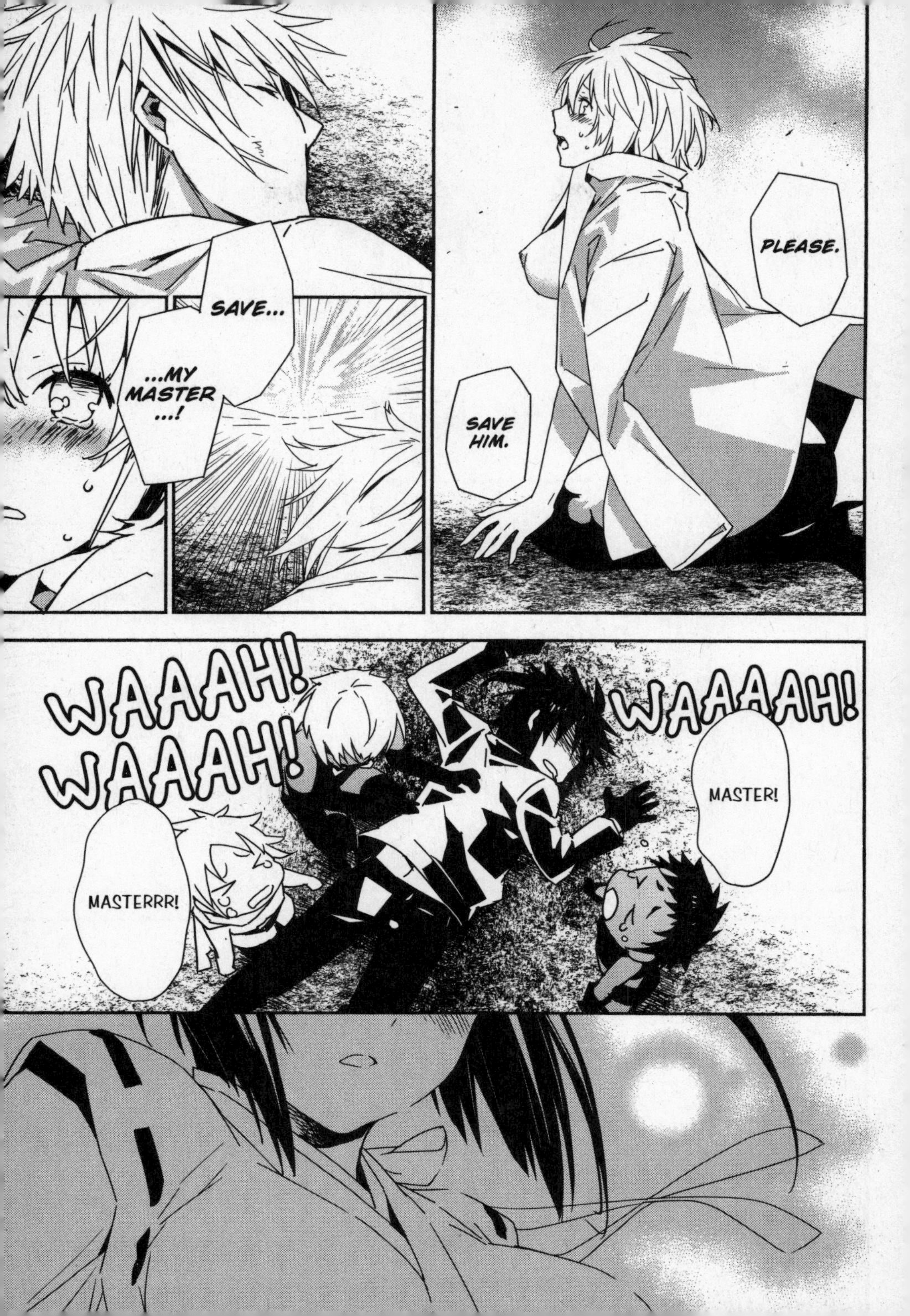
PLEASE.
SAVE HIM.
SAVE...
...MY MASTER ...!
WAAAAH!
MASTER!
WAAAH! WAAAH!
MASTERRR!

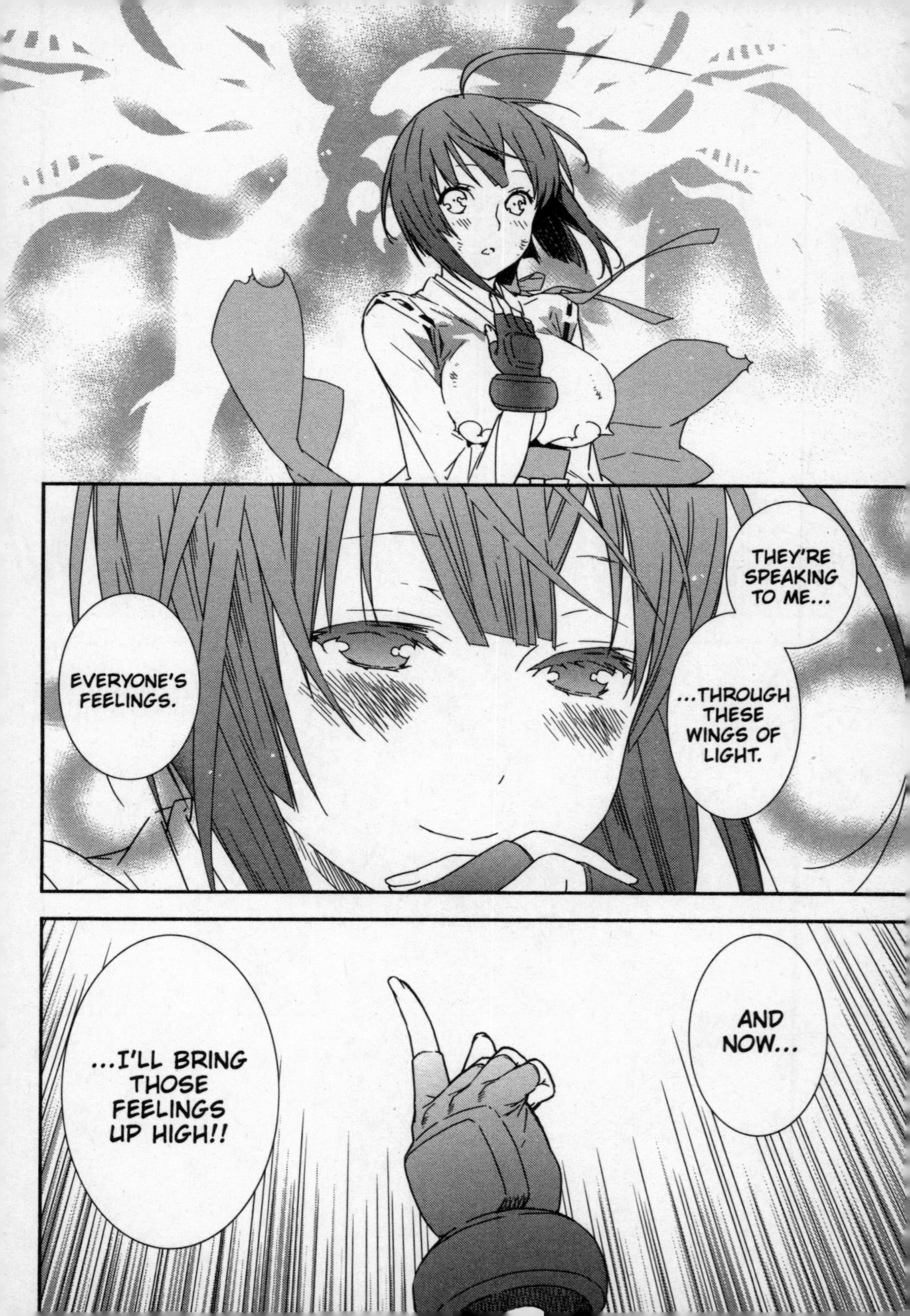
THEY'RE SPEAKING TO ME...
...THROUGH THESE WINGS OF LIGHT.
EVERYONE'S FEELINGS.
AND NOW...
...I'LL BRING THOSE FEELINGS UP HIGH!!

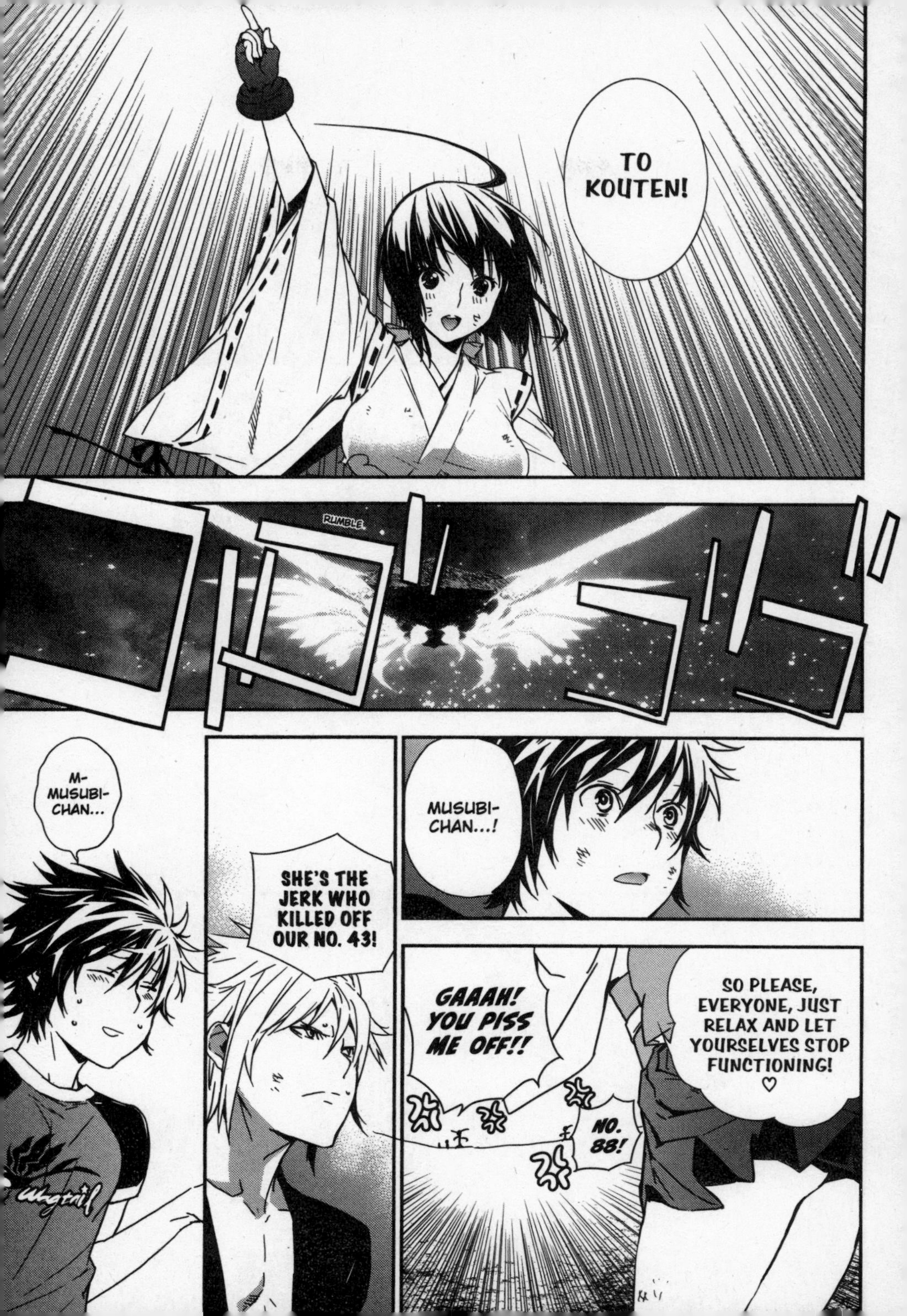
TO KOUTEN!
RUMBLE
MUSUBI-CHAN...!
SO PLEASE, EVERYONE, JUST RELAX AND LET YOURSELVES STOP FUNCTIONING! ♡
GAAAH! YOU PISS ME OFF!!
NO. 88!
SHE'S THE JERK WHO KILLED OFF OUR NO. 43!
M-MUSUBI-CHAN...

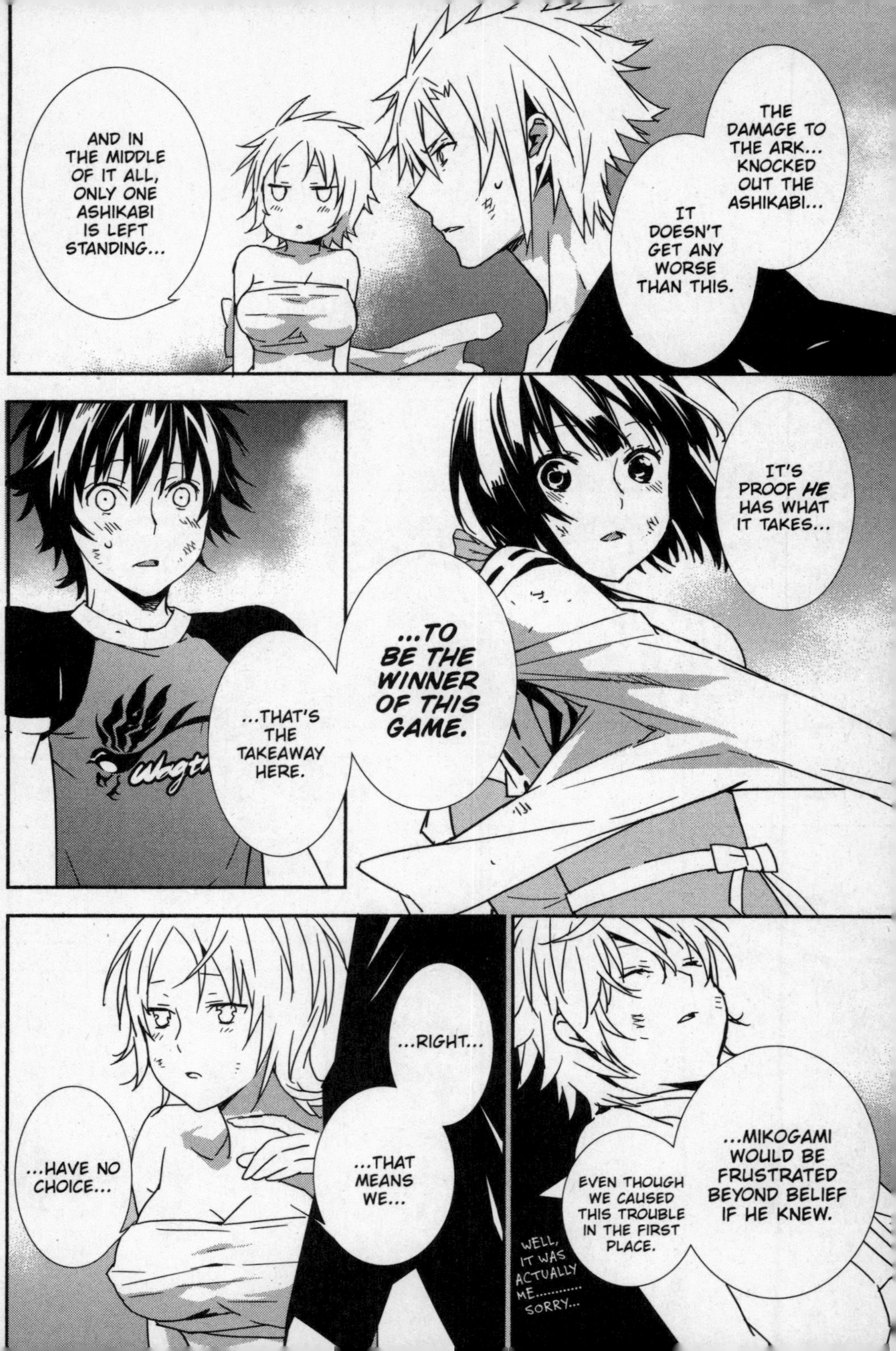
THE DAMAGE TO THE ARK... KNOCKED OUT THE ASHIKABI...
IT DOESN'T GET ANY WORSE THAN THIS.
AND IN THE MIDDLE OF IT ALL, ONLY ONE ASHIKABI IS LEFT STANDING...
IT'S PROOF *HE* HAS WHAT IT TAKES...
...TO BE THE WINNER OF THIS GAME.
...THAT'S THE TAKEAWAY HERE.
...MIKOGAMI WOULD BE FRUSTRATED BEYOND BELIEF IF HE KNEW.
EVEN THOUGH WE CAUSED THIS TROUBLE IN THE FIRST PLACE.
WELL, IT WAS ACTUALLY ME.......... SORRY...
...RIGHT...
...THAT MEANS WE...
...HAVE NO CHOICE...

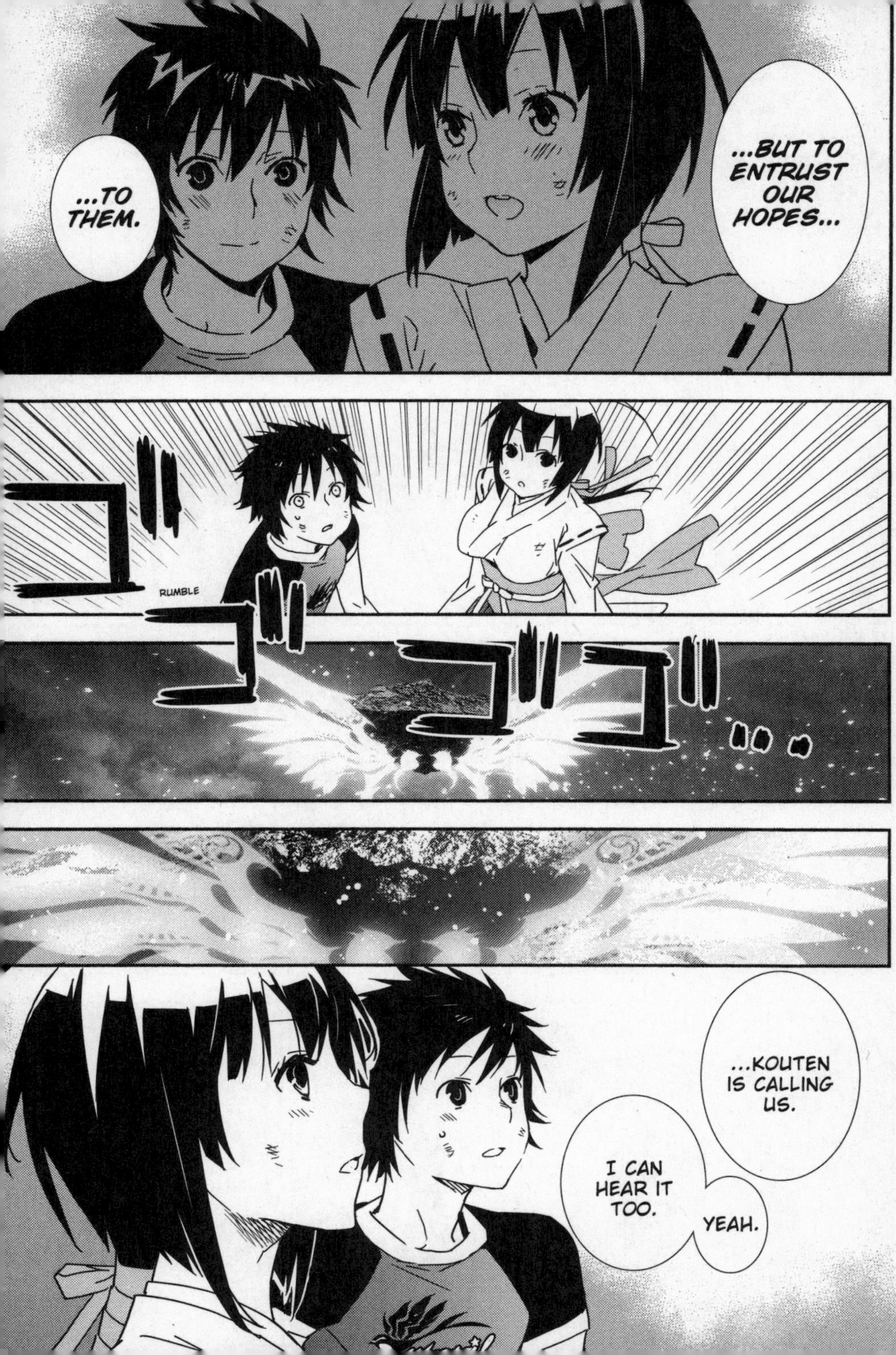
...BUT TO ENTRUST OUR HOPES...
...TO THEM.
RUMBLE
...KOUTEN IS CALLING US.
I CAN HEAR IT TOO.
YEAH.

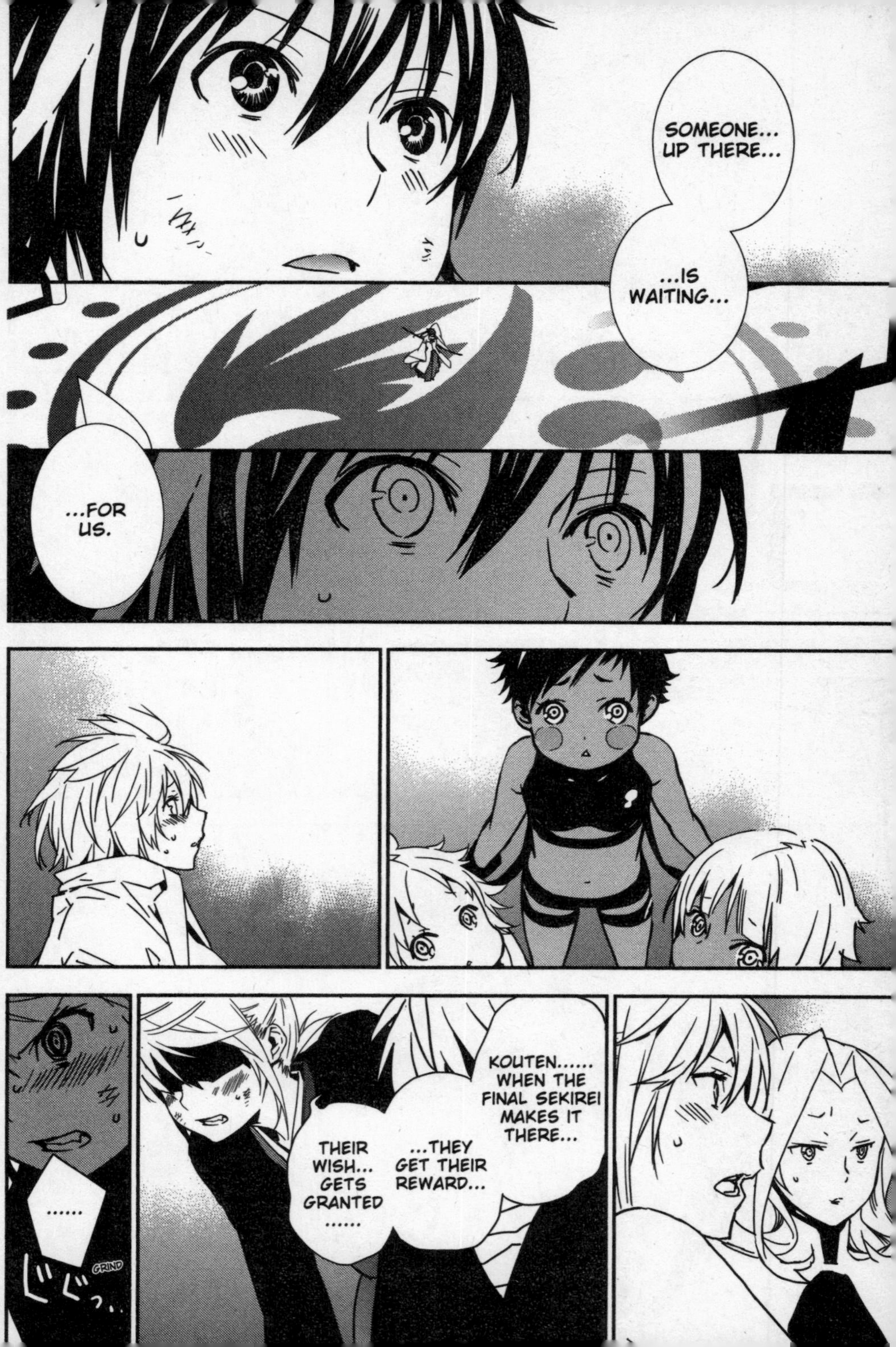
SOMEONE... UP THERE...
...IS WAITING...
...FOR US.
KOUTEN...... WHEN THE FINAL SEKIREI MAKES IT THERE...
...THEY GET THEIR REWARD...
THEIR WISH... GETS GRANTED ......
......
GRIND

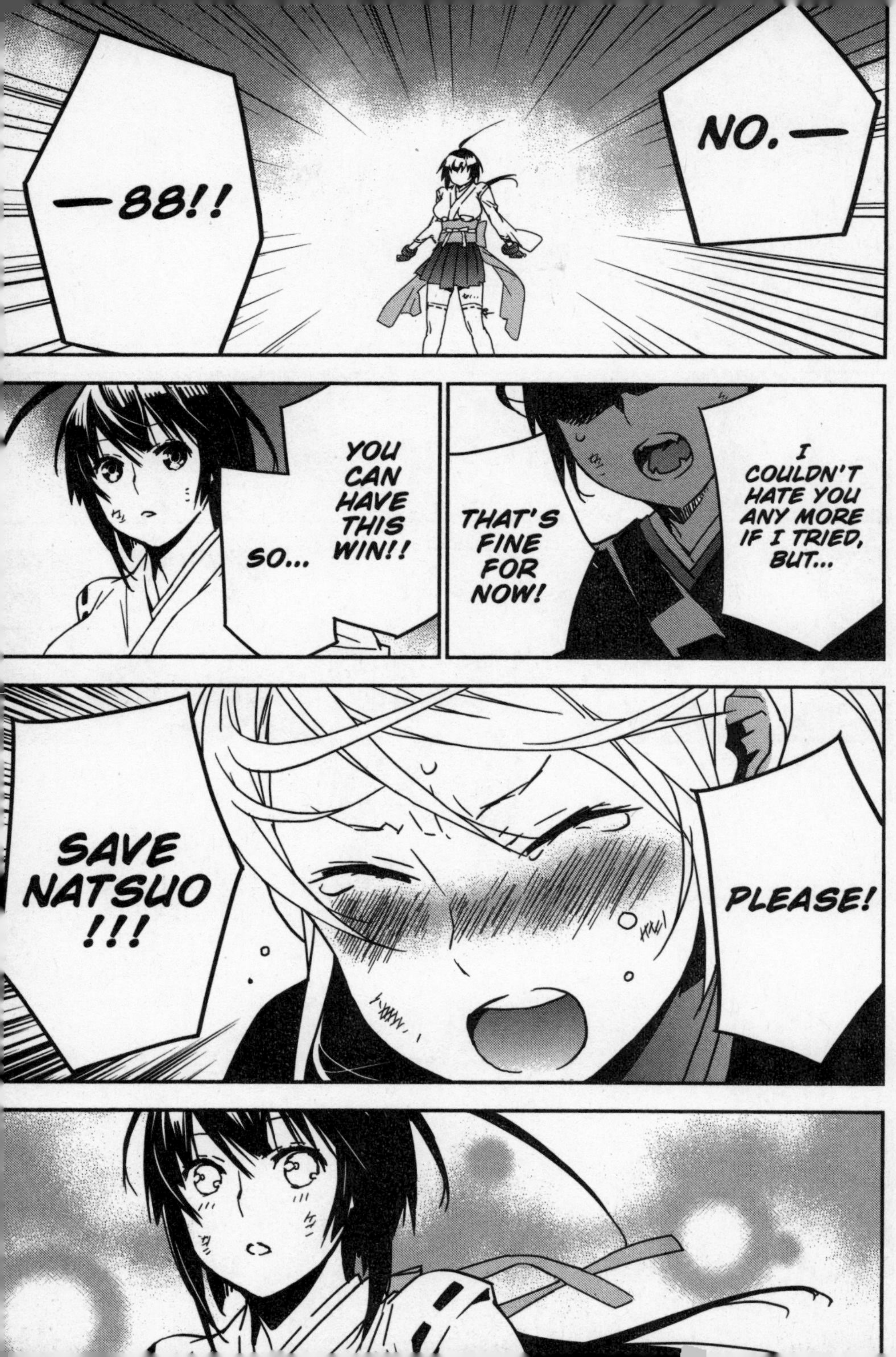
NO.—
—88!!
I COULDN'T HATE YOU ANY MORE IF I TRIED, BUT...
THAT'S FINE FOR NOW!
YOU CAN HAVE THIS WIN!!
SO...
PLEASE!
SAVE NATSUO!!!

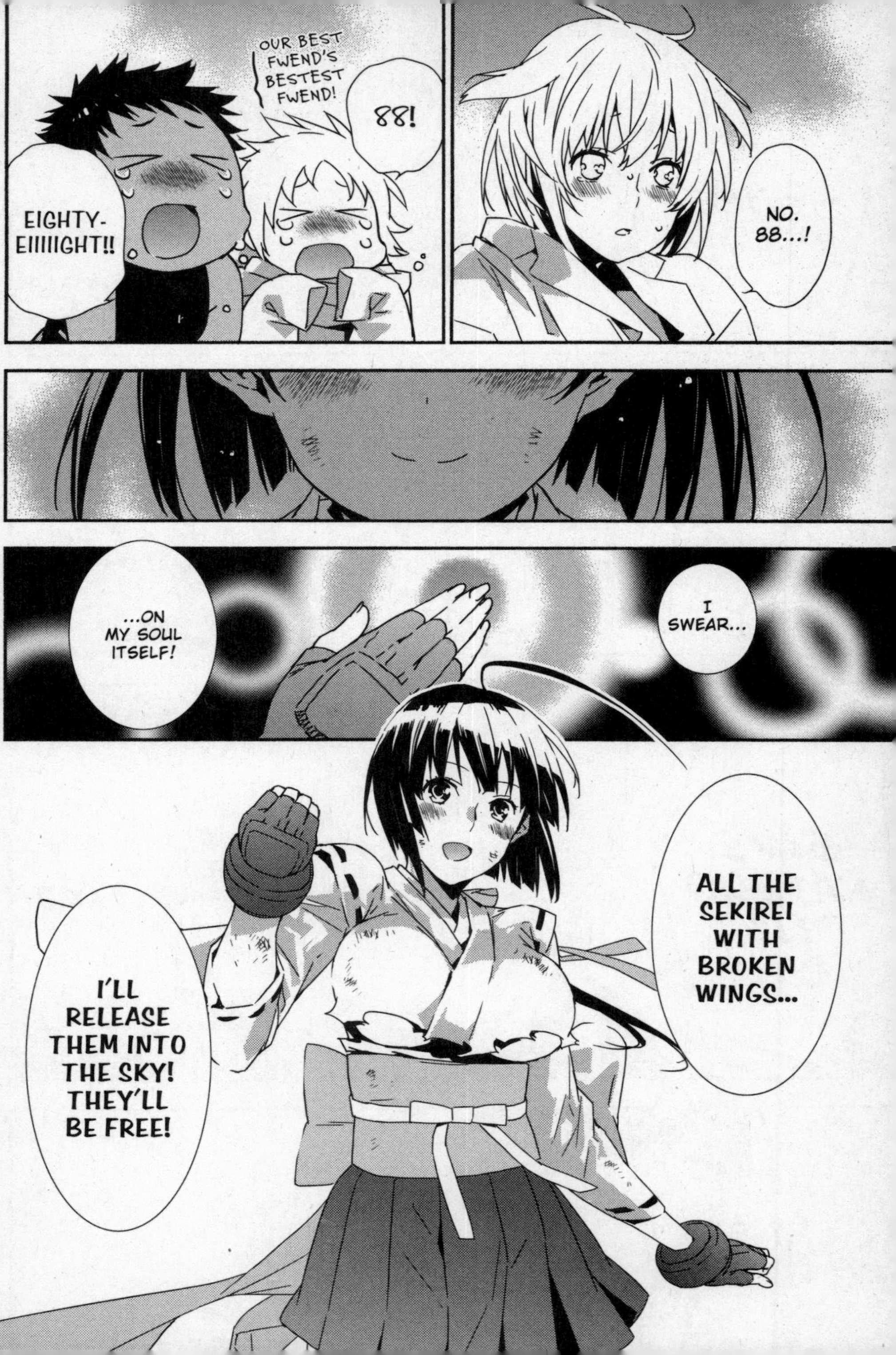
NO. 88...!
OUR BEST FWEND'S BESTEST FWEND!
88!
EIGHTY-EIIIIIGHT!!
I SWEAR...
...ON MY SOUL ITSELF!
ALL THE SEKIREI WITH BROKEN WINGS...
I'LL RELEASE THEM INTO THE SKY! THEY'LL BE FREE!

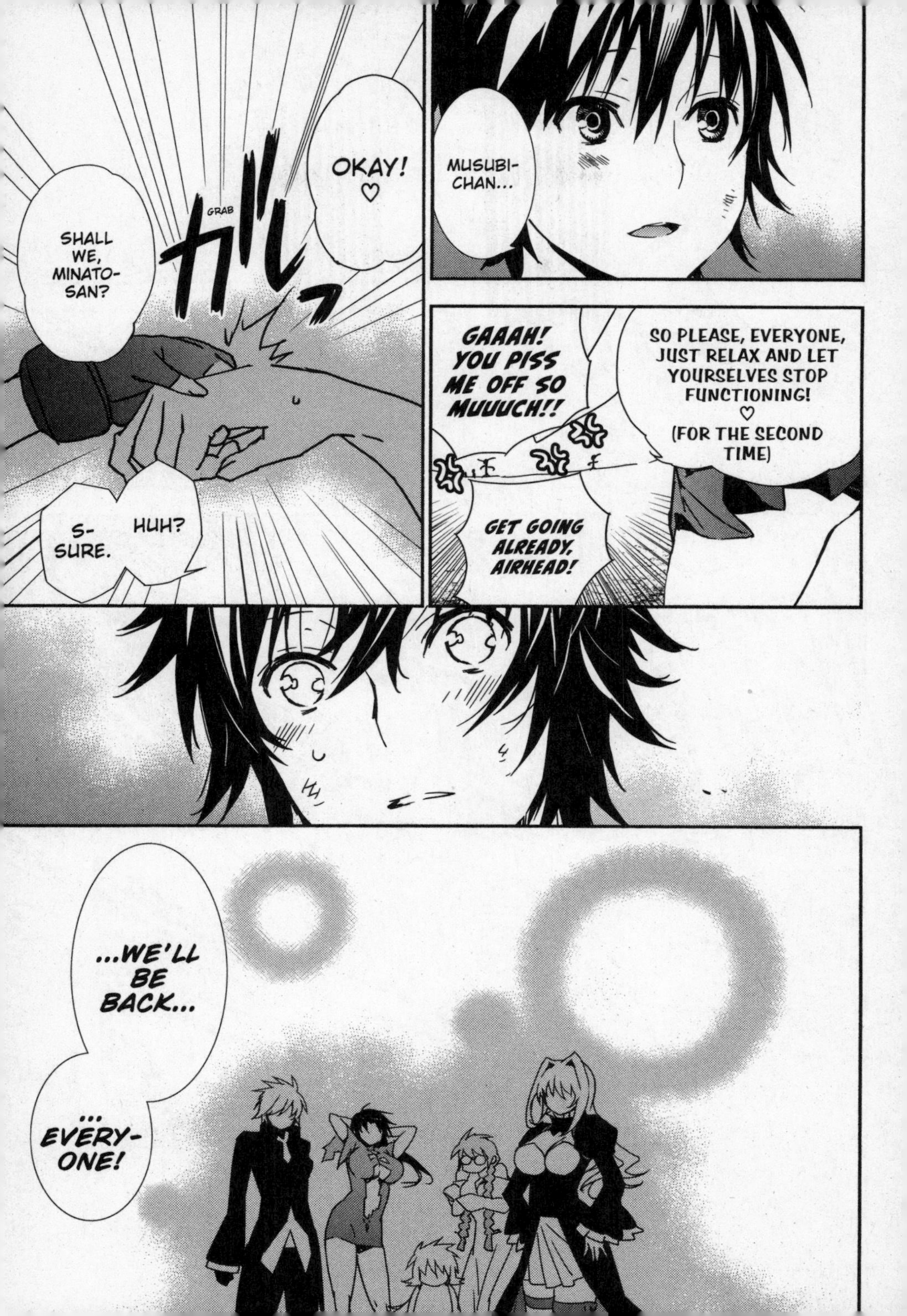
MUSUBI-CHAN...
SO PLEASE, EVERYONE, JUST RELAX AND LET YOURSELVES STOP FUNCTIONING! ♡ (FOR THE SECOND TIME)
GAAAH! YOU PISS ME OFF SO MUUUCH!!
GET GOING ALREADY, AIRHEAD!
OKAY! ♡
SHALL WE, MINATO-SAN?
GRAB
HUH?
S-SURE.
...WE'LL BE BACK...
...EVERYONE!

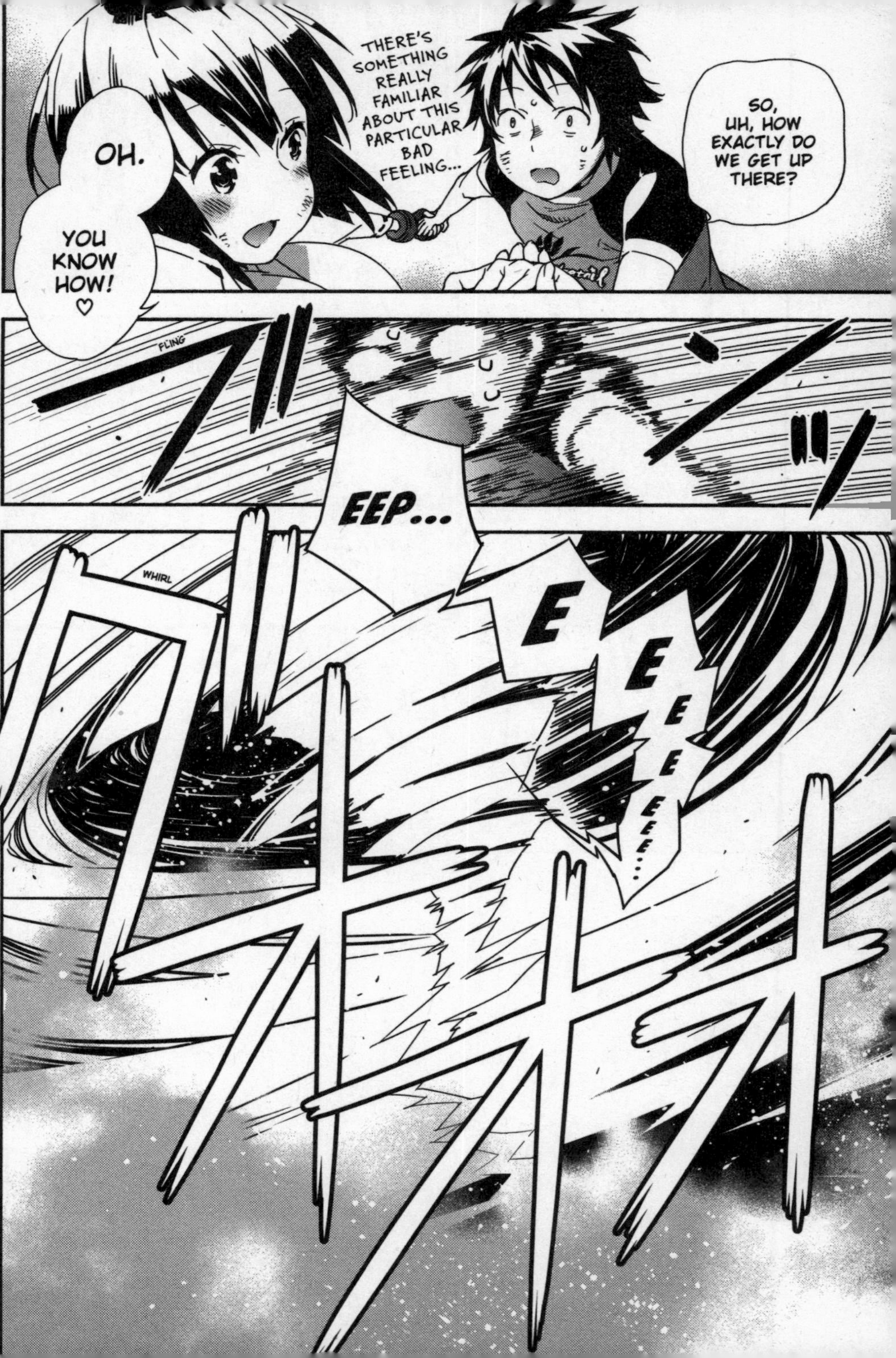
SO, UH, HOW EXACTLY DO WE GET UP THERE?
THERE'S SOMETHING REALLY FAMILIAR ABOUT THIS PARTICULAR BAD FEELING...
OH.
YOU KNOW HOW! ♡
FLING
EEP...
WHIRL
EEEEEEE...

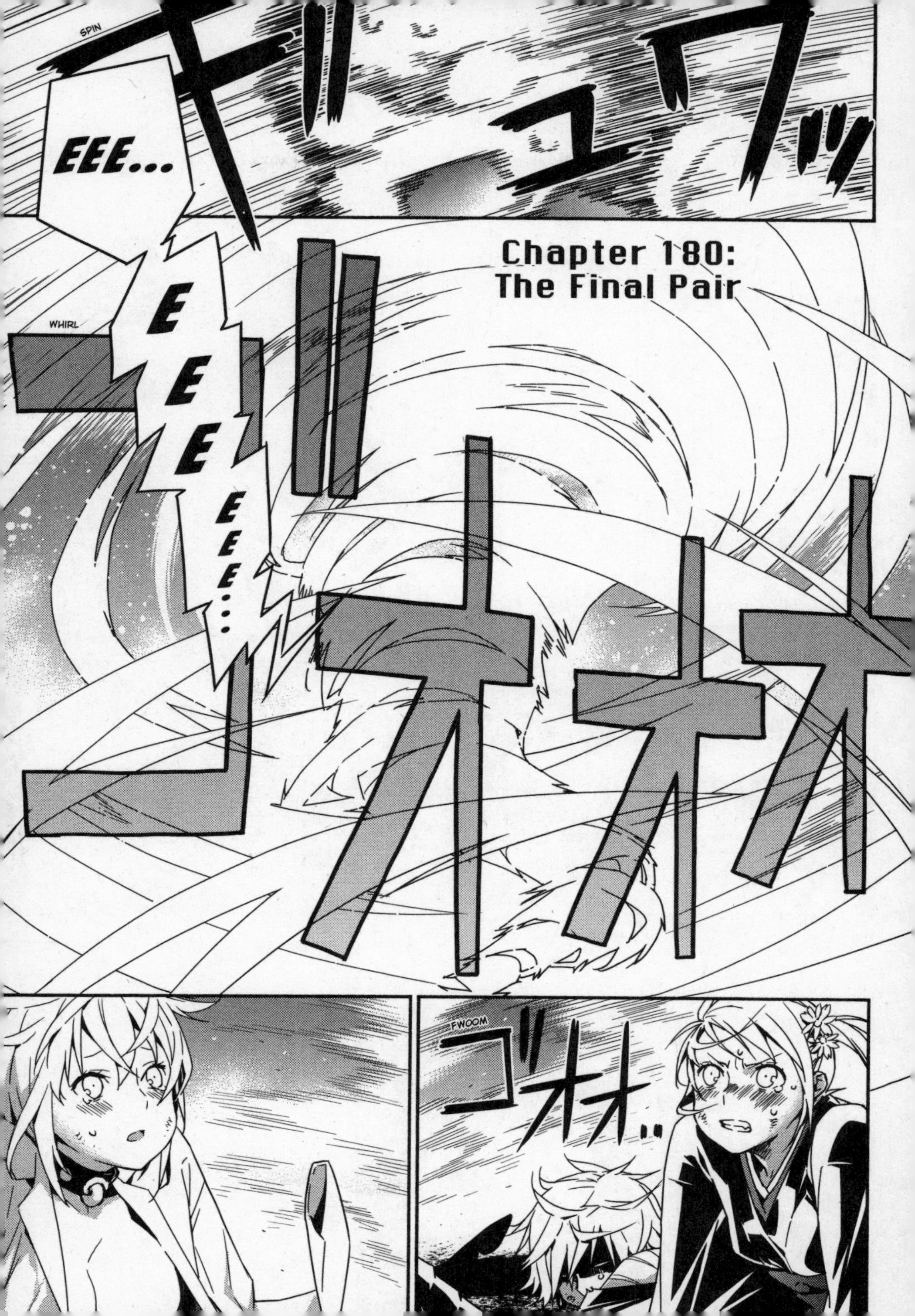
SPIN
EEE...
Chapter 180:
The Final Pair
WHIRL
EEEEEEE...
FWOOM

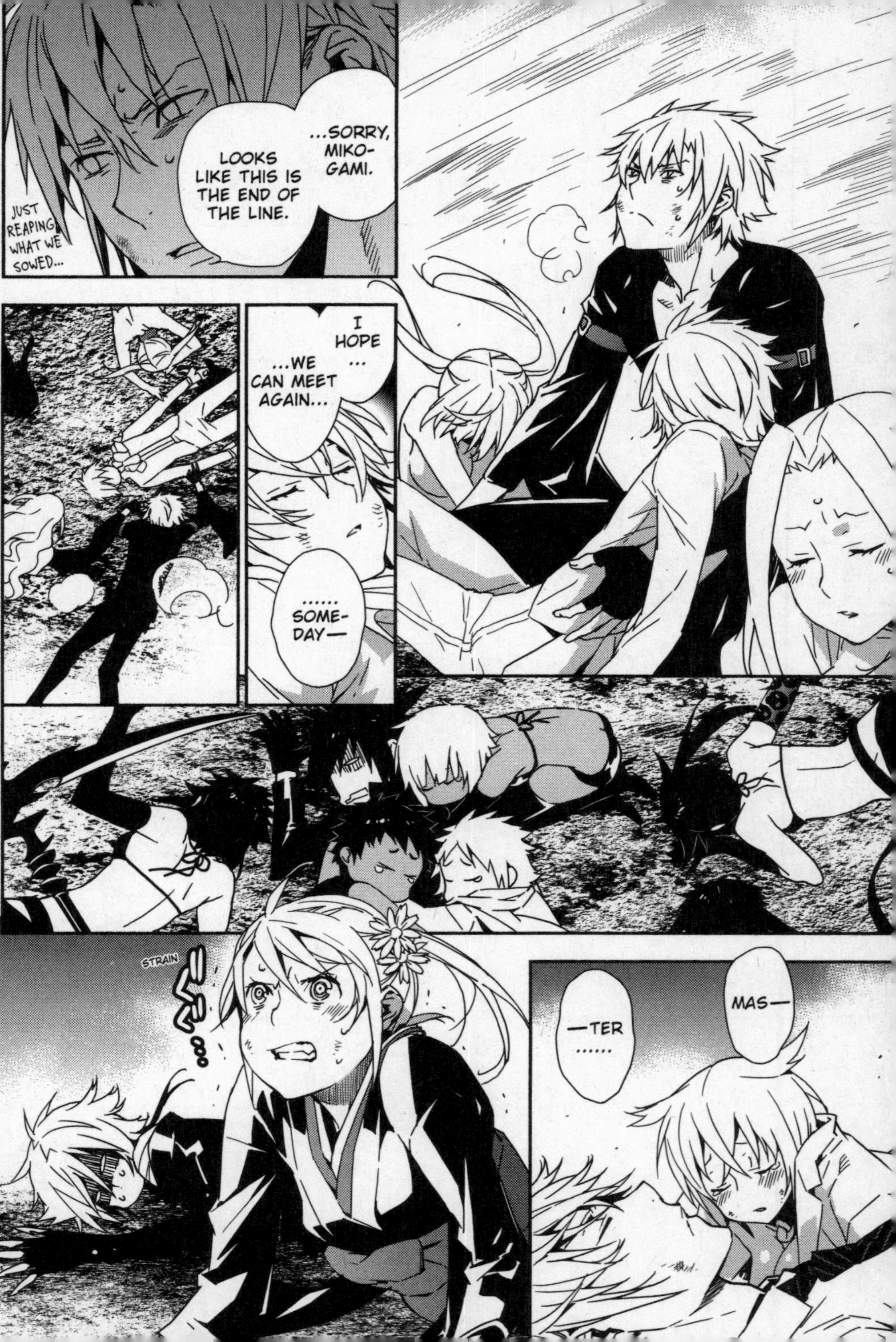
...SORRY, MIKO-GAMI.
LOOKS LIKE THIS IS THE END OF THE LINE.
JUST REAPING WHAT WE SOWED...
I HOPE ...
...WE CAN MEET AGAIN...
...... SOME-DAY—
MAS—
—TER ......
STRAIN

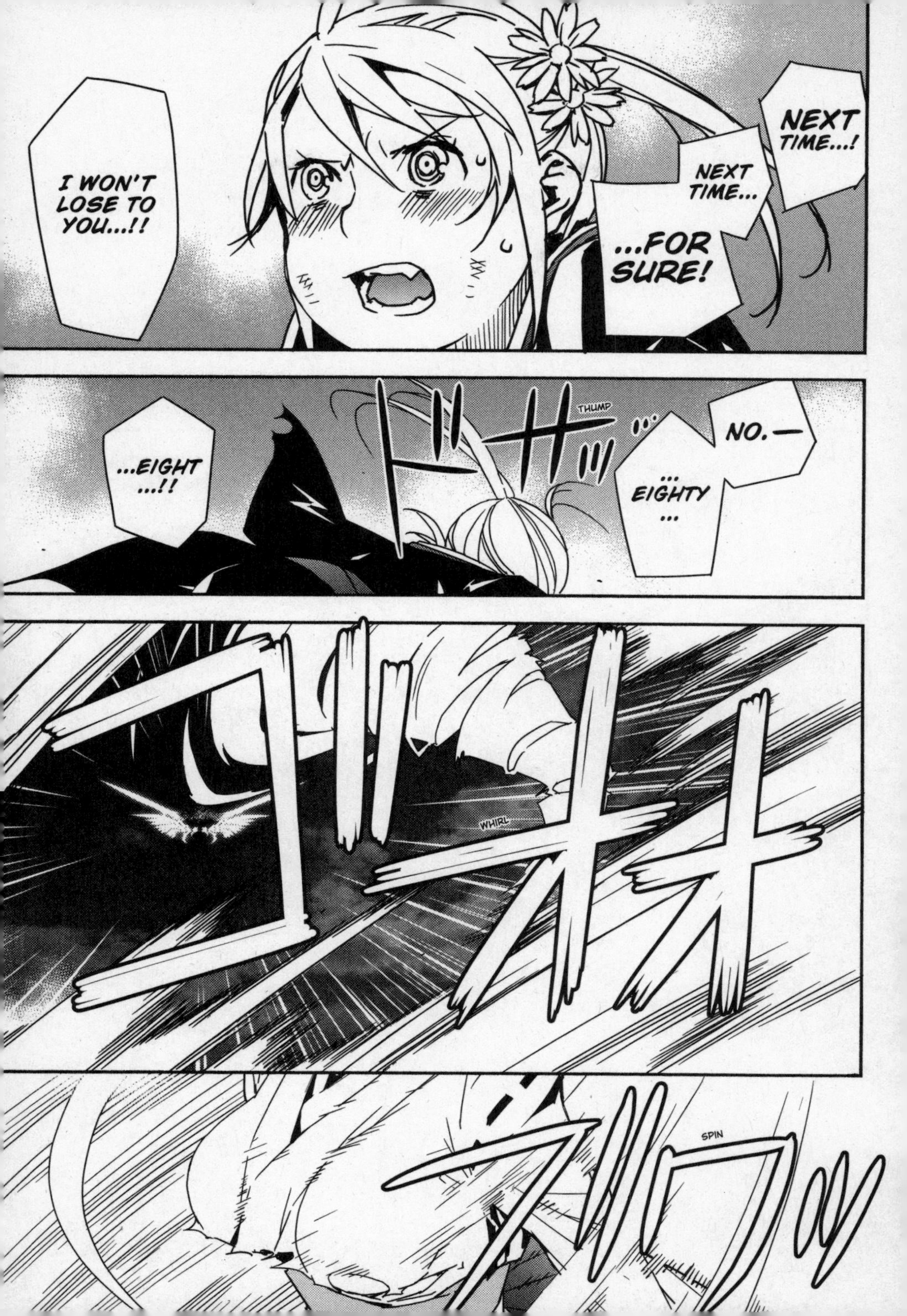
NEXT TIME...!
NEXT TIME...
...FOR SURE!
I WON'T LOSE TO YOU...!!
NO.—
...EIGHTY...
THUMP
...EIGHT...!!
WHIRL
SPIN

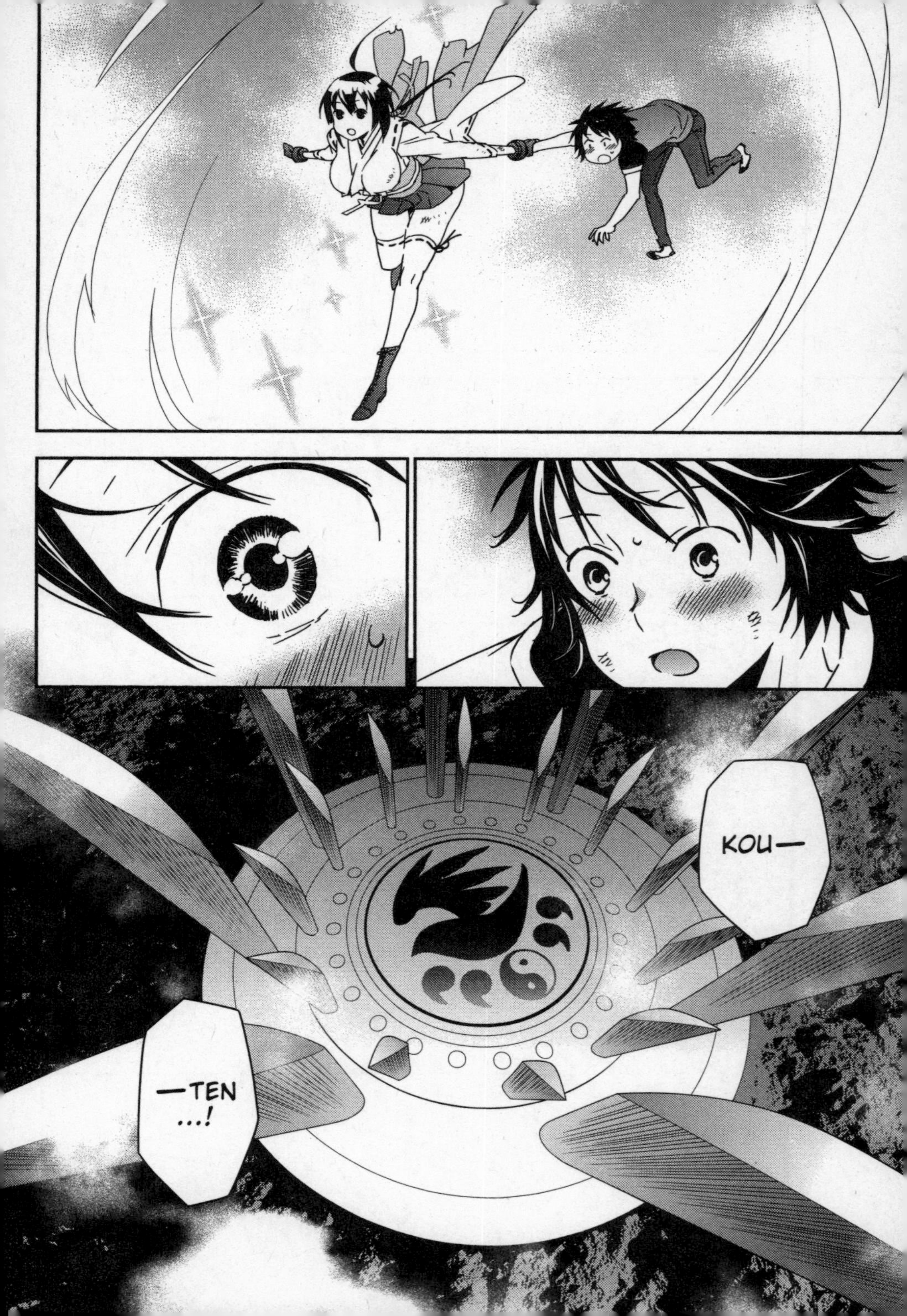
KOU—
—TEN
...!

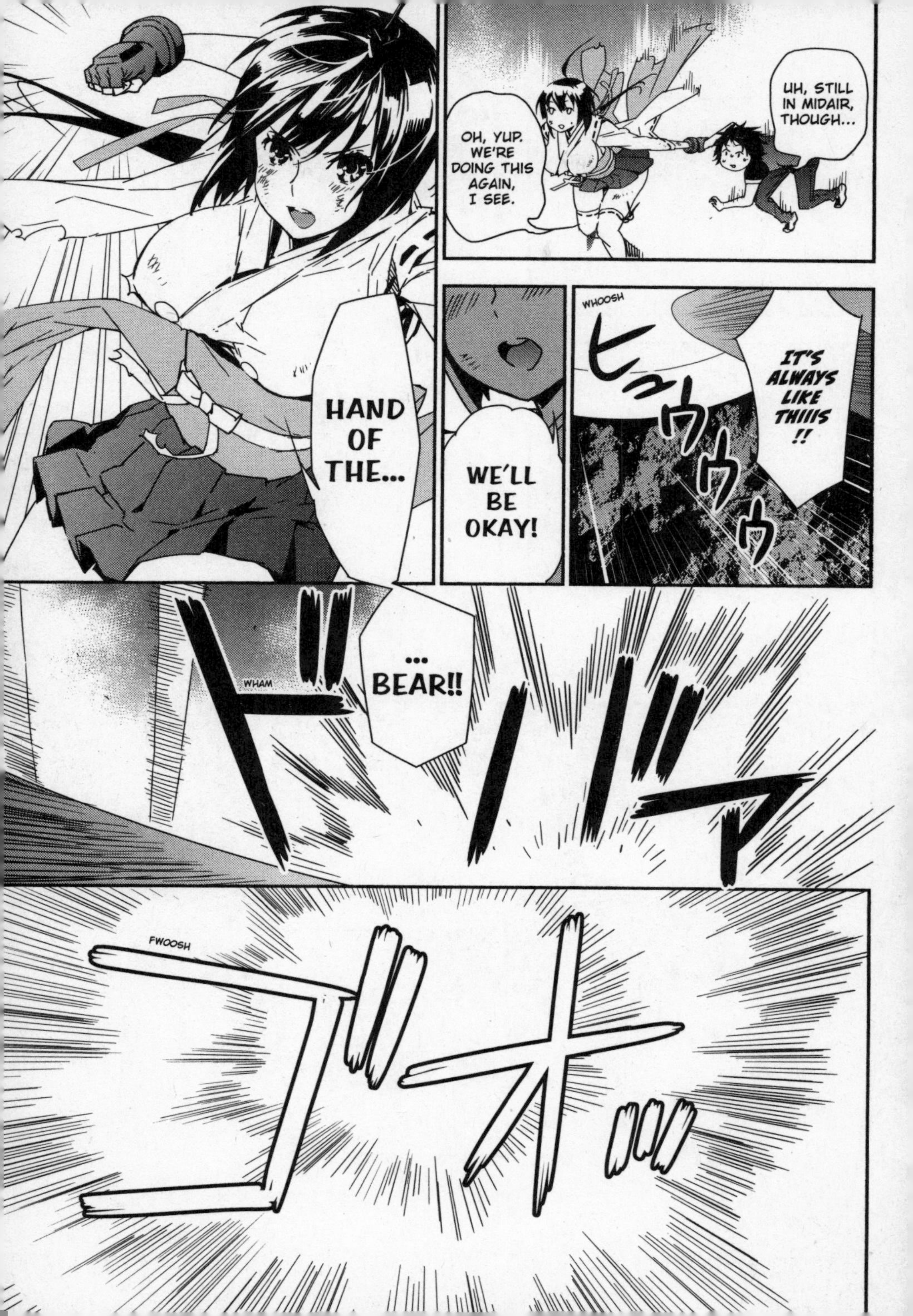
UH, STILL IN MIDAIR, THOUGH...
OH, YUP. WE'RE DOING THIS AGAIN, I SEE.
WHOOSH
IT'S ALWAYS LIKE THIIIS!!
WE'LL BE OKAY!
HAND OF THE...
WHAM
...BEAR!!
FWOOSH

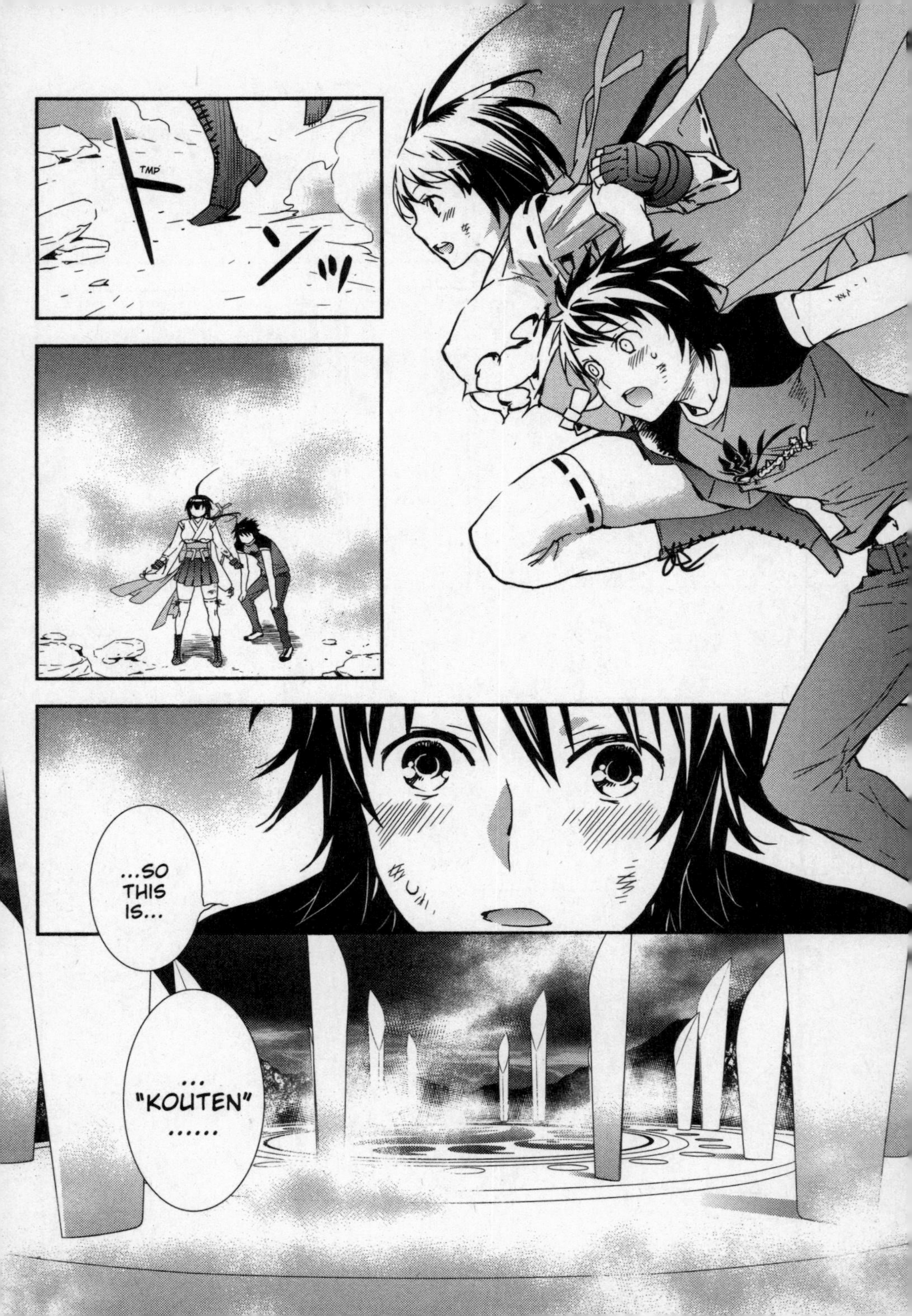
TMP
トンッ
...SO THIS IS...
... "KOUTEN" ......

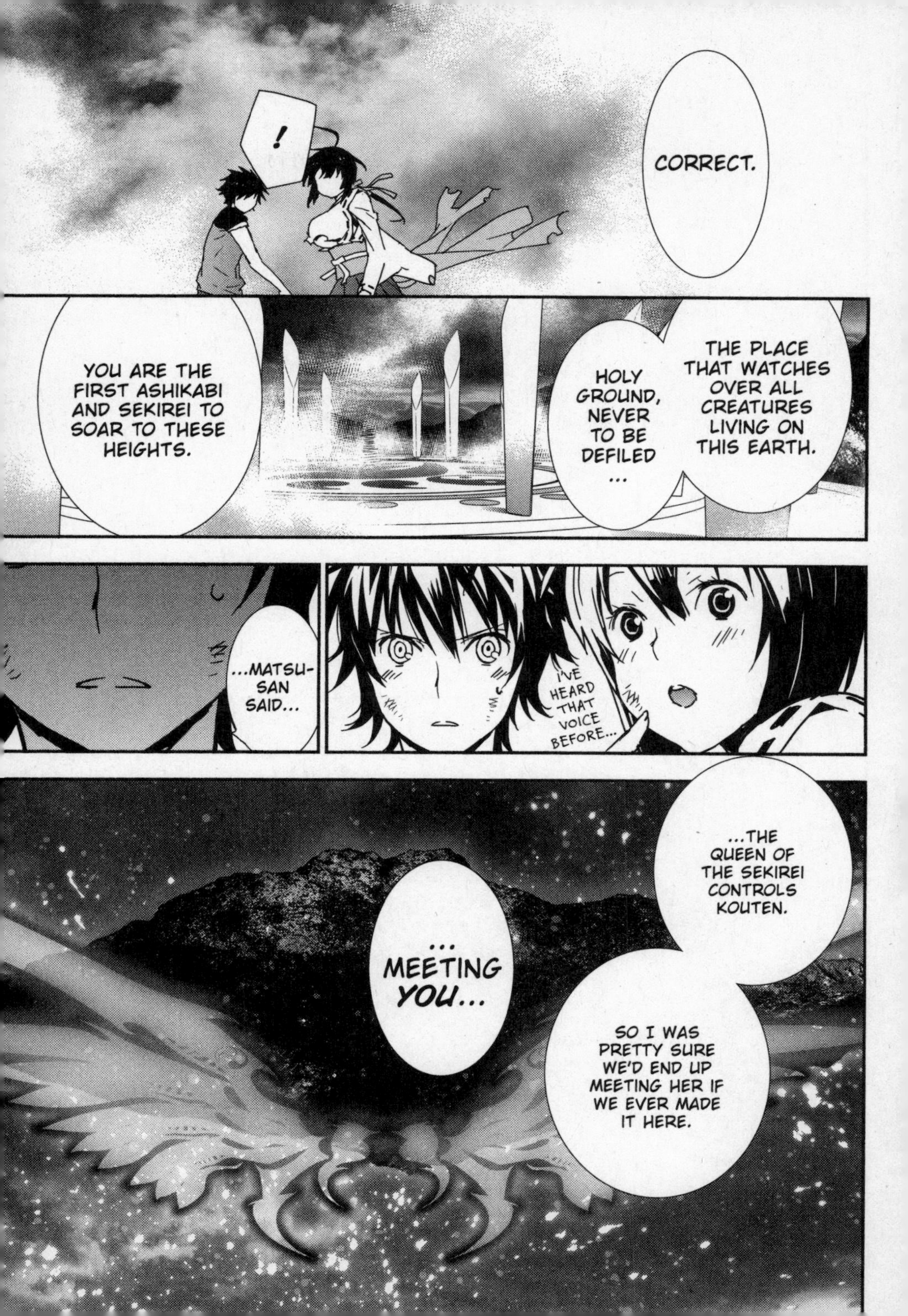
CORRECT.
!
THE PLACE THAT WATCHES OVER ALL CREATURES LIVING ON THIS EARTH.
HOLY GROUND, NEVER TO BE DEFILED ...
YOU ARE THE FIRST ASHIKABI AND SEKIREI TO SOAR TO THESE HEIGHTS.
I'VE HEARD THAT VOICE BEFORE...
...MATSU-SAN SAID...
...THE QUEEN OF THE SEKIREI CONTROLS KOUTEN.
SO I WAS PRETTY SURE WE'D END UP MEETING HER IF WE EVER MADE IT HERE.
... MEETING *YOU*...

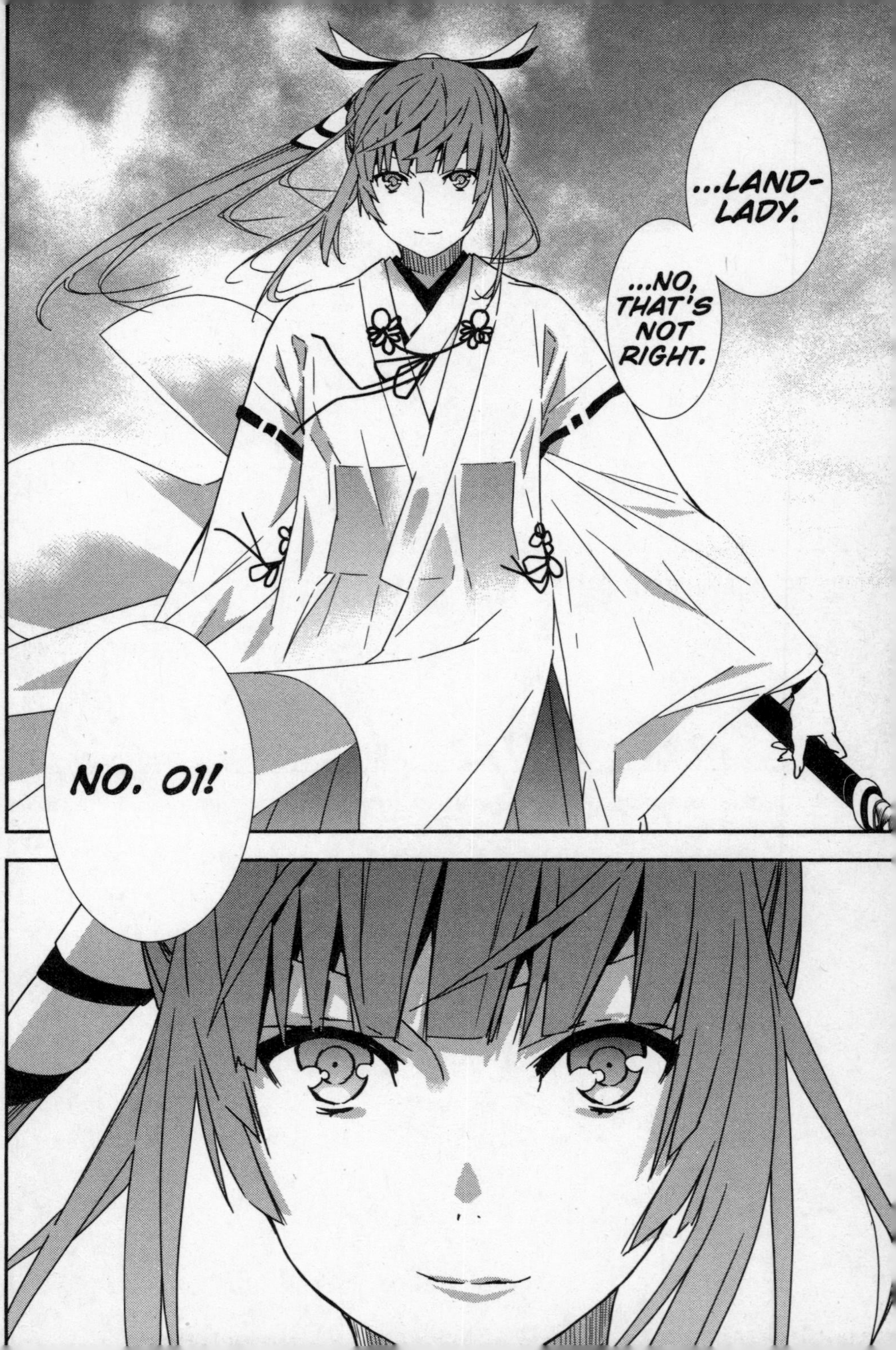
...LAND-LADY.
...NO, THAT'S NOT RIGHT.
NO. 01!

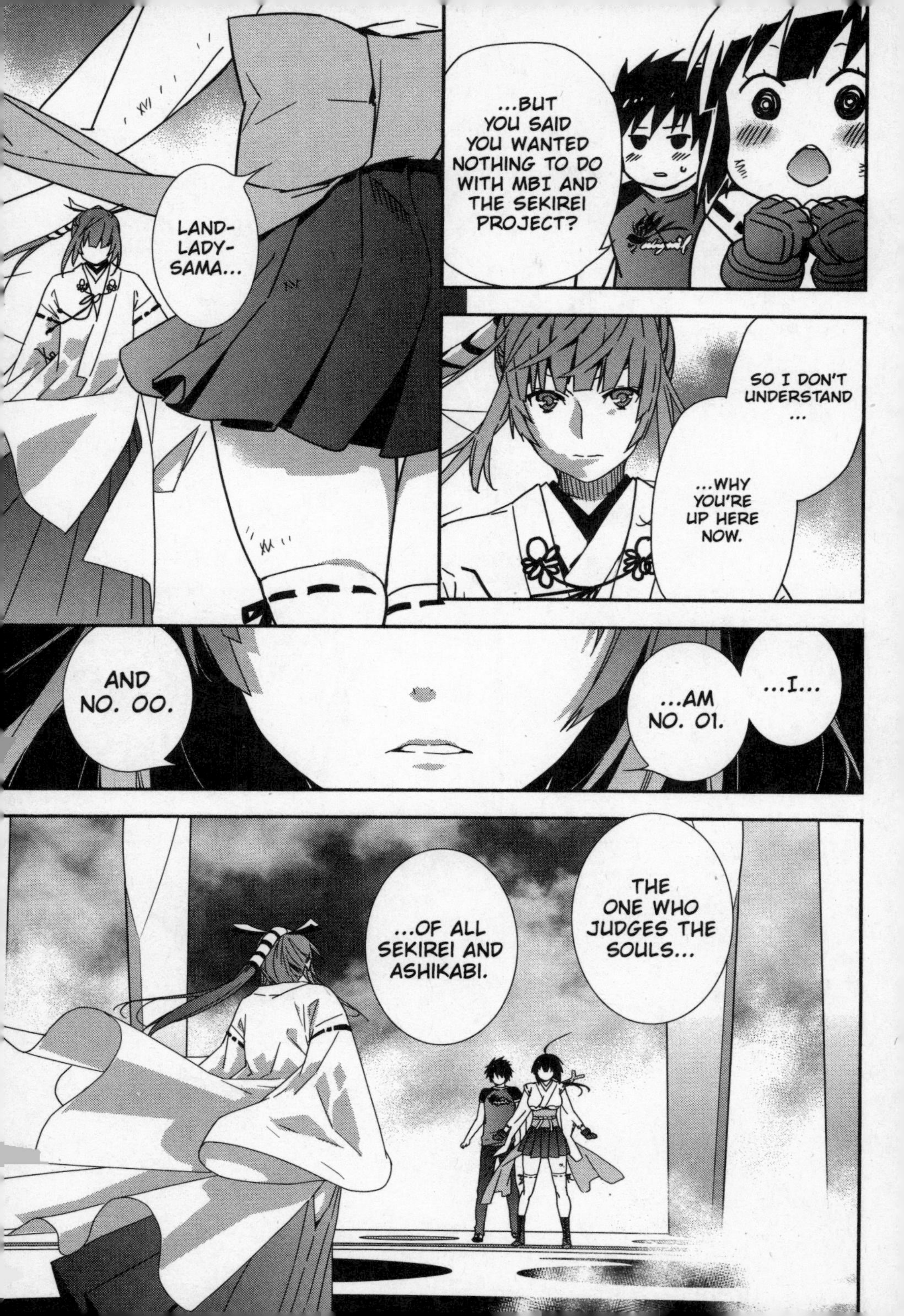
...BUT YOU SAID YOU WANTED NOTHING TO DO WITH MBI AND THE SEKIREI PROJECT?
SO I DON'T UNDERSTAND ...
...WHY YOU'RE UP HERE NOW.
LAND-LADY-SAMA...
...I...
...AM NO. 01.
AND NO. 00.
THE ONE WHO JUDGES THE SOULS...
...OF ALL SEKIREI AND ASHIKABI.

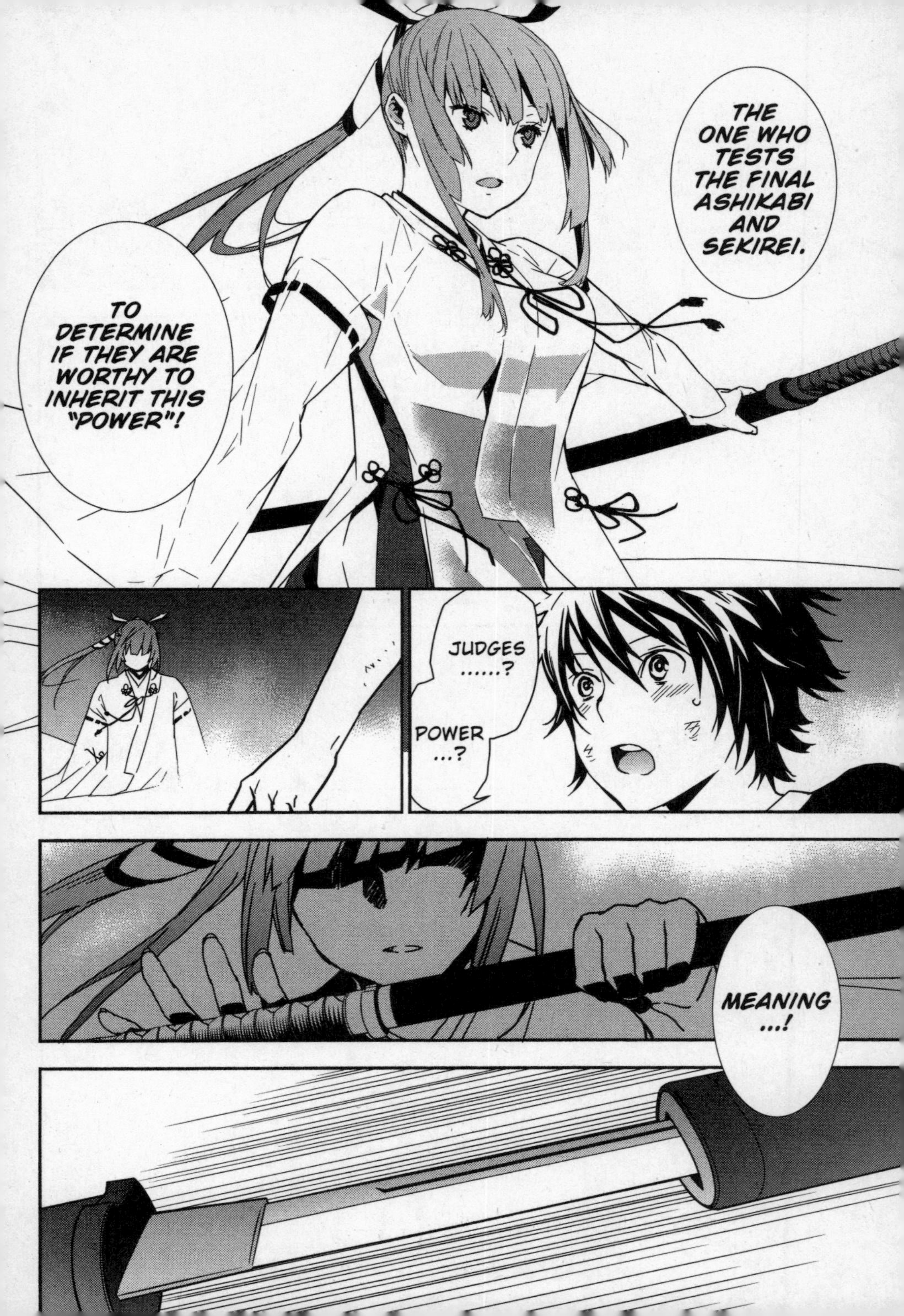
THE ONE WHO TESTS THE FINAL ASHIKABI AND SEKIREI.
TO DETERMINE IF THEY ARE WORTHY TO INHERIT THIS "POWER"!
JUDGES ......?
POWER ...?
MEANING ...!

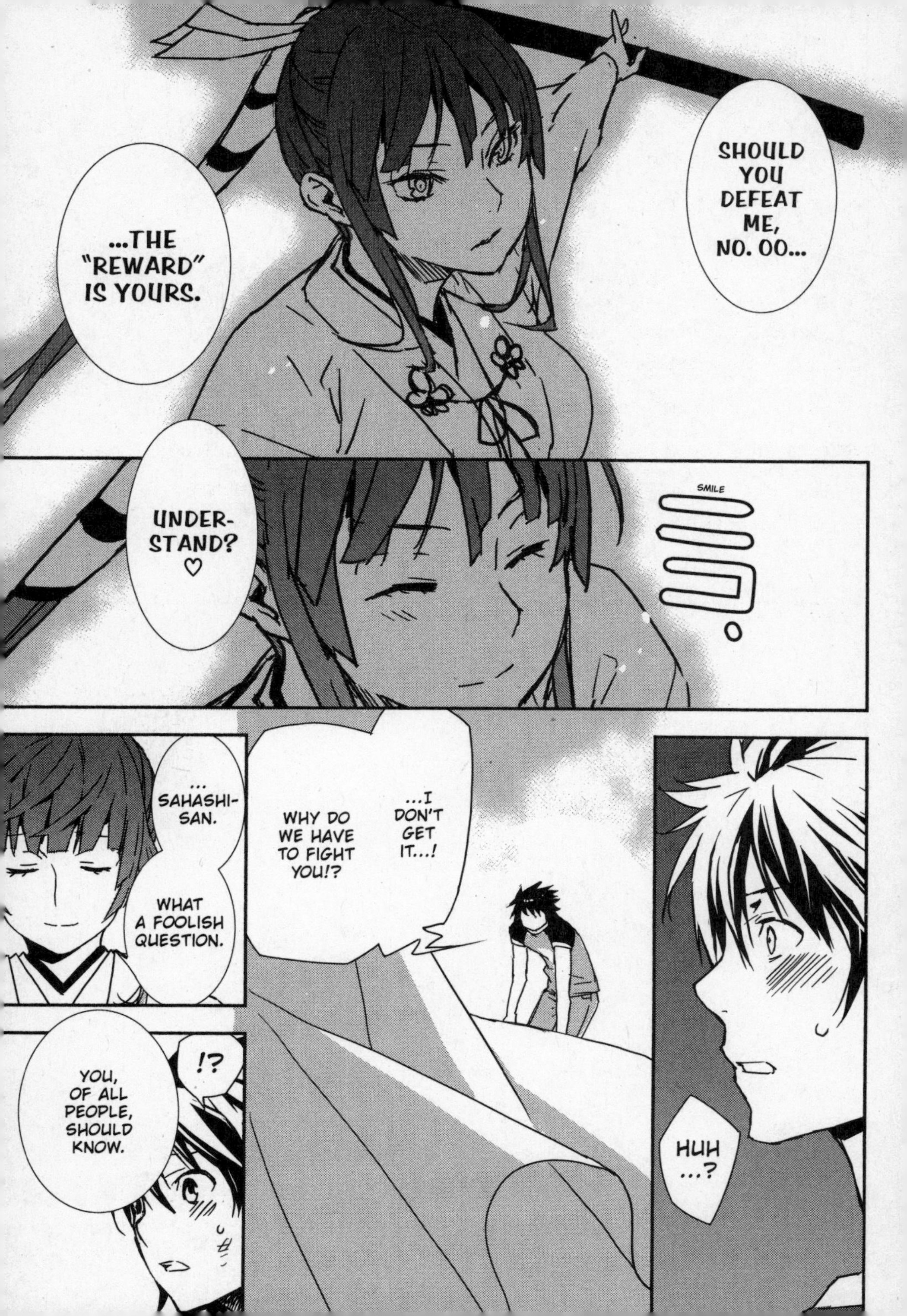
SHOULD YOU DEFEAT ME, NO. OO...
...THE "REWARD" IS YOURS.
SMILE
UNDERSTAND? ♡
HUH ...?
...I DON'T GET IT...!
WHY DO WE HAVE TO FIGHT YOU!?
...SAHASHI-SAN.
WHAT A FOOLISH QUESTION.
!?
YOU, OF ALL PEOPLE, SHOULD KNOW.

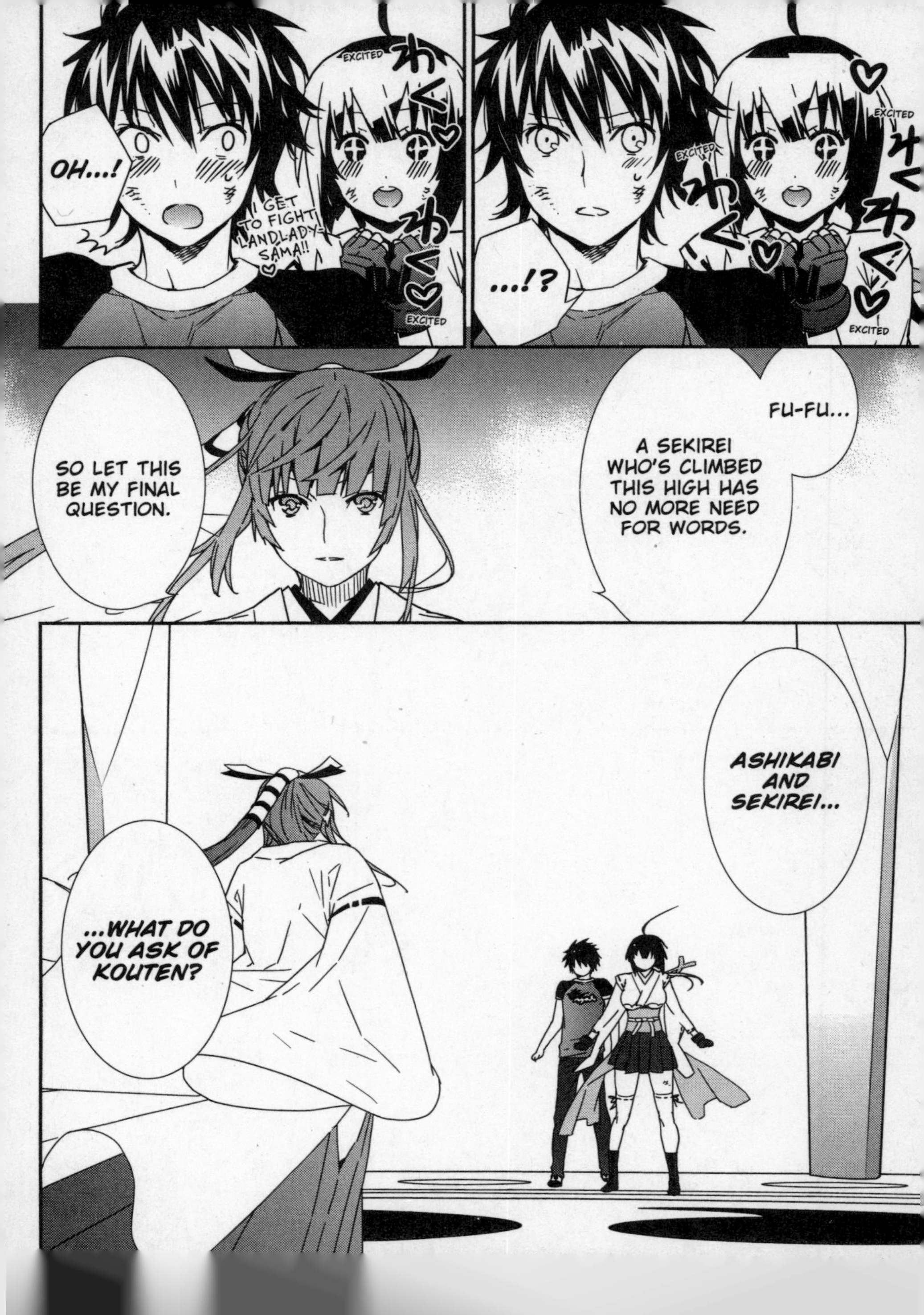
EXCITED
EXCITED
...!?
EXCITED
EXCITED
OH...!
I GET TO FIGHT LANDLADY-SAMA!!
EXCITED
FU-FU...
A SEKIREI WHO'S CLIMBED THIS HIGH HAS NO MORE NEED FOR WORDS.
SO LET THIS BE MY FINAL QUESTION.
ASHIKABI AND SEKIREI...
...WHAT DO YOU ASK OF KOUTEN?

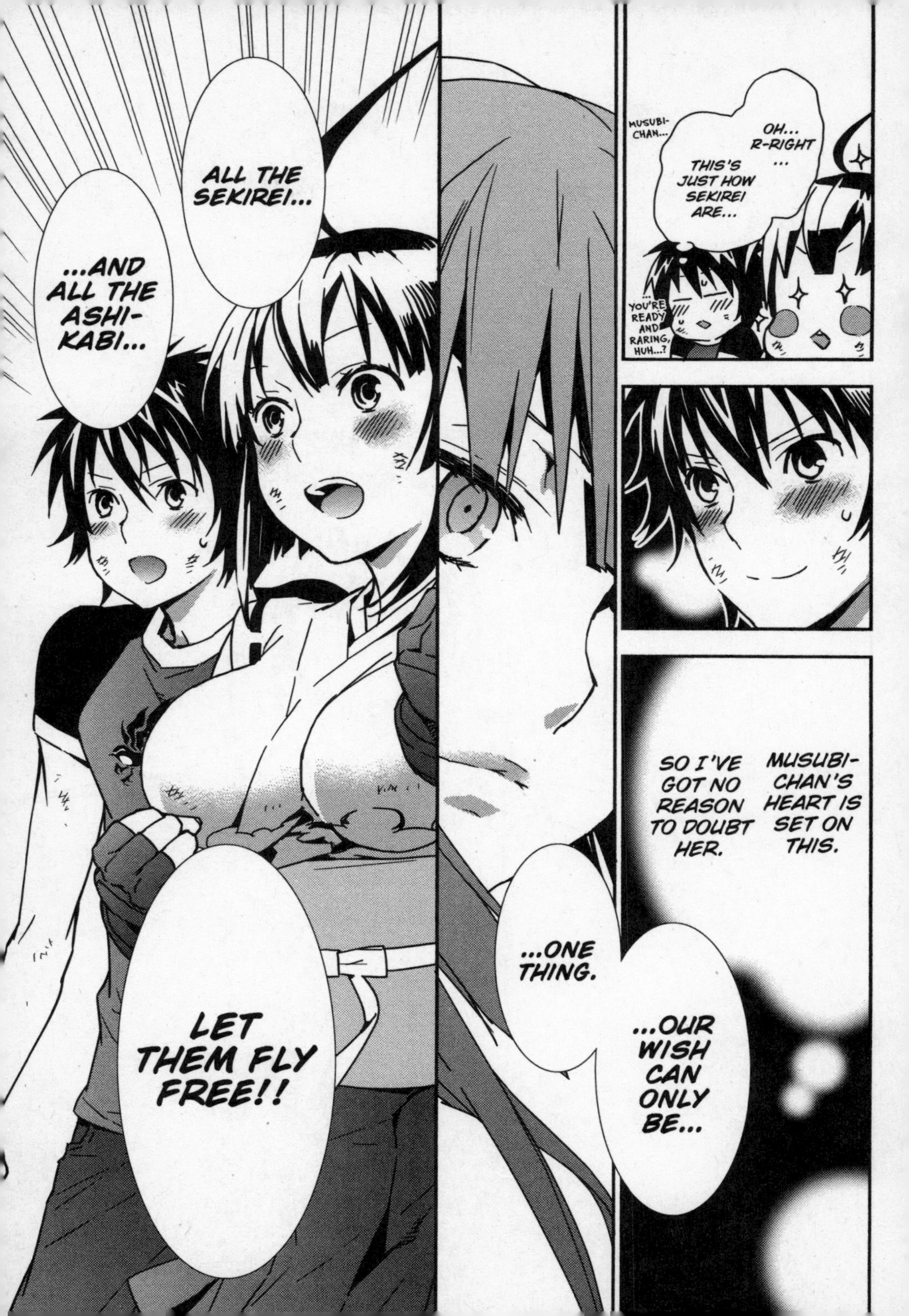
OH... R-RIGHT...
THIS'S JUST HOW SEKIREI ARE...
MUSUBI-CHAN...
...YOU'RE READY AND RARING, HUH...?
MUSUBI-CHAN'S HEART IS SET ON THIS.
SO I'VE GOT NO REASON TO DOUBT HER.
...OUR WISH CAN ONLY BE...
...ONE THING.
ALL THE SEKIREI...
...AND ALL THE ASHI-KABI...
LET THEM FLY FREE!!

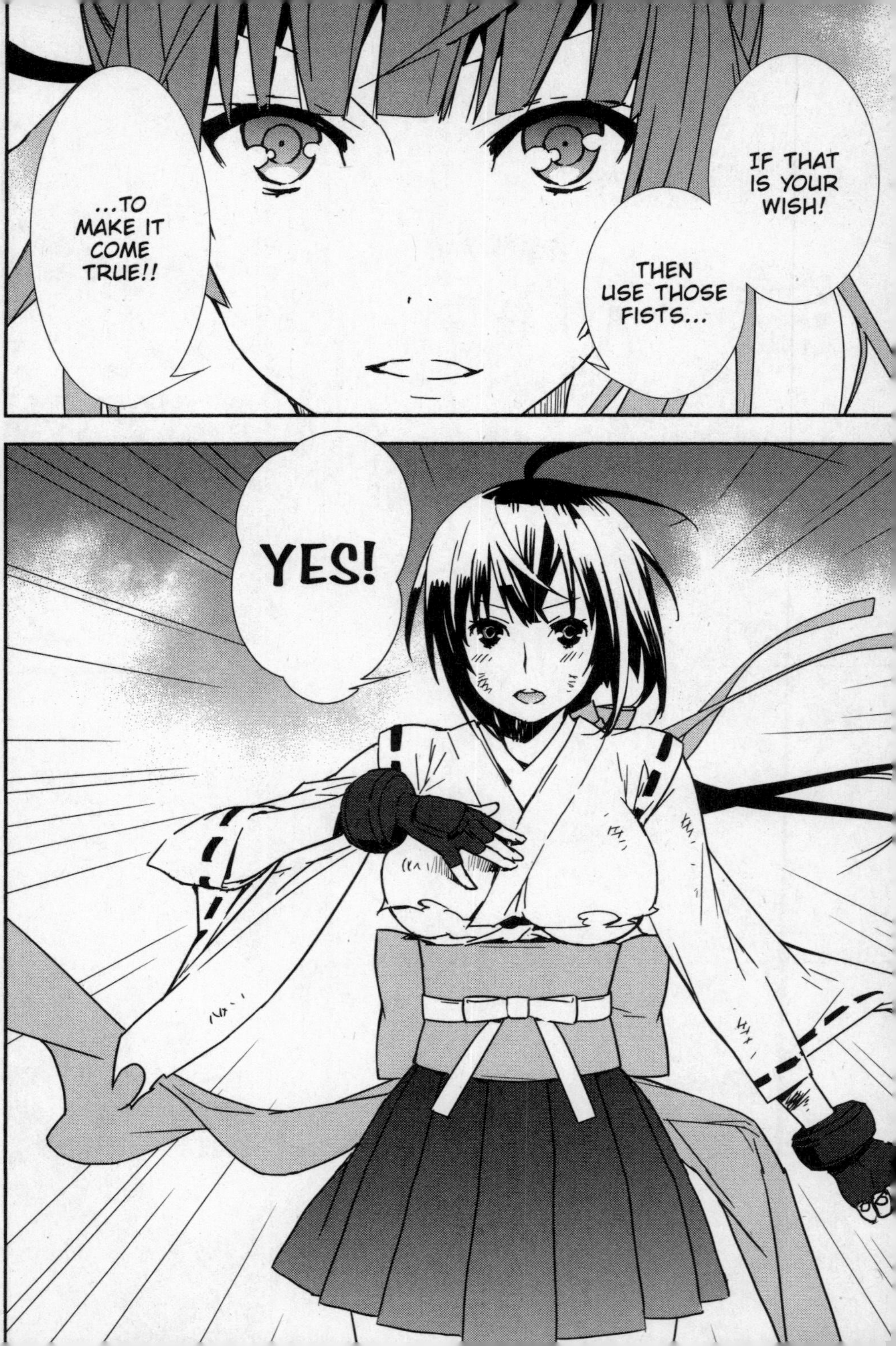
IF THAT IS YOUR WISH!
THEN USE THOSE FISTS...
...TO MAKE IT COME TRUE!!
YES!

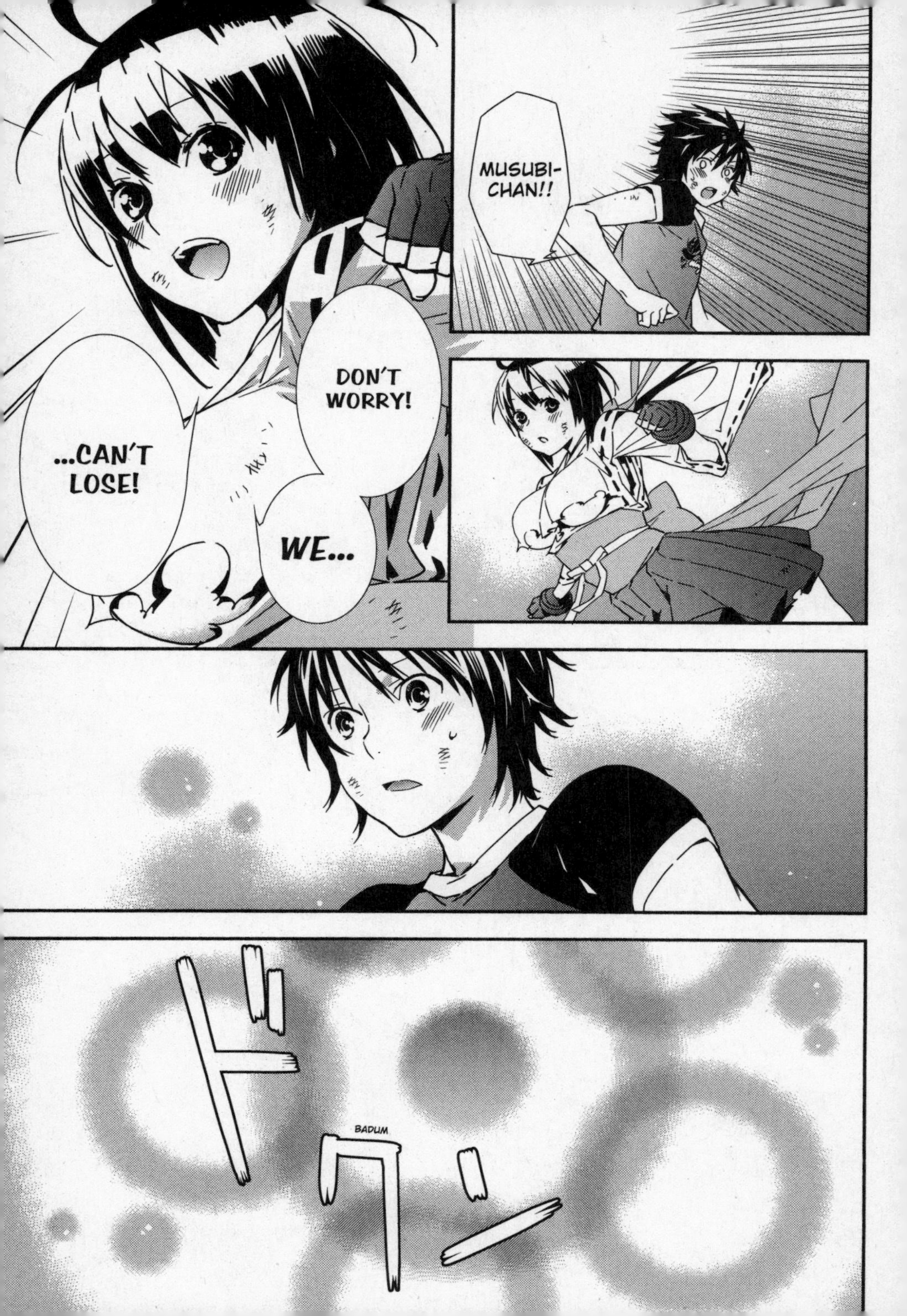
MUSUBI-CHAN!!
DON'T WORRY!
WE...
...CAN'T LOSE!
ドクン
BADUM

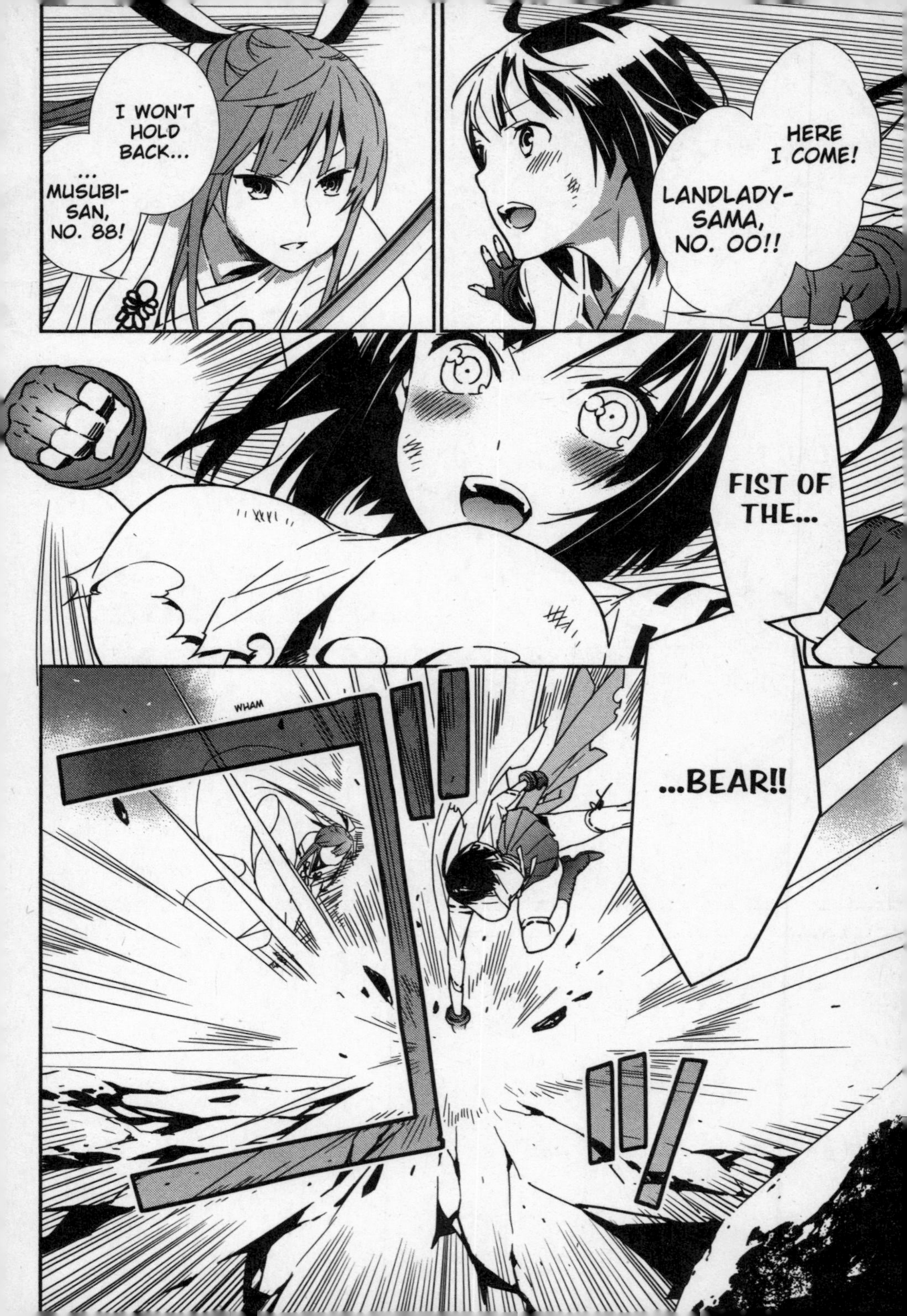
HERE I COME!
LANDLADY-SAMA, NO. 00!!
I WON'T HOLD BACK...
...MUSUBI-SAN, NO. 88!
FIST OF THE...
WHAM
...BEAR!!

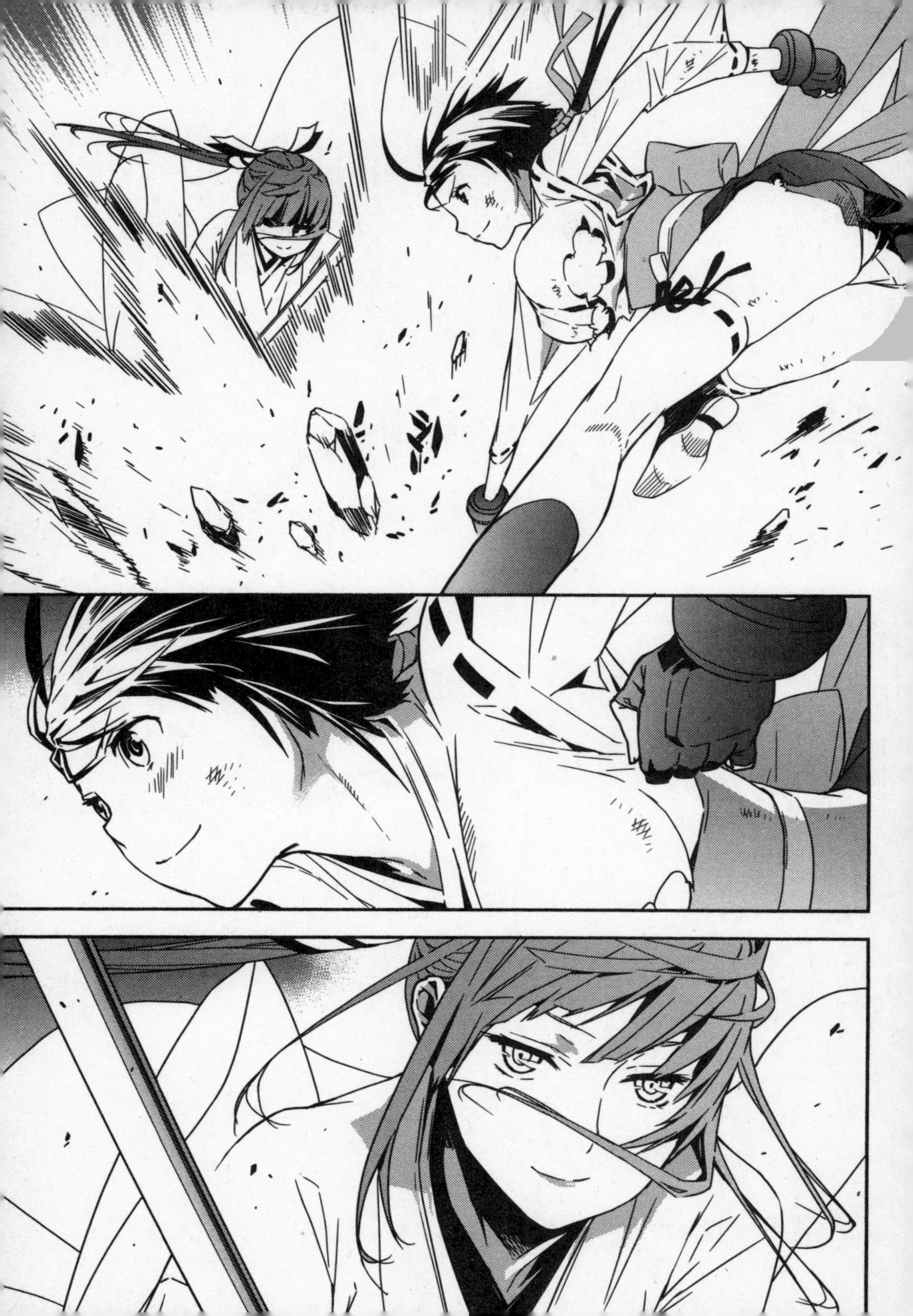

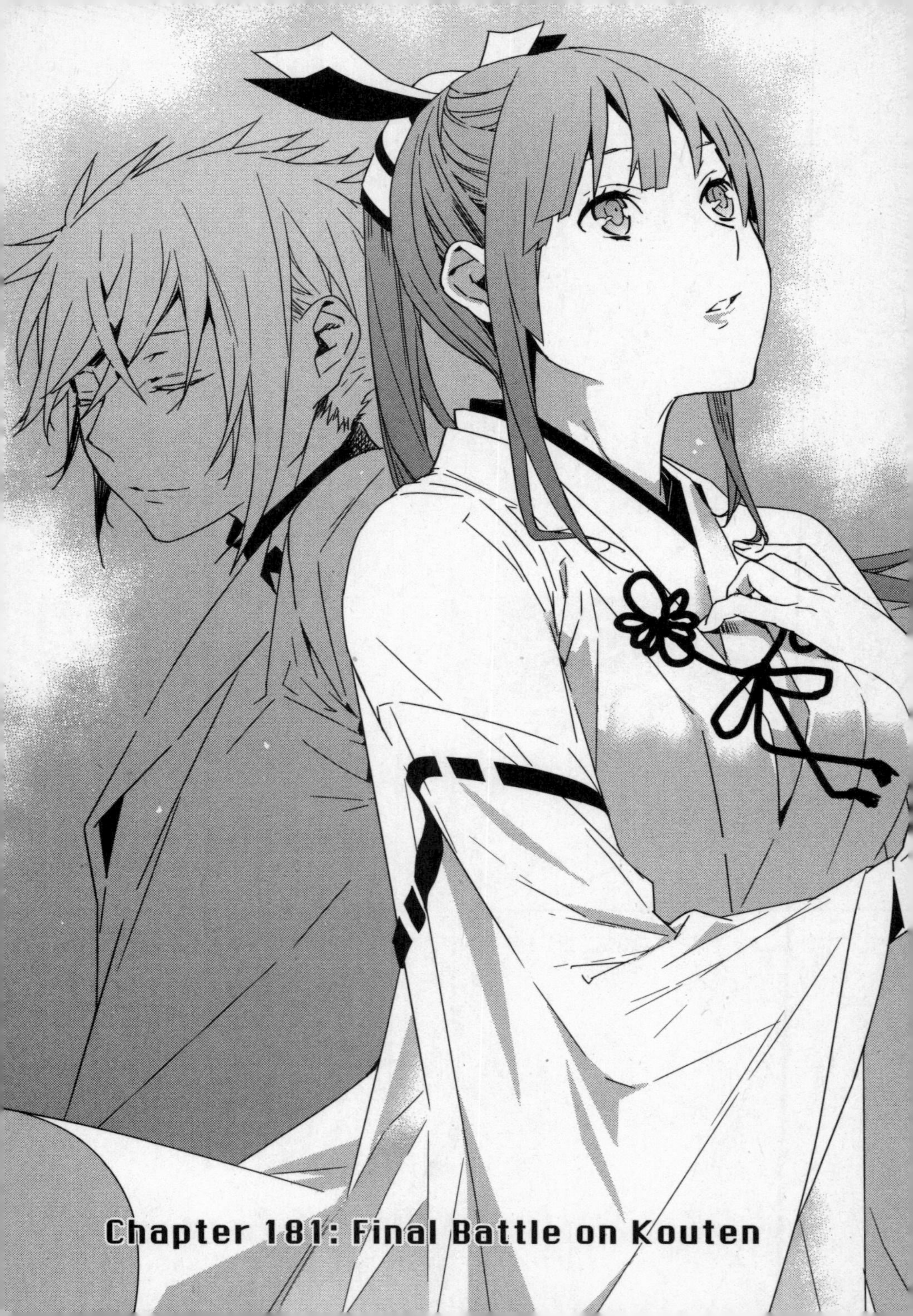

Chapter 181: Final Battle on Kouten

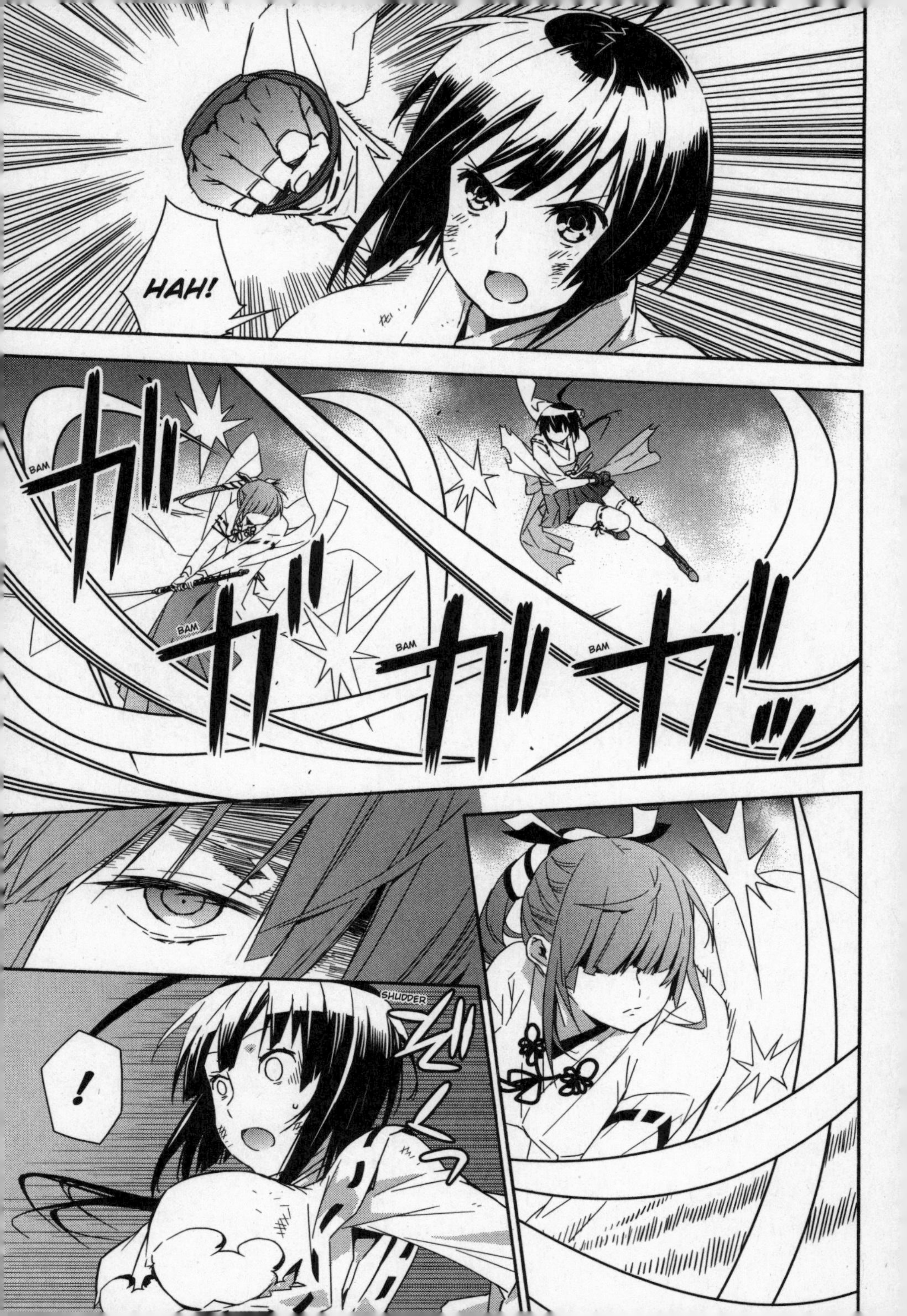
HAH!
BAM
BAM
BAM
BAM
SHUDDER
!

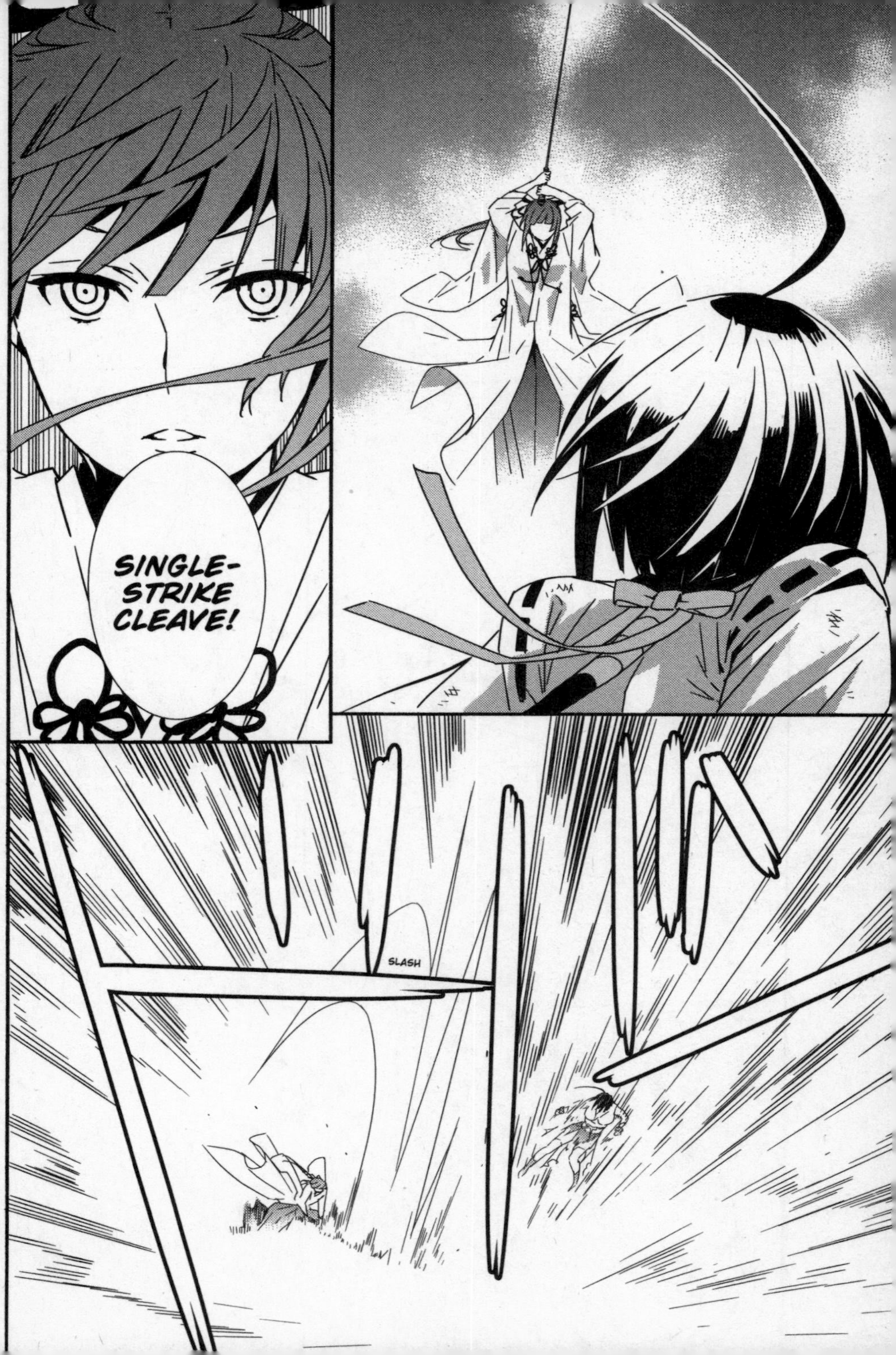
SINGLE-STRIKE CLEAVE!
SLASH

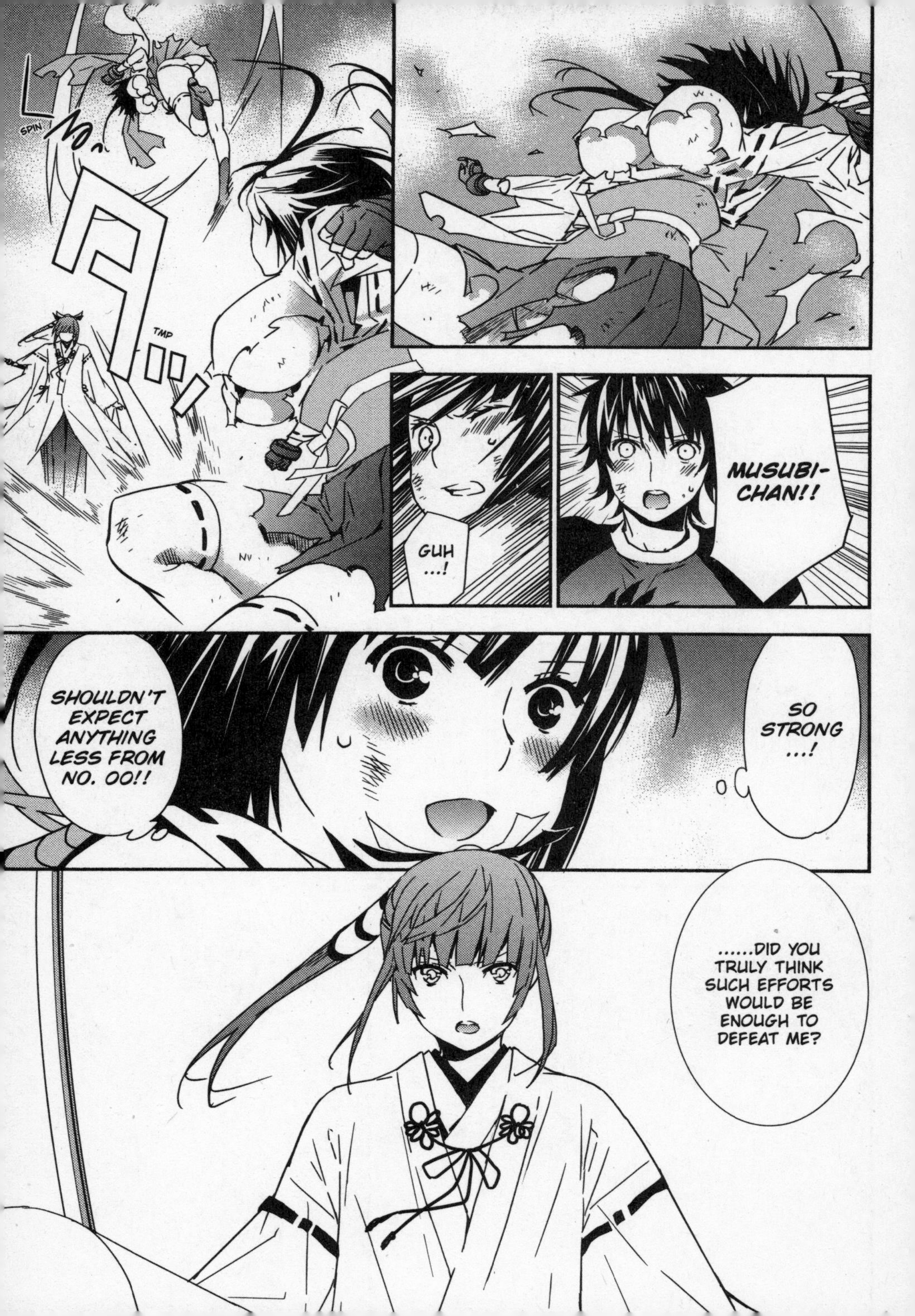
MUSUBI-
CHAN!!
GUH
...!
SPIN
TMP
SO
STRONG
...!
SHOULDN'T
EXPECT
ANYTHING
LESS FROM
NO. 00!!
......DID YOU
TRULY THINK
SUCH EFFORTS
WOULD BE
ENOUGH TO
DEFEAT ME?

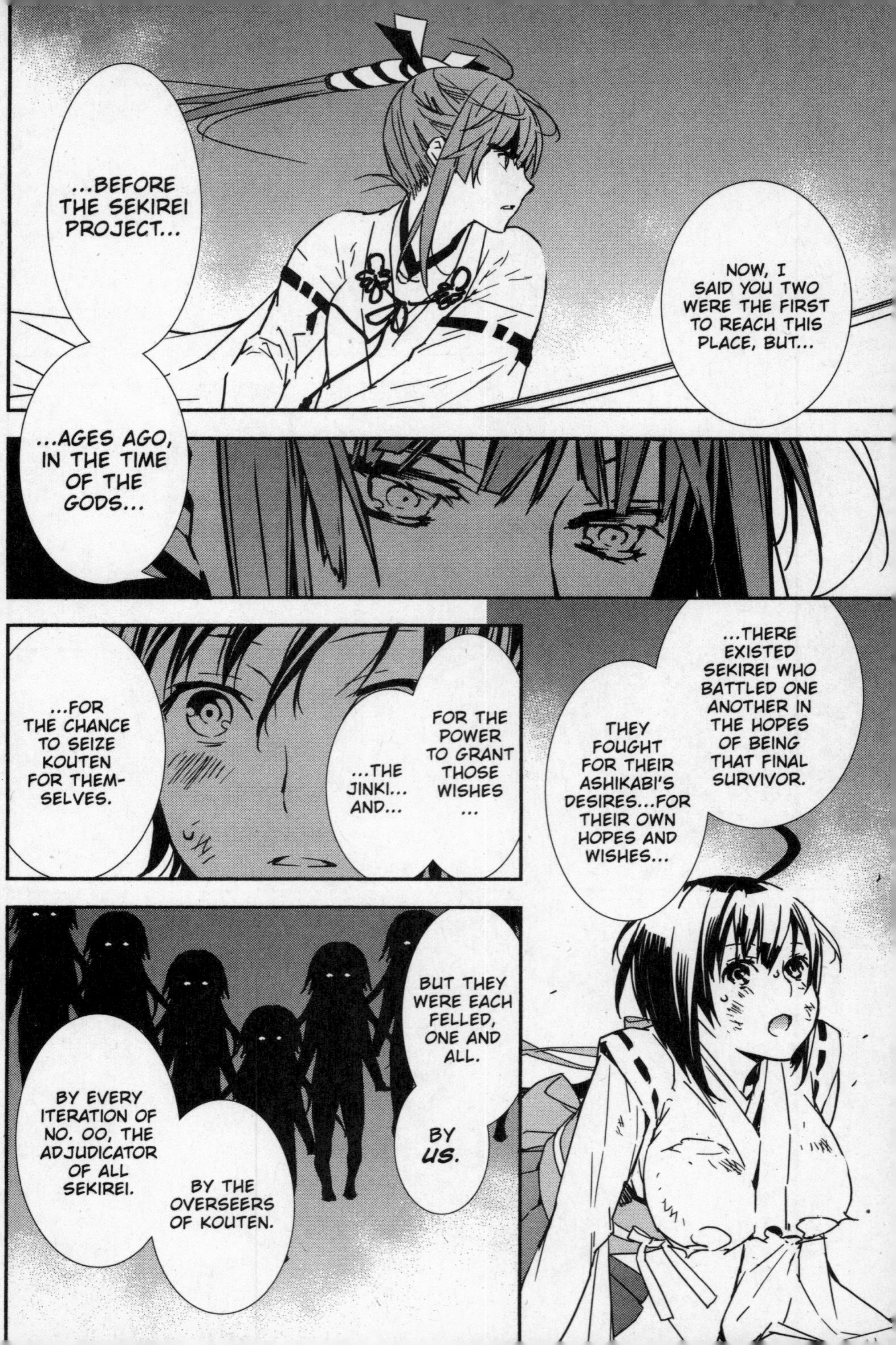
NOW, I SAID YOU TWO WERE THE FIRST TO REACH THIS PLACE, BUT...
...BEFORE THE SEKIREI PROJECT...
...AGES AGO, IN THE TIME OF THE GODS...
...THERE EXISTED SEKIREI WHO BATTLED ONE ANOTHER IN THE HOPES OF BEING THAT FINAL SURVIVOR.
THEY FOUGHT FOR THEIR ASHIKABI'S DESIRES...FOR THEIR OWN HOPES AND WISHES...
FOR THE POWER TO GRANT THOSE WISHES ...
...THE JINKI... AND...
...FOR THE CHANCE TO SEIZE KOUTEN FOR THEM-SELVES.
BUT THEY WERE EACH FELLED, ONE AND ALL.
BY *US*.
BY THE OVERSEERS OF KOUTEN.
BY EVERY ITERATION OF NO. 00, THE ADJUDICATOR OF ALL SEKIREI.

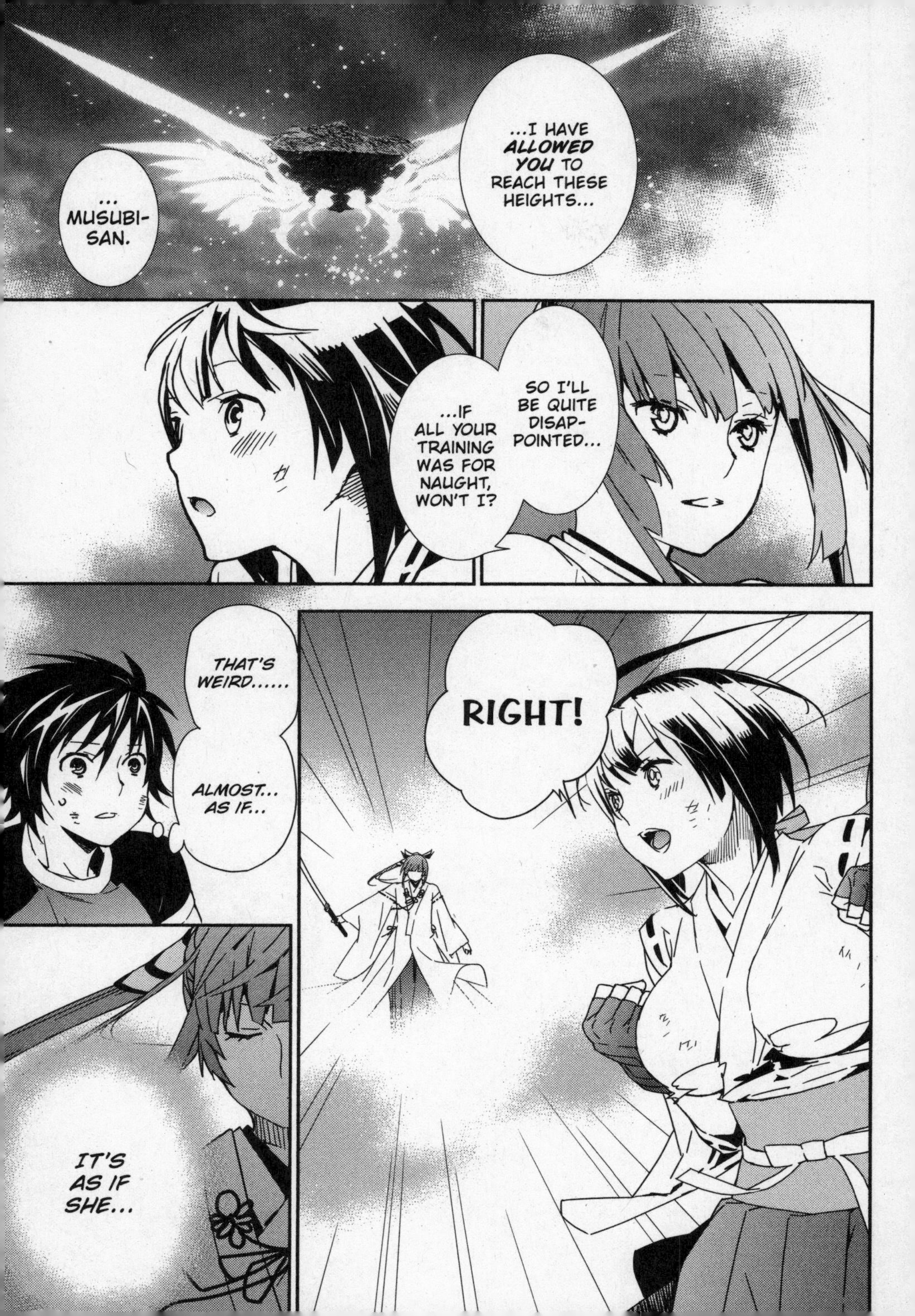
...I HAVE ALLOWED YOU TO REACH THESE HEIGHTS...
...MUSUBI-SAN.
SO I'LL BE QUITE DISAPPOINTED...
...IF ALL YOUR TRAINING WAS FOR NAUGHT, WON'T I?
RIGHT!
THAT'S WEIRD......
ALMOST... AS IF...
IT'S AS IF SHE...

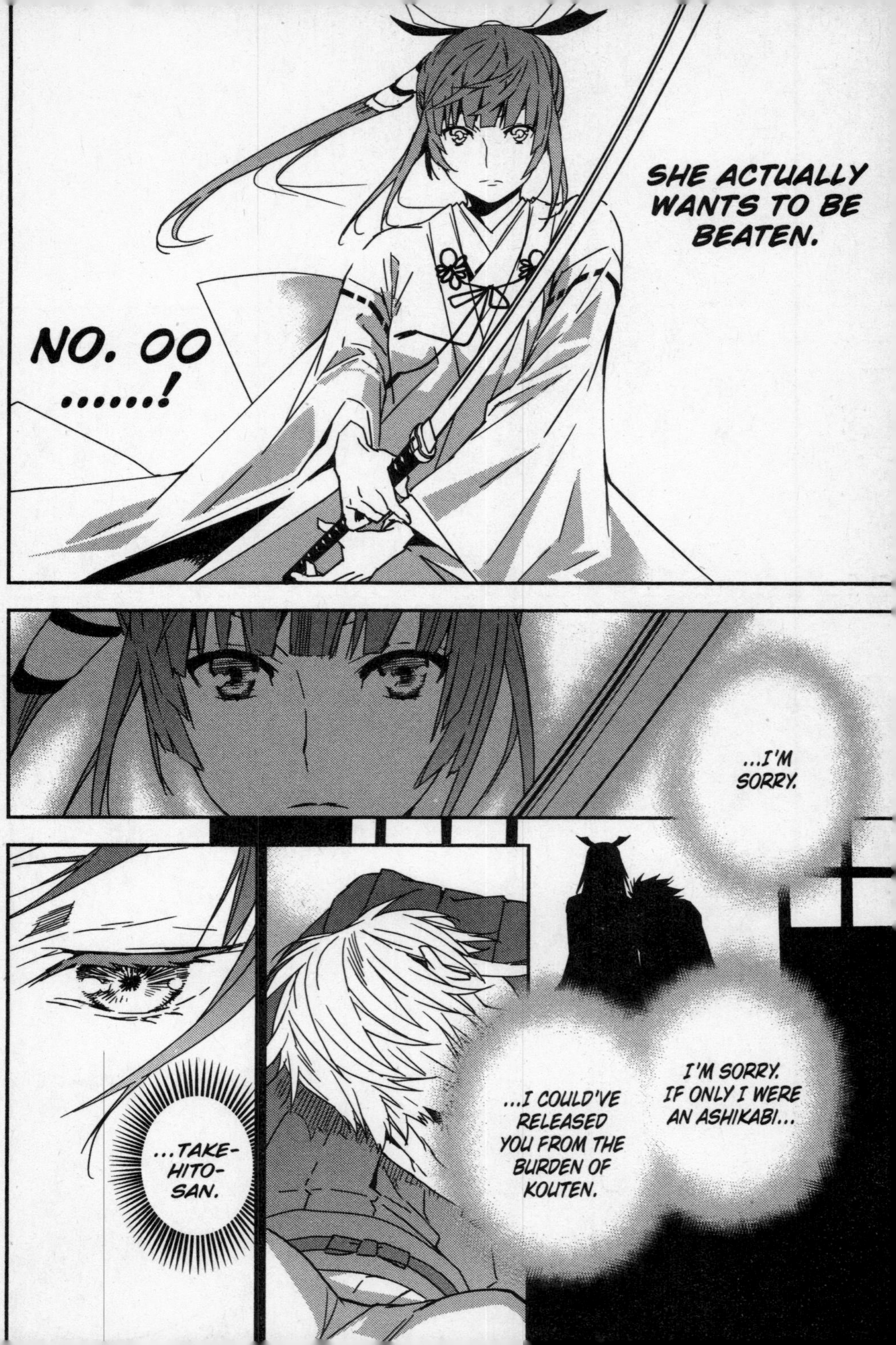
SHE ACTUALLY WANTS TO BE BEATEN.
NO. 00 ......!
...I'M SORRY.
I'M SORRY. IF ONLY I WERE AN ASHIKABI...
...I COULD'VE RELEASED YOU FROM THE BURDEN OF KOUTEN.
...TAKE-HITO-SAN.

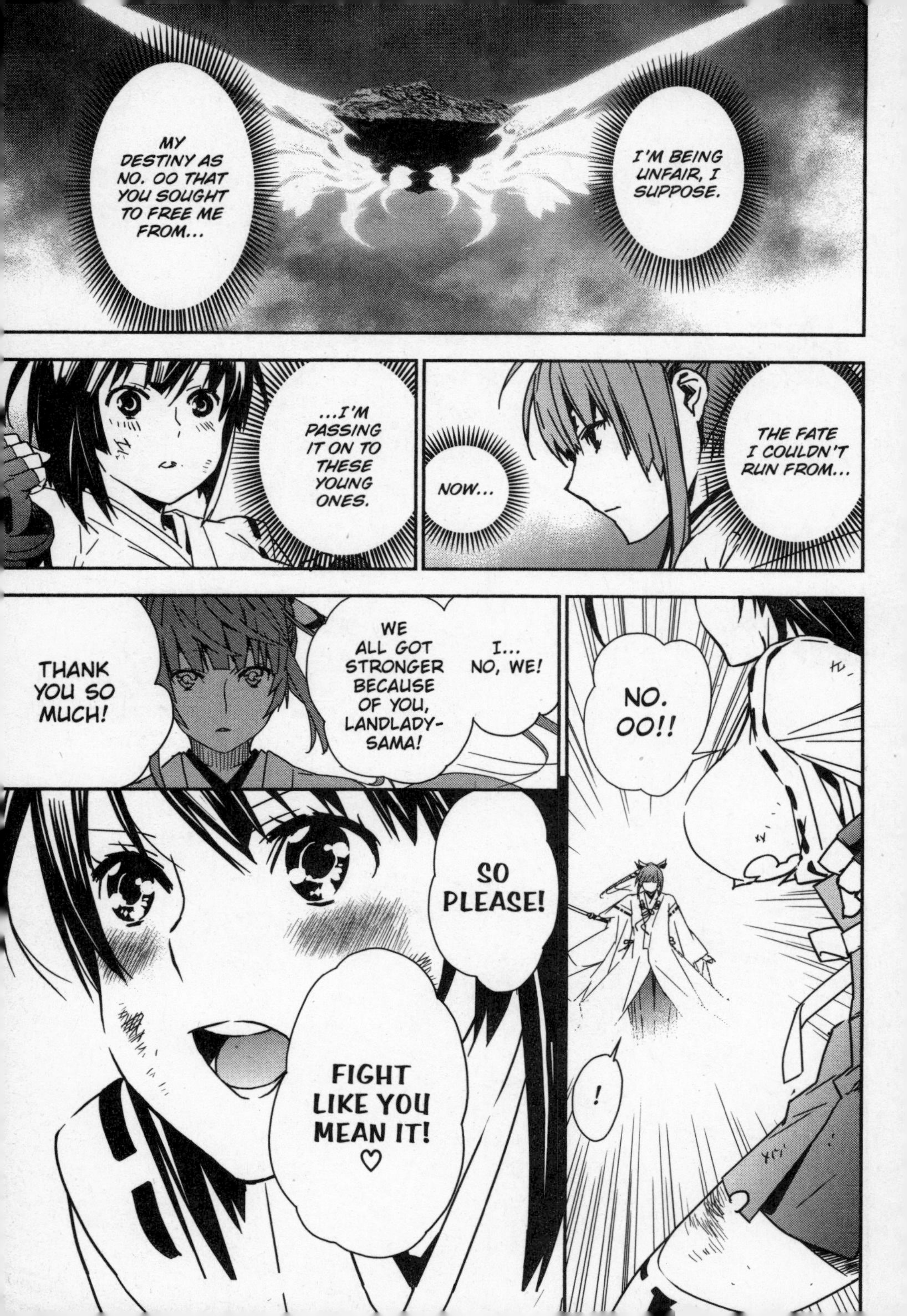
I'M BEING UNFAIR, I SUPPOSE.
MY DESTINY AS NO. 00 THAT YOU SOUGHT TO FREE ME FROM...
THE FATE I COULDN'T RUN FROM...
NOW...
...I'M PASSING IT ON TO THESE YOUNG ONES.
NO. 00!!
!
I... NO, WE!
WE ALL GOT STRONGER BECAUSE OF YOU, LANDLADY-SAMA!
THANK YOU SO MUCH!
SO PLEASE!
FIGHT LIKE YOU MEAN IT! ♡

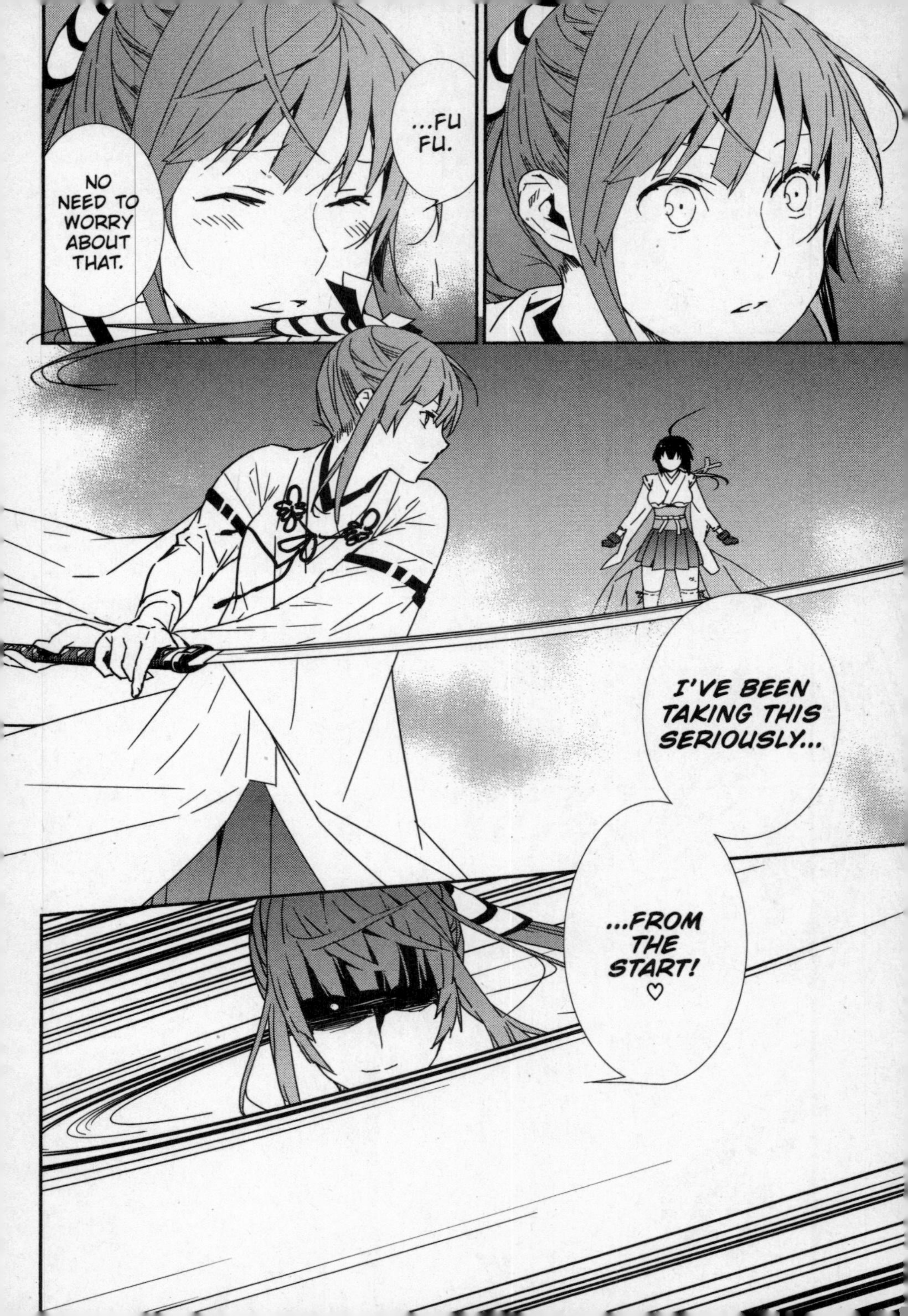
...FU FU.
NO NEED TO WORRY ABOUT THAT.
I'VE BEEN TAKING THIS SERIOUSLY...
...FROM THE START! ♡

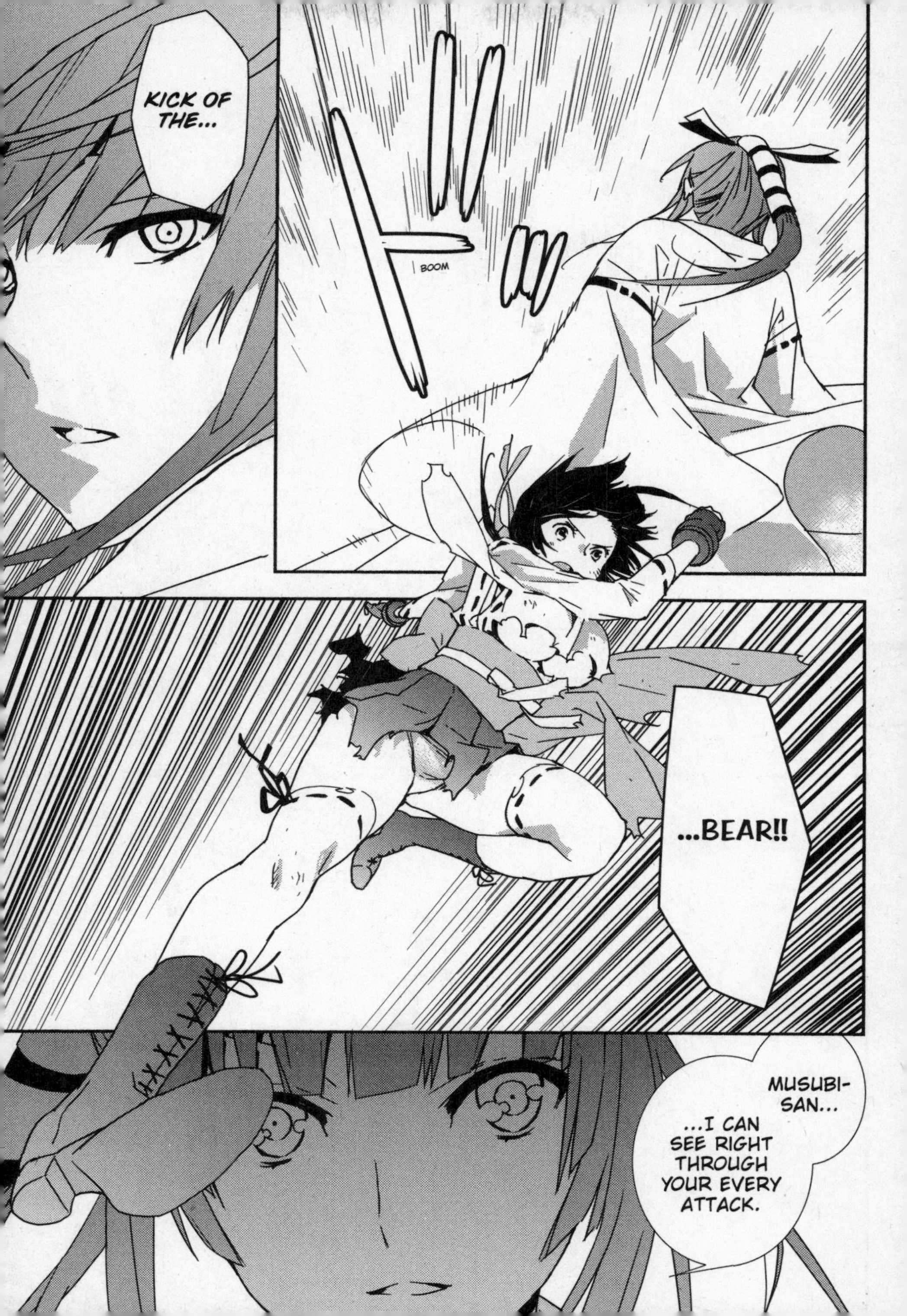
BOOM
KICK OF THE...
...BEAR!!
MUSUBI-SAN...
...I CAN SEE RIGHT THROUGH YOUR EVERY ATTACK.

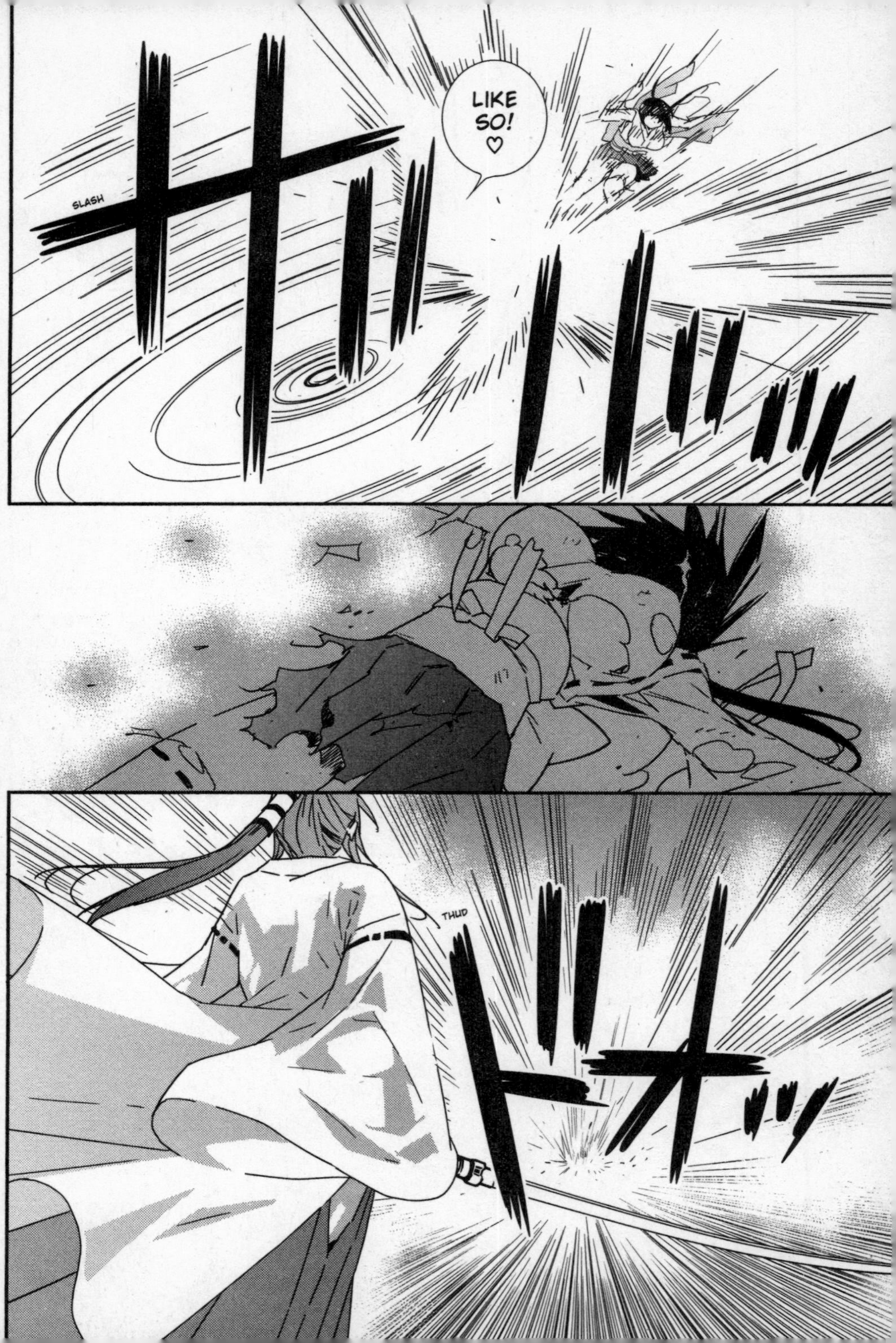
LIKE SO! ♡
SLASH
THUD

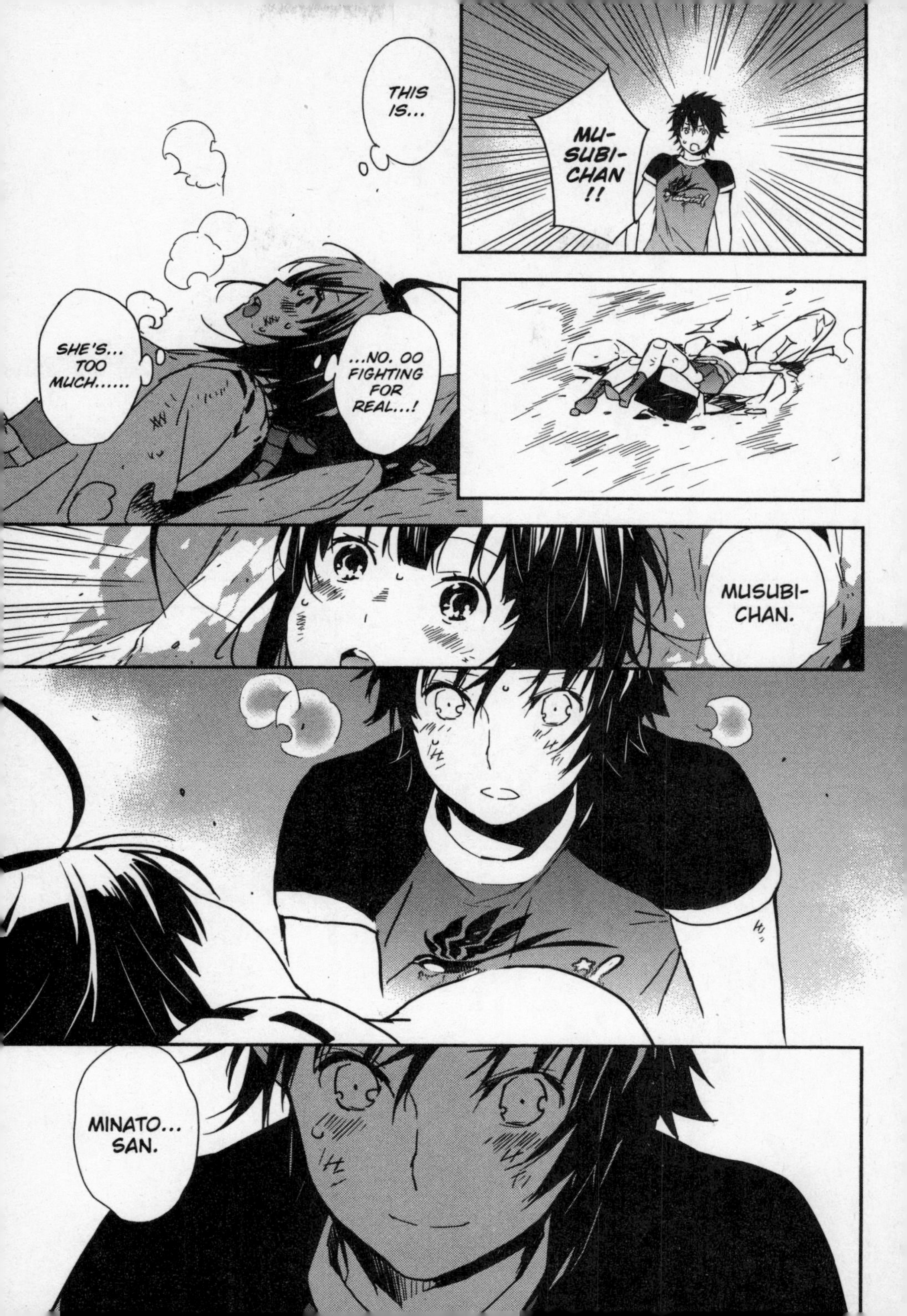
MU-SUBI-CHAN!!
THIS IS...
...NO. OO FIGHTING FOR REAL...!
SHE'S... TOO MUCH......
MUSUBI-CHAN.
MINATO... SAN.

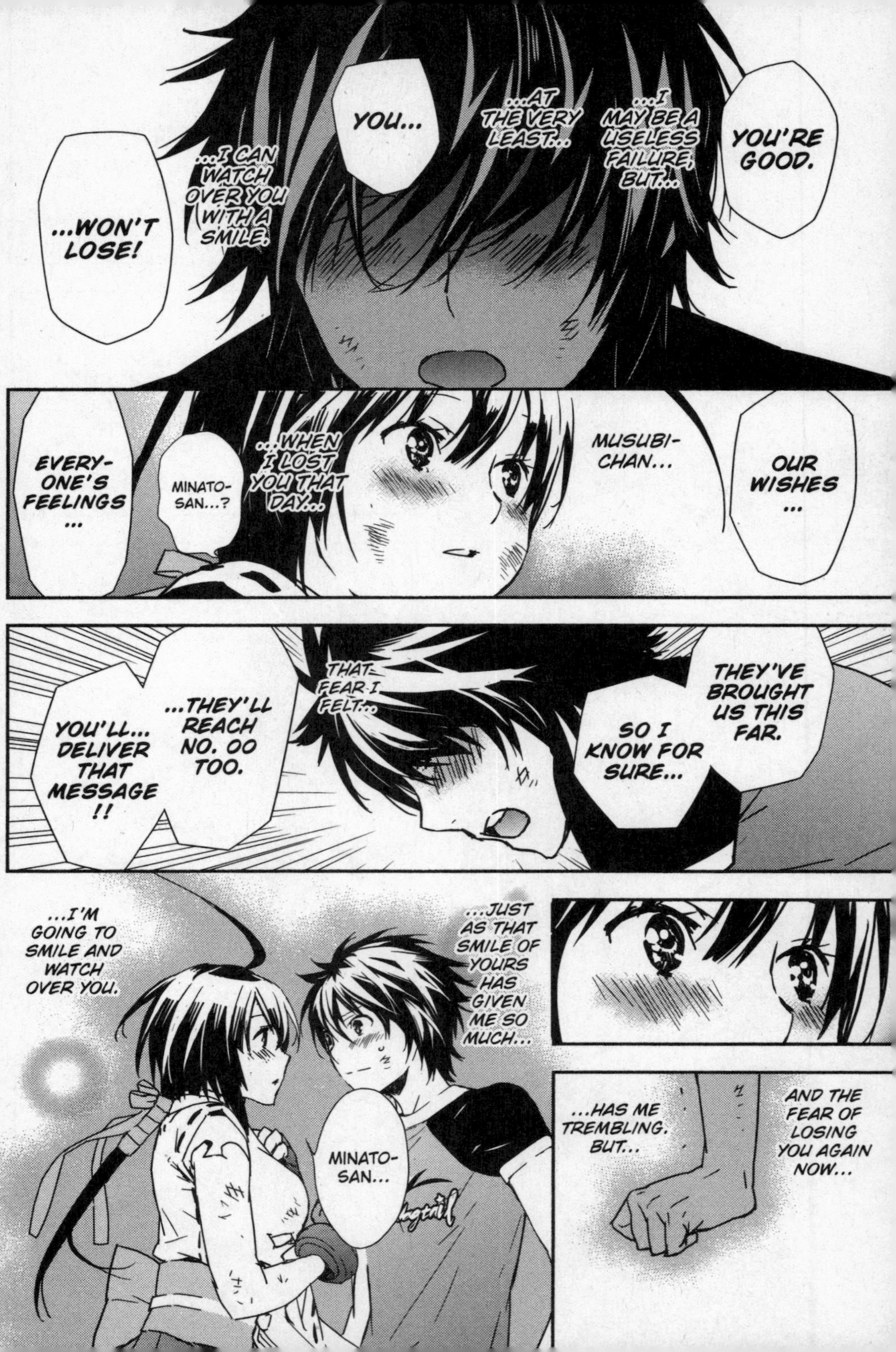
YOU'RE GOOD.
...I MAY BE A USELESS FAILURE, BUT...
...AT THE VERY LEAST...
YOU...
...I CAN WATCH OVER YOU WITH A SMILE.
...WON'T LOSE!
OUR WISHES ...
MUSUBI-CHAN...
...WHEN I LOST YOU THAT DAY...
MINATO-SAN...?
EVERY-ONE'S FEELINGS ...
THEY'VE BROUGHT US THIS FAR.
SO I KNOW FOR SURE...
THAT FEAR I FELT...
...THEY'LL REACH NO. 00 TOO.
YOU'LL... DELIVER THAT MESSAGE !!
AND THE FEAR OF LOSING YOU AGAIN NOW...
...HAS ME TREMBLING. BUT...
...JUST AS THAT SMILE OF YOURS HAS GIVEN ME SO MUCH...
...I'M GOING TO SMILE AND WATCH OVER YOU.
MINATO-SAN...

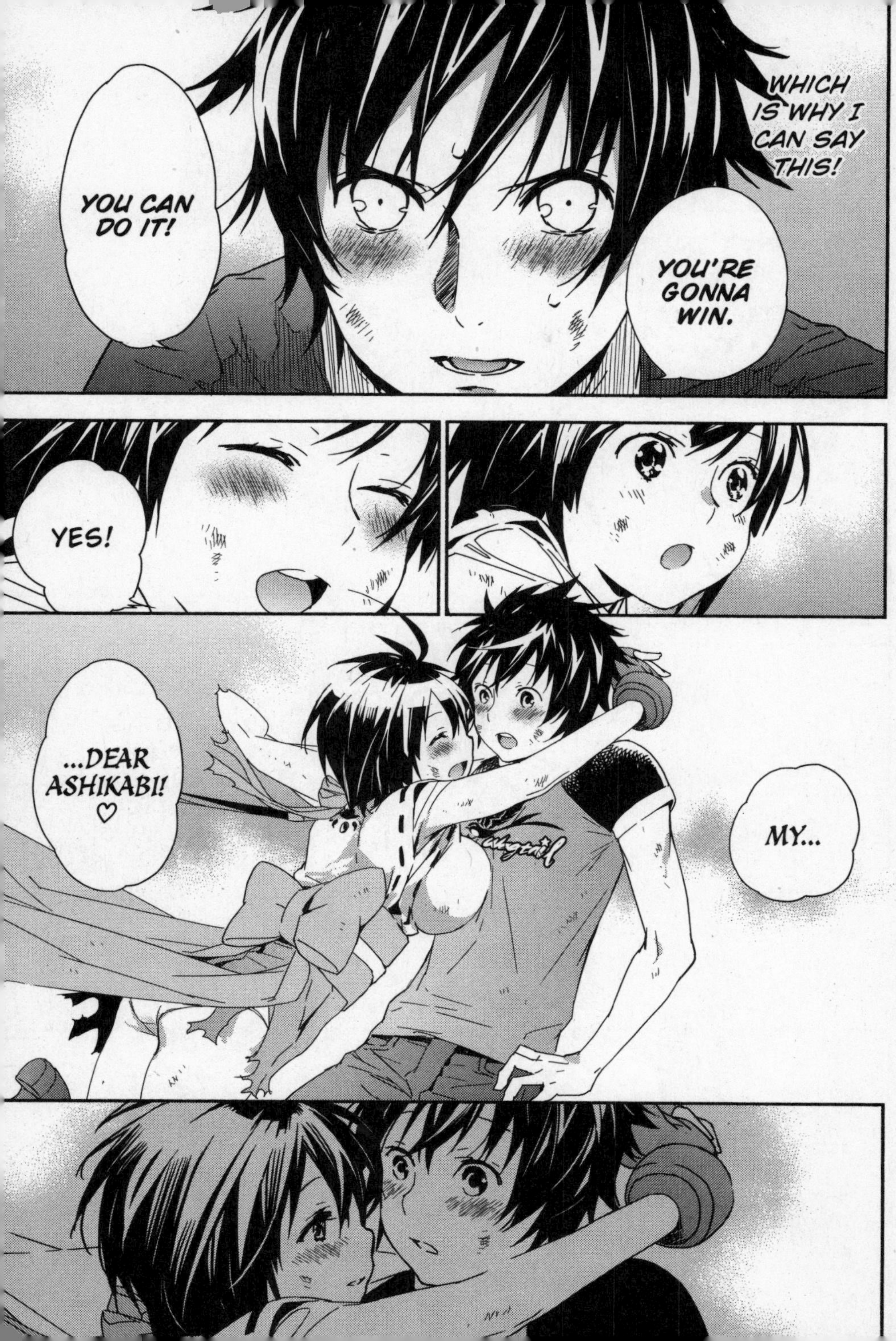
WHICH IS WHY I CAN SAY THIS!
YOU'RE GONNA WIN.
YOU CAN DO IT!
YES!
MY...
...DEAR ASHIKABI! ♡

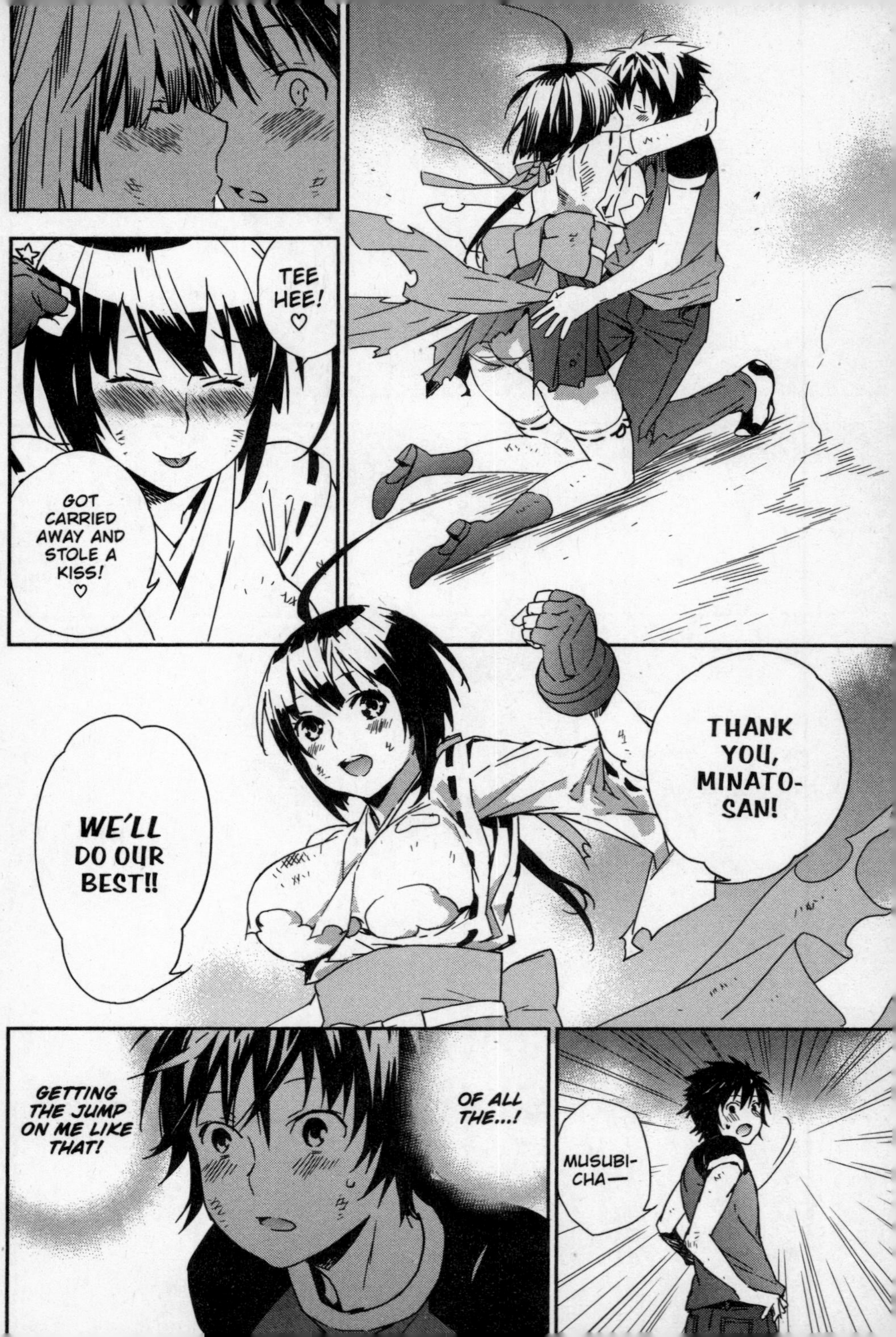
TEE HEE! ♡
GOT CARRIED AWAY AND STOLE A KISS! ♡
THANK YOU, MINATO-SAN!
WE'LL DO OUR BEST!!
MUSUBI-CHA—
OF ALL THE...!
GETTING THE JUMP ON ME LIKE THAT!

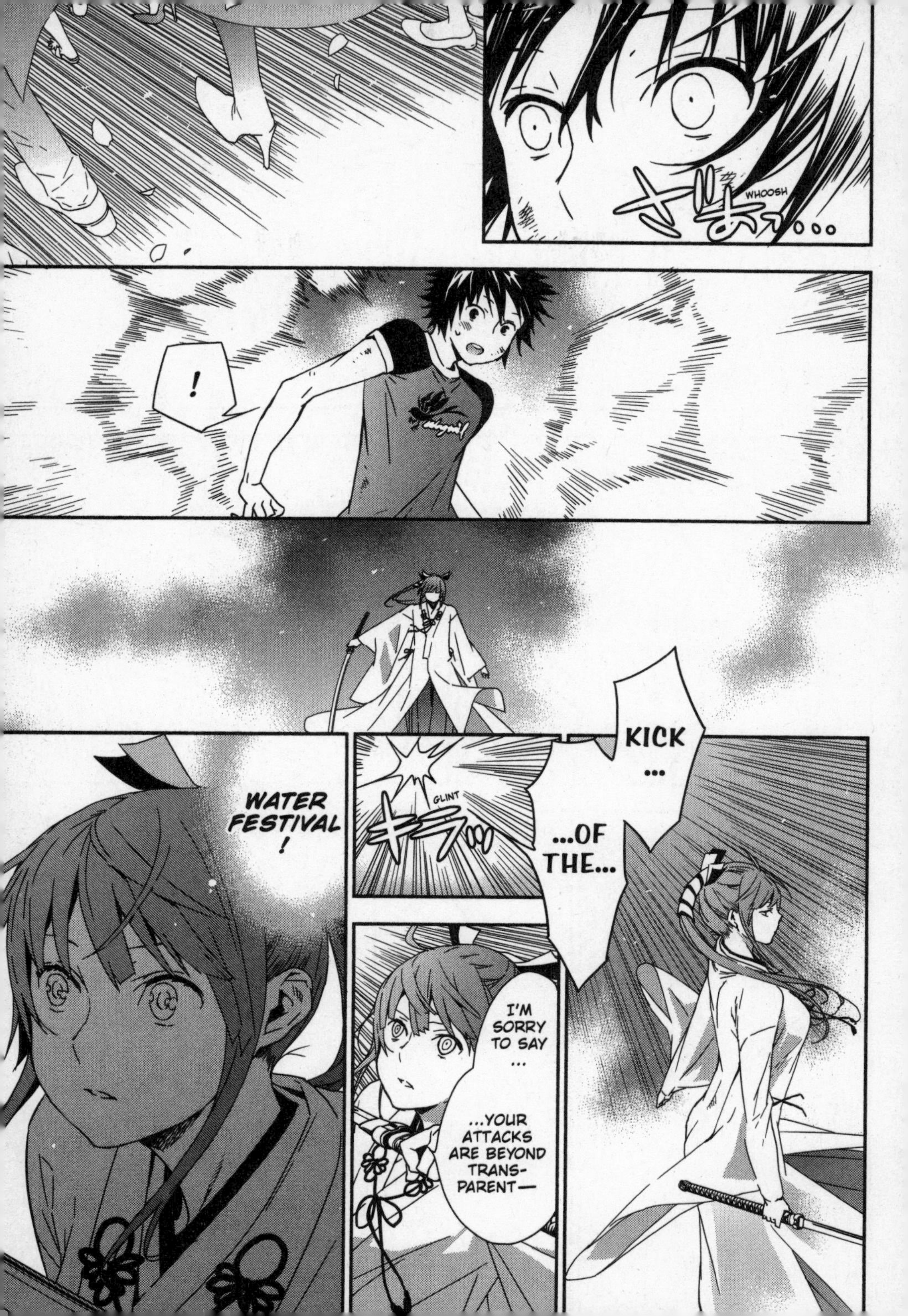
WHOOSH
!
KICK ...
...OF THE...
GLINT
I'M SORRY TO SAY ...
...YOUR ATTACKS ARE BEYOND TRANS-PARENT—
WATER FESTIVAL !

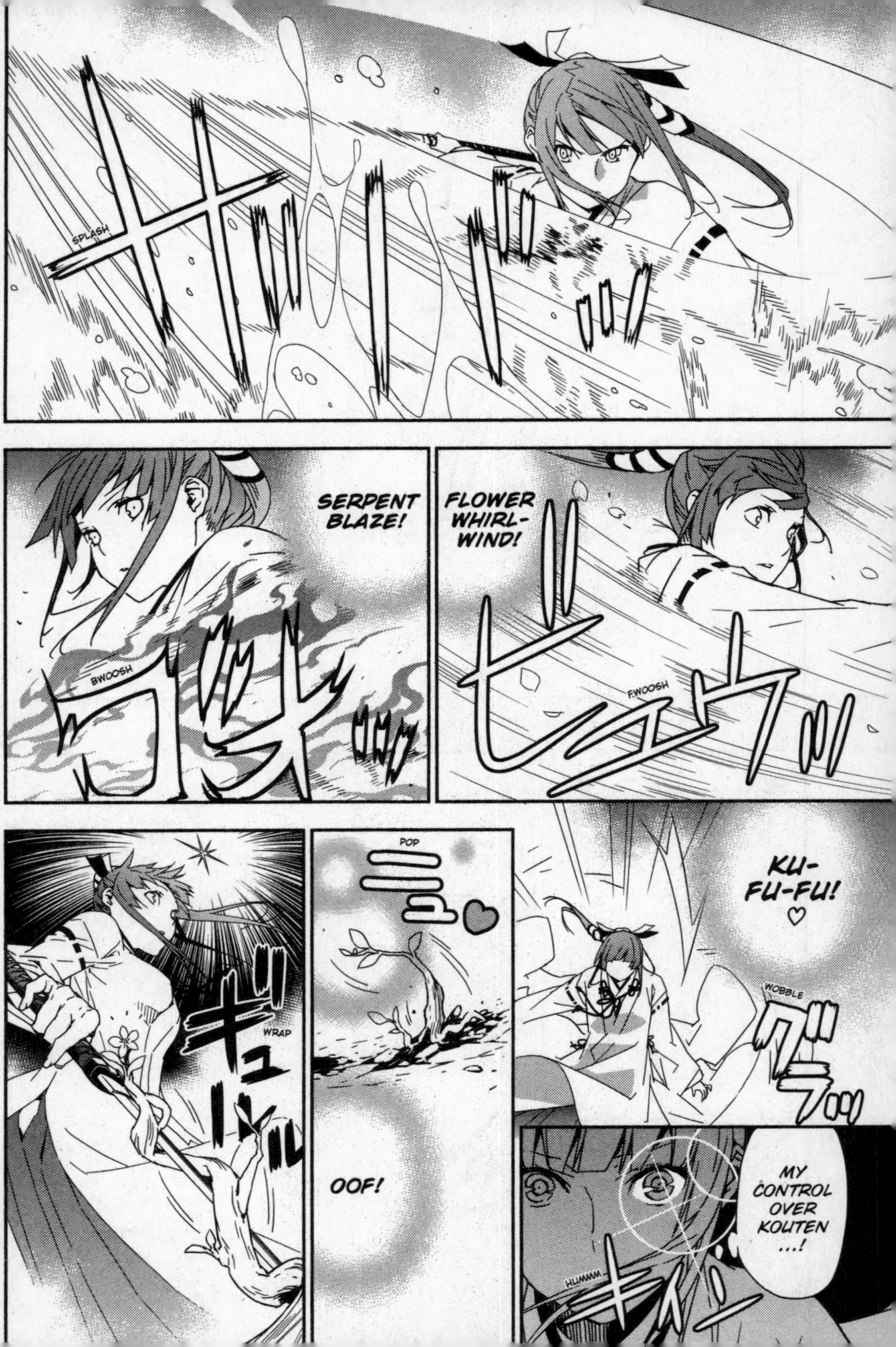
SPLASH
FLOWER WHIRL-WIND!
FWOOSH
SERPENT BLAZE!
BWOOSH
KU-FU-FU! ♡
WOBBLE
MY CONTROL OVER KOUTEN ...!
HUMMM
POP
OOF!
WRAP

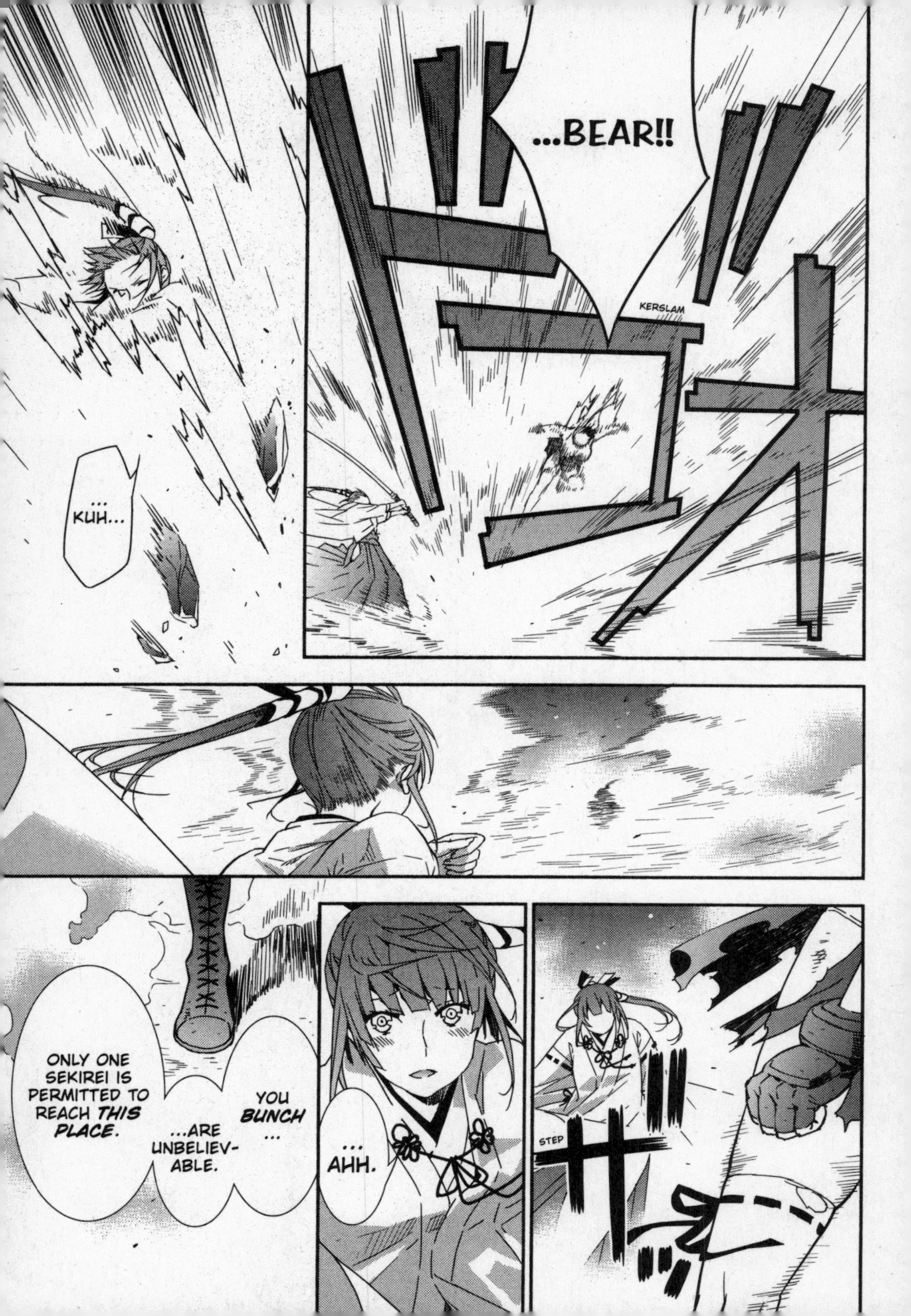
...BEAR!!
KERSLAM
... KUH...
STEP
... AHH.
YOU BUNCH ...
...ARE UNBELIEVABLE.
ONLY ONE SEKIREI IS PERMITTED TO REACH *THIS PLACE*.

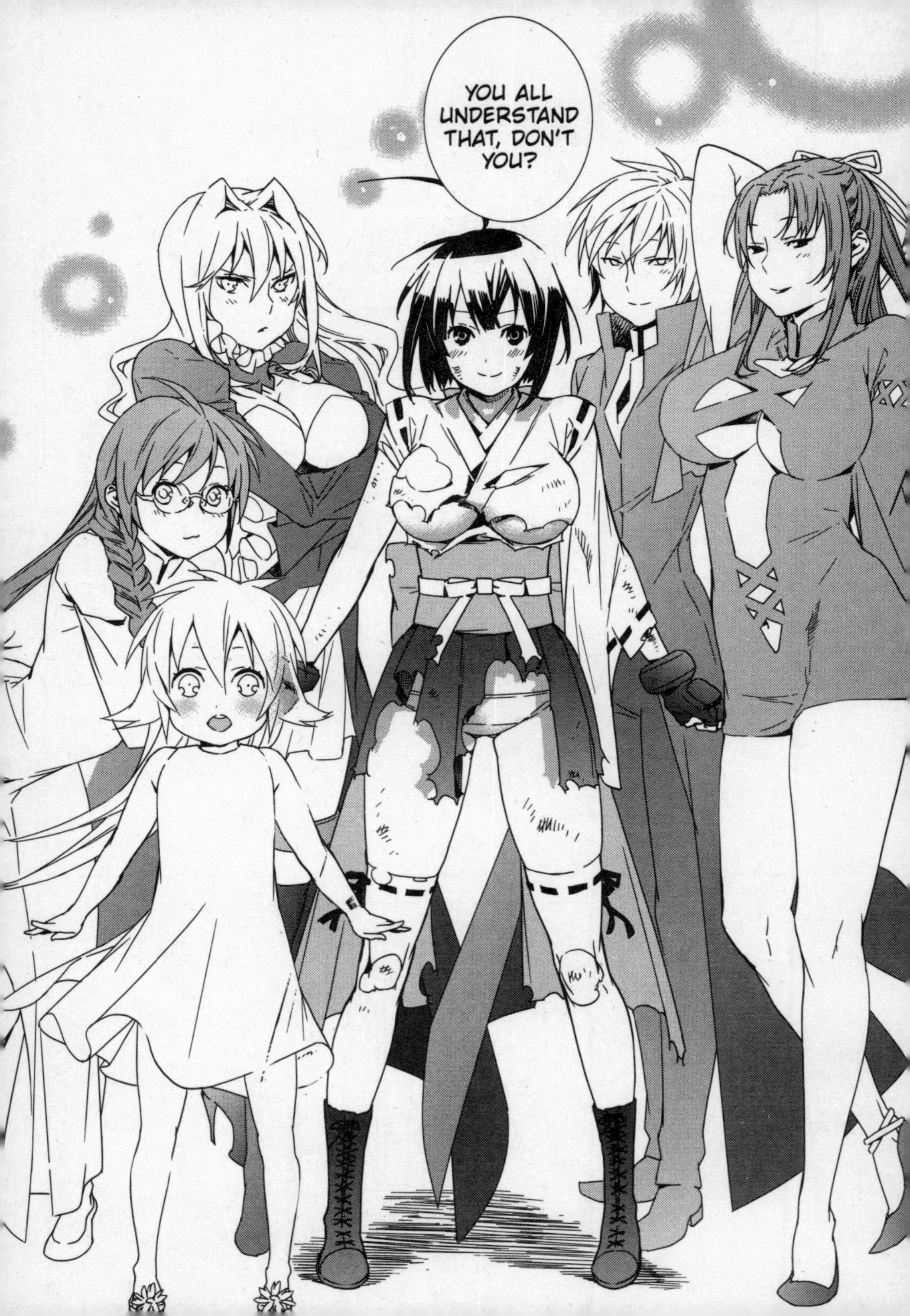
YOU ALL UNDERSTAND THAT, DON'T YOU?

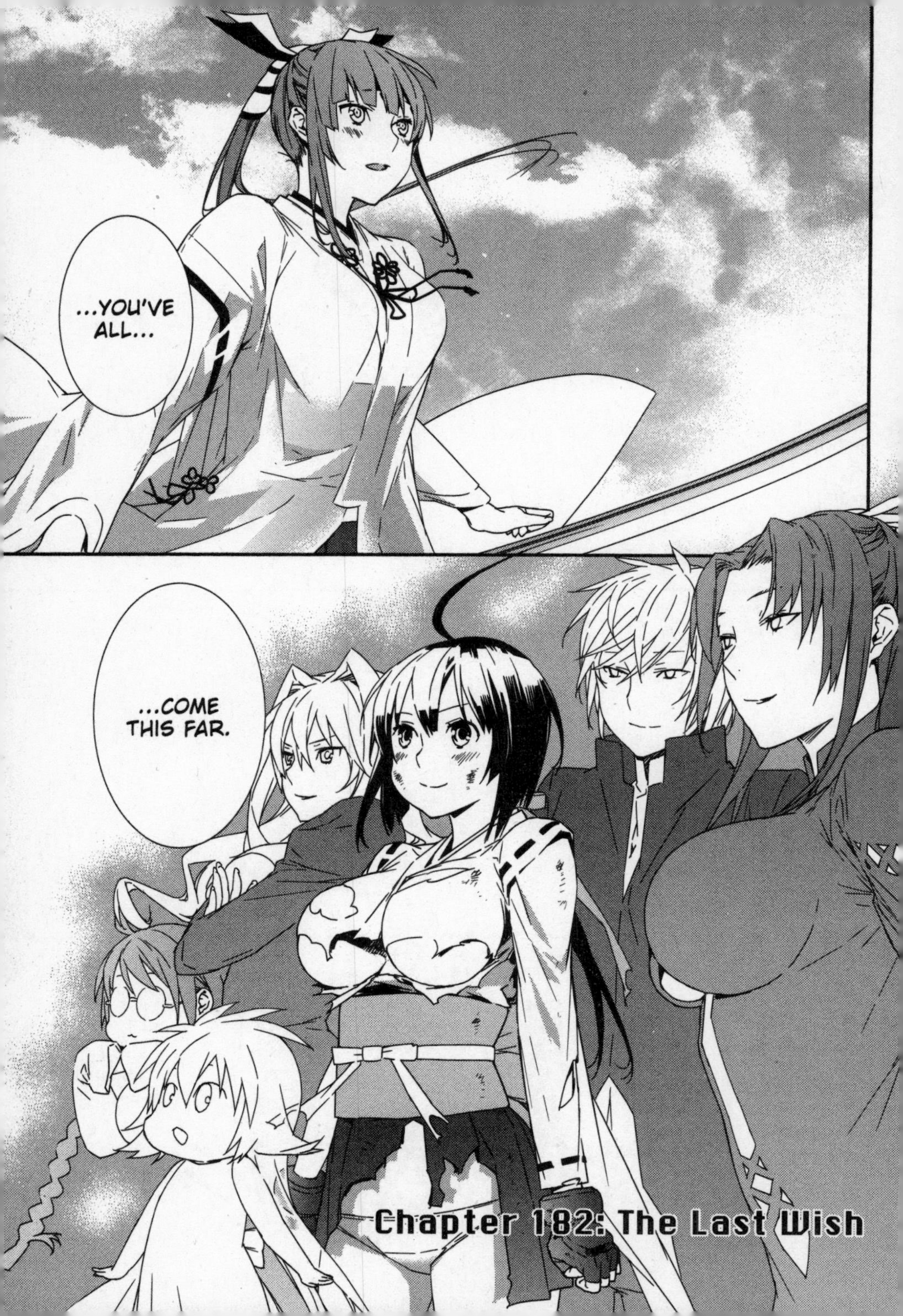
...YOU'VE ALL...
...COME THIS FAR.
Chapter 182: The Last Wish

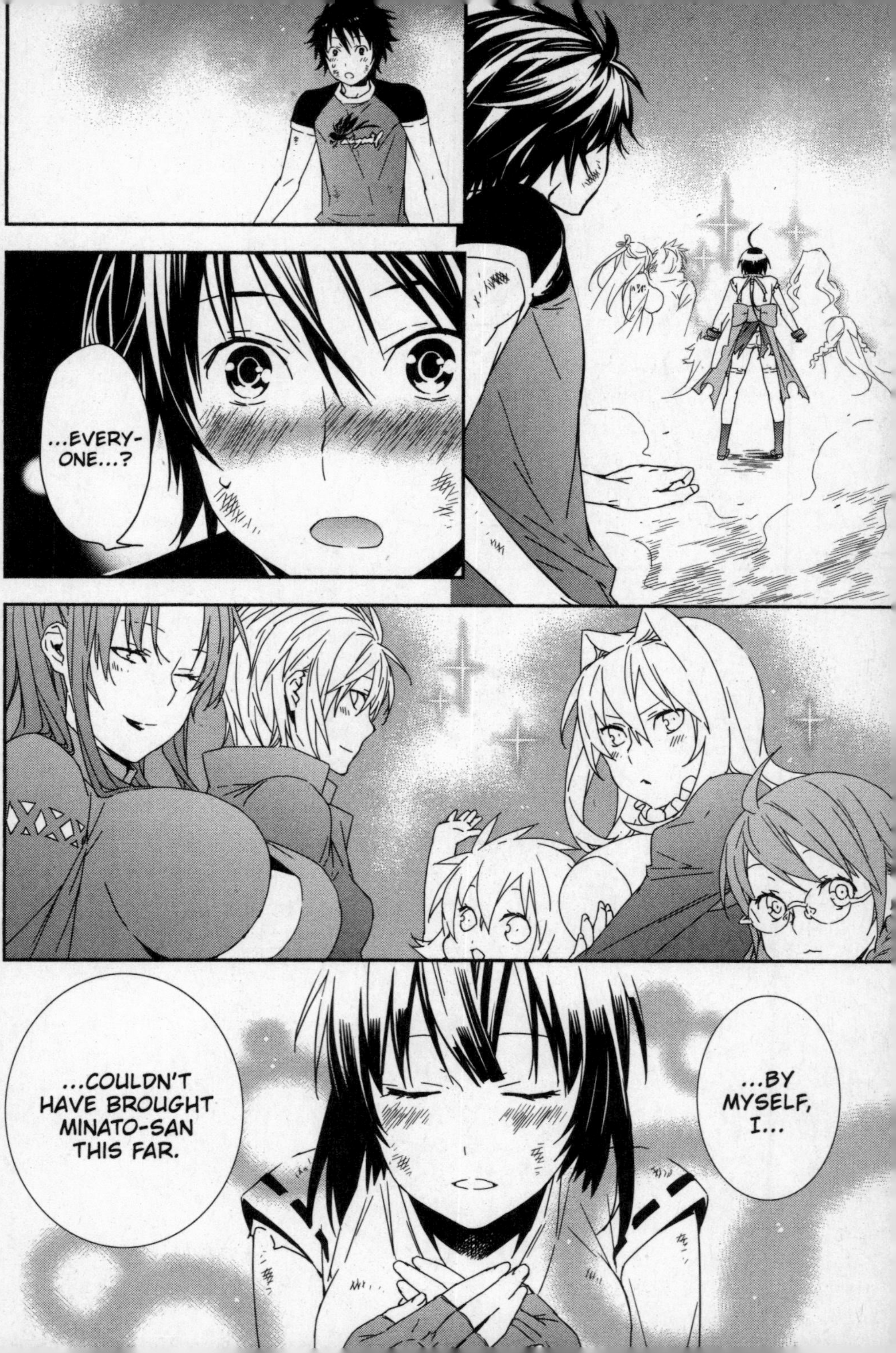
...EVERY-ONE...?
...BY MYSELF, I...
...COULDN'T HAVE BROUGHT MINATO-SAN THIS FAR.

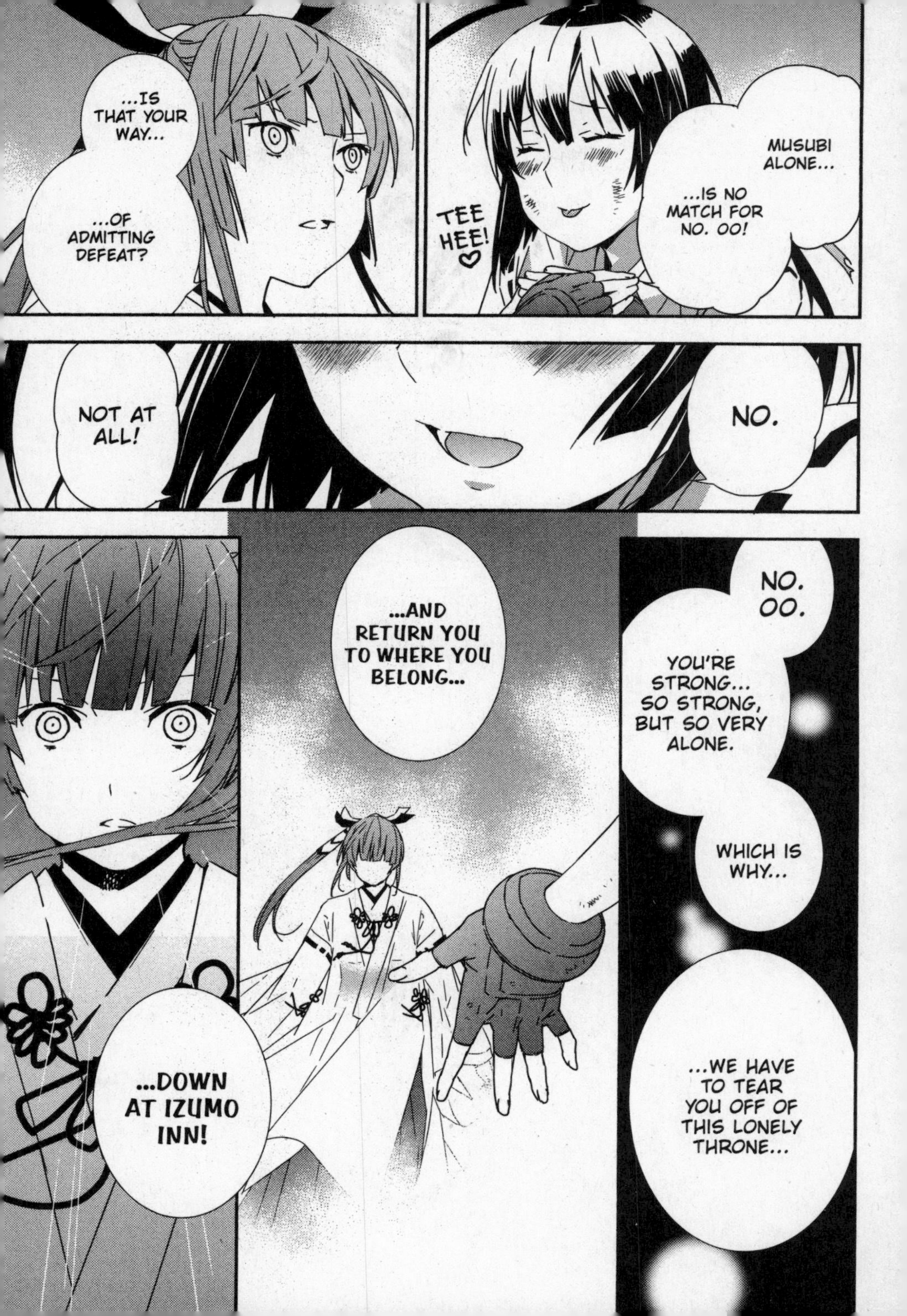
MUSUBI ALONE...
...IS NO MATCH FOR NO. 00!
TEE HEE! ♥
...IS THAT YOUR WAY...
...OF ADMITTING DEFEAT?
NO.
NOT AT ALL!
NO. 00.
YOU'RE STRONG... SO STRONG, BUT SO VERY ALONE.
WHICH IS WHY...
...WE HAVE TO TEAR YOU OFF OF THIS LONELY THRONE...
...AND RETURN YOU TO WHERE YOU BELONG...
...DOWN AT IZUMO INN!

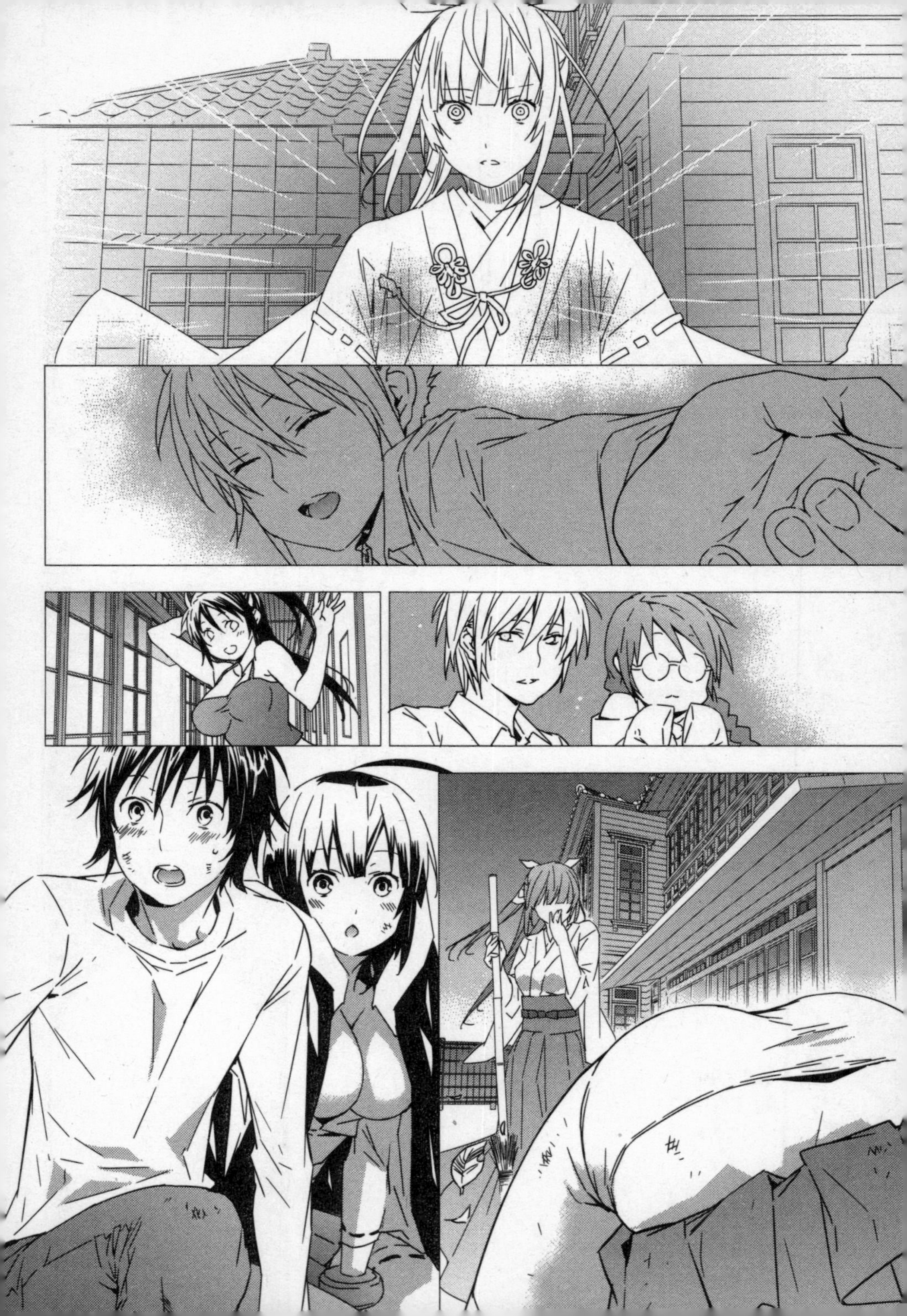

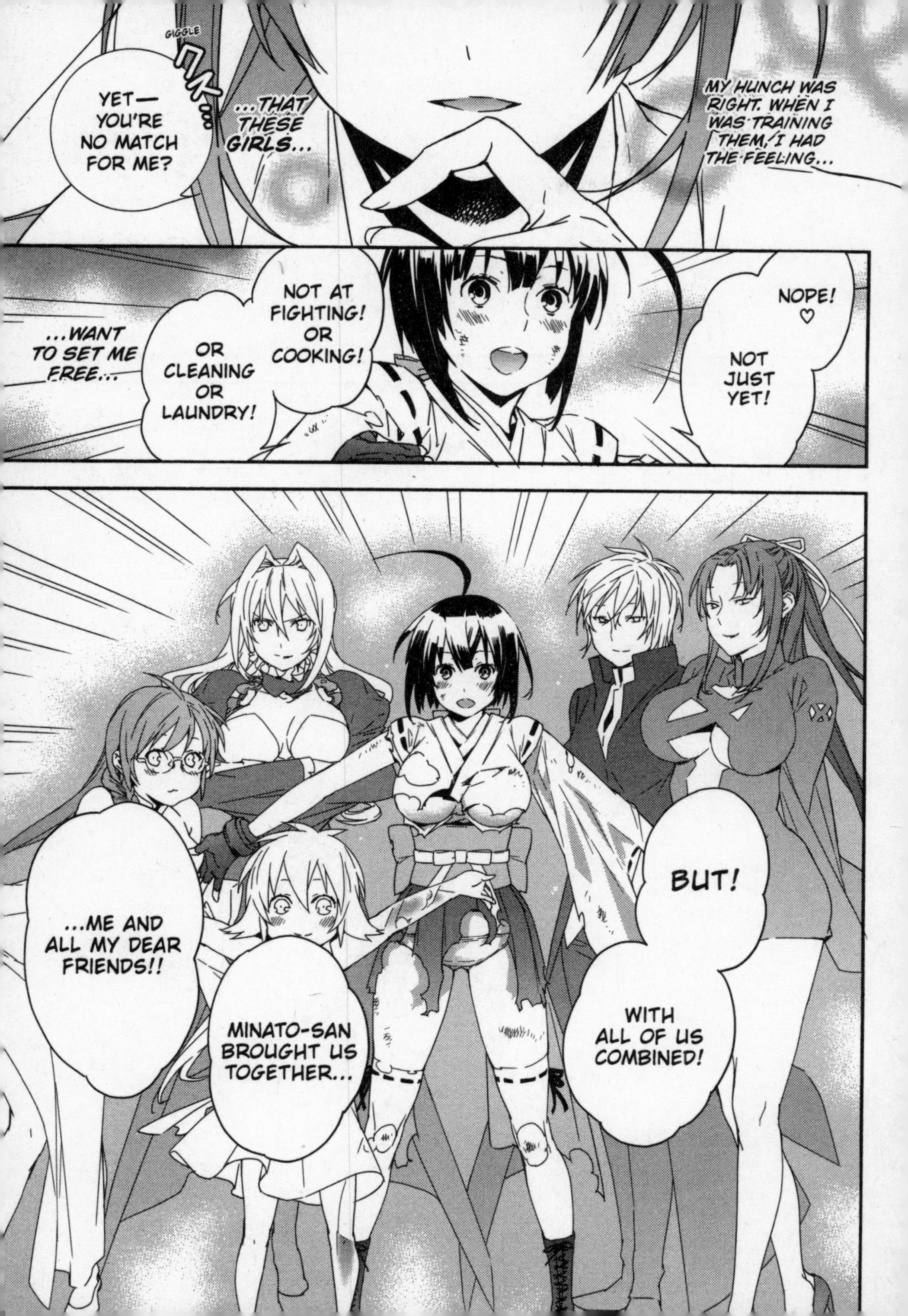
MY HUNCH WAS RIGHT. WHEN I WAS TRAINING THEM, I HAD THE FEELING...
...THAT THESE GIRLS...
GIGGLE
YET— YOU'RE NO MATCH FOR ME?
NOPE! ♡
NOT JUST YET!
NOT AT FIGHTING! OR COOKING!
OR CLEANING OR LAUNDRY!
...WANT TO SET ME FREE...
BUT!
WITH ALL OF US COMBINED!
MINATO-SAN BROUGHT US TOGETHER...
...ME AND ALL MY DEAR FRIENDS!!

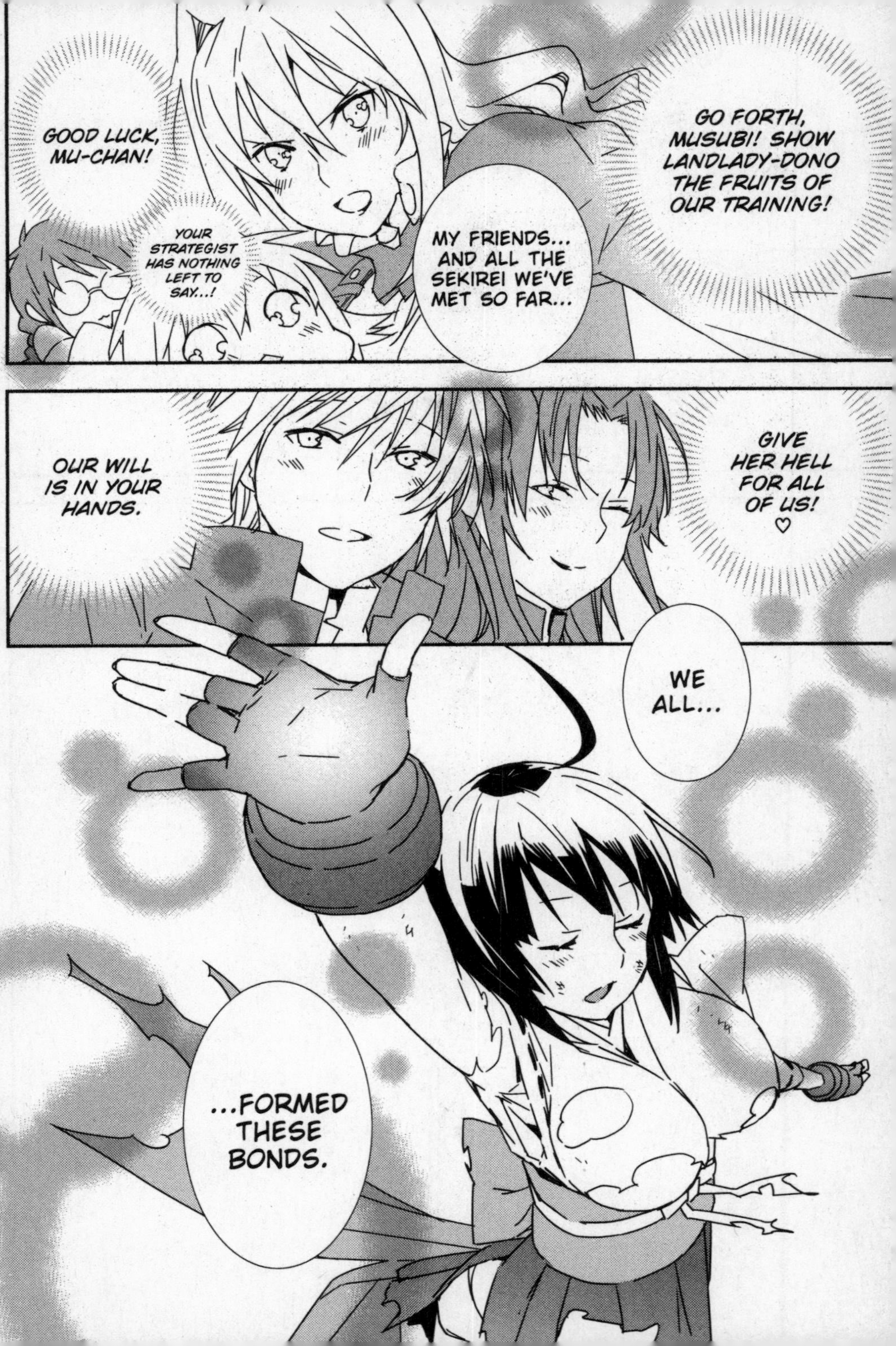
GO FORTH, MUSUBI! SHOW LANDLADY-DONO THE FRUITS OF OUR TRAINING!
GOOD LUCK, MU-CHAN!
YOUR STRATEGIST HAS NOTHING LEFT TO SAY...!
MY FRIENDS... AND ALL THE SEKIREI WE'VE MET SO FAR...
GIVE HER HELL FOR ALL OF US! ♡
OUR WILL IS IN YOUR HANDS.
WE ALL...
...FORMED THESE BONDS.

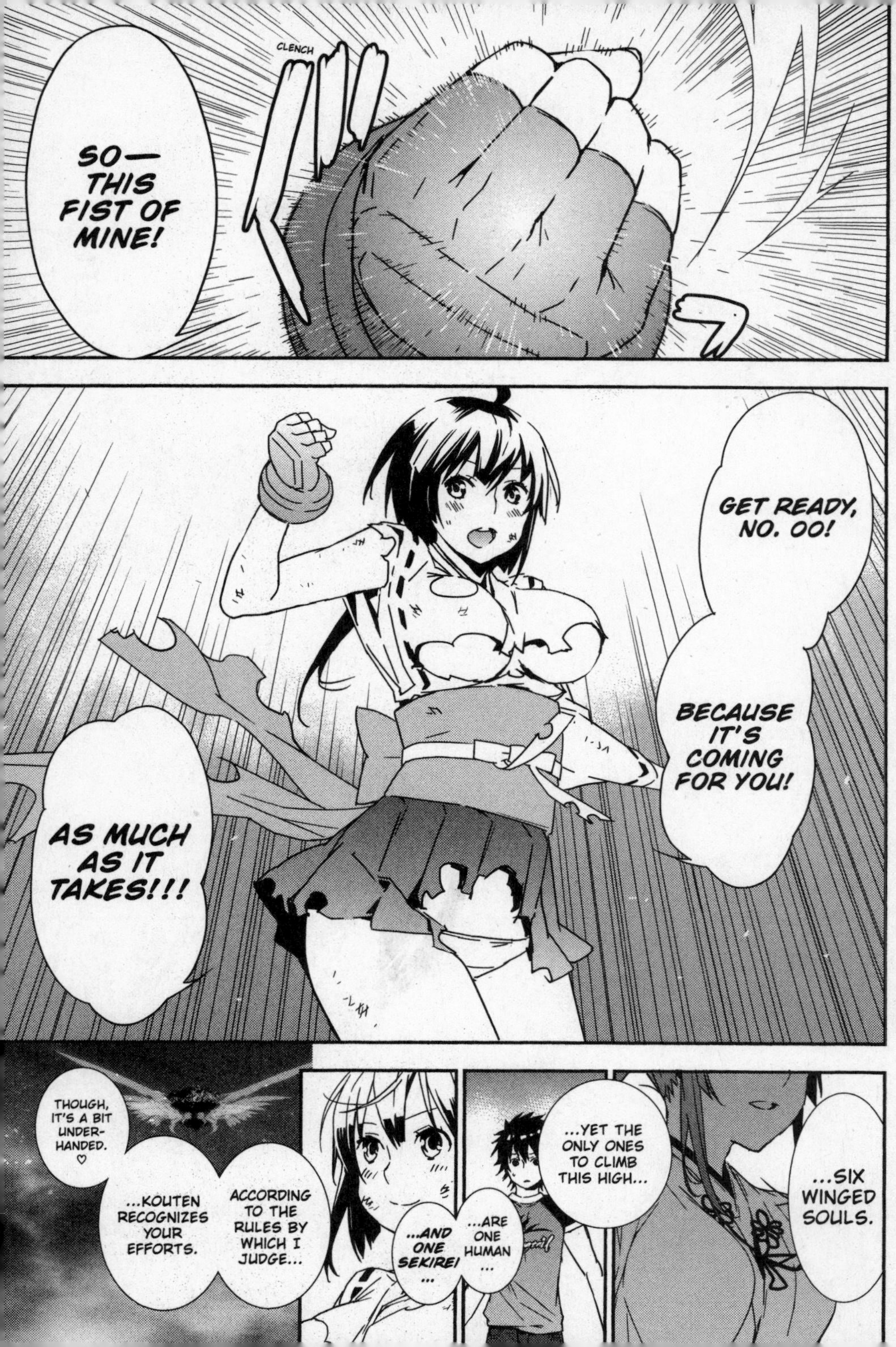
CLENCH
SO— THIS FIST OF MINE!
GET READY, NO. 00!
BECAUSE IT'S COMING FOR YOU!
AS MUCH AS IT TAKES!!!
...SIX WINGED SOULS.
...YET THE ONLY ONES TO CLIMB THIS HIGH...
...ARE ONE HUMAN ...
...AND ONE SEKIREI ...
ACCORDING TO THE RULES BY WHICH I JUDGE...
...KOUTEN RECOGNIZES YOUR EFFORTS.
THOUGH, IT'S A BIT UNDER-HANDED. ♡

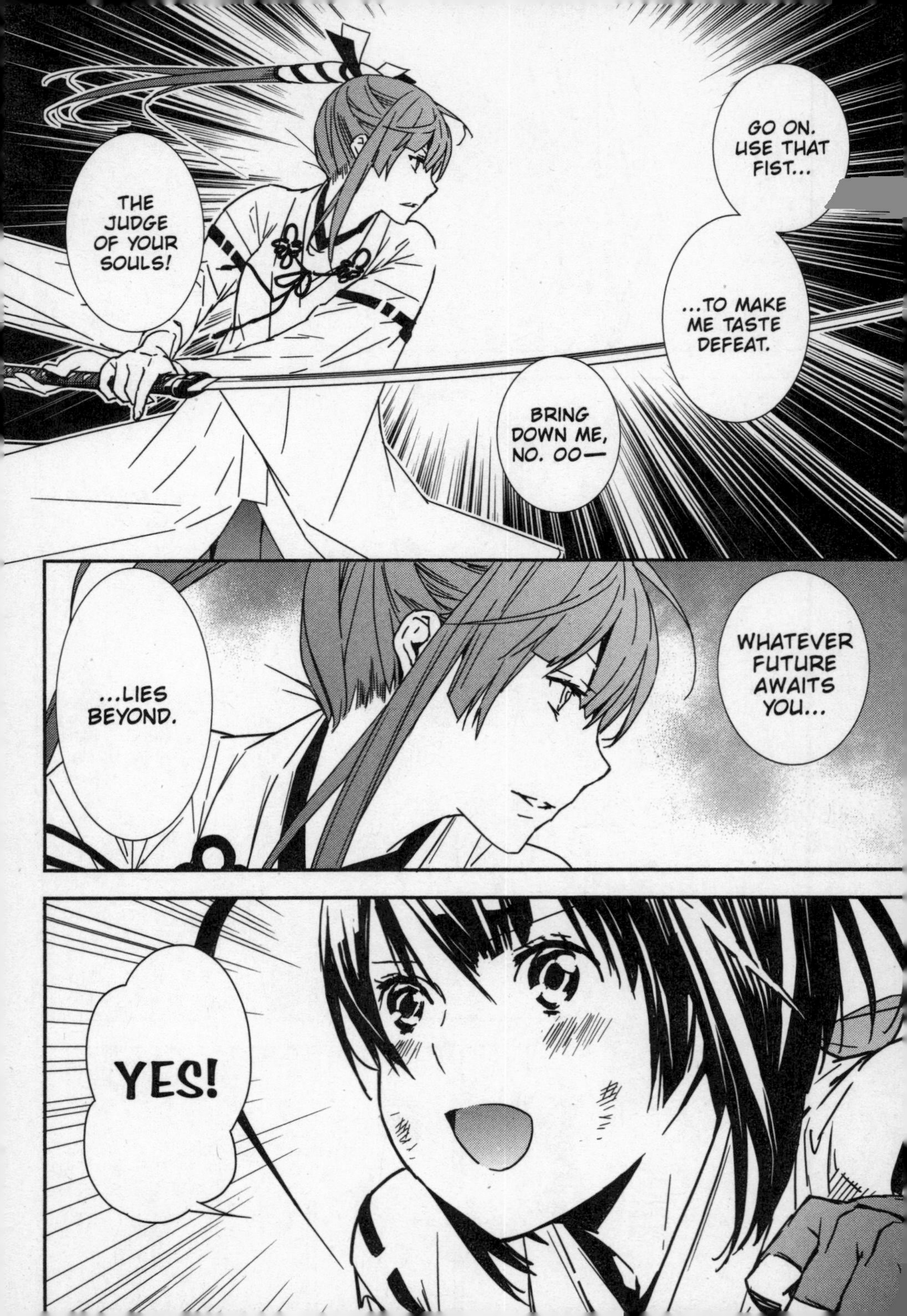
GO ON. USE THAT FIST...
...TO MAKE ME TASTE DEFEAT.
BRING DOWN ME, NO. OO—
THE JUDGE OF YOUR SOULS!
WHATEVER FUTURE AWAITS YOU...
...LIES BEYOND.
YES!

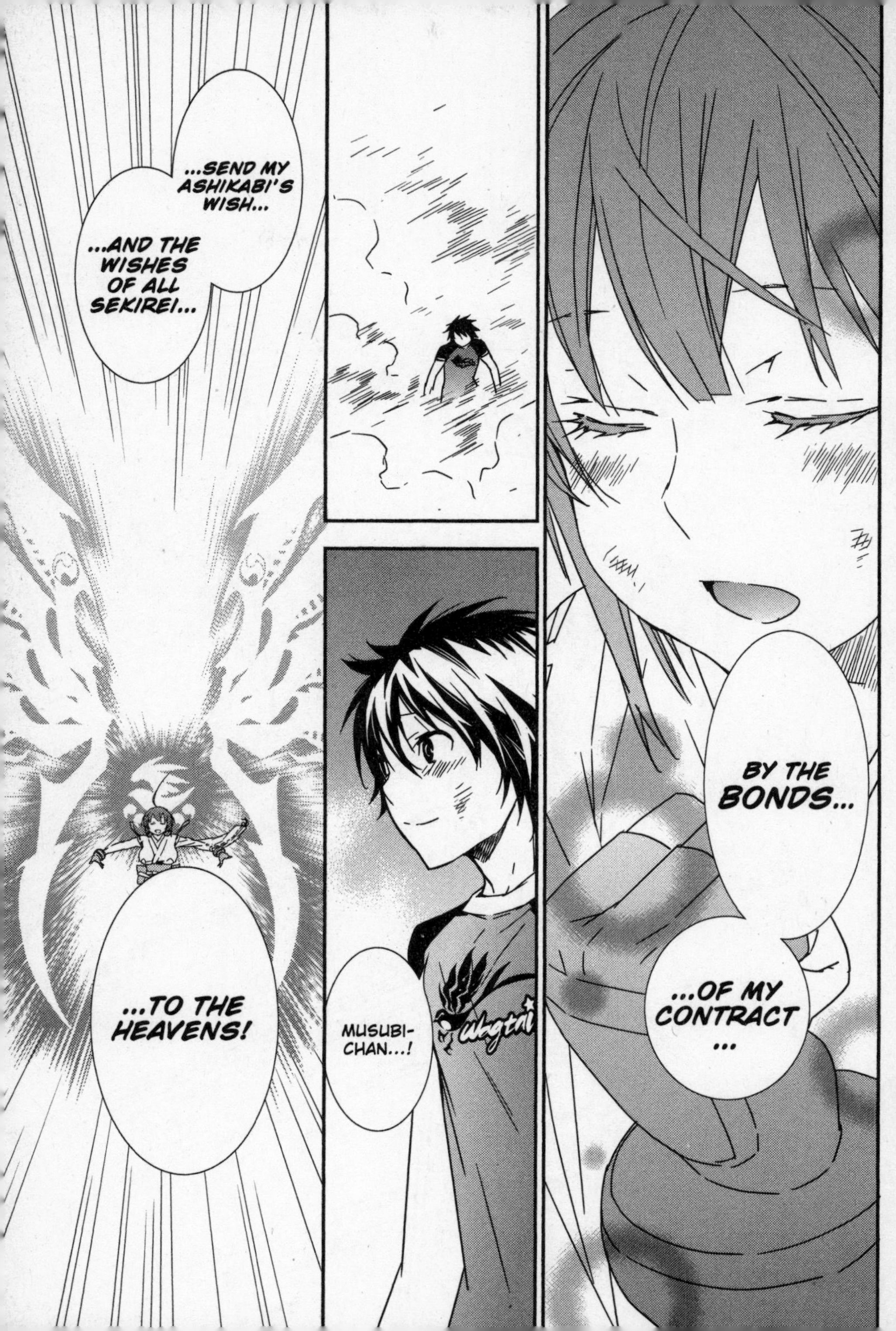
BY THE BONDS...
...OF MY CONTRACT ...
MUSUBI-CHAN...!
...SEND MY ASHIKABI'S WISH...
...AND THE WISHES OF ALL SEKIREI...
...TO THE HEAVENS!

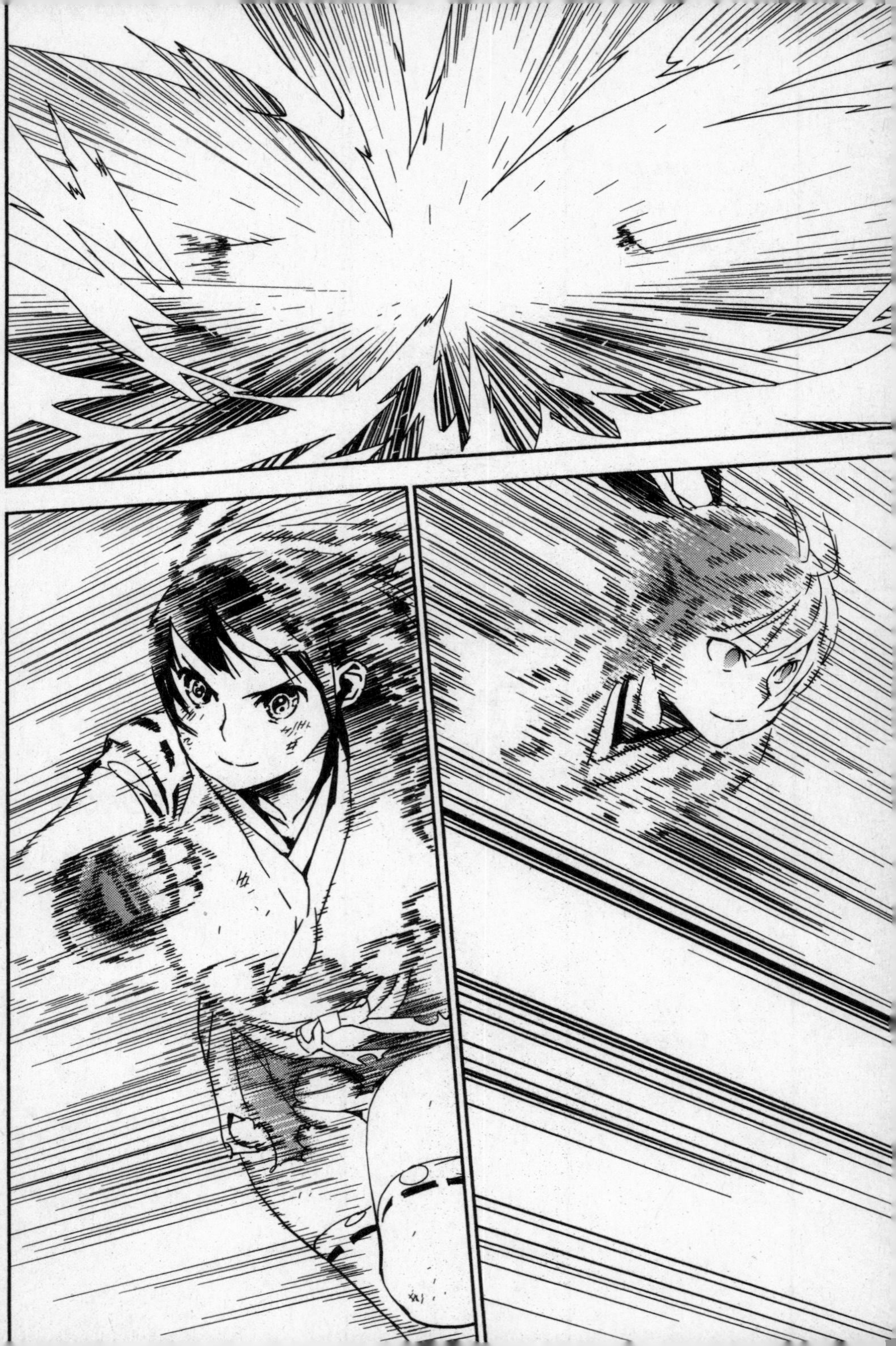

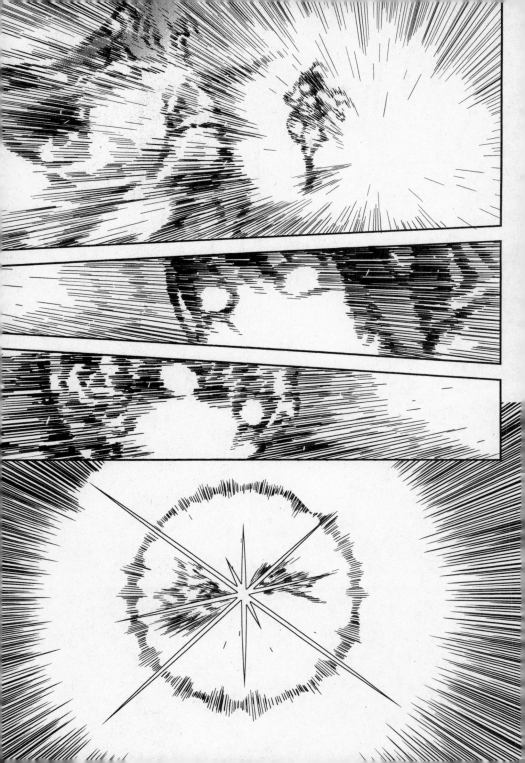

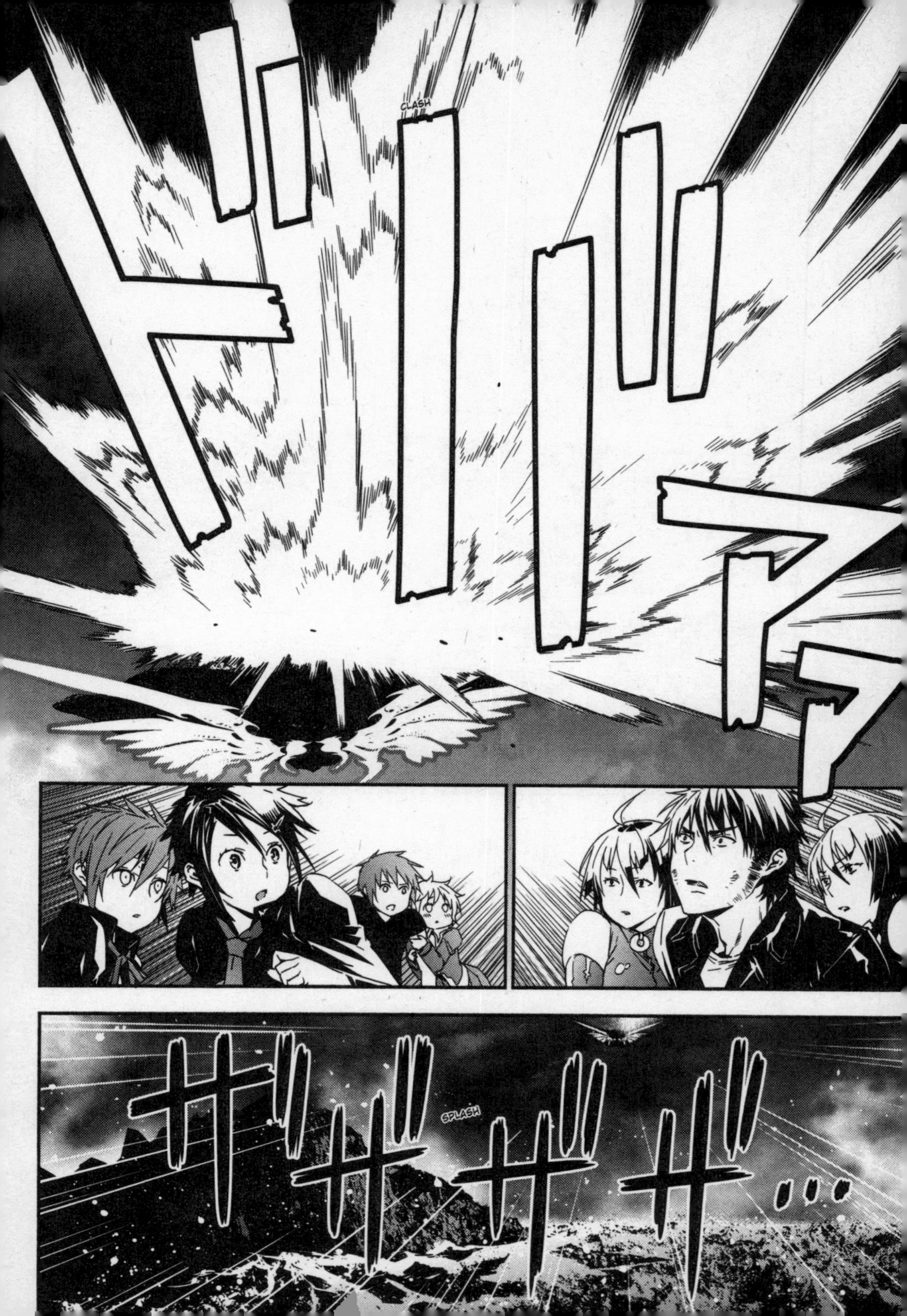
CLASH
SPLASH

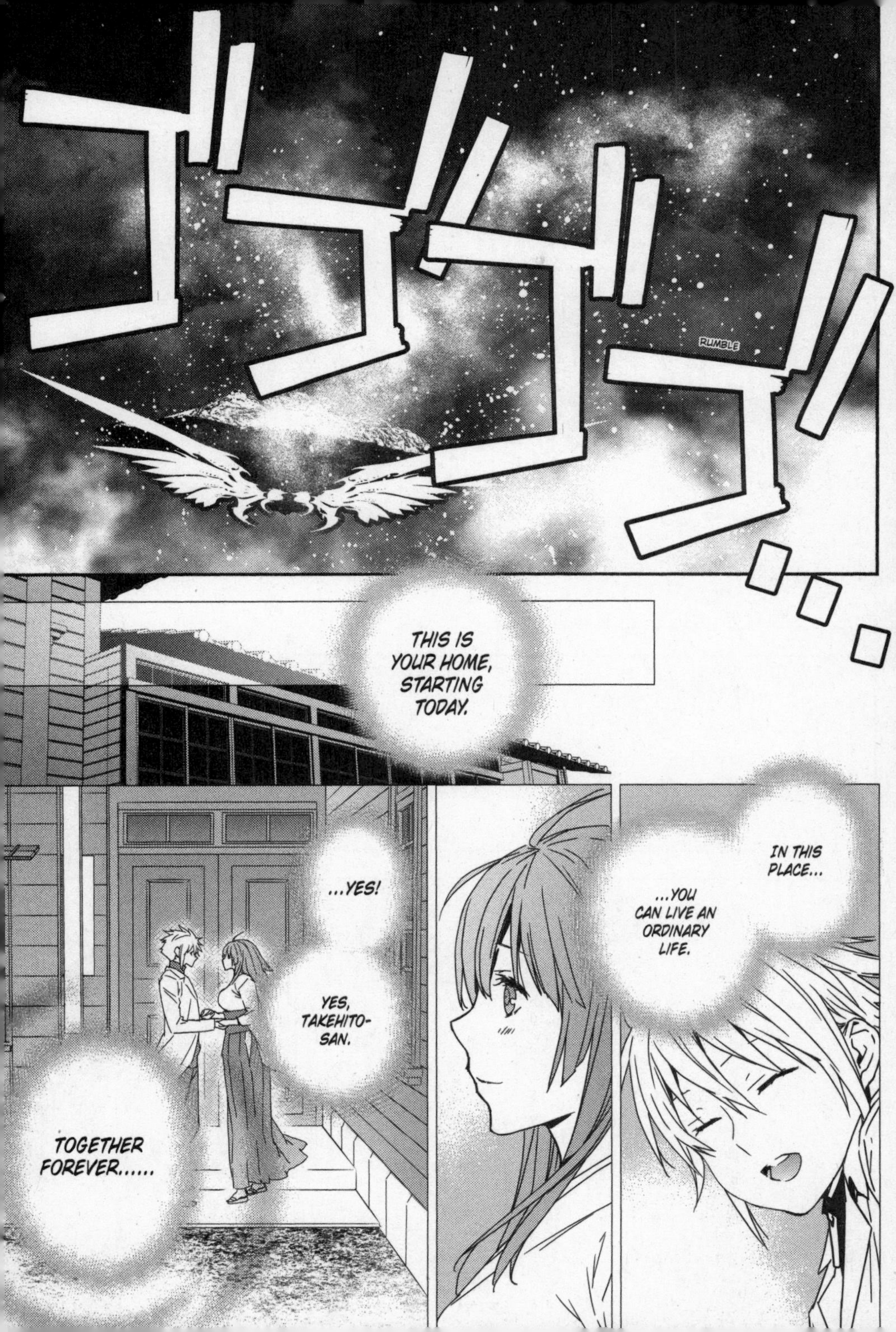
ゴゴゴゴ...
RUMBLE
THIS IS YOUR HOME, STARTING TODAY.
IN THIS PLACE...
...YOU CAN LIVE AN ORDINARY LIFE.
...YES!
YES, TAKEHITO-SAN.
TOGETHER FOREVER......

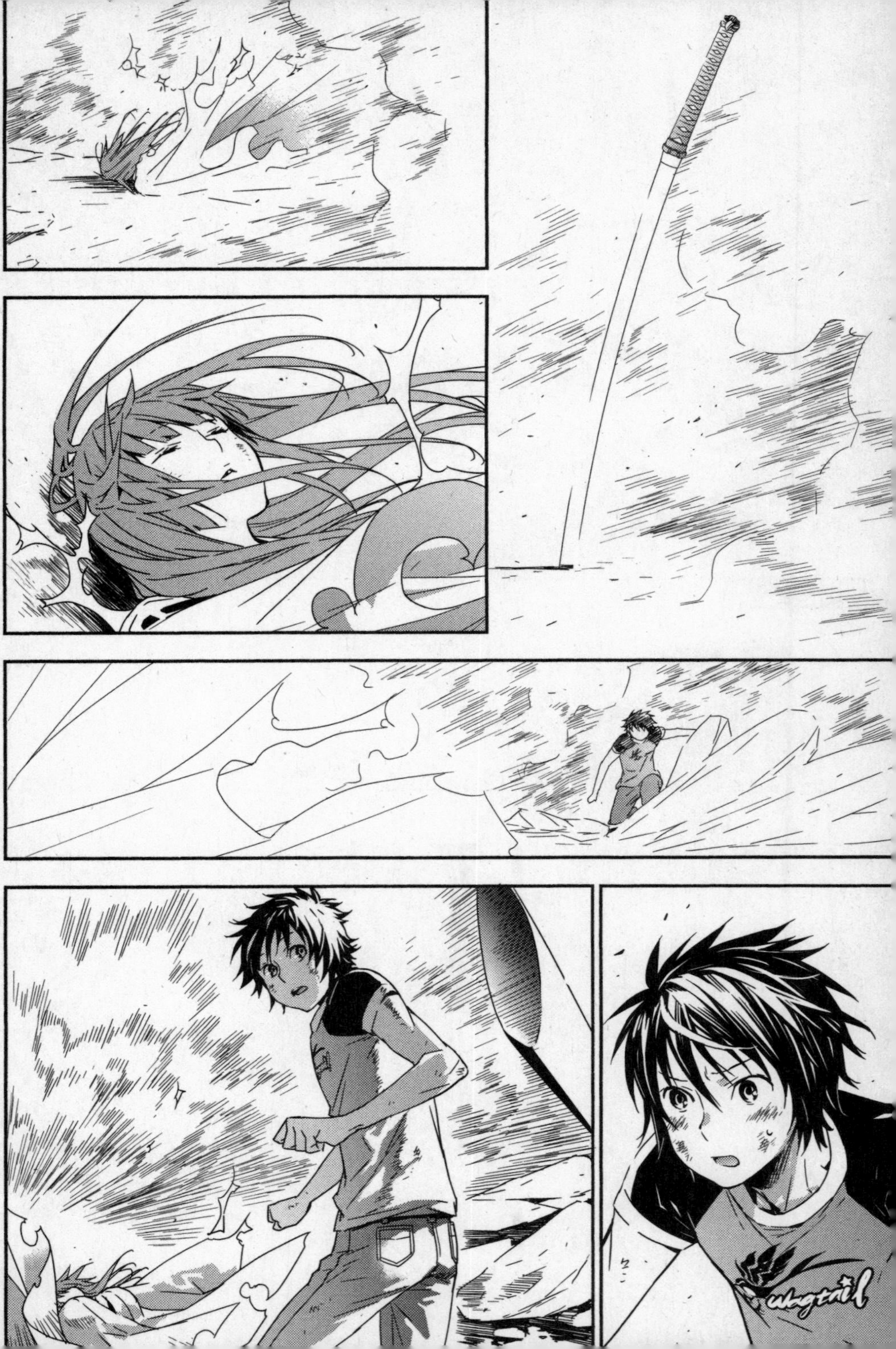

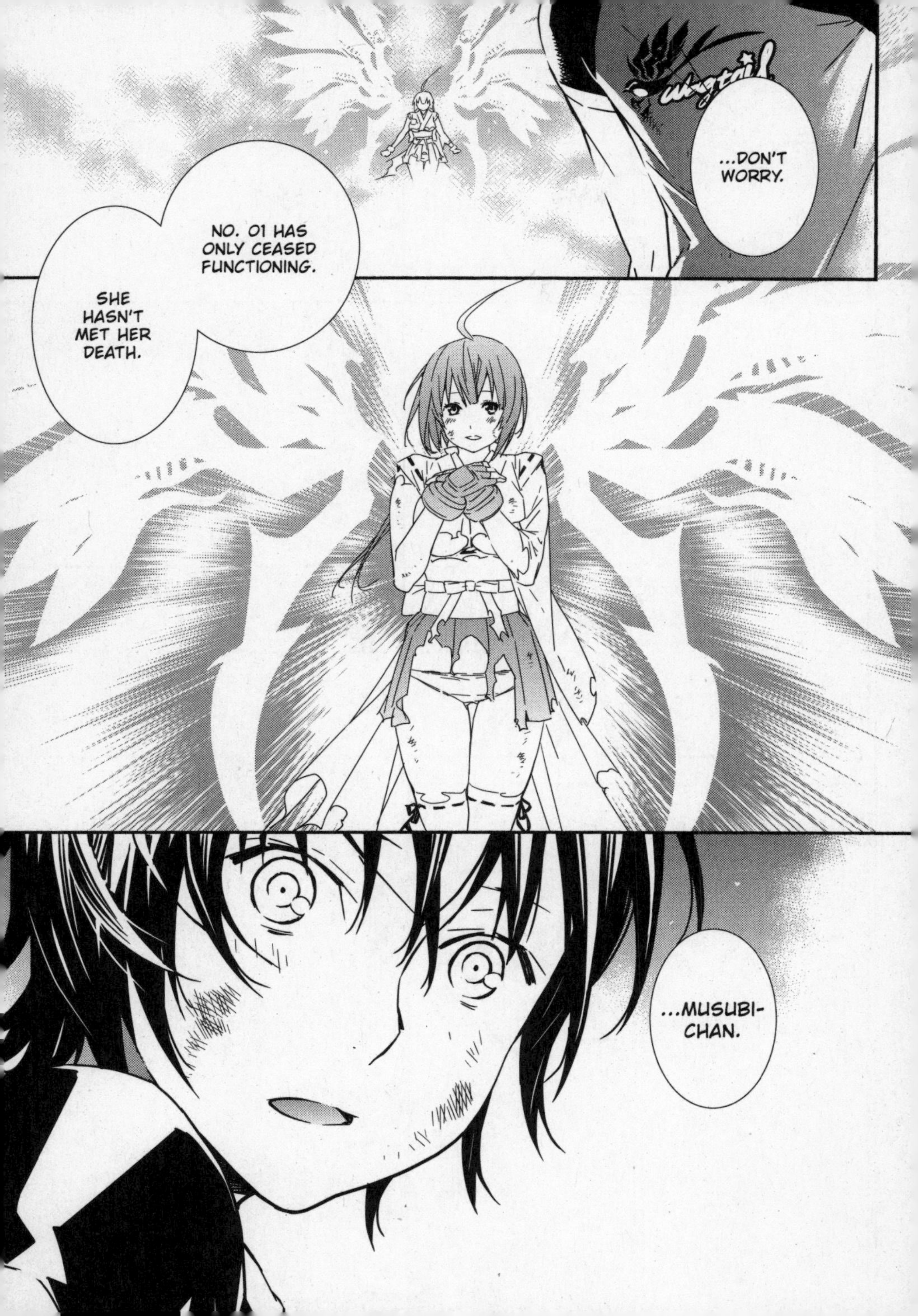
...DON'T WORRY.
NO. 01 HAS ONLY CEASED FUNCTIONING.
SHE HASN'T MET HER DEATH.
...MUSUBI-CHAN.

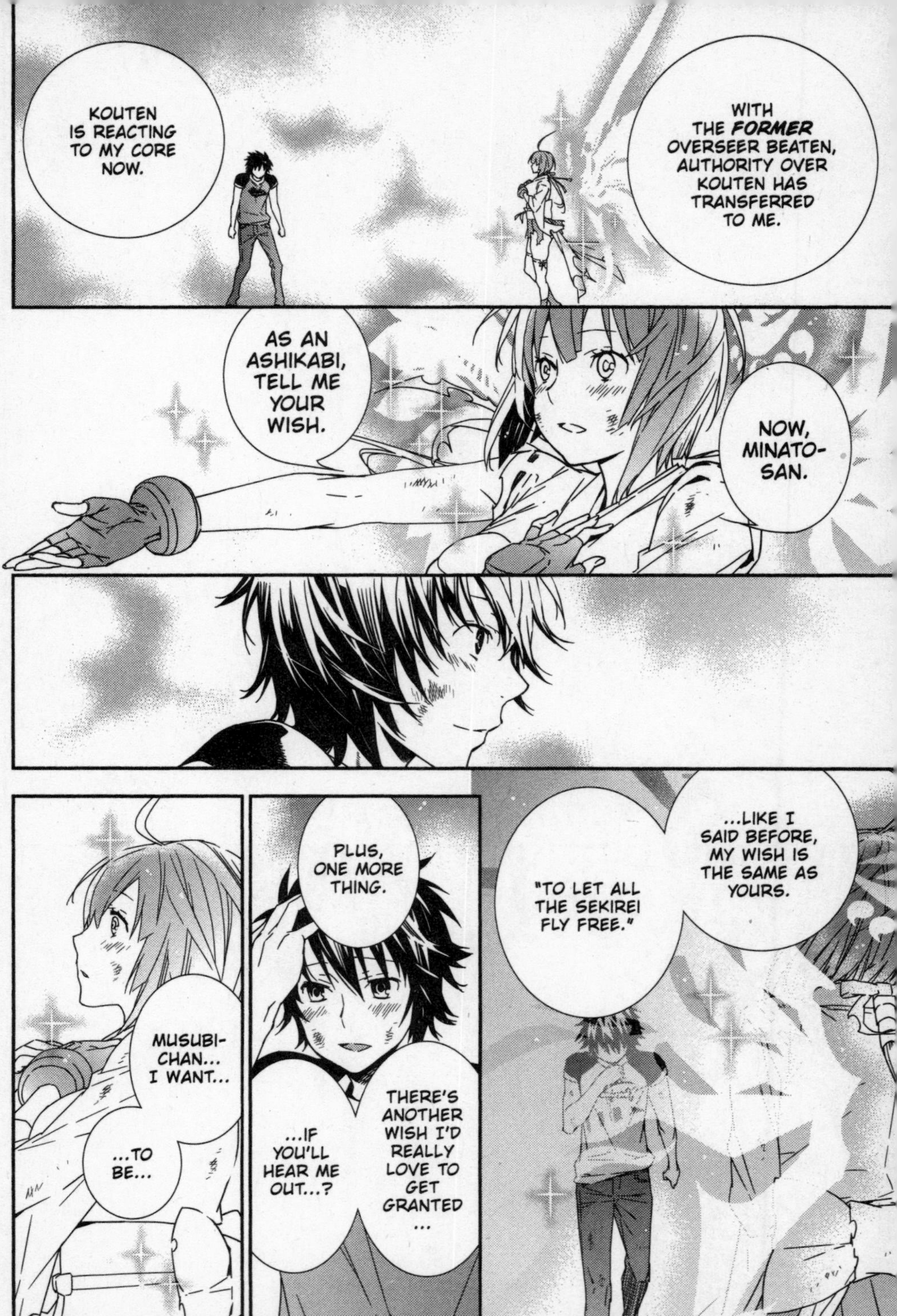
WITH THE FORMER OVERSEER BEATEN, AUTHORITY OVER KOUTEN HAS TRANSFERRED TO ME.
KOUTEN IS REACTING TO MY CORE NOW.
NOW, MINATO-SAN.
AS AN ASHIKABI, TELL ME YOUR WISH.
...LIKE I SAID BEFORE, MY WISH IS THE SAME AS YOURS.
"TO LET ALL THE SEKIREI FLY FREE."
PLUS, ONE MORE THING.
THERE'S ANOTHER WISH I'D REALLY LOVE TO GET GRANTED...
...IF YOU'LL HEAR ME OUT...?
MUSUBI-CHAN... I WANT...
...TO BE...

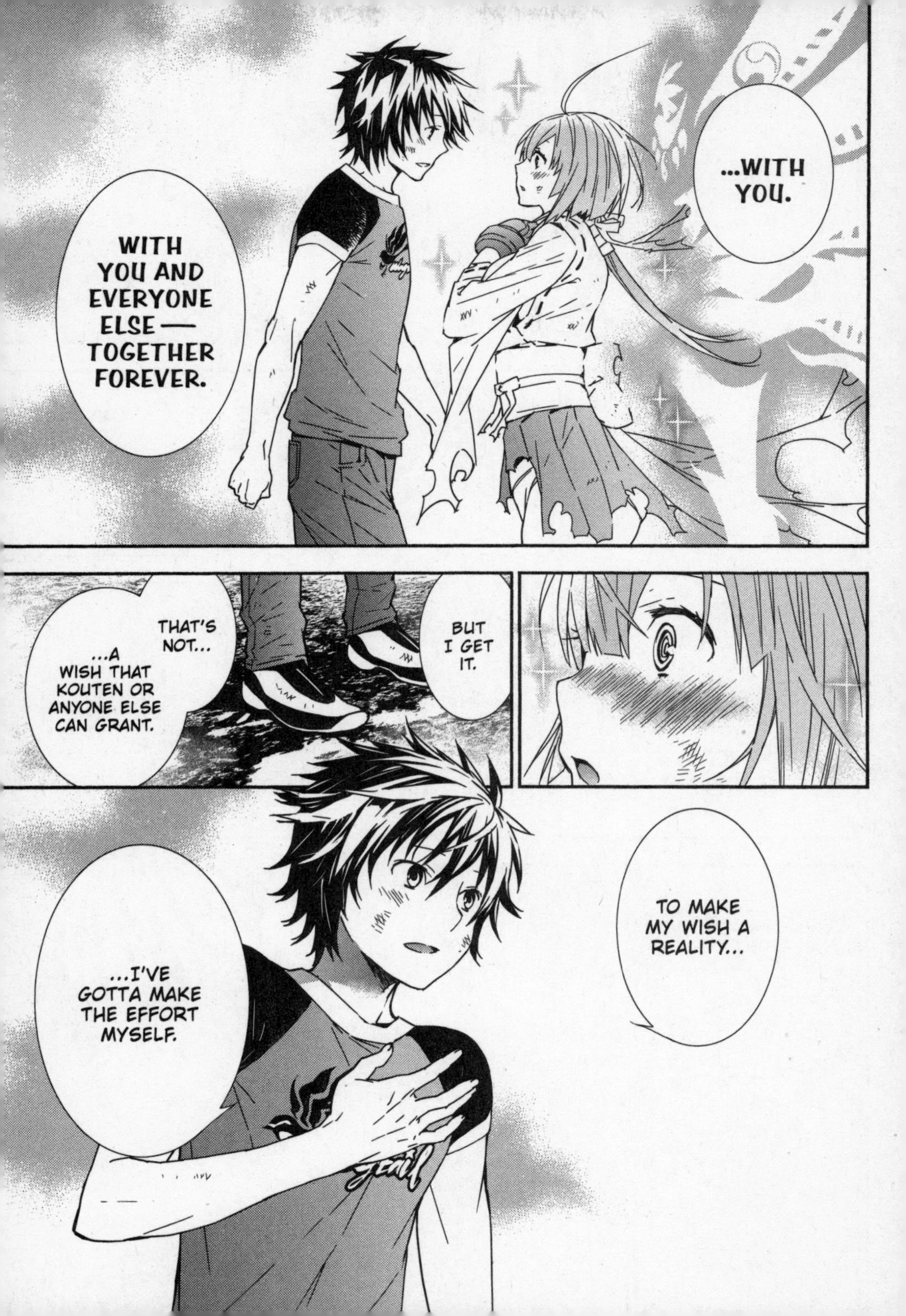
...WITH YOU.
WITH YOU AND EVERYONE ELSE—TOGETHER FOREVER.
BUT I GET IT.
THAT'S NOT...
...A WISH THAT KOUTEN OR ANYONE ELSE CAN GRANT.
TO MAKE MY WISH A REALITY...
...I'VE GOTTA MAKE THE EFFORT MYSELF.

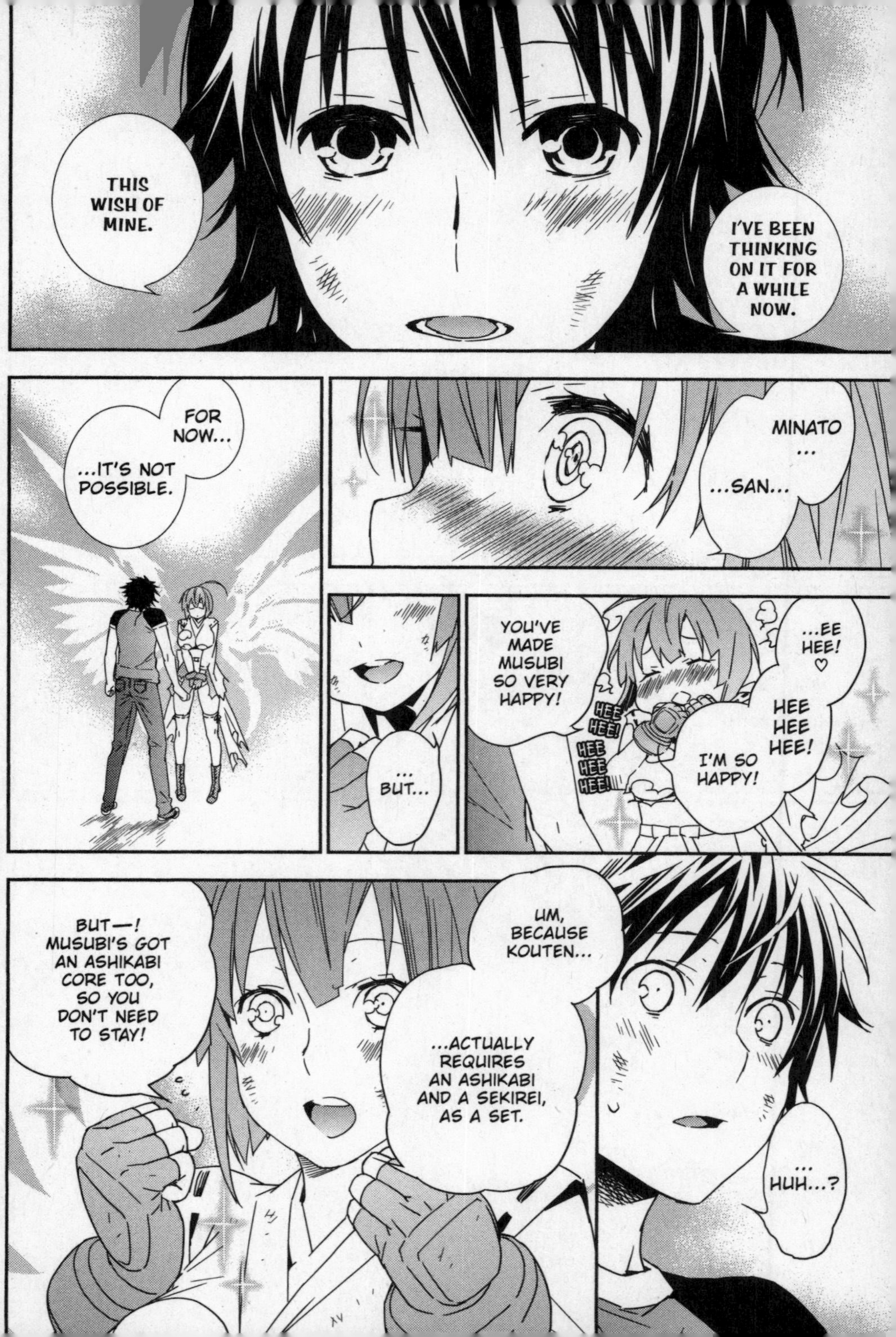
I'VE BEEN THINKING ON IT FOR A WHILE NOW.
THIS WISH OF MINE.
MINATO ... ...SAN...
...EE HEE! ♡
HEE HEE HEE!
I'M SO HAPPY!
YOU'VE MADE MUSUBI SO VERY HAPPY!
HEE HEE!
HEE HEE HEE!
... BUT...
FOR NOW...
...IT'S NOT POSSIBLE.
... HUH...?
UM, BECAUSE KOUTEN...
...ACTUALLY REQUIRES AN ASHIKABI AND A SEKIREI, AS A SET.
BUT—! MUSUBI'S GOT AN ASHIKABI CORE TOO, SO YOU DON'T NEED TO STAY!

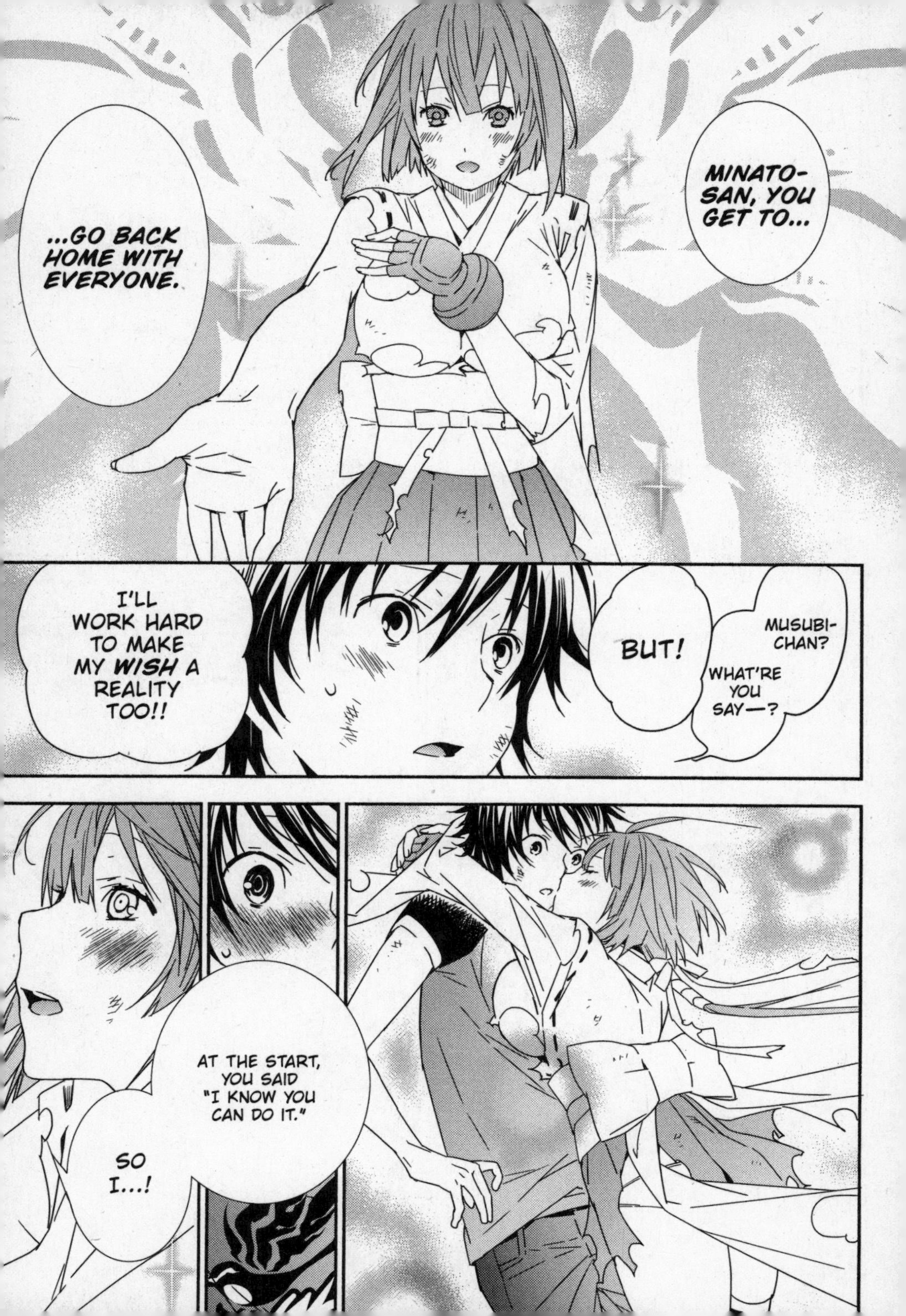
MINATO-SAN, YOU GET TO...
...GO BACK HOME WITH EVERYONE.
MUSUBI-CHAN? WHAT'RE YOU SAY—?
BUT!
I'LL WORK HARD TO MAKE MY WISH A REALITY TOO!!
AT THE START, YOU SAID "I KNOW YOU CAN DO IT."
SO I...!

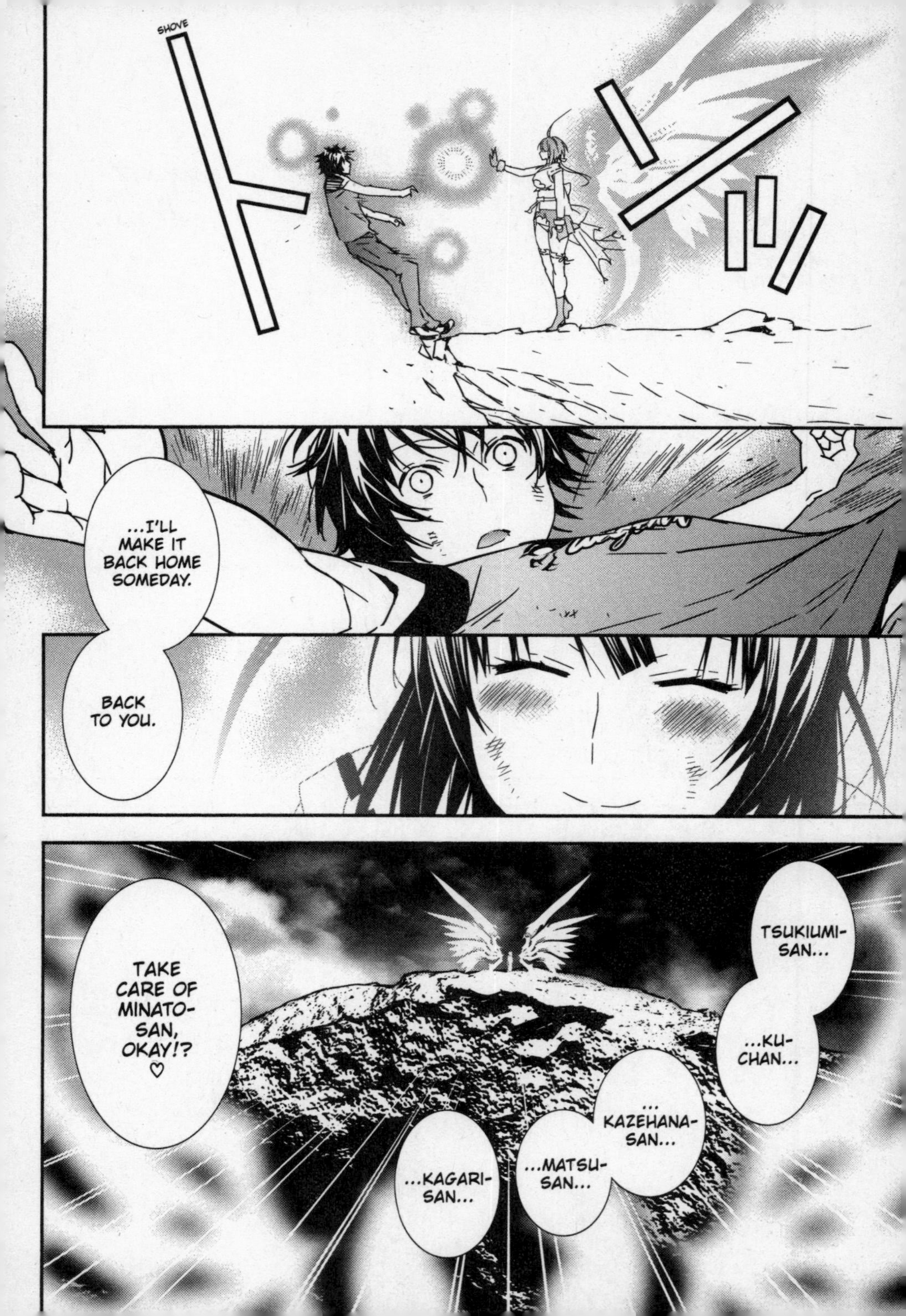
SHOVE
...I'LL MAKE IT BACK HOME SOMEDAY.
BACK TO YOU.
TSUKIUMI-SAN...
...KU-CHAN...
...KAZEHANA-SAN...
...MATSU-SAN...
...KAGARI-SAN...
TAKE CARE OF MINATO-SAN, OKAY!? ♡

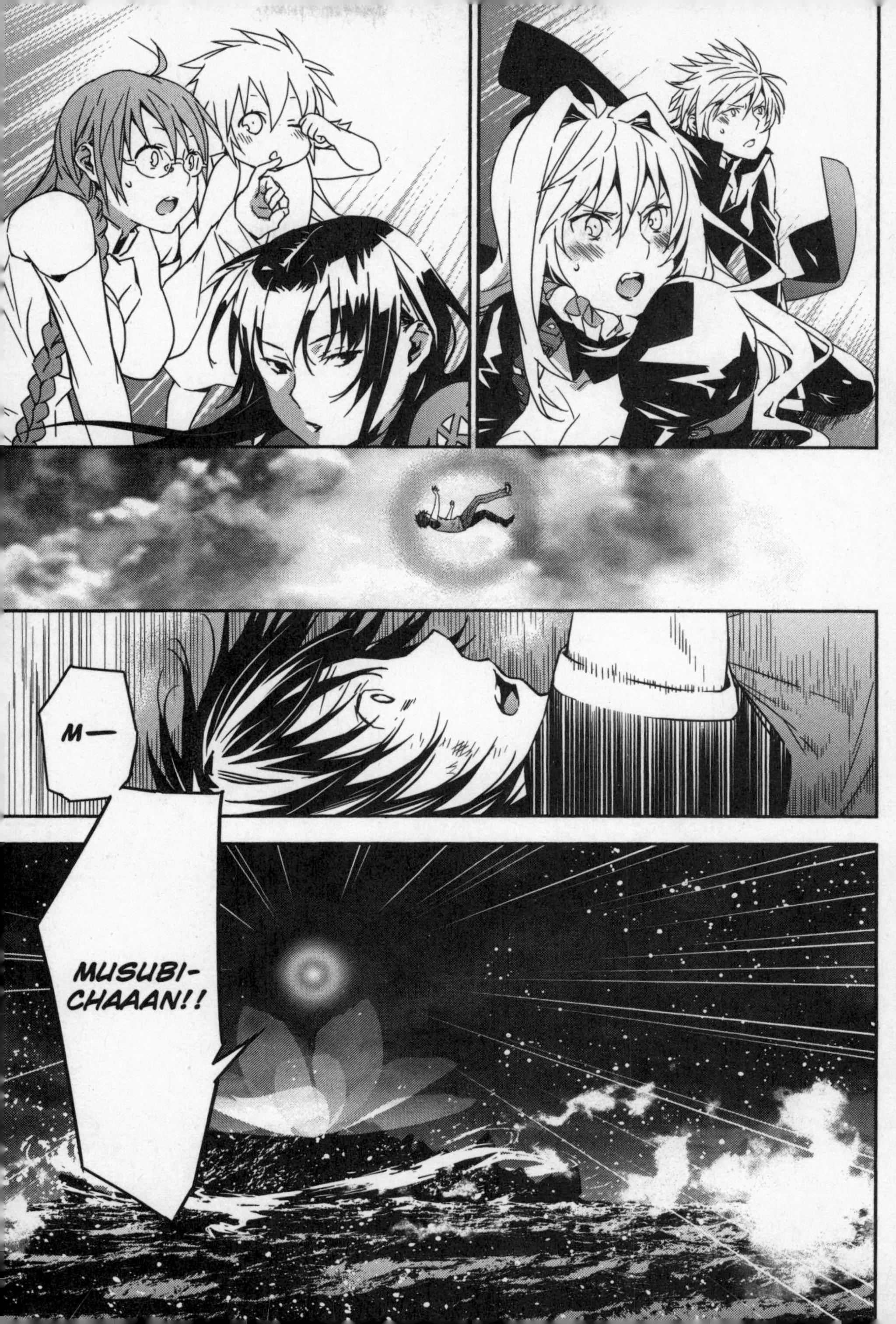
M—
MUSUBI-
CHAAAN!!

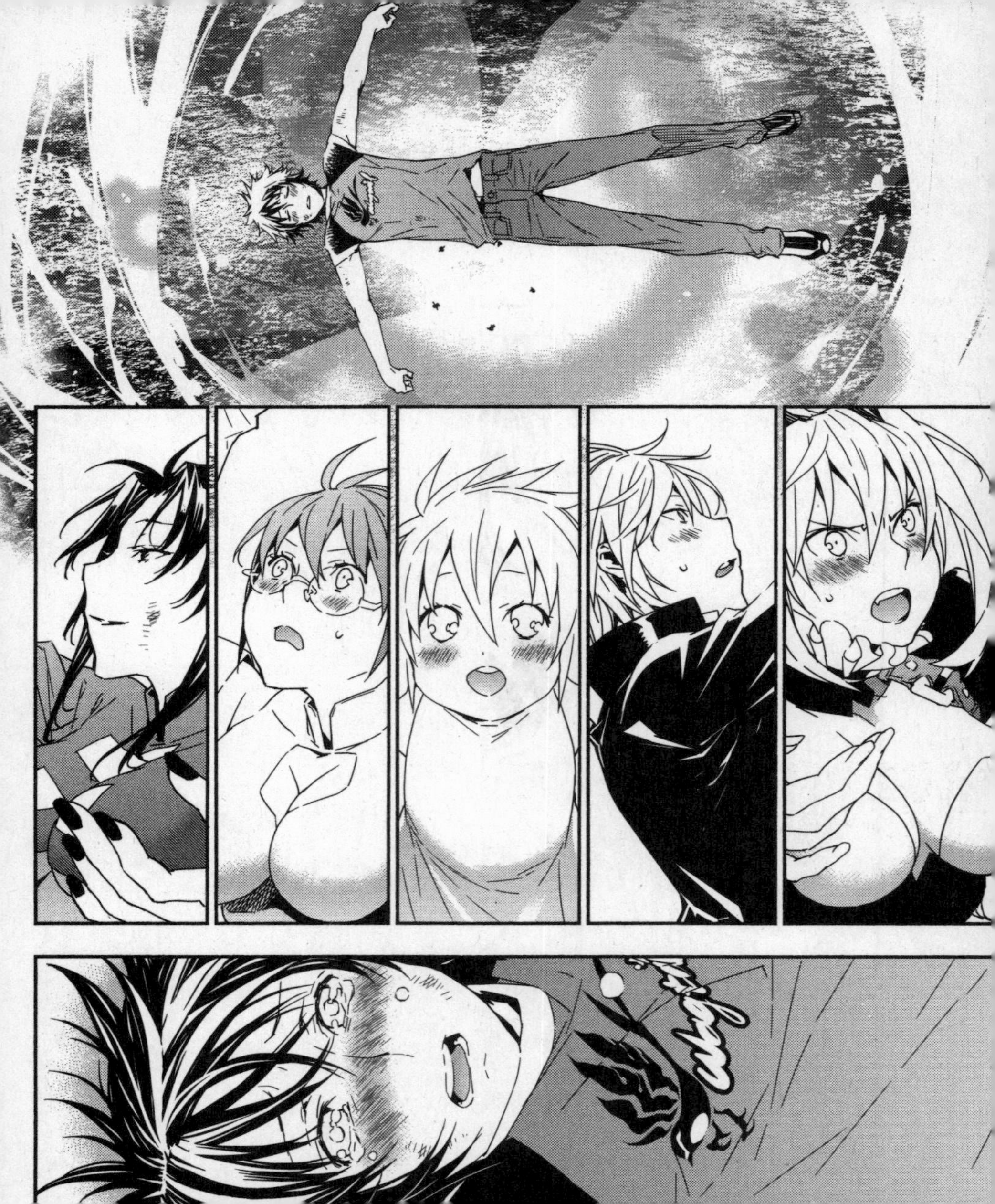

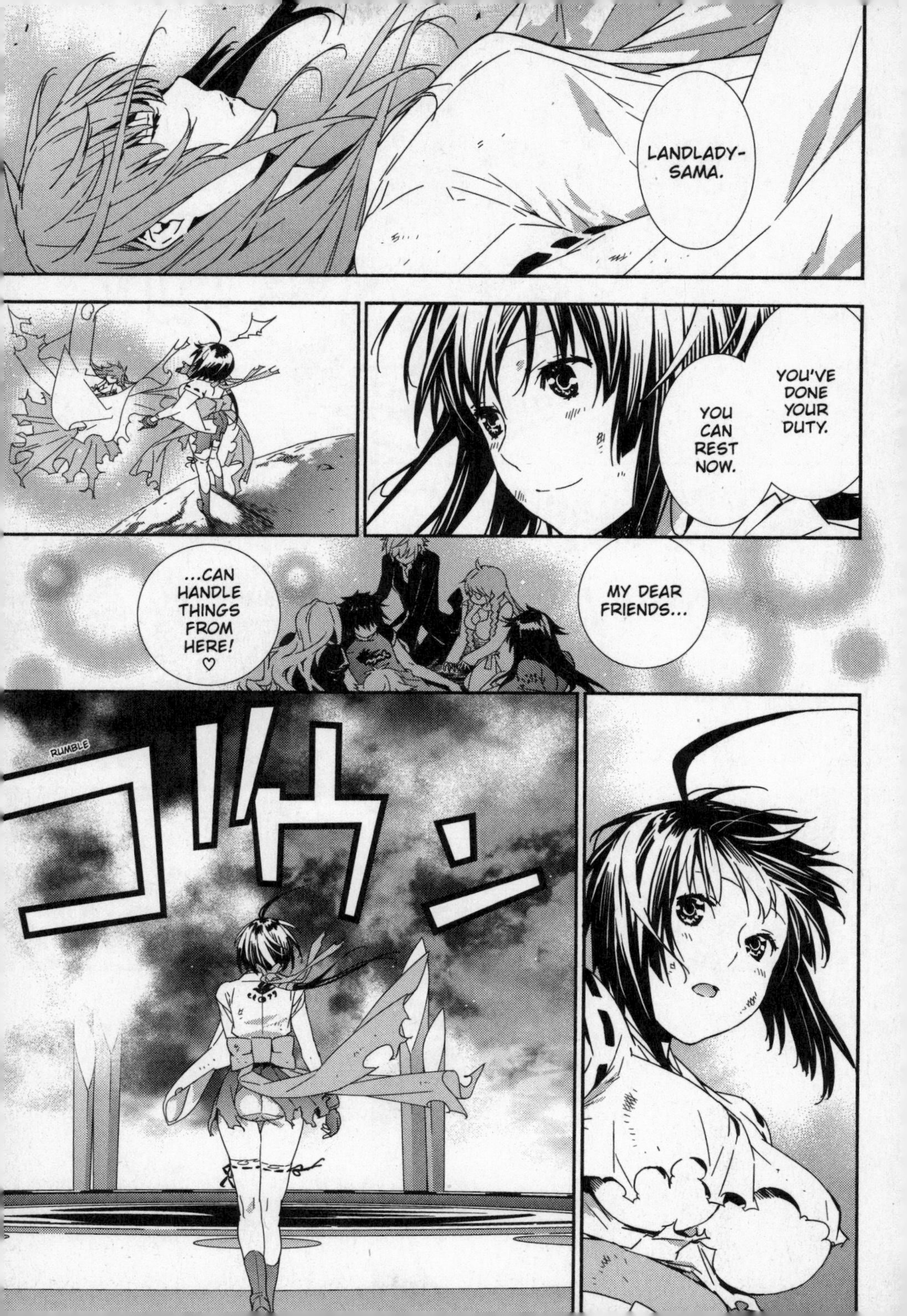
LANDLADY-SAMA.
YOU'VE DONE YOUR DUTY.
YOU CAN REST NOW.
MY DEAR FRIENDS...
...CAN HANDLE THINGS FROM HERE! ♡
RUMBLE

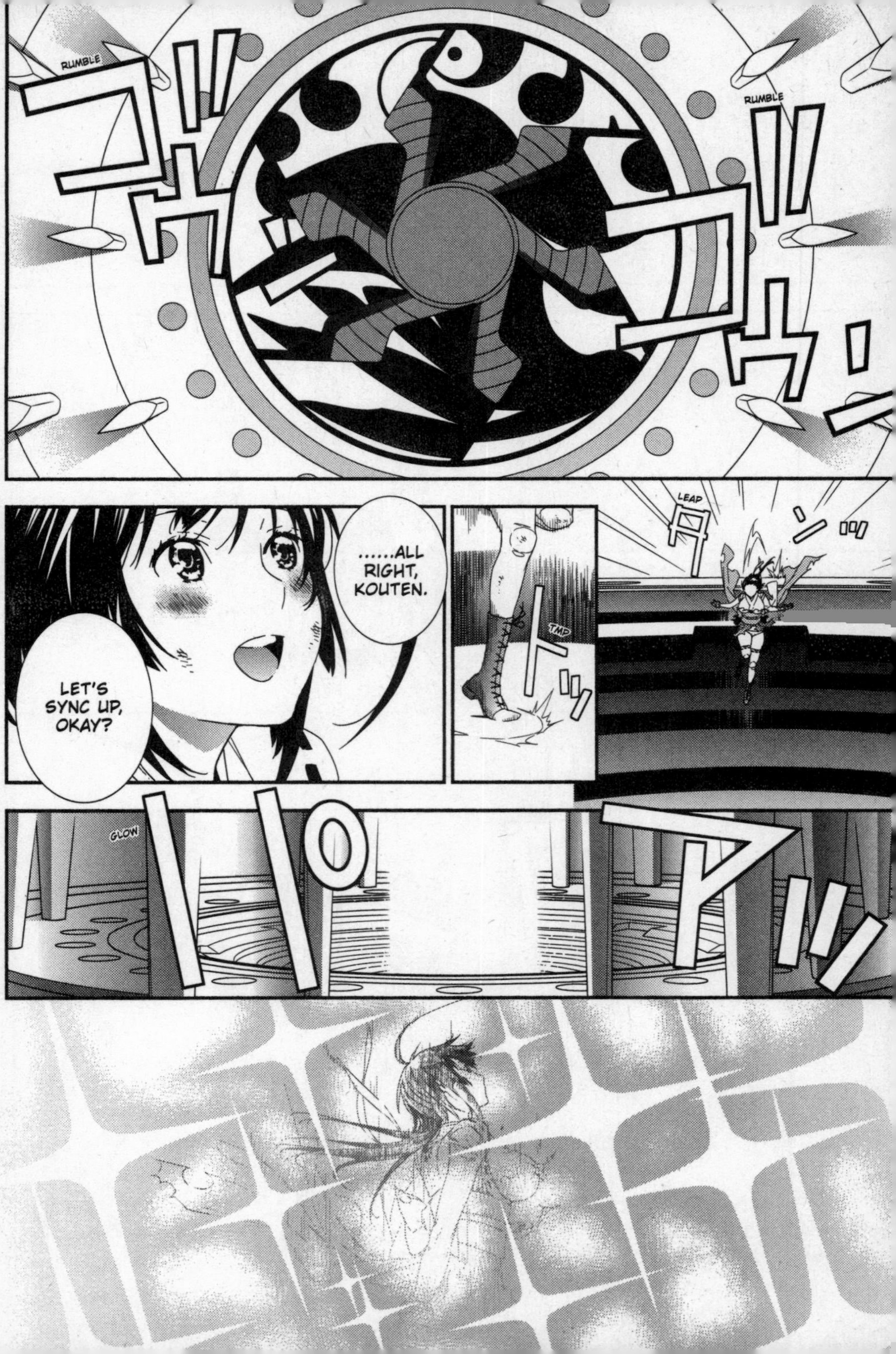
RUMBLE
RUMBLE
LEAP
TMP
......ALL RIGHT, KOUTEN.
LET'S SYNC UP, OKAY?
GLOW

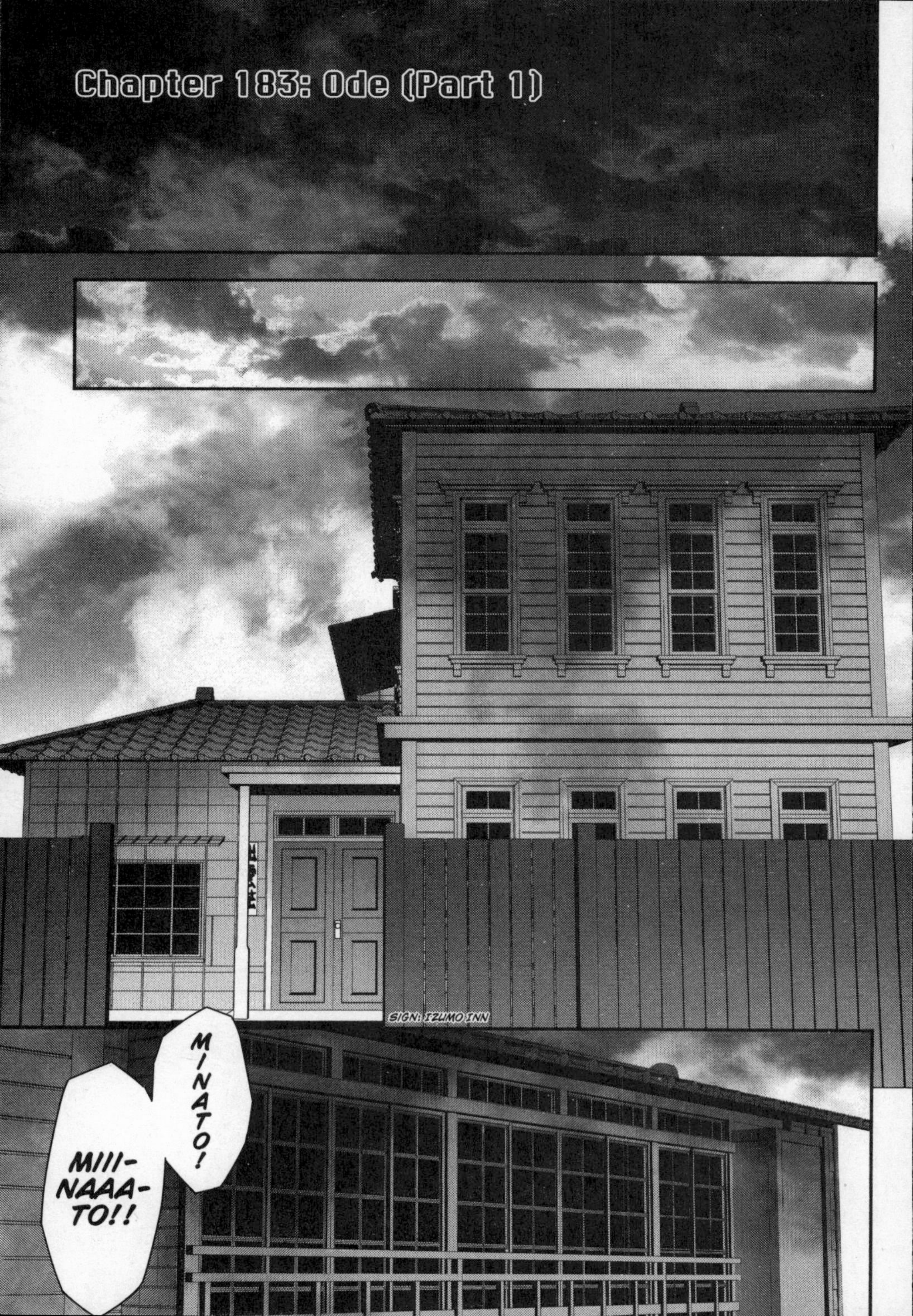
Chapter 183: Ode (Part 1)
SIGN: IZUMO INN
MINATO!
MIII-NAAAA-TO!!

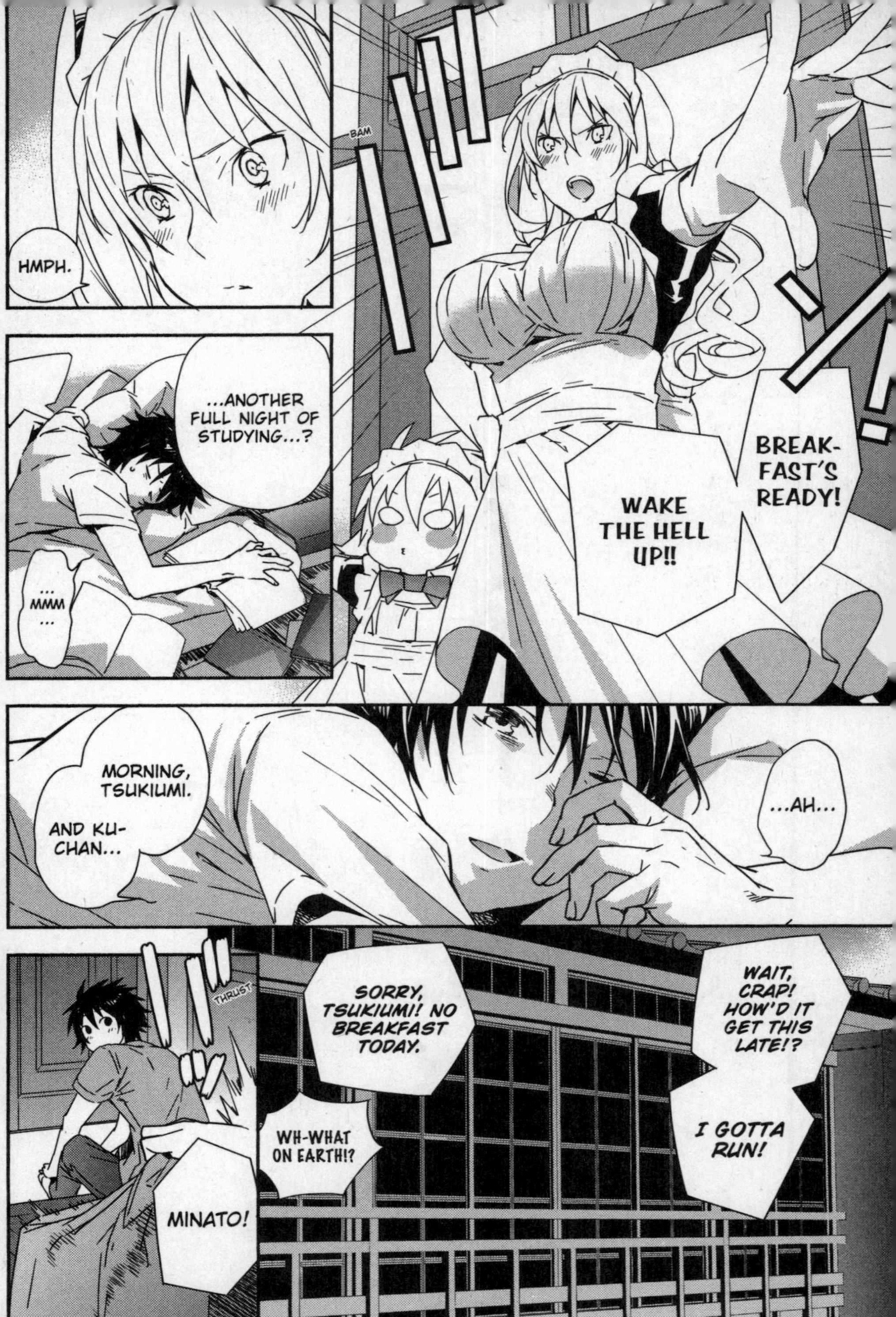
BAM
BREAK-FAST'S READY!
WAKE THE HELL UP!!
HMPH.
...ANOTHER FULL NIGHT OF STUDYING...?
...MMM...
...AH...
MORNING, TSUKIUMI.
AND KU-CHAN...
WAIT, CRAP! HOW'D IT GET THIS LATE!?
I GOTTA RUN!
SORRY, TSUKIUMI! NO BREAKFAST TODAY.
WH-WHAT ON EARTH!?
THRUST
MINATO!

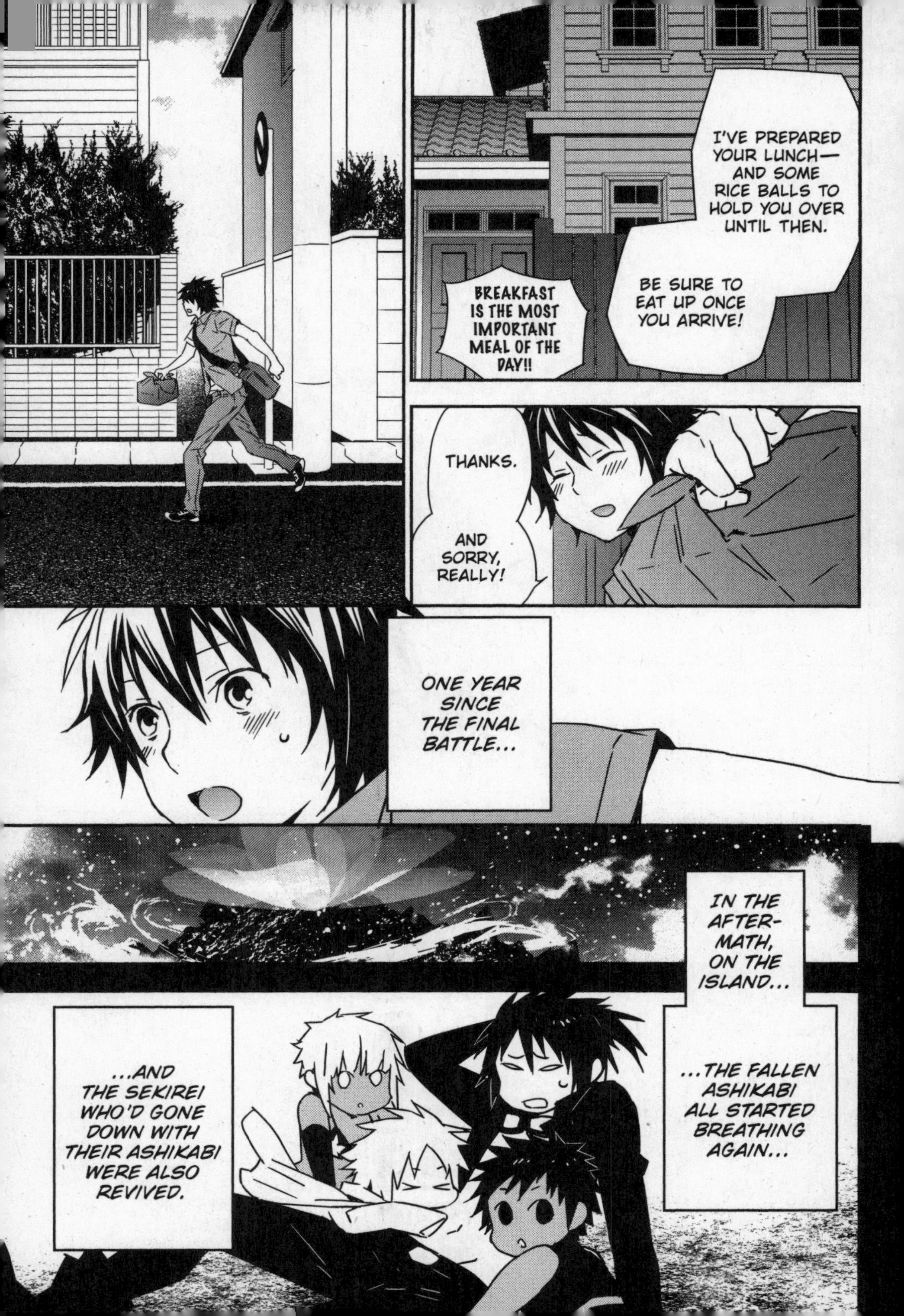
I'VE PREPARED YOUR LUNCH—AND SOME RICE BALLS TO HOLD YOU OVER UNTIL THEN.
BE SURE TO EAT UP ONCE YOU ARRIVE!
BREAKFAST IS THE MOST IMPORTANT MEAL OF THE DAY!!
THANKS.
AND SORRY, REALLY!
ONE YEAR SINCE THE FINAL BATTLE...
IN THE AFTER-MATH, ON THE ISLAND...
...THE FALLEN ASHIKABI ALL STARTED BREATHING AGAIN...
...AND THE SEKIREI WHO'D GONE DOWN WITH THEIR ASHIKABI WERE ALSO REVIVED.

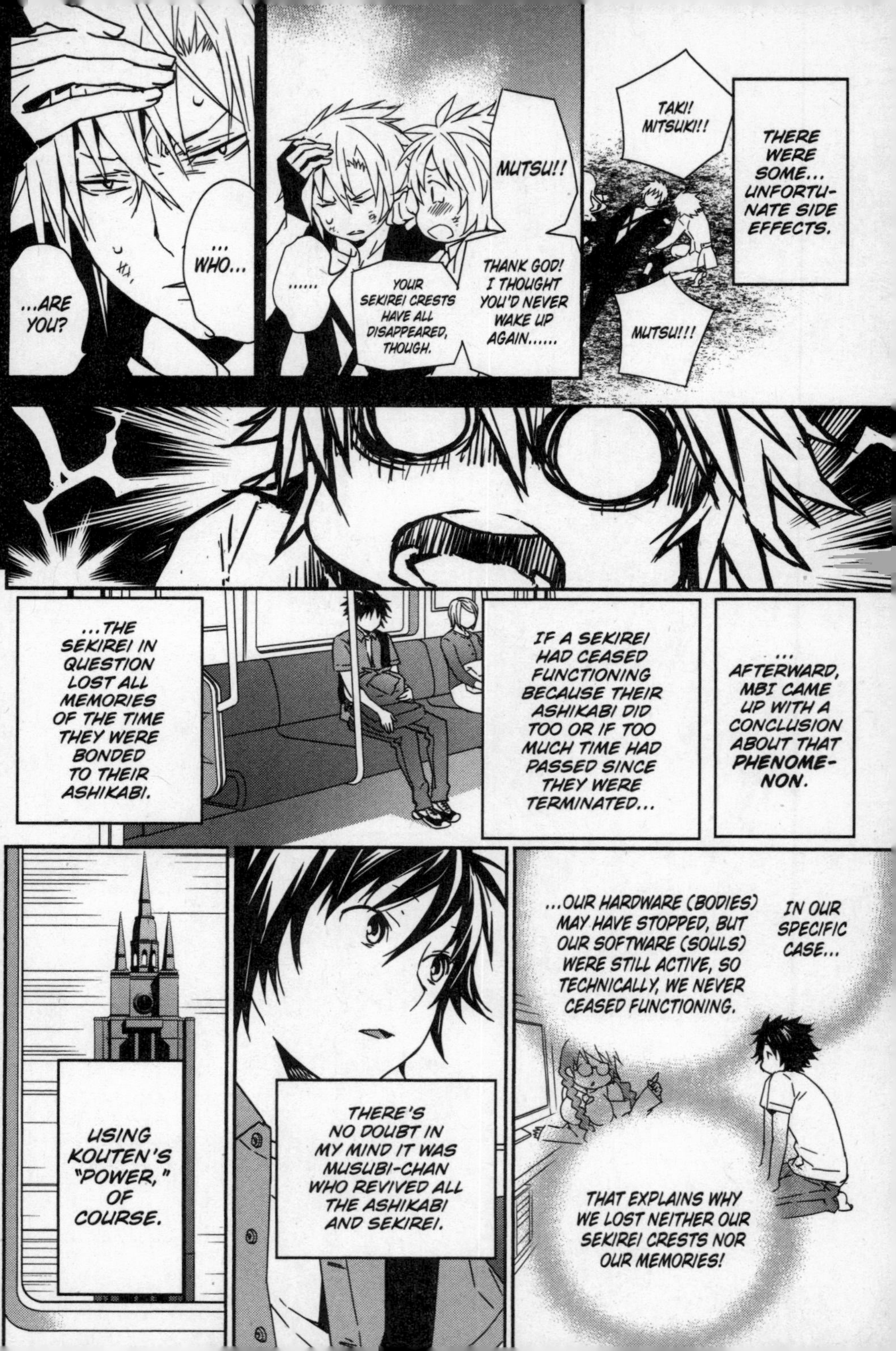
THERE WERE SOME... UNFORTUNATE SIDE EFFECTS.
TAKI! MITSUKI!!
MUTSU!!!
MUTSU!!
THANK GOD! I THOUGHT YOU'D NEVER WAKE UP AGAIN......
YOUR SEKIREI CRESTS HAVE ALL DISAPPEARED, THOUGH.
......
... WHO...
...ARE YOU?
... AFTERWARD, MBI CAME UP WITH A CONCLUSION ABOUT THAT PHENOMENON.
IF A SEKIREI HAD CEASED FUNCTIONING BECAUSE THEIR ASHIKABI DID TOO OR IF TOO MUCH TIME HAD PASSED SINCE THEY WERE TERMINATED...
...THE SEKIREI IN QUESTION LOST ALL MEMORIES OF THE TIME THEY WERE BONDED TO THEIR ASHIKABI.
IN OUR SPECIFIC CASE...
...OUR HARDWARE (BODIES) MAY HAVE STOPPED, BUT OUR SOFTWARE (SOULS) WERE STILL ACTIVE, SO TECHNICALLY, WE NEVER CEASED FUNCTIONING.
THAT EXPLAINS WHY WE LOST NEITHER OUR SEKIREI CRESTS NOR OUR MEMORIES!
THERE'S NO DOUBT IN MY MIND IT WAS MUSUBI-CHAN WHO REVIVED ALL THE ASHIKABI AND SEKIREI.
USING KOUTEN'S "POWER," OF COURSE.

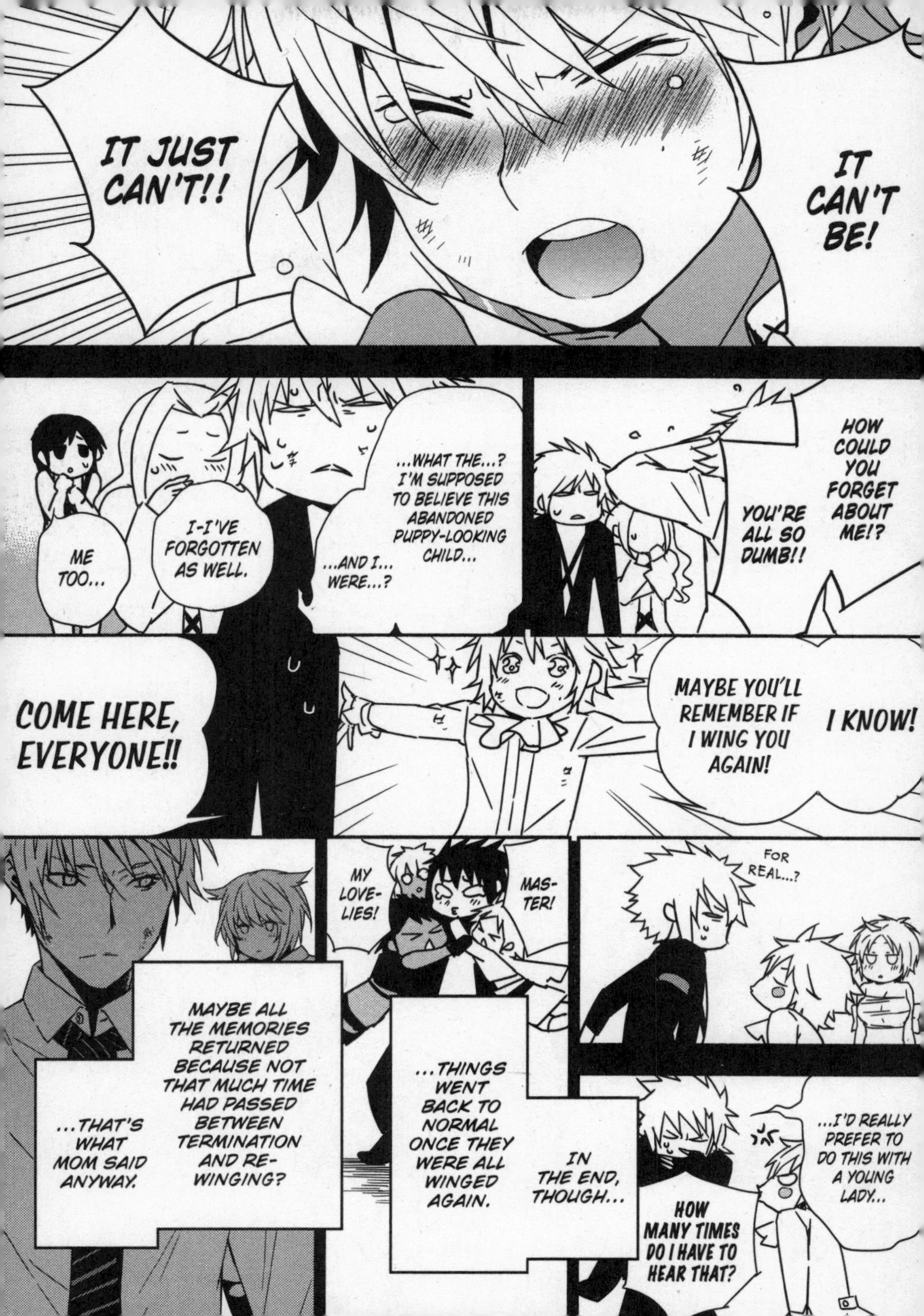
IT CAN'T BE!
IT JUST CAN'T!!
HOW COULD YOU FORGET ABOUT ME!?
YOU'RE ALL SO DUMB!!
...WHAT THE...? I'M SUPPOSED TO BELIEVE THIS ABANDONED PUPPY-LOOKING CHILD...
...AND I... WERE...?
I-I'VE FORGOTTEN AS WELL.
ME TOO...
I KNOW!
MAYBE YOU'LL REMEMBER IF I WING YOU AGAIN!
COME HERE, EVERYONE!!
FOR REAL...?
MASTER!
MY LOVELIES!
...I'D REALLY PREFER TO DO THIS WITH A YOUNG LADY...
HOW MANY TIMES DO I HAVE TO HEAR THAT?
IN THE END, THOUGH...
...THINGS WENT BACK TO NORMAL ONCE THEY WERE ALL WINGED AGAIN.
MAYBE ALL THE MEMORIES RETURNED BECAUSE NOT THAT MUCH TIME HAD PASSED BETWEEN TERMINATION AND RE-WINGING?
...THAT'S WHAT MOM SAID ANYWAY.

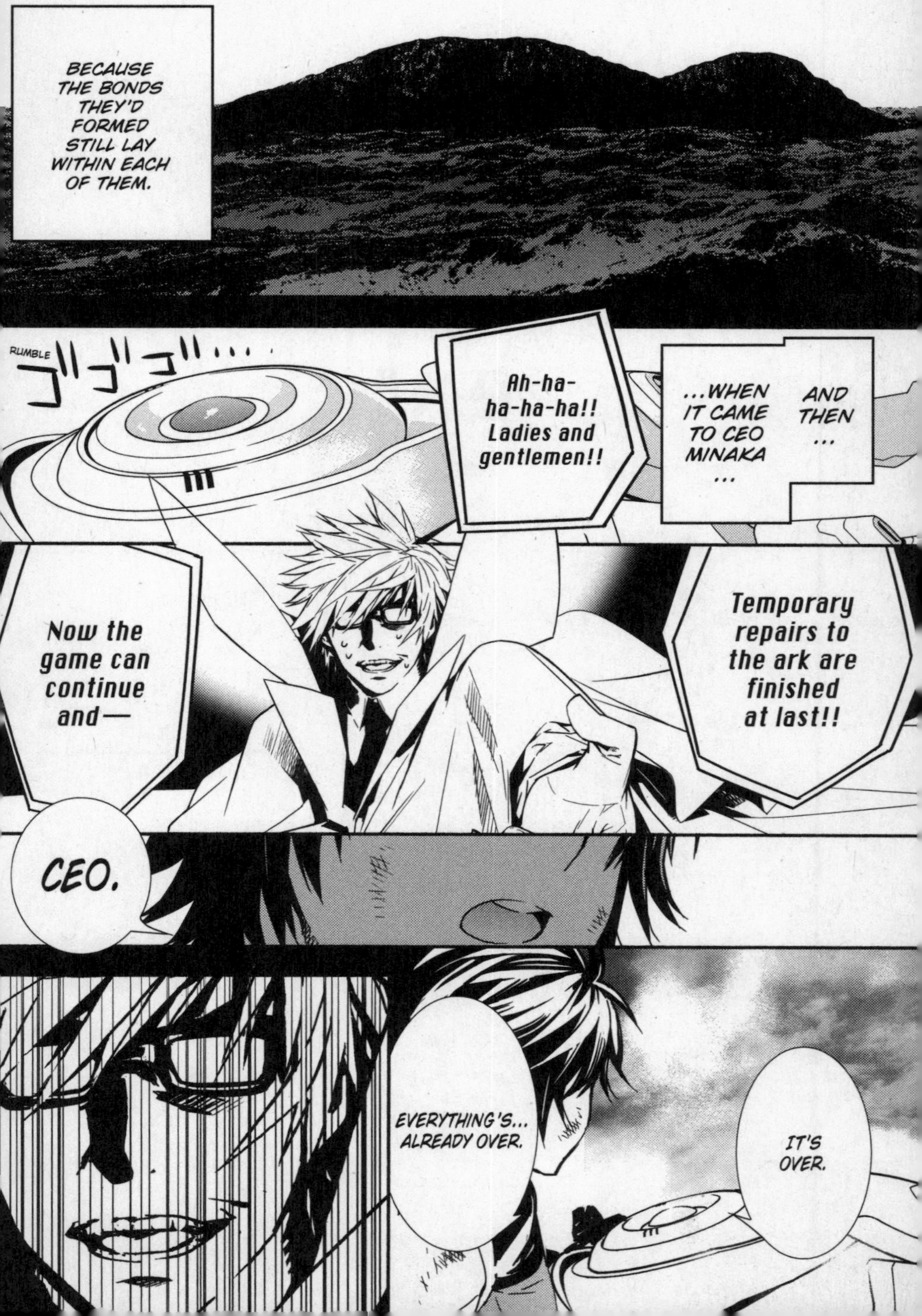
BECAUSE THE BONDS THEY'D FORMED STILL LAY WITHIN EACH OF THEM.
AND THEN ...
...WHEN IT CAME TO CEO MINAKA ...
Ah-ha-ha-ha-ha!! Ladies and gentlemen!!
RUMBLE
ゴゴゴ...
Temporary repairs to the ark are finished at last!!
Now the game can continue and—
CEO.
IT'S OVER.
EVERYTHING'S... ALREADY OVER.

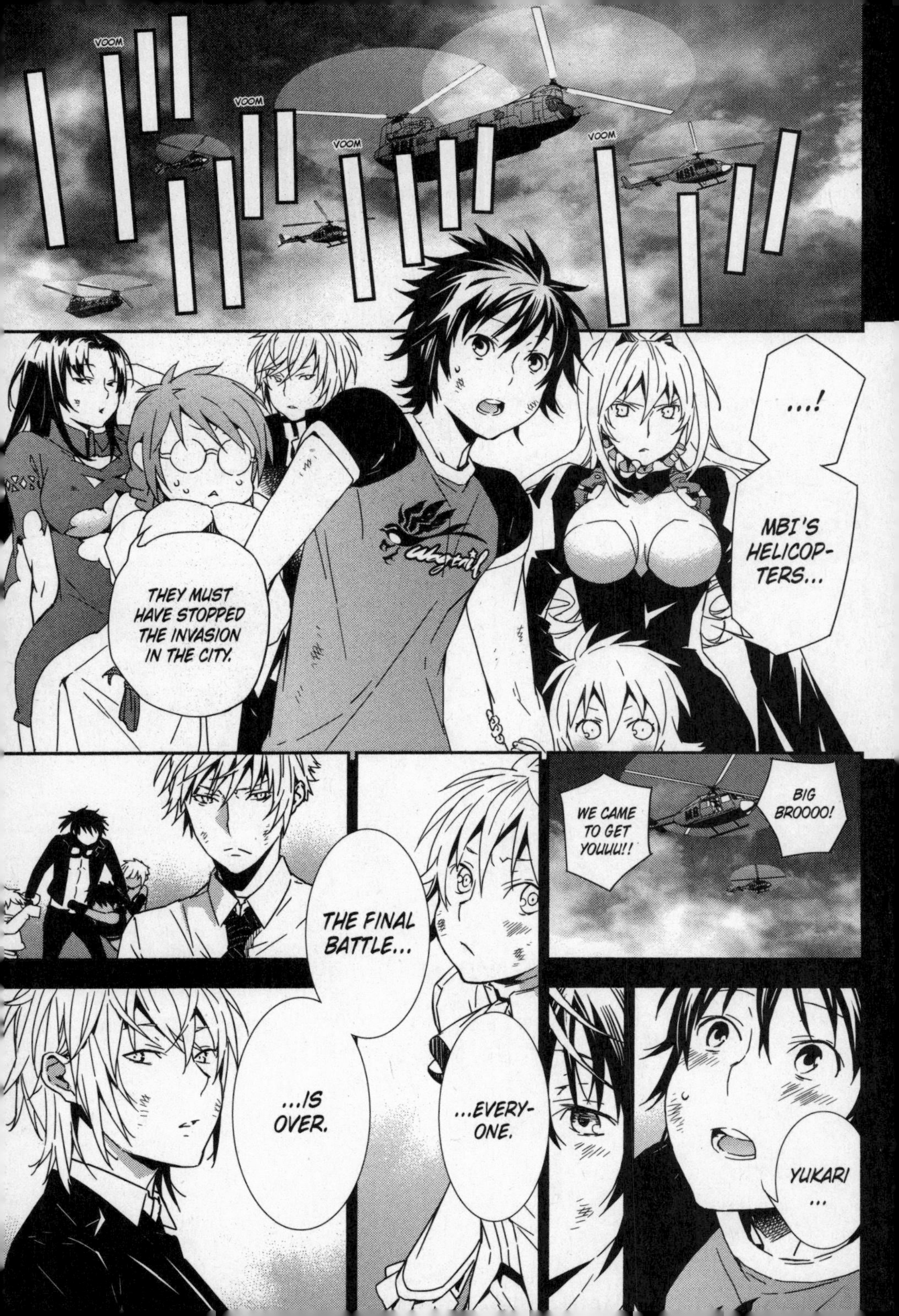
VOOM
VOOM
VOOM
VOOM
...!
MBI'S HELICOP-TERS...
THEY MUST HAVE STOPPED THE INVASION IN THE CITY.
BIG BROOOO!
WE CAME TO GET YOUUU!!
THE FINAL BATTLE...
YUKARI ...
...EVERY-ONE.
...IS OVER.

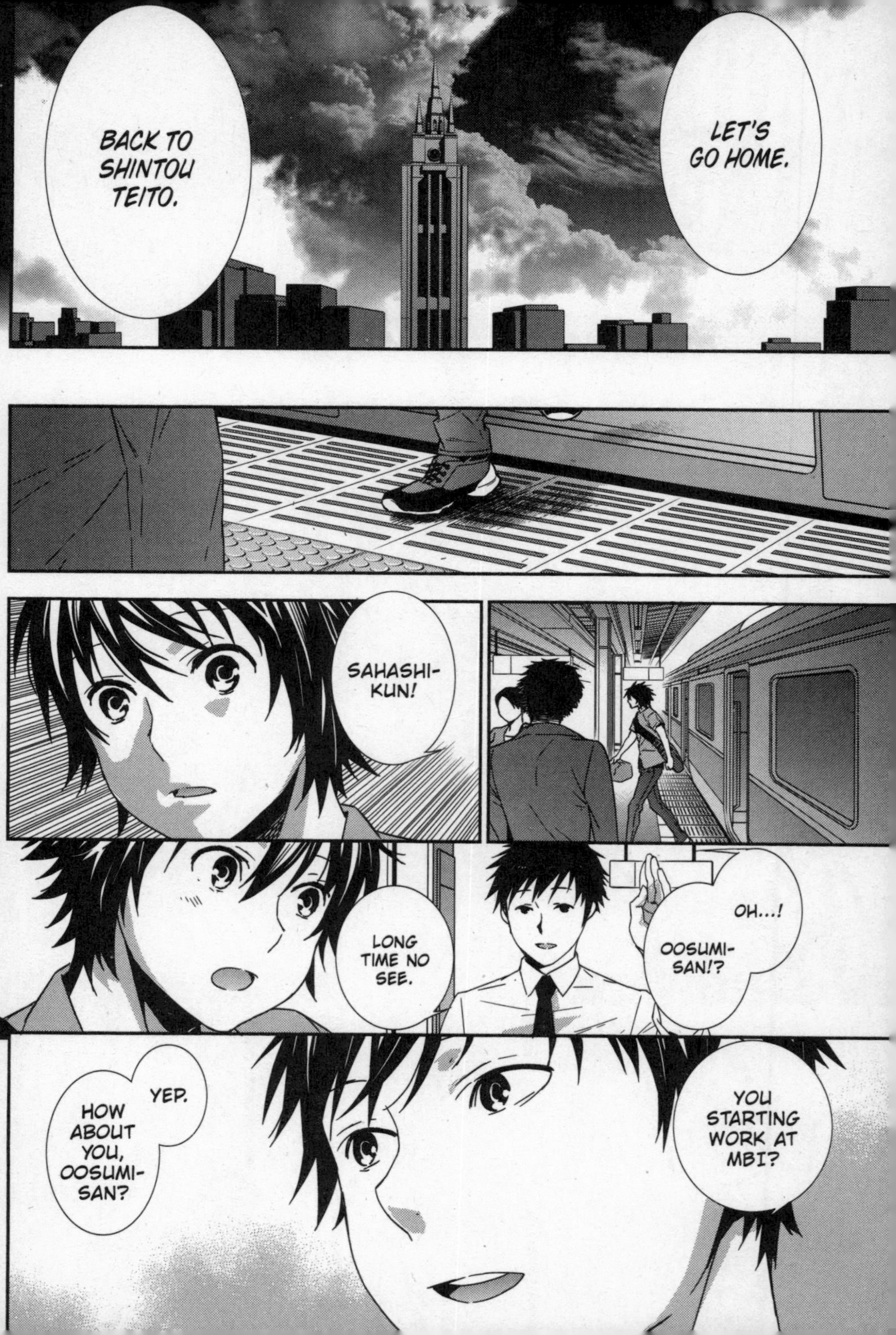
LET'S GO HOME.
BACK TO SHINTOU TEITO.
SAHASHI-KUN!
OH...!
OOSUMI-SAN!?
LONG TIME NO SEE.
YOU STARTING WORK AT MBI?
YEP.
HOW ABOUT YOU, OOSUMI-SAN?

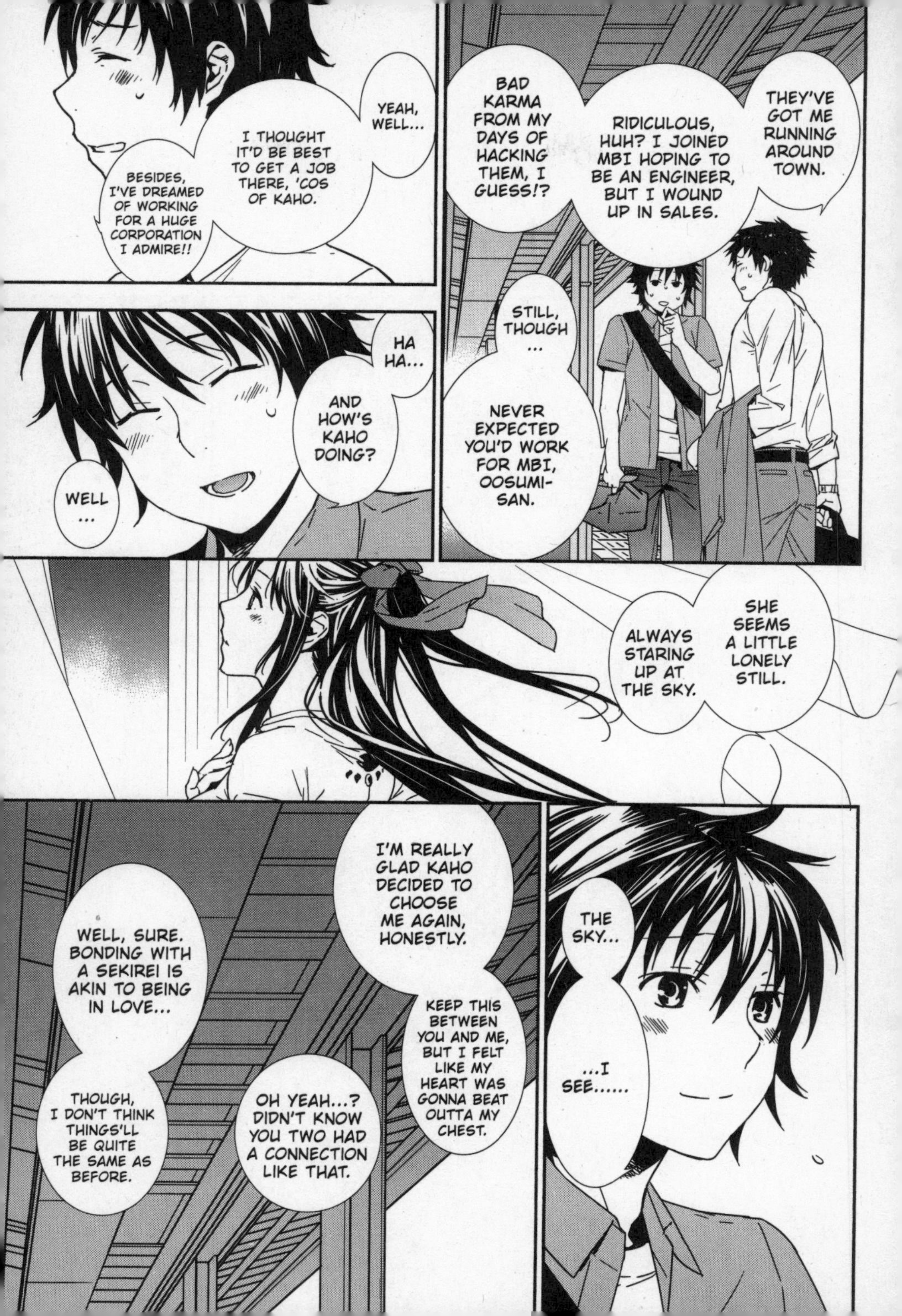
THEY'VE GOT ME RUNNING AROUND TOWN.
RIDICULOUS, HUH? I JOINED MBI HOPING TO BE AN ENGINEER, BUT I WOUND UP IN SALES.
BAD KARMA FROM MY DAYS OF HACKING THEM, I GUESS!?
STILL, THOUGH ...
NEVER EXPECTED YOU'D WORK FOR MBI, OOSUMI-SAN.
YEAH, WELL...
I THOUGHT IT'D BE BEST TO GET A JOB THERE, 'COS OF KAHO.
BESIDES, I'VE DREAMED OF WORKING FOR A HUGE CORPORATION I ADMIRE!!
HA HA...
AND HOW'S KAHO DOING?
WELL ...
SHE SEEMS A LITTLE LONELY STILL.
ALWAYS STARING UP AT THE SKY.
THE SKY...
...I SEE......
I'M REALLY GLAD KAHO DECIDED TO CHOOSE ME AGAIN, HONESTLY.
KEEP THIS BETWEEN YOU AND ME, BUT I FELT LIKE MY HEART WAS GONNA BEAT OUTTA MY CHEST.
OH YEAH...? DIDN'T KNOW YOU TWO HAD A CONNECTION LIKE THAT.
WELL, SURE. BONDING WITH A SEKIREI IS AKIN TO BEING IN LOVE...
THOUGH, I DON'T THINK THINGS'LL BE QUITE THE SAME AS BEFORE.

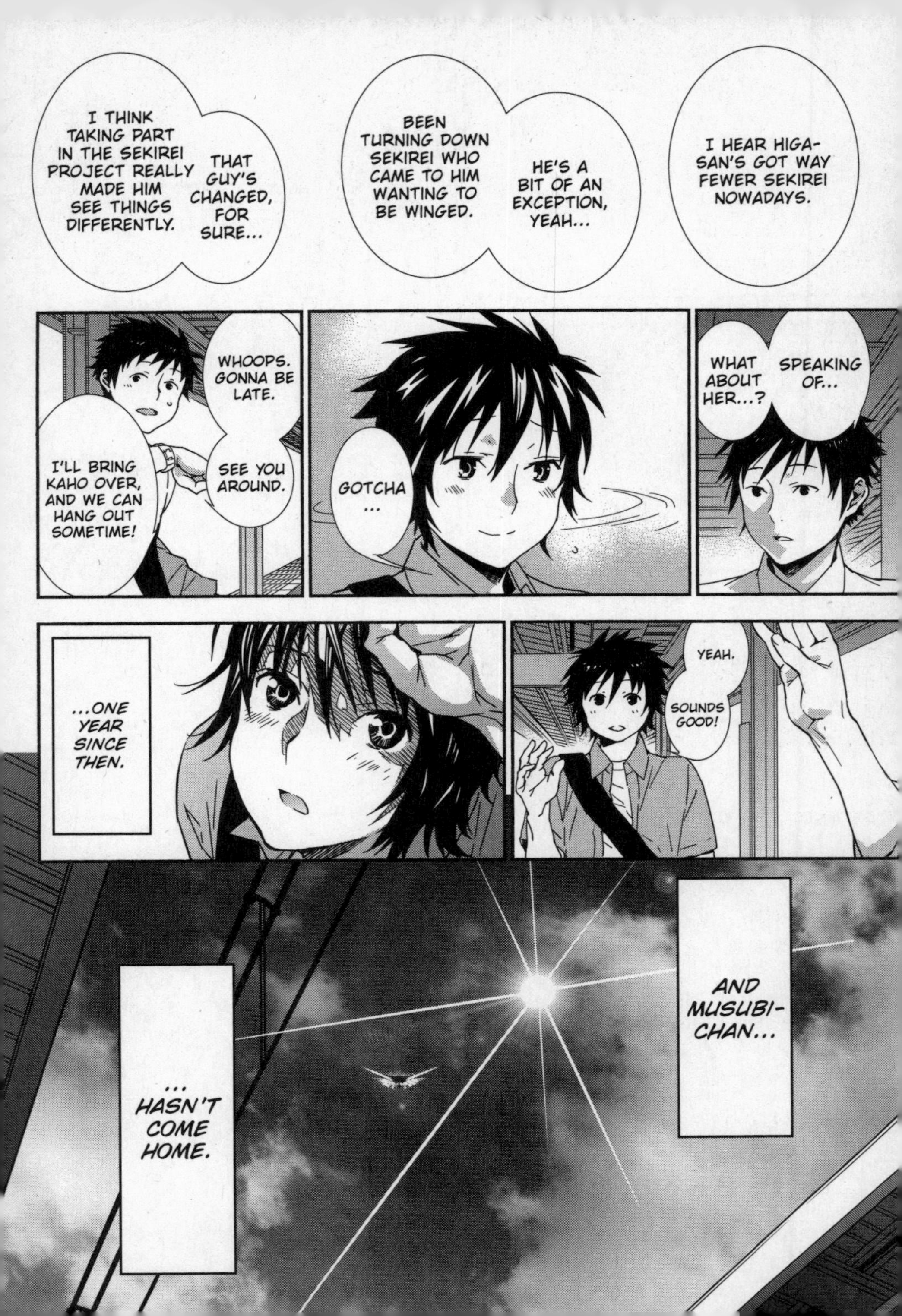
I HEAR HIGA-SAN'S GOT WAY FEWER SEKIREI NOWADAYS.
HE'S A BIT OF AN EXCEPTION, YEAH...
BEEN TURNING DOWN SEKIREI WHO CAME TO HIM WANTING TO BE WINGED.
THAT GUY'S CHANGED, FOR SURE...
I THINK TAKING PART IN THE SEKIREI PROJECT REALLY MADE HIM SEE THINGS DIFFERENTLY.
SPEAKING OF...
WHAT ABOUT HER...?
GOTCHA...
WHOOPS. GONNA BE LATE.
SEE YOU AROUND.
I'LL BRING KAHO OVER, AND WE CAN HANG OUT SOMETIME!
YEAH.
SOUNDS GOOD!
...ONE YEAR SINCE THEN.
AND MUSUBI-CHAN...
...HASN'T COME HOME.

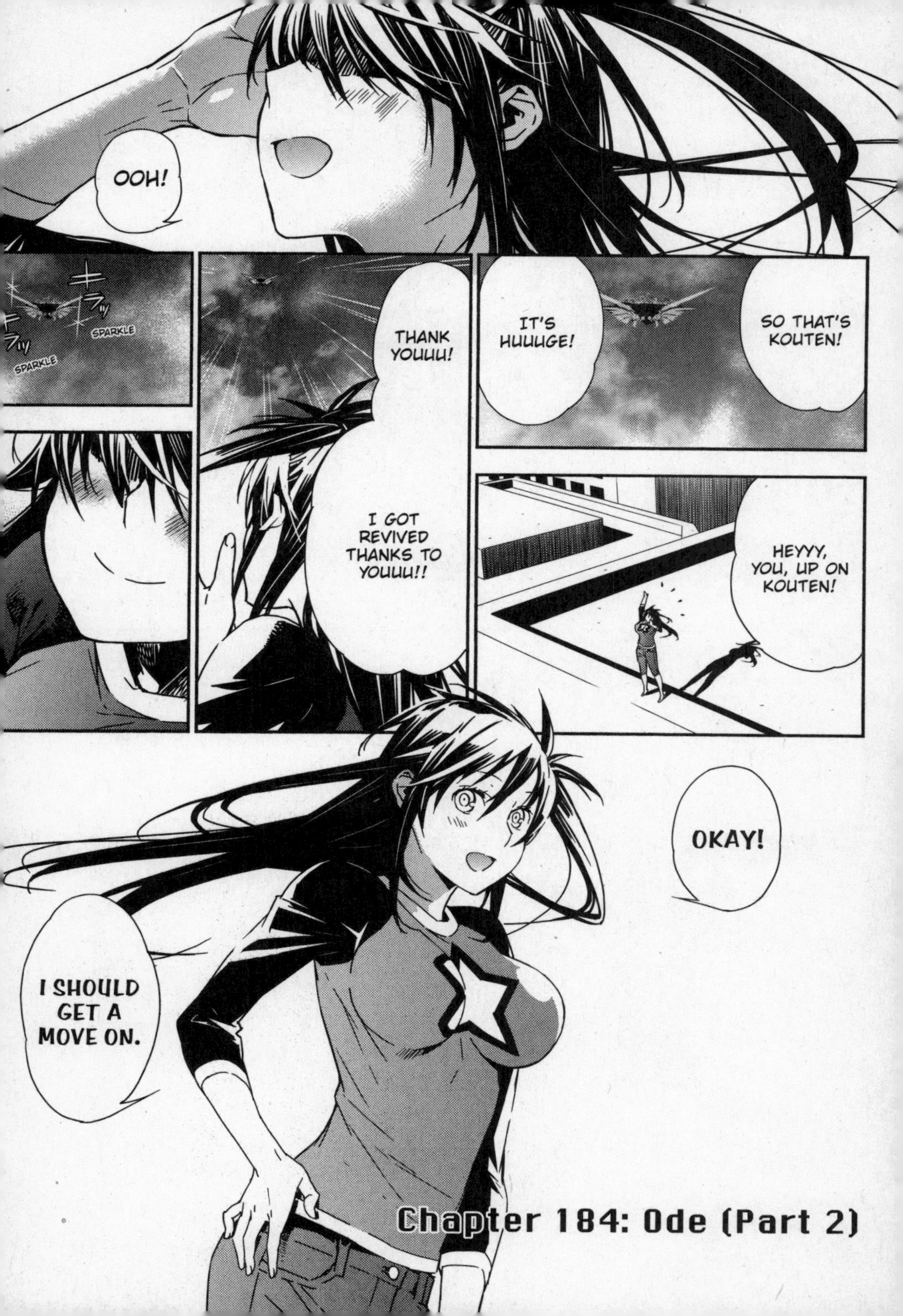
OOH!
SO THAT'S KOUTEN!
IT'S HUUUGE!
HEYYY, YOU, UP ON KOUTEN!
THANK YOUUU!
I GOT REVIVED THANKS TO YOUUU!!
SPARKLE
SPARKLE
OKAY!
I SHOULD GET A MOVE ON.

Chapter 184: Ode (Part 2)

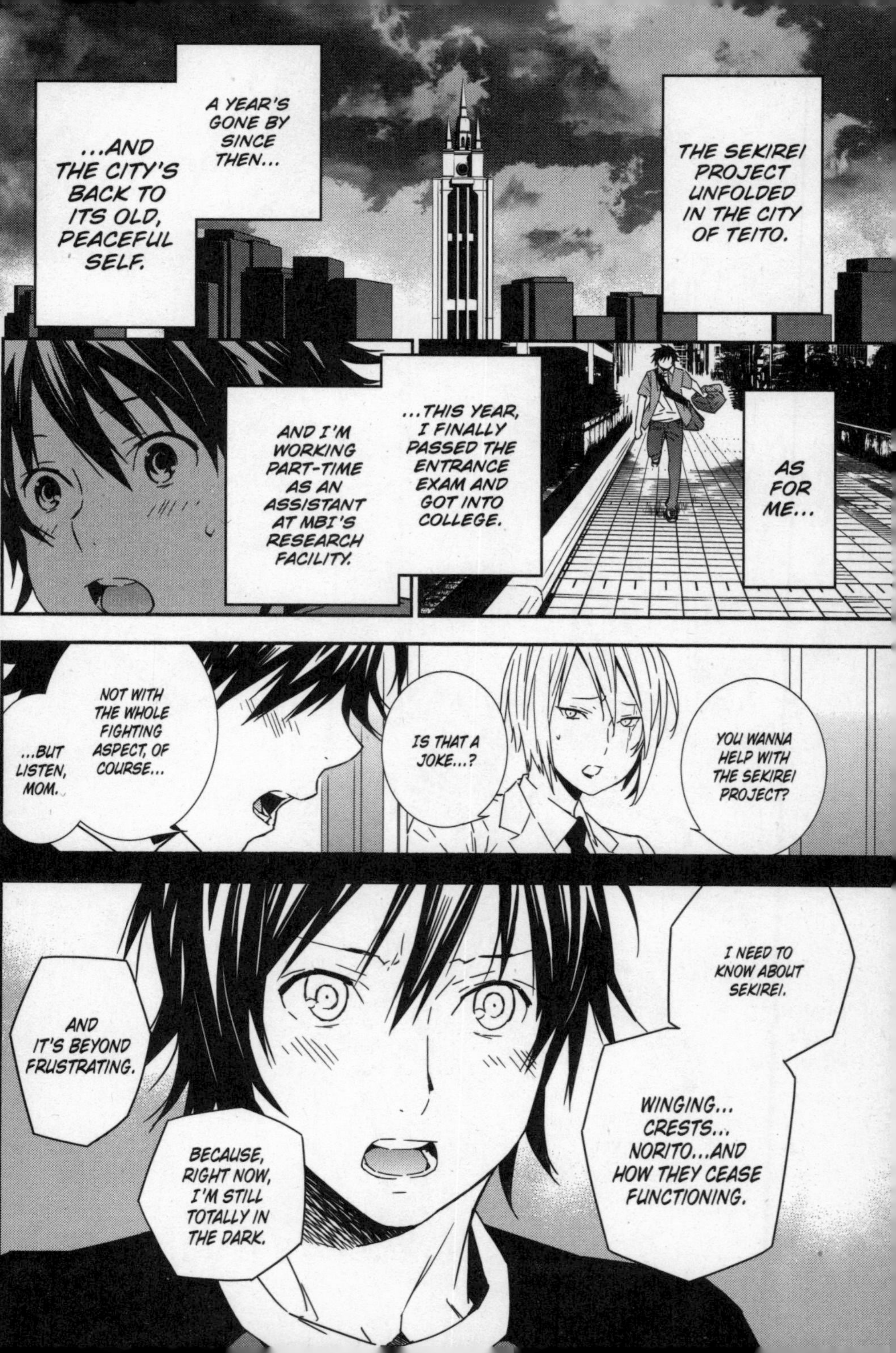
THE SEKIREI PROJECT UNFOLDED IN THE CITY OF TEITO.
A YEAR'S GONE BY SINCE THEN...
...AND THE CITY'S BACK TO ITS OLD, PEACEFUL SELF.
AS FOR ME...
...THIS YEAR, I FINALLY PASSED THE ENTRANCE EXAM AND GOT INTO COLLEGE.
AND I'M WORKING PART-TIME AS AN ASSISTANT AT MBI'S RESEARCH FACILITY.
YOU WANNA HELP WITH THE SEKIREI PROJECT?
IS THAT A JOKE...?
NOT WITH THE WHOLE FIGHTING ASPECT, OF COURSE...
...BUT LISTEN, MOM.
I NEED TO KNOW ABOUT SEKIREI.
WINGING... CRESTS... NORITO...AND HOW THEY CEASE FUNCTIONING.
AND IT'S BEYOND FRUSTRATING.
BECAUSE, RIGHT NOW, I'M STILL TOTALLY IN THE DARK.

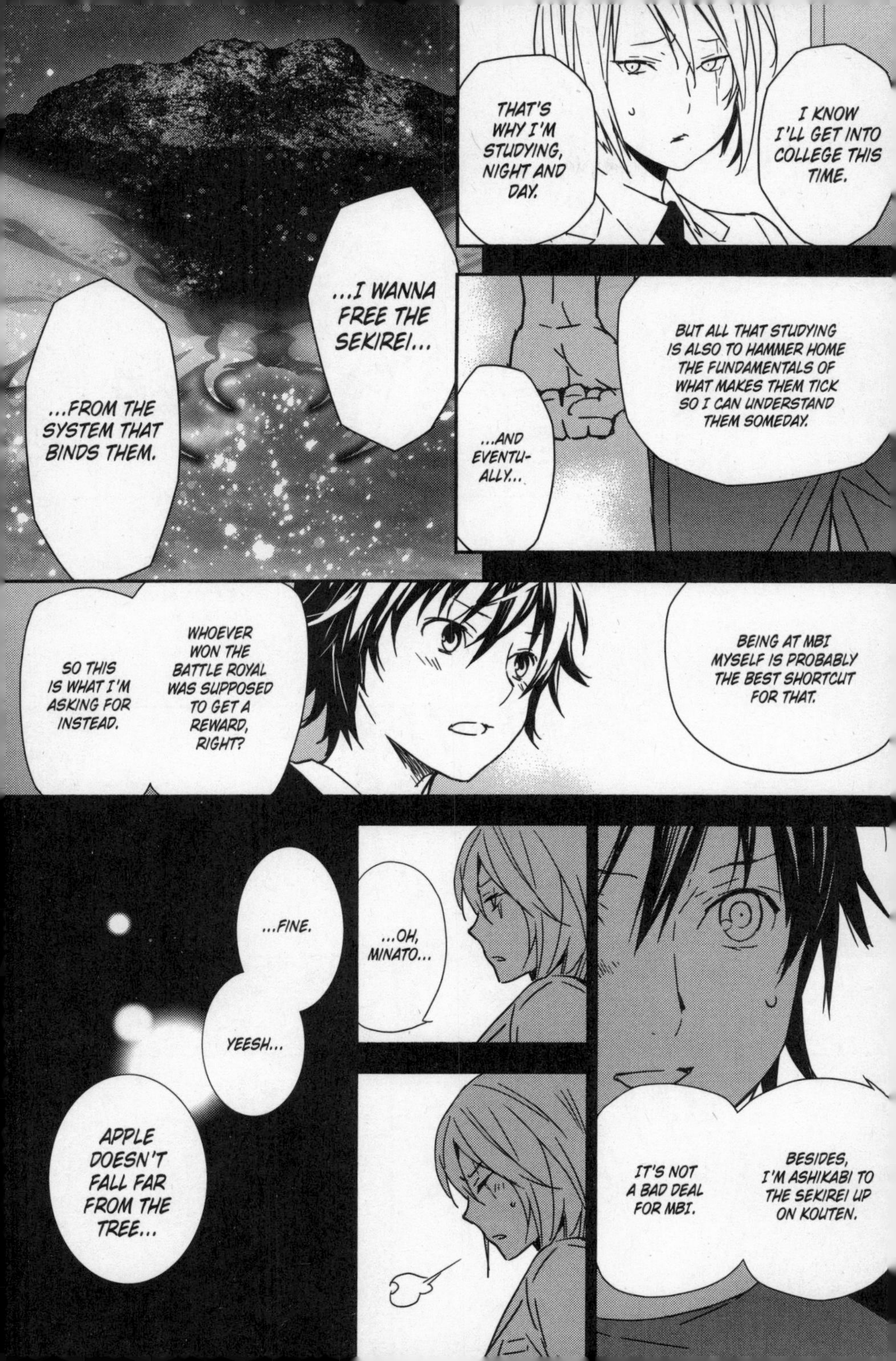
I KNOW I'LL GET INTO COLLEGE THIS TIME.
THAT'S WHY I'M STUDYING, NIGHT AND DAY.
BUT ALL THAT STUDYING IS ALSO TO HAMMER HOME THE FUNDAMENTALS OF WHAT MAKES THEM TICK SO I CAN UNDERSTAND THEM SOMEDAY.
...AND EVENTU-ALLY...
...I WANNA FREE THE SEKIREI...
...FROM THE SYSTEM THAT BINDS THEM.
BEING AT MBI MYSELF IS PROBABLY THE BEST SHORTCUT FOR THAT.
WHOEVER WON THE BATTLE ROYAL WAS SUPPOSED TO GET A REWARD, RIGHT?
SO THIS IS WHAT I'M ASKING FOR INSTEAD.
BESIDES, I'M ASHIKABI TO THE SEKIREI UP ON KOUTEN.
IT'S NOT A BAD DEAL FOR MBI.
...OH, MINATO...
...FINE.
YEESH...
APPLE DOESN'T FALL FAR FROM THE TREE...

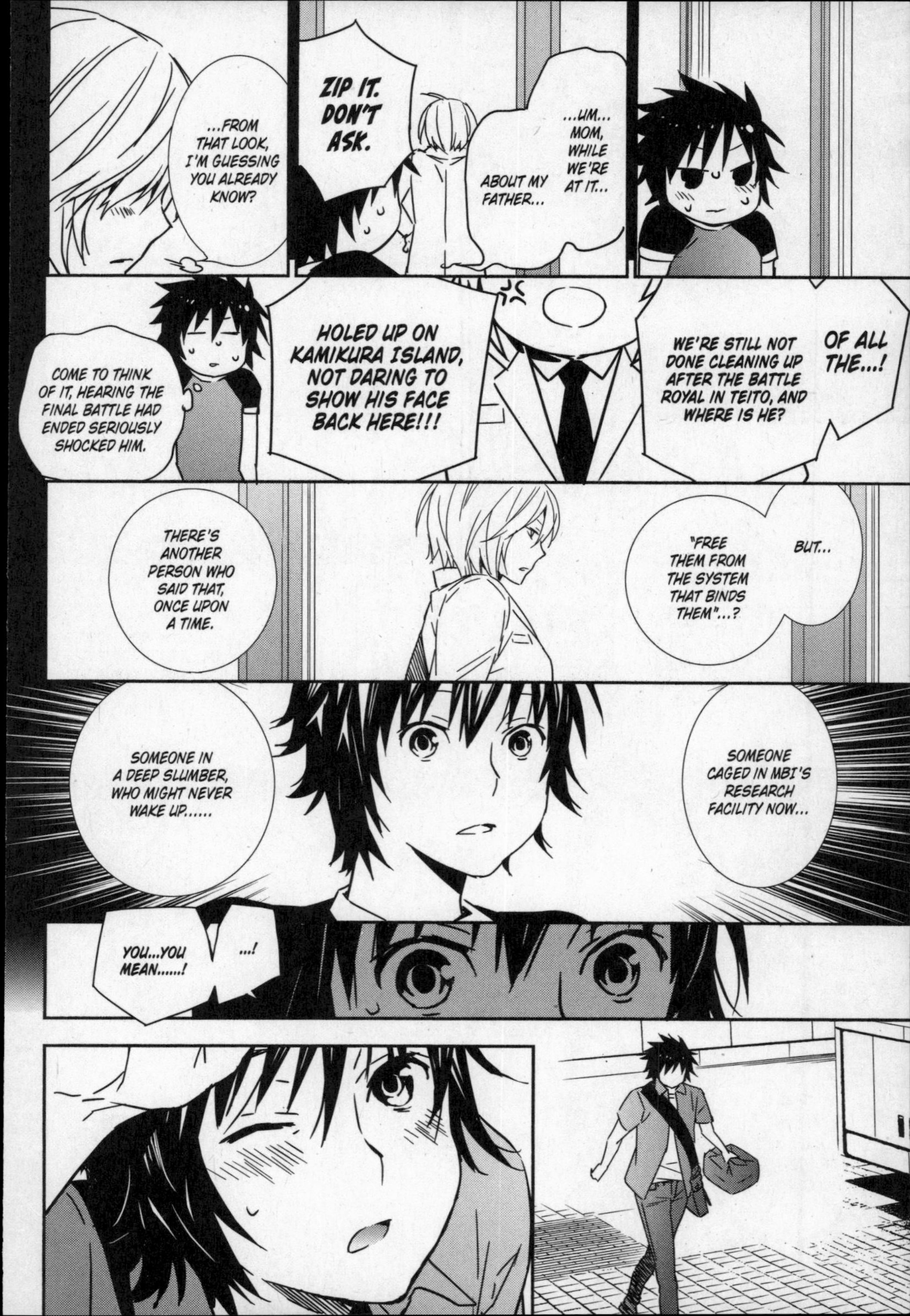
...UM... MOM, WHILE WE'RE AT IT...
ABOUT MY FATHER...
ZIP IT. DON'T ASK.
...FROM THAT LOOK, I'M GUESSING YOU ALREADY KNOW?
OF ALL THE...!
WE'RE STILL NOT DONE CLEANING UP AFTER THE BATTLE ROYAL IN TEITO, AND WHERE IS HE?
HOLED UP ON KAMIKURA ISLAND, NOT DARING TO SHOW HIS FACE BACK HERE!!!
COME TO THINK OF IT, HEARING THE FINAL BATTLE HAD ENDED SERIOUSLY SHOCKED HIM.
BUT...
"FREE THEM FROM THE SYSTEM THAT BINDS THEM"...?
THERE'S ANOTHER PERSON WHO SAID THAT, ONCE UPON A TIME.
SOMEONE CAGED IN MBI'S RESEARCH FACILITY NOW...
SOMEONE IN A DEEP SLUMBER, WHO MIGHT NEVER WAKE UP......
...!
YOU...YOU MEAN......!

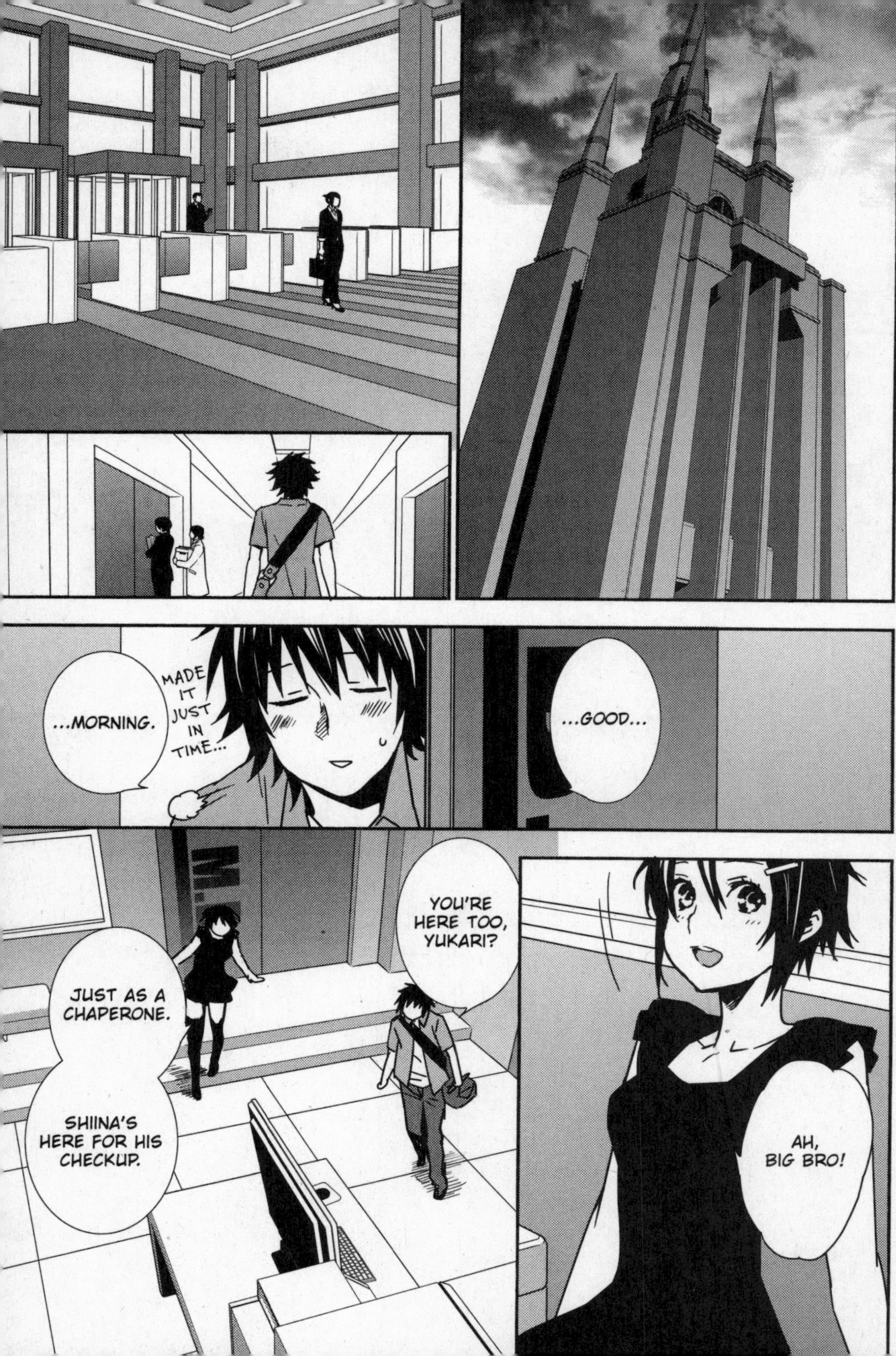
...GOOD...
...MORNING.
MADE IT JUST IN TIME...
AH, BIG BRO!
YOU'RE HERE TOO, YUKARI?
JUST AS A CHAPERONE.
SHIINA'S HERE FOR HIS CHECKUP.

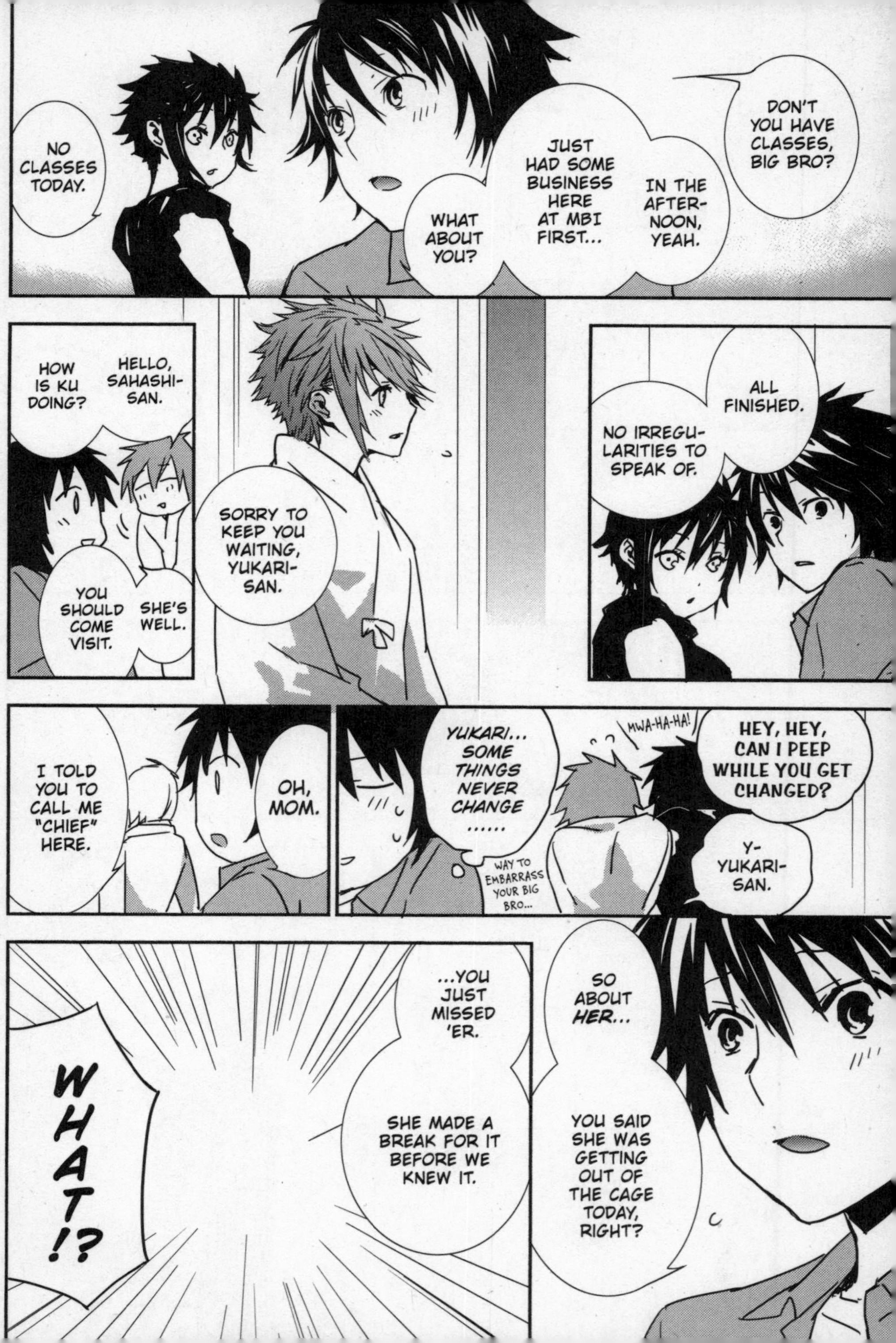
DON'T YOU HAVE CLASSES, BIG BRO?
IN THE AFTERNOON, YEAH.
JUST HAD SOME BUSINESS HERE AT MBI FIRST...
WHAT ABOUT YOU?
NO CLASSES TODAY.
ALL FINISHED.
NO IRREGULARITIES TO SPEAK OF.
SORRY TO KEEP YOU WAITING, YUKARI-SAN.
HELLO, SAHASHI-SAN.
HOW IS KU DOING?
SHE'S WELL.
YOU SHOULD COME VISIT.
MWA-HA-HA!
HEY, HEY, CAN I PEEP WHILE YOU GET CHANGED?
Y-YUKARI-SAN.
YUKARI... SOME THINGS NEVER CHANGE ......
WAY TO EMBARRASS YOUR BIG BRO...
OH, MOM.
I TOLD YOU TO CALL ME "CHIEF" HERE.
SO ABOUT *HER*...
YOU SAID SHE WAS GETTING OUT OF THE CAGE TODAY, RIGHT?
...YOU JUST MISSED 'ER.
SHE MADE A BREAK FOR IT BEFORE WE KNEW IT.
WHAT!?

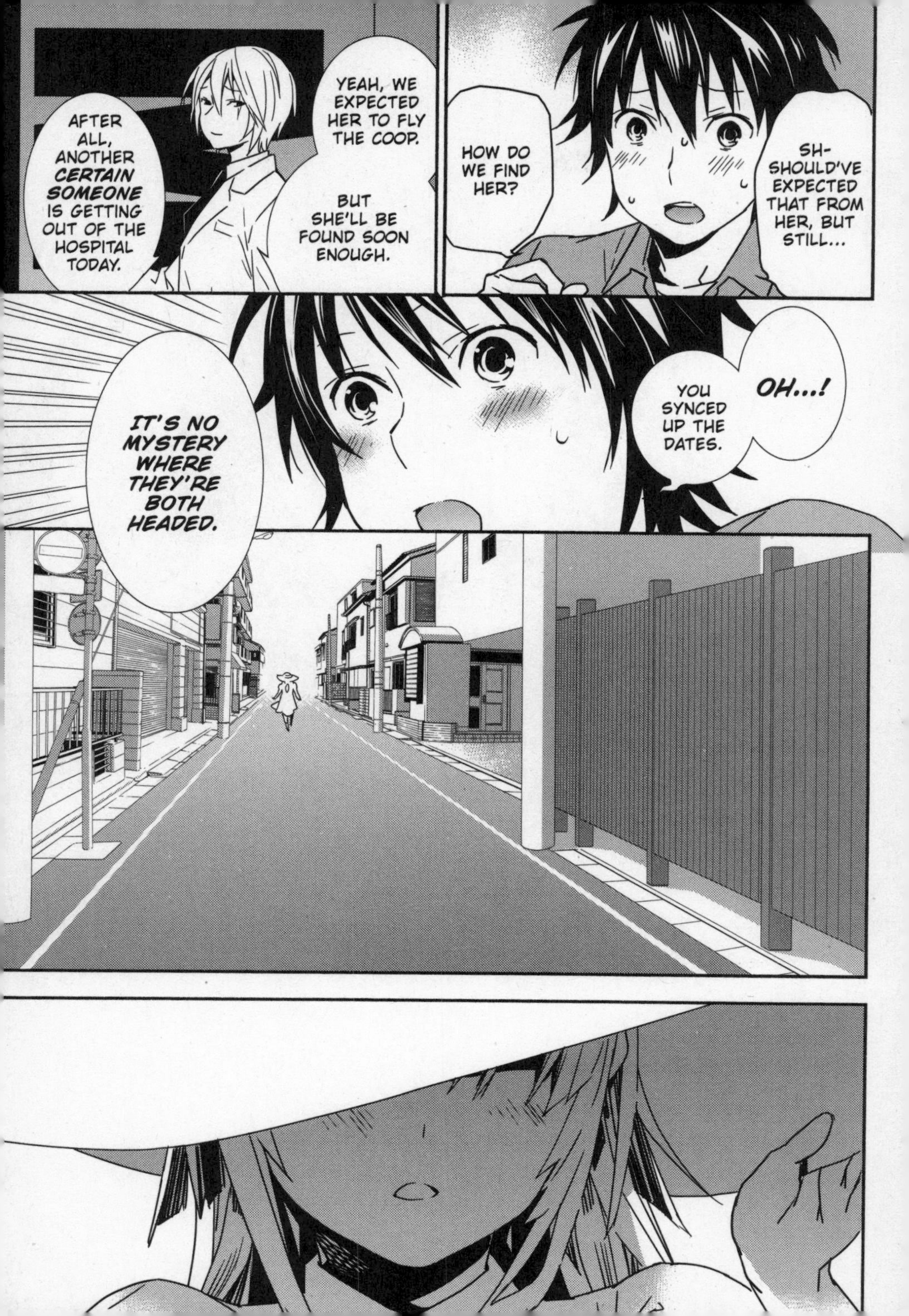
SH-SHOULD'VE EXPECTED THAT FROM HER, BUT STILL...
HOW DO WE FIND HER?
YEAH, WE EXPECTED HER TO FLY THE COOP.
BUT SHE'LL BE FOUND SOON ENOUGH.
AFTER ALL, ANOTHER *CERTAIN SOMEONE* IS GETTING OUT OF THE HOSPITAL TODAY.
OH...!
YOU SYNCED UP THE DATES.
IT'S NO MYSTERY WHERE THEY'RE BOTH HEADED.

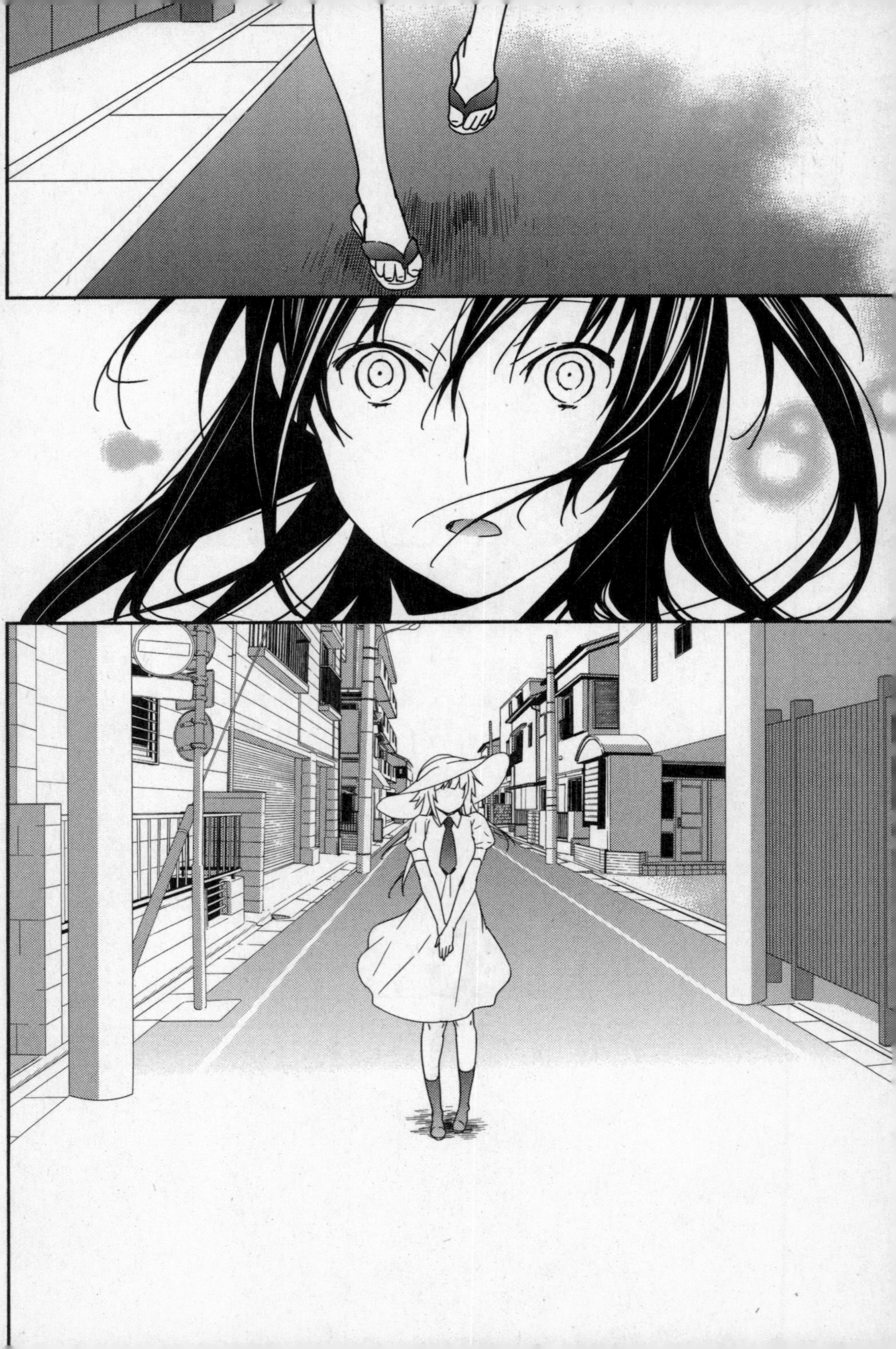

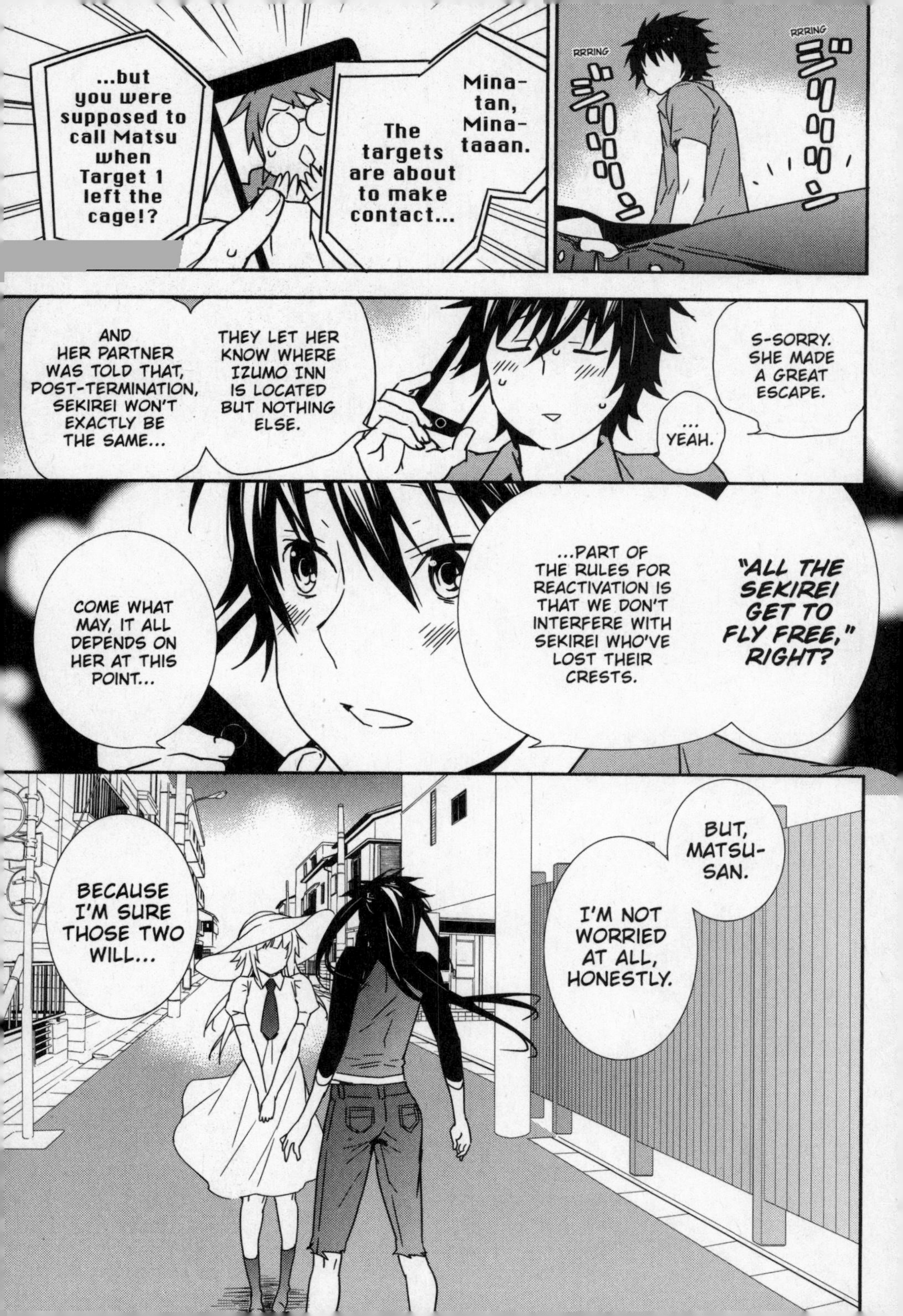
RRRING
RRRING
Mina-tan, Mina-taaan.
The targets are about to make contact...
...but you were supposed to call Matsu when Target 1 left the cage!?
S-SORRY. SHE MADE A GREAT ESCAPE.
...YEAH.
THEY LET HER KNOW WHERE IZUMO INN IS LOCATED BUT NOTHING ELSE.
AND HER PARTNER WAS TOLD THAT, POST-TERMINATION, SEKIREI WON'T EXACTLY BE THE SAME...
"ALL THE SEKIREI GET TO FLY FREE," RIGHT?
...PART OF THE RULES FOR REACTIVATION IS THAT WE DON'T INTERFERE WITH SEKIREI WHO'VE LOST THEIR CRESTS.
COME WHAT MAY, IT ALL DEPENDS ON HER AT THIS POINT...
BUT, MATSU-SAN.
I'M NOT WORRIED AT ALL, HONESTLY.
BECAUSE I'M SURE THOSE TWO WILL...

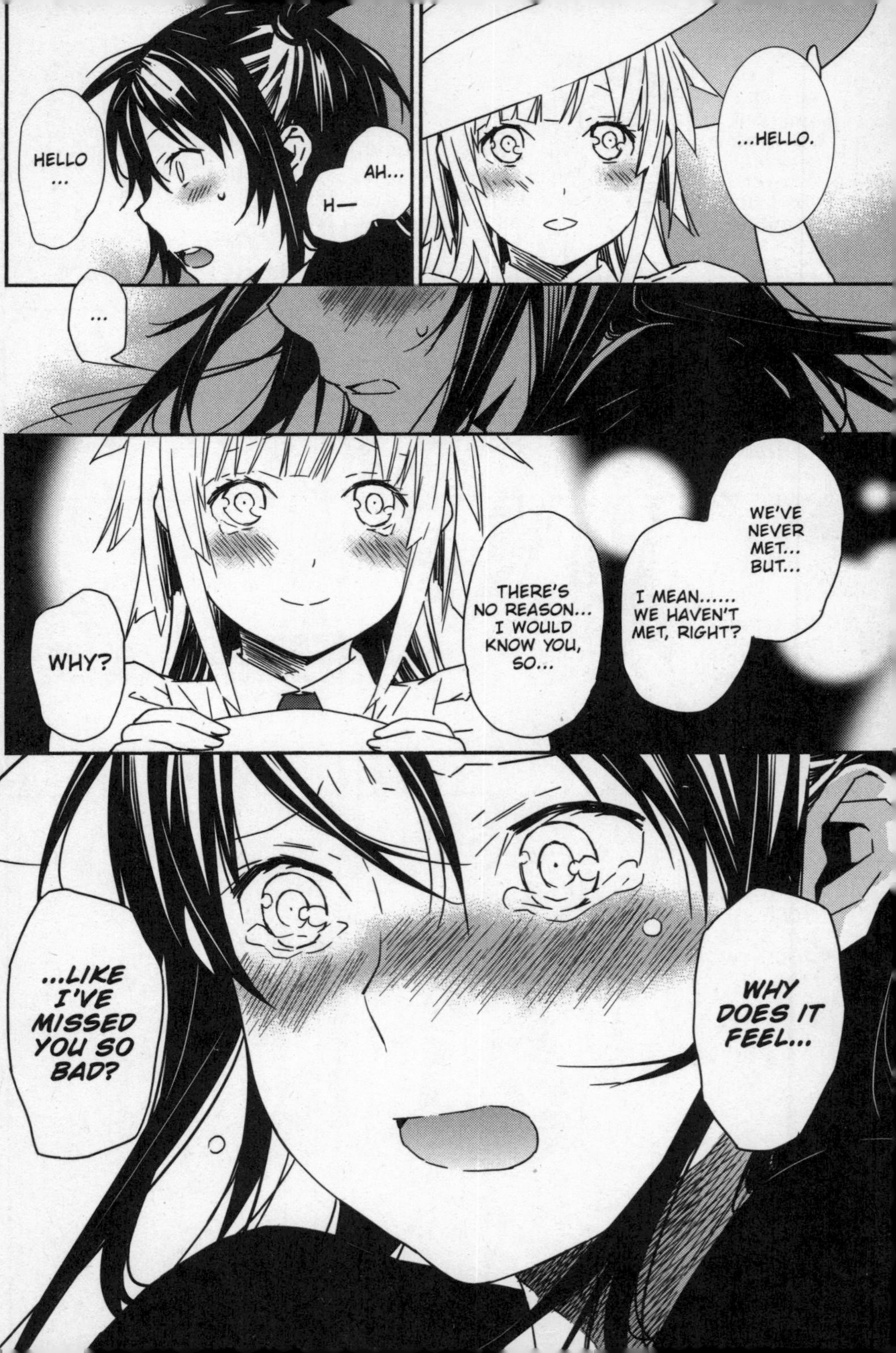
...HELLO.
AH... H—
HELLO ...
...
WE'VE NEVER MET... BUT...
I MEAN...... WE HAVEN'T MET, RIGHT?
THERE'S NO REASON... I WOULD KNOW YOU, SO...
WHY?
WHY DOES IT FEEL...
...LIKE I'VE MISSED YOU SO BAD?

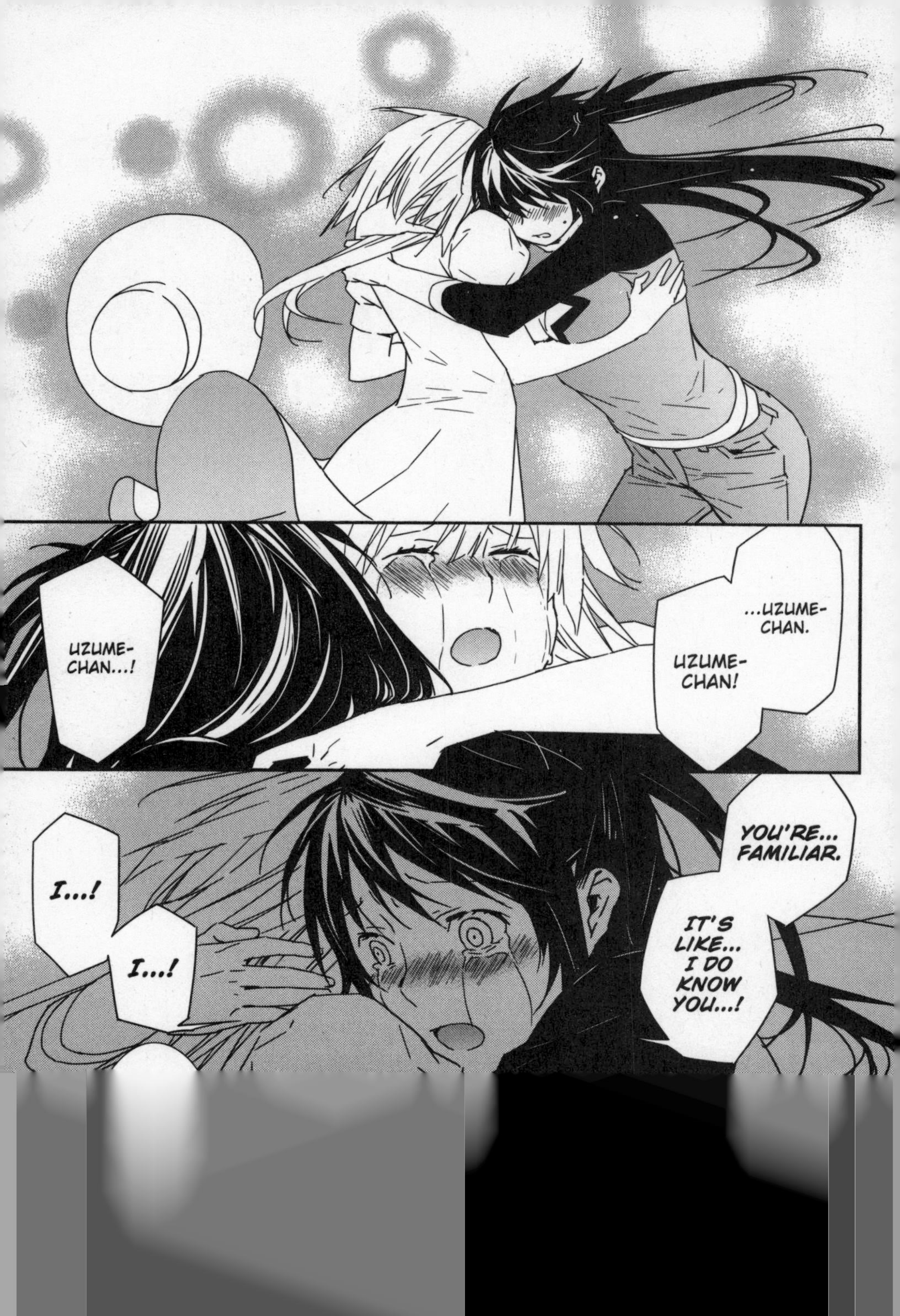
...UZUME-CHAN.
UZUME-CHAN!
UZUME-CHAN...!
YOU'RE... FAMILIAR.
IT'S LIKE... I DO KNOW YOU...!
I...!
I...!

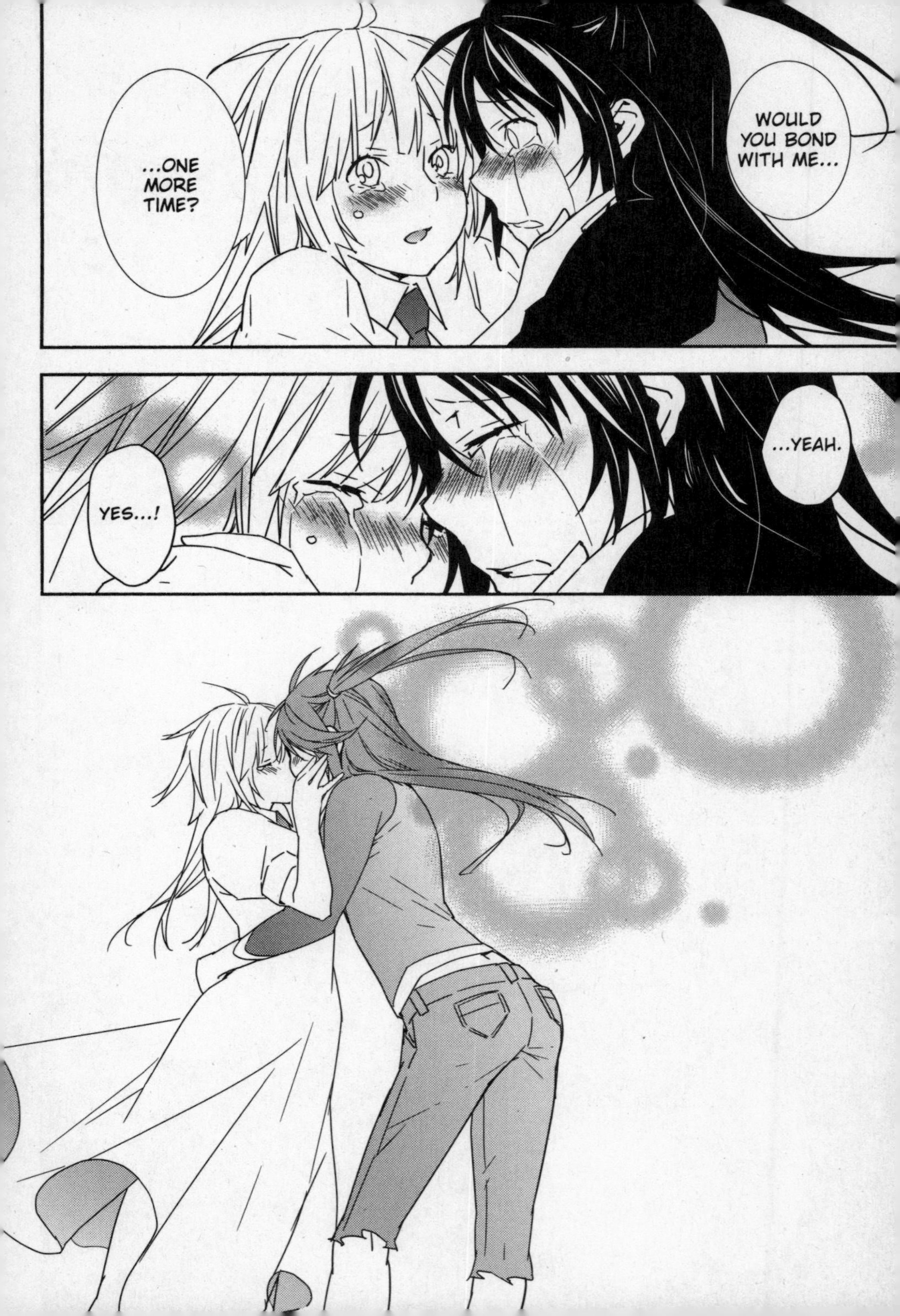
WOULD YOU BOND WITH ME...
...ONE MORE TIME?
...YEAH.
YES...!

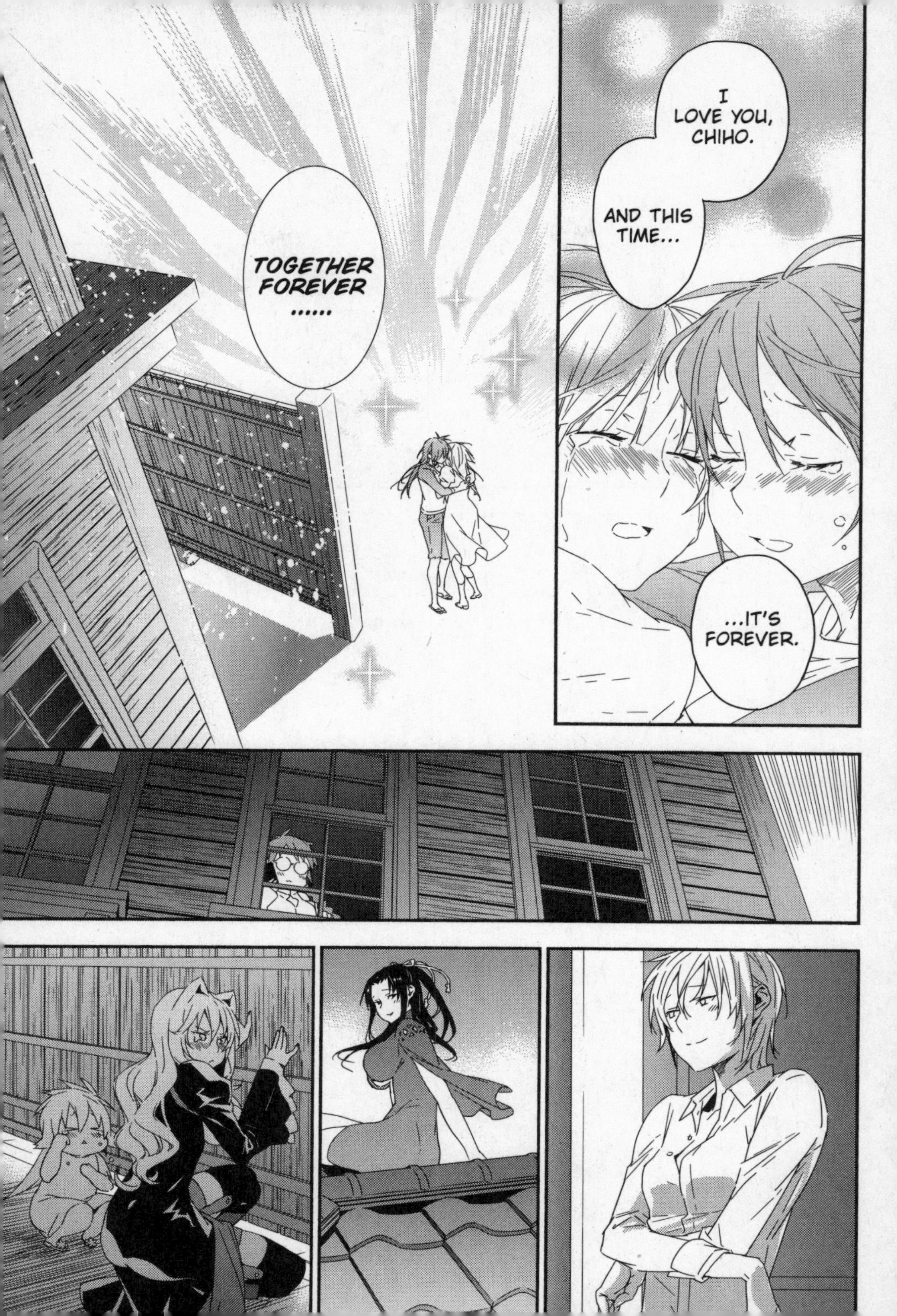
I LOVE YOU, CHIHO.
AND THIS TIME...
...IT'S FOREVER.
TOGETHER FOREVER ......

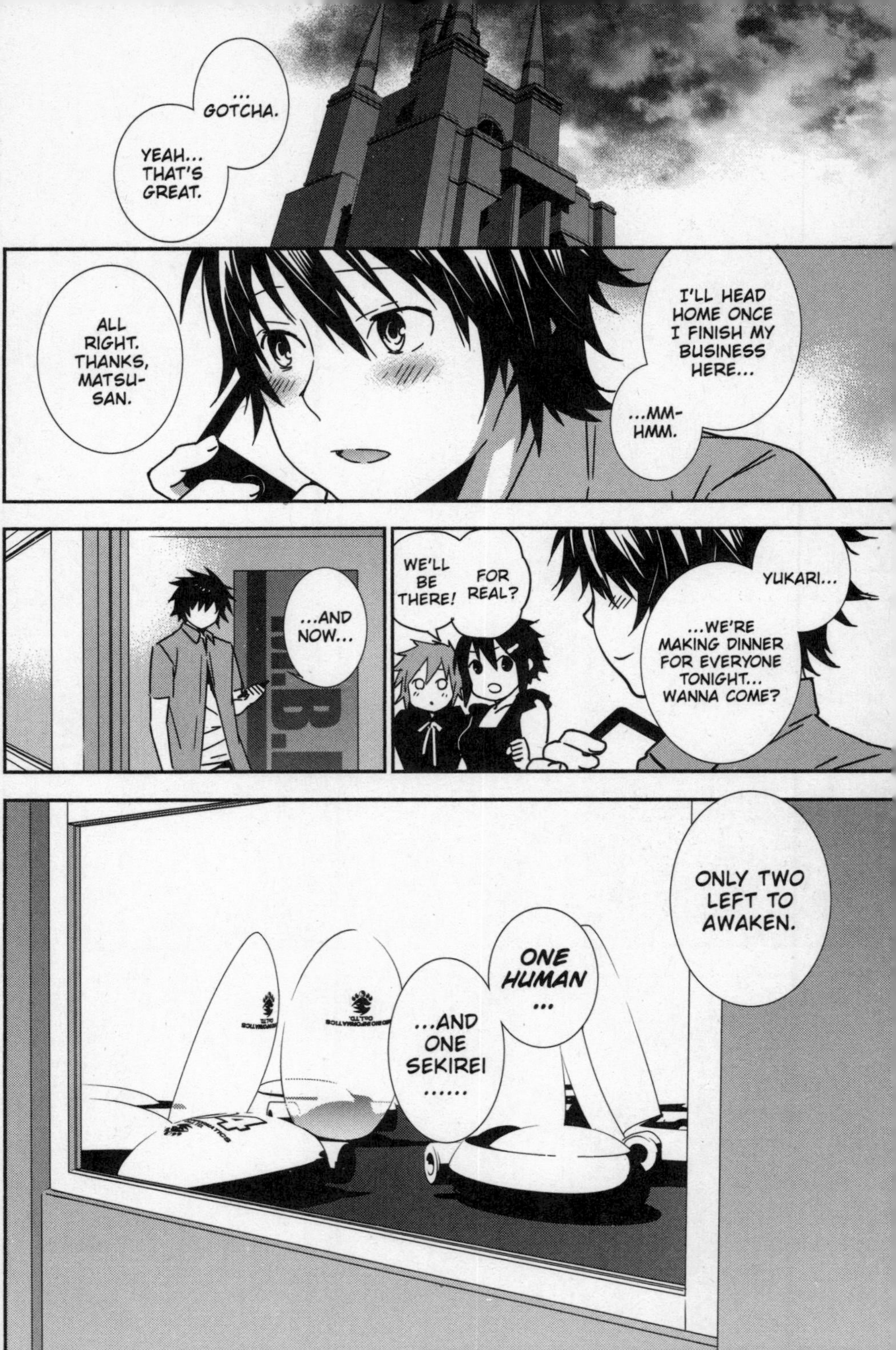
...GOTCHA.
YEAH... THAT'S GREAT.
I'LL HEAD HOME ONCE I FINISH MY BUSINESS HERE...
...MM-HMM.
ALL RIGHT. THANKS, MATSU-SAN.
YUKARI...
...WE'RE MAKING DINNER FOR EVERYONE TONIGHT... WANNA COME?
FOR REAL?
WE'LL BE THERE!
...AND NOW...
ONLY TWO LEFT TO AWAKEN.
ONE HUMAN...
...AND ONE SEKIREI......

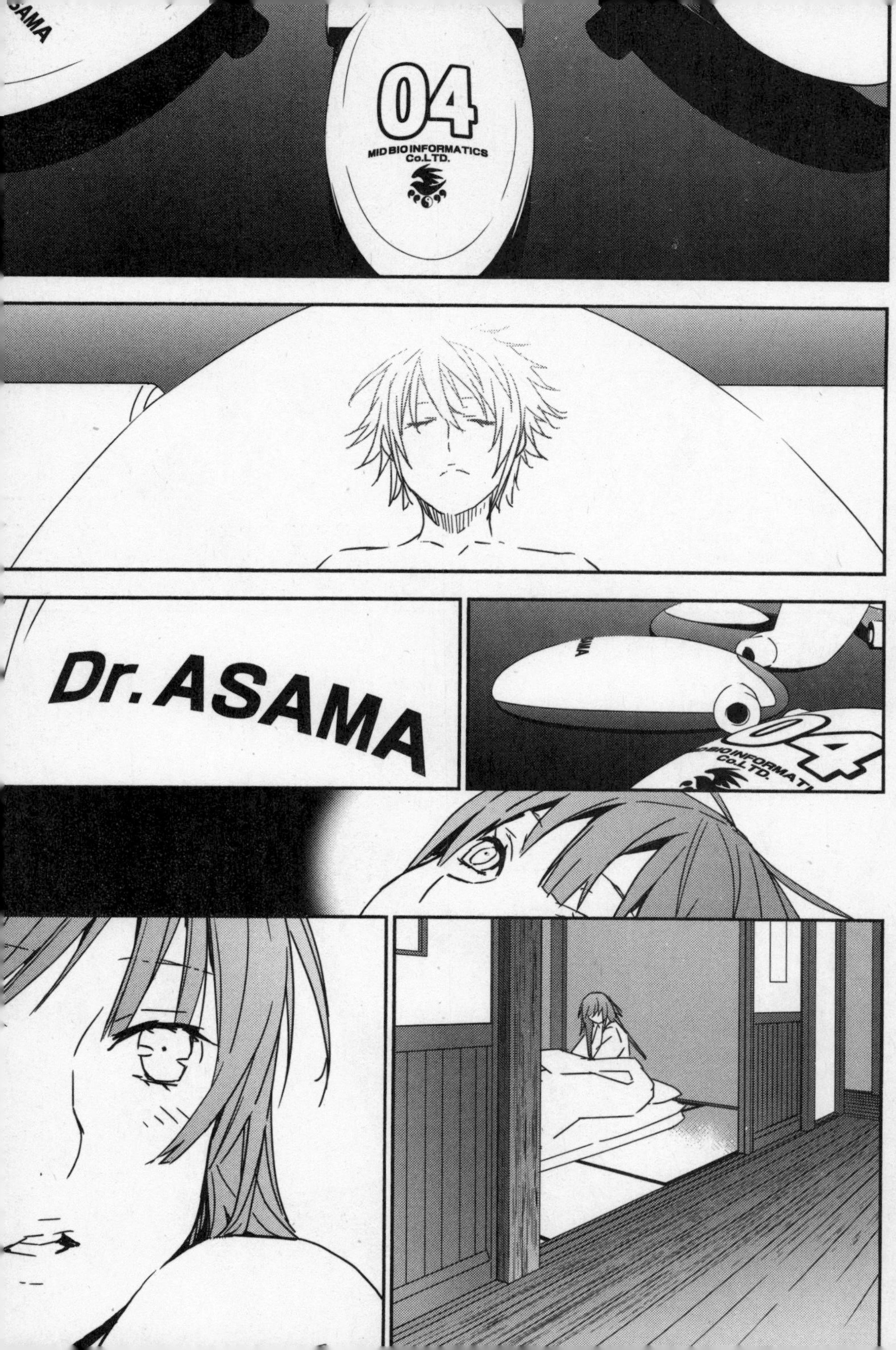
04
MID BIO INFORMATICS
Co.LTD.
Co.LTD.
Dr. ASAMA

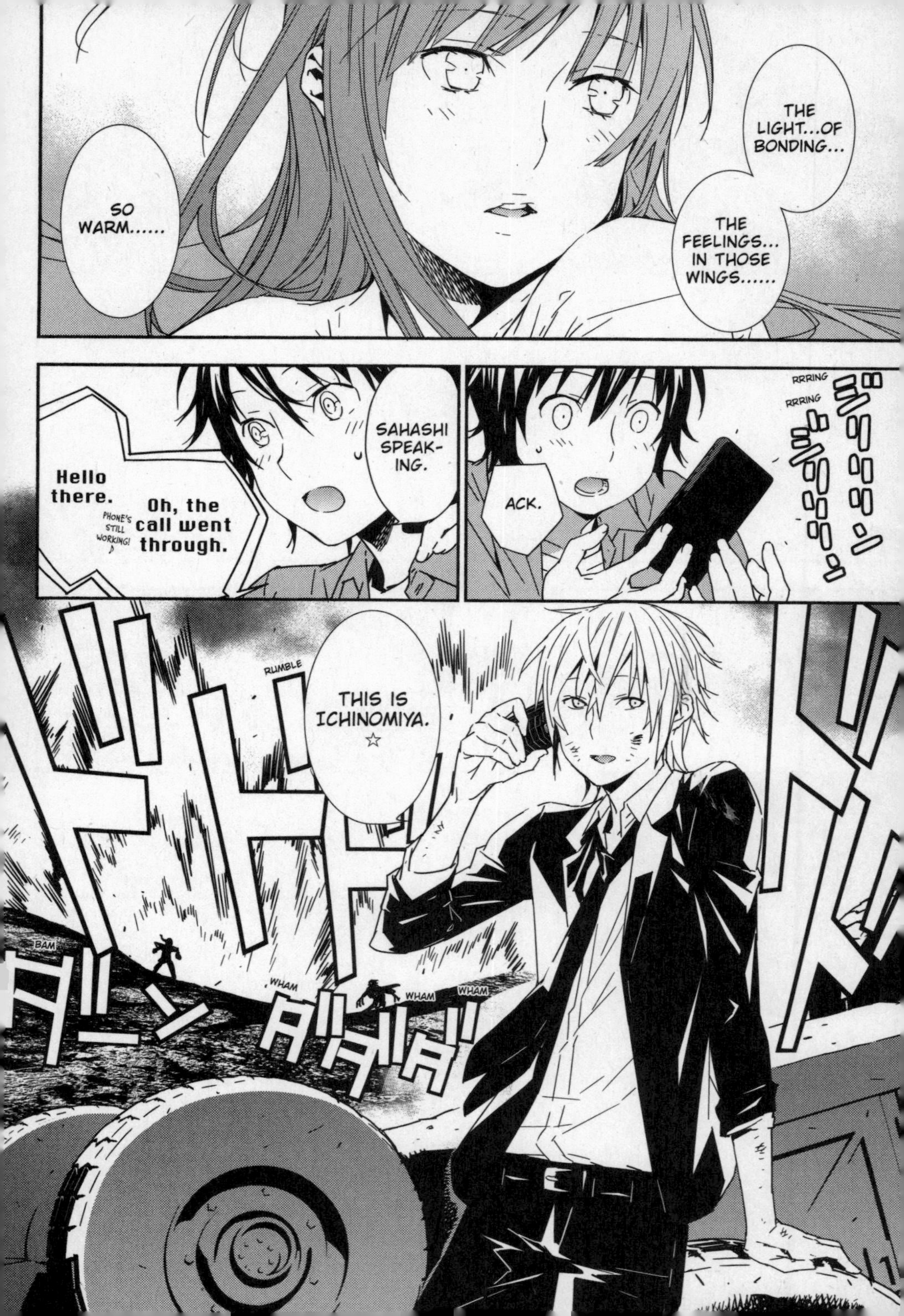
THE LIGHT...OF BONDING...
THE FEELINGS... IN THOSE WINGS......
SO WARM......
RRRING
RRRING
ACK.
SAHASHI SPEAK-ING.
Oh, the call went through.
Hello there.
PHONE'S STILL WORKING! ♪
RUMBLE
THIS IS ICHINOMIYA. ☆
WHAM
WHAM
WHAM
BAM

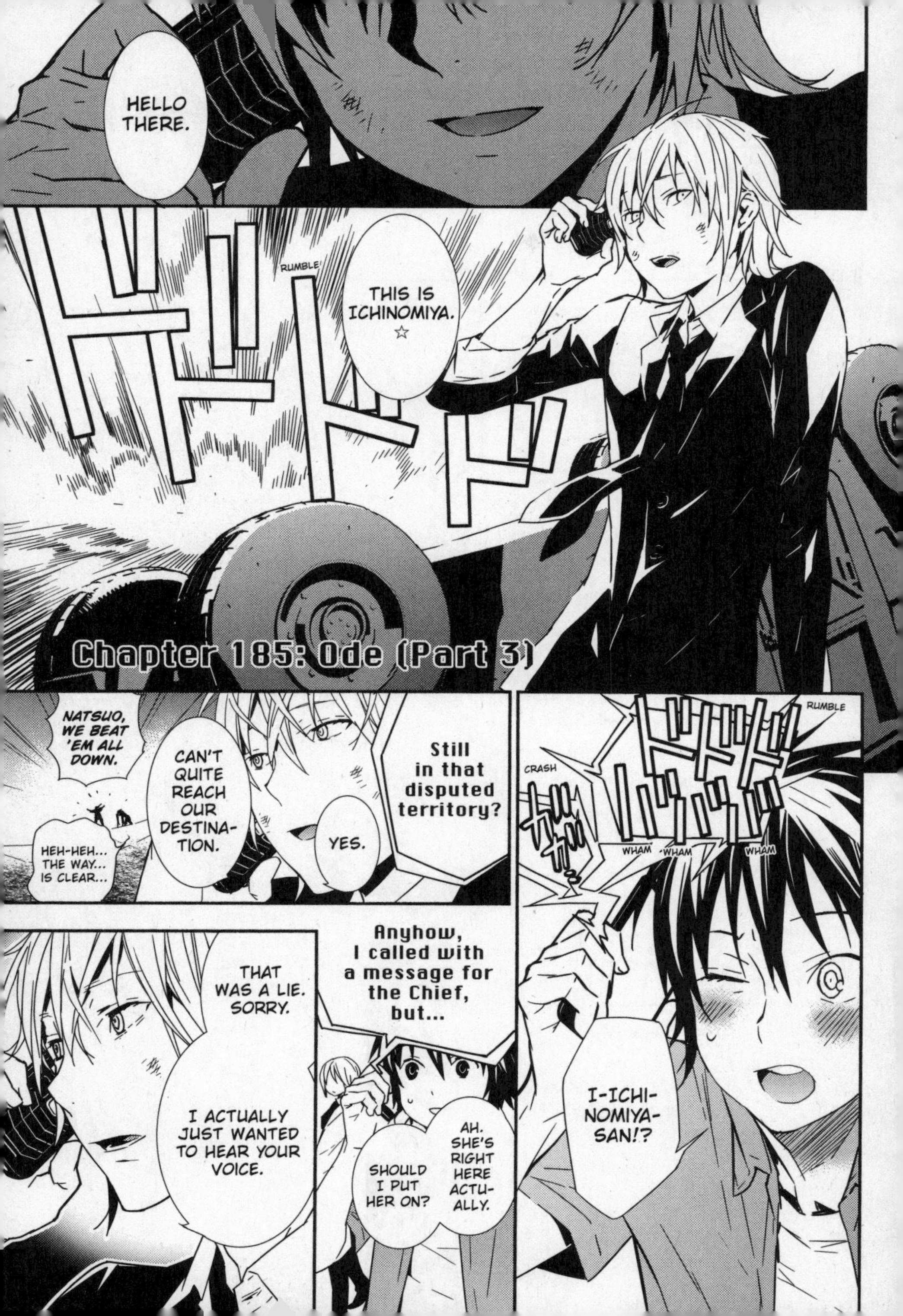
HELLO THERE.
RUMBLE
THIS IS ICHINOMIYA. ☆
Chapter 185: Ode (Part 3)
RUMBLE
CRASH
WHAM
WHAM
WHAM
I-ICHI-NOMIYA-SAN!?
Still in that disputed territory?
YES.
CAN'T QUITE REACH OUR DESTINATION.
NATSUO, WE BEAT 'EM ALL DOWN.
HEH-HEH... THE WAY... IS CLEAR...
Anyhow, I called with a message for the Chief, but...
AH. SHE'S RIGHT HERE ACTU-ALLY.
SHOULD I PUT HER ON?
THAT WAS A LIE. SORRY.
I ACTUALLY JUST WANTED TO HEAR YOUR VOICE.

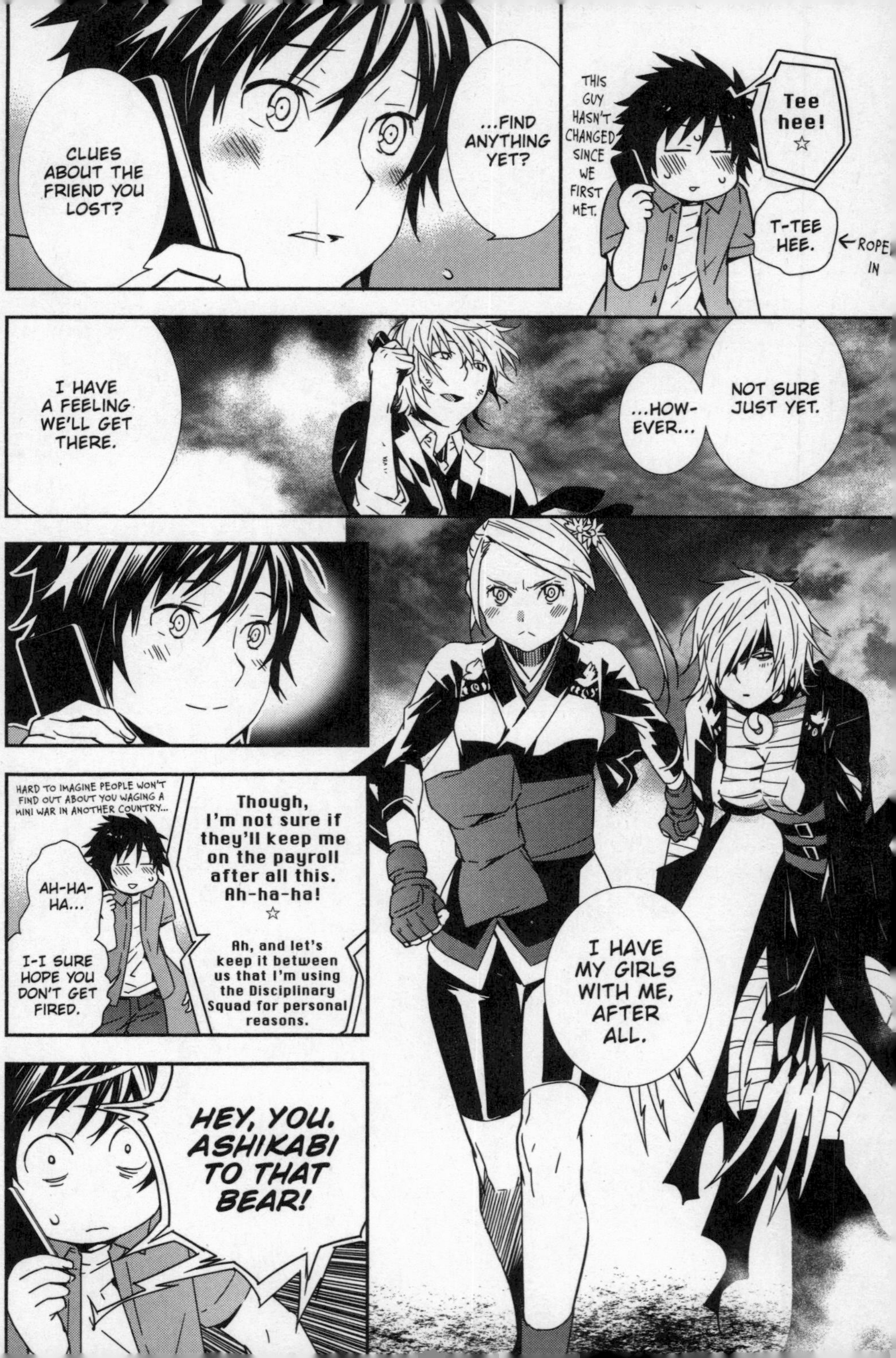
Tee hee! ☆
THIS GUY HASN'T CHANGED SINCE WE FIRST MET.
T-TEE HEE.
← ROPE IN
...FIND ANYTHING YET?
CLUES ABOUT THE FRIEND YOU LOST?
NOT SURE JUST YET.
...HOW-EVER...
I HAVE A FEELING WE'LL GET THERE.
I HAVE MY GIRLS WITH ME, AFTER ALL.
Though, I'm not sure if they'll keep me on the payroll after all this. Ah-ha-ha! ☆
Ah, and let's keep it between us that I'm using the Disciplinary Squad for personal reasons.
HARD TO IMAGINE PEOPLE WON'T FIND OUT ABOUT YOU WAGING A MINI WAR IN ANOTHER COUNTRY...
AH-HA-HA...
I-I SURE HOPE YOU DON'T GET FIRED.
HEY, YOU. ASHIKABI TO THAT BEAR!

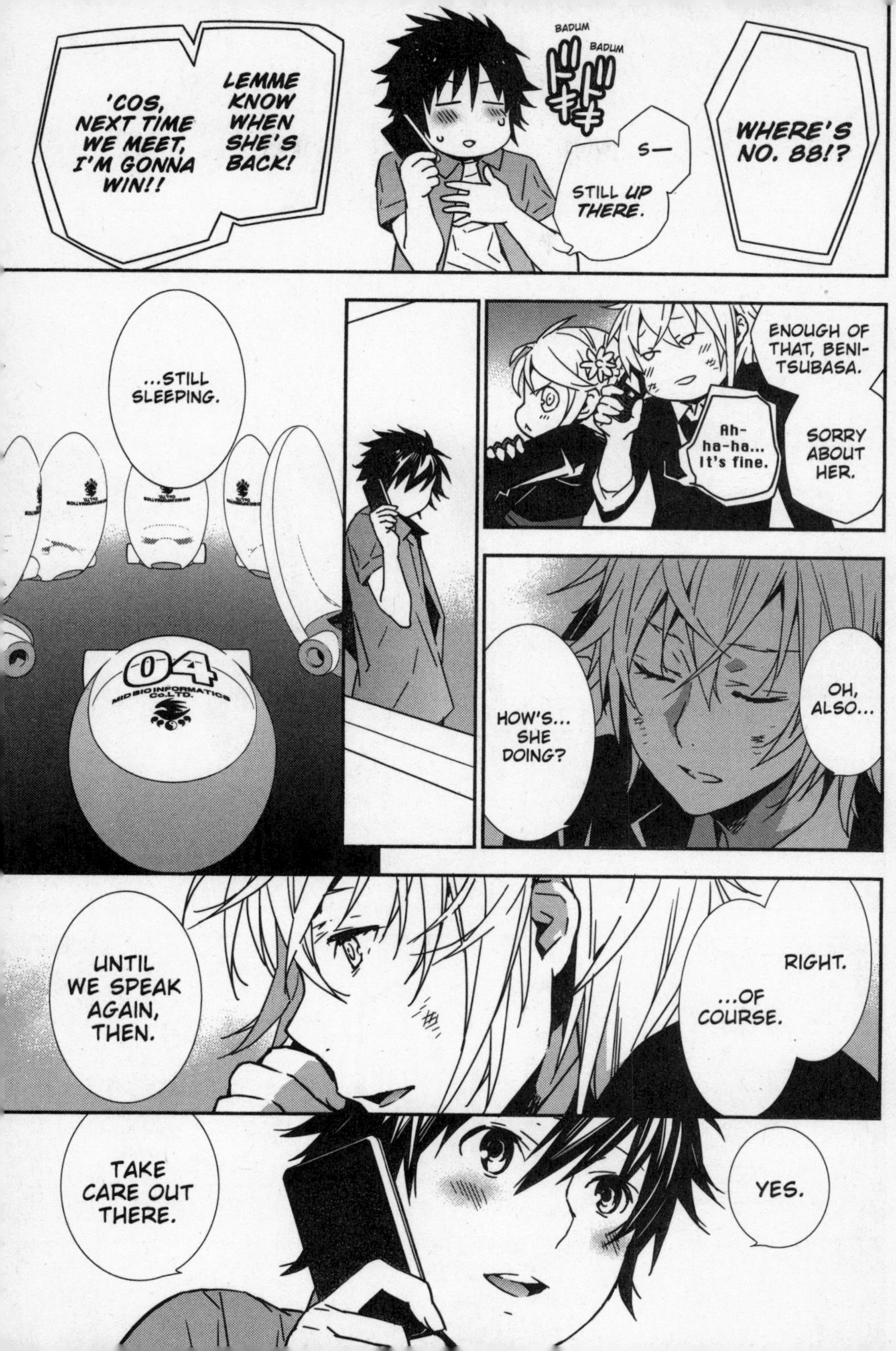
WHERE'S NO. 88!?
S—
STILL UP THERE.
BADUM BADUM
ドキドキ
LEMME KNOW WHEN SHE'S BACK!
'COS, NEXT TIME WE MEET, I'M GONNA WIN!!
ENOUGH OF THAT, BENI-TSUBASA.
SORRY ABOUT HER.
Ah-ha-ha... It's fine.
OH, ALSO...
HOW'S... SHE DOING?
...STILL SLEEPING.
04
MID BIG INFORMATICS Co.LTD.
RIGHT.
...OF COURSE.
UNTIL WE SPEAK AGAIN, THEN.
YES.
TAKE CARE OUT THERE.

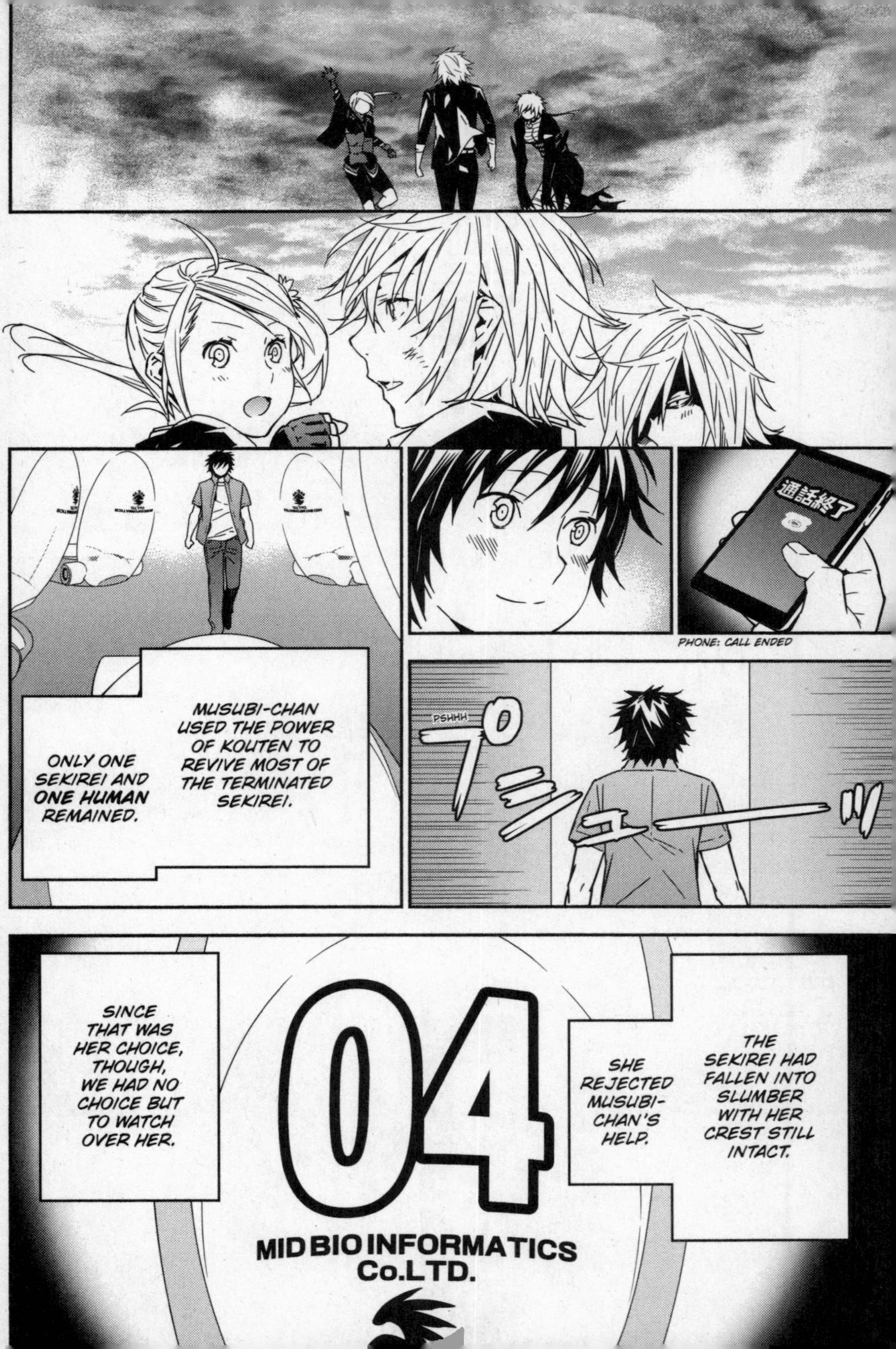
通話終了
PHONE: CALL ENDED
PSHHH
MUSUBI-CHAN USED THE POWER OF KOUTEN TO REVIVE MOST OF THE TERMINATED SEKIREI.
ONLY ONE SEKIREI AND ONE HUMAN REMAINED.
THE SEKIREI HAD FALLEN INTO SLUMBER WITH HER CREST STILL INTACT.
SHE REJECTED MUSUBI-CHAN'S HELP.
04
MID BIO INFORMATICS Co.LTD.
SINCE THAT WAS HER CHOICE, THOUGH, WE HAD NO CHOICE BUT TO WATCH OVER HER.

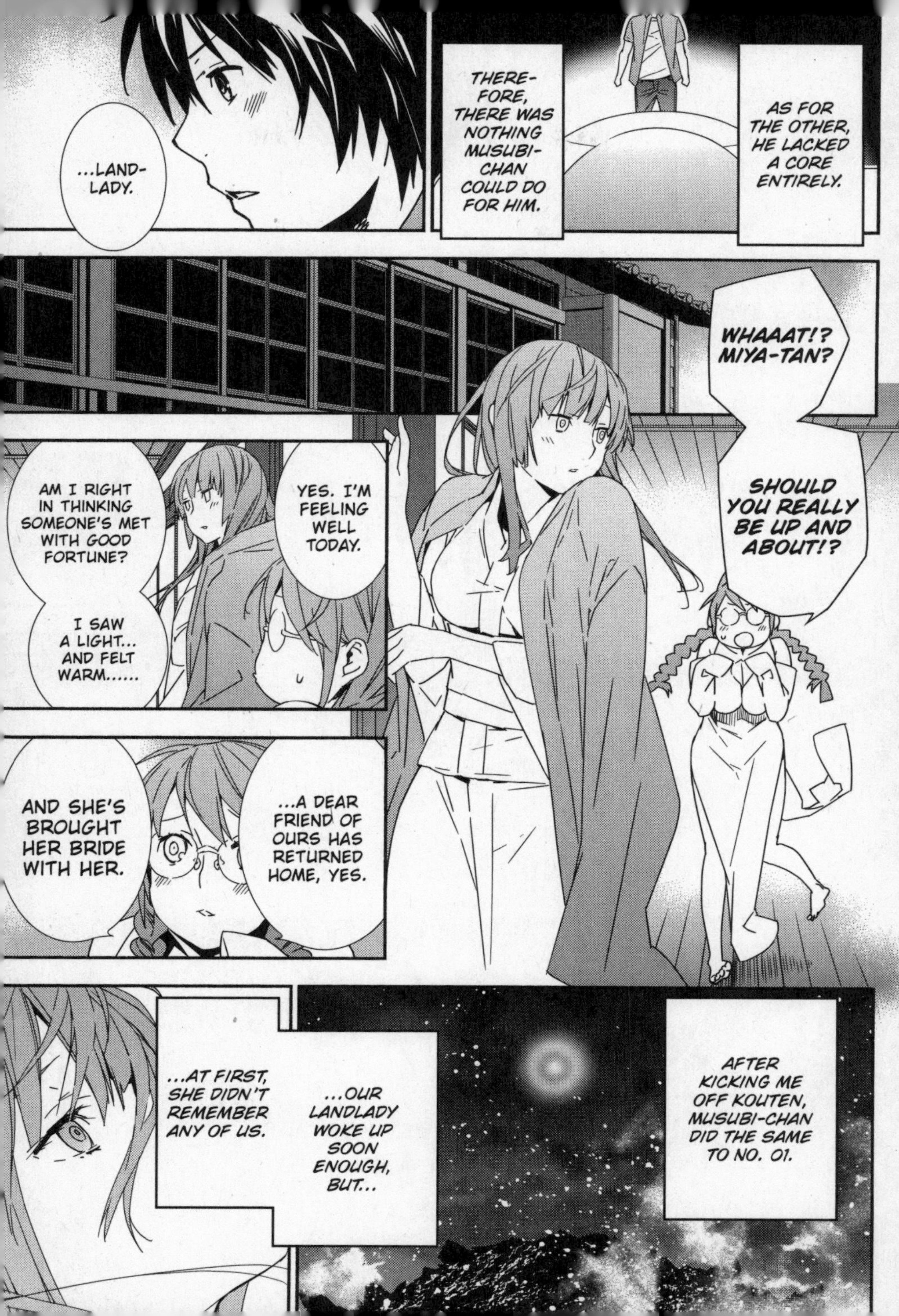
AS FOR THE OTHER, HE LACKED A CORE ENTIRELY.
THERE-FORE, THERE WAS NOTHING MUSUBI-CHAN COULD DO FOR HIM.
...LAND-LADY.
WHAAAT!? MIYA-TAN?
SHOULD YOU REALLY BE UP AND ABOUT!?
YES. I'M FEELING WELL TODAY.
AM I RIGHT IN THINKING SOMEONE'S MET WITH GOOD FORTUNE?
I SAW A LIGHT... AND FELT WARM......
...A DEAR FRIEND OF OURS HAS RETURNED HOME, YES.
AND SHE'S BROUGHT HER BRIDE WITH HER.
AFTER KICKING ME OFF KOUTEN, MUSUBI-CHAN DID THE SAME TO NO. 01.
...OUR LANDLADY WOKE UP SOON ENOUGH, BUT...
...AT FIRST, SHE DIDN'T REMEMBER ANY OF US.

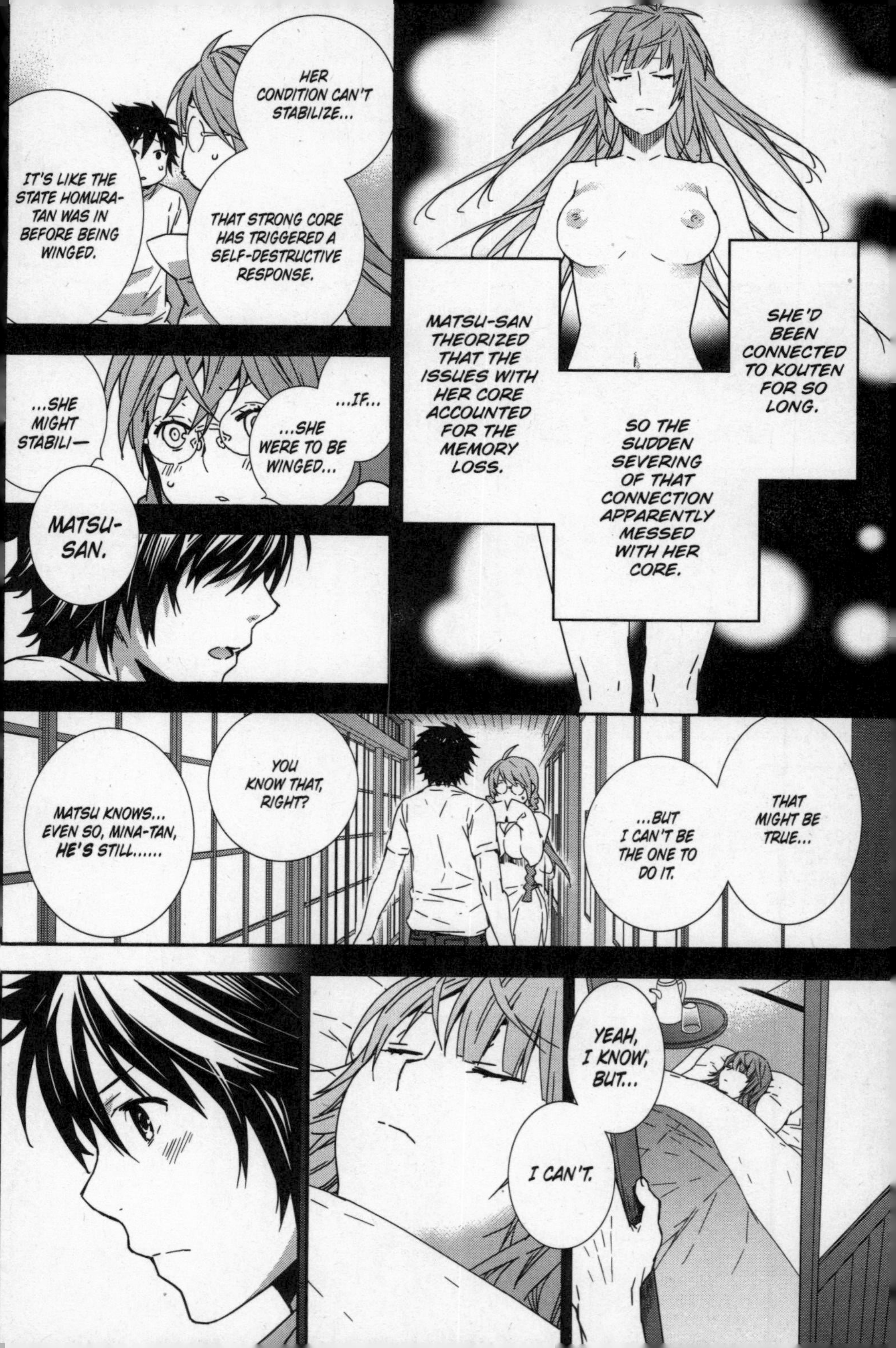
SHE'D BEEN CONNECTED TO KOUTEN FOR SO LONG.
SO THE SUDDEN SEVERING OF THAT CONNECTION APPARENTLY MESSED WITH HER CORE.
MATSU-SAN THEORIZED THAT THE ISSUES WITH HER CORE ACCOUNTED FOR THE MEMORY LOSS.
HER CONDITION CAN'T STABILIZE...
THAT STRONG CORE HAS TRIGGERED A SELF-DESTRUCTIVE RESPONSE.
IT'S LIKE THE STATE HOMURA-TAN WAS IN BEFORE BEING WINGED.
...IF...
...SHE WERE TO BE WINGED...
...SHE MIGHT STABILI—
MATSU-SAN.
THAT MIGHT BE TRUE...
...BUT I CAN'T BE THE ONE TO DO IT.
YOU KNOW THAT, RIGHT?
MATSU KNOWS... EVEN SO, MINA-TAN, HE'S STILL......
YEAH, I KNOW, BUT...
I CAN'T.

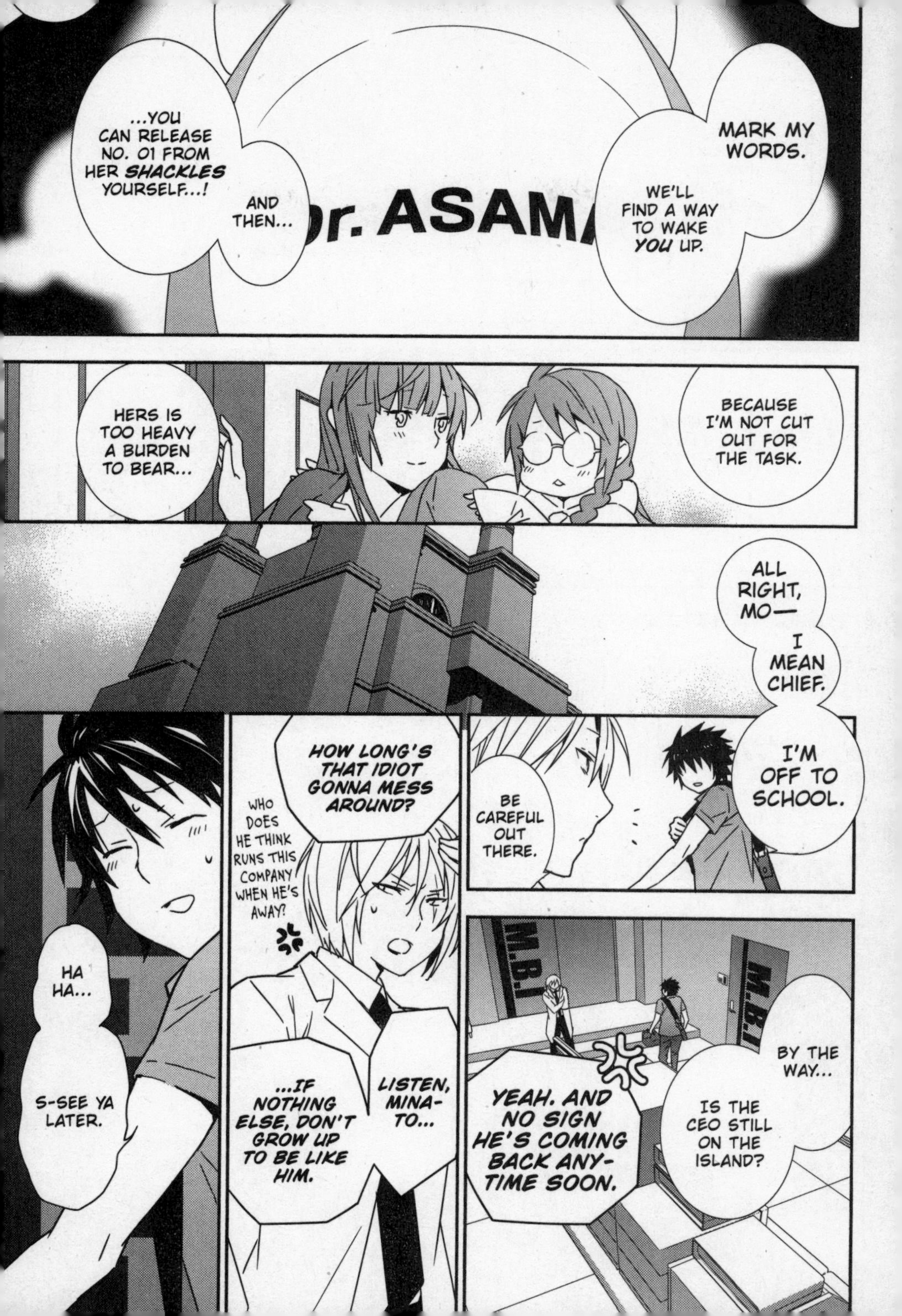
MARK MY WORDS.
WE'LL FIND A WAY TO WAKE *YOU* UP.
AND THEN...
...YOU CAN RELEASE NO. 01 FROM HER *SHACKLES* YOURSELF...!
Dr. ASAMA
BECAUSE I'M NOT CUT OUT FOR THE TASK.
HERS IS TOO HEAVY A BURDEN TO BEAR...
ALL RIGHT, MO—
I MEAN CHIEF.
I'M OFF TO SCHOOL.
BE CAREFUL OUT THERE.
BY THE WAY...
IS THE CEO STILL ON THE ISLAND?
YEAH. AND NO SIGN HE'S COMING BACK ANY-TIME SOON.
HOW LONG'S THAT IDIOT GONNA MESS AROUND?
WHO DOES HE THINK RUNS THIS COMPANY WHEN HE'S AWAY?
LISTEN, MINA-TO...
...IF NOTHING ELSE, DON'T GROW UP TO BE LIKE HIM.
HA HA...
S-SEE YA LATER.

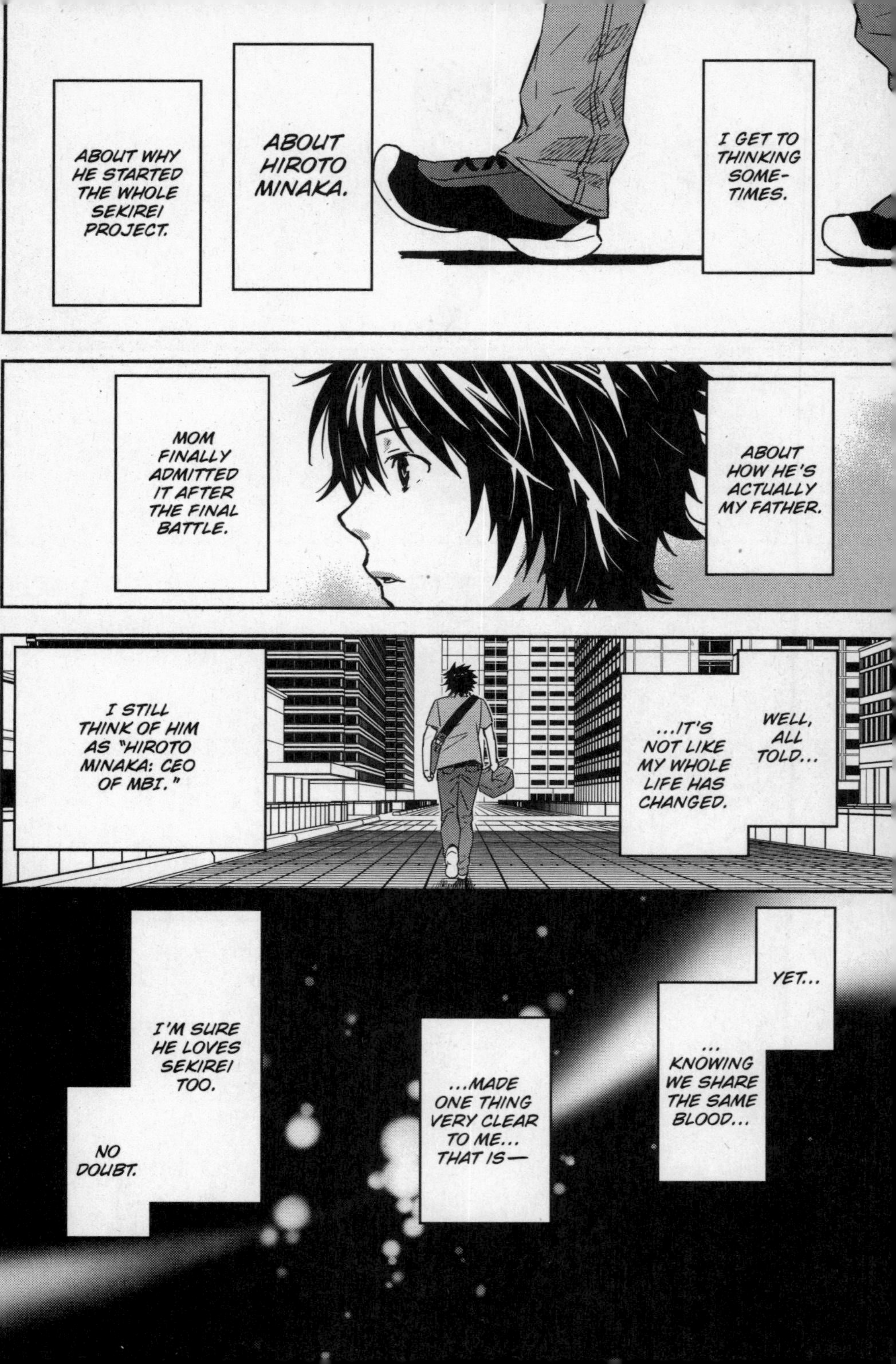
I GET TO THINKING SOME-TIMES.
ABOUT HIROTO MINAKA.
ABOUT WHY HE STARTED THE WHOLE SEKIREI PROJECT.
ABOUT HOW HE'S ACTUALLY MY FATHER.
MOM FINALLY ADMITTED IT AFTER THE FINAL BATTLE.
WELL, ALL TOLD...
...IT'S NOT LIKE MY WHOLE LIFE HAS CHANGED.
I STILL THINK OF HIM AS "HIROTO MINAKA: CEO OF MBI."
YET...
...KNOWING WE SHARE THE SAME BLOOD...
...MADE ONE THING VERY CLEAR TO ME... THAT IS—
I'M SURE HE LOVES SEKIREI TOO.
NO DOUBT.

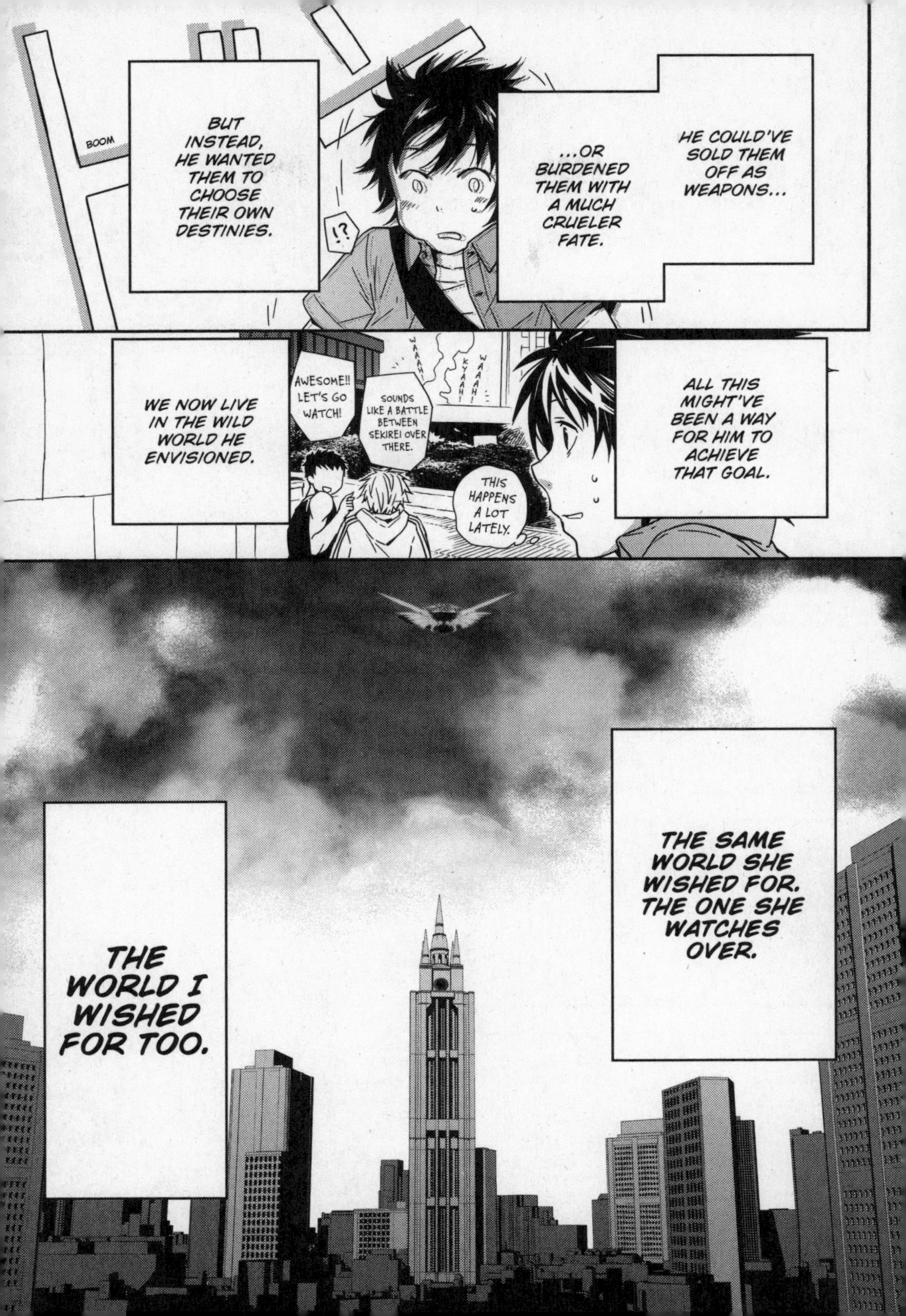
HE COULD'VE SOLD THEM OFF AS WEAPONS...
...OR BURDENED THEM WITH A MUCH CRUELER FATE.
BUT INSTEAD, HE WANTED THEM TO CHOOSE THEIR OWN DESTINIES.
BOOM
!?
ALL THIS MIGHT'VE BEEN A WAY FOR HIM TO ACHIEVE THAT GOAL.
THIS HAPPENS A LOT LATELY.
WAAAH!
KYAAAH!
WAAAH!
SOUNDS LIKE A BATTLE BETWEEN SEKIREI OVER THERE.
AWESOME!! LET'S GO WATCH!
WE NOW LIVE IN THE WILD WORLD HE ENVISIONED.
THE SAME WORLD SHE WISHED FOR. THE ONE SHE WATCHES OVER.
THE WORLD I WISHED FOR TOO.

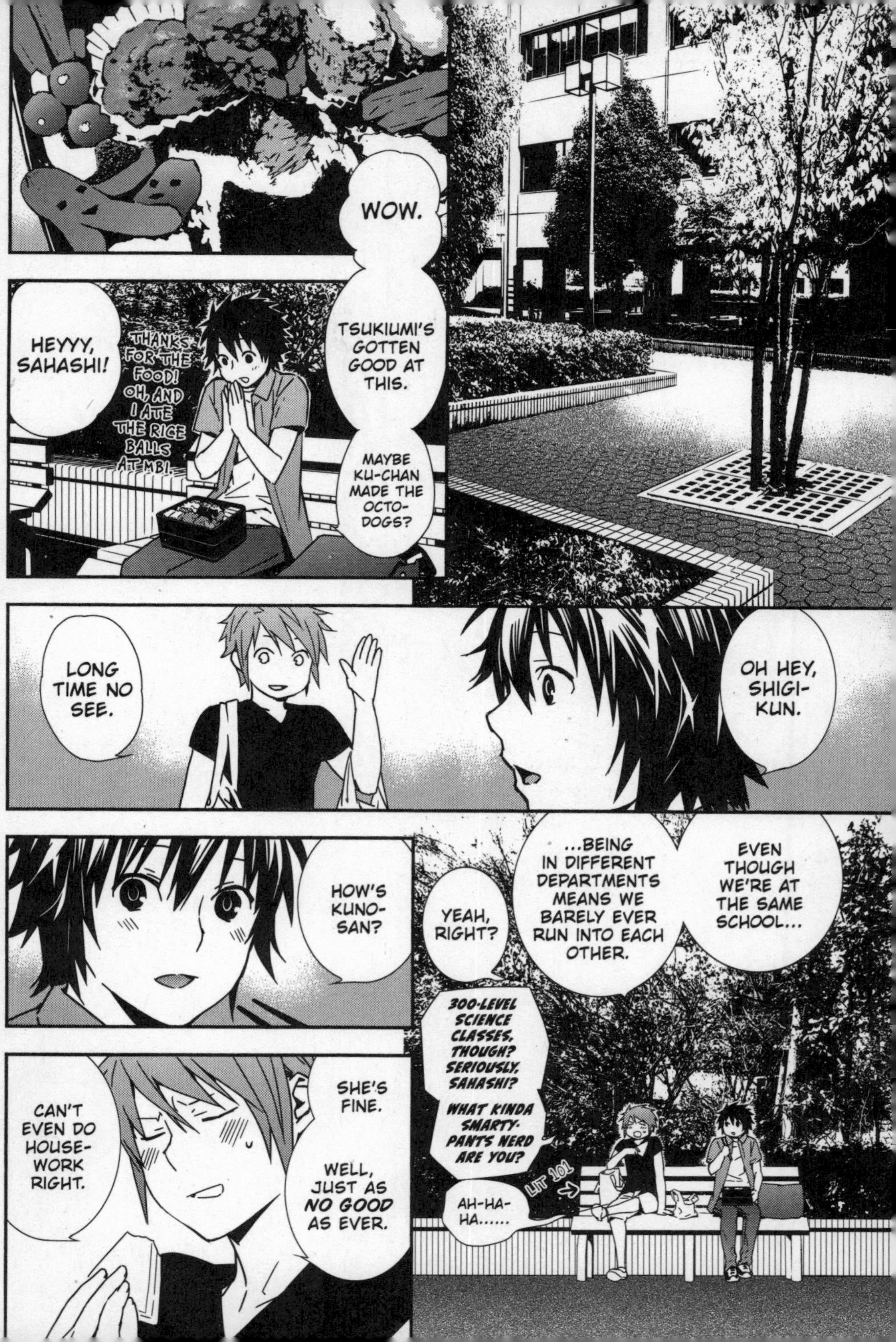
WOW.
TSUKIUMI'S GOTTEN GOOD AT THIS.
MAYBE KU-CHAN MADE THE OCTO-DOGS?
HEYYY, SAHASHI!
THANKS FOR THE FOOD! OH, AND I ATE THE RICE BALLS AT MBI.
OH HEY, SHIGI-KUN.
LONG TIME NO SEE.
EVEN THOUGH WE'RE AT THE SAME SCHOOL...
...BEING IN DIFFERENT DEPARTMENTS MEANS WE BARELY EVER RUN INTO EACH OTHER.
YEAH, RIGHT?
300-LEVEL SCIENCE CLASSES, THOUGH? SERIOUSLY, SAHASHI?
WHAT KINDA SMARTY-PANTS NERD ARE YOU?
AH-HA-HA......
LIT 101
HOW'S KUNO-SAN?
SHE'S FINE.
WELL, JUST AS NO GOOD AS EVER.
CAN'T EVEN DO HOUSE-WORK RIGHT.

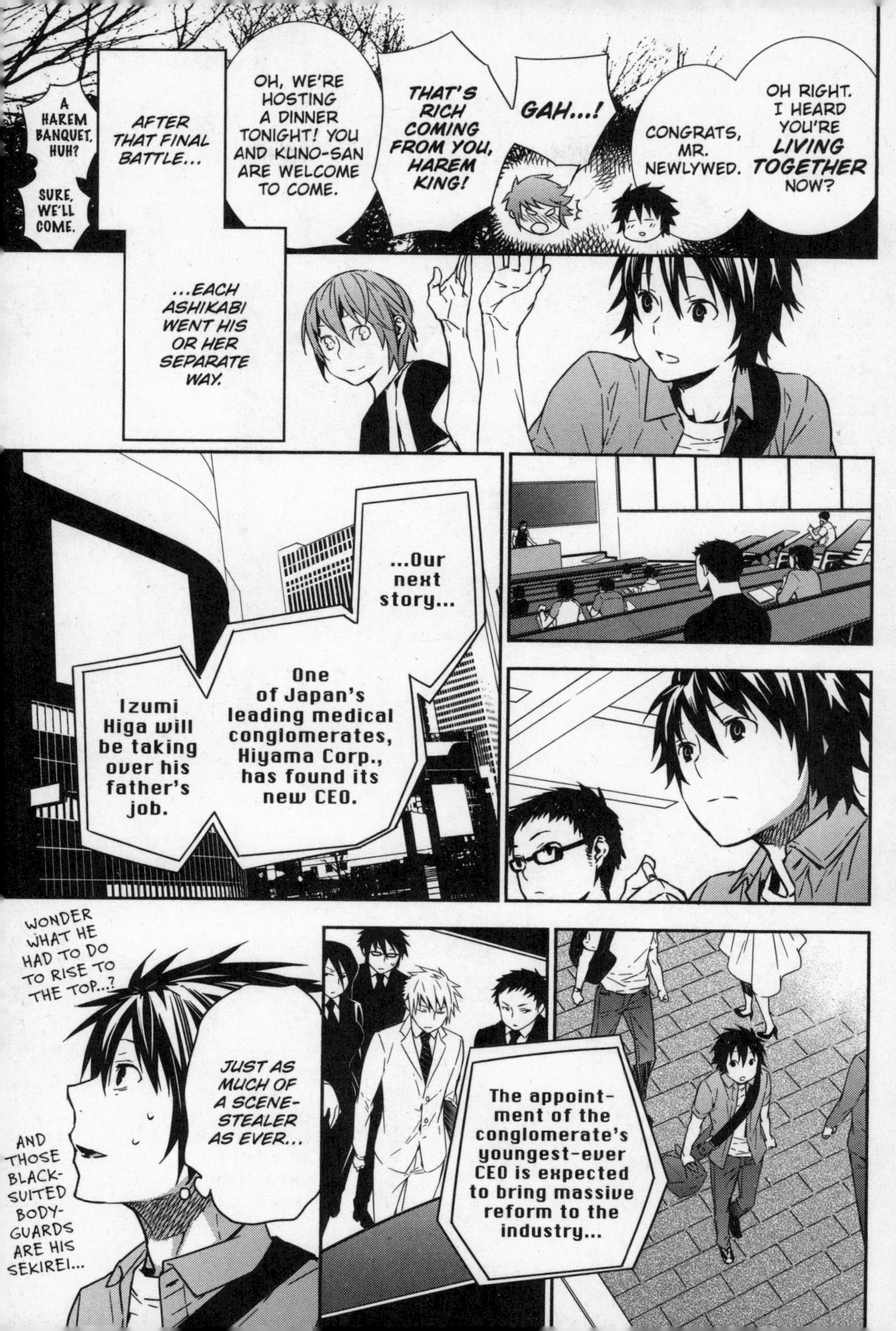
OH RIGHT. I HEARD YOU'RE LIVING TOGETHER NOW?
CONGRATS, MR. NEWLYWED.
GAH...!
THAT'S RICH COMING FROM YOU, HAREM KING!
OH, WE'RE HOSTING A DINNER TONIGHT! YOU AND KUNO-SAN ARE WELCOME TO COME.
AFTER THAT FINAL BATTLE...
A HAREM BANQUET, HUH?
SURE, WE'LL COME.
...EACH ASHIKABI WENT HIS OR HER SEPARATE WAY.
...Our next story...
One of Japan's leading medical conglomerates, Hiyama Corp., has found its new CEO.
Izumi Higa will be taking over his father's job.
The appoint-ment of the conglomerate's youngest-ever CEO is expected to bring massive reform to the industry...
JUST AS MUCH OF A SCENE-STEALER AS EVER...
WONDER WHAT HE HAD TO DO TO RISE TO THE TOP...?
AND THOSE BLACK-SUITED BODY-GUARDS ARE HIS SEKIREI...

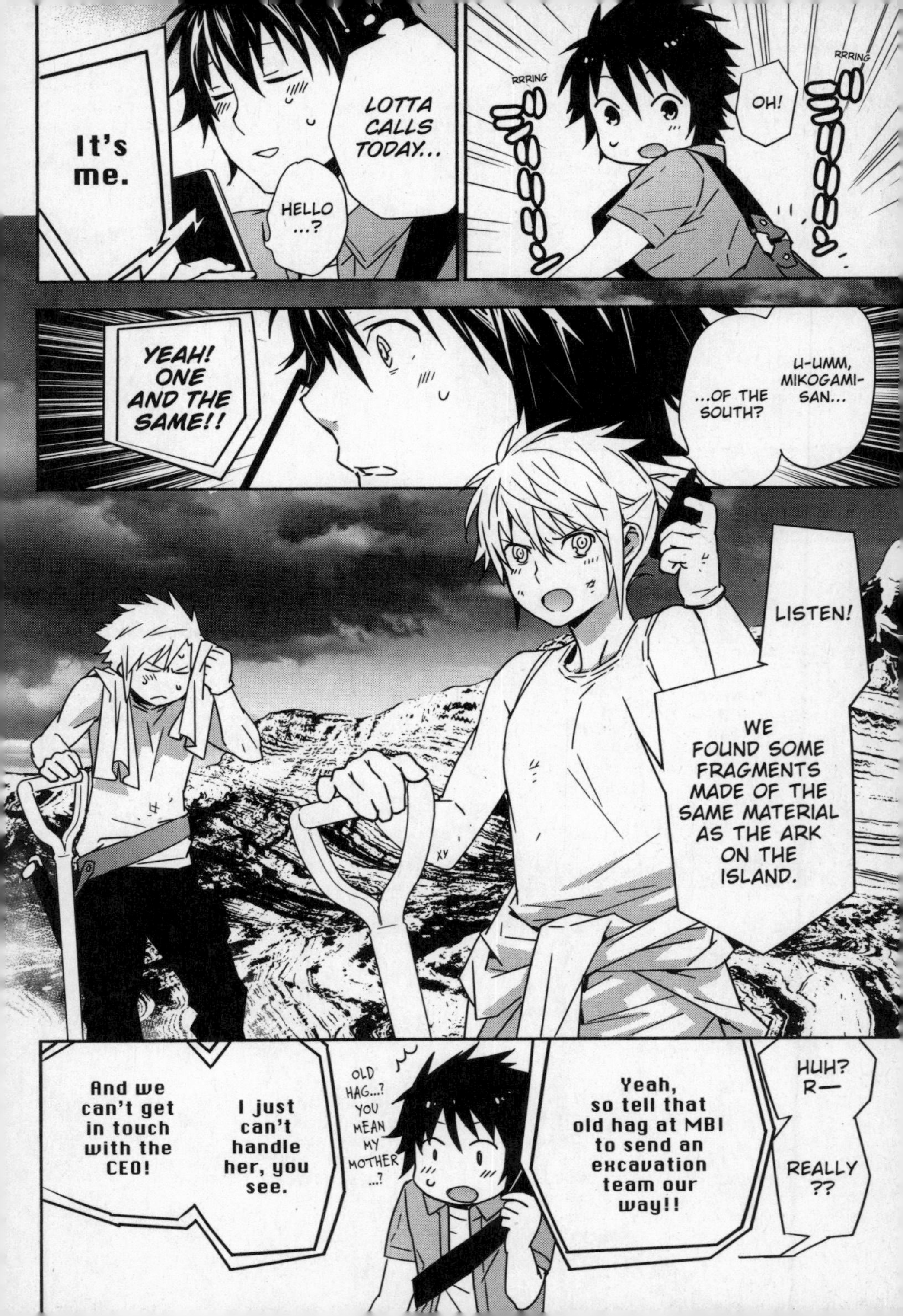
RRRING
OH!
RRRING
LOTTA CALLS TODAY...
HELLO ...?
It's me.
U-UMM, MIKOGAMI-SAN...
...OF THE SOUTH?
YEAH! ONE AND THE SAME!!
LISTEN!
WE FOUND SOME FRAGMENTS MADE OF THE SAME MATERIAL AS THE ARK ON THE ISLAND.
HUH? R—
REALLY ??
Yeah, so tell that old hag at MBI to send an excavation team our way!!
OLD HAG...? YOU MEAN MY MOTHER ...?
I just can't handle her, you see.
And we can't get in touch with the CEO!

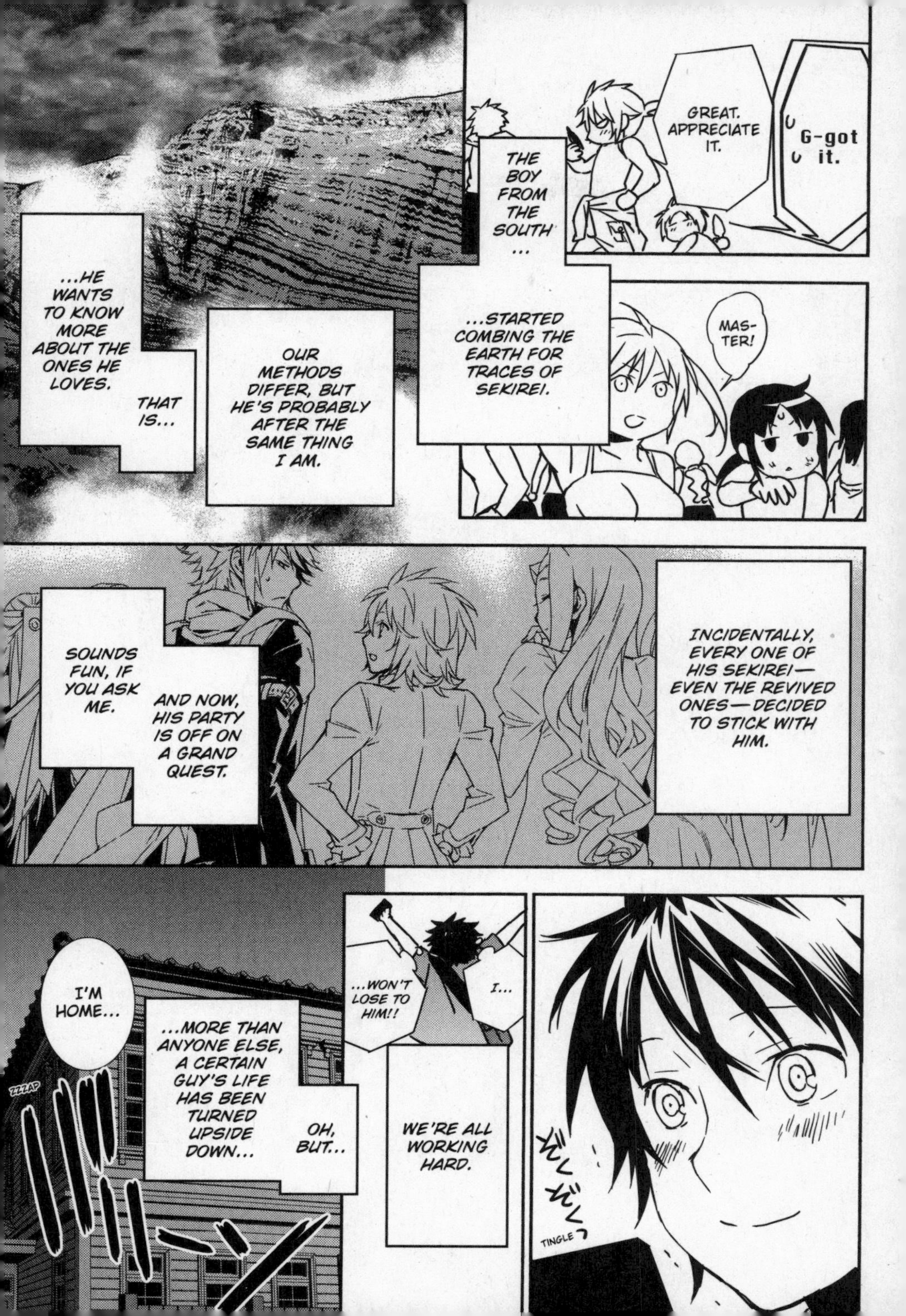
G-got it.
GREAT. APPRECIATE IT.
THE BOY FROM THE SOUTH...
...STARTED COMBING THE EARTH FOR TRACES OF SEKIREI.
MAS-TER!
OUR METHODS DIFFER, BUT HE'S PROBABLY AFTER THE SAME THING I AM.
...HE WANTS TO KNOW MORE ABOUT THE ONES HE LOVES.
THAT IS...
INCIDENTALLY, EVERY ONE OF HIS SEKIREI—EVEN THE REVIVED ONES—DECIDED TO STICK WITH HIM.
AND NOW, HIS PARTY IS OFF ON A GRAND QUEST.
SOUNDS FUN, IF YOU ASK ME.
TINGLE
I...
...WON'T LOSE TO HIM!!
WE'RE ALL WORKING HARD.
OH, BUT...
...MORE THAN ANYONE ELSE, A CERTAIN GUY'S LIFE HAS BEEN TURNED UPSIDE DOWN...
I'M HOME...
ZZZAP

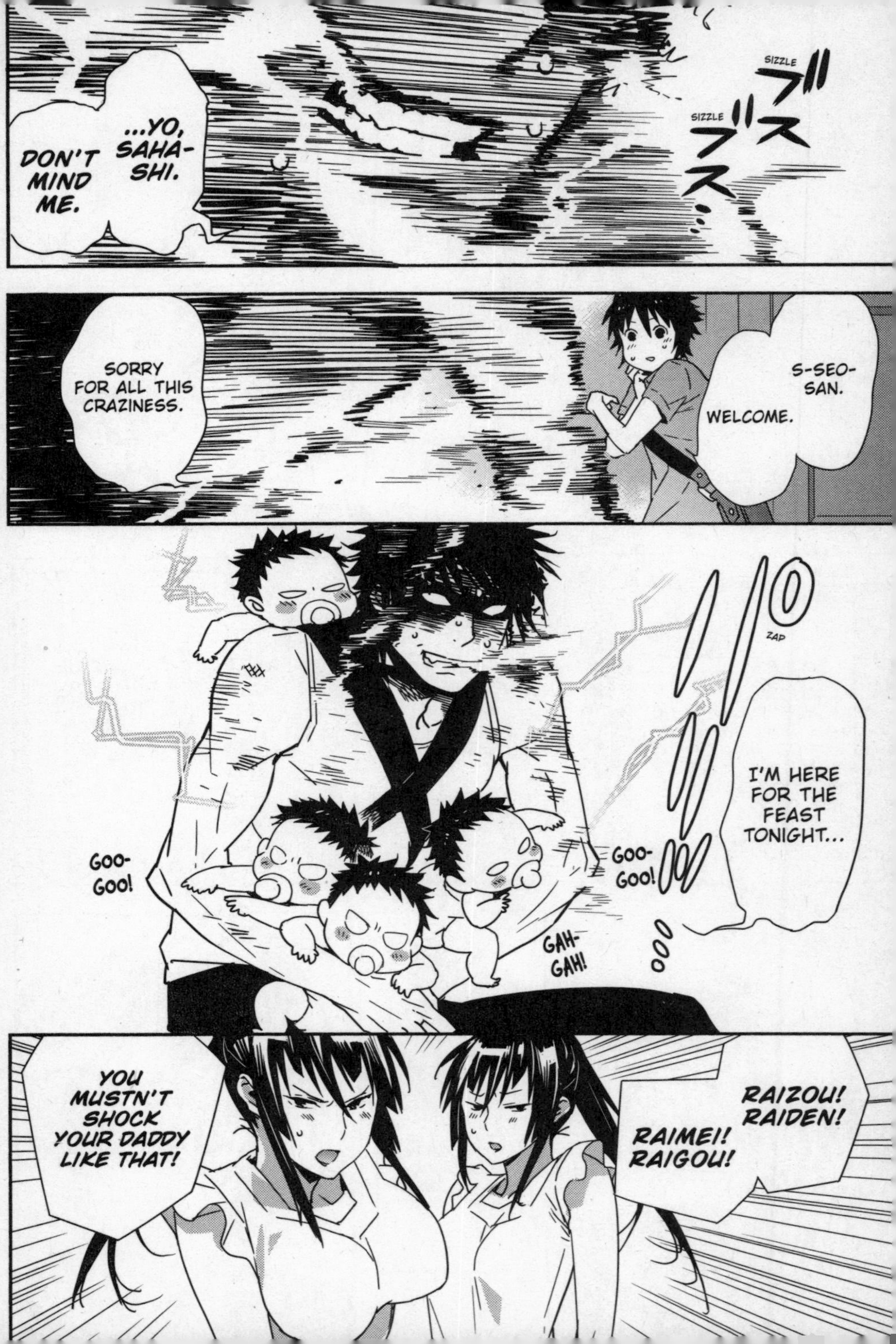
SIZZLE
ブス
SIZZLE
ブス
...YO, SAHA-SHI.
DON'T MIND ME.
S-SEO-SAN.
WELCOME.
SORRY FOR ALL THIS CRAZINESS.
ZAP
I'M HERE FOR THE FEAST TONIGHT...
GOO-GOO!
GAH-GAH!
GOO-GOO!
RAIZOU! RAIDEN!
RAIMEI! RAIGOU!
YOU MUSTN'T SHOCK YOUR DADDY LIKE THAT!

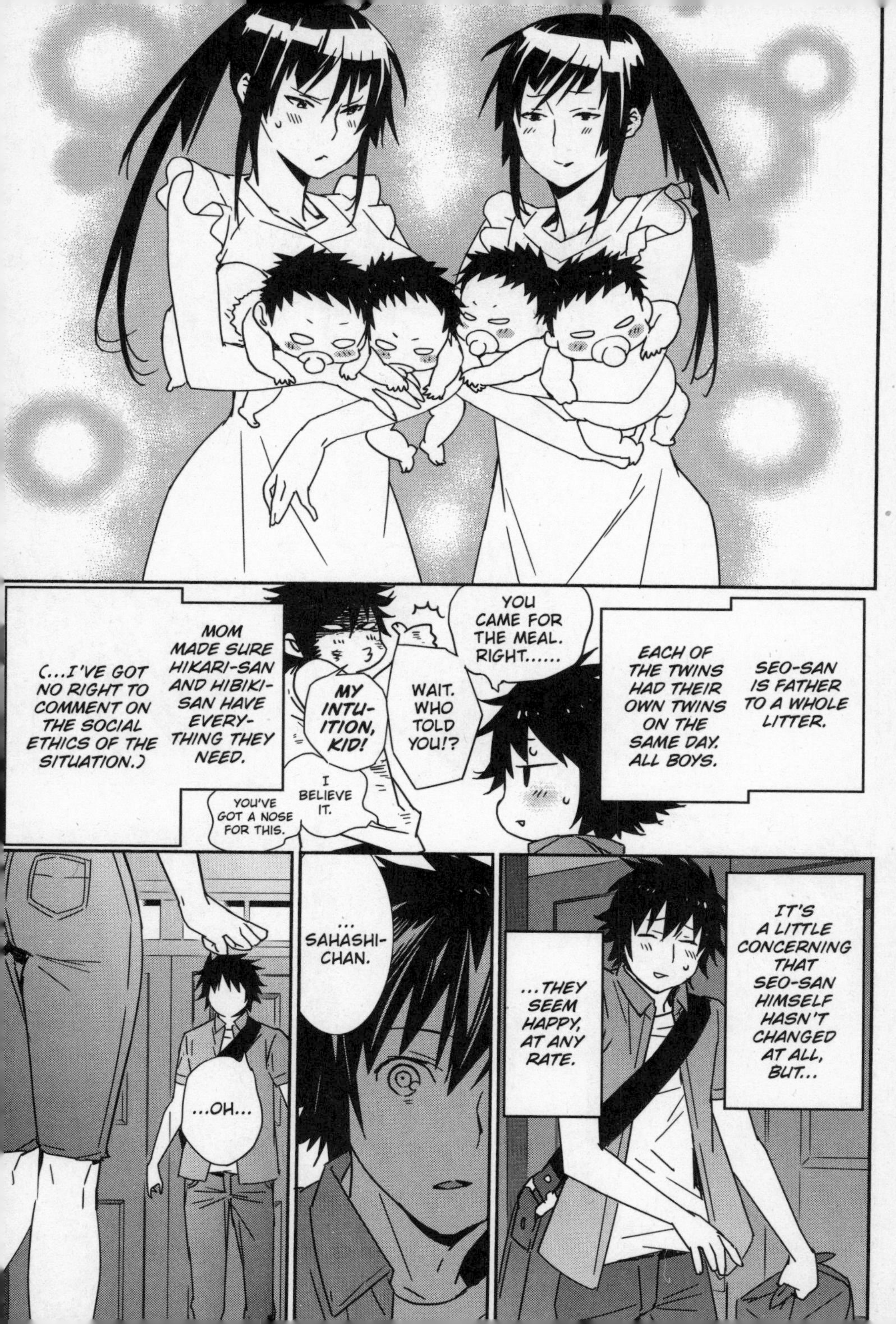
SEO-SAN IS FATHER TO A WHOLE LITTER.
EACH OF THE TWINS HAD THEIR OWN TWINS ON THE SAME DAY. ALL BOYS.
YOU CAME FOR THE MEAL. RIGHT......
WAIT. WHO TOLD YOU!?
MY INTUITION, KID!
I BELIEVE IT.
YOU'VE GOT A NOSE FOR THIS.
MOM MADE SURE HIKARI-SAN AND HIBIKI-SAN HAVE EVERY-THING THEY NEED.
(...I'VE GOT NO RIGHT TO COMMENT ON THE SOCIAL ETHICS OF THE SITUATION.)
IT'S A LITTLE CONCERNING THAT SEO-SAN HIMSELF HASN'T CHANGED AT ALL, BUT...
...THEY SEEM HAPPY, AT ANY RATE.
... SAHASHI-CHAN.
...OH...

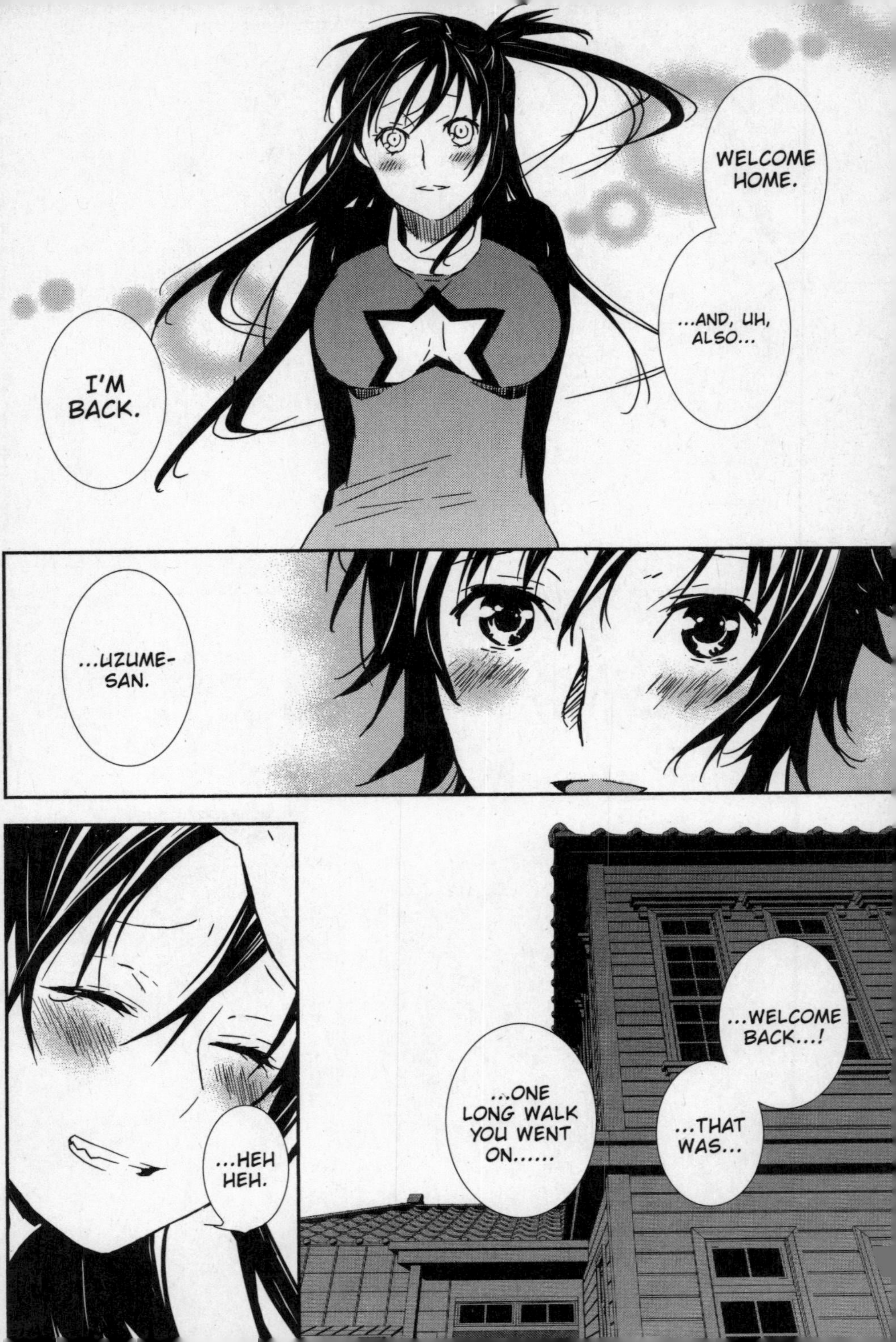
WELCOME HOME.
...AND, UH, ALSO...
I'M BACK.
...UZUME-SAN.
...WELCOME BACK...!
...THAT WAS...
...ONE LONG WALK YOU WENT ON......
...HEH HEH.

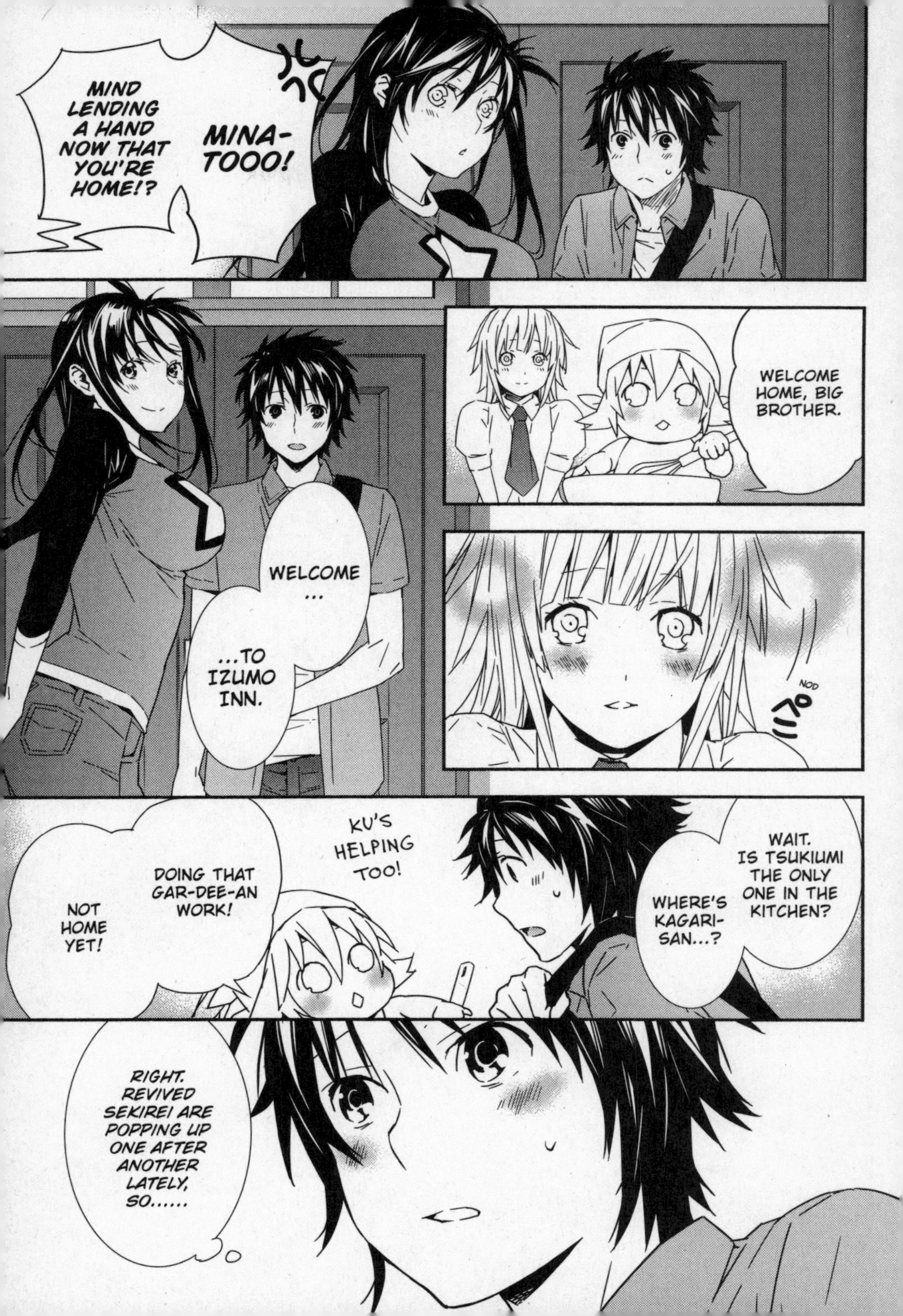
MINA-TOOO!
MIND LENDING A HAND NOW THAT YOU'RE HOME!?
WELCOME HOME, BIG BROTHER.
NOD
WELCOME ...
...TO IZUMO INN.
WAIT. IS TSUKIUMI THE ONLY ONE IN THE KITCHEN?
WHERE'S KAGARI-SAN...?
KU'S HELPING TOO!
DOING THAT GAR-DEE-AN WORK!
NOT HOME YET!
RIGHT. REVIVED SEKIREI ARE POPPING UP ONE AFTER ANOTHER LATELY, SO......

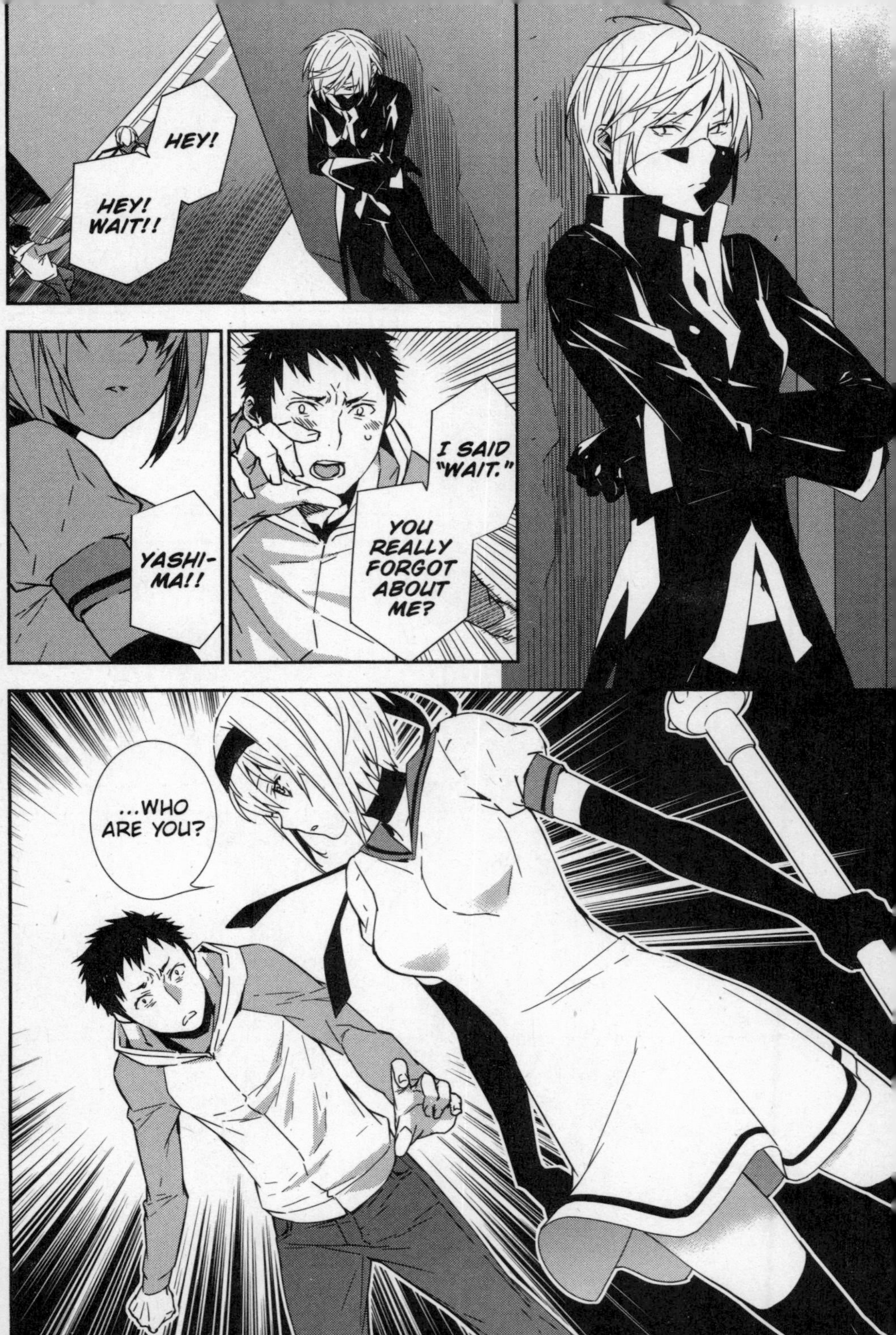
HEY!
HEY! WAIT!!
I SAID "WAIT."
YOU REALLY FORGOT ABOUT ME?
YASHIMA!!
...WHO ARE YOU?

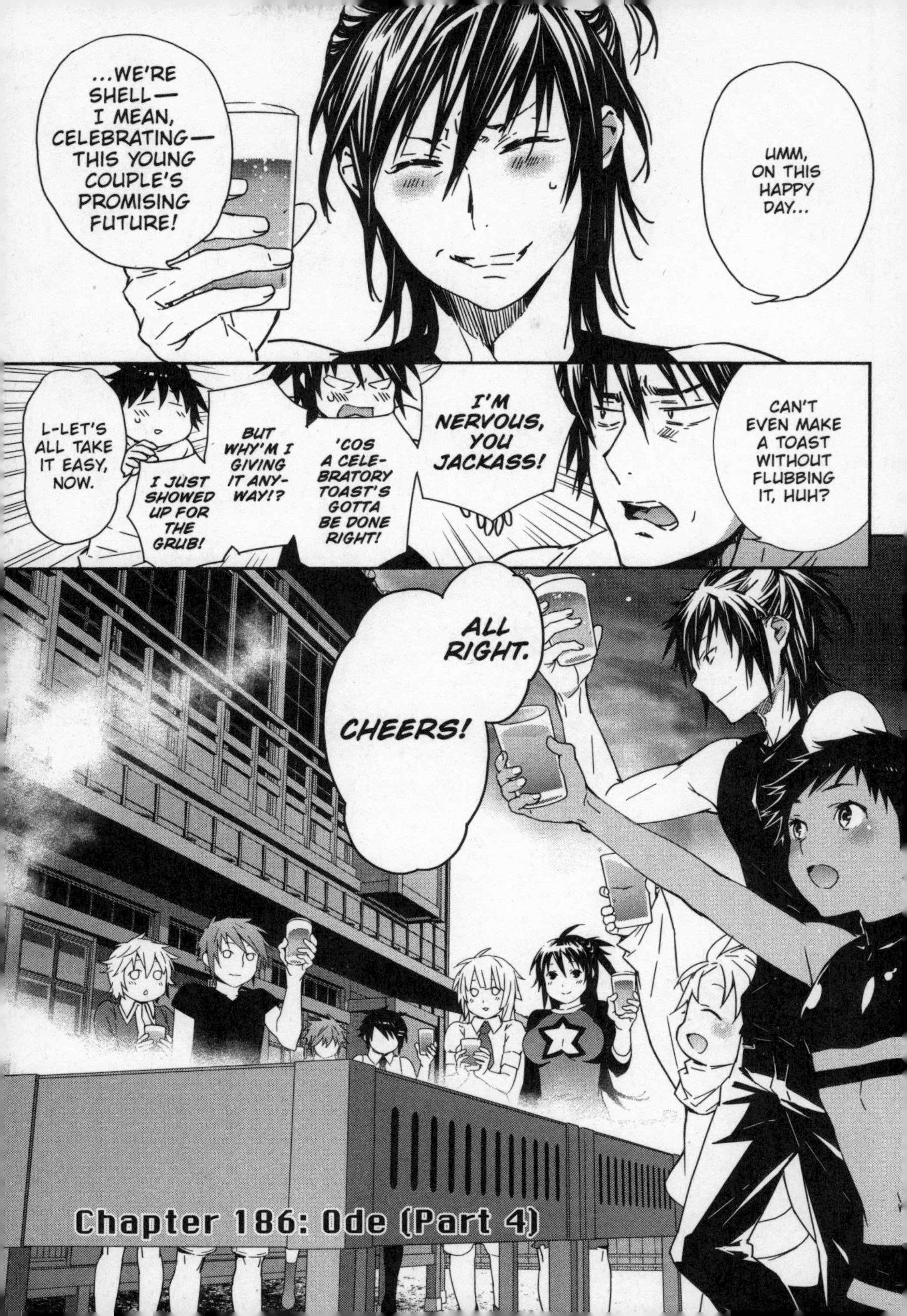
UMM, ON THIS HAPPY DAY...
...WE'RE SHELL— I MEAN, CELEBRATING— THIS YOUNG COUPLE'S PROMISING FUTURE!
CAN'T EVEN MAKE A TOAST WITHOUT FLUBBING IT, HUH?
I'M NERVOUS, YOU JACKASS!
'COS A CELEBRATORY TOAST'S GOTTA BE DONE RIGHT!
BUT WHY'M I GIVING IT ANYWAY!?
I JUST SHOWED UP FOR THE GRUB!
L-LET'S ALL TAKE IT EASY, NOW.
ALL RIGHT.
CHEERS!
Chapter 186: Ode (Part 4)

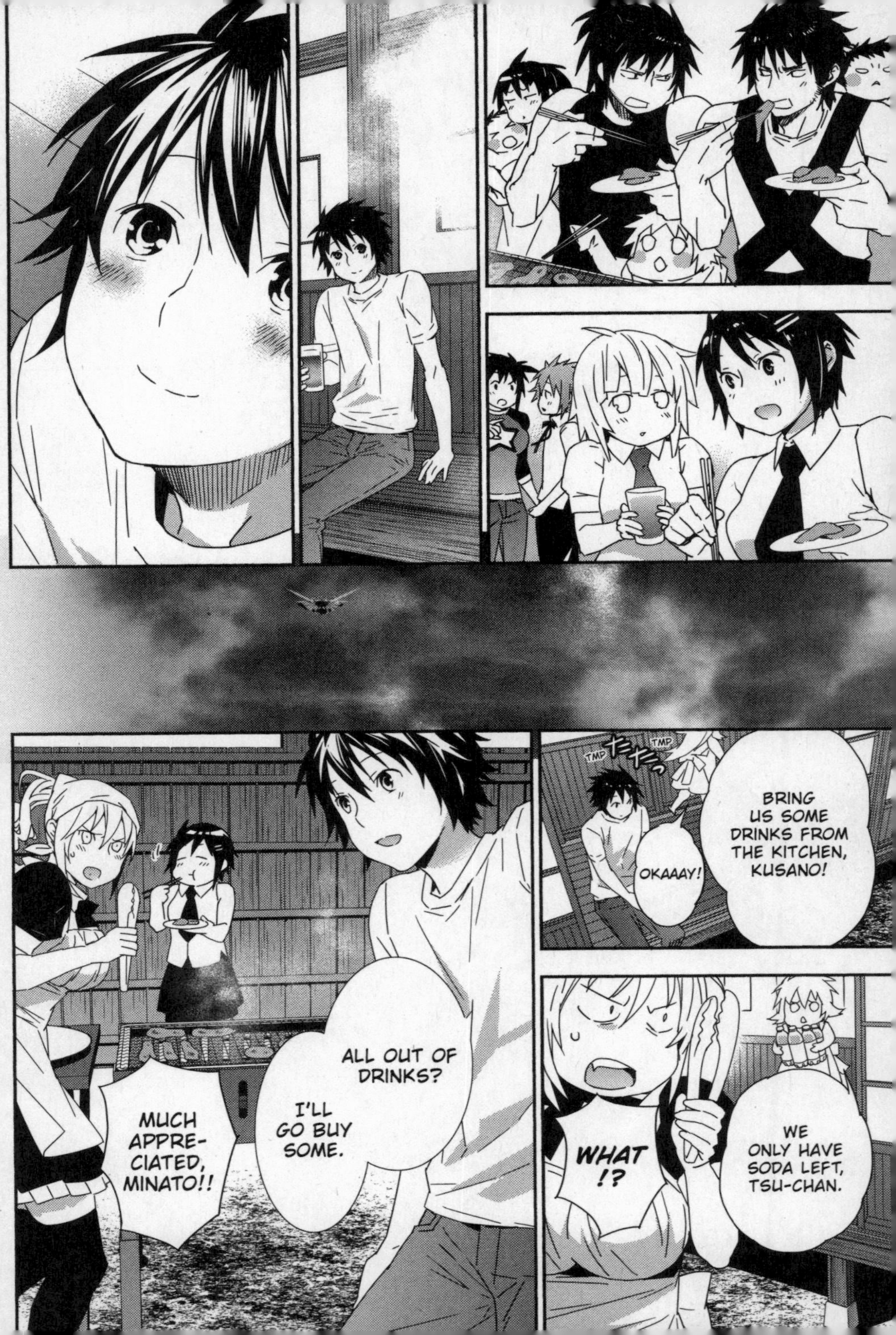
TMP
TMP
BRING US SOME DRINKS FROM THE KITCHEN, KUSANO!
OKAAAY!
WE ONLY HAVE SODA LEFT, TSU-CHAN.
WHAT!?
ALL OUT OF DRINKS?
I'LL GO BUY SOME.
MUCH APPRECIATED, MINATO!!

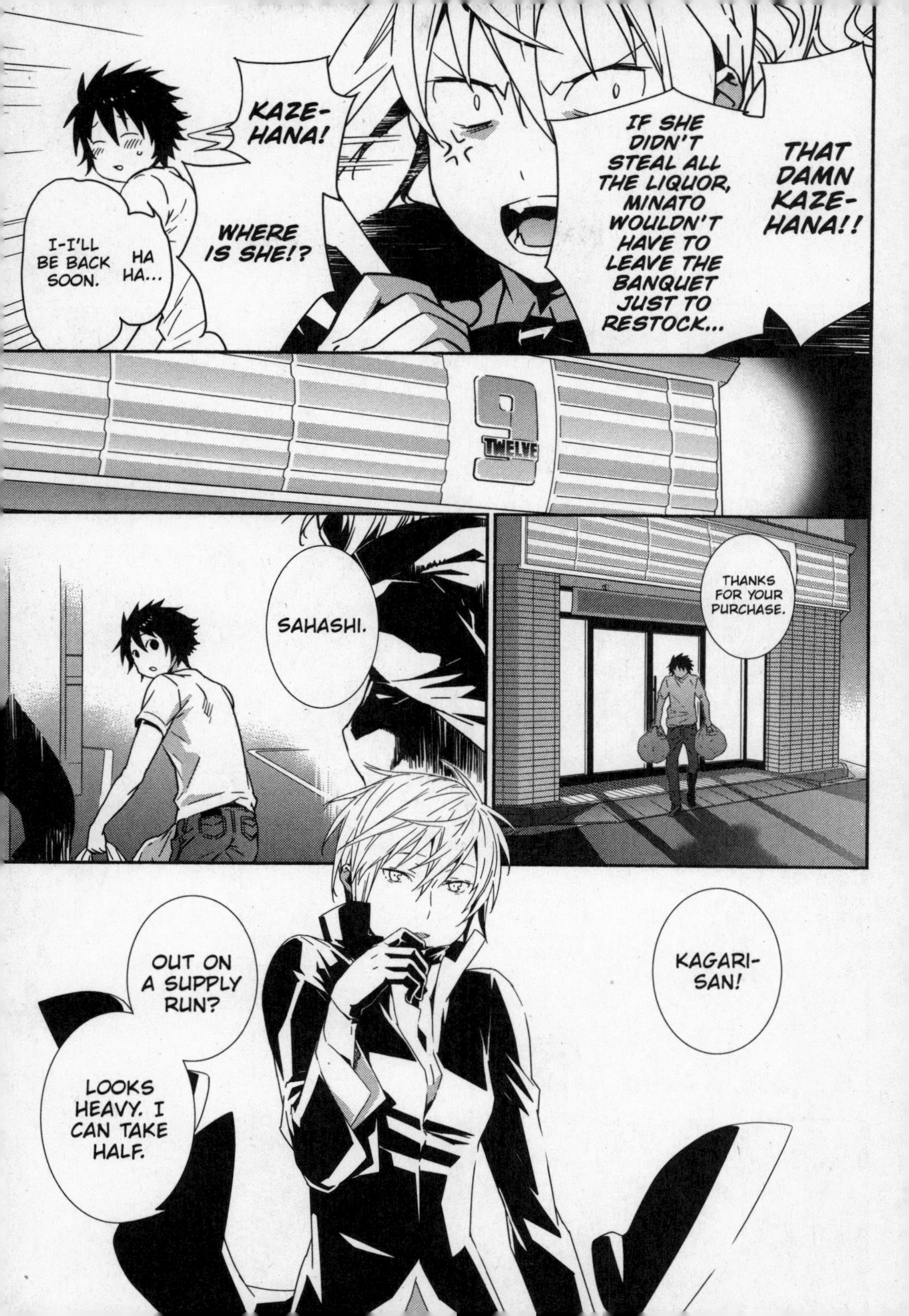
THAT DAMN KAZE-HANA!!
IF SHE DIDN'T STEAL ALL THE LIQUOR, MINATO WOULDN'T HAVE TO LEAVE THE BANQUET JUST TO RESTOCK...
KAZE-HANA!
WHERE IS SHE!?
HA HA...
I-I'LL BE BACK SOON.
9 TWELVE
THANKS FOR YOUR PURCHASE.
SAHASHI.
KAGARI-SAN!
OUT ON A SUPPLY RUN?
LOOKS HEAVY. I CAN TAKE HALF.

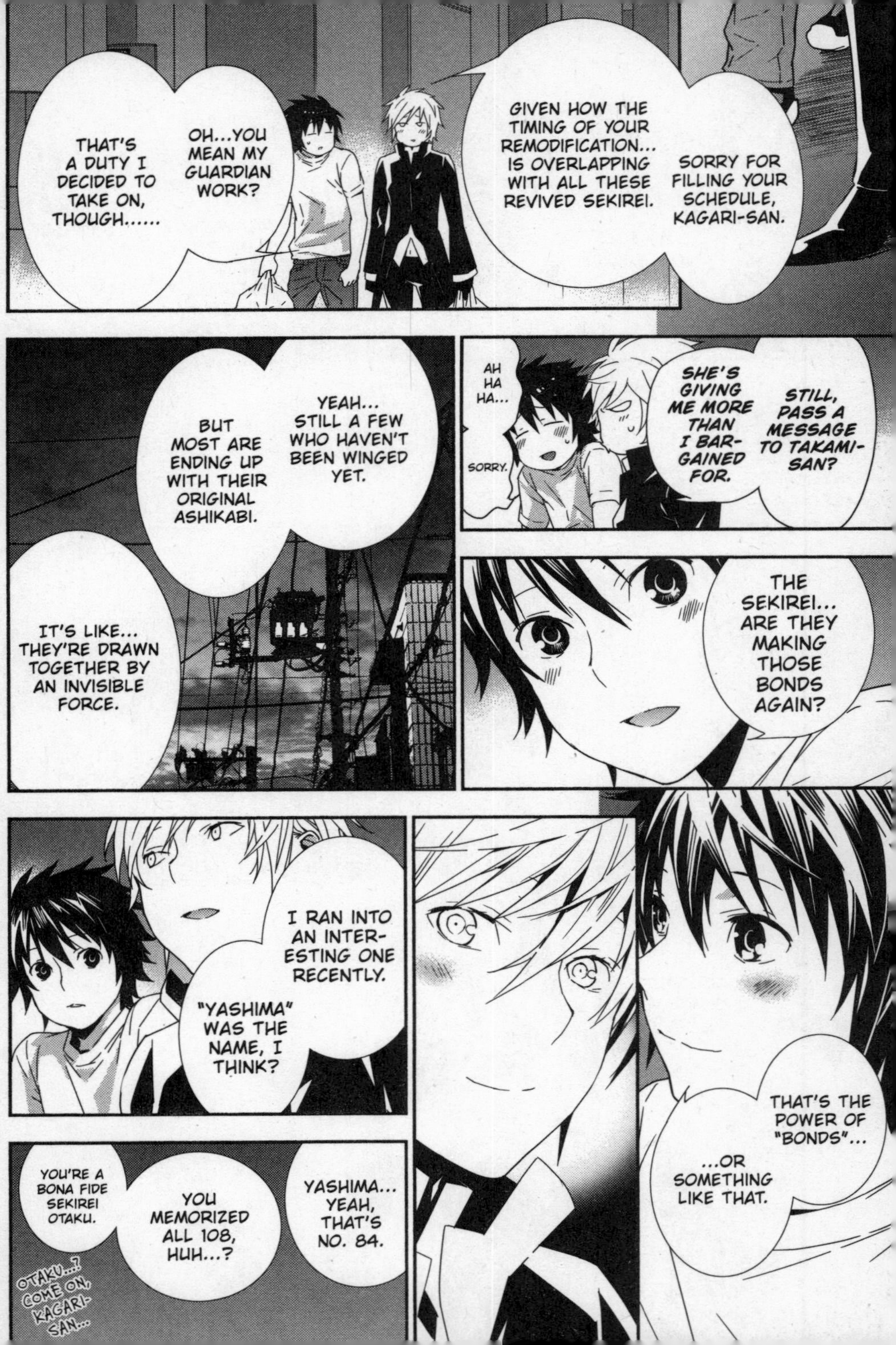
SORRY FOR FILLING YOUR SCHEDULE, KAGARI-SAN.
GIVEN HOW THE TIMING OF YOUR REMODIFICATION... IS OVERLAPPING WITH ALL THESE REVIVED SEKIREI.
OH...YOU MEAN MY GUARDIAN WORK?
THAT'S A DUTY I DECIDED TO TAKE ON, THOUGH......
STILL, PASS A MESSAGE TO TAKAMI-SAN?
SHE'S GIVING ME MORE THAN I BARGAINED FOR.
AH HA HA...
SORRY.
THE SEKIREI... ARE THEY MAKING THOSE BONDS AGAIN?
YEAH... STILL A FEW WHO HAVEN'T BEEN WINGED YET.
BUT MOST ARE ENDING UP WITH THEIR ORIGINAL ASHIKABI.
IT'S LIKE... THEY'RE DRAWN TOGETHER BY AN INVISIBLE FORCE.
THAT'S THE POWER OF "BONDS"...
...OR SOMETHING LIKE THAT.
I RAN INTO AN INTERESTING ONE RECENTLY.
"YASHIMA" WAS THE NAME, I THINK?
YASHIMA... YEAH, THAT'S NO. 84.
YOU MEMORIZED ALL 108, HUH...?
YOU'RE A BONA FIDE SEKIREI OTAKU.
OTAKU...? COME ON, KAGARI-SAN...

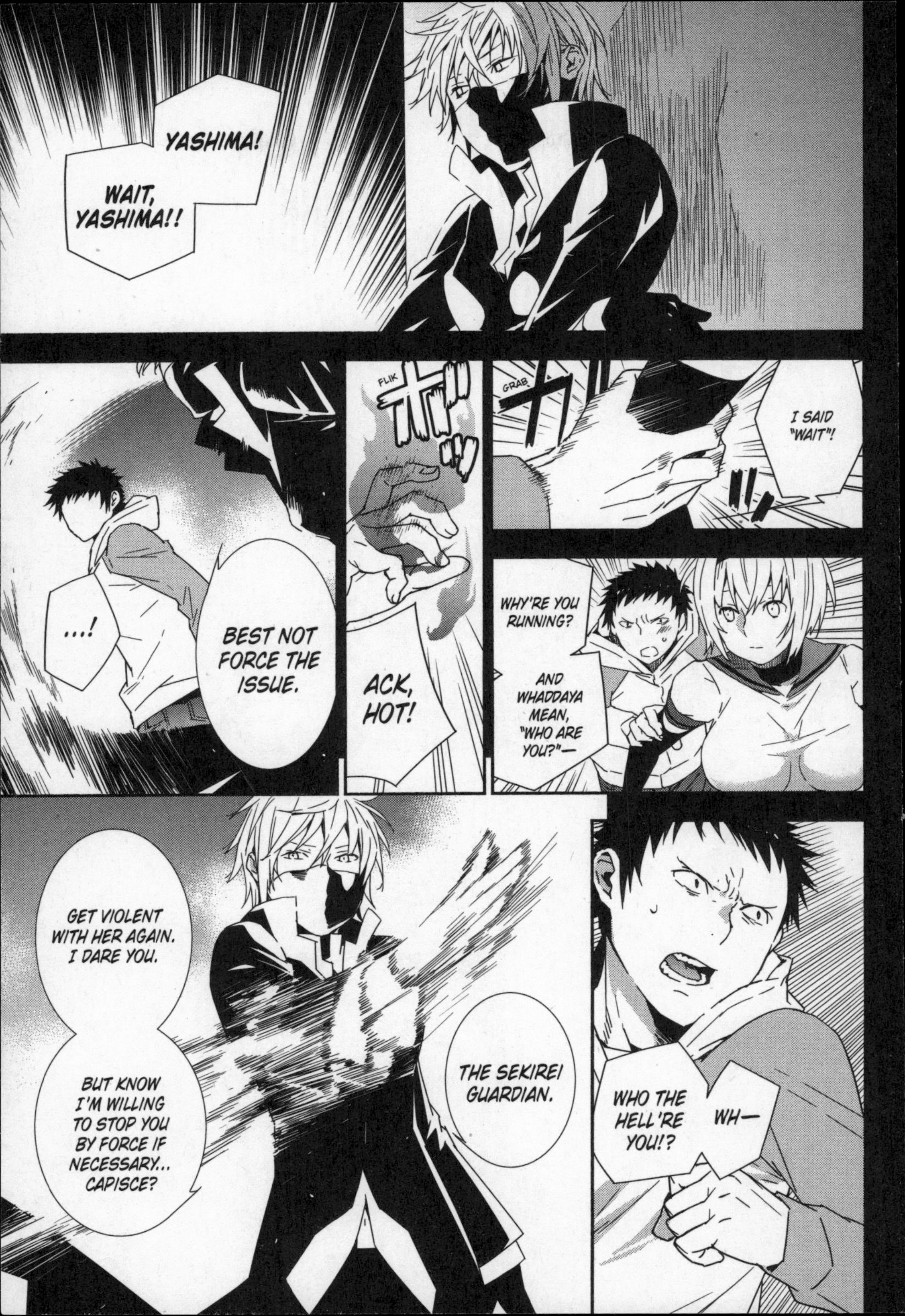
YASHIMA!
WAIT, YASHIMA!!
GRAB
I SAID "WAIT"!
WHY'RE YOU RUNNING?
AND WHADDAYA MEAN, "WHO ARE YOU?"—
FLIK
ACK, HOT!
BEST NOT FORCE THE ISSUE.
...!
WH—
WHO THE HELL'RE YOU!?
THE SEKIREI GUARDIAN.
GET VIOLENT WITH HER AGAIN. I DARE YOU.
BUT KNOW I'M WILLING TO STOP YOU BY FORCE IF NECESSARY... CAPISCE?

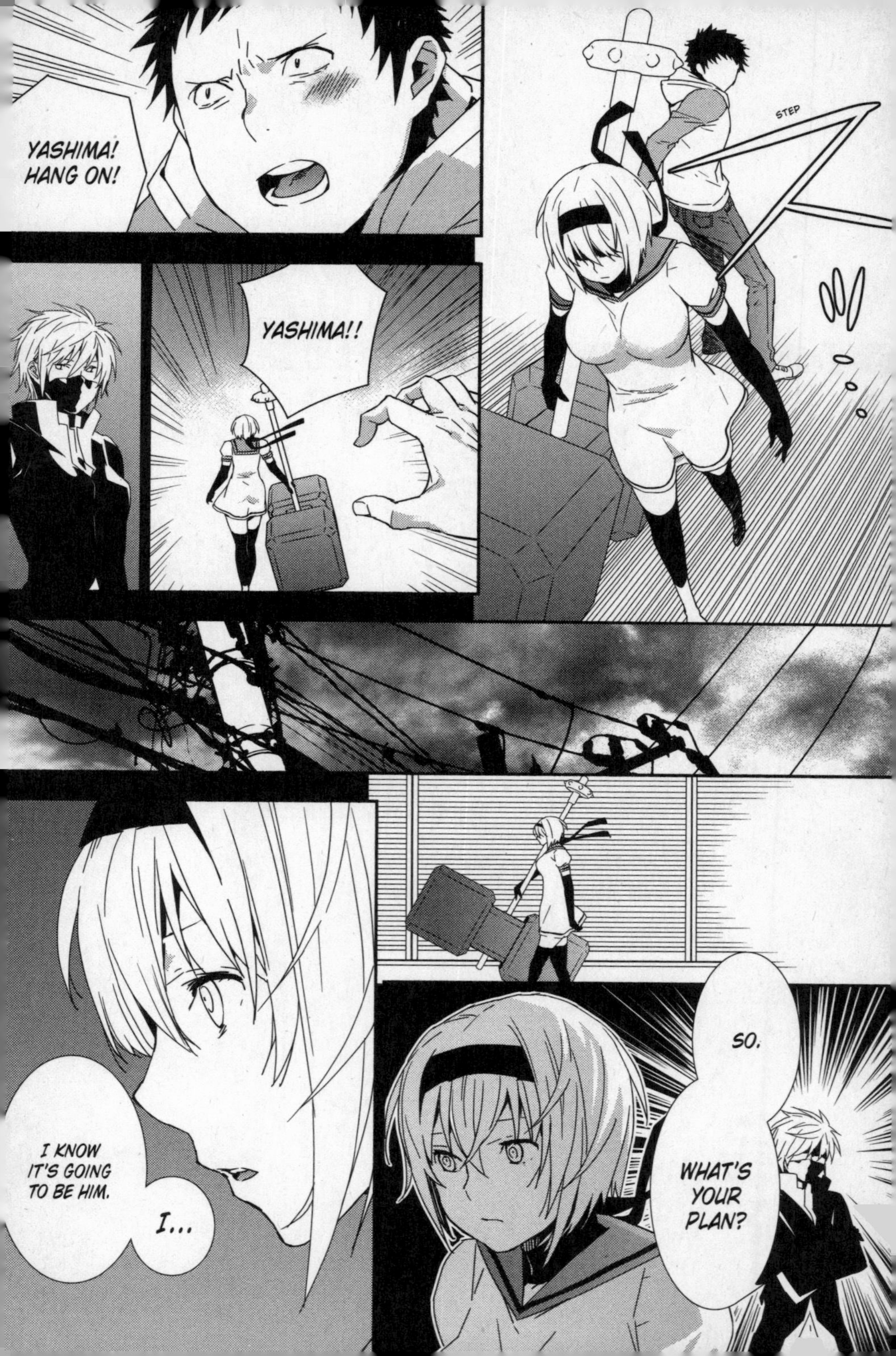
STEP
YASHIMA! HANG ON!
YASHIMA!!
SO.
WHAT'S YOUR PLAN?
I KNOW IT'S GOING TO BE HIM.
I...

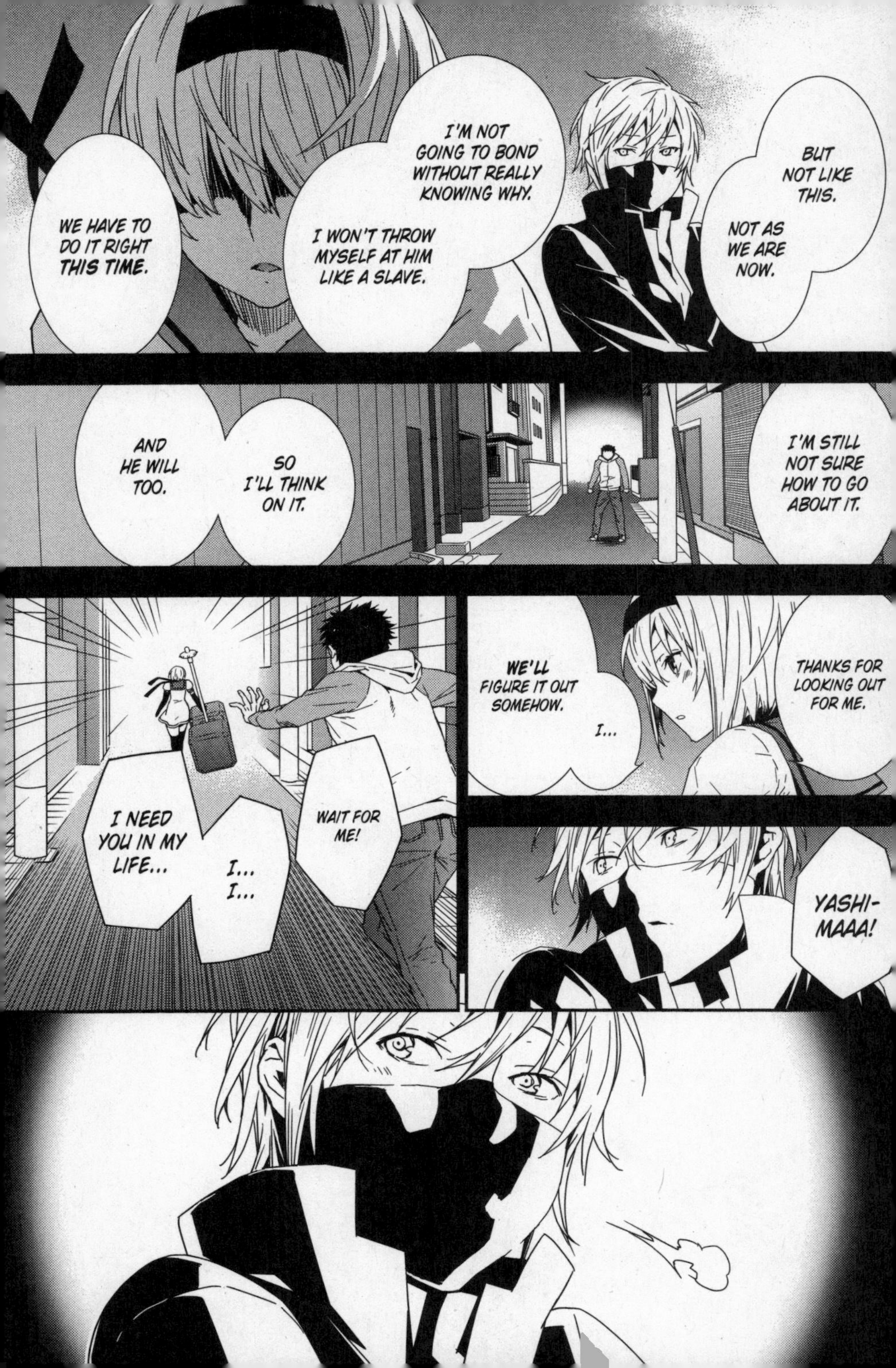
BUT NOT LIKE THIS.
NOT AS WE ARE NOW.
I'M NOT GOING TO BOND WITHOUT REALLY KNOWING WHY.
I WON'T THROW MYSELF AT HIM LIKE A SLAVE.
WE HAVE TO DO IT RIGHT THIS TIME.
I'M STILL NOT SURE HOW TO GO ABOUT IT.
SO I'LL THINK ON IT.
AND HE WILL TOO.
THANKS FOR LOOKING OUT FOR ME.
I...
WE'LL FIGURE IT OUT SOMEHOW.
YASHI-MAAA!
WAIT FOR ME!
I... I...
I NEED YOU IN MY LIFE...

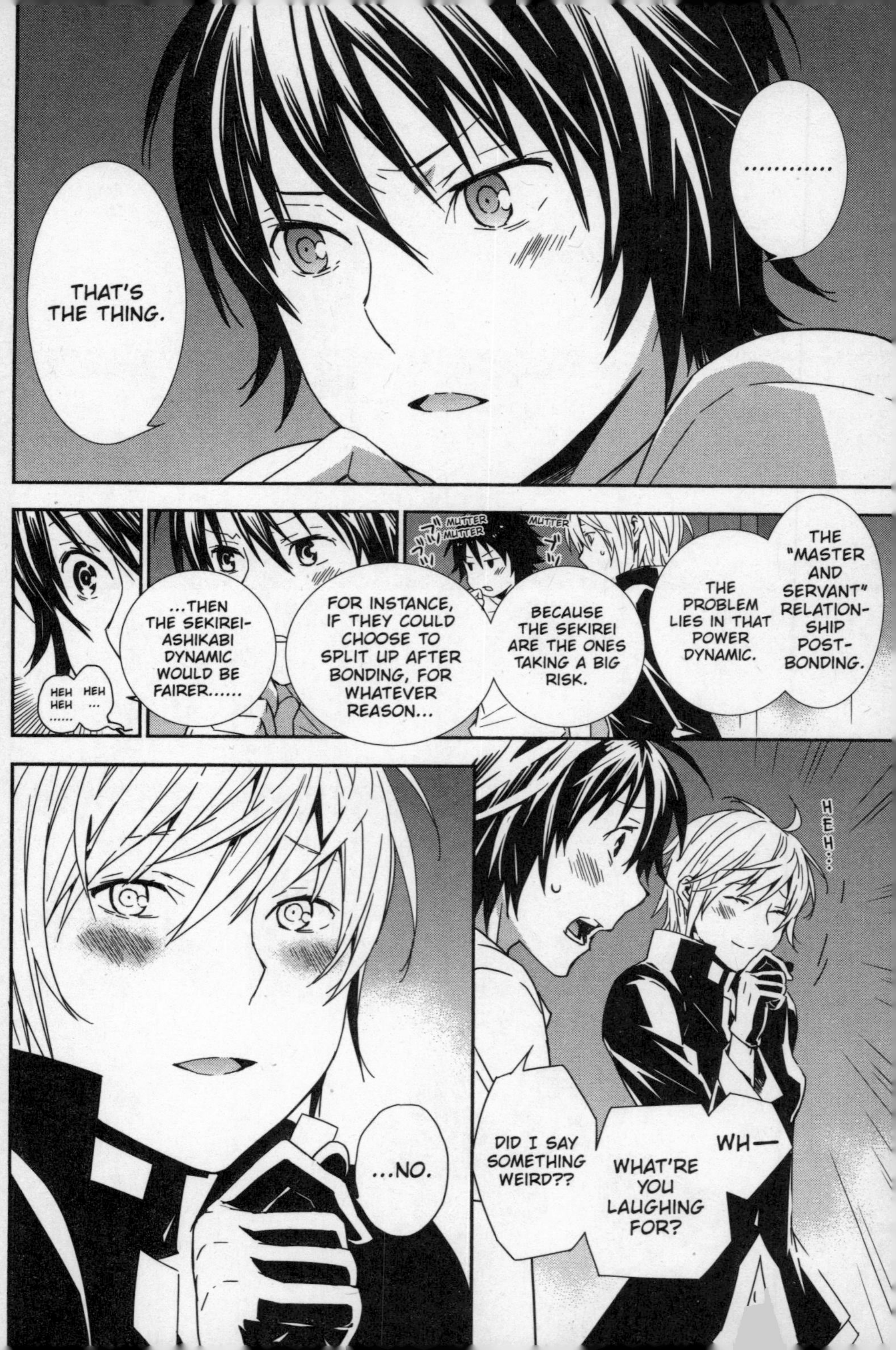
....
THAT'S THE THING.
THE "MASTER AND SERVANT" RELATIONSHIP POST-BONDING.
THE PROBLEM LIES IN THAT POWER DYNAMIC.
MUTTER
MUTTER MUTTER
BECAUSE THE SEKIREI ARE THE ONES TAKING A BIG RISK.
FOR INSTANCE, IF THEY COULD CHOOSE TO SPLIT UP AFTER BONDING, FOR WHATEVER REASON...
...THEN THE SEKIREI-ASHIKABI DYNAMIC WOULD BE FAIRER......
HEH ...
HEH HEH ......
HEH...
WH— WHAT'RE YOU LAUGHING FOR?
DID I SAY SOMETHING WEIRD??
...NO.

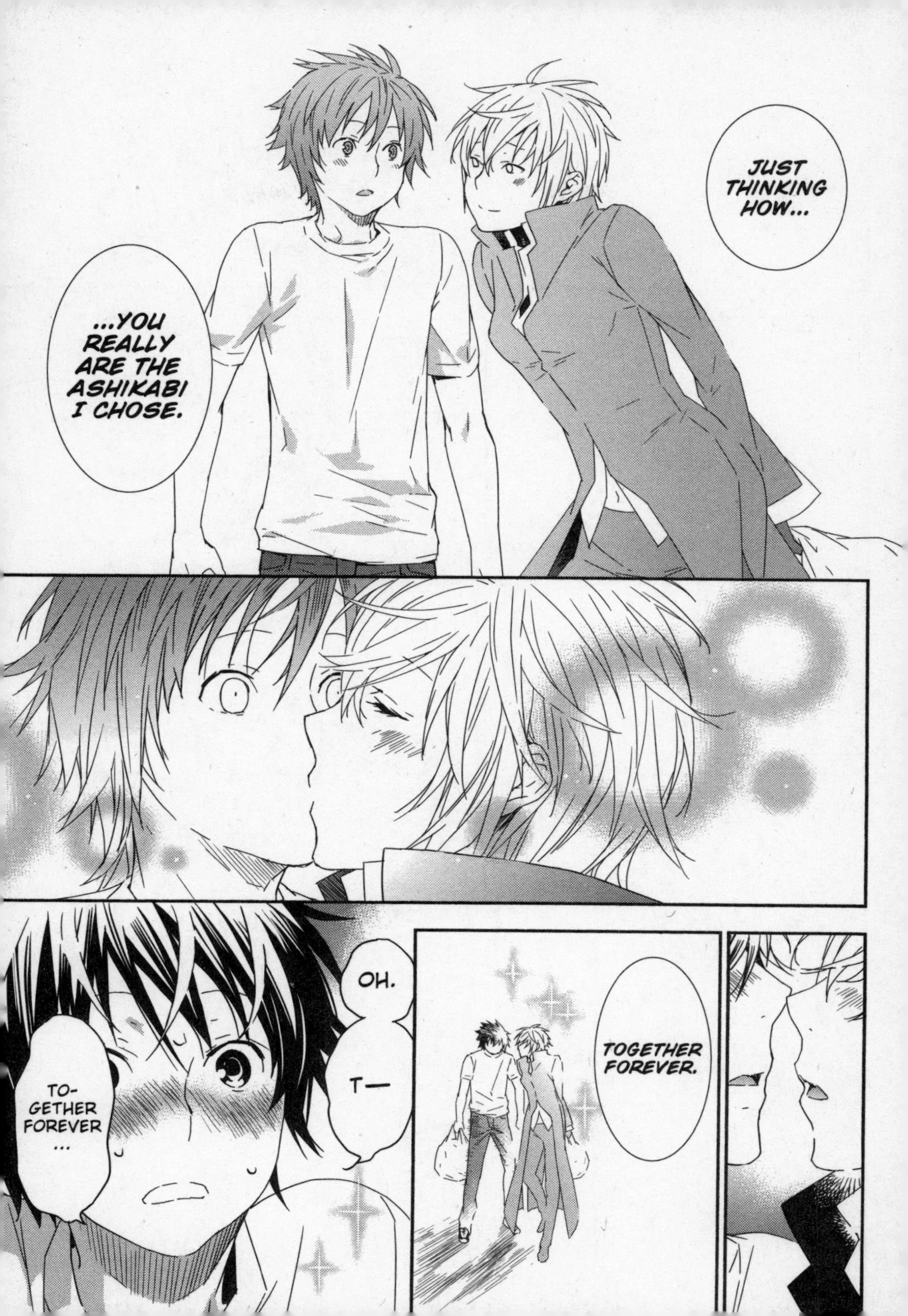
JUST THINKING HOW...
...YOU REALLY ARE THE ASHIKABI I CHOSE.
TOGETHER FOREVER.
OH.
T—
TO-GETHER FOREVER ...

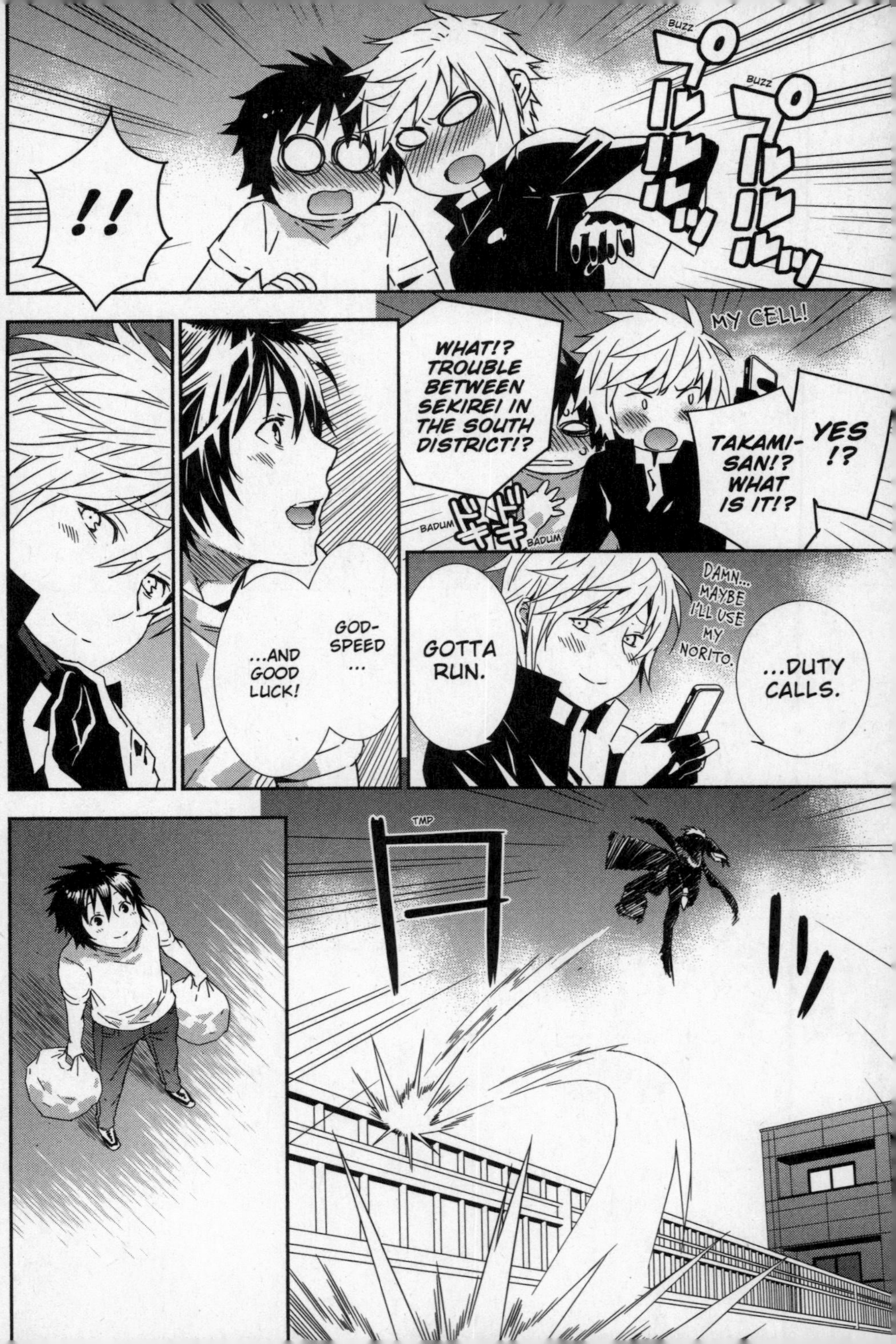
BUZZ
プルルルッ
BUZZ
プルルルッ
!!
MY CELL!
YES !?
TAKAMI-SAN!? WHAT IS IT!?
WHAT!? TROUBLE BETWEEN SEKIREI IN THE SOUTH DISTRICT!?
BADUM ドキ
BADUM ドキ
...DUTY CALLS.
DAMN... MAYBE I'LL USE MY NORITO.
GOTTA RUN.
GOD-SPEED ...
...AND GOOD LUCK!
TMP
タッ

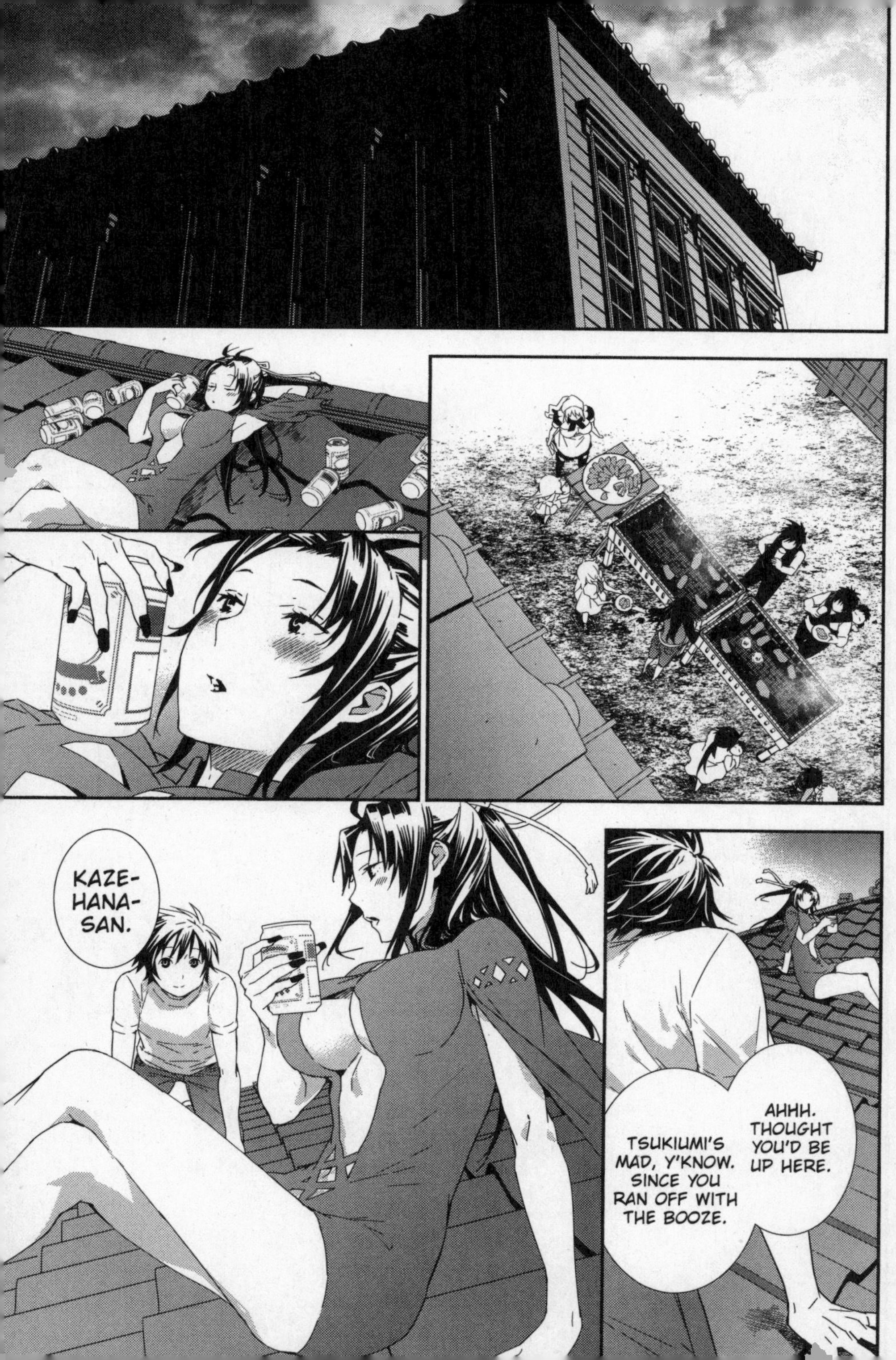
AHHH. THOUGHT YOU'D BE UP HERE.
TSUKIUMI'S MAD, Y'KNOW. SINCE YOU RAN OFF WITH THE BOOZE.
KAZE-HANA-SAN.

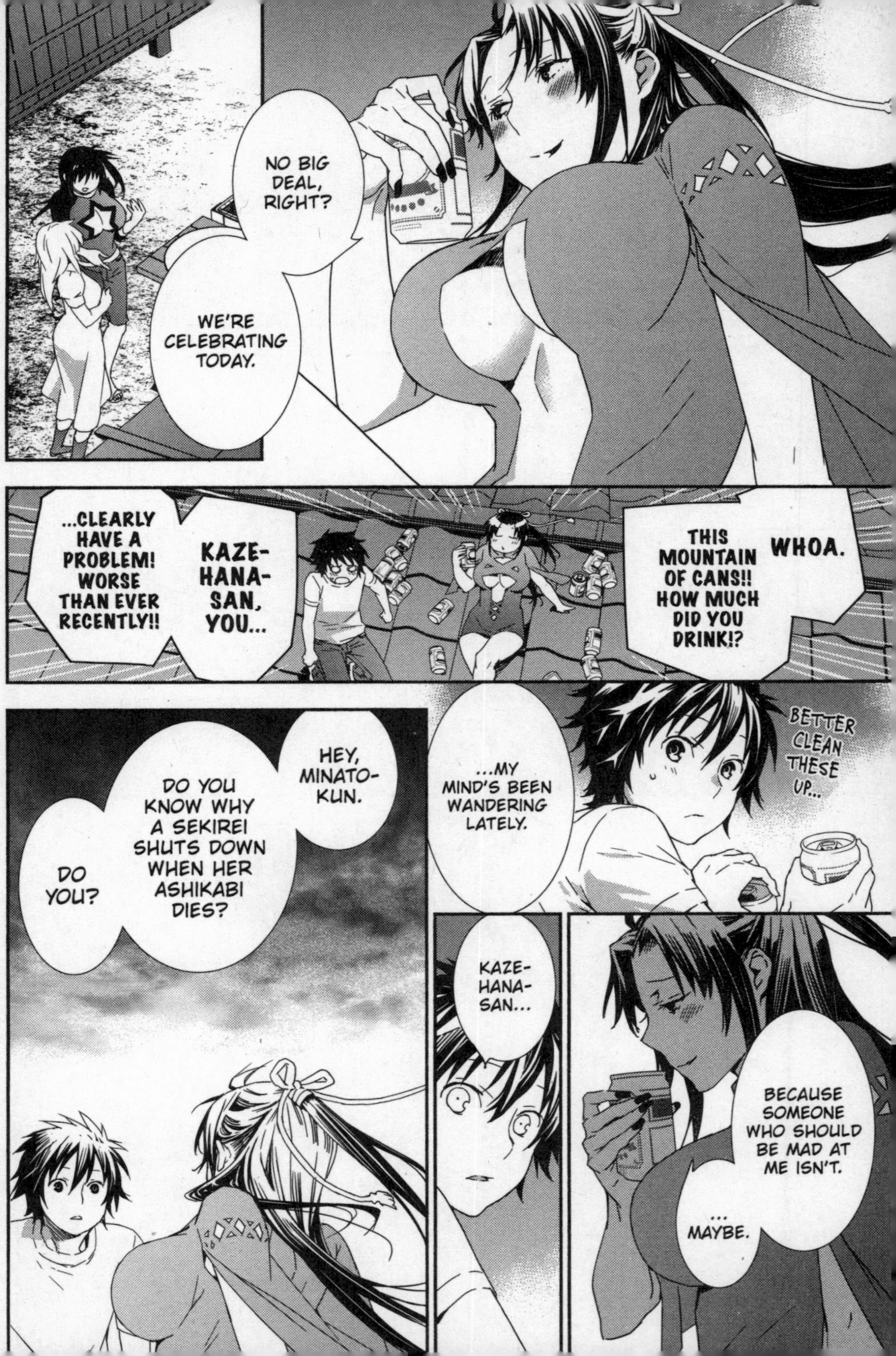
NO BIG DEAL, RIGHT?
WE'RE CELEBRATING TODAY.
WHOA.
THIS MOUNTAIN OF CANS!! HOW MUCH DID YOU DRINK!?
KAZE-HANA-SAN, YOU...
...CLEARLY HAVE A PROBLEM! WORSE THAN EVER RECENTLY!!
BETTER CLEAN THESE UP...
...MY MIND'S BEEN WANDERING LATELY.
BECAUSE SOMEONE WHO SHOULD BE MAD AT ME ISN'T.
... MAYBE.
KAZE-HANA-SAN...
HEY, MINATO-KUN.
DO YOU KNOW WHY A SEKIREI SHUTS DOWN WHEN HER ASHIKABI DIES?
DO YOU?

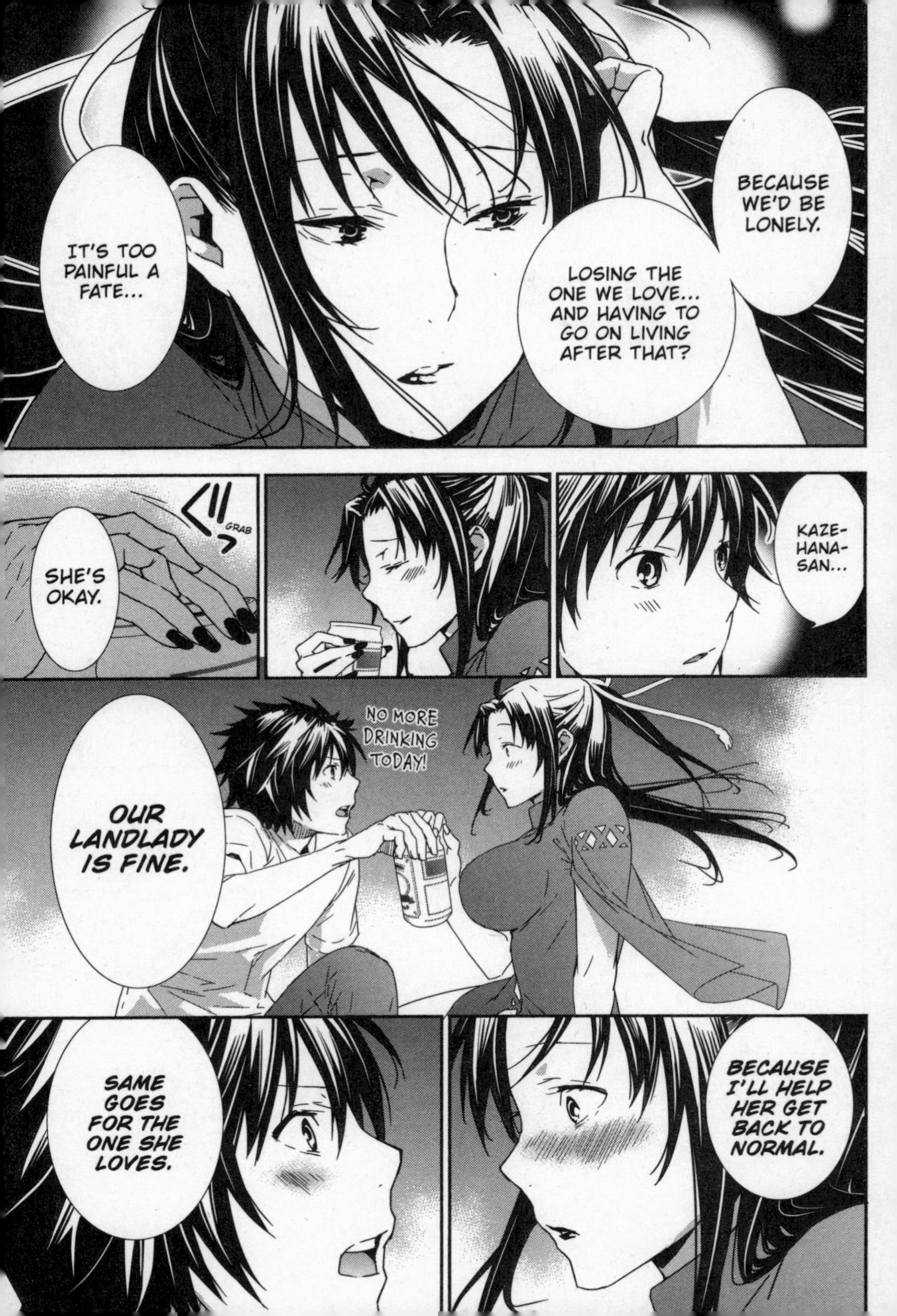
BECAUSE WE'D BE LONELY.
LOSING THE ONE WE LOVE... AND HAVING TO GO ON LIVING AFTER THAT?
IT'S TOO PAINFUL A FATE...
KAZE-HANA-SAN...
GRAB
SHE'S OKAY.
NO MORE DRINKING TODAY!
OUR LANDLADY IS FINE.
BECAUSE I'LL HELP HER GET BACK TO NORMAL.
SAME GOES FOR THE ONE SHE LOVES.

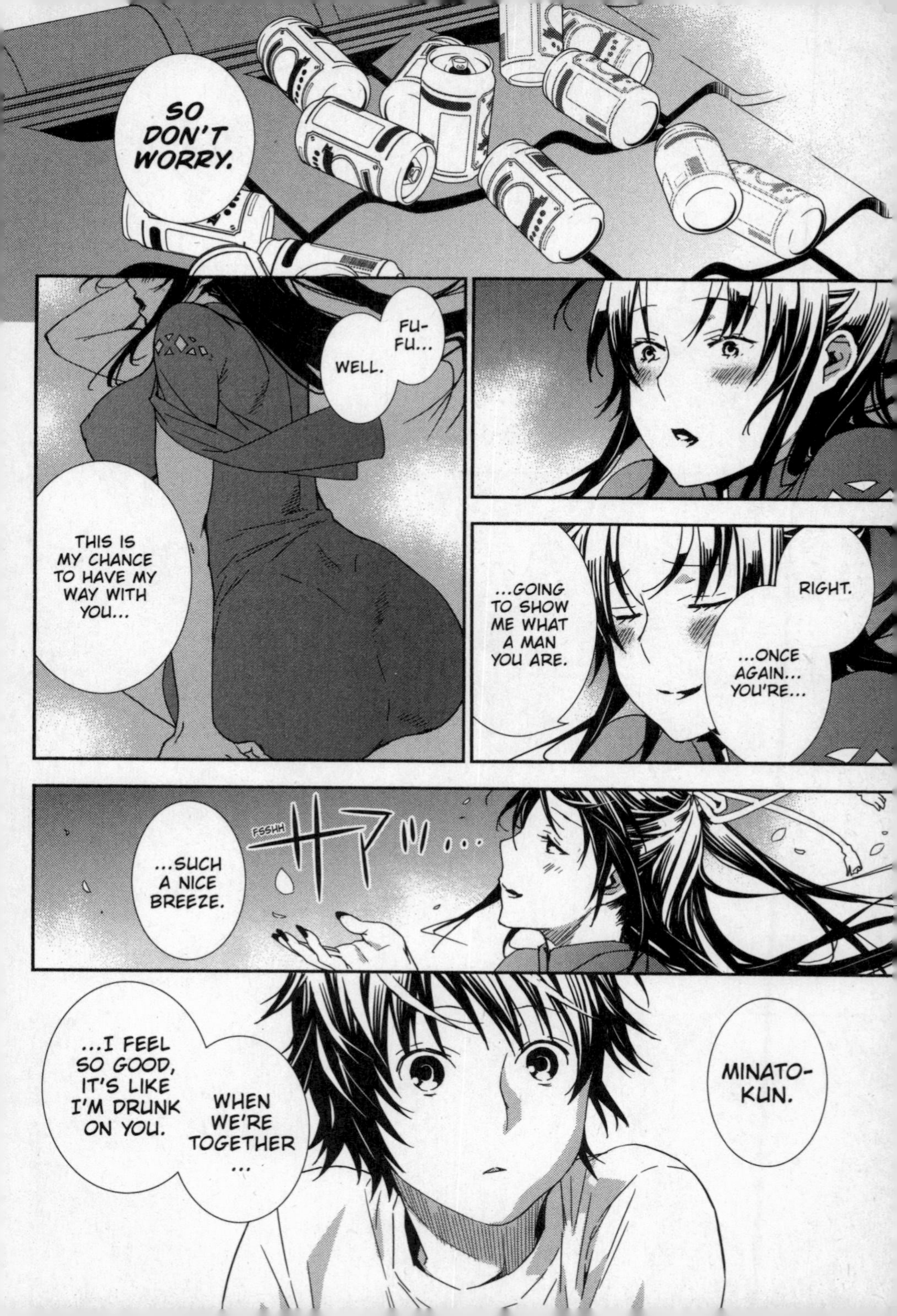
SO DON'T WORRY.
RIGHT.
...ONCE AGAIN... YOU'RE...
...GOING TO SHOW ME WHAT A MAN YOU ARE.
FU-FU... WELL.
THIS IS MY CHANCE TO HAVE MY WAY WITH YOU...
FSSHH
...SUCH A NICE BREEZE.
MINATO-KUN.
WHEN WE'RE TOGETHER...
...I FEEL SO GOOD, IT'S LIKE I'M DRUNK ON YOU.

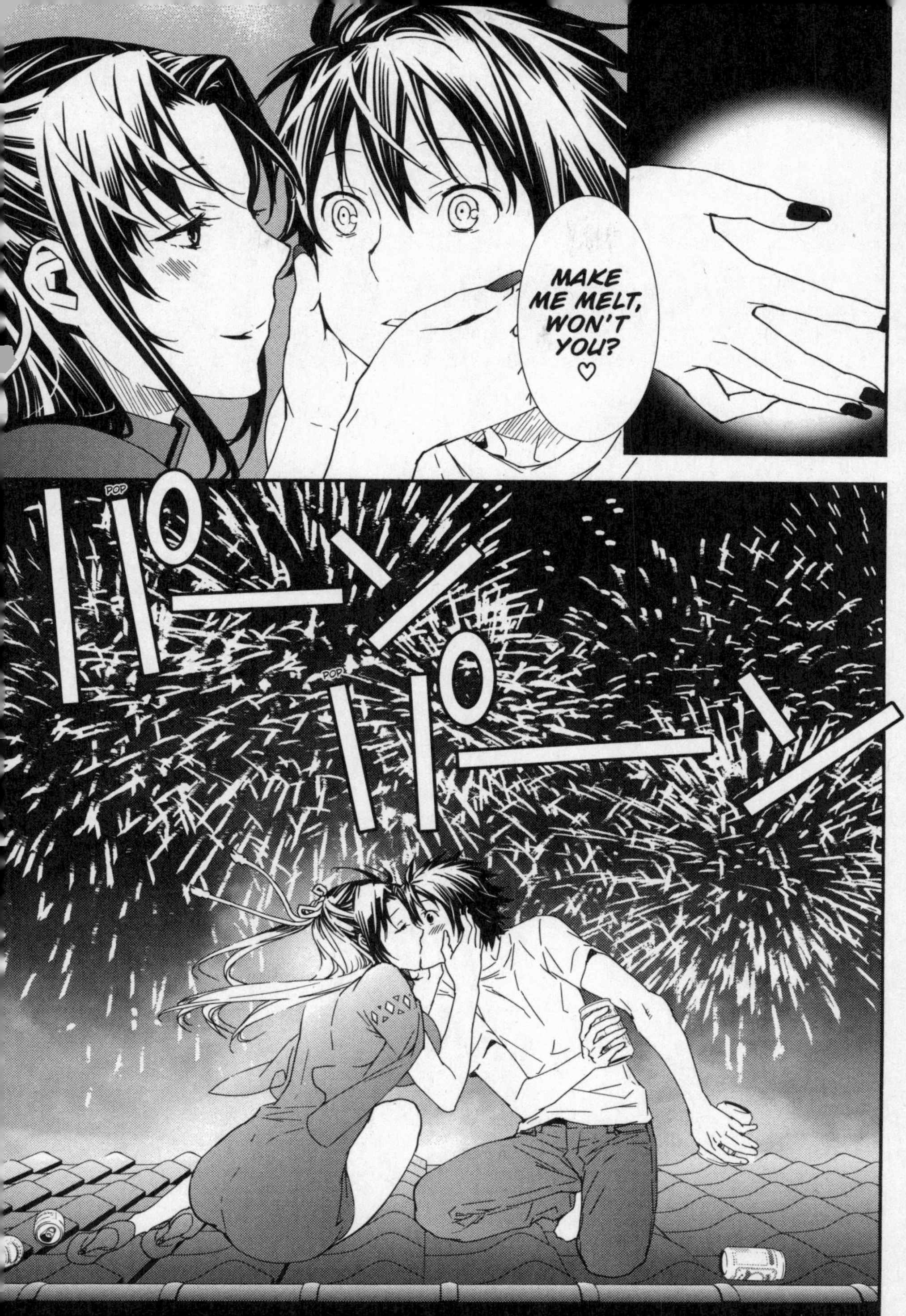
MAKE ME MELT, WON'T YOU? ♡
POP
パーン
POP
パーン

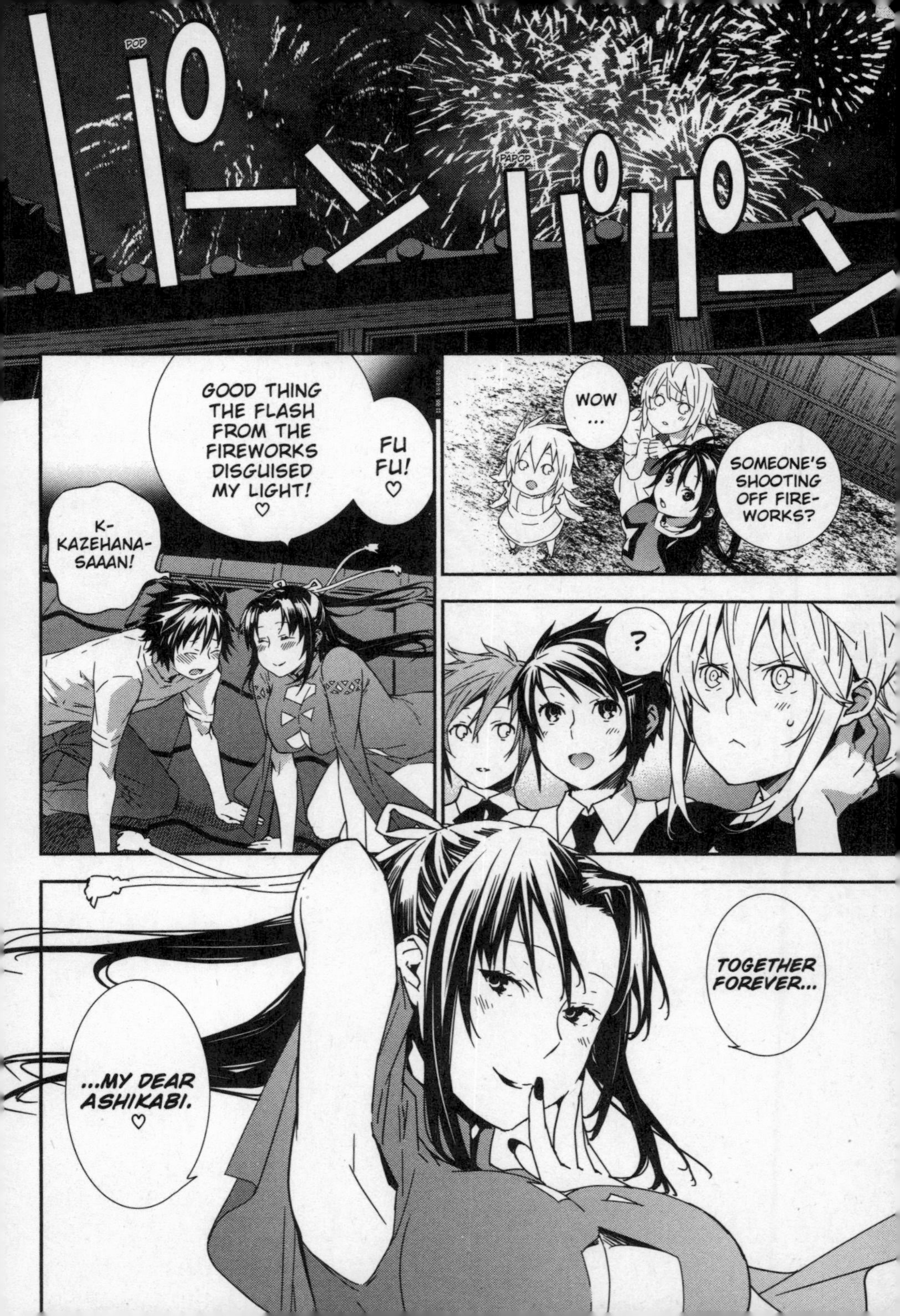
POP
PAPOP
WOW ...
SOMEONE'S SHOOTING OFF FIRE-WORKS?
GOOD THING THE FLASH FROM THE FIREWORKS DISGUISED MY LIGHT! ♡
FU FU! ♡
K-KAZEHANA-SAAAN!
?
TOGETHER FOREVER...
...MY DEAR ASHIKABI. ♡

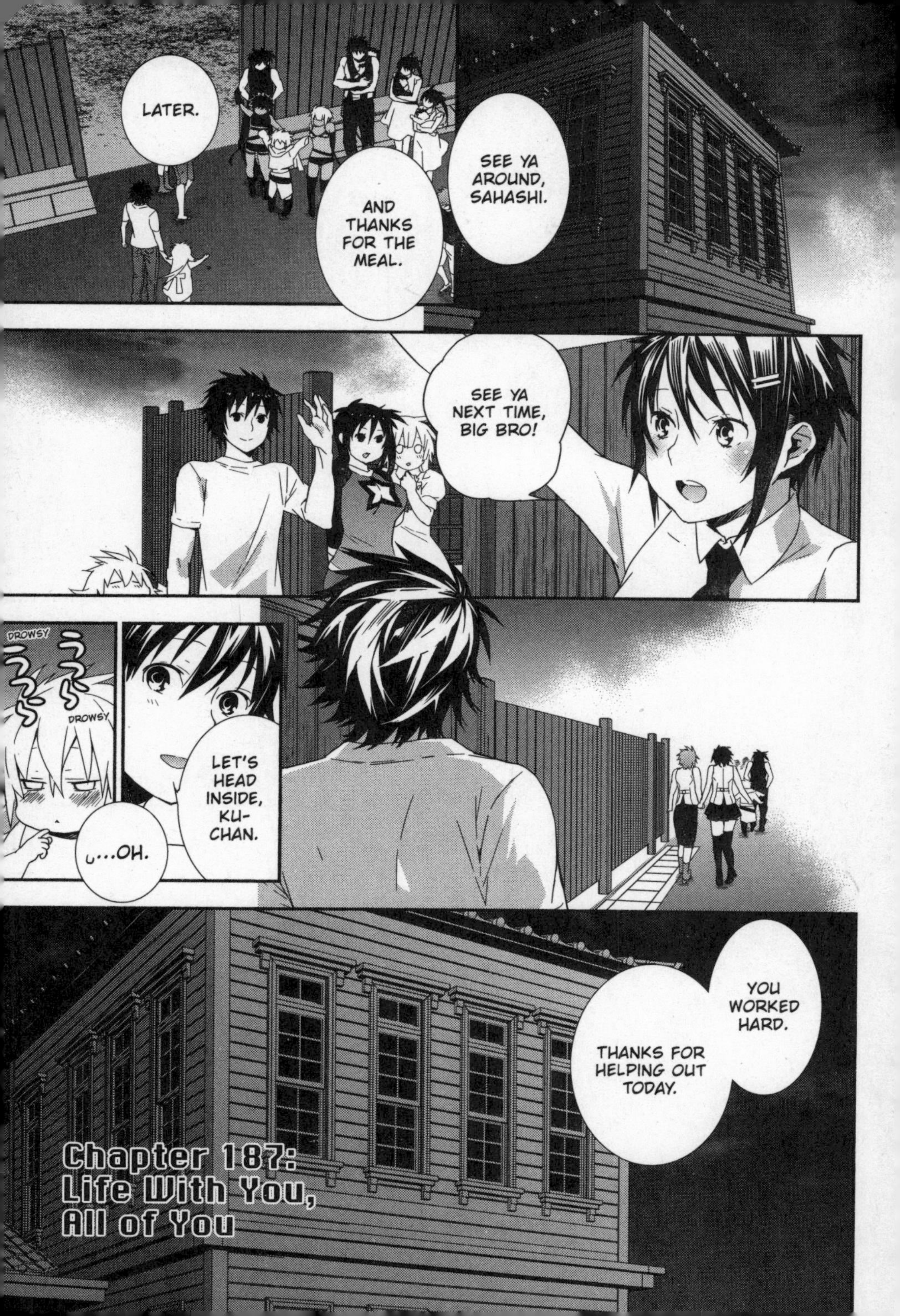
SEE YA AROUND, SAHASHI.
AND THANKS FOR THE MEAL.
LATER.
SEE YA NEXT TIME, BIG BRO!
LET'S HEAD INSIDE, KU-CHAN.
DROWSY
DROWSY
...OH.
YOU WORKED HARD.
THANKS FOR HELPING OUT TODAY.

Chapter 187: Life With You, All of You

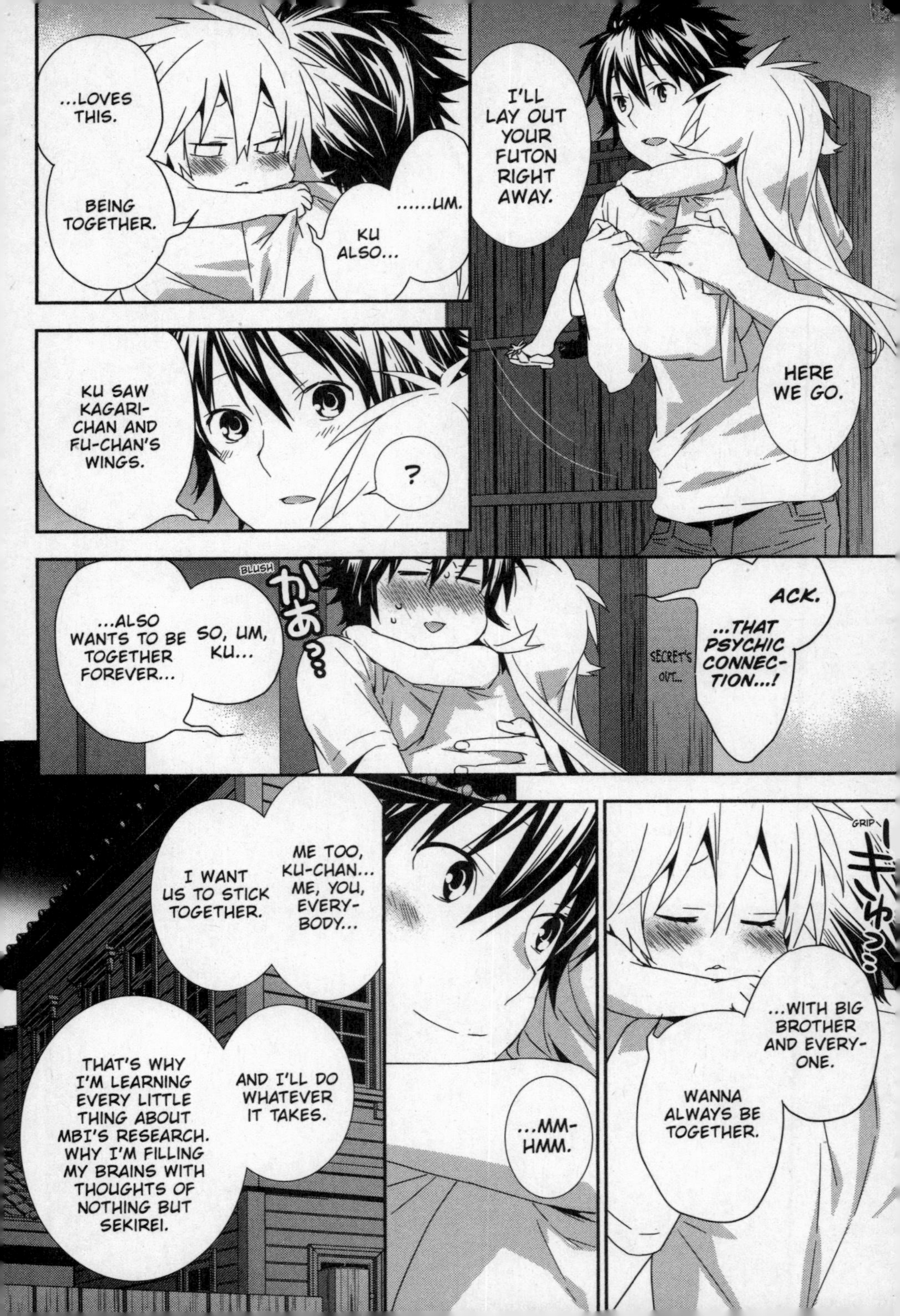
I'LL LAY OUT YOUR FUTON RIGHT AWAY.
HERE WE GO.
......UM.
KU ALSO...
...LOVES THIS.
BEING TOGETHER.
?
KU SAW KAGARI-CHAN AND FU-CHAN'S WINGS.
ACK.
...THAT PSYCHIC CONNECTION...!
SECRET'S OUT...
BLUSH
SO, UM, KU...
...ALSO WANTS TO BE TOGETHER FOREVER...
GRIP
...WITH BIG BROTHER AND EVERYONE.
WANNA ALWAYS BE TOGETHER.
...MM-HMM.
ME TOO, KU-CHAN... ME, YOU, EVERYBODY...
I WANT US TO STICK TOGETHER.
AND I'LL DO WHATEVER IT TAKES.
THAT'S WHY I'M LEARNING EVERY LITTLE THING ABOUT MBI'S RESEARCH. WHY I'M FILLING MY BRAINS WITH THOUGHTS OF NOTHING BUT SEKIREI.

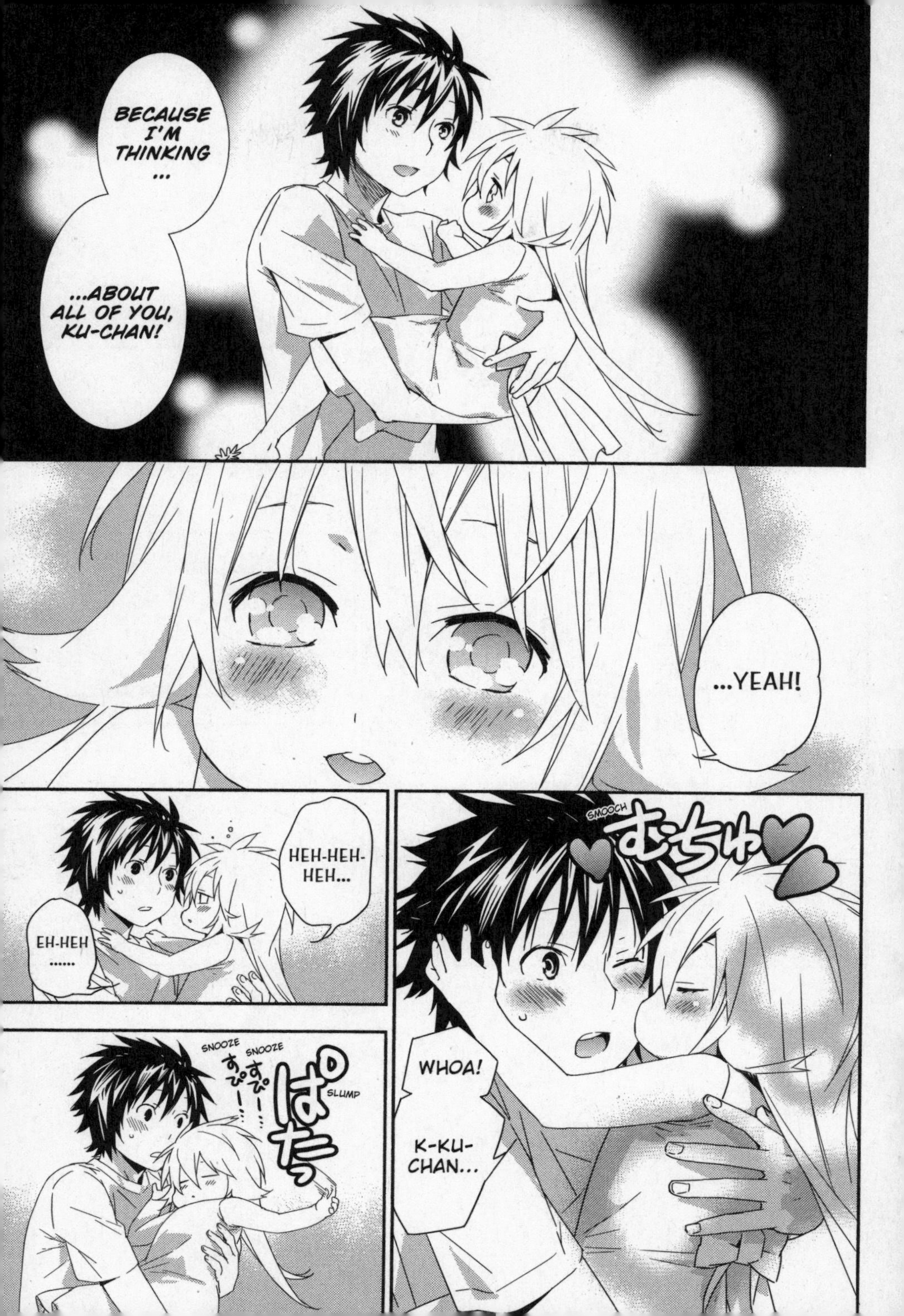
BECAUSE I'M THINKING ...
...ABOUT ALL OF YOU, KU-CHAN!
...YEAH!
SMOOCH
むちゅ
WHOA!
K-KU-CHAN...
HEH-HEH-HEH...
EH-HEH ......
SNOOZE SNOOZE
すぴー…すぴー…
ぱたっ
SLUMP

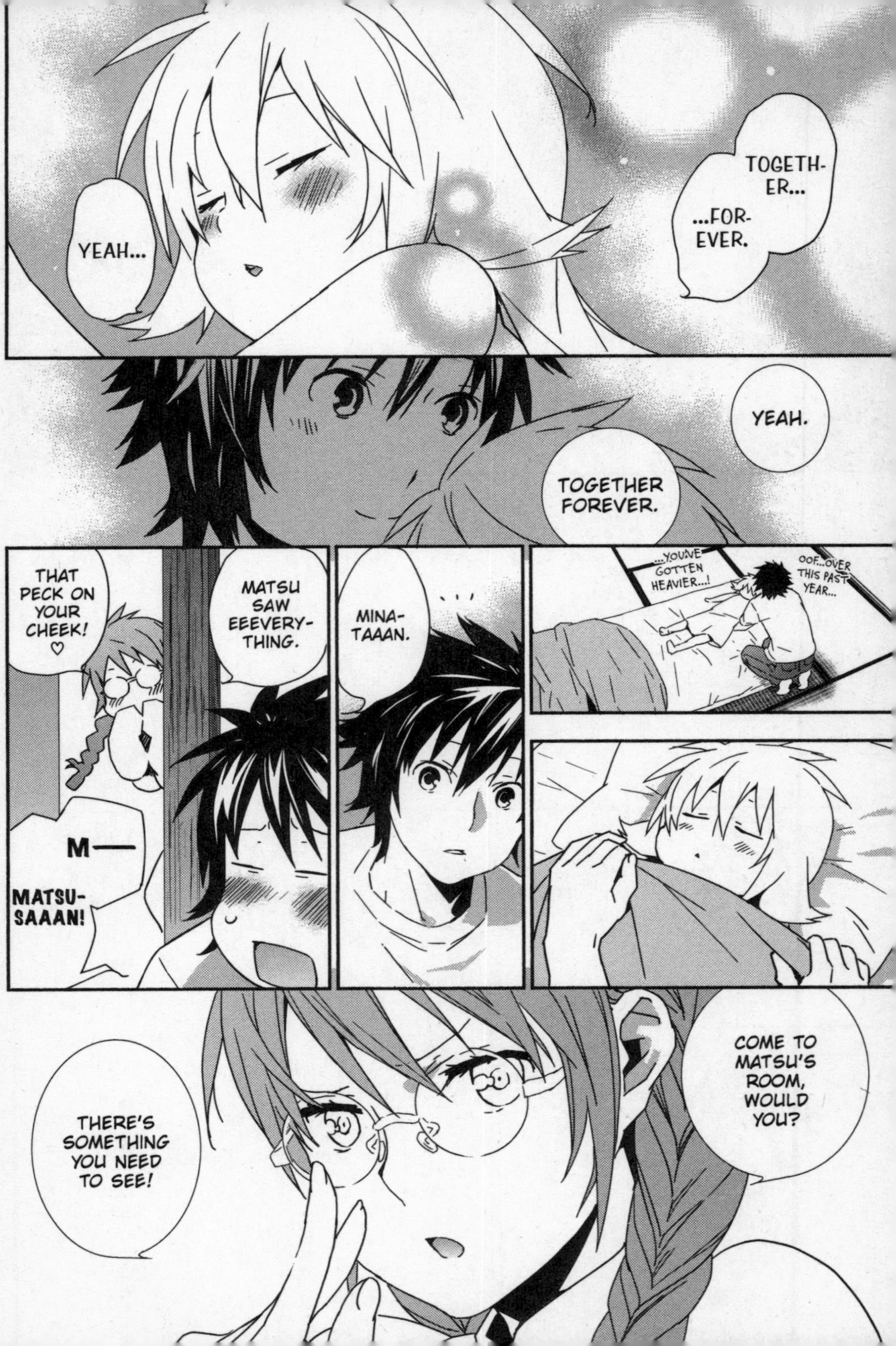
TOGETH-ER...
...FOR-EVER.
YEAH...
YEAH.
TOGETHER FOREVER.
OOF...OVER THIS PAST YEAR...
...YOU'VE GOTTEN HEAVIER...!
MINA-TAAAN.
...
MATSU SAW EEEVERY-THING.
THAT PECK ON YOUR CHEEK! ♡
M—
MATSU-SAAAN!
COME TO MATSU'S ROOM, WOULD YOU?
THERE'S SOMETHING YOU NEED TO SEE!

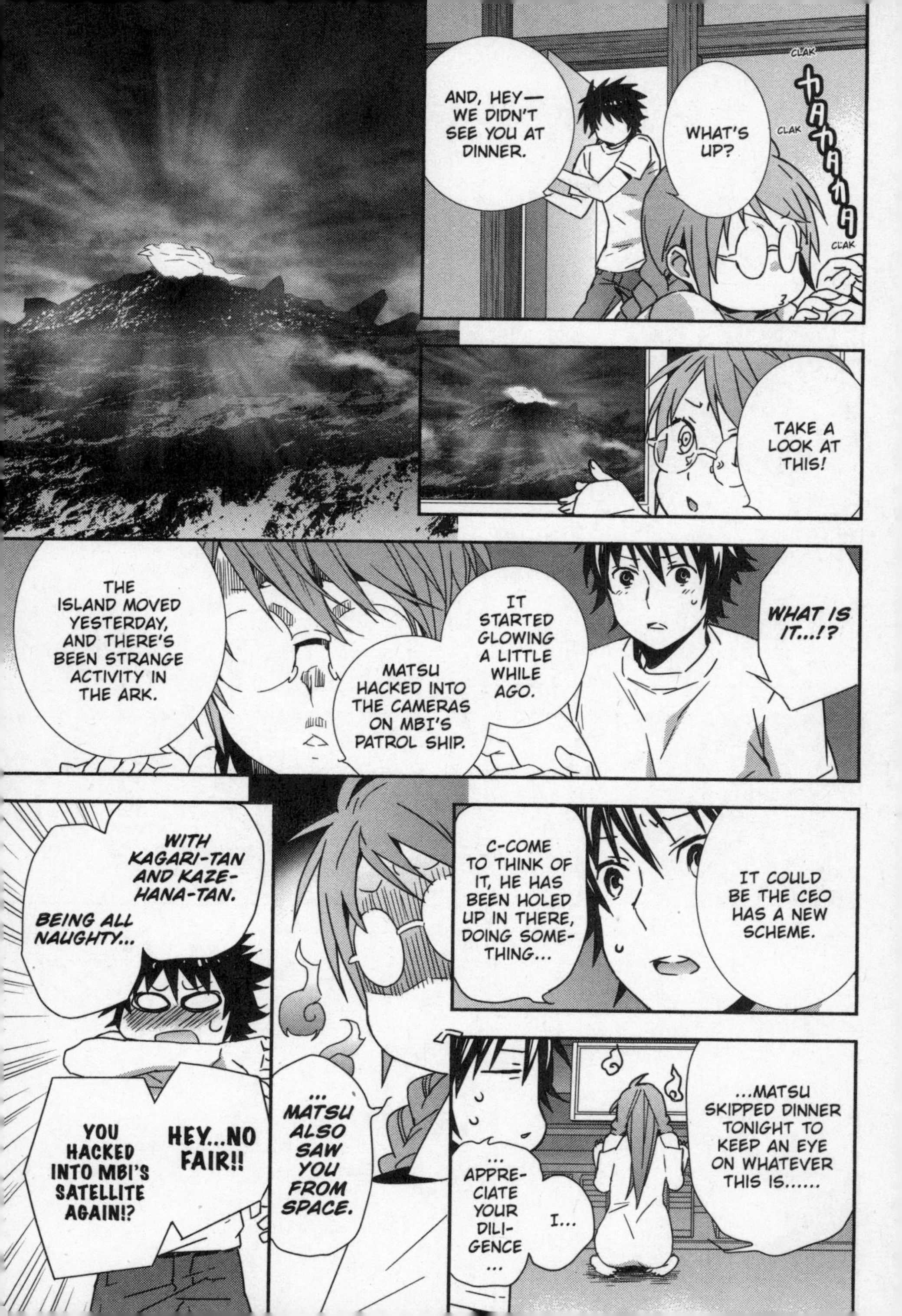
CLAK
CLAK
CLAK
WHAT'S UP?
AND, HEY— WE DIDN'T SEE YOU AT DINNER.
TAKE A LOOK AT THIS!
WHAT IS IT...!?
IT STARTED GLOWING A LITTLE WHILE AGO.
MATSU HACKED INTO THE CAMERAS ON MBI'S PATROL SHIP.
THE ISLAND MOVED YESTERDAY, AND THERE'S BEEN STRANGE ACTIVITY IN THE ARK.
IT COULD BE THE CEO HAS A NEW SCHEME.
C-COME TO THINK OF IT, HE HAS BEEN HOLED UP IN THERE, DOING SOME-THING...
...MATSU SKIPPED DINNER TONIGHT TO KEEP AN EYE ON WHATEVER THIS IS......
I...
...APPRE-CIATE YOUR DILI-GENCE...
...MATSU ALSO SAW YOU FROM SPACE.
WITH KAGARI-TAN AND KAZE-HANA-TAN.
BEING ALL NAUGHTY...
HEY...NO FAIR!!
YOU HACKED INTO MBI'S SATELLITE AGAIN!?

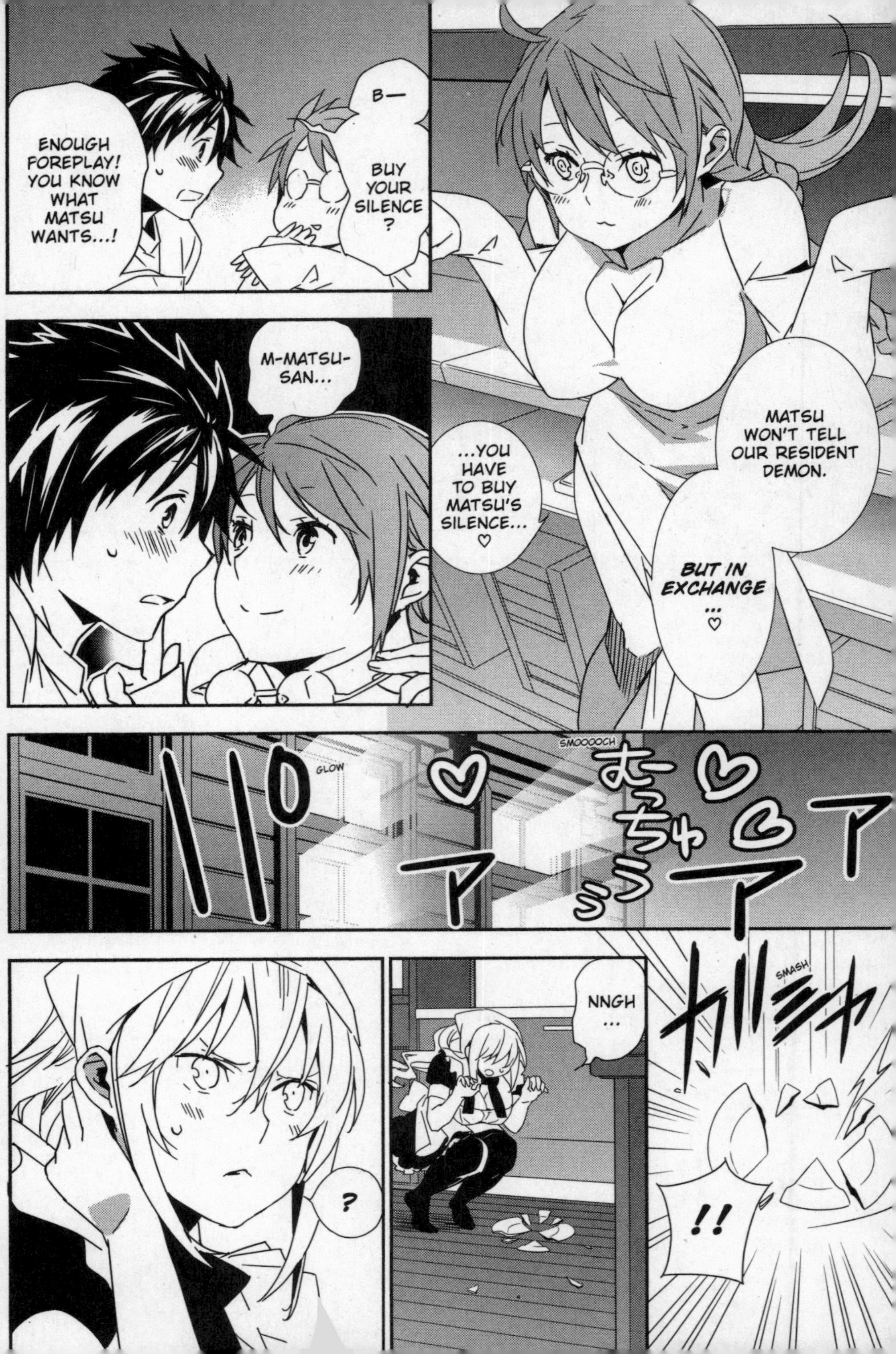
MATSU WON'T TELL OUR RESIDENT DEMON.
BUT IN EXCHANGE ... ♡
...YOU HAVE TO BUY MATSU'S SILENCE... ♡
B—
BUY YOUR SILENCE ?
ENOUGH FOREPLAY! YOU KNOW WHAT MATSU WANTS...!
M-MATSU-SAN...
SMOOOOCH
GLOW
SMASH
!!
NNGH ...
?

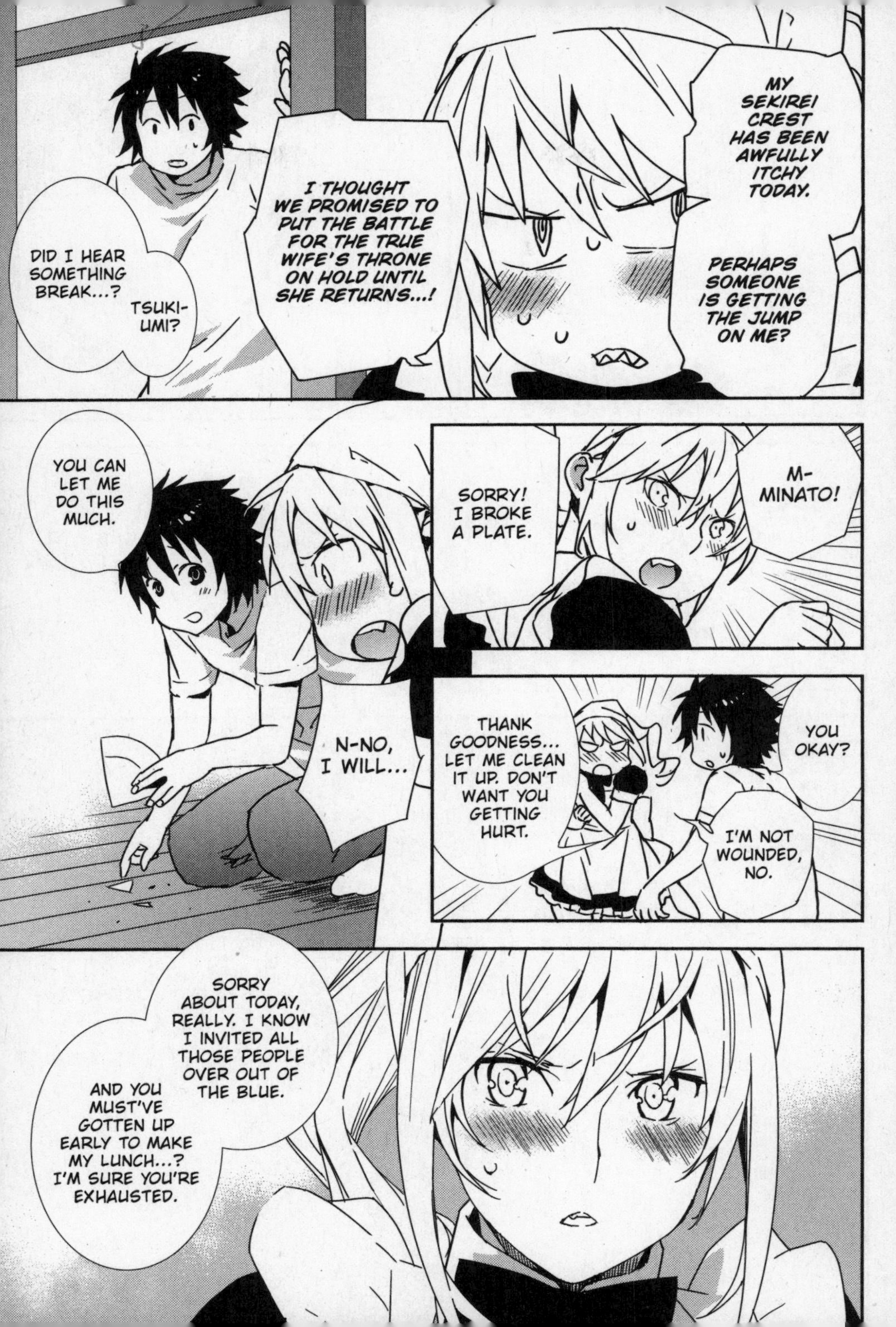
MY SEKIREI CREST HAS BEEN AWFULLY ITCHY TODAY.
PERHAPS SOMEONE IS GETTING THE JUMP ON ME?
I THOUGHT WE PROMISED TO PUT THE BATTLE FOR THE TRUE WIFE'S THRONE ON HOLD UNTIL SHE RETURNS...!
DID I HEAR SOMETHING BREAK...?
TSUKI-UMI?
M-MINATO!
SORRY! I BROKE A PLATE.
YOU OKAY?
I'M NOT WOUNDED, NO.
THANK GOODNESS... LET ME CLEAN IT UP. DON'T WANT YOU GETTING HURT.
N-NO, I WILL...
YOU CAN LET ME DO THIS MUCH.
SORRY ABOUT TODAY, REALLY. I KNOW I INVITED ALL THOSE PEOPLE OVER OUT OF THE BLUE.
AND YOU MUST'VE GOTTEN UP EARLY TO MAKE MY LUNCH...? I'M SURE YOU'RE EXHAUSTED.

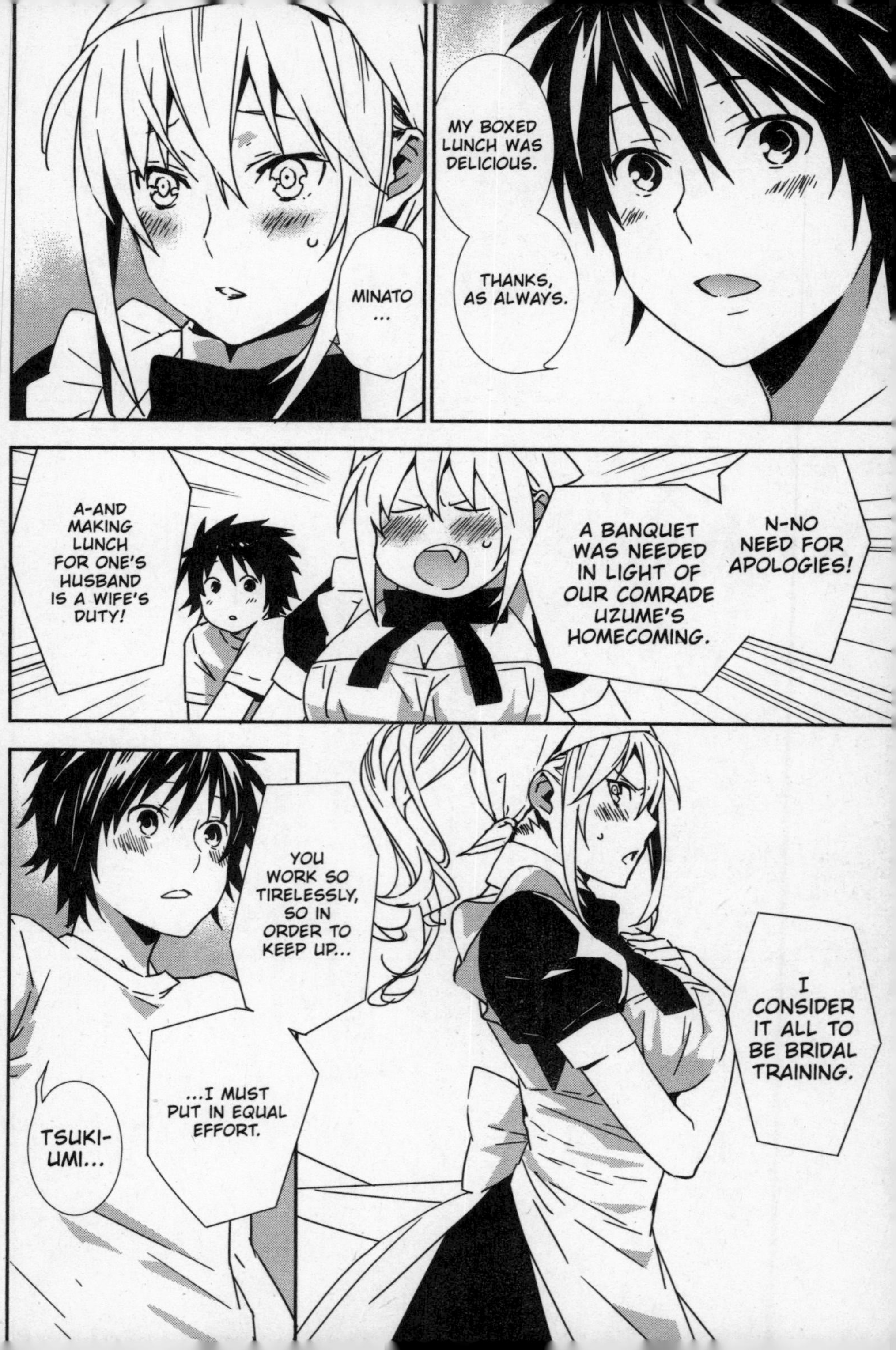
MY BOXED LUNCH WAS DELICIOUS.
THANKS, AS ALWAYS.
MINATO ...
N-NO NEED FOR APOLOGIES!
A BANQUET WAS NEEDED IN LIGHT OF OUR COMRADE UZUME'S HOMECOMING.
A-AND MAKING LUNCH FOR ONE'S HUSBAND IS A WIFE'S DUTY!
I CONSIDER IT ALL TO BE BRIDAL TRAINING.
YOU WORK SO TIRELESSLY, SO IN ORDER TO KEEP UP...
...I MUST PUT IN EQUAL EFFORT.
TSUKI-UMI...

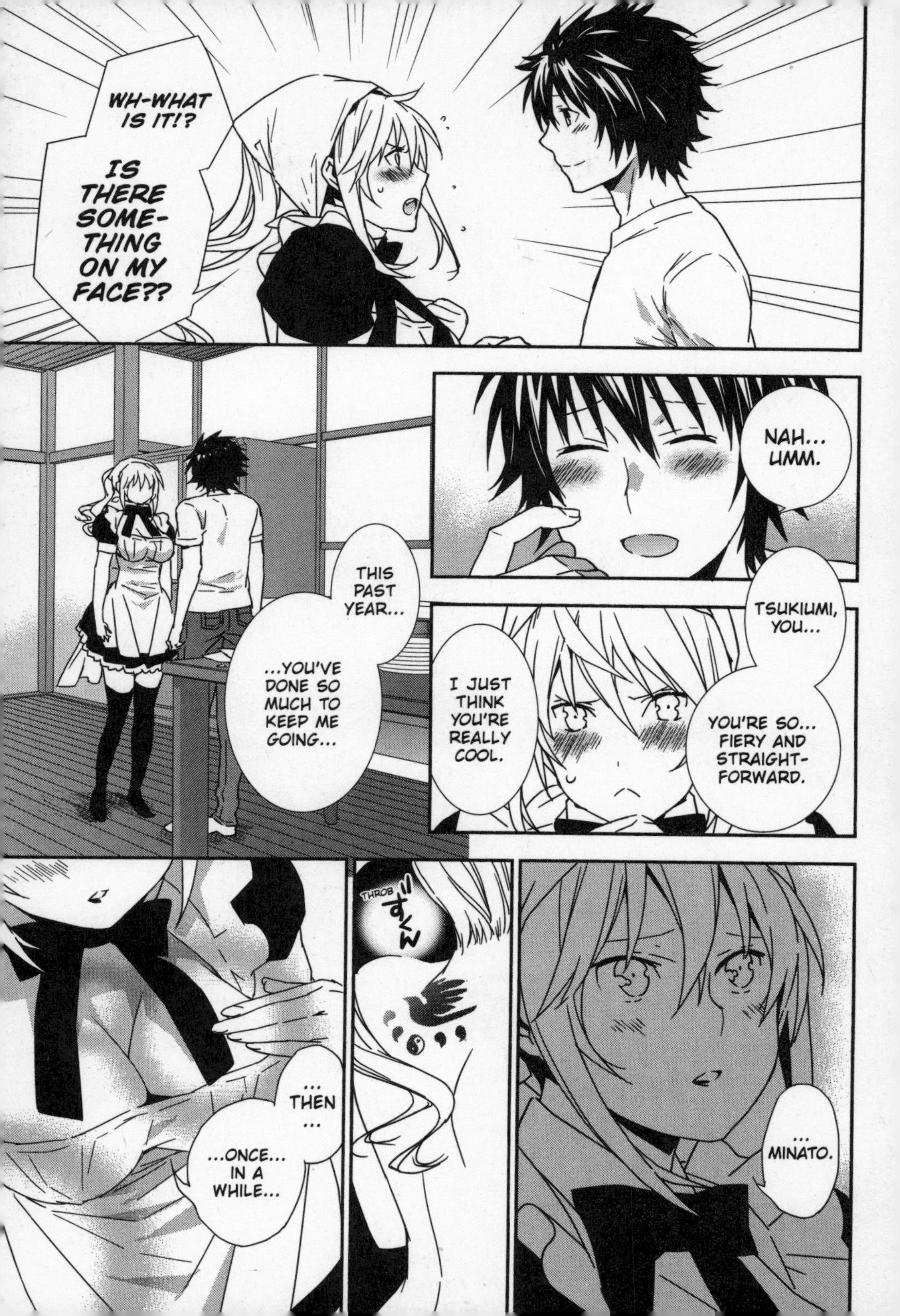
WH-WHAT IS IT!?
IS THERE SOME-THING ON MY FACE??
NAH... UMM.
TSUKIUMI, YOU...
YOU'RE SO... FIERY AND STRAIGHT-FORWARD.
I JUST THINK YOU'RE REALLY COOL.
THIS PAST YEAR...
...YOU'VE DONE SO MUCH TO KEEP ME GOING...
...MINATO.
THROB
...THEN...
...ONCE... IN A WHILE...

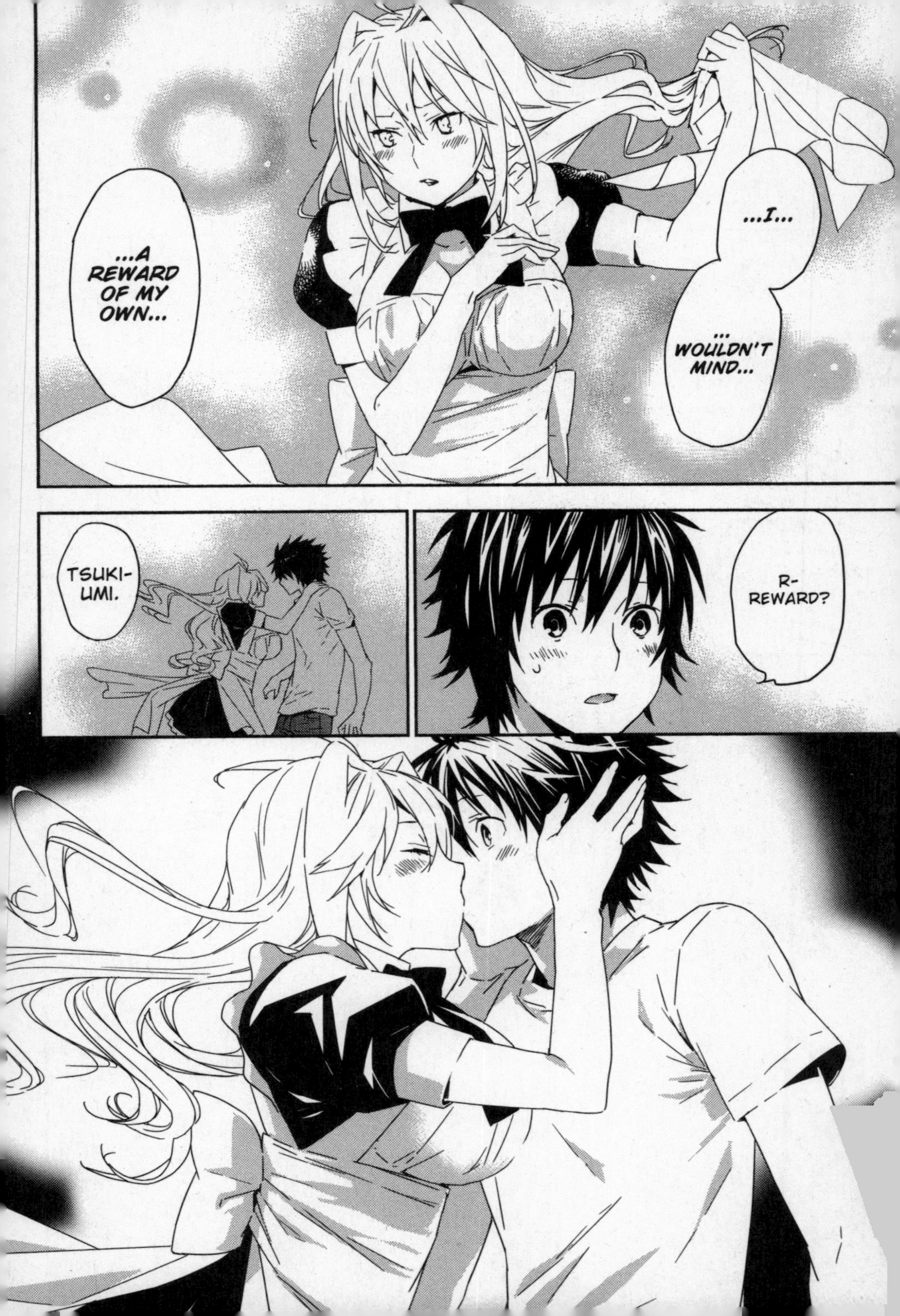
...I...
...WOULDN'T MIND...
...A REWARD OF MY OWN...
R-REWARD?
TSUKI-UMI.

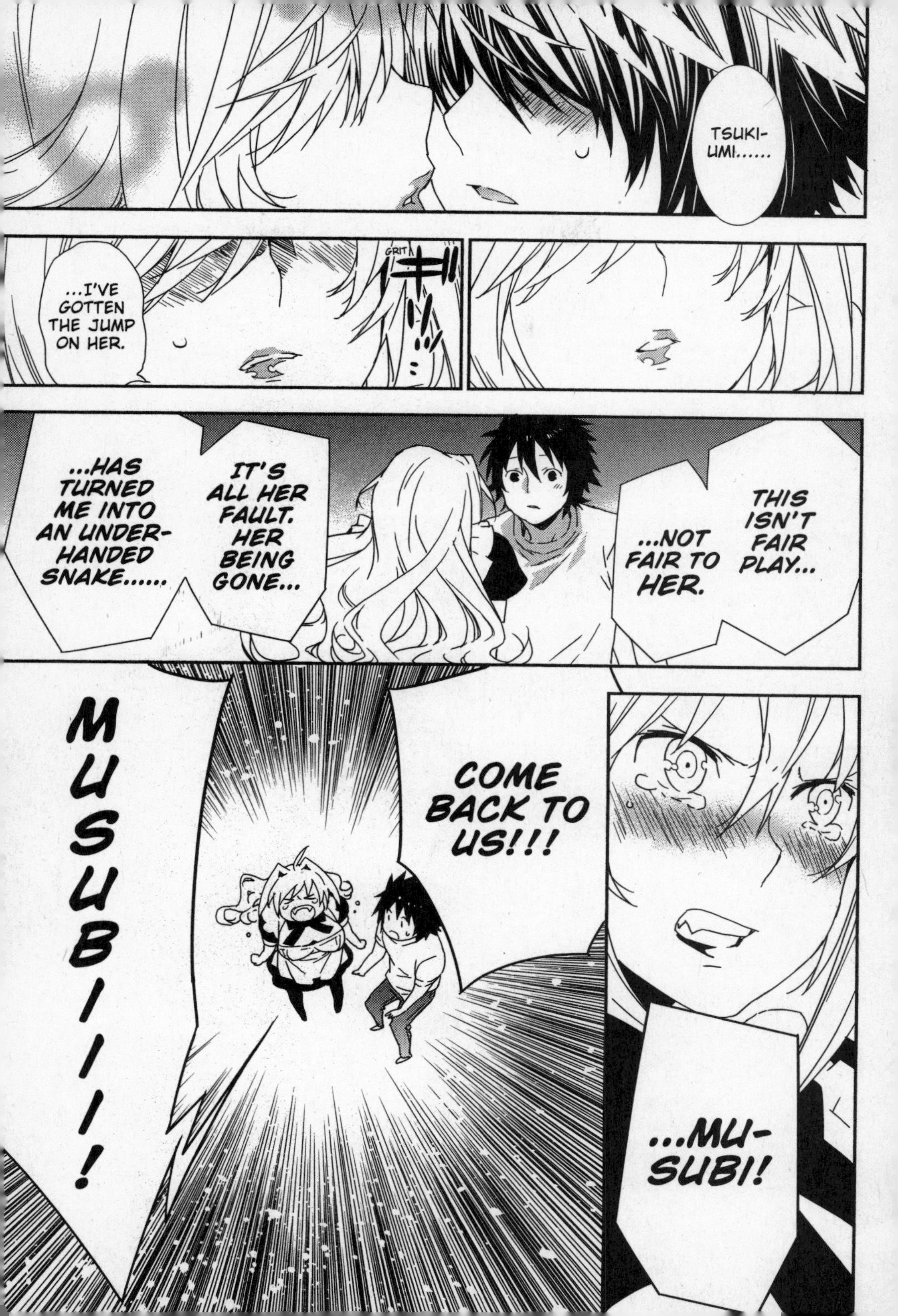
TSUKI-UMI......
GRIT
...I'VE GOTTEN THE JUMP ON HER.
THIS ISN'T FAIR PLAY...
...NOT FAIR TO HER.
IT'S ALL HER FAULT. HER BEING GONE...
...HAS TURNED ME INTO AN UNDER-HANDED SNAKE......
...MU-SUBI!
COME BACK TO US!!!
MUSUBIIII!

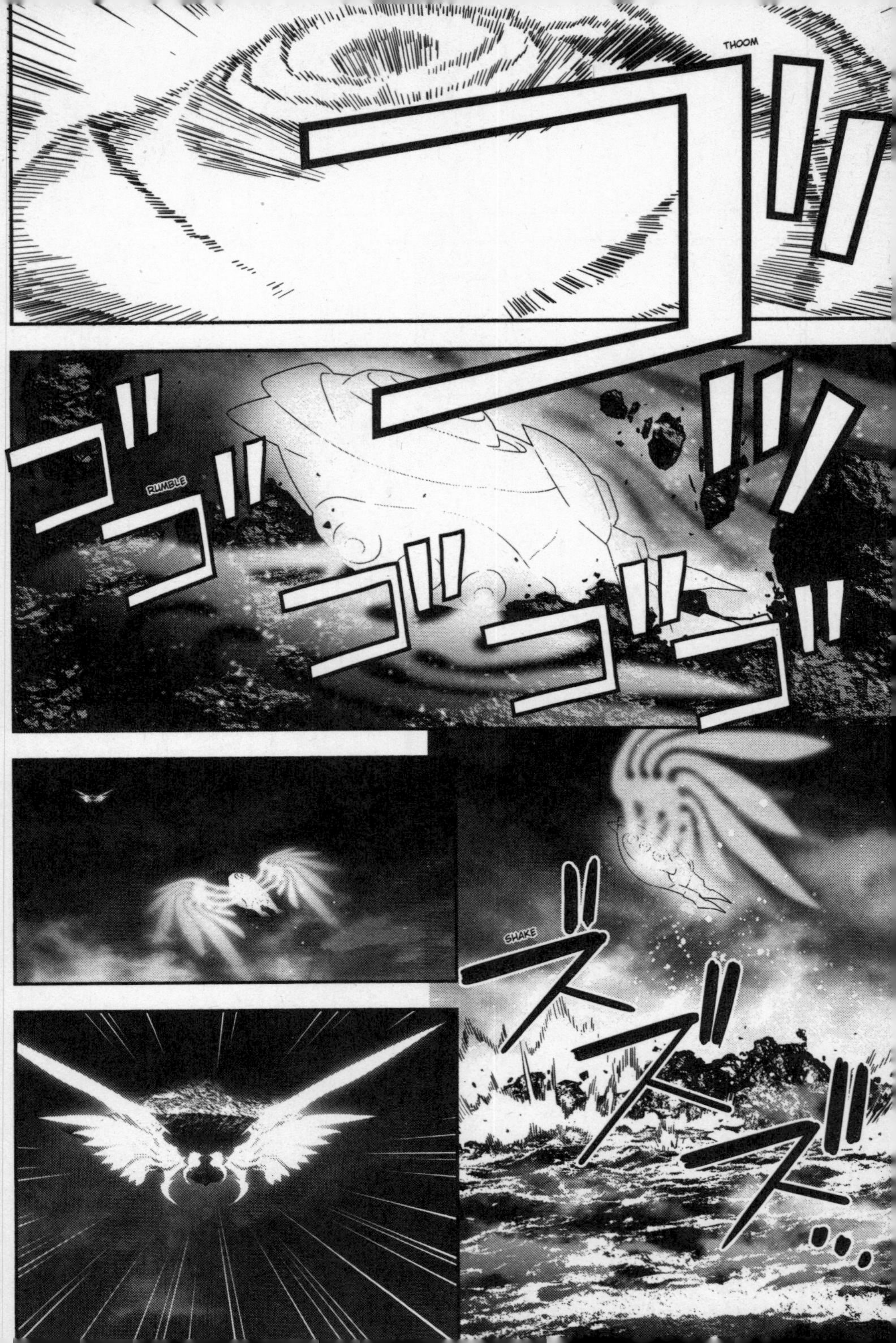
THOOM
RUMBLE
SHAKE

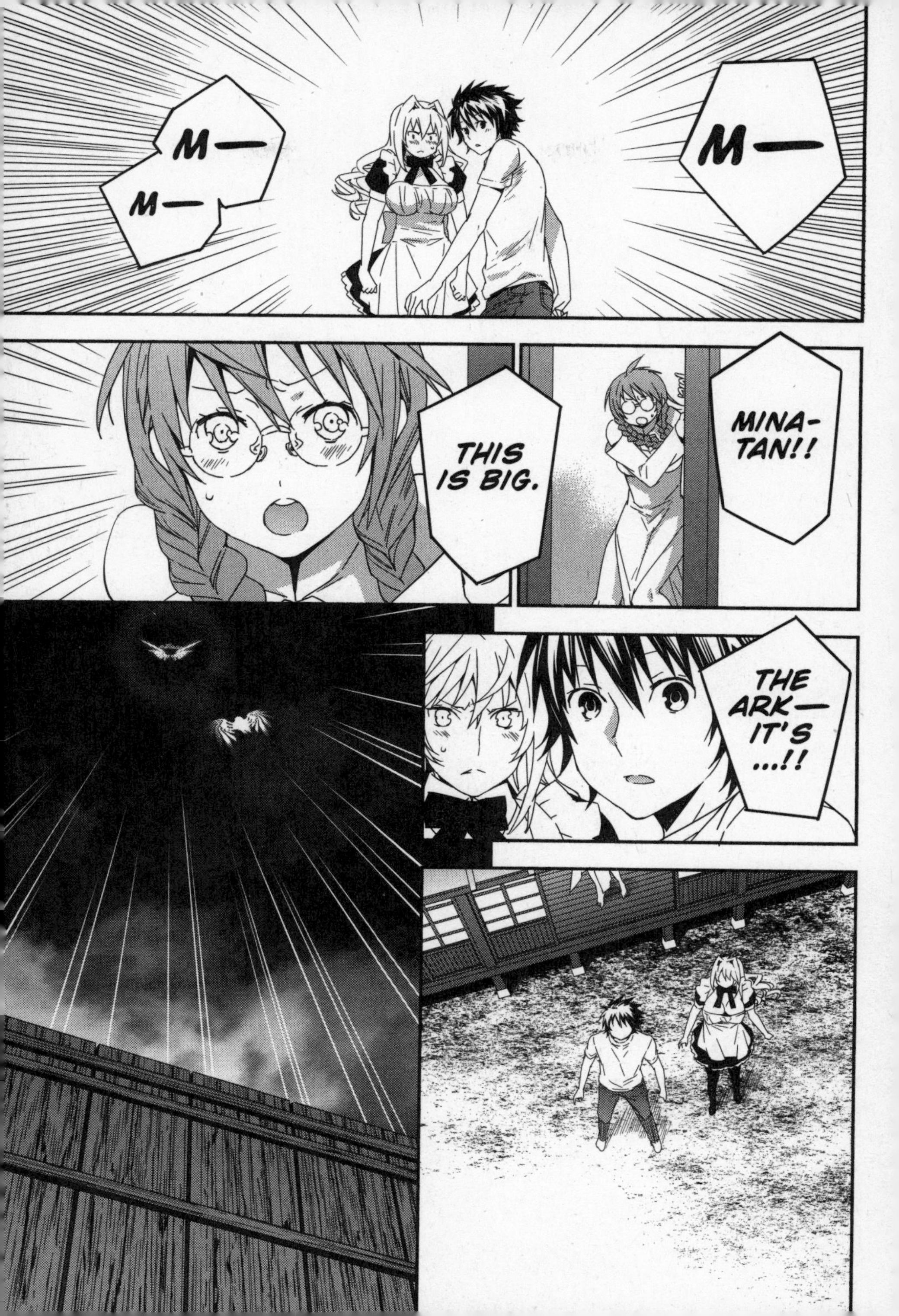
M—
M—
M—
MINA-TAN!!
THIS IS BIG.
THE ARK— IT'S ...!!

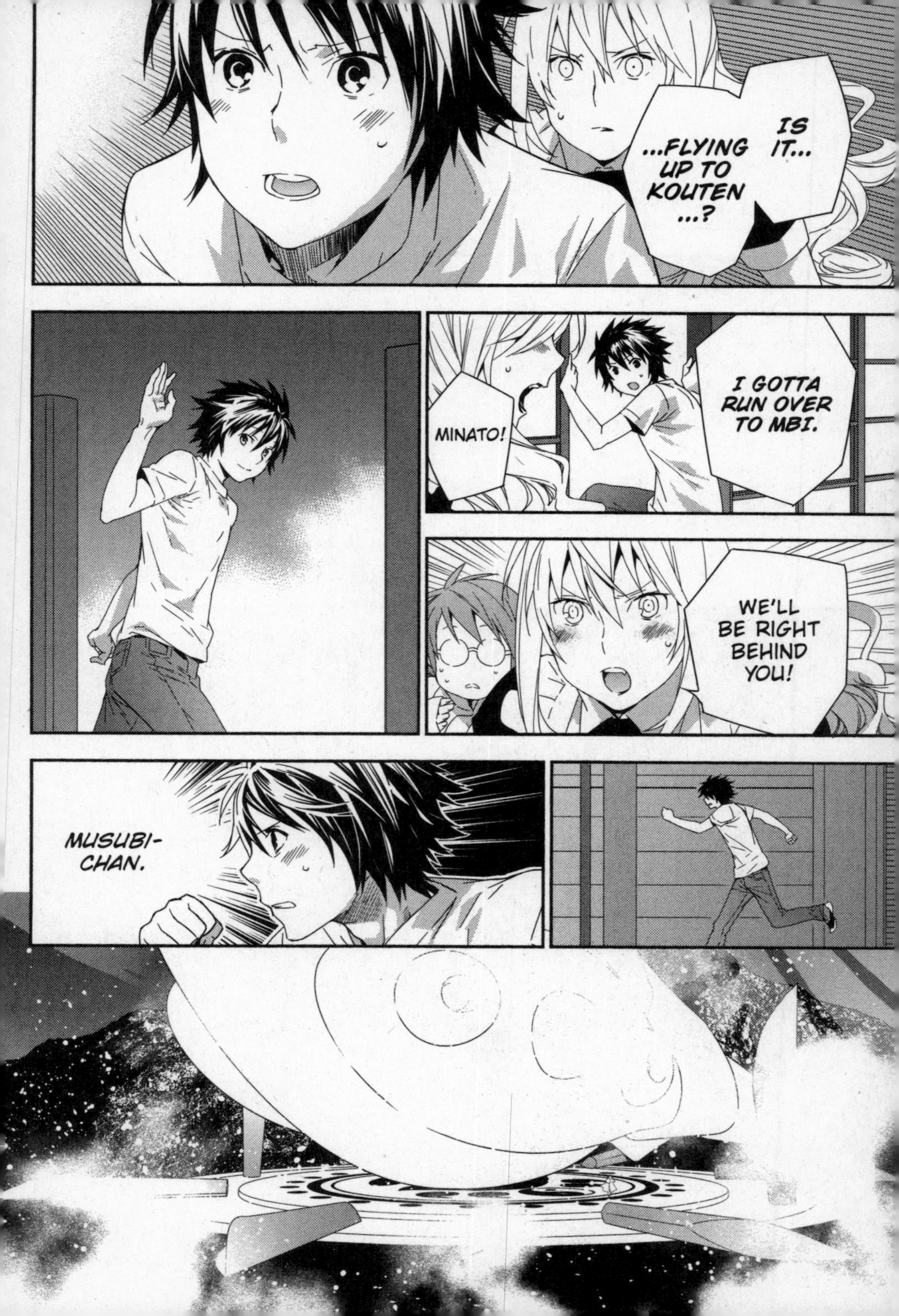
IS IT... ...FLYING UP TO KOUTEN ...?
I GOTTA RUN OVER TO MBI.
MINATO!
WE'LL BE RIGHT BEHIND YOU!
MUSUBI-CHAN.

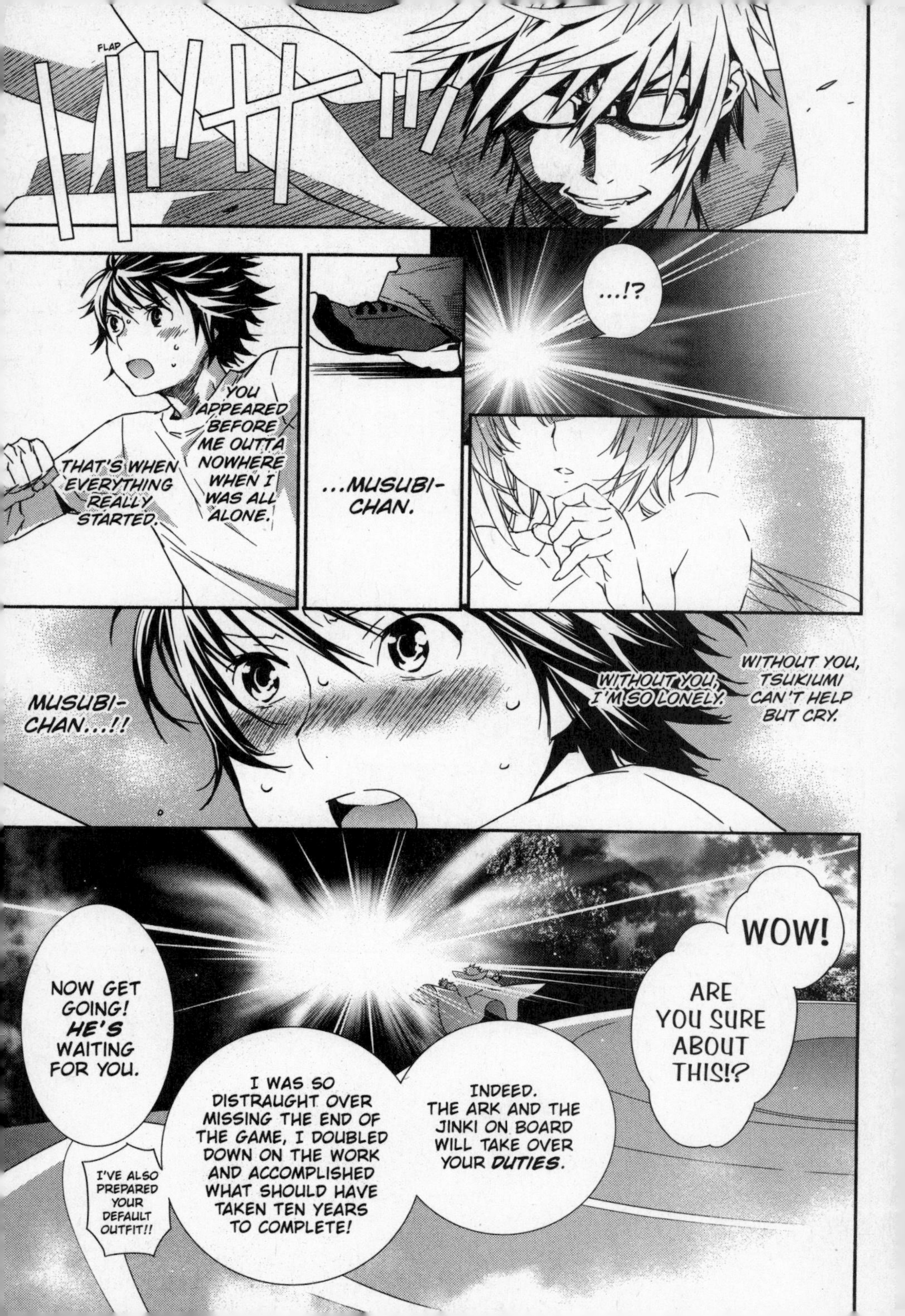
FLAP
...!?
...MUSUBI-CHAN.
YOU APPEARED BEFORE ME OUTTA NOWHERE WHEN I WAS ALL ALONE.
THAT'S WHEN EVERYTHING REALLY STARTED.
WITHOUT YOU, TSUKIUMI CAN'T HELP BUT CRY.
WITHOUT YOU, I'M SO LONELY.
MUSUBI-CHAN...!!
WOW!
ARE YOU SURE ABOUT THIS!?
INDEED. THE ARK AND THE JINKI ON BOARD WILL TAKE OVER YOUR DUTIES.
NOW GET GOING! HE'S WAITING FOR YOU.
I WAS SO DISTRAUGHT OVER MISSING THE END OF THE GAME, I DOUBLED DOWN ON THE WORK AND ACCOMPLISHED WHAT SHOULD HAVE TAKEN TEN YEARS TO COMPLETE!
I'VE ALSO PREPARED YOUR DEFAULT OUTFIT!!

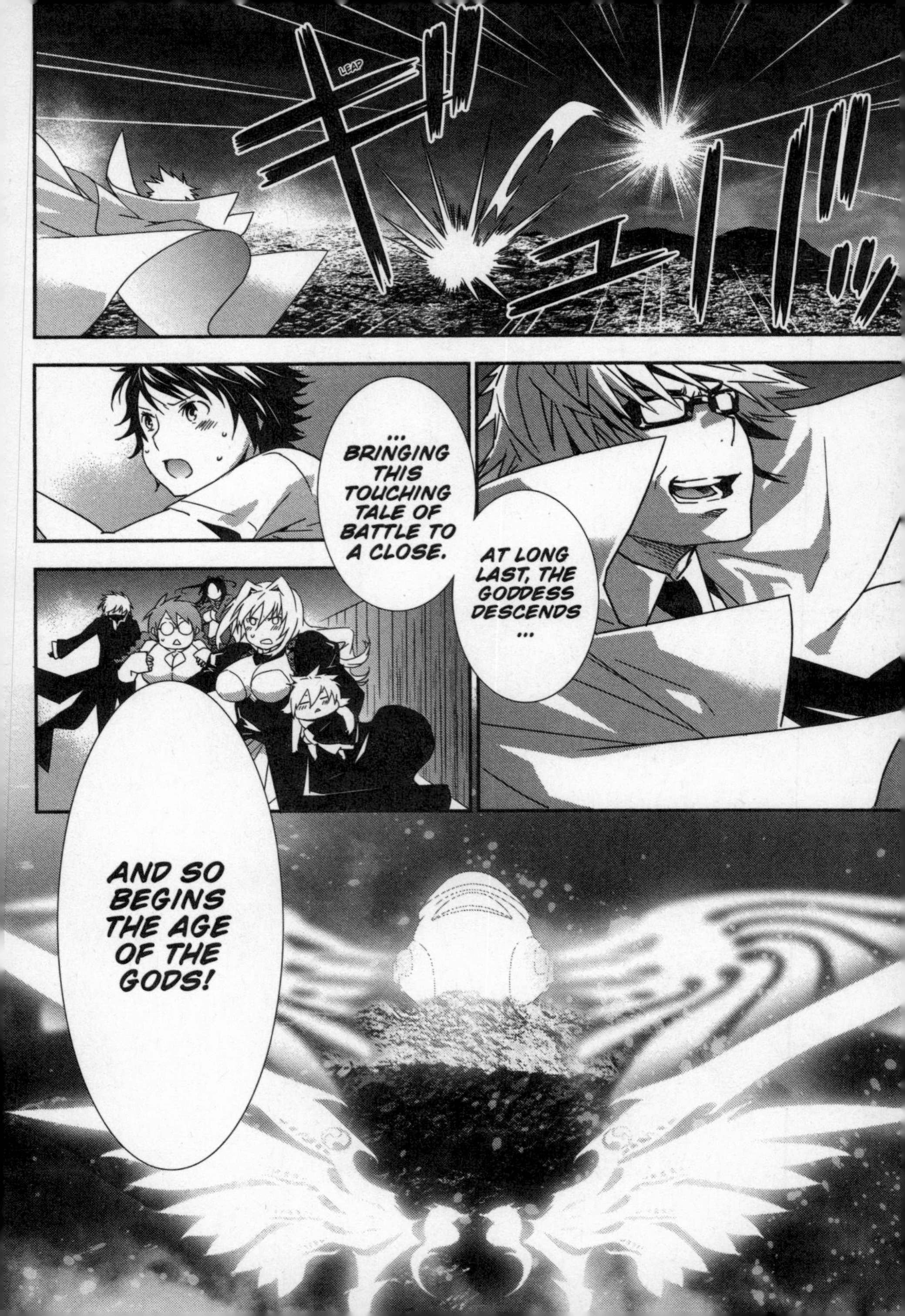
LEAP
AT LONG LAST, THE GODDESS DESCENDS ...
... BRINGING THIS TOUCHING TALE OF BATTLE TO A CLOSE.
AND SO BEGINS THE AGE OF THE GODS!

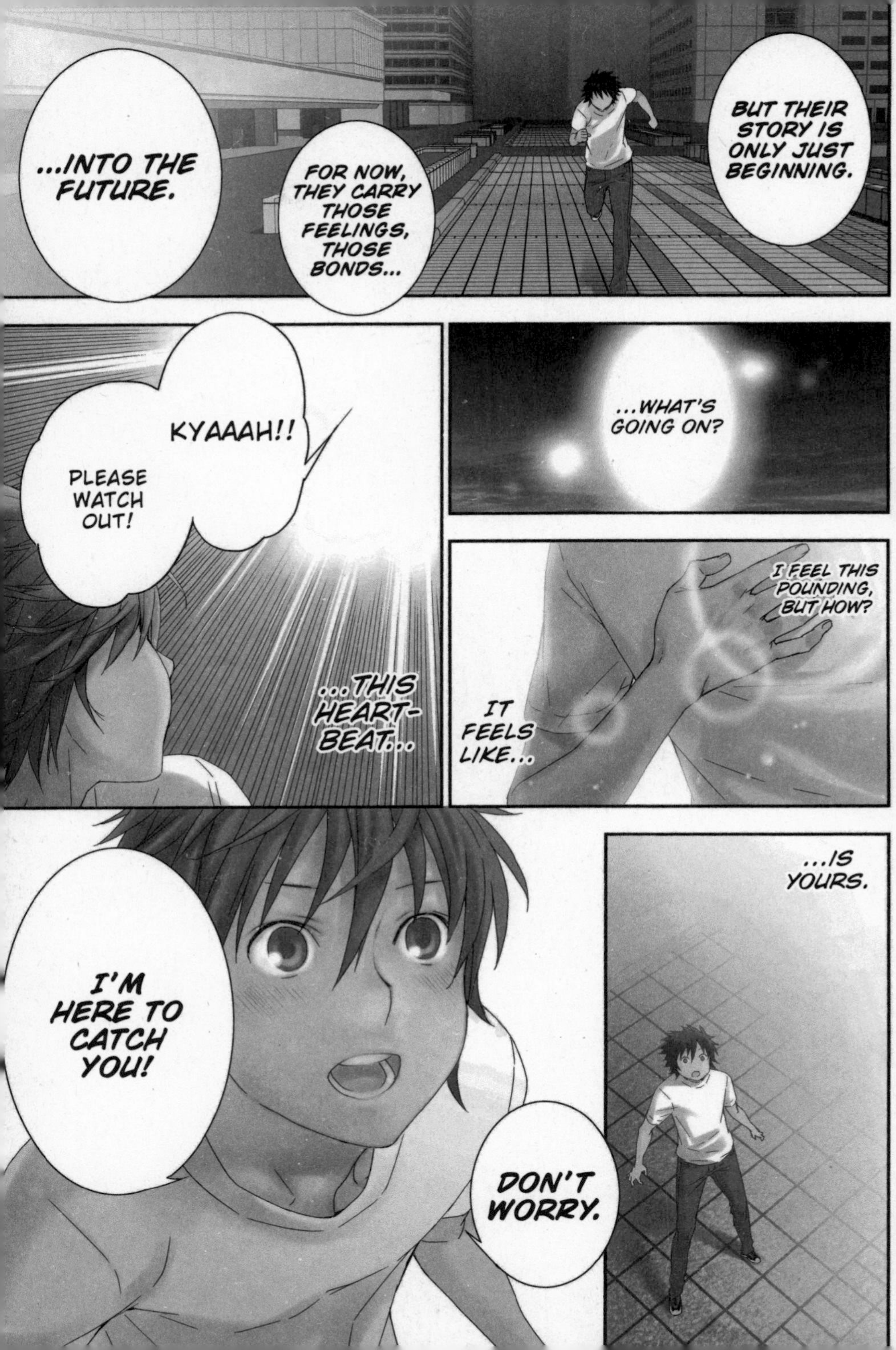
BUT THEIR STORY IS ONLY JUST BEGINNING.
FOR NOW, THEY CARRY THOSE FEELINGS, THOSE BONDS...
...INTO THE FUTURE.
...WHAT'S GOING ON?
I FEEL THIS POUNDING, BUT HOW?
IT FEELS LIKE...
KYAAAH!!
PLEASE WATCH OUT!
...THIS HEART-BEAT...
...IS YOURS.
DON'T WORRY.
I'M HERE TO CATCH YOU!

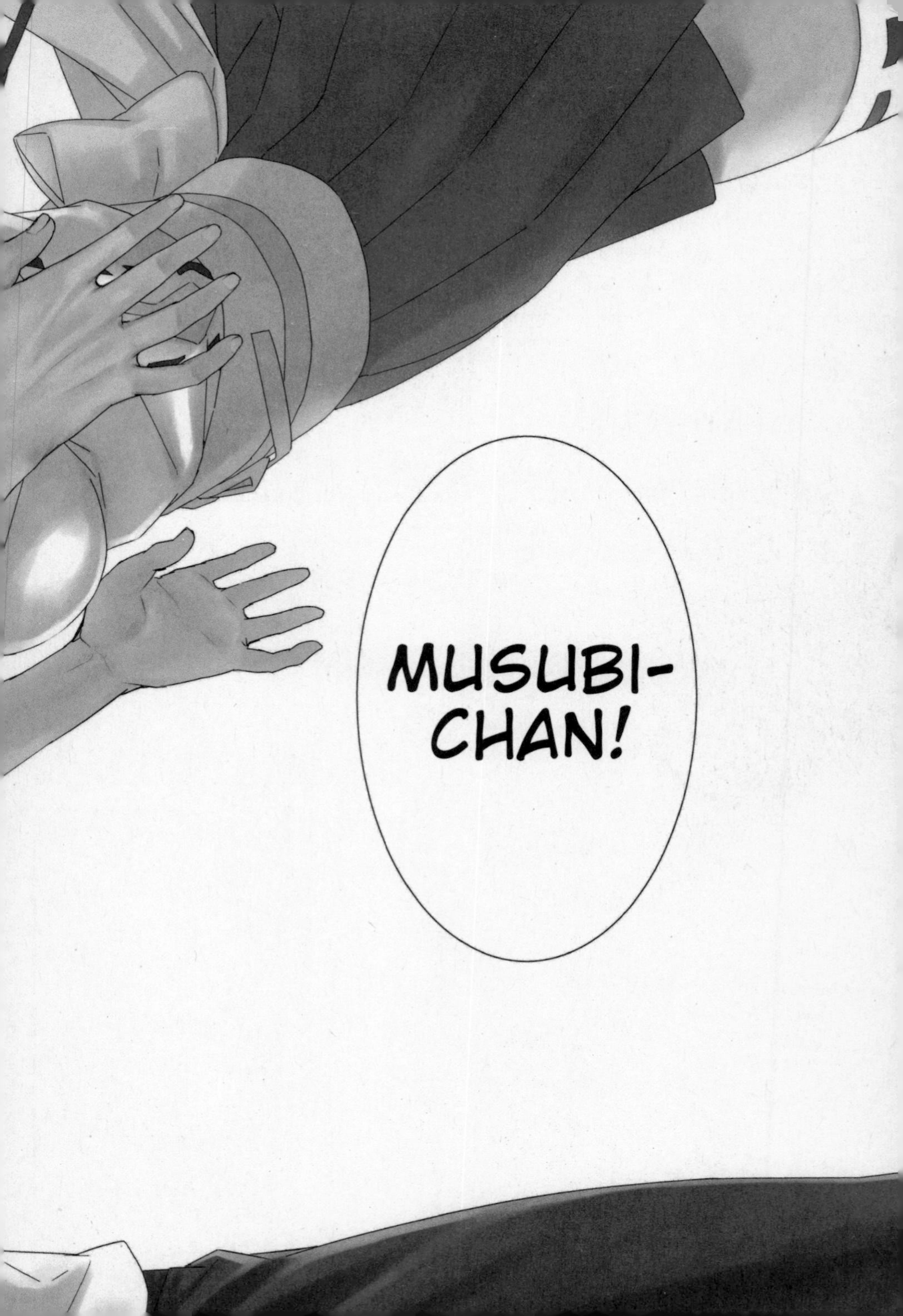
MUSUBI-CHAN!

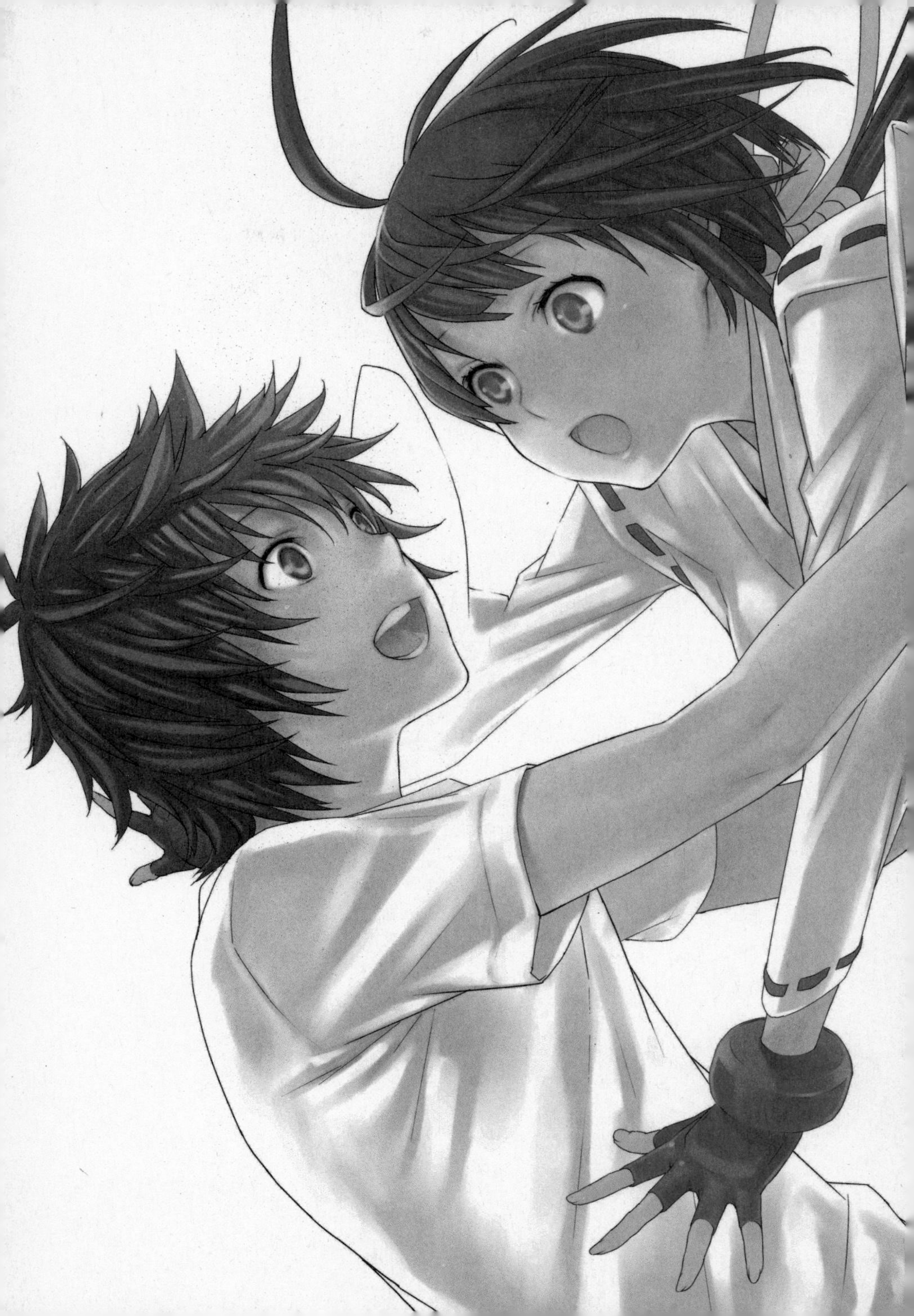

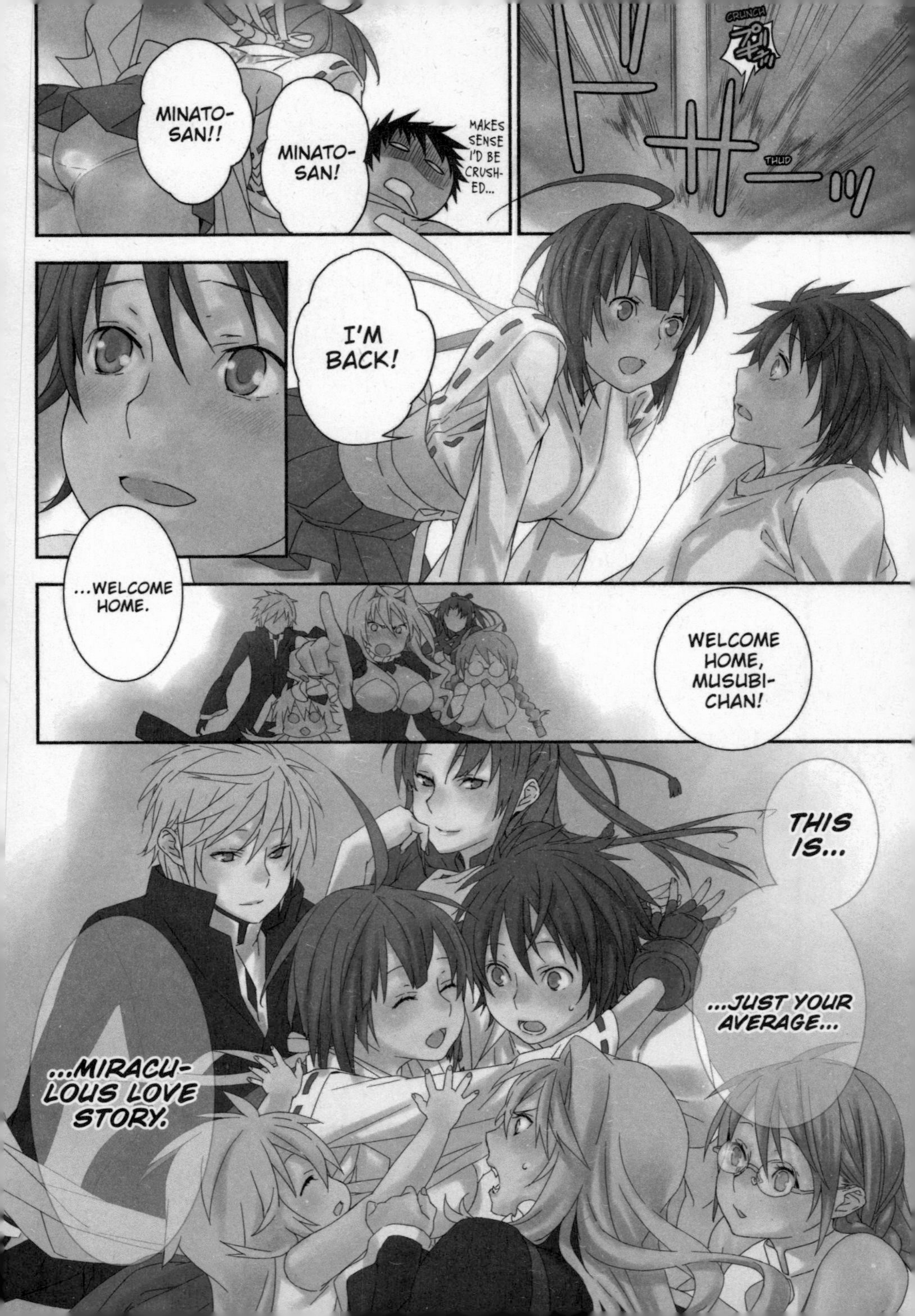
CRUNCH
THUD
MAKES SENSE I'D BE CRUSH-ED...
MINATO-SAN!
MINATO-SAN!!
I'M BACK!
...WELCOME HOME.
WELCOME HOME, MUSUBI-CHAN!
THIS IS...
...JUST YOUR AVERAGE...
...MIRACU-LOUS LOVE STORY.

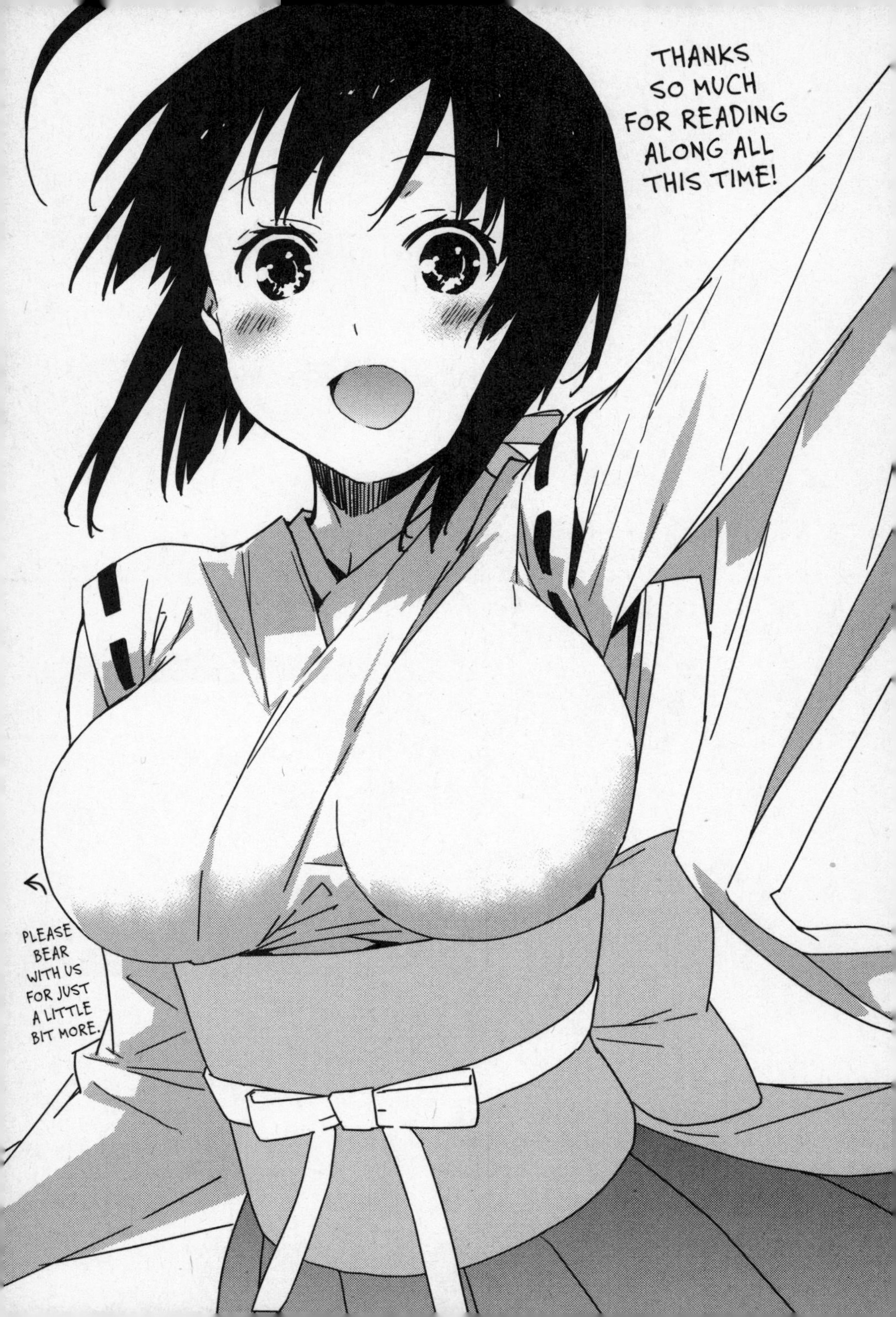
THANKS SO MUCH FOR READING ALONG ALL THIS TIME!
PLEASE BEAR WITH US FOR JUST A LITTLE BIT MORE.

JUST THEN, AT IZUMO INN...

MATSU-SAN...
I'M THIRSTY.
WOULD YOU MIND BRINGING ME SOME WATER...?
...MATSU-SAN?
WAFT
OF COURSE.
HERE YOU GO.

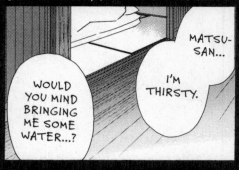

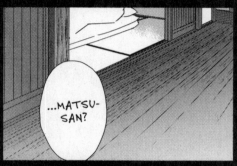

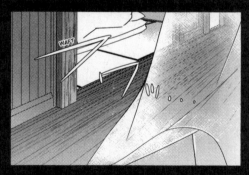

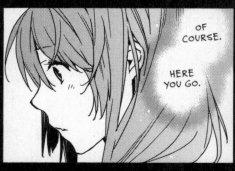

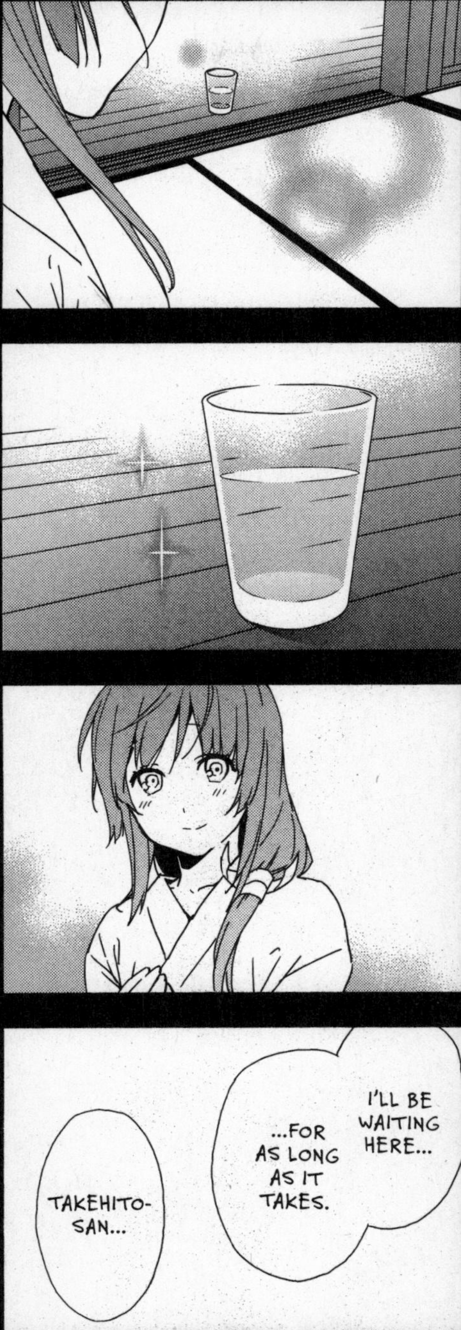
I'LL BE WAITING HERE...
...FOR AS LONG AS IT TAKES.
TAKEHITO-SAN...

END ♡

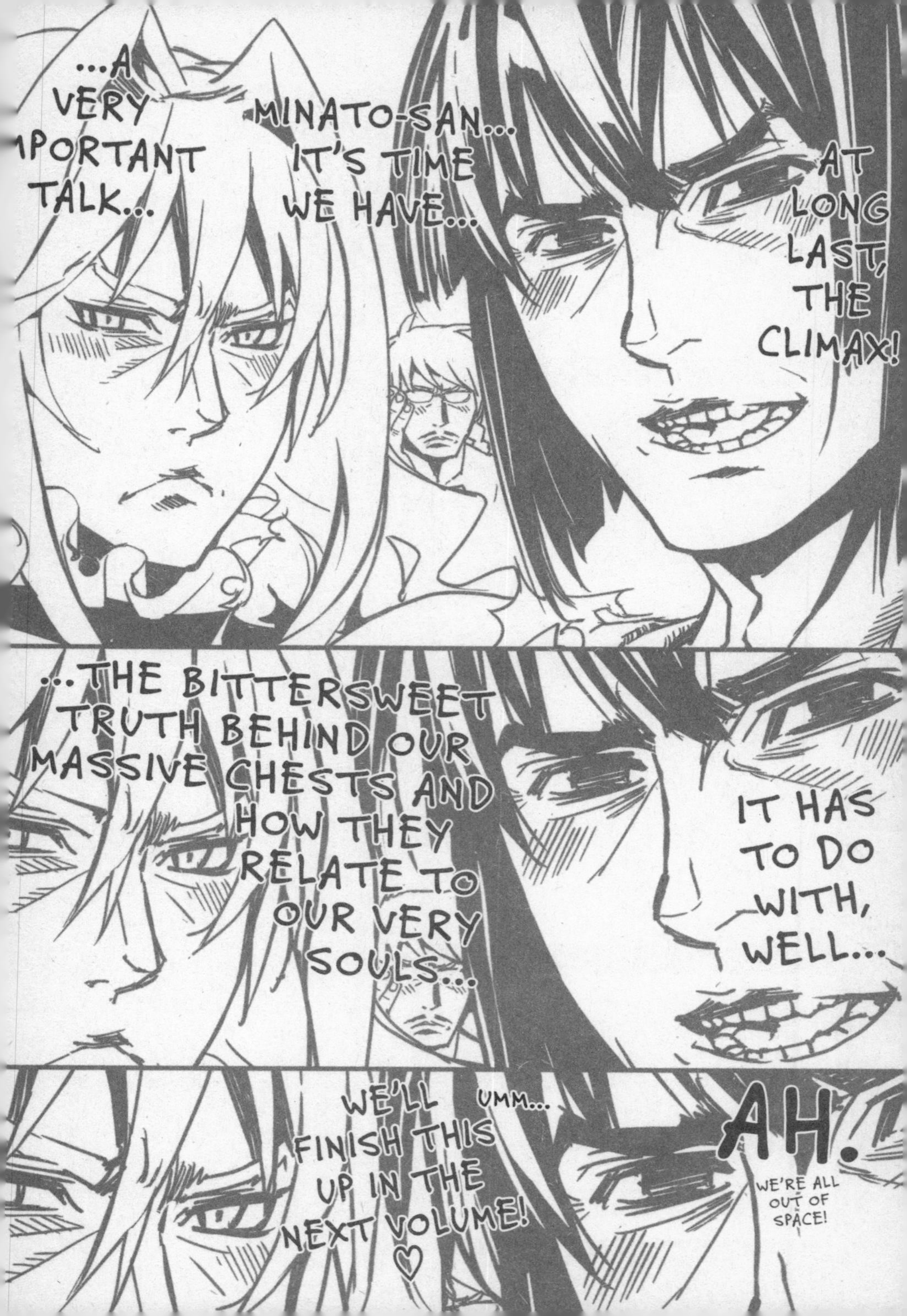
AT LONG LAST, THE CLIMAX!
MINATO-SAN... IT'S TIME WE HAVE...
...A VERY IMPORTANT TALK...
IT HAS TO DO WITH, WELL...
...THE BITTERSWEET TRUTH BEHIND OUR MASSIVE CHESTS AND HOW THEY RELATE TO OUR VERY SOULS...
AH.
WE'RE ALL OUT OF SPACE!
UMM...
WE'LL FINISH THIS UP IN THE NEXT VOLUME! ♡

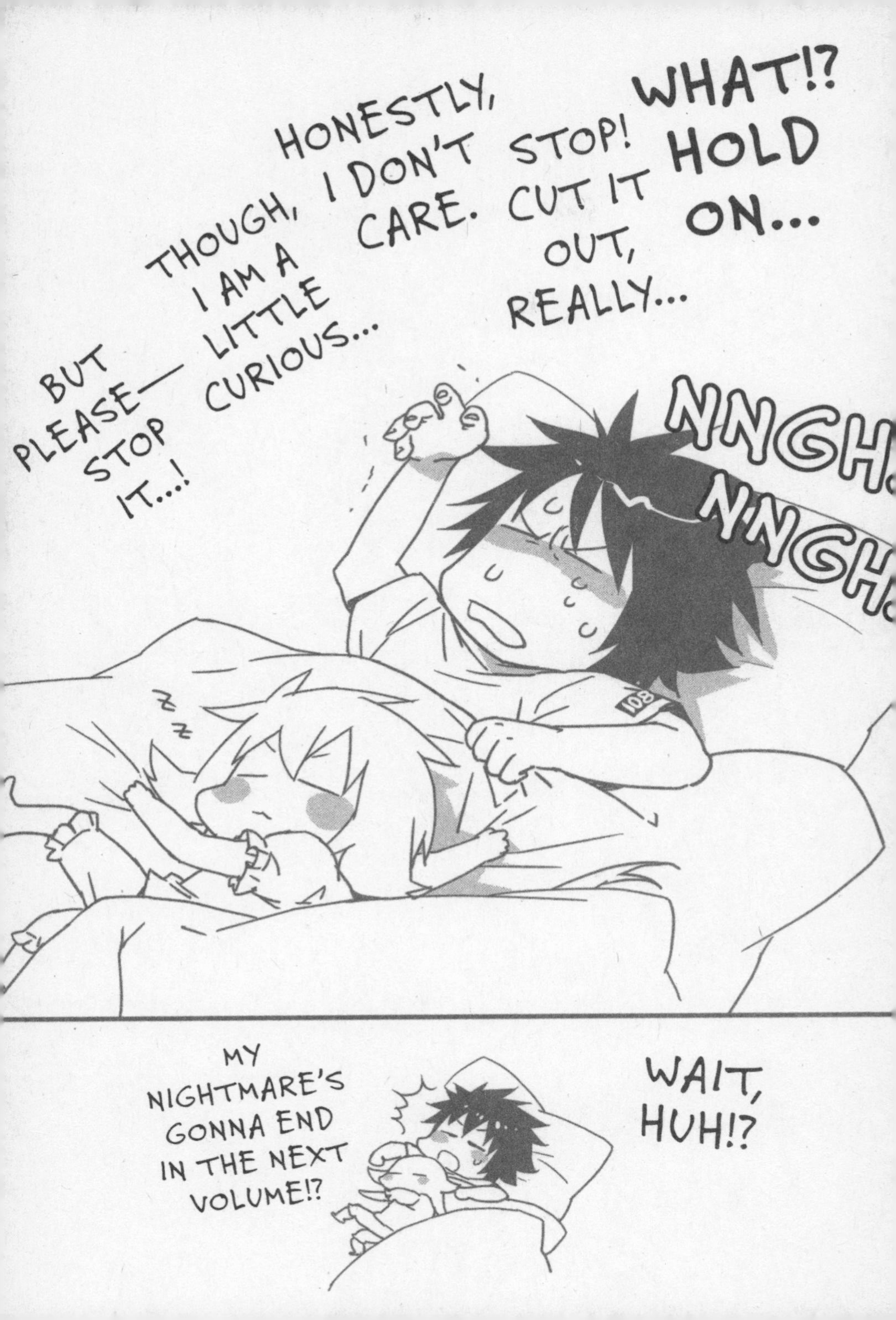
WHAT!? HOLD ON...
NNGH. NNGH.
STOP! CUT IT OUT, REALLY...
HONESTLY, THOUGH, I DON'T CARE.
I AM A LITTLE CURIOUS...
BUT PLEASE— STOP IT...!
WAIT, HUH!?
MY NIGHTMARE'S GONNA END IN THE NEXT VOLUME!?

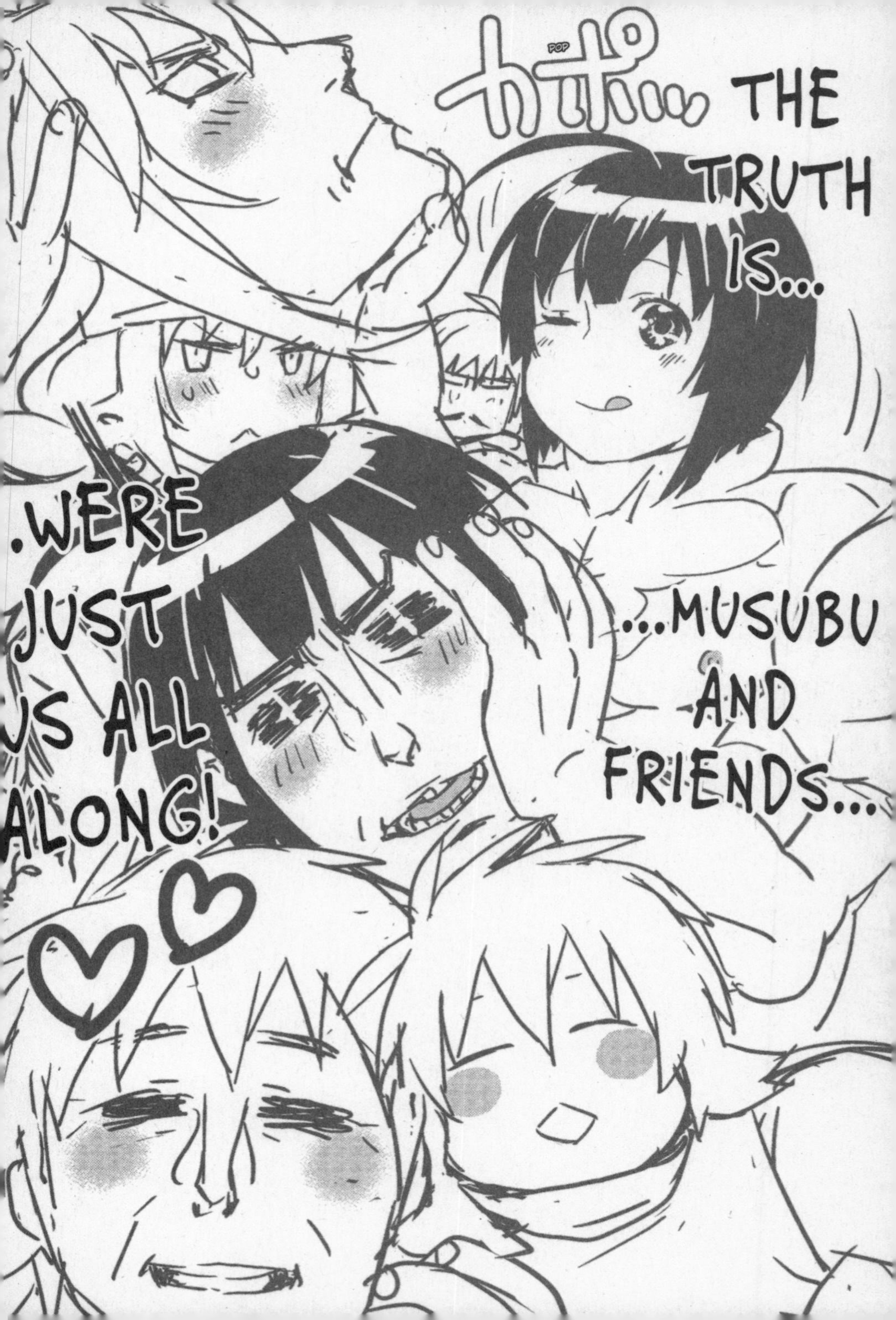
カポ…
POP
THE TRUTH IS...
...MUSUBU AND FRIENDS...
.WERE JUST US ALL ALONG!

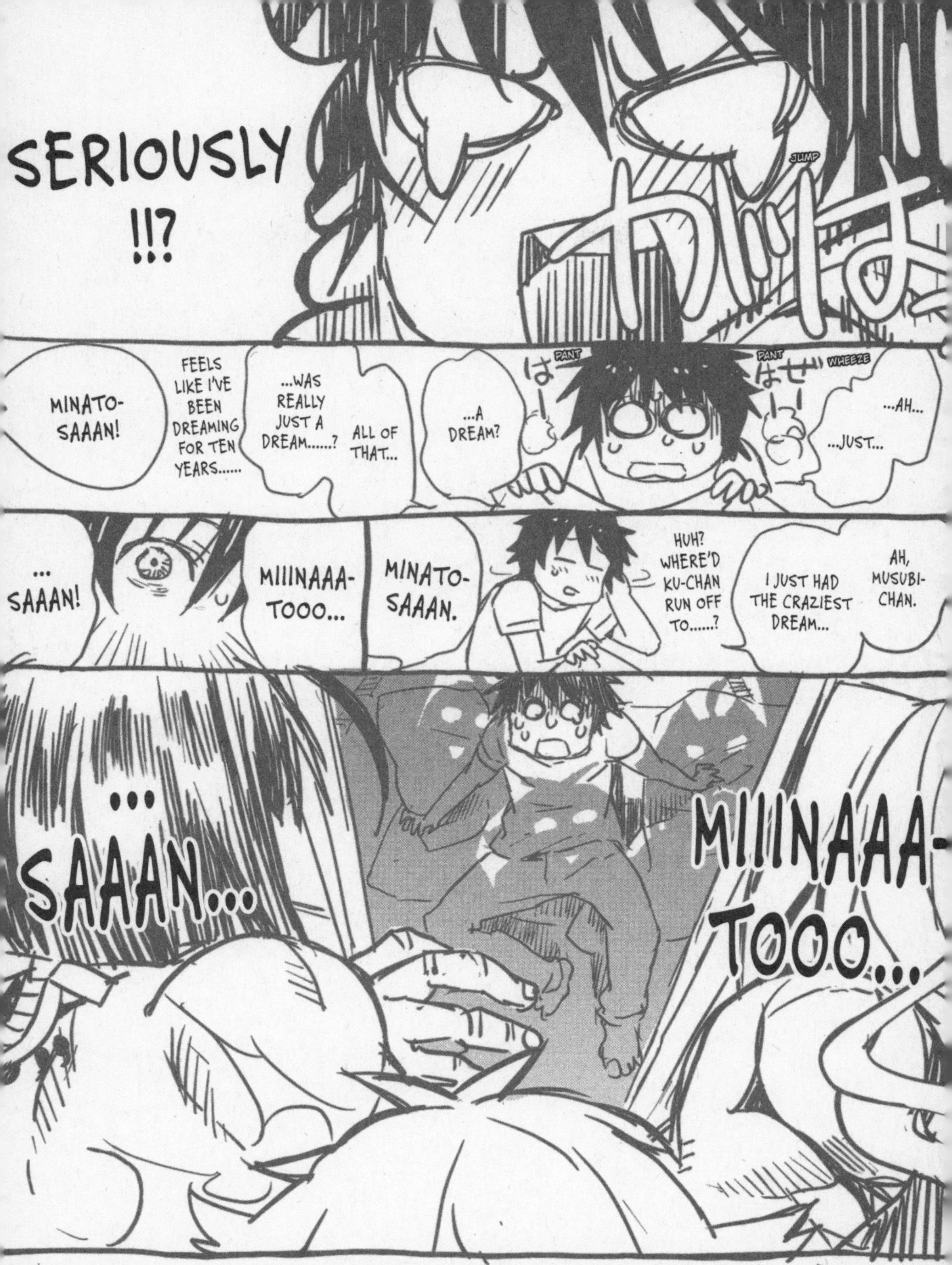
JUMP
SERIOUSLY !!?
...AH...
...JUST...
PANT
WHEEZE
PANT
...A DREAM?
ALL OF THAT...
...WAS REALLY JUST A DREAM......?
FEELS LIKE I'VE BEEN DREAMING FOR TEN YEARS......
MINATO-SAAAN!
AH, MUSUBI-CHAN.
I JUST HAD THE CRAZIEST DREAM...
HUH? WHERE'D KU-CHAN RUN OFF TO......?
MINATO-SAAAN.
MIIINAAA-TOOO...
... SAAAN!
MIIINAAA-TOOO...
... SAAAN...

GYAAAH...! MINATO SAHASHI'S NIGHTMARE CONTINUES......

Translation Notes

COMMON HONORIFICS
no honorific: Indicates familiarity or closeness; if used without permission or reason, addressing someone in this manner would constitute an insult.
-san: The Japanese equivalent of Mr./Mrs./Miss. If a situation calls for politeness, this is the fail-safe honorific.
-sama: Conveys great respect; may also indicate that the social status of the speaker is lower than that of the addressee.
-dono: A more archaic form of address similar to -sama.
-kun: Used most often when referring to boys, this indicates affection or familiarity. Occasionally used by older men among their peers, but it may also be used by anyone referring to a person of lower standing.
-chan: An affectionate honorific indicating familiarity used mostly in reference to girls; also used in reference to cute persons or animals of either gender.
-tan: A more cutesy version of -chan.

Page 8 - Minato's wagtail T-shirt
The Japanese wagtail is a common species of bird that prefers freshwater environments. The Japanese name for it, *sekirei*, also happens to be the title of the series.

Page 249 - Rounin
Though *rounin* once referred to masterless samurai, in modern Japanese society, it's used to denote prospective college students who've failed their entrance exams and exist in a sort of societal limbo.

Page 372 - Kuno/No good
Kuno's name sounds very similar to *munou*, which means "incompetence."

Page 376 - Raizou, Raiden, Raimei, Raigou
All of these baby names start with *Rai-*, meaning "lightning."

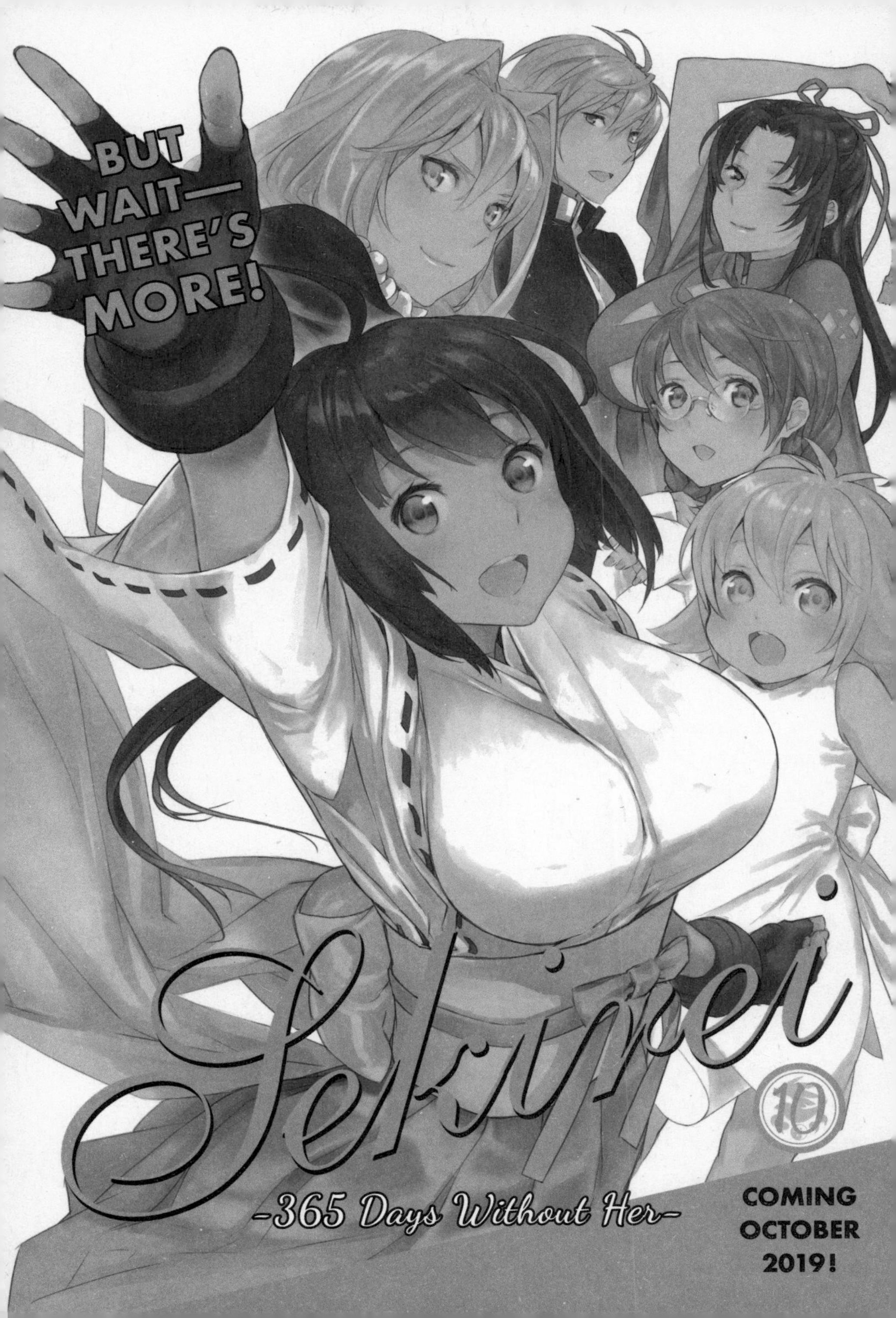
BUT WAIT—THERE'S MORE!
Sekirei
10
-365 Days Without Her-
COMING OCTOBER 2019!

RED IS THE NEW BLACK IN THIS BLOODY, ACTION-PACKED SERIES ABOUT A GROUP OF RIGHTEOUS ASSASSINS!

Teenage country bumpkin Tatsumi dreams of earning enough money for his impoverished village by working in the Capital—but his short-lived plans go awry when he's robbed by a buxom beauty upon arrival! Penniless, Tatsumi is taken in by the lovely Miss Aria, but just when his Capital dreams seem in reach yet again, Miss Aria's mansion is besieged by Night Raid—a team of ruthless assassins who targets high-ranking members of the upper class! As Tatsumi is quick to learn, appearances can be deceiving in the Capital, and this team of assassins just might be... the good guys?!

Akame ga KILL!

FULL SERIES AVAILABLE NOW!

For more information, visit www.yenpress.com

Yen Press

©Takahiro, Tetsuya Tashiro/SQUARE ENIX

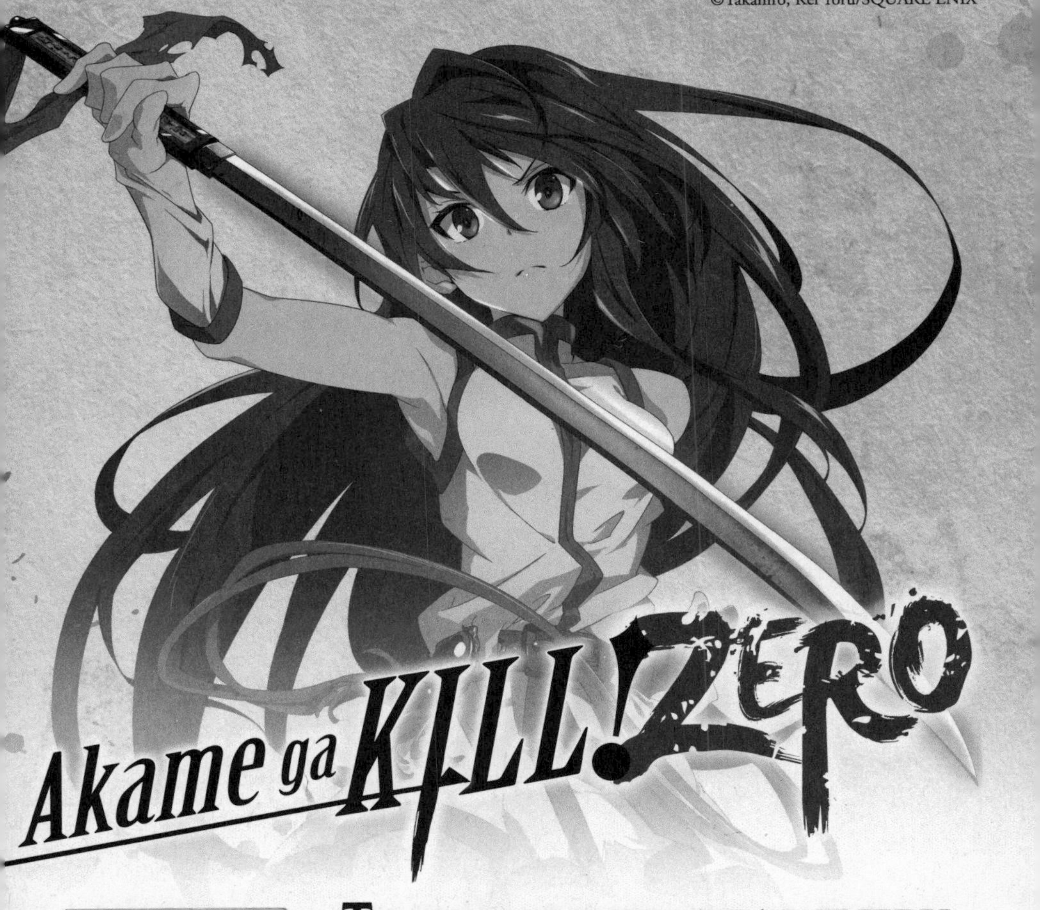
Akame ga KILL! ZERO

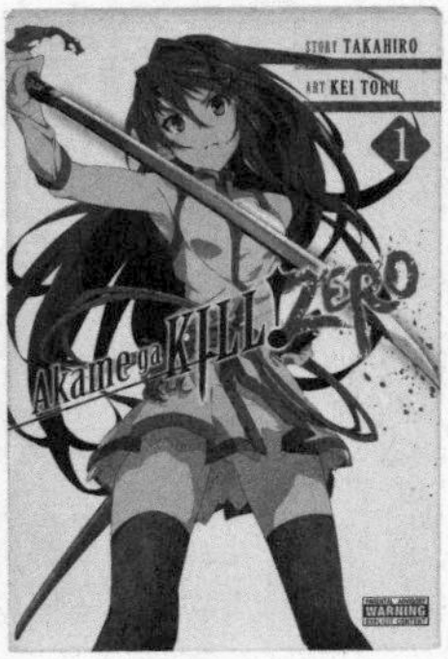
STORY TAKAHIRO
ART KEI TORU
1
Akame ga KILL! ZERO
WARNING

VOLUMES 1-7 AVAILABLE NOW!

Yen Press

THEY BELIEVED THAT EVERY TIME THEY TOOK A LIFE, THEY BROUGHT HAPPINESS TO ANOTHER...

Before becoming Night Raid's deadliest ally, Akame was a young girl bought by the Empire and raised as an assassin whose sole purpose was to slaughter everything in her path. Because that's what makes people happy...right? Discover Akame's shocking past in *Akame ga KILL! Zero*, the prequel to the hit series *Akame ga KILL!*

For more information, visit www.yenpress.com

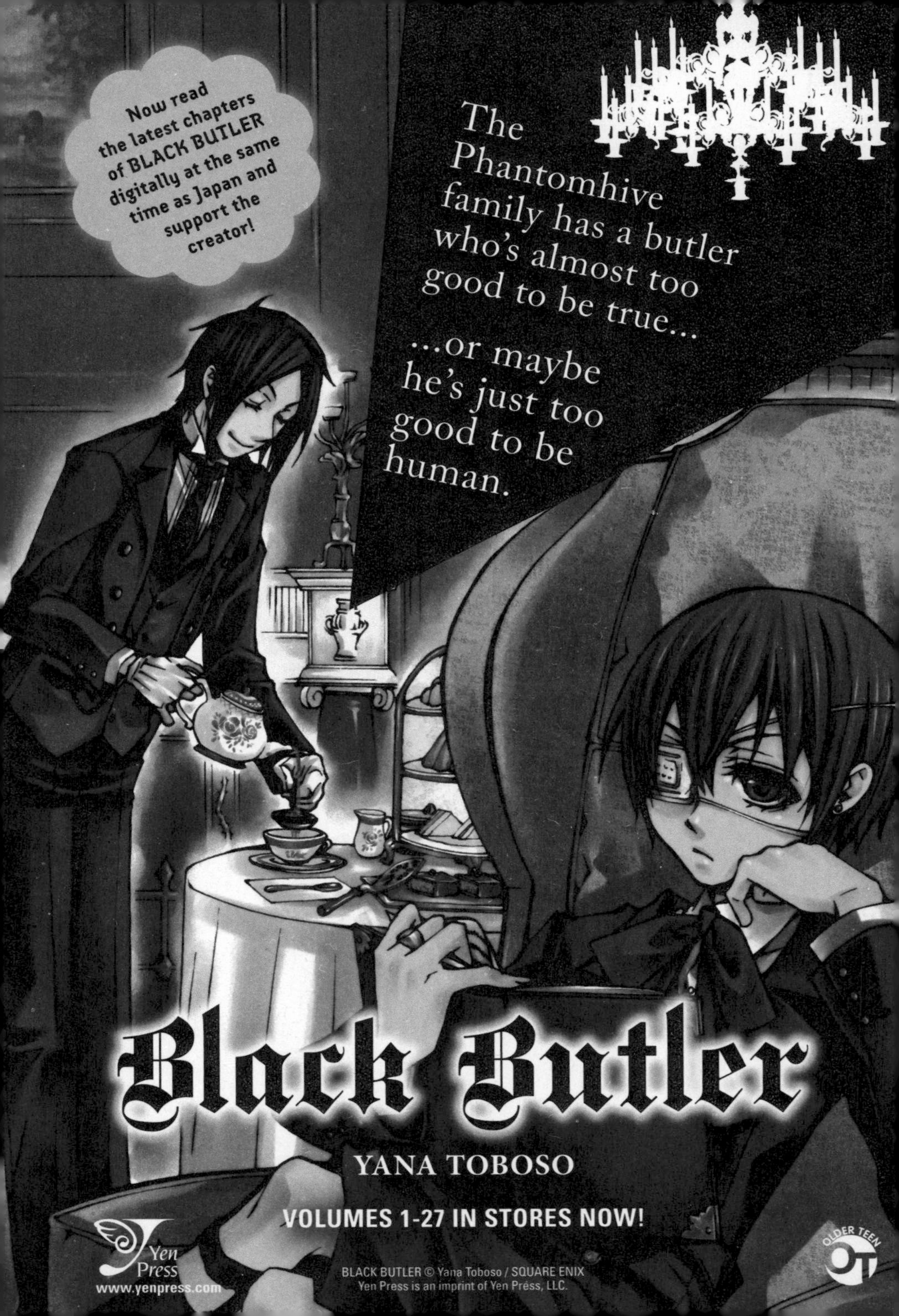
Now read the latest chapters of BLACK BUTLER digitally at the same time as Japan and support the creator!
The Phantomhive family has a butler who's almost too good to be true...
...or maybe he's just too good to be human.
Black Butler
YANA TOBOSO
VOLUMES 1-27 IN STORES NOW!
Yen Press
www.yenpress.com
BLACK BUTLER © Yana Toboso / SQUARE ENIX
Yen Press is an imprint of Yen Press, LLC.
OLDER TEEN
OT

HE DOES NOT LET ANYONE ROLL THE DICE.

A young Priestess joins her first adventuring party, but blind to the dangers, they almost immediately find themselves in trouble. It's Goblin Slayer who comes to their rescue—a man who has dedicated his life to the extermination of all goblins by any means necessary. A dangerous, dirty, and thankless job, but he does it better than anyone. And when rumors of his feats begin to circulate, there's no telling who might come calling next...

Light Novel V. 1-6 Available Now!

Check out the simul-pub manga chapters every month!

Goblin Slayer © Kumo Kagyu / Noboru Kannatuki / SB Creative Corp.

www.yenpress.com

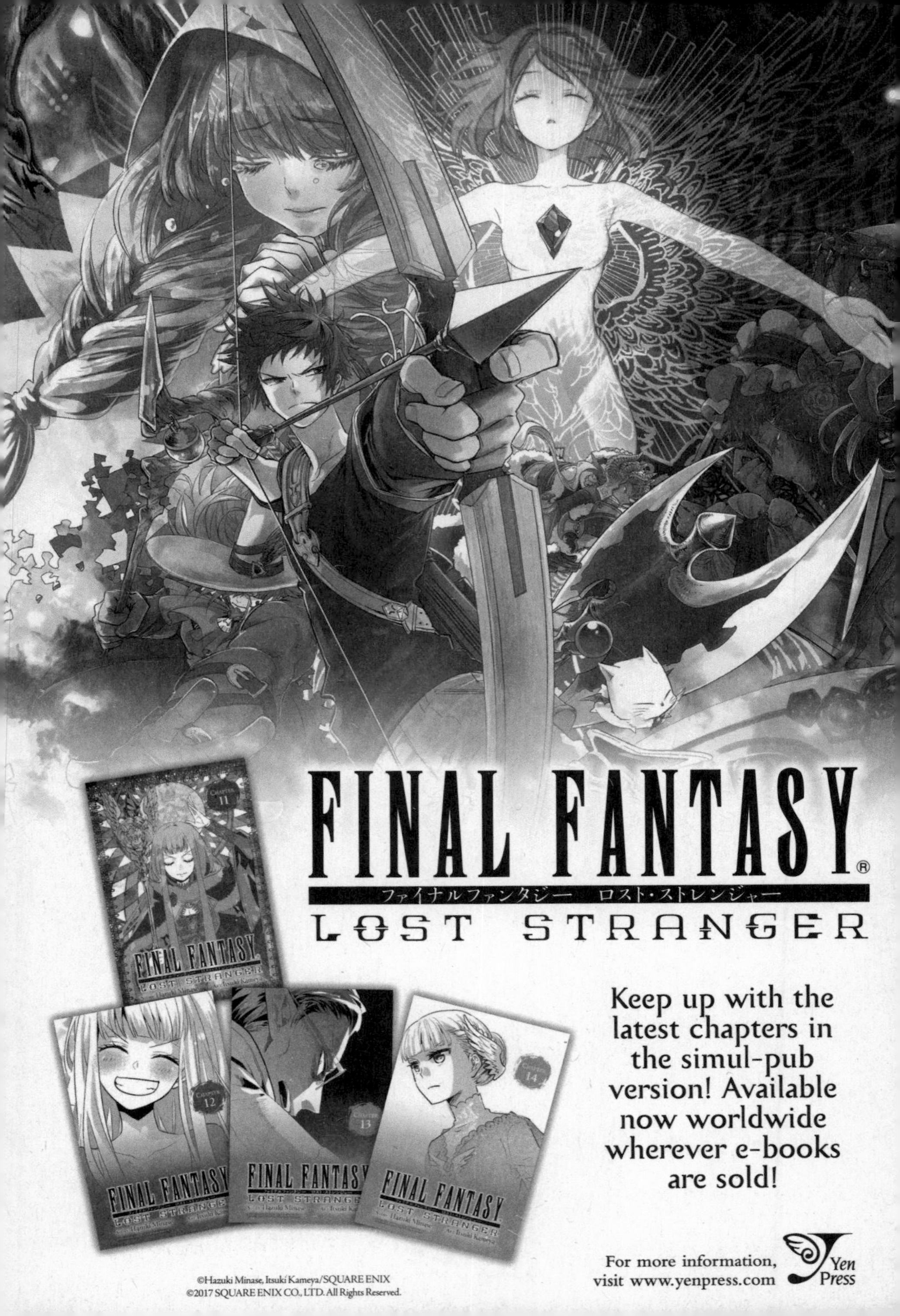
FINAL FANTASY®
ファイナルファンタジー　ロスト・ストレンジャー
LOST STRANGER
Keep up with the latest chapters in the simul-pub version! Available now worldwide wherever e-books are sold!
For more information, visit www.yenpress.com
Yen Press
©Hazuki Minase, Itsuki Kameya/SQUARE ENIX
©2017 SQUARE ENIX CO., LTD. All Rights Reserved.

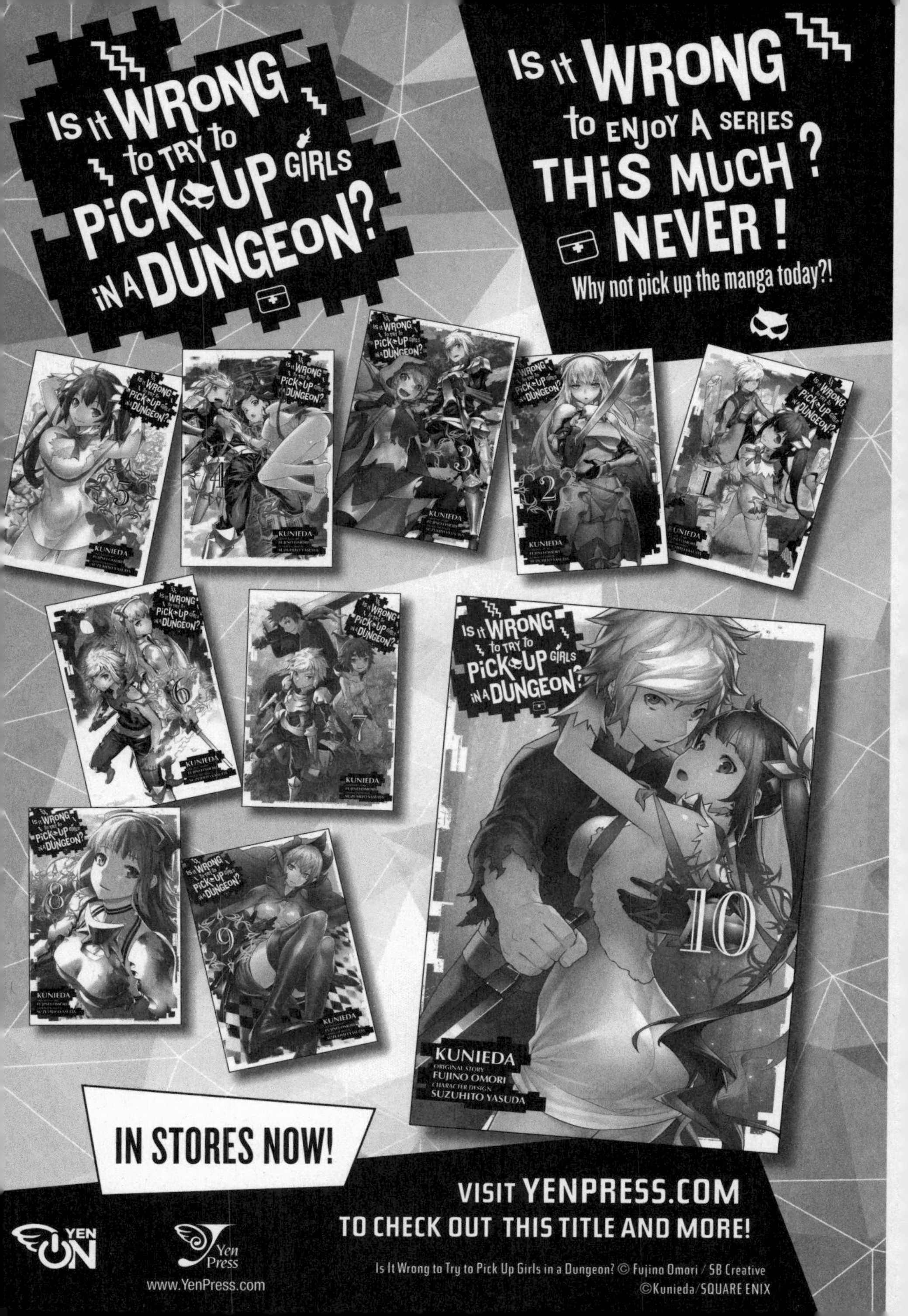
Is it WRONG to try to PiCK UP GiRLS iN A DUNGEON?
Is it WRONG to ENJOY A SERIES THIS MUCH?
NEVER!
Why not pick up the manga today?!
KUNIEDA
ORIGINAL STORY
FUJINO OMORI
CHARACTER DESIGN
SUZUHITO YASUDA
IN STORES NOW!
VISIT YENPRESS.COM
TO CHECK OUT THIS TITLE AND MORE!
YEN ON
Yen Press
www.YenPress.com
Is It Wrong to Try to Pick Up Girls in a Dungeon? © Fujino Omori / SB Creative
©Kunieda/SQUARE ENIX

Soul Eater ©Atsushi Ohkubo/SQUARE ENIX

SOUL EATER

THE COMPLETE SERIES AVAILABLE NOW!

(25 VOLUMES IN ALL!)

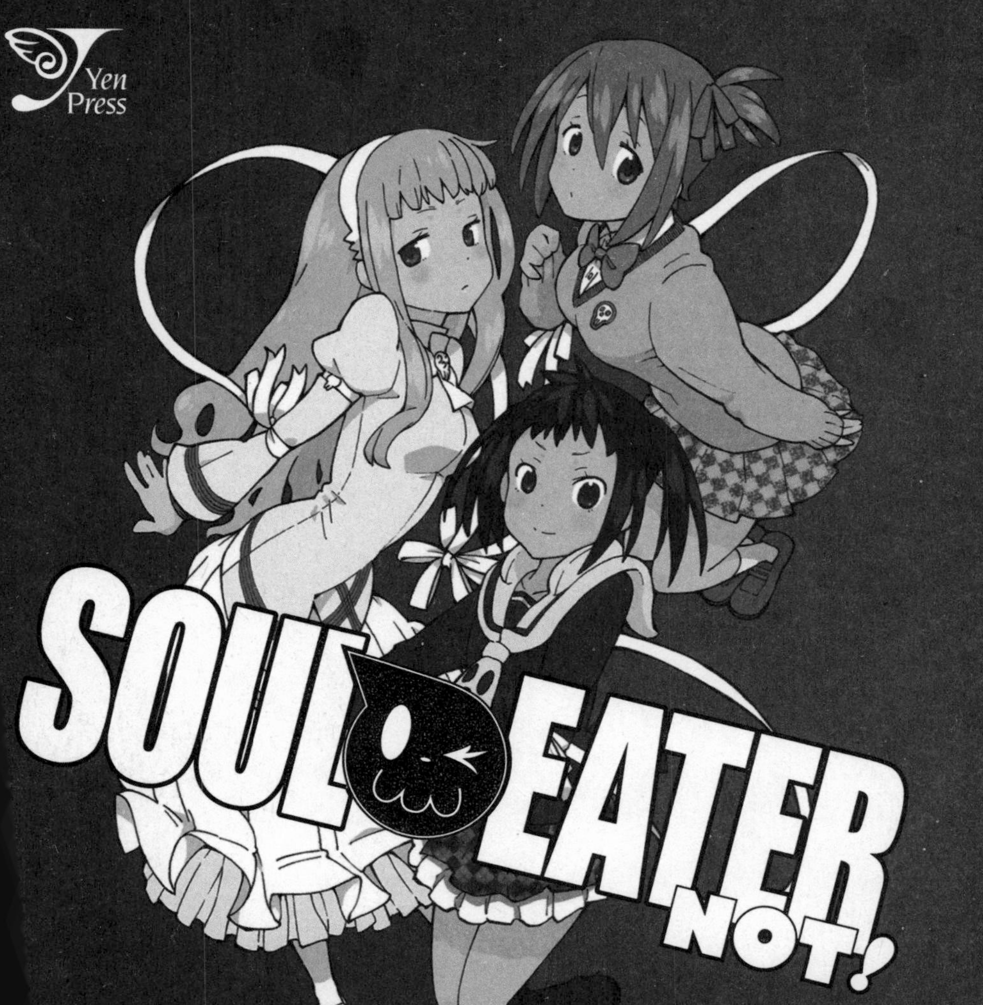
Yen Press
SOUL EATER NOT!

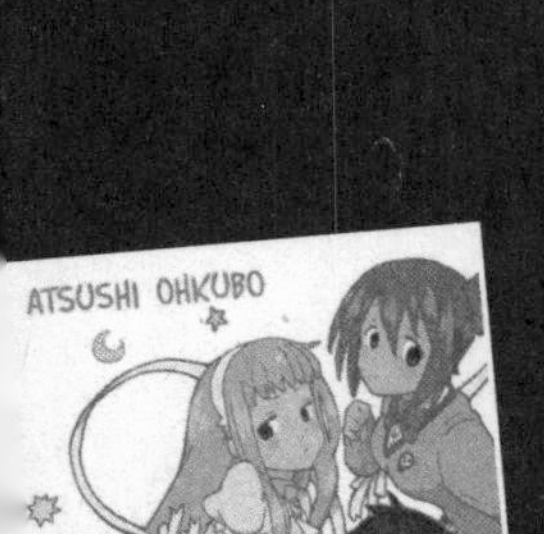
ATSUSHI OHKUBO
SOUL EATER NOT!

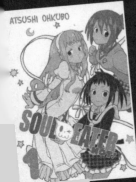

FINAL FANTASY TYPE - 0

AVAILABLE NOW AT BOOKSELLERS
EVERYWHERE!

Yen
Press
www.YenPress.com

FINAL FANTASY TYPE-0
©2012 Takatoshi Shiozawa / SQUARE ENIX
©2011 SQUARE ENIX CO.,LTD.
All Rights Reserved.

Art: TAKATOSHI SHIOZAWA
Character Design: TETSUYA NOMURA
Scenario: HIROKI CHIBA

The cadets of Akademeia's Class Zero are legends, with strength and magic unrivaled, and crimson capes symbolizing the great Vermilion Bird of the Dominion. But will their elite training be enough to keep them alive when a war breaks out and the Class Zero cadets find themselves at the front and center of a bloody political battlefield?!

Sekirei 9

SAKURAKO GOKURAKUIN

TRANSLATION: CALEB D. COOK   LETTERING: PHIL CHRISTIE

This book is a work of fiction. Names, characters, places, and incidents are the product of the author's imagination or are used fictitiously. Any resemblance to actual events, locales, or persons, living or dead, is coincidental.

SEKIREI Volumes 17 & 18 ©2015 Sakurako Gokurakuin/SQUARE ENIX CO., LTD.
First published in Japan in 2015 by SQUARE ENIX CO., LTD. English translation rights arranged with SQUARE ENIX CO., LTD. and Yen Press, LLC through Tuttle-Mori Agency, Inc., Tokyo.

English translation © 2019 by SQUARE ENIX CO., LTD.

Yen Press, LLC supports the right to free expression and the value of copyright. The purpose of copyright is to encourage writers and artists to produce the creative works that enrich our culture.

The scanning, uploading, and distribution of this book without permission is a theft of the author's intellectual property. If you would like permission to use material from the book (other than for review purposes), please contact the publisher. Thank you for your support of the author's rights.

Yen Press
150 West 30th Street, 19th Floor
New York, NY 10001

Visit us at yenpress.com
facebook.com/yenpress
twitter.com/yenpress
yenpress.tumblr.com
instagram.com/yenpress

First Yen Press Print Edition: July 2019
The volumes in this omnibus were originally published as ebooks in July 2018 and September 2018 by Yen Press.

Yen Press is an imprint of Yen Press, LLC.
The Yen Press name and logo are trademarks of Yen Press, LLC.

The publisher is not responsible for websites (or their content) that are not owned by the publisher.

Library of Congress Control Number: 2017939213

ISBN: 978-0-316-44767-6 (paperback)

10 9 8 7 6 5 4 3 2 1

WOR

Printed in the United States of America